The Handbook of Project Management

This practice-oriented handbook presents practitioners and students with a comprehensive overview of the essential knowledge and current best practices in project management. It includes the most up-to-date thinking in the discipline, describing recent developments in a way that practitioners can immediately use in their work.

The Handbook of Project Management was the first "APM Body of Knowledge Approved" title for the Association for Project Management. Over the course of six editions, *The Handbook of Project Management* has become the definitive desk reference for project management practitioners. The team of expert contributors, selected to introduce the reader to the knowledge and skills required to manage projects, includes many of the most experienced and highly regarded international writers and practitioners. The book is divided into six parts: Projects; Performance; Process; People; Portfolio; and Perspectives. Including over 25 completely new chapters, this sixth edition provides a fully up-to-date encyclopaedia for the discipline and profession of project management.

The book will be of use to all project management practitioners, from those starting out in the profession to people with advanced experience. It is also highly relevant to students, with earlier editions being used as a set or recommended text on Masters' courses in project management.

Martina Huemann is a Professor for Major Infrastructure Delivery at BSSC, University College London and Professor at WU Vienna. Martina is Editor-in-Chief of the *International Journal of Project Management* and Founding Editor-in-Chief of *Project Leadership and Society*. As co-founder of enable2change, she believes in co-creation between practitioners, policy makers, and scholars.

Rodney Turner is a Visiting Professor at the University of Leeds. He is the author or editor of 18 books and editor of the *International Journal of Project Management* from 1993 to 2018. His research covers governance, stakeholder experience, and megaproject management. In 2004, he received a research achievement award from PMI and in 2012 from IPMA.

The Handbook of Project Management

Sixth Edition

Edited by Martina Huemann
and Rodney Turner

Routledge
Taylor & Francis Group
LONDON AND NEW YORK

Designed cover image: Getty Images / AlexSava

Sixth edition published 2024
by Routledge
4 Park Square, Milton Park, Abingdon, Oxon, OX14 4RN

and by Routledge
605 Third Avenue, New York, NY 10158

Routledge is an imprint of the Taylor & Francis Group, an informa business

First edition published by Gower 1987
Fifth edition published by Gower 2014, and Routledge 2016

British Library Cataloguing-in-Publication Data
A catalogue record for this book is available from the British Library

Library of Congress Cataloging-in-Publication Data
Names: Huemann, Martina, 1969- editor. | Turner, J. Rodney
(John Rodney), 1953– editor. | Turner, J. Rodney (John Rodney),
1953– Gower handbook of project management.
Title: The handbook of project management /
edited by Martina Huemann and Rodney Turner.
Description: Sixth edition. | Abingdon, Oxon; New York, NY: Routledge, 2024. |
Includes bibliographical references. |
Identifiers: LCCN 2023041287 (print) | LCCN 2023041288 (ebook) |
ISBN 9781032227634 (hardback) | ISBN 9781032227627 (paperback) |
ISBN 9781003274179 (ebook)
Subjects: LCSH: Project management.
Classification: LCC HD69.P75 .H35436 2024 (print) |
LCC HD69.P75 (ebook) | DDC 658.4/04—dc23/eng/20230907
LC record available at https://lccn.loc.gov/2023041287
LC ebook record available at https://lccn.loc.gov/2023041288

ISBN: 978-1-032-22763-4 (hbk)
ISBN: 978-1-032-22762-7 (pbk)
ISBN: 978-1-003-27417-9 (ebk)

DOI: 10.4324/9781003274179

Typeset in Bembo
by codeMantra

Yvonne Schoper
9th September 1965–22nd April 2023
Sadly missed

Contents

Figures

Tables

Notes on contributors

Editors

Martina Huemann

Martina Huemann is a Professor for Major Infrastructure Delivery at BSSC, University College London and Professor at WU Vienna University of Economics and Business. She has published widely on topics such as project careers, stakeholder engagement, sustainability, and project management. For her research on Human Resource Management in Project-oriented Organizations, she received the IPMA Research Award. Martina is Editor-in-Chief of the *International Journal of Project Management* and Founding Editor-in-Chief of *Project Leadership and Society*. Martina Huemann has over 20 years of experience in research, teaching, and consulting. She believes in co-creation between practitioners and scholars and is a co-founder of enable2change a network of independent experts to translate strategy into action.

Rodney Turner

Rodney Turner is a Visiting Professor at the University of Leeds, and the University of Warwick. Recently he was a Professor at SKEMA Business School, Lille France, the Politecnico di Milano, and Professor and High-End Foreign Expert at Shanghai University. Rodney is the author or editor of 18 books, and he was editor of *The International Journal of Project Management* from 1993 to 2018. His research covers the relationship between governance and decision-making, stakeholders and customer experience, and megaproject management. In 2004 he received a lifetime research achievement award from the Project Management Institute, and in 2012 from the International Project Management Association.

Contributors

Monique Aubry

Monique Aubry is an Honorary Professor in the Department of Management at ESG UQAM in Montréal, Canada. Now retired from full professorship, she pursues her research on two main topics: the development of megaprojects and organizing for projects. She founded the Lab for Transfer on Innovative Practices in Project Context at ESG UQAM. In 2020, she was awarded the PMI Research Achievement Award recognizing her legacy in the field, and, in 2012, she received the IPMA Research Award for her research on Project Management Offices. Over the last few years, she has acted as an external adviser on the management of public projects for several ministries and public organizations in Quebec, Canada

Hans Bakker

Hans Bakker is a Full Professor of Management of Engineering Projects at the Faculty of Civil Engineering and Geosciences, Delft University of Technology. The chair is sponsored by the NAP Network, a knowledge network of the Dutch Process Industry. Prior to becoming a professor, he has been working for Royal Dutch Shell for almost 30 years. His education clearly seeks the relation with the practical applications and the research is focused on measurably improving the performance of project management as well in the construction as in process industry. In his academic endeavours the focus is on the human element: people are key.

Marian Bosch-Rekveldt

Marian Bosch-Rekveldt holds a PhD in project management from Delft University of Technology. As an associate professor in the group Infrastructure Design and Management at the Faculty of Civil Engineering and Geoscience of the Delft University of Technology, she is involved in education (BSc, MSc, and professional education, on campus as well as online) and research in the field of project management of large (infrastructure) projects. Her research focuses on managing complexity and the development of fit-for-purpose project management to create value by projects. Knowing that people are key, investigating collaboration is one of her key interests.

Lynn Crawford

Lynn Crawford is a Professor in the School of Project Management and John Grill Institute for Project Leadership at The University of Sydney and has extensive experience assisting leading corporations and government agencies in developing project management capability. She is an Honorary Fellow of the APM (UK) and recipient of their Sir Monty Finniston award for contribution to project management practice and research; Life Fellow of AIPM; Honorary Fellow of IPMA; recipient of the 2011 IPMA Research Achievement Award. She and her team won an IPMA Global Outstanding Research Contribution Award for their research into project-based work and careers.

Darren Dalcher

Darren Dalcher is a Professor in Strategic Project Management at Lancaster University Management School, and a Visiting International Scholar at InnoLab, University of Vaasa. He is the founder and Director of the National Centre for Project Management and co-editor of the APM Body of Knowledge. He is Editor-in-Chief of the *Journal of Software: Evolution and Process*, published by Wiley, and Editor of the Routledge Frontiers in Project Management series of research books. His research focuses on rethinking project success; repositioning the concept of agility in connection to strategy, sustainability, and innovation; and, understanding the impacts of morality, complexity, and reflective practice.

Hemanta Doloi

Hemanta Doloi is currently an Associate Professor in Construction Management at the Faculty of Architecture, Building, and Planning at the University of Melbourne, Australia. He is the Director of the Smart Villages Lab (SVL) which focuses on data-driven research in the area of "rural construction and development" under the auspice of the smart villages program. He leads the trans-disciplinary research in smart villages for developing solutions for affordable housing and infrastructure systems, generating new theories for education and governance, and empowering rural communities. Hemanta won the Australian Institute of Quantity Surveyor's Infinite Value Award in teaching and research – recognizing the excellence of scholarships impacting the wider community in the profession. He serves as an editorial member of a few prestigious journals including the *International Journal of Project Management, Built Environment Project and Asset Management* and *Construction Innovation: Information, Process, Management.* He is a founding Chair of the *International Conference on Smart Villages and Rural Development (COSVARD).* He has widely published in the areas of project management, infrastructure planning and policy, construction economics and management, and smart villages.

Ali Eshraghi

Ali Eshraghi is a Postdoctoral Research Associate in project leadership at the School of Project Management at the University of Sydney. His research interests are at the intersection of business management and digital innovation. Ali's doctoral degree from the University of Edinburgh (UK) in 2017 utilized a sociological lens to explore the development and use of IT innovations in a voluntary organization. He has held research positions in Sharif University of Technology and Sydney Business School, looking at the role of informalities in reshaping complex innovation projects; and examining how end-users collectively experiment with novel and malleable workplace technologies.

Pernille Eskerod

Dr. Pernille Eskerod is a Professor at Webster Vienna Private University where she is the area coordinator for Management and Organizational Behavior in the Department of Business and Management. Before joining Webster, she worked at the University of Southern Denmark. Her book (2016, with Dr. Anna Lund Jepsen), Project Stakeholder Management, is utilized across the globe. She has received international research grants. In 2020, she published A Stakeholder Perspective: Origins and Core Concepts in the Oxford Research Encyclopedia of Business and Management. She believes in progress through education – and serves for The Cyprus Agency of Quality Assurance and Accreditation in Higher Education.

Bent Flyvbjerg

Bent Flyvbjerg is the first BT Professor and inaugural Chair of Major Program Management at the University of Oxford, the Villum Kann Rasmussen Professor and Chair at the IT University of Copenhagen, and a Senior Research Fellow at St Anne's College, the University of Oxford. He is the most cited scholar in the world in project management. His books and articles have been translated into 20 languages. Flyvbjerg received the Project Management Institute Research Achievement Award, two Fulbright Scholarships, and a knighthood. He serves as an advisor to 10 Downing Street, the U.S. and Chinese governments, and Fortune 500 companies. His most recent book is *How Big Things Get Done* (with Dan Gardner).

Carlos Galera-Zarco

Dr. Carlos Galera-Zarco is a Lecturer (Assistant Professor) in Project Management and Business Analytics at UCL. He holds a PhD in Servitization and Digitalization and an MSc in Economics and International Management. He is also a Visiting Lecturer at Aston Business School. He has a background in Civil Engineering (MEng) and practical experience working on different infrastructure projects for a global engineering company (Sacyr). He is interested in the strategic challenges that data management is creating for both organizations and customers. His research tries to shed light on data-driven value creation and capture, and the implementation of smart services in the construction sector. He has published articles in specialized scientific journals (ABS/JCR) and presented his research works at several international conferences.

Hans Georg Gemünden

Jörg Gemünden is a Professor Emeritus of technology and innovation management at Technische Universität Berlin; Germany and professor emeritus of project management of BI Norwegian Business School in the Department of Leadership and Organization in Oslo. He holds a diploma and a doctorate in Business Administration from the University of the Saarland in Saarbrücken, and a habilitation degree and an honorary doctorate from the University of Kiel. He has received several awards of excellence for his research (e.g., the IPMA Research Achievement Award, IPMA Research Award). His work has been published in various journals, including *Organization Science*, *Research Policy*, *Journal of Product Innovation Management*, *IEEE Transactions on Engineering Management*, *R&D Management*, *Creativity and Innovation Management*, *International Journal of Project Management*, and *Project Management Journal*.

Marcel Hertogh

Marcel Hertogh is a Full Professor of Infrastructure Design and Management at Delft University of Technology and Resilience Convergence and Design at Erasmus University. He studied Civil Engineering in Delft and economics at Erasmus University Rotterdam. He did his PhD at Erasmus University and ETH Zurich. The focus of his research is on the integrated design and management of major programs. The current challenges in our complex environment, the integration of disciplines, and collaboration with partners (quadruple) are key to obtaining support and creating impact (triple bottom line). Current examples are the city of the future and the integration of infrastructures in the urban environment.

David Hillson

David Hillson, The Risk Doctor, is a thought leader and expert practitioner who speaks and writes widely on risk management. David has a well-deserved reputation as an excellent speaker on risk, blending thought leadership with practical application, presented in an accessible style that combines clarity with humour. David has advised major organizations, governments, and charities in 60 countries on how to create value from risk, and his wisdom and insights are in high demand. David has received many awards for his ground-breaking work in risk management, and he has developed significant innovations that are now widely accepted as best practices.

Lavagnon Ika

Professor Ika is a Professor of Project Management and founding Director of the Major Projects Observatory at the Telfer School of Management, University of Ottawa. He is an Associate Editor of the *International Journal of Project Management* and a member of the Academic Boards of the international project management associations PMI and IPMA. Professor Ika's research has been published in prestigious journals such as *IEEE Transactions on Engineering Management, Production Planning and Control, International Journal of Project Management, Project Management Journal, and World Development*. Professor Ika won the IPMA Research Award in 2017.

Helgi Thor Ingason

Helgi Thor Ingason is a Professor at Reykjavik University in Iceland. He finished his PhD degree in process metallurgy from NTNU in Norway, an MSc degree in mechanical and industrial engineering from the University of Iceland, and a SAPM certification from Stanford University. Helgi Thor is the author and co-author of several books on project management and quality management. He is a Certified Senior Project Manager and has served as a management consultant for many organizations in Iceland. Some of his posts external to academia include serving as the Research Coordinator of IPMA, interim CEO of Reykjavik Energy, and SORPA bs.

Anna Y. Khodijah

Anna Y. Khodijah is a Lecturer and researcher in Information Systems and Strategic IT Management at the University of Duisburg-Essen (UDE), Germany. She completed her master's program at the International University of Japan and currently pursuing her doctorate at the UDE. Her areas of interest are cultural diversity and project management. For almost 20 years, Anna has been working as a project manager in prestigious organizations such as IBM, Mitsubishi, and Deloitte Consulting. Her recent responsibility was managing a project for a city government in North Rhine-Westphalia, Germany, to evaluate the acceptance of the city government's employees and managers on the mobile office, as part of the smart city and digitization initiatives.

Alexander Kock

Alexander Kock is a Full Professor of technology and innovation management at the Technische Universität Darmstadt, Germany. His research interests include organizational issues of innovation and project management, especially the management of project portfolios, highly innovative projects, the front end of innovation, and university–industry collaboration. He received the IPMA Research Award for his project portfolio benchmarking studies. His work has been published in various journals, including *Research Policy*, *Journal of Product Innovation Management*, *IEEE Transactions on Engineering Management*, *R&D Management*, *International Journal of Project Management*, and *Project Management Journal*.

Ruth Christine Lechler

Ruth Christine Lechler is a Research Associate at Zurich University of Applied Sciences and a doctoral candidate at WU Vienna University of Economics and Business. She researches and lectures on motivation in projects, project management, and organizational design. Ruth holds a degree in Management, Organizational Studies, and Cultural Theory from the University of St. Gallen. As a trained Design Thinker, she applied Design Thinking in strategy consulting and led transformation and digitalization projects in the industrial sector.

Patrick Lehner

Patrick Lehner, Dr. leads the Center of Organizational Design & Processes at Zurich University of Applied Sciences. Patrick teaches and researches organizational development and project management and is a member of the research team multiprojectmanagement.org. Previously, Patrick spent 16 years in the industry as a manager and as a project leader of various organizational development projects and technical projects.

Beverley Lloyd-Walker

Beverley is a research fellow within the School of Property, Construction, and Project Management, RMIT University, Melbourne. During the last few years, her research has concentrated on "people in temporary organizations". This research has been conducted within the project-based Australian economy, exploring new project procurement approaches, and careers in project management. Recently, issues around policies and practices in projectified workplaces, especially within more collaborative forms of project delivery alliances and integrated project delivery, have become a major focus of her research. This research has explored the professional skills required for successful project leadership within alliances and other relationship-based procurement forms. Beverley's interest in collaborative forms of project procurement led to her researching the range of forms used globally, and thus to her role in researching and writing the book "Collaborative Project Procurement Arrangements" published in 2015. Beverley has had over 50 refereed items published, has co-authored three editions of a human resource management book, and has co-authored an industry report. She has supervised 11 doctoral theses; one master's by thesis, and eight master's theses.

Mauro Mancini

Mauro Mancini is a Full Professor of project management at the Department of Management Economics and Industrial Engineering at Politecnico di Milano and Associate Dean of Corporate Education at PoliMi Graduate School of Management. He is the Director of an international Master in Project Management (IMPM) and of an Executive Master in Business Administration (EMBA). He is responsible for research and consultancy projects in the construction, oil and gas, military, and services sectors (e.g., insurance and digital payments). His main international publications regard Project Management, Project Governance, Risk Management, Megaprojects, Nuclear Energy, Construction, Modularization, and Building Information Modeling (BIM).

Costanza Mariani

Costanza Mariani is PhD candidate in Management Engineering at Politecnico di Milano and she leads the IPMA Special Interest Group on Artificial Intelligence. Her research topic concerns the application of Artificial Intelligence and predictive machine learning algorithms in project management. Costanza is also a teaching assistant for the Industrial Project Management and Project and Program Management courses at the Department of Management Engineering at Politecnico di Milano. She also teaches Project Management Fundamentals at the Politecnico di Milano School of Management.

Miia Martinsuo

Miia Martinsuo is a Professor of Industrial Management at Tampere University. Her field of research and teaching is project and service business. Prof. Martinsuo has 20 years of academic experience in project and service business, and nine years of industrial experience, particularly in organization and process development in the metal and engineering industry. Her current research interests include: Project-based organizing; steering and selecting product development project portfolios; the autonomy and control of projects; managing manufacturing and process innovations; industrial service operations and innovations; and organizational transformation towards service business.

Harvey Maylor
Harvey Maylor is an Associate Professor at the Saïd Business School, University of Oxford. He teaches at the Major Projects Leadership Academy and the Saïd MSc in Major Program Management. He was previously Director of the International Centre for Program Management at Cranfield.

His work is widely published in management journals and is highly cited. His main text (*Project Management*, Pearson, fifth edition 2022) is Europe's best-selling PM text and has been translated into five different languages.

His main research interests are in organizational systems design and complexity in major projects, and the (non-)adoption of promising practices.

Eunice Maytorena-Sanchez
Eunice is a Senior Lecturer in Project Management at Alliance Manchester Business School. Her research interests are in project and program management across a range of sectors (construction, utility, defence, IT/IS), and is a co-author of Strategic Project Organizing (Oxford, 2022). She has over 15 years of experience in Higher Education teaching at undergraduate, master's, MBA, and executive levels. She has developed expertise in assisting project organizations develop their capabilities in stakeholder management, strategic project management and risk, uncertainty, and complexity management. She has worked with many organizations in the public, private, and not-for-profit sectors in the UK and overseas.

Jack Meredith
Jack Meredith is Professor of Management and Broyhill Distinguished Scholar, Emeritus at Wake Forest University. He received undergraduate degrees in engineering and mathematics and his PhD and MBA from the University of California, Berkeley. Previously he worked for Hewlett-Packard Corp., Douglas Aircraft Company, and TRW Systems Group. His research has been published in the *International Journal of Project Management, Project Management Journal, Journal of Operations Management, Management Science, Sloan Management Review,*

Strategic Management Journal, California Management Review, etc. He co-authors the textbooks *Project Management: A Managerial Approach*, *Operations Management for MBAs*, and *Project Management in Practice*. He was the Editor-in-Chief of the *Journal of Operations Management* and founding Editor of *Operations Management Research*.

Ralf Müller

Ralf Müller is a Professor of Project Management at BI Norwegian Business School and an Adjunct Professor at the University of Technology Sydney, and Dalian University, China. He is the Editor-in-Chief of the *Project Management Journal®*. His research, concepts, and theories on leadership, governance, and organizational project management appeared in more than 300 scientific publications, including 18 books. In recent years, IPMA, PMI, and other institutions acknowledged his work with many awards, including several fellow and lifetime achievement awards. Stanford University ranked him as among the top 2% of the most influential scientists worldwide. Before joining academia, he spent 30 years in the industry, including a time as Worldwide Director of Project Management at NCR Corporation.

Ruth Murray-Webster

Ruth is recognized as a leader of project-based organizational change and risk management, performing roles as a practitioner, adviser, facilitator, researcher, and author across most sectors for more than 30 years. She researched organizational change from the perspective of the recipients of change for an executive doctorate at Cranfield School of Management.

Vadake K. Narayanan

Vadake K. Narayanan is currently the Deloitte & Touché Jones Stubbs Professor of Strategy and Entrepreneurship at Drexel University, Philadelphia, PA. He had formerly served as the founding Associate Dean for Research in the Le Bow College of Business (2005–2015), as the Director of the Center for Management of Technology (1995–2000), and as the Associate Dean for Academic Affairs in the School of Business at the University of Kansas (KU) (1992–1995). He has been the recipient of several awards including the Albert Nelson Marquis Lifetime Achievement Award by Marquis Who's Who. Until December 2019, Narayanan served on the Academic Advisory Board of Project Management Institute (PMI). He was the (founding) Chair of the Strategy Process Interest Group at the Strategic

Management Society. He also served as the chair of the Teaching Committee (2000–2001), and the Secretary-Treasurer of the Technology & Innovation Management Division of the National Academy of Management (1995–1998). Since 1988 till 2000, he has been on the editorial board of *Organization Science*. Narayanan has published five books and monographs: His articles have appeared in leading professional journals. Narayan has been a consultant to large pharmaceutical and high technology companies and science-related government agencies, primarily in the areas of strategy execution and corporate innovation.

Eleni Papadonikolaki

Dr. Eleni Papadonikolaki, ARB, MAPM, SFHEA, is an Associate Professor in Digital Innovation and Management at the Bartlett School of Construction and Project Management at University College London. Eleni has a PhD in the alignment of digital technologies with supply chain management, from TU Delft, Netherlands, an MSc, and a Dipl.-Eng. Bringing practical experience working as an architect engineer and design manager on a number of complex and international projects in Europe and the Middle East, she is researching and helping teams manage the interfaces between digital technology and projects. She is the author of over 80 peer-reviewed publications, e.g., in the *International Journal of Project Management*, *Project Management Journal,* and others. She has won and delivered collaborative research projects as Principal and Co-Investigator funded by European and UK research councils. Eleni is the Founding Director of the MSc in Digital Engineering Management at UCL where she develops the new generation of project leaders for digital transformation.

Beverly Pasian

Beverly's occupancy in the world of project management has extended for almost 30 years. Initially focusing on education, managing e-learning projects led to her first master's degree, in open-distance education. Books and her first PhD followed, focusing on e-learning project management. Satisfied for many years as a project management researcher and teacher, she wanted to be a more socially responsible digital citizen. Turning her attention to the impact of projects on the quality of life in smart cities, her understanding of projects as choices in urban innovation has increased dramatically. A second PhD and leadership roles in IPMA and IEEE have followed. Working with cities and companies to understand smart city projects is her ongoing interest.

Ossi Pesämaa

Ossi Pesämaa holds a PhD from the Luleå University of Technology. His research interests involve identifying the roles of motivation, choices, and conditions in strategic management for various performance outcomes. Ossi offers classes at all levels involving topics such as methods, project management, and other related aspects of management. He has previously published in journals such as *International Journal of Project Management, Project Management Journal, International Journal of Managing Projects in Business, Journal of Management in Engineering, Construction Management and Economics, Journal of Business Research, Journal of Management Control, Entrepreneurship & Regional Development, and Industrial Marketing Management.*

Jeffrey Pinto

Professor Pinto is the Andrew Morrow and Elizabeth Lee Black Chair in Management Technology with the Black School of Business, Penn State, the Behrend College, Erie, PA, USA. He is the author or editor of more than 25 books and some 200 other publications. His research has been published in *Management Science, Research Policy, Journal of Management, Expert Systems with Applications, Sloan Management Review, Journal of Management Studies, Journal of Product Innovation Management,* and the *IEEE Transactions on Engineering Management.* Professor Pinto has received both the PMI and IPMA Research Achievement Awards for his lifetime contributions.

Shankar Sankaran

Shankar Sankaran PhD is a Professor of Organizational Project Management at the University of Technology Sydney (UTS) Australia. He teaches courses on Organizational Project Management at UTS, Tongji University, and BI Fudan University in China. He has published books, book chapters, and journal articles that have been published in ranked journals and won research awards. He has edited books and written book chapters in them including the *Cambridge Handbook of Organizational Project Management* and *Organizational Project Management: Theory and Implementation.*

Ron Schipper

Ron Schipper is the Program Manager of Sustainability at the Municipality of Waddinxveen (Netherlands) and an independent researcher. Different projects for a better life capture his drive, and finding possibilities for sustainability transitions in every project and portfolio is his daily business. Today he is one of the well-known recognized experts in the field of sustainability in project management with over a dozen papers and several books published and various practical contributions towards organizations adopting this topic. Ron is also an external examiner in the Master of Project Management in HU University of Applied Science in the Netherlands.

Yvonne Schoper

Yvonne Schoper was a professor of International Management with a focus on International Project Management at HTW University of Applied Sciences Berlin, Germany. She holds a PhD in Industrial Engineering from Cranfield University (UK) and has 12 years of work experience as a project manager for BMW for several international car development projects. Her research interests were the projectification of economies and its impact on societies, intercultural project management, and careers in project management.

She was a board member of GPM, the German Association for Project Management, and served as Vice President for the International Project Management Association (IPMA).

Natalya Sergeeva

Natalya Sergeeva is an Associate Professor in the Management of Projects at the Bartlett School of Sustainable Construction, University College London.

Natalya is an academic and consultant in the areas of project management and leadership, innovation management, and strategic management. Her contribution is in deepening understanding of the ways in which leaders craft, communicate, and maintain project narratives, identity narratives, and narratives about innovation, sustainability, and digital transformation. Her research has been published in the *International Journal of Project Management*, *Project Management Journal*, *International Journal of Managing Projects in Business*, *Project Leadership and Society*, *Construction Economics and Management*, *Industrial Marketing Management*, *International Journal of Innovation Management*, and *European Journal of Innovation Management*.

Aaron Shenhar

Aaron Shenhar is a Professor and Educator of Project Management, the first recipient of the PMI Research Achievement Award, and IEEE's Engineering Manager of the Year Award. Following a career in defence, he was a tenured professor, building several academic programs in project and technology management. His research is used in the curriculum of many corporate and university programs throughout the world. His book, *Reinventing Project Management,* HBSP was among the best five business books of 2007. He is currently CEO of The SPL Group, a consulting and education firm focusing on aligning business and technology in industry and government.

Gilbert Silvius

Gilbert Silvius is an expert in project management and information management, with engagements at several universities across Europe. Gilbert has authored several books and over 50 academic journal articles, with a main research focus on sustainability in project management. For his work on this topic, Gilbert received the GPM 2013 sustainability award and the 2020 outstanding contribution IPMA Research Award. As a practitioner, Gilbert has over 30 years of experience in organizational change and IT projects and is a member of the international enable2change network of project management experts.

Dagmar Silvius-Zuchi

Dagmar Silvius-Zuchi is an experienced consultant and trainer, and founder of the enable2change network of project and change management experts. Her experience spans different industries and change types. Next to her professional experience, she holds an Honorary Professorship from IMC Krems, and lectures at SKEMA Business School in Paris and Lille, Vienna University of Economics and Business, and several other universities. Dagmar's professional certifications include IPMA Level B, PMI PMP, PRINCE2 Practitioner, and Scrum Master. Because of her in-depth knowledge of project management standards she has participated in the development of several ISO standards related to project management.

Christine Unterhitzenberger

Christine Unterhitzenberger is an Associate Professor in Project Management at the University of Leeds and a Chartered Project Professional. Her research explores perceptions of fairness in projects and their impact on individuals, projects, and organizations. She is also interested in how governance can influence desired behaviour in project contexts. She has won multiple awards for her research and educational practice, is a leading member of the project research community at BAM and EURAM, and is an active volunteer with APM. Prior to her academic career, she was a senior project management consultant in the construction industry.

Reinhard Wagner

Reinhard Wagner has been active for more than 35 years in project-related leadership in a wide range of societal sectors. As Managing Director of Tiba Managementberatung GmbH, a leading PM Consultancy in Germany, he supports senior executives in transforming their corporations into project-oriented, adaptive, and sustainably successful organizations. During more than 20 years of voluntary engagement, Reinhard served the German as well as the International Project Management Association (IPMA) in a range of leadership roles (including President and Chairman). He is a Senior Lecturer at Alma Mater Europaea and is dedicated to researching the project society.

Derek Walker

Derek is an emeritus professor at RMIT University, Melbourne. Derek is also co-editor with Professor Steve Rowlinson from Hong Kong University on 'The Routledge Handbook of Integrated Project delivery' 2020, a 28-chapter book co-authored with a range of world experts on aspects of integrated project delivery. He mainly collaborates with colleagues from Scandinavia, the UK, and other Universities in Australia. He has been an active researcher and has written and co-written over 70 book chapters, 11 books, and 120 refereed journal papers. He has supervised 29 doctoral candidates to successful completion. His fields of interest include: strategic project management; collaboration; organizational learning; innovation diffusion; and project governance. He was the founding editor of the *International Journal of Managing Projects in Business* and editor for its first decade. In 2018 he was awarded the IPMA (International Project Management Association) Lifetime Research Achievement.

Jennifer Whyte

Jennifer Whyte is the Head of the School of Project Management and Director of the John Grill Institute for Project Leadership at the University of Sydney. Her main research interests are in major projects, systems integration, and how digital information is transforming their delivery. She also has research interests in pragmatist approaches to future making and innovation. She is also a Professor at Imperial College London, has previously been a Shimizu Visiting Professor at Stanford University, and sat on the UK Construction Leadership Council. Her research has a real-world impact, and she works closely with project practitioners and government policy makers.

Graham M Winch

Graham is a Professor of Project Management at Alliance Manchester Business School, a role he has held since 2004. He was Academic Director for Executive Education at AMBS, including project leadership programs such as Managing Projects for BP, and Leading Complex Projects Programs and Portfolios for BAE Systems. He is the author of *Managing Construction Projects* (Wiley-Blackwell, 2010), co-author of *Strategic Project Organizing* (OUP, 2022), and co-editor of the *Research Handbook of Complex Project Organizing* (Edward Elgar, 2023). He has published over 60 refereed journal articles, complemented by numerous book chapters, conference papers, and research reports.

Ofer Zwikael

Ofer Zwikael is a Professor of Project Management at the Australian National University. His four books and more than 250 scholarly peer-reviewed papers have been recognized through research awards from the Academy of Management, British Academy of Management, Project Management Institute, International Project Management Association, Emerald, and the Australian Institute of Project Management. As one of the world's leading project management scholars, Professor Zwikael was named by Stanford University and Elsevier to be among the top 2% of international scientists. His research on project benefits management has been funded by major organizations, including the Australian Department of Defence and the Project Management Institute (U.S.).

Foreword

Unlocking Success through Innovative and Effective Project Management

In today's fast-paced and ever-evolving world, organizations of all sizes and industries face increasingly complex challenges. Challenges are interconnected to the fact that we live in a project society where projects shape people, organizations, and society (Lundin et al., 2015). In this particular context, projects often act as agents of change that drive innovation and transformation required to tackle economic, environmental, societal, managerial, and technological challenges. Projects not only deliver changes but also create the future (Huemann, 2022). A future which requires more complex solutions, using a variety of viewpoints from different skills and expertise to create a fairer, more sustainable, more united world. To stay ahead of the curve, project managers must develop the capability to continually adapt to respond to these needs to deliver successful projects that create value.

Project management research has evolved over the past decades and is now a more mature disciplinary field (Locatelli et al., 2023). Project management enables businesses to navigate the dynamic landscape with innovation and agility. It provides a structured framework and a set of best practices that empower individuals and teams to plan, execute, and deliver projects on time, within budget, and to the highest quality standards. Project management is also the strategic means for generating value through the delivery of projects. The increasing role of project management and projects in society calls for a better understanding of the criticality and competencies required to manage and deliver projects. Researchers have the duty to develop practical knowledge to help practitioners constantly renew themselves.

It is with great pleasure that I introduce this Handbook on Project Management—a comprehensive compendium that will equip practitioners with the essential knowledge and skills to excel in this field. Whether you are just entering the realm of project management, or someone seeking to enhance their understanding of the discipline, this Handbook is an invaluable resource that will enhance your capabilities and empower your journey towards project management excellence.

Within these pages, you will embark on a transformative learning experience. The new edition of the Handbook is thoughtfully crafted to take you on a step-by-step journey through its six parts providing practical insights and actionable strategies to maximize project success. It covers a wide array of topics, ranging from the various elements of project management and its successful implementation, the functions a project manager has to perform to execute the project and deliver performance to the processes that need to be followed to deliver project outputs and benefits. Furthermore, it explores the best models of project management, the ways to better capture the issues of managing multiple projects and finally, it looks at the perspective of projects and their management.

One of the key strengths of this Handbook is its ability to cater to both traditional and innovative project management approaches. It recognizes the importance of adapting to changing business environments and introduces innovative principles and methodologies to complement the established project management methodologies. Moreover, this Handbook places a strong emphasis on the human element of project management, the resilience needed in the face of adversity, the digitalization concerns, and the management of value in projects. It recognizes that successful project delivery relies not only on technical skills but also on effective collaboration and leadership. It underlines the importance of being vigilant and sensitive to the evolution of project management practices. It also highlights the role played by projects in the implementation of sustainable and fair decisions and actions. These insights will not only elevate your project management capabilities but also enrich your professional interactions and relationships.

The contributors to this Handbook are a distinguished group of academics, each with extensive experience and a deep understanding of the challenges and opportunities inherent in project management. Their collective wisdom, shared through the pages of this book, will ignite your imagination, challenge your assumptions, and inspire you to push the boundaries of what you thought was possible. As you embark on this journey, I encourage you to approach each chapter with an open mind and a willingness to learn. Engage with the material, reflect on your own experiences, and envision how the principles and models discussed can be applied to your own projects. Remember, project management is not merely a technical discipline—it is an art that requires creativity, adaptability, and the ability to navigate uncertainty. Practitioners may not realize it but the most important aspects of what they manage are projects as agents of change to build a better society.

I trust that this Handbook will serve as your trusted companion, providing the guidance and inspiration you need to navigate the complexities of modern project environments. May it empower you to unlock your full potential and exceed your expectations.

Nathalie Drouin PhD, MBA, LLB
Chairholder of the Research Chair INFRA-S on Social Value of Infrastructures
Professor, Université du Québec à Montréal
Adjunct Professor, UTS, Sydney, Australia
Editor-in-chief, *International Journal of Managing Projects in Business*

Preface

Welcome to the sixth edition of the Handbook of Project Management. This is the fourth edition edited by Rodney, but we welcome Martina as part of the natural progression. The scope of this book is quite different from the fifth edition. In moving from the fourth to the fifth edition, Rodney kept many of the chapters similar, just changed the authors. In this sixth edition, there is quite a different set of chapters. You might think that is the influence of Martina. Martina has brought a fresh approach, but Rodney is also well aware that project management is changing.

We have reintroduced the part on managing people. It was dropped from the fifth edition because there was a Gower Handbook on managing people on projects. But managing people is an essential part of project management, thus we brought it back.

What might raise eyebrows are the things we have left out of this edition. Chapters 7 and 8 cover the management of scope. But there are no explicit chapters on managing time, cost, schedule, or quality explicitly. However, Chapter 14 considers managing cost and schedule from a data analytics perspective and Chapter 32 offers a discussion on behavioural bias.

What people want to know about in a handbook of project management is the new ideas pushing new boundaries and giving us a new understanding of how to manage projects. Similarly, Rodney was going to write a chapter on project start-up, but we decided we had said everything we wanted to say about start-up in our Chapter 9 on project organization. Also, Chapter 20 on feasibility and Chapter 26 on teams cover start-up. In the preface to the third edition, Rodney said he was sad there wasn't a chapter on close-out. He said it made it look as though project managers enjoyed the chase more than the finish. Start-ups and close-outs are things that were well explored in the 1980s. People now know how to do them. We have included in this handbook topics which are the subject of more temporary research.

As with previous editions, Rodney and Martina do not necessarily share the views of all the authors. There is nothing we violently disagree with, but we have a range of authoritative views. Project management is a social construct, so we would not say anything is wrong, but people can have different ways of viewing the same thing.

Each chapter has a list of references and further reading. We told the authors that they were writing a handbook for practitioners, so they could say what they believed, and not support every claim with a reference. We said there were three purposes for references. The most important was to guide readers where to look for further information on the topic. The second is to acknowledge the source of somebody else's material. The third is for the author to blow their own trumpet. Books primarily satisfy the first purpose, though research articles in the leading research journals, which are readily accessible can be useful.

Again we have tried to use the original English spelling program (with the same root as diagram and epigram). When you realize all the grief about whether it is a program or programme is caused by the Victoria affectation of theatre owners wanting to make the theatre programs look posh by using the French spelling, you do think, "Give it a rest, keep it simple".

Finally, we would like to thank Helga Baumschabl for her help in editing the book.

Martina Huemann
London and Vienna
m.huemann@ucl.ac.uk

Rodney Turner
East Horsley
rodneyturner@europrojex.co.uk

Chapter 1

A handbook for project management practitioners

Martina Huemann and Rodney Turner

The relevance of projects

We understand projects as temporary organizations and agents for change (Huemann, 2022). Thus with projects, project sequences, and programs, we deliver economic, environmental, and social value to the project owner organization, stakeholders, and the society in general. Projects are not exceptions but they are a common design element in private and public organizations to enable them to fulfil their purpose. Contemporary projects come in different types and are performed in different contexts. They have a wide range of sizes, from small software development projects to digital transformation programs, international development programs to mega projects or programs to enhance infrastructure and our living in cities.

We are living in a project society!

Engagement between research and practice

Because of the importance of projects to deliver bespoken products and services and to deliver change. We see them contribute to solving problems and challenges in organizations to allow for developing their future as well as contributing to solving grand challenges (Lavagnon & Lauchlan, 2022).

DOI: 10.4324/9781003274179-1

We see a need for mutual engagement between project directors, project professionals, decision-makers, and project scholars and experts important to co-create knowledge to advance the successful delivery of projects.

In this handbook, we provide a comprehensive and contemporary understanding of Managing Projects to translate recent research and developments into chapters for practitioners. We invited leading experts and researchers to share their understanding of a topic enriched by their own research but written for a practitioner audience. In this starting chapter, we provide an overview of the book and relate it to four professional bodies of knowledge.

The six parts of the handbook

The book consists of six parts:

1 The first describes projects and their management, and considers various elements of project management and its successful implementation.
2 The second part describes the functions that a project manager has to perform to execute the project, and how they deliver performance.
3 The third part describes the processes that need to be followed to deliver the project's output and its desired benefits.
4 The fourth part considers people working on projects, and exploring different models of management.
5 The fifth part describes various issues relating to the management of multiple projects.
6 The sixth part considers a few perspectives on projects and their management.

Part I: Projects

Chapter 2: Rodney and Martina explain what we understand by projects and their management. They describe several features of projects and introduce management, leadership, governance, and governmentality.

Chapter 3: V.K. Narayanan explores how to link projects to strategy through strategic initiatives. By that, he stresses the importance of creating and recreating the future of the company based on a strategic perception of projects and programs.

Chapter 4: Jeff Pinto and Lavignon Ika address the changing nature of project success, unravelling the surprising complexity that underlies a comprehensive understanding of success, and as well, pointing to a number of important paradoxes and challenges in success.

Chapter 5: Rodney and Martina describe the nature of complexity in projects. Complex projects require different approaches to their management from simpler projects. While simpler projects can be managed using deductive approaches to solve problems, complex projects need inductive approaches to create narratives to explore mysteries.

Chapter 6: Martina introduces auditing as a method to govern projects and programs and organize learning.

Part II: Performance

Chapter 7: Ossi Pesämaa introduces principles, issues, and concepts for measuring project performance. The chapter offers hands-on qualitative definitions and diagnostics of empirical observations.

Chapter 8: Focusing on requirements, scope, and configuration, Hemanta Doloi highlights the elements of the three interrelated dimensions, which are ….

Chapter 9: Rodney and Martina describe the creation of the project organization, making people feel they are part of the project, and defining their roles and responsibilities. They share their thoughts on the traditional design of project organizations and enrich these with contemporary design elements.

Chapter 10: Graham Winch explores the role of the project owner organization. Without the owner identifying the need for a new asset, developing a value proposition, and then ensuring beneficial use, the investment cycle does not work.

Chapter 11: A project starts with the development of a business case, and ends with benefit realization. Jack Meredith and Ofer Zwikael discuss the need for a senior manager who will have the overall accountability for these.

Chapter 12: Miia Martinsuo introduces three main processes of managing value in projects: making the value proposition, planning and managing value streams, and delivering value outcomes.

Chapter 13: Derek Walker and Beverley Lloyd-Walker explain how integrated project delivery leads to superior performance.

Chapter 14: Eleni Papadonikolaki and Carlos Galera-Zarco conceptualize the relation between projects, information, and data, and discuss key application areas of data analytics in projects, for instance scheduling and costing. They then present the state-of-the-art applications, means, and tools of data analytics in key areas of project management.

Chapter 15: Project delivery increasingly uses digital infrastructures. They comprise complex and evolving sets of interconnected software packages and applications. Jennifer Whyte and Ali Eshraghi discuss some practical lessons and considerations for project managers.

Chapter 16: Our ability to manage risk is directly proportional to our chances of successfully delivering our project. David Hillson explains why, starting from first principles.

Chapter 17: Christine Unterhitzenberger suggests that enhanced resilience will enable the project to recover better from the crisis by facilitating desirable structures and behaviours prior to the occurrence of a crisis.

Chapter 18: Gilbert Silvius, Ron Schipper, and Martina Huemann identify the areas of impact of sustainability on project management. They cover examples and instruments for the integration of sustainability into project management. They consider the integration of Sustainability in Project Management a scope as well as a mind shift.

Part III: Process

Chapter 19: Rodney and Martina describe the processes of project management. There are three types of processes: the investment process, the project process, and the project management process.

Chapter 20: Marian Bosch-Rekveldt, Hans Bakker and Marcel Hertogh explore how the feasibility and planning phases could benefit from a more flexible approach, specifically focusing on interaction, collaboration, and adopting a change mindset.

Chapter 21: Today's projects need to solve wicked problems. Ruth Lechler, Martina Huemann and Patrick Lehner introduce design thinking as an agile project approach to develop product and services in co-creation with end users.

Chapter 22: Dagmar Silvius-Zuchi and Gilbert Silvius discuss the characteristics of predictive, adaptive, and hybrid approaches to projects, and develop a set of criteria to assess the suitability of an approach for a given project within an organizational context.

Chapter 23: Rodney and Martina describe scenario planning and future planning as ways of taking a more experimental, descriptive, and innovative approach to manage projects.

Part IV: People

Chapter 24: Lynn Crawford identifies what project managers do, how they become project managers and develop their competence, the personal characteristics they bring to the role, and how this interacts with the many different contexts within which they operate.

Chapter 25: Lynn Crawford provides greater clarity on the nature of the sponsor role, the governance and support responsibilities, what they do, what it takes to develop the skills to be effective, and tailor actions and behaviours to suit the needs of each project.

Chapter 26: Reinhard Wagner reveals why projects are a suitable organizational form for people to fulfil their basic needs, namely autonomy, competence, and relatedness when selecting team members for a project. He suggests paying attention to their motivation and fit.

Chapter 27: Pernille Eskerod and Martina Huemann offer a comprehensive understanding of project stakeholder engagement.

Chapter 28: Natalya Sergeeva, Graham Winch, and Eunice Maytorena-Sanchez present a new Project Leadership Model, which focuses on how leaders make sense of their project, and thereby create narratives to build knowledge and understanding of the project.

Chapter 29: Ralf Müller addresses balanced leadership in projects. More specifically, leadership approaches, their particularities in a project context, and the need to balance different leadership approaches in situational contingency over time.

Chapter 30: Martina Huemann and Ruth Lechler examine what motivates young project professionals to work on projects. They argue that projects provide an appealing work environment that aligns with the career aspirations of these professionals.

Chapter 31: Anna Khodijah describes how diversity, in particular cultural diversity, influences the project and how the project manager (and project team) should deal with the effect of diversity to reach high performance.

Chapter 32: Bent Flyvbjerg identifies the most important behavioural biases for project management, including political and cognitive bias. Specifically, the chapter focuses on strategic misrepresentation, optimism bias, uniqueness bias, the planning fallacy, overconfidence bias, and the base-rate fallacy.

Chapter 33: Darren Dalcher provides managers with the vocabulary, practical tools, and frameworks needed to address ethical and moral challenges. He identifies the importance of ethics, before providing a snapshot of ethical challenges and attitudes and presenting some of the key pressures on professionals.

Part V: Portfolio

Chapter 34: Is this piece of work a project or a program? Harvey Maylor and Ruth Murray-Webster describe an alternative pragmatism.

Chapter 35: Hans Georg Gemünden and Alexander Kock describe project portfolio management main objectives, highlighting its essential role for organizations as the central link between strategy and projects.

Chapter 36: Hans Georg Gemünden and Alexander Kock address the issue of managing sequences of projects that build on each other, and create, develop, or terminate paths of innovation development and innovation exploitation or paths of organizational transformation.

Chapter 37: Costanza Mariani and Mauro Mancini provide an overview of methods currently used to select projects. They highlight how to apply supervised and unsupervised machines to project portfolio selection to forecast the outcomes of projects, classifying and clustering upcoming projects in a predictive way.

Chapter 38: Shankar Sankaran explains the Organizational Project Management model, which can help organizations integrate all project management-related activities in an organizational hierarchy or network to ensure that projects create value for stakeholders.

Chapter 39: Martina describes the model of the Project-oriented Organization and its specific features expressed in its strategy, structure, and culture. The model offers a theoretical perspective applicable to any organization that performs projects.

Chapter 40: Ralf Müller addresses the governance of projects from an intra-organizational and inter-organizational perspective. Good governance considers contextual contingency and synchronizes between the organization's project, program, portfolio, corporate, and inter-organizational layers to accomplish its benefits.

Chapter 41: Monique Aubry offers a PMO toolbox for those who are designing a new project management office (PMO) or wish to update or modify existing ones specific to an organizational context.

Part VI: Perspectives

Chapter 42: Yvonne Schoper and Helgi Thor Ingason describe the projectification of society. They define projectification as the economic trend of an increasing diffusion of projects as a form of business organization.

Chapter 43: Beverly Pasian and Aaron Shenhar describe the periodization of quality of life and citizen engagement in smart cities.

Chapter 44: To conclude this book, Rodney gives some personal reflections on the evolution of project management.

Invitation

In compiling this book, we made choices about what to include. We have tended to focus on topics reflecting recent developments in the subject, guiding readers to the new areas they need to be aware of, and ignoring some of the more traditional areas that we believe are rather well understood.

We invite you to engage in the chapters and take out for you what resonates with you. We invite you to make the knowledge fit your contexts and apply it in your projects.

References and further reading

Huemann, M., 2022. Celebrating the power of projects and their management, *International Journal of Project Management*, 40(1), 1–3.

Lavagnon, A.I., and Lauchlan, T.M., 2022. Tackling grand challenges with projects: Five insights and a research agenda for project management theory and practice, *International Journal of Project Management*, 40(6), 601–607.

Part I

Projects

In Part I, we consider the nature of projects and their management. We describe how they help organizations achieve their strategic objectives, and how we define and measure success. Complex projects need their management adapted to deal with the complexity. We show how that can be achieved. Finally, we describe the auditing of projects and programs.

Chapter 2: Projects and their management

Rodney and Martina explain what we understand by projects and their management. A project is a temporary organization to which resources are assigned to deliver beneficial change. This definition captures the essential features of a project. It describes a project as a temporary organization. Other definitions call a project a temporary endeavour. It is an endeavour that lasts a limited period of time to deliver objectives. On one level those objectives are to deliver a beneficial outcome that provides value. On the other, it is to use resources to do work to deliver an output. If the project is to be profitable, the value must exceed the cost, so the project should be completed and the output delivered at a time and cost that makes the value worthwhile. The project needs to be managed and governed. Governance is a strategic-level process that provides direction. Management is an operational-level activity to guide the doing of the work. Management and governance are institutional-oriented processes. Alongside are people-oriented ones, leadership, and governmentality.

Chapter 3: Linking strategy and projects through strategic initiatives

V. K. Narayanan explores how projects can be linked to strategy through strategic initiatives. Strategic initiatives represent a type of program that actualizes strategy implementation. They represent groups of interdependent projects which contribute to the strategy of a company, require significant coordination between top and middle managers, and thus offer a bridge between strategy and program

DOI: 10.4324/9781003274179-2

management. They usually emerge from strategy redirection and unfold over time. Being the designated architects of a firm's strategy, senior management must fulfil six additional interlinked roles in strategic initiatives: alignment, choosing their leaders, sponsorship, mentoring, leverage of institutional capital, and dealing with legacy systems. The leaders of strategic initiatives face contexts (a) characterized by conflicts, (b) where their responsibility exceeds their authority, (c) with ongoing alignment, and (d) that demand extreme flexibility. Because alignment is a dynamic concept, the leaders need to continually negotiate the boundaries of their tasks, and manage the expectations of senior management and other power brokers in the organization. Resource bricolage, negotiation with internal markets, and continual aligning are central to their success. Human resource functions in the organization have a central role to play in the development of leaders of strategic initiatives.

Chapter 4: Project success

Despite decades of research on project-based work, the nature of and our ability to comprehensively and clearly define what we mean by "project success" remains a surprisingly elusive challenge. Contradictions and complications abound in identifying the standards for a successful project, often with negative consequences for project organizations that misidentify critical elements in these new initiatives. As our knowledge of project theory deepens and projects in ever-wider arenas of technical and commercial settings are developed, our understanding of what constitutes a successful project has undergone a similar evolutionary development. Jeff Pinto and Lavignon Ika address the changing nature of project success, unravelling the surprising complexity that underlies a comprehensive understanding of success, and as well, pointing to a number of important paradoxes and challenges in success. Finally, we offer several recommendations for practicing project managers as they manage for success.

Chapter 5: Managing project complexity

Rodney and Martina describe the nature of the complexity of projects. We describe the dimensions of complexity. We consider the practitioner view with six dimensions and the academic view with two dimensions. With the academic view, we meet for the first time the concept that conventional project management cannot manage complex projects. We then consider the nature of uncertainty and how it leads to bounded rationality and bounded manageability. It also leads to the difference between puzzles and mysteries. Complex projects are mysteries which require innovation. Conventional project management is not good at innovation. We then consider what has been written over the years about planning under uncertainty. We end with some views on megaprojects.

Chapter 6: Auditing projects and programs

Martina introduces auditing as a method to govern projects and programs and organize learning. We offer a systematic way of auditing and describe the audit process, methods, roles, and values to ensure audits and reviews provide meaningful learning opportunities to project and program teams and to the project-oriented organization. We conceptualize the audit as a communication system, which stresses the need for clear roles, and communication policies. Finally, the chapter discusses the responsibility of the PMO and provides tips for successfully performing project management audits.

Chapter 2

Projects and their management

Rodney Turner and Martina Huemann

Introduction

In this chapter, we consider what we understand by projects and their management. A project is a temporary organization to which resources are assigned to deliver beneficial change. This definition captures the essential features of a project. It describes a project as a temporary organization. Other definitions call a project a temporary endeavour. It is an endeavour that lasts a limited period of time to deliver objectives. On one level those objectives are to deliver a beneficial outcome that provides value. On the other, it is to use resources to do work to deliver an output. If the project is to be profitable, the value must exceed the cost, so the project should be completed and the output delivered at a time and cost that makes the value worthwhile. The project needs to be managed and governed. Governance is a strategic-level process that provides direction. Management is an operational-level activity to guide the doing of the work. Management and governance are institutional-oriented processes. Alongside are people-oriented ones, leadership, and governmentality.

Projects

There are several related definitions of projects. We start with the main one we want to use, that by Rodney and Ralf Müller (Turner, 2014; Turner & Müller, 2003).

DOI: 10.4324/9781003274179-X

> A project is a temporary organization to which resources are assigned to deliver beneficial change.

There are three elements to this definition, which we discuss below:

1 The project is a temporary organization
2 That organization is an agency for assembling resources to do work
3 That work will deliver a change which we expect will provide a benefit – the organization is an agency for change

The Project Management Institute (2021) in the seventh edition of its body of knowledge defines a project as:

> A project is a temporary effort to create value through a unique product, service, or result.

This defines the project as a temporary effort rather than a temporary organization, so it focuses on the work rather than the organization. It does not mention the resources but they are implied to undertake the effort. It describes the change as a product service or result. It emphasizes that the product, service, or results should provide value. There has been a change from PMI's sixth edition to the seventh edition. The definition in the sixth edition (PMI, 2017), was more like Association for Project Management's (APM) below, saying the purpose of the project was to deliver the product service or result. Little mention was made of the value or benefit desired. PMI in the introduction to the seventh edition says the focus on value is an important change. The PMI definition also mentions the dreaded word unique, which we discuss further below.

The APM, 2019 gives a definition for project management, but from that definition, we can draw out a definition of a project:

> A project is an endeavour to deliver specific objectives subject to defined acceptance criteria, and those objectives should be delivered within constraints of time and cost.

This focuses just on the deliverables the project will produce, the change, or product, service, or results, but that deliverable is subject to performance criteria (quality) and time and cost, the dreaded triple constraint.

So the third objective is different from the first two. The first two say the primary objective is to produce a result that works to deliver value or benefit. The second just says that the primary objective is to produce a result. In Chapter 4, Jeff Pinto and Lavignon Ika describe project success. Throughout the chapter we write we use two dimensions of success (Turner & Xue, 2018):

1 Project success is that the project deliverable, the change, product, service, or result, should work and be operated to deliver the expected value or benefit
2 Project management success is that the deliverable, the change, product, service, or result, is delivered subject to the performance criteria (quality) and constraints of time and cost.

So there are four features of a project which we discuss n turn:

1 The beneficial change, that is the product, service, or result and the value it delivers
2 The temporary organization: indeed we describe three organizations associated with a project
3 The resources
4 The dreaded uniqueness.

Beneficial change

We consider projects as agents for change (Huemann, 2022; Huemann & Silvius, 2017).

Figure 2.1 shows that a project delivers results over three levels:

1 the output
2 the outcome
3 goals

The output: this is the change, product, service, or results delivered by the project. The output may be concrete or more abstract in nature. It may be a new building, road, or tunnel. It may be a new computer system. It may be a new product and the machinery to make that product. A more abstract output may be a new way of working or a new service provided to people. The success of achieving the output to the desired constraints will be judged on the last day of the project.

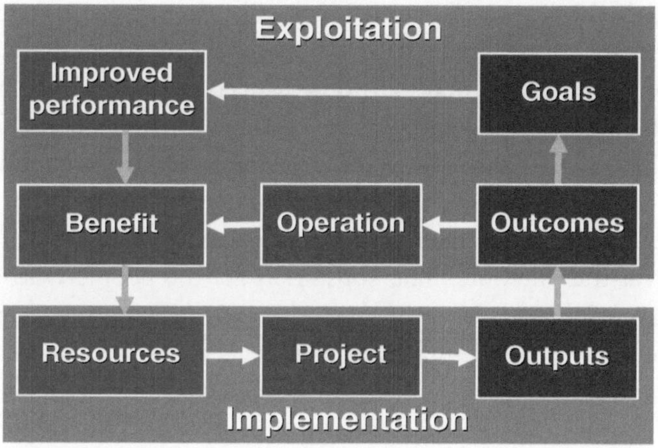

Figure 2.1: Results-based view of the beneficial change from projects

The output introduces the role of the investor and the owner. The investor is the organization that decides it is worthwhile to build the output, and sources the resources to do it. They benefit from either owning and operating the output or selling it. They expect that the benefit will repay the cost of building the output. The owner is the organization that owns and operates the output post-project and gets benefit from its operation, which either repays the cost of buying it or building it. The investor and the owner roles can held by one organization. In Chapter 10, Graham Winch uses the word owner to describe an organization that is effectively the investor. But he is focusing on that organization's need to define and own the business case pre- and during the project and to ensure the benefits are achieved. In Chapter 7, Ofer Zwikael and Jack Meredith use the term "project owner" to describe an individual working for that organization who leads on those responsibilities. So that is compatible with what we have said but is focusing on the need to own the business case pre- and during the project. They are interested in the success of the investment. Project owner and project sponsor as individual roles are often used synonymously. In Chapter 25, Lynn Crawford comprehensively discusses the project sponsor, which is considered an individual role or a group role.

The outcome: The outcome relates to the investment. It is a longer-term perspective, going beyond the single project. The delivery of the investment is often performed by a sequence of projects or a combination of projects and programs. The output will provide the owner organization with new competencies, the ability to do new things. That is the project outcome. The operation of those competencies will provide the value or benefit. The benefit will usually be financial but may be non-financial, such as social and ecologic-related benefits. We give examples of non-financial benefits below. The success of achieving the outcome, and the value or benefits the project produces, will be judged in the months following the project.

Two further roles are identified. The operators are the people who operate the output to deliver the outcome. The consumers are the people who consume the service or product produced by the operation of the outcome, paying for it to provide the benefit, or benefiting from it in other non-financial ways. They are also called end users.

The goal: The goal also relates to the investment. With time higher level goals may be obtained. The success of achieving the goals and their profitability will be judged in the years following the project.

We think there is some value in giving examples of the output, outcome, and goals. We describe what they mean for each type of project using examples from Turner (2020).

Example of an IT Project: It needed several attempts to computerize the despatch of ambulances in London. The fourth project was a successful attempt. The *project output* was a computer system. The system had three main components:

- Call receipt: A 999 call would be received. An operator would use the computer system to locate the call on a map.
- Vehicle location: The computer system would locate the nearest free vehicle. It may not be the nearest in distance but the nearest in time.
- Vehicle despatch: The system would send a message to the vehicle to answer the call.

National standards had been set for how quickly calls should be answered, which London Ambulance was failing to achieve. The *outcome* related to the main non-financial benefit that the London Ambulance Service could meet the national standards. But there would also be non-financial benefits in terms of improved patient health and lives saved. Productivity should also improve enabling the same number of people to handle more calls. The *goals* were that with time the health of the population of London should improve, and the faith of the people of London in the system should improve.

Example of a Construction Project: The construction project is the construction of a north-south metro line in the city of Amsterdam. The *output* is a railway line, consisting of track, signalling, stations, and rolling stock. The *outcome* is reflected in the stated desired benefits which are to:

- connect the north and south of the city, and both to the city centre.
- improve the efficiency of the transport system.
- reduce traffic.
- support economic development and tourism.

Interestingly these are all non-financial. There is no mention of making profits from selling tickets. The purpose of the sale of tickets is to pay for the project. The fourth objective is effectively the *goal*. With time the economy of Amsterdam will improve and tourists will be better served, hopefully increasing the number of visitors.

Example of an Organizational change project: The objective of this project is to improve antibiotic sustainability in nine European countries. The objective of the project is not to achieve antibiotic sustainability, which is impossible, but to better manage it. The *outputs* of the projects are procedures for managing antibiotic sustainability in hospitals and other health facilities, measures of their use, and courses for training people in their use. There is also a desire to create an international network of experts. The desired benefits are to improve antibiotic use in the nine European countries, with the potential goal of achieving antibiotic sustainability.

All three projects have non-financial benefits.

Temporary organization

Of the three definitions above, only Turner and Müller (2003) call a project a temporary organization. PMI (2021) and APM (2019) both call the project a temporary activity. Turner and Müller suggest that the investor wants to undertake an investment, and so transfers resources to a temporary organization to do the work of the project to deliver the investment. PMI and APM suggest that the work could be done by a group of people working within the routine organization. Müller and Turner differentiate between a temporary organization and a temporary task undertaken by a routine organization.

In talking about project organization, (Chapter 10), we suggest that a project might give a package of work to the routine organization. Is it a project, or is it a task undertaken by the routine organization? The answer to that question is how the parent organization wants to represent it. In his book (Turner, 2014), Rodney gives the example of a former student of his, who was a maintenance engineer with a telecommunications company. He was doing a lot of maintenance tasks, every one of which was different. Rodney wanted to say that was routine work, but the student wanted to say every task was a project. Who is Rodney to say? If it helps the student view his work as a series of projects, then that is the way forward. Crawford et al. (2005) say that in categorizing projects, an organization will develop its own vocabulary and decide what it wants to call projects. Martina Huemann takes a slightly different view. What is called a project must be viable, it needs to involve a certain complexity and it needs to bring meaning. Calling a simple task a project, because a certain person is doing it the first time, might not be adding much value and we end up in a projectitis, calling every task with a temporary aspect a project.

Rolf Lundin & Anders Söderholm (1995) first developed the idea of the project as a temporary organization. In the same issue of the journal, Johann Packendorf further developed the concept, saying that viewing the project as a temporary organization might improve the rigour of project management research. Rene Bakker, Robert DeFillippi, and Jörg Sydow (2016) organized a track on temporary organizing at the EGOS conference in 2015, which resulted in a special issue of the journal organization studies. As the title of their editorial suggests, they looked at promises, processes, and problems of temporary organizing. They identified three key issues:

1 How to theorize and deal with time. This was a key issue for Lundin and Söderholm (1995). Time is a central variable and not just a boundary condition.
2 How to explore and relate what is "permanent" and what is "temporary". This is a fuzzy issue and as we will explore a bit more below, it is a social construct.
3 How to empirically study temporary organizing. One of Packendorf's (1995) aims was to make project management research more rigorous. Most of the papers in the special issue were qualitative case studies, but Bakker et al. suggest alternative methodologies. My paper with Ralf Müller at the EGOS conference was not included in the special issue and was used in structural equation modelling (Müller et al., 2016).

There is fuzziness about what is permanent and what is temporary. The oldest organization is the Roman Catholic Church at 2,000 years old. There are several Japanese and South Korean organizations more than 1,000 years old. They are permanent on timescales that matter. The project with the longest duration from first work to commissioning was the Rhine to Danube canal. Work was started by Charlemagne in 792, and it was commissioned in 1992. The average life of a Fortune 500 company is 60 years. What is permanent and what is temporary is a social construct. An investing organization which views itself as permanent wants to develop a beneficial change, and so creates an organization which it views as temporary to undertake the change. Usually, the project finishes and the investor enjoys the investment. There are examples of projects which outlive the investor, and a new investing organization has to take them over.

Carroll (1995) suggests that the success of an organizational form depends on its ability to attract resources. Projects are very effective at attracting resources because they are an effective way of managing change. They can deliver change in a fast and flexible way, in ways that cannot be achieved in a routine organization. They can also be used to prototype new ways of working. Turner and Müller (2003) describe projects as agencies for change. Carroll also suggests that an organization's longevity is an indication of its efficiency. Projects are effective at delivering change but are an inefficient way of working, so as soon as the change is delivered the project should be disbanded and routine management adopted to manage the new asset delivered.

Graham Winch (2014) suggests there are three organizations involved in the management of projects, Figure 2.2:

1 The project is a temporary organization that delivers the beneficial change.
2 The investor is a permanent organization that wants the beneficial change, and so creates the temporary organization to assign resources to, to do the work. The investor may be a routine organization or a project-based or project-oriented organization.
3 The investor often does not own the resources needed to do the work of the project, and so hires the resources from a contractor.

Resources

The project is an agency for assembling resources to do the work to deliver the project output. The main resources are people, materials, and money, but can

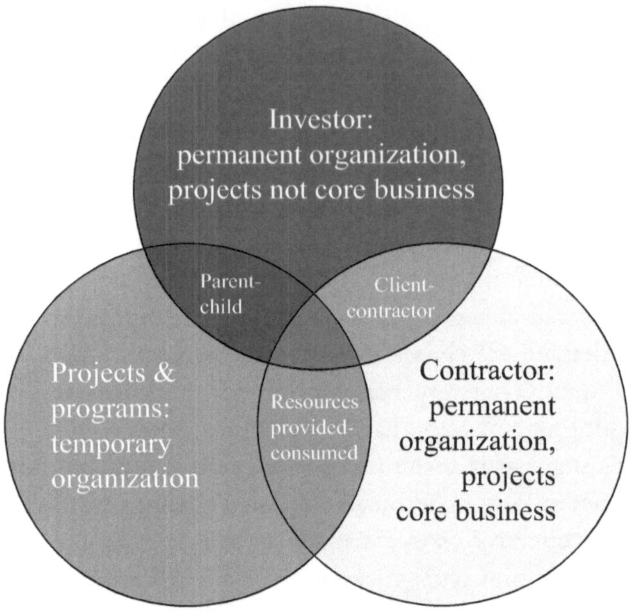

Figure 2.2: Three organizations involved in the management of projects, after Winch (2014)

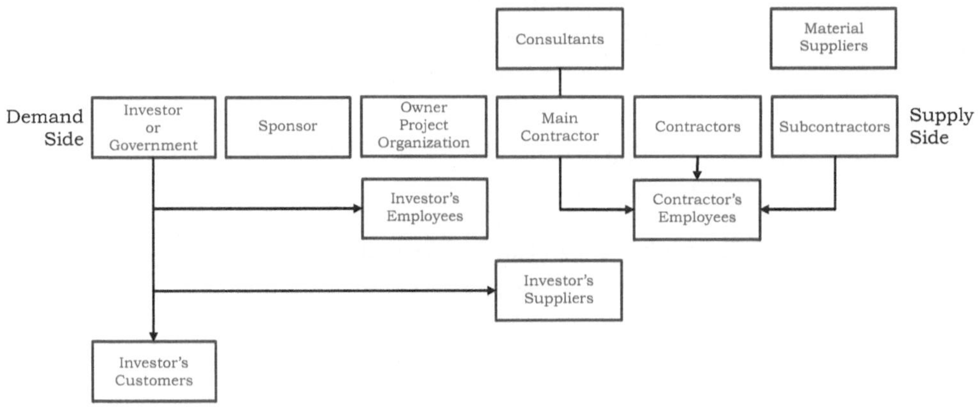

Figure 2.3: Internal stakeholders who provide the resources to do the work of the project

include other things such as information or political support. Above we met contractors who provide people to the investor to do the work of the project. Other contractors include sub-contractors and material suppliers. Figure 2.3 shows a range of internal stakeholders, and organizations who provide the resources to do the work of the project. They range from the supply side, those organizations who primarily supply resources, to the demand side, those who use them. Shown are:

- material suppliers.
- sub-contractors.
- contractors.
- consultants.
- the main contractor responsible for the design and delivery.
- the investors' project organization responsible for the overall management of the project.
- the sponsor discussed further below.
- the investor.

Also shown are employees in many of these organizations, who are the main people resources involved.

Uniqueness

Rodney in his books (Turner, 2014), has tended to say that projects are unique, novel, and transient. They are transient, the organization is temporary, and the work to deliver the beneficial change lasts a limited amount of time. The concepts of uniqueness and novelty were important to us in the early days of project management when we were trying to differentiate projects from routine operations, but it is less important now. Many of the definitions of projects talk about the temporary organization being unique, or the work unique. Of the definitions above, only PMIs use the word unique and it suggests the project's output is unique. In Chapter 32, Bent Flyvbjerg suggests that people abuse the concept of uniqueness. He gives examples of people who say because my project is unique I have nothing to learn from other projects. Clearly, that attitude is extremely short-sighted. No two organizations, whether temporary or permanent are identical. Every organization is unique. However, organizations have similarities, and there is a lot to learn by building on the similarities. No two human beings are identical, but we have a lot to learn from similarities. We suggest there are a range of project types:

- repeaters: virtually routine batch processing.
- runners: quite similar to previous projects.

- strangers: essentially different from previous projects but with some common elements.
- aliens: unlike anything we have done before.

But we can always gain experience from what people have done in the past, and we can conduct experiments to improve our understanding. The Gotthard Base Tunnel (Drouin & Turner, 2022) is the deepest railway tunnel ever built, at the time of construction the longest tunnel ever built, and drilled through rocks that had not been drilled through before. But they learnt a lot from previous tunnels and conducted test drilling. The concept of uniqueness has really served its purpose. No two organizations, temporary or permanent, are identical. But we should all know we can learn from what other people do.

Multiple projects

In the early days of project management, people only researched and wrote about projects undertaken individually. However, since the early 1990s, people have recognized that projects often take place in groups of projects. The two main forms are programs and portfolios, though many forms are now recognized, including networks, sequences, and the project-based or project-oriented organization (Miterev et al., 2017; Turner & Miterev, 2019). A program is a collection of projects with a common objective. Often the objective is to introduce change, which can be poorly defined at the outset. The program is broken into smaller projects, which have clearly defined objectives. The completion of the early projects refines the understanding of the program objective. A portfolio is a collection of projects sharing resources. A portfolio is often a collection of projects to achieve an organization's strategic objectives. A project-oriented organization is one that does most of its work as projects. Different forms of multiple projects are described in later chapters of this book.

Management and governance

In its definition of project management, APM (2019) says management is the application of processes, methods, skills, knowledge, and experience to the achievement of the project's objectives. PMI (2021) gives a very similar definition, saying project management is the use of specific knowledge, skills, tools, and techniques to deliver something of value to people. Both suggest that management is the use of knowledge and skills, to apply processes, methods, and systems to the achievement of the project's objectives. Rodney in his book (Turner, 2014) emphasises the process (Chapter 20).

It is now common to also talk about governance. Some people unfortunately say governance when they mean management because they think it adds gravitas to their work.

Table 2.1 suggests that governance is a strategic-level activity which steers the organization. It is the systems, processes, and procedures which:

- provide direction to the organization, defining and balancing goals.
- define how work will be monitored and controlled.
- define the roles, responsibilities, and rights of and relationships between stakeholders.

Management is an operational-level activity to direct the doing of the work, through which objectives are achieved. According to Müller et al. (2020), it is a means to an end, executed within the boundaries set by governance.

Governance and management are institutional activities. Alongside each are people-oriented activities, governmentality, and leadership, respectively. Governmentality is the human side of governance. Dean (2010) suggests it is the overarching mechanism from which governance flows, and so is a policy-level

Table 2.1 Positioning governance, governmentality, management, and leadership (after Müller, 2019)

	Human agency	*Structure*
Steering	**Governmentality:** The way governors interact with those they govern. • Mentalities, rationalities, ways of interaction Ways chosen by those in governance roles to implement, maintain, and change the governance structure	**Governance:** Framework for managers to do work • Structures, policies, processes, etc. • Ways managers are held accountable for their work
Executing	**Leadership:** People-oriented activity to accomplish organizational objectives	**Management:** Goal and task-oriented activity to accomplish organizational objectives

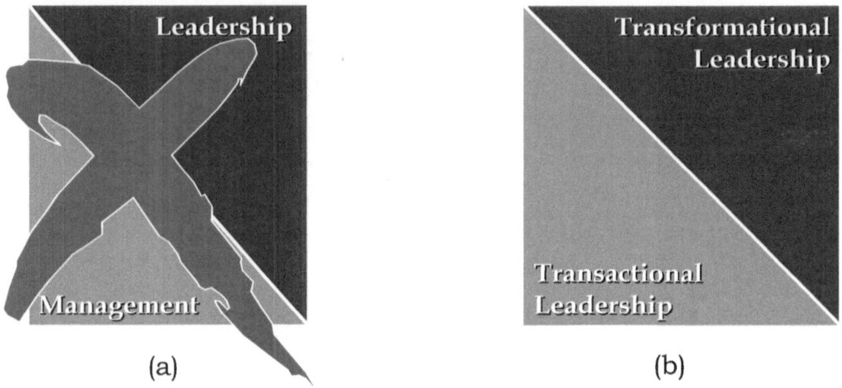

Figure 2.4: Leadership and management must operate together

activity. Governmentality defines how governors interact with those that they govern. Leadership is the human side of management. It is an operational-level activity, by which people are guided as to how to achieve their objectives.

Some people draw figures like Figure 2.4(a) with two dimensions. They draw a diagonal and say the bottom left is management and the top right is leadership. This is complete nonsense. You need both leadership and management. Henry Mintzberg (2013) says leadership without management is dysfunctional. It leads to lots of activity with no outcome. He says management without leadership is mediocre, it will function adequately. In fact the two dimensions are transactional leadership and transformational leadership, Bass (1990), Figure 2.4(b).

This book is about projects and their management and governance. We are not going to steal our thunder by saying more at this point.

Conclusion

This chapter aimed to set the ground for the handbook.

References and further reading

Bakker, R, DeFillippi, R & Sydw, J. (2016). Temporary organizing: promises, processes, problems. *Organization Studies,* 37(12), 1703–1719.

Bass, BM. (1990). From transactional to transformational leadership: learning to share the vision. *Organisational Dynamics,* 18(3), 19–31.

Carroll, GR. (1995). "On the organizational ecology of Chester I Barnard." In OE Williamson, (ed.), *Organizational Theory: From Chester Barnard to the Present and Beyond.* Oxford: Oxford University Press.

Crawford, LH, Hobbs, JB & Turner, JR. (2005). *Project Categorization Systems: Aligning Capability with Strategy for Better Results.* Project Management Institute.

Dean, M. (2010). *Governmentality: Power and Rule in Modern Society.* Thousand Oaks, CA: Sage.

Drouin, N & Turner, JR. (2022). *The Elgar Advanced Introduction to Megaprojects.* Cheltenham, and Northampton, MA: Edward Elgar.

Huemann, M. (2022). Celebrating the power of projects and their management. *International Journal of Project Management,* 40(1), 1–3.

Huemann, M & Silvius, G. (2017). Projects to create the future: managing projects meets sustainable development. *International Journal of Project Management,* 35(6), 1066–1070.

Lundin, RA & Söderholm, A. (1995). A theory of the temporary organization. *Scandinavian Journal of Management,* 11(4), 437–455.

Mintzberg, H. (2013). *Simply Managing.* Harlow, London, New York, Boston, MA, San Francisco, CA, Toronto, Sydney, Auckland, Singapore, Hong Kong, Tokyo, Seoul, Taipei, New Delhi, Cape Town Sao Paolo, Mexico City, Madrid, Amsterdam, Munich, Paris, Milan: FT Publishing International.

Miterev, M, Mancini, M & Turner, JR. (2017). Towards a design for the project-based organization. *International Journal of Project Management,* 35(3), 479–491.

Müller, R. (2019). Governance, governmentality and project performance: the role of sovereignty. *International Journal of Information Systems and Project Management,* 7(2), 5–17.

Müller, R, Drouin, N & Sankaran, S. (2020). *Organizational Project Management: Theory and Implementation.* Cheltenham and Northampton, MA: Edward Elgar.

Müller, R, Turner, JR, Shao, J, Andersen, ES & Kvalnes, O. (2016). Governance and ethics in temporary organizations: the mediating role of corporate governance. *Project Management Journal,* 47(6), 7–23.

Murray-Webster, R & Dalcher, D. (2019). *APM Body of Knowledge,* 7th Edition. Prince Risborough: Association for Project Management.

OECD. (2015). *G20/OECD Principles of Corporate Governance.* Paris: OECD Publishing.

Packendorf, J. (1995). Inquiring into the temporary organization: new directions for project management researc. *Scandinavian Journal of Management,* 11(4), 319–333.

Project Management Institute. (2017). *A Guide to the Project Management Body of Knowledge (PMBOK® Guide),* 6th Edition. Newtown Square, PA: Project Management Institute.

Project Management Institute. (2021). *A Guide to the Project Management Body of Knowledge (PMBOK® Guide),* 7th Edition. Newtown Square, PA: Project Management Institute.

Turner, JR. (2014). *The Handbook of Project-Based Management: Leading Strategic Change in Organizations,* 4th Edition. New York: McGraw-Hill.

Turner, JR. (2020). Investigating how governmentality and governance influence decision making on projects. *Project Leadership and Society,* 1, December, article 100003.

Turner, JR & Miterev, M. (2019). The organizational design of the project-based organization. *Project Management Journal,* 50(4), 487–498.

Turner, JR & Müller, R. (2003). On the nature of the project as a temporary organization. *International Journal of Project Management,* 21(1), 1–8.

Turner, JR & Xue, Y. (2018). On the success of megaprojects. *International Journal of Managing Projects in Business*, 11(3), 783–805.

Winch, GM. (2014). Three domains of project organising. *International Journal of Project Management,* 32(5), 721–731.

Xue, Y. (2009). *A Results-Based Monitoring and Evaluation System for Key Infrastructure Projects*, unpublished PhD Thesis, Lille School of Management, Lille, France.

Chapter 3

Linking strategy and projects through strategic initiatives

Vadake K. Narayanan

Introduction

- Eighteen Canadian major ports, all members of Green Marine (GM) a North American voluntary environmental certification organization for the marine industry, have been working proactively to improve port sustainability through a variety of initiatives, which have been considered important for the success of the ports (Hossain, Adams, & Walker, 2019).
- ALPHA, a rollout of an electronic road-tolling scheme, was a joint venture with three principal stakeholders (a mobile telephony provider, an automotive company, and an infrastructure firm) striving to enter the rapidly developing telematics market in the first few years after the turn of the millennium. The scheme was designed to put its parent organizations in a leadership position for future road-tolling initiatives (Klingebiel & De Meyer, 2013).
- During the 1990s, fast cycle approaches were introduced in the pharmaceutical industry, as pharmaceutical firms grasped the importance of being the first to reach the market with a new drug. Fast cycle capability and agility became core capabilities for firms but developing them involved many different paths. One path involved employing a set of experimental fast cycle projects with the understanding that lessons for these projects could be codified and transferred to other projects (Narayanan & DeFIllippi, 2012).

DOI: 10.4324/9781003274179-4

Although the above three cases may on the surface appear very dissimilar, each exemplifies what we would term a "strategic initiative," an initiative that is a special case of a program, (Chapter 34), and is central to the success of a strategy as conceived by the top management of an organization – be it private, nonprofit, or governmental. Strategic initiatives have in recent years emerged as major tools of strategy implementation.

Recent project management scholarship (e.g., Geraldi, Teerikangas, & Birollo, 2022) has emphasized the role of project, program, and portfolio management as a dynamic decision-making process where a particular organization may undertake a group of *interdependent* projects rather than a single independent project to accomplish organizational objectives. Indeed, today's projects typically take place as one of a group of projects, either a program or a portfolio of projects, unlike traditional project management which describes projects as delivering well-defined independent objectives. Some estimates suggest that the latter kind of project only accounts for less than 10% of all project activity. Indeed, strategic initiatives resemble a program of projects, because they represent a group of initiatives which contribute to the strategy of a company. SIs require significant coordination between top and middle managers and thus offer a bridge between strategic and program management. strategic initiatives have become significant for a company because the turbulence of their environments is pushing them into an era of strategic experimentation (Narayanan, Buche, & Kemmerer, 2003) beyond the four stages of strategic management originally conceptualized by McKinsey consultants (Gluck, Kaufman, & Walleck, 1982).

In this chapter, I will summarize the characteristics of strategic initiatives as a tool for strategy implementation. Strategic initiatives are deployed in widely different contexts, and their applicability extends beyond projectified organizations (Clegg & Courpasson, 2004) or project management organizations (Chinowsky, Diekmann, & O'Brien, 2010). This chapter is organized as follows: First, I will define SI, touching upon a wide range of contexts in which SIs are deployed but summarizing the central role of coordination between top and middle managers for their successful conduct. Second, drawing upon the literatures on program management, I will describe the major characteristics of strategic initiatives, distinguishing them from strategies and projects. Third, I will highlight the different roles of senior managers and leaders in this endeavor. A fourth section will suggest the central role of the Human Resources Department

(HRD) in the success of a strategic initiative. Finally, I will conclude with a call for more grounded research in this area that requires academic-industry collaboration.

Strategic initiatives: what are they?

Strategic initiatives are "temporary, coordinated undertakings for renewing or expanding the capabilities of an organization that has the potential to substantially impact its evolution and performance" (Lechner & Kreutzer, 2010). Unlike the concept of strategy that focuses on an organization's match with its environment, strategic initiatives are specific programs such as new business creation, new product development, or development of a specific capability. They have captured the attention not only of academics but also large corporations such as General Electric, Intel, Siemens, Helvetia, and Deutsche Bank to name a few.

Strategic initiatives tend to be very diverse, and this diversity is traceable to the tasks involved in completing a strategic initiative. As can be seen from the examples summarized in the introduction, on the surface, there is little in common between a sustainability initiative, the rollout of an electronic road-tolling scheme, and being a project in a fast cycle initiative. What makes each initiative 'strategic' is that each is considered necessary for the success of the respective organization's strategy and hence crucial to its *implementation.* Strategic initiatives may not resemble one another even within the same organization. Strategic initiatives operate in a change-filled context and hence are somewhat ambiguous with respect to objectives, timelines, and success criteria. The parameters of their success are negotiated and ill-defined, and hence *socially constructed.*

Strategic initiatives require coordination across organizational levels and sometimes (as in the case of ALPHA) external entities. Senior managers remain involved, along with middle and lower-level managers, and strategic initiatives activities substantially affect other parts of an organization, i.e., they are not self-contained. In the example of the fast cycle program above, the goal was to build fast cycle capability in the organization and hence the designated project teams had a significant responsibility to disseminate fast cycle principles across their organization (in addition to drug development). The managers of strategic initiatives have thus to be focused on problem-solving, problems that could be technical/scientific but more often involve dealing with organizational and political challenges.

Key differences between strategy, strategic initiatives and projects

As illustrated above, strategic initiatives typically involve *several* projects orchestrated under either a *technological or conceptual umbrella*, and these projects usually have significant organizational implications. In many cases, building significant organizational capabilities such as agility is initiated by senior management of a company as a strategic initiative, and is decomposed into a set of projects, sometimes termed heavyweight projects. When an initiative is charged with improving an existing capability, the initiative will be largely compatible with the knowledge, skills, technology, systems, values, and norms embedded in the organization's existing capabilities. The intent is to integrate what is learned within the group into the organization's existing capabilities in order to improve them; this form of learning can be called 'single-loop learning' (Argyris & Schön, 1978) or learning that reinforces established knowledge. However, to the extent the changes sought are intended to develop new capabilities, there will be fewer opportunities to draw on the knowledge, skills, and technology associated with existing capabilities. In such cases, the goal is to broaden the repertoire of organizational capabilities available to the organization. Because it often involves pursuing ideas or ways of doing things that are inconsistent with established practice, this is akin to prior double-loop learning (Argyris & Schön, 1978) or learning that 'challenges' established knowledge.

Strategic initiatives share several characteristics with programs:

1 The objectives of strategic initiative are broad and less defined and may change over time.
2 A strategic initiative project is *interdependent* with other projects in the SI in terms of operational activities.
3 Strategic initiatives have to *share* resources (funding and people primarily) with other strategic initiatives and the operating organization.

However, strategic initiatives are distinct in three major ways:

1 In cases where external partners are involved (as in the first example in the beginning), leaders of strategic initiatives are positioned to *shape* the objectives of the joint effort.
2 When a strategic initiative is oriented toward capability building, the strategic initiative will have to *interface* with other parts of the organization (i.e., not

merely the various elements of strategic initiatives), their internal customers who are likely to be affected by the output of the strategic initiative.

3 Strategic initiatives need to work in an *ongoing* manner with middle and senior management who are ultimately driving the strategy.
4 Senior management may appoint leaders of a strategic initiative for political *viability* rather than technical expertise or experience.

Strategic initiatives usually emerge from a strategy redirection, and they unfold over time. As we have seen, they resemble projects because they must operate within timelines; however, they are different from both strategies and projects in several ways. In Table 3.1, I have summarized the key differences among strategy, strategic initiatives and projects.

As summarized in Table 3.1, strategic initiatives are tools of strategy implementation, and hence they typically originate from the top of an organization. Although strategy often seeks competitive advantage, strategic initiatives, being focused on implementation, typically focus on capability building and are thus one step removed from the pursuit of competitive advantage. Strategy effectiveness is often measured in the long run, but the time horizons for a strategic initiative's completion are typically short to medium-term. They require coordination across organizational levels, as upper echelons will rely on lower levels to accomplish several tasks necessary for implementation. Strategy formulation and strategic initiatives both require a holistic view of an organization. At least in theory, strategy determines an organization's structures and systems, but strategic initiatives must work *within* existing structures and systems. Strategy confronts both uncertainty and ambiguity, and the criteria of strategy success are somewhat socially constructed; strategic initiatives are also riddled with ambiguity in their criteria of assessment and metrics of success. Both generation and deployment of resources are central tasks in strategy, but in the case of strategic initiatives, resources are typically raised over time as and when deemed necessary.

The way strategic initiative differ from strategies also points to their differences from typical projects. The latter have *relatively* specific and self-contained tasks, with clear deadlines, but strategic initiatives have flexible timelines and must be adaptable in terms of accomplishing their goals. The budget, cost, and time objectives that characterize a project are more difficult to establish in a strategic

Table 3.1 Differences among three concepts: strategy, strategic initiative, project

	Strategy	*Strategic initiative*	*Project*
Focus	Competitive Advantage	Strategy Implementation Capability Building	Specific projects
Time Frame	Long run, often undefined	Short to medium Flexible time boundaries	Clear time boundaries
Characteristics of the task	Uncertain and ambiguous	High levels of ambiguity	Relatively clear
Organizational conception	Systemic	Interdependent with existing structures and systems	Relatively self-contained
Existing structures and systems	As a dependent variable that can be changed	1 Existing structures as a given 2 Internal structure linked to a larger organization	1 Existing structures as a given 2 Relatively self-contained except in matrix
Resources	Focus on both generation and utilization	Flexible allocation over the initiative	More or less specified in the beginning
Metrics of success	Socially constructed	Ambiguous	Relatively clear

initiative, where most of these objectives must be viewed much more flexibly. Both work *within* existing organizational structures and systems, but strategic initiatives typically will be called upon to take a system-wide perspective on its activities. Whereas resources are typically negotiated at the beginning of a project, in the case of strategic initiatives resource negotiation extends over its life span.

From a human resource perspective, strategic initiative offers both challenges and opportunities. A leader must be capable of placating multiple constituencies with somewhat differing or even conflicting goals; their constituencies extend beyond the leaders' senior management and dedicated teams to include external partners and stakeholders. Strategic initiatives also offer their leaders and team members access and visibility to top managers that a typical project may not. Viewed either way, the *socio-political* component of the job is significantly more substantive in the case of strategic initiatives than in the case of project leaders.

The tasks to be performed in a strategic initiative

Strategic initiatives require *multilevel* coordination, I will outline the key tasks to be performed by (1) senior management and (2) leaders of strategic initiative and their teams, as well as the coordination between the two levels (Figure 3.1).

Senior management

Being the designated architects of a firm's strategy, senior management has the ultimate responsibility for strategy implementation and hence also for the crafting of requisite strategic initiatives, monitoring their progress, and when needed their disbanding. Although classical management roles continue to be important, because of the unique characteristics of strategic initiatives, senior management must fulfill six (additional) interlinked roles:

1 *Alignment.* Unlike projects, which are typically self-contained, strategic initiatives are linked to other facets of implementation. Hence a key role of the senior management is to keep the progress of a strategic initiative aligned to other activities in strategy implementation. Alignment often requires adaptive planning of strategic initiatives and brings with it the need to modify their activities along the way. For example, in multi-partner initiatives such as the rollout of an electronic road-tolling scheme (see introduction), when the objectives or the commitments of a partner change, strategic initiatives will have to adapt to the changes.

2 *Choice of leaders of strategic initiatives.* In the case of strategic initiatives, senior managers often get involved in the selection of team leaders, a task that is not left to a PMO (if an organization has one). Ease of achieving alignment and hence 'cultural' and 'social fit' may play major roles in selection, especially in an organization with a pool of qualified team leaders. In the fast cycle initiative (summarized in the introduction) in an organization with many capable project leaders, some of the leaders were chosen from statistical analysis and project management groups over other individuals with significant drug development leadership experience in biochemical fields.

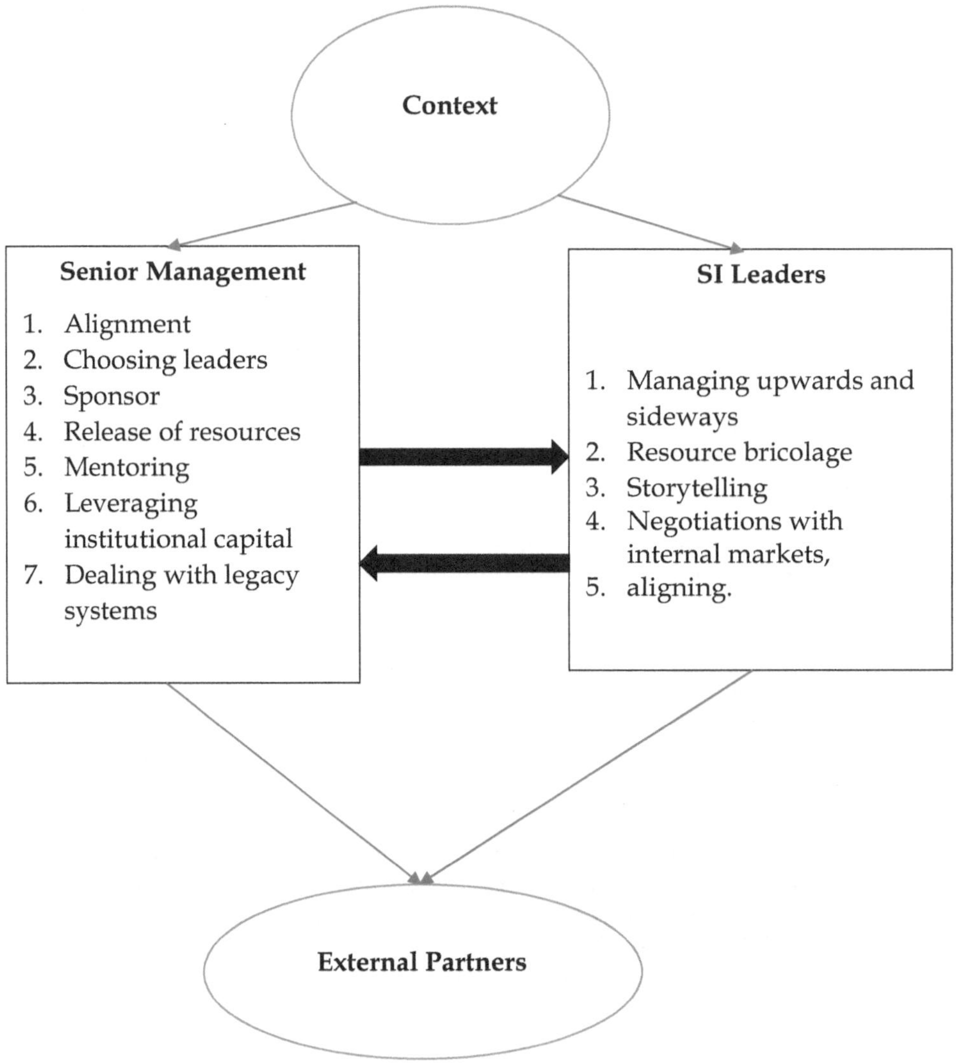

Figure 3.1: Multilevel tasks in strategic initiatives

3 *Sponsoring*. A major role played by senior management, sponsorship involves advocating for the strategic initiative and assuring adequate resources (money, power, and attention) flow into them as and when necessary. As I noted earlier, resource requirements for strategic initiatives are continually negotiated. Sponsors not only screen resource requests to ensure alignment but because

of their closer proximity to power bases in their organizations, they are better positioned to justify their need for resource providers.

4 *Mentoring.* Mentoring involves shepherding leaders of strategic initiatives in appropriate directions and provides a major mechanism for alignment. Because leaders generally tend to be seasoned leaders themselves, mentoring involves less actual teaching but more making sure the leaders are aware of the resources, pockets of resistance and support, as well as political sensitivities of key senior management actors.
5 *Leveraging institutional capital.* Senior managers can facilitate this activity, by (a) encouraging project leaders to tap institutional knowledge by referring them to individuals who can help; (b) establishing systems to promote access, use, collection, and preservation of data; and (c) enabling a supportive culture. Senior managers are probably more informed than project leaders about individuals in the organizations' centralized units and in other parts that may be useful sources of information about how the company handled a similar initiative or challenge. Putting people in touch with each other – knowledge brokering – not only enables tapping into institutional knowledge but also sends a powerful signal that the activity is recognized and valued in the organization.
6 *Dealing with legacy systems.* Legacy systems such as IT, human resource data records, or even budgetary systems can block the progress of a strategic initiative. For example, access to data (for decisions) is often determined by IT departments with limited consideration of the broader implications, and this may serve as a hindrance when someone wants to mount an urgent search for individuals with specialized knowledge. In a global organization, budgetary constraints designed for the control of normal operations may preclude the leader from seeking in-person counsel from someone else in another country. Such legacy systems can also facilitate a search. Human resource professionals can assist senior managers in centralized functions or centers of excellence to understand how they can promote access to and the utilization of knowledge. The senior managers are uniquely positioned to address the challenges of legacy systems.

Leaders of strategic initiatives

Leaders with project management experience have a set of skill sets that are useful for strategic initiative implementation: the ability to break down a complex task into simpler assignable tasks, set up and maintain timelines, coordinate across assigned tasks, and bring attention to resources both monetary and human. However, as the above discussion suggests, strategic initiatives present them with more uncertain situations than in the case of relatively self-contained projects, situations that demand attention to alignment, higher levels of flexibility, agility in problem-solving, ambiguous effectiveness criteria, and coordination with many other parts of an organization. I will outline their challenges in terms of (1) The context, (2) Enablers of success, (3) Major tasks, and (4) Opportunities.

The context. Many individuals are saddled with leadership of a strategic initiative *on top* of their ongoing jobs and hence they may have more than one superior (much like in a matrix organization). They may also have to lead individuals who are not direct reports. Additionally, alignment with strategy is an ongoing demand in any initiatives of this nature. The context is thus:

1 *Filled with potential for conflicts.* Unlike in many matrix organizations, where there are reasonably understood conflict resolution mechanisms, strategic initiatives demand ongoing conflict management processes. Thus, leaders often must work with competing and conflicting demands from different superiors and stakeholders.
2 *Responsibility without authority.* leaders will have to work both with team members and the larger organization over whom they have limited authority. The context necessitates attentiveness to others' concerns and compromises.
3 *Ongoing alignment and problem-solving.* The primary criterion of effectiveness in a strategic initiative is its congruence with the intended strategy, which itself is an evolving and sometimes elusive concept. These criteria are often socially constructed, that is, they depend upon human judgments without any specifiable linkage to objective criteria.
4 *Need for flexibility.* The context also promotes the need for flexibility. To use a sports analogy, strategic initiatives resemble soccer more than (US) football, where clearly executed plans are typical.

The context faced by leaders of strategic initiative and teammates is thus ambiguous and fluid and promotes the need to pay attention to the social and political factors in an organization, in addition to the substantive solutions to various challenges.

Enablers of success. The leader needs to maintain at least three perceptions in order to be regarded as successful in this context. I have deliberately used the term 'perceptions' because the focus is on how judgments are made about the leader by *other* individuals, primarily senior management, and not always necessarily tied to objective measurable metrics:

1 *Commitment.* From the senior management's point of view, a primary source of confidence in the leaders is their demonstrated commitment to the strategy that underlies the strategic initiative. Strategic initiatives are seen as tools to implement strategies; commitment would be judged in terms of alignment and concrete metrics such as time cost and budget, although important, are likely to be viewed as operational metrics. In the example of fast cycle teams above, one of the project teams recommended disbanding the drug development project on the grounds that the project created inadequate value. Although the recommendation was unusual for the company, the team was judged to be highly effective in its contribution to the strategic initiative: a focus on building organizational capability instead of commercializing the drug.
2 *Credibility.* Because of the ambiguities inherent in strategic initiatives, a critical marker of success is the credibility of the leader and their team. Because strategic initiatives and their teams are like to be chosen by senior management, in the beginning, they may enjoy credibility, but this credibility needs to be nurtured over the course of the initiative. Credibility extends beyond 'truth' as popularly conceived: Senior managers often pay attention to members of the larger organization (or external partners) in terms of how they see strategic initiatives progressing. Leaders of strategic initiatives are expected to account for the larger organizational concerns in their proposed options, to avoid roadblocks that could be erected during an alternative's rollout. Thus, credibility may also depend on the leader's competence in execution and its ability to get other players on board during the rollout.
3 *Communication.* Because of the shifting needs of alignment, a strategic initiative involves continual negotiations with senior management, other parts of the organization, and external partners (if involved). Leaders and members must be capable of communicating with a wide array of individuals. And hence a marker of their success will be the ease with which they are intelligible to their audiences who may not have the same grasp of project and initiative details as the strategic initiative team.

Major tasks. In addition to problem-solving skills, project leaders will need to accomplish five major tasks:

1 *Managing upwards and sideways.* Unlike typical projects, strategic initiatives are unlikely to be clearly defined in the beginning. Because alignment is a dynamic concept, leaders will not only have to continually negotiate the boundaries of their tasks and manage the expectations of the senior management but also other power brokers in their organizations.
2 *Resource bricolage.* Strategic initiatives being perennially under-resourced, leaders often have to find creative ways to identify and utilize resources. This may also involve 'leaning' on other resource holders to accomplish tasks. Resource bricolage is an unwritten function of the leaders.
3 *Negotiations with internal markets.* Sometimes, leaders are expected to identify individuals who could be part of their teams. In these circumstances, the leaders will need to have some awareness of the internal markets (including useful teammates and helpful others). Their success in recruiting appropriate team members may determine the fate of their initiative.
4 *Perpetual aligning.* As I have earlier noted several times, the trajectory of a strategic initiative is not likely to be straightforward, because strategy implementation itself is filled with surprises (Mintzberg, 1978). Leaders and members will have to continually revise their plans to be in sync with the changing realities of strategy implementation.
5 *Storytelling.* One of the central functions of a leader is communication. In dealing with senior management, external partners, and team members, the leaders will need to communicate their ideas to audiences with widely differing familiarity with their goals and accomplishments. Creating a credible narrative and delivering it, or storytelling, is a major part of their toolkit.

In sum, the leaders' tasks are ambiguous and demand higher levels of collaboration with senior managers. Although they are generally more involving and perhaps more stressful than a typical project, they also come with significant rewards.

Opportunities. Being invited to be part of a strategic initiative is a token of recognition, although the tasks are often piled on top of regular work commitments. Selection to be the leader of a strategic initiative is typically not random or an afterthought but the output of a deliberative process among senior managers. In turn, this offers high visibility to the chosen individuals with an opportunity to build strong relationships with some senior managers. Three opportunities may be awaiting them on successful completion of the strategic initiative:

1 In some cases, leadership positions are testing grounds for advancement in management ranks. The visibility they gain, the relationships they build, and the credibility they gather are all useful for fulfillment in their future senior roles.
2 In almost all cases, a strategic initiative provides individuals with a broader view of their organizations than the ones they would have had before. This is particularly useful because they are likely to garner prestige in their current positions.
3 External markets are likely to notice when a strategic initiative and their teams have had remarkable accomplishments. This in turn suggests that the leaders will often have career enhancements possible outside of their own organizations.

As can be seen from the above, during strategy implementation, strategic initiatives are often instituted for building organizational capabilities and technical infrastructure. Many tasks labeled 'projects' fall under the umbrella of a strategic initiative, but these 'projects' are somewhat different from the typical projects as sketched in Table 3.1. Nonetheless, strategic initiatives provide a crucial bridge between strategy and projects.

Role of human resource development in strategic initiatives

In the last couple of decades, there has been a concerted advocacy for the role of human resources in project management (Huemann, Keegan, & Turner, 2007). HR also plays (or should play) a significant role in strategic initiatives; I will summarize four ways in which HR should be engaged with strategic initiatives:

1 *Selection of leaders and members*. Although leaders are typically chosen by the senior managers, HR can add a dimension to their deliberations, by reinforcing the need for attention to the soft skills of the leaders (as emphasized in this chapter).
2 *Mentoring*. HR can be a significant aid to the senior managers in the mentoring of the leaders of strategic initiatives. While senior managers are generally likely to be task-focused, HR can 'educate' leaders on such skill sets as storytelling.
3 *Institutional capital*. HR probably has broad access to individuals in an organization. They are therefore a rich resource for leveraging institutional capital. Additionally, they can also assist leaders in finding talent within their organizations (Internal labor markets).

4 *Post SI utilization of talent.* Both leaders and team members have not merely shown their ability to perform during a strategic initiative, but they also have acquired significant skill sets and institutional knowledge. HR can play a role in ensuring these knowledge gains are utilized after the completion of strategic initiatives.

HR can thus enhance the performance of organizations not merely by their functional expertise but by ensuring the fit between the individuals and the tasks. Few functional areas are better fitted than HR to ensure the need for soft skills among leaders and team members.

Conclusion

As I have articulated, strategic initiatives provide a bridge between strategy and projects, and offer a major stepping stone for individuals in their careers. The concept of a strategic initiative is relatively new, and both industry and academic practitioners are in the process of deepening their knowledge of strategic initiatives. As we move forward, we will gain greater clarity in how strategic initiatives benefit from project skills and how they enable project managers in their career progression. This process of knowledge creation can be accelerated by collaborative research between practicing managers and research-focused scholars. So, I end with a call for programmatic research in a strategic initiative that links academic researchers and leaders. Of strategic initiatives.

References and further reading

Argyris, C., & Schön, D. A. (1978). *Organizational Learning: A Theory of Action Perspective.* Reading, MA: Addison-Wesley.

Chinowsky, P. S., Diekmann, J., & O'Brien, J. (2010). Project organizations as social networks. *Journal of Construction Engineering and Management, 136*(4), 452–458.

Clegg, S., & Courpasson, D. (2004). Political hybrids: Tocquevillean views on project organizations. *Journal of Management Studies, 41*(4), 525–547.

Geraldi, J., Teerikangas, S., & Birollo, G. (2022). Project, program and portfolio management as modes of organizing: Theorizing at the intersection between mergers and acquisitions and project studies. *International Journal of Project Management,* 439–452.

Gluck, F., Kaufman, S., & Walleck, A. S. (1982). The four phases of strategic management. *The Journal of Business Strategy, 2*(3), 9.

Hossain, T., Adams, M., & Walker, T. R. (2019). Sustainability initiatives in Canadian ports. *Marine Policy, 106*, 103519.

Huemann, M., Keegan, A. E., & Turner, J. R. (2007). Human resource management in the project-oriented company: A review. *International Journal of Project Management, 25*, 315–323.

Klingebiel, R., & De Meyer, A. (2013). Becoming aware of the unknown: Decision making during the implementation of a strategic initiative. *Organization Science, 24*(1), 133–153.

Lechner, C, and Kreutzer, M. (2010). Coordinating growth initiatives in multi-unit firms. *Long Range Planning 43*(1), 6–32.

Mintzberg, H. (1978). Patterns in strategy formation. *Management Science, 24*(9), 934–948.

Narayanan, V. K. (2019). Using institutional knowledge to answer puzzling questions about novel challenges and opportunities. *Strategy & Leadership, 47*(6), 15–23.

Narayanan, V. K., Buche, M. W., & Kemmerer, B. (2003). From strategic management to strategic experimentation: The convergence of IT, knowledge management, and strategy. In *IT-Based Management: Challenges and Solutions* (pp. 30–49). IGI Global.

Narayanan, V. K., & Defillippi, R. (2012). The influence of strategic context on project management system: A senior management perspective. In *Project Governance* (Eds. Terry M. Williams and Knut Samset). Palgrave Macmillan.

Chapter 4

Project success

Jeffrey Pinto and Lavagnon Ika

Introduction

Understanding what we mean by "success" in projects presents a surprisingly complicated challenge. In situations where there is clear evidence to support a nearly unqualified success, as in the case of the Panama Canal expansion, it seems relatively easy to point to its success on many levels as a testimony to careful planning, hard work, and sound results. The project, when opened in 2016, included new sets of locks, the widening and deepening of the canal, sustainable water drainage technologies, and the capacity for the canal to carry nearly twice the capacity it had previously possessed.

Contrastingly, organizations are often confronted with equally clear examples of failed projects, in which a variety of technical, behavioral, and commercial decisions interacted to create expensive and embarrassing failures. For example, Zillow, the online real estate app decided to enter the market for house flipping in the U.S., recognizing that a hot real estate market could offer them the opportunity to use a modified version of their software to identify, purchase, and resell houses electronically. "Zillow Offers" began in 2018 and quickly unraveled, as the company underestimated the complexities of using their software to predict housing prices and demand. When finally shut down in the fall of 2021, Zillow was left holding hundreds of houses it could not quickly sell, having taken a nearly $400 million-dollar loss, while laying off 25% of its workforce (Kirschner, 2021).

DOI: 10.4324/9781003274179-5

Thus, taking the project view (Pinto & Slevin, 1987) and not the differing perspectives of stakeholders (Davis, 2017), it is often easy to highlight clear examples of success and failure, allowing us to learn valuable lessons both about what (and what not) to do when faced with similar challenges in managing our own projects.

But what about the much more numerous cases where success or failure is not so clear-cut or even results in disputes among different stakeholders? How are we to understand everyday situations where our projects present us with choices among murky trade-offs, the need to sacrifice one key project feature to retain another or the often-competing demands of project stakeholders, all holding us accountable for project results? In short, how do professionals best understand the manner in which project goals can be realized and ultimate project success understood? It is ironic that a discipline focused on the delivery of organizational value through the use of project and project management techniques still appears mired in conceptual confusion around such basic principles as consistent, generally accepted definitions of "success." For many practitioners, identifying a successful project comes to resemble U.S. Supreme Court Justice Potter Stewart's famous description of pornography – "I know it when I see it." But is such a nebulous and subjective analysis beneficial for project professionals? Identifying a successful project *post hoc*, assuming it matches some pre-determined set of criteria, is a dangerous and self-defeating perspective, as it offers little guidance for professionals to best manage their future projects toward a clear set of goals. Moreover, such opaque guidance opens the door to misinterpretation and ambiguity about initiating and delivering projects.

Consider, for example, the Boston Artery/Tunnel project, often referred to as the "Big Dig." Begun in 1991 and officially completed at the end of 2007, this megaproject rerouted miles of I-93, a busy interstate highway that had run through the city center, into a series of tunnels and reconfigured thoroughfares. Originally pegged at $1.6 billion, the project's final bill (including interest) has been estimated at $24.3 billion by the time of its completion, a decade past the original schedule. Moreover, design failures and poor engineering led to multiple commuter deaths during its first years of use, begging the question: can one view the Big Dig as a success? A failure?

Clearly, the answer lies somewhere between these two poles. Years late and massively over-budget, yet fulfilling its goals of rechannelling a smoggy, congested traffic pattern most efficiently, the Big Dig illustrates the difficulty in identifying and applying simplistic labels to complex challenges in delivering successful projects.

From these examples, it seems clear that gaining a clear understanding of what constitutes "success" for projects is a complicated and critically important issue for a number of reasons. First, establishing, at the outset, a clear baseline for expectations (what we intend to measure) provides guidelines for the project team, especially when faced with competing, trade-off decisions (e.g., if project safety is paramount, decisions to cut corners in order to save time will be rejected). Second, establishing the key dimensions of project success (that is, groupings of related success criteria) provides a basis for project team members' performance evaluation. When the most important features of a project are clearly identified (e.g., time to market), it sends clear guidance to the project team that speed is the highest priority, and their individual performance will be evaluated against this standard.

This chapter will address the idea of project success, examining its evolution as a guiding project management principle, unraveling the complexity that underlies a comprehensive understanding of success, and, along the way, showing that the more we seem to know about success, the more a variety of paradoxes emerge. These tensions must be understood and adequately addressed if we are to better comprehend how the critical notion of project success underscores project-based activities. One cannot expect to continuously hit a moving target; we may get lucky now and then; but the more our standards for success remain in flux – poorly understood and changing – the more difficult it is to posit a general theory of effective project management practice. Simply put, project success constitutes the endpoint or the achievement of the target goal toward which all our managerial activities are aimed. Unless we clearly understand what "success" means or come to grips with its shifting goalposts, we have, at best, merely a general idea of how we can best do our jobs as project professionals.

Our evolving understanding of success

As project-based work has risen in popularity in both public and private organizations, our understanding of critical elements – including success – has undergone a concomitant and continuous reassessment and adjustment to new realities. Specifically, the manner in which we measure project success has evolved steadily over time. Initially, parsimony tended to oversimplify projects and how to measure success. Researchers nowadays, however, reject the more simplistic models in preference for greater accuracy. Indeed, projects have gotten more complicated and the world has become more complex. Globalization, faster time to market, shorter product development cycles, increased technical integration, and broadening societal concerns offer a few examples of such trends. Therefore, there is an increasing need to foster a deeper understanding of these multiple pressures to paint a more comprehensive and accurate picture of success.

There have been some important historical analyses of the changing nature of project success (e.g., Jugdev & Muller, 2005; Ika, 2009). Let us briefly consider the critical stages and additions to project success metrics over the years.

The iron triangle

The earliest work theorizing the elements of project success has been generally attributed to Martin Barnes (1969), who first posited the "iron triangle," consisting of time, cost, and quality. Conceptually pleasing, the iron triangle formed the basis for most standard success measurements for nearly two decades. For instance, identifying and measuring schedule and cost performance indices based on completed "value," earned value management (EVM) demonstrates the lasting legacy of the iron triangle. In spite of its common usage to determine project success, several scholars pointed to important shortcomings with the model. For example, in a well-cited paper, Atkinson (1999) criticized the iron triangle suggesting that time and cost represented merely two "best guesses" with quality akin to a "phenomenon;" that is, something discovered after the fact far more often than a goal contemplated at the inception of the project. More specifically, as we become more fully aware of the myriad external systems and dynamics within which projects operate, we objected to a fully "inward-looking" success measure that focused solely on the project itself, as if external events or stakeholders had no role in either shaping or being affected by project outcomes. A case in point, megaprojects may fail to meet their time and cost targets yet finally deliver organizational benefits and satisfy public needs (Turner & Xue, 2018).

Stakeholders matter

By the late 1980s, sufficient pushback against the iron triangle had led to a reshaping of success metrics. In 1987, Pinto and Slevin proposed a modification to Barnes' triple constraint, by adding stakeholder satisfaction to the iron triangle, arguing that a success measure absent external client validation was seriously compromised. Their work coincided with a scholarly movement within the project management milieu to address stakeholders (Cleland, 1986) as both a critical success factor (causal variable) and a key performance indicator (effect). Practice, in effect, suggested that success achievement involved a serious understanding of the role that numerous stakeholder groups can play in smoothing project development. Stakeholder perceptions may have little to do with project delivery within time, cost, and quality constraints but often make disparate judgments over time on the project's success (Turner & Zolin, 2012; Davis, 2017). For example, while project managers tend to concentrate on project *management* success, senior executives generally focus on *business case success*, as they seek value for money after completion. Indeed, research clearly suggested that, for nearly all project classes (e.g., software/IT), any approach to improving the likelihood of success had to closely align with stakeholders' expectations. In fact, the logical offshoot of this realization was captured in the rise of agile project management, with its focus on capturing "user stories," Scrum, and sprints (Serrador & Pinto, 2015).

Contingency is critical

Although Pinto and Slevin (1987) pointed to a variety of complicated issues in assessing project success, including the ideas that success depends on "when" we ask these questions and "who" (which stakeholders) we ask, it took 20 years to fully highlight this contingency. Specifically, Shenhar and Dvir (2007) argued that new product development project "complexity" yielded implications for different project classes, particularly in terms of the time frame when the project was evaluated. Their success dimensions included: efficiency (immediate assessment during execution or at completion), impact on the team (months after completion), impact on customer (months after completion), business and direct success (often one or two years after completion), and preparation for the future (likely three or five years after completion). Sustainability considerations may even take decades or centuries (Maltzman & Shirley, 2015). As Zwikael and Meredith (2021) suggest, the problematic nature of time also reflects a number of false negatives and/or positives; that is, the understanding that, as time passes, projects that were originally thought to be failures can be reconsidered as successes and *vice versa*.

Commercial success and the business case

A critical innovation in our understanding of success was forwarded by de Wit (1988), who first distinguished between *project management* success or the short-term delivery of the project within the internal, "iron triangle" metrics, and *project* success, which referred to the business case targets and longer-term achievement of project goals. In effect, if we borrow words from Peter Drucker, de Wit's conceptualization asked us to distinguish between "doing the project right" and "doing the right project," with the latter putting emphasis on external evaluative criteria, like commercial profitability or improved business processes. Another way this distinction is made is by differentiating project management success and "deliverable success" (Ika, 2018) or "project investment success" (Zwikael & Meredith, 2021), which we call here "business case success." Both project management success and business case success constitute two sides of the same coin, the first focusing on "tactical" delivery targets and the second "strategic," or longer-term commercial outcomes (Slevin & Pinto, 1987). However, though they are correlated (Serrador & Pinto, 2015), the former may not necessarily lead to the latter, perhaps due to such things as uncertainty, as complexity theory teaches us (Ika, 2018).

Benefits realization

The expansion of project success to include external criteria, business cases, and commercial outcomes found its logical connection to a broader understanding of project "benefits." Also refuting the sole focus on the efficient delivery of project outputs, Zwikael and Smyrk (2019) echoed the argument that such a view does not support broader project effectiveness. In fact, the role of projects in the creation of strategic value should be aptly recognized (Shenhar & Dvir, 2007). Notably, value means the sum of economic and wider social benefits to be accrued minus the costs incurred. This argument accepts that organizations invest in projects with the specific objective of realizing identified target benefits, referred to as "the flows of value that arise from a project." Benefits realization casts a wide net to address the myriad ways, both economic and social, that projects can provide value for their constituents/stakeholders.

Green success and sustainability

In line with the emphases on net zero emissions and broader societal goals of sustainability in both activities and outcomes, a modern explanation of project success is expected to highlight an additional emphasis on "green success". As a logical extension of the benefits realization model, sustainability in projects invites us to consider the societal impacts of project development, both positive and damaging, expected and unexpected. Moreover, it aligns more directly with corporate social responsibility guidelines or United Nations Sustainable Development Goals. In other words, we expect that there will be more emphasis on sustainability as a critical measure of project success (e.g., Carvalho & Rabechini, 2017). Green success in projects pushes out the boundaries of what criteria we may use to address project success, but also creates some logical conundrums regarding project sponsors and managers and their agency; that is, the broader, more long-term, and more external the criteria employed to assess success, the greater are our obvious concerns about self-efficacy on the part of the project team. In effect, the question to be asked is the degree to which project organizations can hold project managers responsible for a series of success criteria that could be reasonably argued to be beyond their immediate or direct control. Put another way, while we can train project managers to address tactical criteria of time, cost, and quality, do we run the risk of their disengagement by raising the stakes (and success measures) to aspects or time frames that may be too broad or far off into the future?

Table 4.1 shows a summary of some of the significant existing models of project success. Note that this table also highlights a key feature, namely, that some success dimensions are specifically heavy project class. While our discussion in this chapter has deliberately focused on generic models of success, without regard to project type, past research within project classes has provided additional insight into success criteria (e.g., the Delone & McLean, 2003 model of Information Systems project success). This table also tends to downplay the contingency variables of time ("When we ask") and stakeholders ("Who we ask") (Pinto & Slevin, 1987; Shenhar & Dvir, 2007). Nevertheless, as a simplified way for highlighting some of the evolution of our understanding of project success, the table offers a useful means for contrasting models over time.

Table 4.1 Seven models of success

Barnes (1969) Generic	*Pinto and Slevin (1987) Generic*	*Delone and McLean (2003) IS*	*Shenhar and Dvir (2007) New product development*	*Maltzman and Shirley (2015) Generic*	*Ika (2018) International development projects*	*Zwikael and Meredith (2021) Generic*
Time, cost, and quality (iron triangle)	Time, cost, and performance Perceived quality Client satisfaction	Information quality System quality Service quality Intention to use Use User satisfaction Net benefits	Efficiency Impact on customer Impact on team Business and direct success Preparation for future	Project management success Project success Green success	Project management success (efficiency time and cost; effectiveness objectives) Deliverable success (relevance country, relevance for beneficiaries, institutional impact; sustainability)	Project management success (time, budget, scope; no undesirable impacts by project manager) Project ownership success (target benefits; business case realized) Project investment success (satisfactory results; investment again by funder; overall success)

Current and unresolved challenges

Our quest for more knowledge about the nature of project success has offered enormous insights into the manner in which projects should be completed as well as charting a "roadmap" for project teams in identifying the most critical priorities for the project and its team, including offering a benchmark for targeting project goals. However, as our knowledge of success has broadened, it has brought with it some concomitant challenges for project-based organizations in reflecting on and resolving some embedded paradoxes in managing success. In this section, we will consider some of these paradoxes and offer thoughts on means to address them most effectively.

The clash of competing success criteria

One of the unique features of project management practice has been the concept of trade-offs with regard to decision-making. In effect, trade-off decisions recognize that many elements of success are themselves often antithetical. As an example, we see the classic "dollar-day" trade-off as an expression of the challenge of resource staffing for project activities; that is, the willingness to apply additional resources (which cost the project more money) as a solution to cutting days off the schedule. Thus, improving the project's delivery date (schedule adherence) can come at the expense of budget disruptions.

In a similar way, we need to consider the implications of trade-offs as they relate to project success measures. One recent example of this conundrum exists with the London Crossrail megaproject, which is being developed to add another East-West line to the congested London Underground system. First approved in 2007 and with construction beginning in 2009, the Elizabeth line is the first of the Crossrail routes scheduled to go into service. A key feature of the Crossrail project is the preservation of archaeological sites from early settlements along the Thames watershed. In fact, this cultural "sustainability" was one of the original charges for the project, with the expectation that tunnel boring discoveries would be fully explored and preserved. The contracts include an obligation that main contractors must provide sufficient time to allow archaeological works to be completed and a minimum 28-day period permitted for excavation of unexpected discoveries. So numerous have been these discoveries and so detailed the archaeological excavations that the impact on project schedule and budget has been significant, with dozens of sites uncovered, program delays costing up to $40,000 per week, and delays in the main works tunneling leading to daily delay damages of $1 million per day (Carver, 2010). The impact of such costs raises the question of responsibility: does the project manager bear the blame for resulting delays outside his purview in situations where one goal target (sustainability) actively militates against other critical targets of schedule and budget adherence? This is no idle issue, as the original head of Crossrail, Simon Wright, was replaced in late 2018, in large part due to significant delays in the project schedule.

The role of the project manager (keeping eyes on the prize)

Some measures of project success involve longer-term or more "macro" evaluations, such as benefits delivery (e.g., marketplace success). The Project Management Institute defines benefits realization as: "an outcome of actions, behaviors, products, or services that provide utility to the sponsoring organization as well as to the program's intended beneficiaries." The expected realization of these benefits typically takes time to emerge and be identified (and in some way linked to value), suggesting that success targets such as benefits delivery can push off the actual performance reckoning of a project (and its responsible personnel) well past the point the project officially finished. While critical concepts, benefits delivery, and commercial success as key metrics, when they are over-emphasized, exposed to the risk of rendering "on the ground" project management (and the project manager) ineffectual. Project classes that depend on developing a business case and that seek commercial success involve lengthy time lags between the completion of the project and its assessment. The longer the time lag, the murkier the relationship between project management behavior and subsequent success. That is, pushing off the day when success is identified too far into the future raises the question of the project manager's actual role in success (to say nothing of the inability to tie rewards to performance, making standard career advancement motivation moot).

Multiple stakeholders and their implications

Research on multiple, polycentric stakeholders has demonstrated the complexity of their often-competing demands, values, and impact on the project's development and success. Not only are many projects characterized by large and diverse stakeholder groups, but a deeper analysis of these dynamics also frames a wicked problem of balancing competing demands. Simply put: when a project experiences demands from multiple, competing stakeholders, who wins? How does the project manager balance the political agendas of these groups in a way that furthers rather than hinders the likelihood of project success? Further, research has also shown that the stakeholders-success equation includes who creates and who captures value and when. The Golden Gate Bridge offers an interesting illustration as its value is captured by contemporary Americans, yet many of them did not participate in the original value-creation process.

The danger of collective amnesia

Large infrastructure projects have long held a curiously compelling place in the minds of scholars and practitioners alike. Notoriously inclined to run past early budget and schedule projections (often to an enormous degree), entire classes (e.g., hydroelectric dams, rail, and IT/software) of these projects have, according to Flyvbjerg (2016), demonstrated consistent patterns of underperformance. About half of these projects do not come in within budget (Love et al., 2019). The irony is that for many of these projects, especially in the public eye, current utility routinely trumps development chaos. As noted earlier, the Big Dig is a case in point, as it underwent massive time and cost overruns, not to mention the tragic effect of a catastrophic failure of ceiling tiles in one tunnel and badly designed guardrails, leading to the death of multiple commuters. And yet, in spite of this checkered history, there is a decidedly positive "immediacy effect" regarding the Big Dig.

Implications of public sentiment

Sentiment analysis is a relatively new methodology for exploring multiple, external stakeholders and their responses to organizational decisions (Wang & Pitsis, 2020; Kundu et al., 2021). A near corollary to our point about collective amnesia is the risk of over-reliance on changing public sentiment to dictate key decision-making or refocus *ex ante* project goals in new directions, particularly when the project is in mid-development. An example is the shifting tide of public opinion regarding the California High-Speed Rail Project, which moved from a decidedly positive public attitude toward one that was increasingly negative until final "semi-cancellation" by California's Governor Gavin Newsom. The implications of allowing public sentiment to adjust or create "moving targets," in the form of constantly reassessed success criteria are profound; it potentially disrupts the project manager and team from gaining a level of expertise with the technical challenges of the project, disrupts the ability to foster long-term positive stakeholder relationships, and puts key project decisions in the hands of elected officials or "intervenor" groups (Cleland, 1986), with the implications of their changeability.

Suggestions when managing for success

Recognize the importance of business case success *and* project management success

We noted earlier that internal measures of project success (time, cost, quality) conform to a standard referred to as project management success; i.e., doing the project right. Additionally (it is important here not to say "alternatively"), successful project delivery consists of doing the right project, what we refer to as "business case success." Business case success *versus* project management success is a useful dichotomy to understand the ideas of strategic and tactical execution of the project, but they are not a substitute for each other, nor should one category be emphasized at the expense of the other, without full acknowledgment *a priori* of the consequences of such a deliberate choice.

Identify relevant success criteria in advance

This chapter has identified a wide assortment of project success criteria and while it is tempting to adopt all of them for determining the success of future projects, managers need to be mindful of fully understanding the manner in which they apply various success metrics to their projects for several reasons. First, are they establishing the wrong criteria; for example, requiring the assessment of project's marketplace benefits for internal projects for which commercial success is very hard to measure? Second, clear goals established at the outset remove the danger of trying to hit a moving target as well as avoiding demotivating behaviors like establishing a set of guidelines at the beginning and changing them midstream. Without clear standards for project success, the end result is likely to leave project managers unclear about how they are to be evaluated, when trade-offs have to be addressed, and what the correct prioritization scheme should be. Third, for parsimony reasons, three to five success dimensions are recommended in practice.

Develop a multi-level responsibility grid

Aligned with the previous points, we know that projects can have a series of goal targets, which contingency theory suggests can change over time or depending on the project's larger goals (e.g., benefits delivery). In situations that involve multiple layers of complexity, it is often helpful to develop a multi-level responsibility matrix that identifies key decision-makers for each level of the project. For example, a project manager may be responsible for short-term, internal, project management decisions, while senior or top management liaises with the project team as more external, macro, or system-level decisions have to be made. In short, assigning the correct resource to correctly address success at the correct level may increase the likelihood of project success.

Create a stakeholder engagement strategy

Large projects, in particular, have large and often complicated stakeholder groups, requiring a careful plan to address multiple, competing priorities and goals. Gil and Pinto (2018) discussed the nature of polycentric governance structures for complex projects and argued for the necessity to identify and develop strategies for engaging these multiple stakeholder groups. At a smaller project level, some well-known stakeholder management strategies include developing influence diagrams or agile methodologies that include users as a critical component of the project team. Research clearly shows the critical nature of effective stakeholder management on subsequent project success (Davis, 2017), but equally important is having a comprehensive strategy for addressing these groups and their impact on project success, in order to turn them into partners rather than adversaries.

Conclusion

Knowledge of project success and its critical components represents a fundamental requirement for both the effective practice of project management and efforts to study project-based phenomena. As our understanding of the critical elements in project management continues to expand and refine, so too has our ability to gain a clearer sense of the goal target toward which projects are deliberately aimed – project success. This chapter offers some of the key elements in the development of a comprehensive understanding of success, including its historical roots and key scholarly developments. Of equal importance, we have offered a set of unresolved questions and paradoxes that continue to spark controversy about what success really consists of. These unresolved questions lead to some practical suggestions for project managers, as they discover that a seemingly fundamental and straightforward idea like "success" is, in fact, far more complicated and requires a great deal of careful planning and monitoring to ensure that we are getting "the right things right."

References and further reading

Atkinson, R. (1999). Project management: Cost, time and quality, two best guesses and a phenomenon, its time to accept other success criteria. *International Journal of Project Management*, **17**(6), 337–342.

Barnes, M. (1969). Email dated 14/12/2005 and interview on January 2006. Quoted in Weaver, Patrick (2007). The origins of modern project management. In the Fourth Annual Project Management Institute College of Scheduling Conference, Vancouver, Canada, 15–18.

Carvalho, M. M., & Rabechini, R. (2017). Can project sustainability management impact project success? An empirical study applying a contingent approach. *International Journal of Project Management*, **35**(6), 1120–1132.

Carver, J. (2010). The urban archaeology of the London Crossrail project approach, organisational management, challenges of integration. 15th International Conference on "Cultural Heritage and New Technologies", Vienna, 518–537.

Cleland, D. I. (1986). Project stakeholder management. *Project Management Journal*, **17**(4), 36–44.

Davis, K. (2017). An empirical investigation into different stakeholder groups perception of project success. *International Journal of Project Management*, **35**(4), 604–617.

DeLone, W. H., & McLean, E. R. (2003). The DeLone and McLean model of information systems success: A ten year update. *Journal of Management Information Systems*, **19**(4), 60–95.

de Wit, A. (1988). Measurement of project success. *Project Management Journal*, **6**(3), 164–170.

Flyvbjerg, B. (2016). The fallacy of beneficial ignorance: A test of Hirschman's Hiding Hand. *World Development*, **84**(1), 176–189.

Gil, N., & Pinto, J. K. (2018). Polycentric organizing and performance: A contingency model and evidence from megaproject planning in the UK. *Research Policy*, **47**(4), 717–734.

Ika, L. (2009). Project success as a topic in project management journals. *Project Management Journal*, **40**(4), 6–19.

Ika, L. A. (2018). Beneficial or detrimental ignorance: The straw man fallacy of Flyvbjerg's test of Hirschman's Hiding Hand. *World Development*, **103**(1), 369–382.

Jugdev, K., & Muller, R. (2005). A retrospective look at our evolving understanding of project success. *Project Management Journal*, **36**(4), 19–31.

Kirschner, A. (2021). Zillow torched $381 million overpaying for houses. *Slate*, November 3; retrieved at: https://slate.com/technology/2021/11/zillow-house-flipping-failure-awesome.html

Kundu, O., James, A. D., & Rigby, J. (2021). Public opinion on megaprojects over time: Findings from four megaprojects in the UK. *Public Management Review*. DOI: 10.1080/14719037.2021.2003107.

Love, P. E. D., Sing, M. C. P., Ika, L. A., & Newton, S. (2019). The cost performance of transportation projects: The fallacy of the planning fallacy account. *Transportation Research Part A: Policy and Practice*, **122**, 1–20.

Maltzman, R., & Shirley, D. (2015). *Driving project, program, and portfolio success: The sustainability wheel*. Boca Raton, FL: CRC Press.

Pinto, J. K., & Slevin, D. P. (1987). Critical factors in successful project implementation. *IEEE Transactions of Engineering Management*, **34**(1), 22–27.

Pinto, J. K. & Slevin, D. P. (1988). Project success: Definitions and measurement techniques. *Project Management Journal*, **19**(1), 67–72.

Serrador, P., & Pinto, J. K. (2015). Does agile work? A quantitative analysis of agile project success. *International Journal of Project Management*, **33**(5), 1040–1051.

Shenhar, A. J., & Dvir, D. (2007). *Reinventing project management. The diamond approach to successful growth and innovations*. Cambridge, MA: Harvard Business School Press.

Slevin, D. P., & Pinto, J. K. (1987). Balancing strategy and tactics in project implementation. *Sloan Management Review*, **Fall Issue**, 33–41.

Turner, J. R., & Xue, Y. (2018). On the success of megaprojects. *International Journal of Managing Projects in Business*, **11**(3), 783–805.

Turner, R., & Zolin, R. (2012). Forecasting success on large projects: Developing reliable scales to predict multiple perspectives by multiple stakeholders over multiple time frames. *Project Management Journal*, **43**(5), 87–99.

Wang, A., & Pitsis, T. S. (2020). Identifying the antecedents of megaproject crises in China. *International Journal of Project Management*, **38**(6), 327–339.

Zwikael, O., & Meredith, J. (2021). Evaluating the success of a project and the performance of its leaders. *IEEE Transactions on Engineering Management*, **68**(6), 1745–1757.

Zwikael, O., & Smyrk, J. R. (2019). *Project management: A benefit realisation approach.* Cham: Springer.

Chapter 5

Managing project complexity

Rodney Turner and Martina Huemann

Introduction

In this chapter, we describe the nature of the complexity of projects. We describe the dimensions of complexity. We consider the practitioner view with six dimensions and the academic view with two dimensions. With the academic view, we meet for the first time the concept that conventional project management cannot manage complex projects. We then consider the nature of uncertainty and how it leads to bounded rationality and bounded manageability. It also leads to the difference between puzzles and mysteries. Complex projects are mysteries which require innovation. Conventional project management is not good at innovation. We then consider what has been written over the years about planning under uncertainty. We end with some views on megaprojects. We were going to have a whole chapter on megaprojects. But one section says all we need to say.

Complexity on projects

Dimensions of complexity

There are many models of project complexity (see for instance Bosch-Rekveldt et al., 2011; Geraldi et al., 2011; Hertogh & Westerweld, 2010; Remington & Pollack, 2007), Kaye Remington and Julien Polack (2007) suggest four dimensions: structural; technical; directional; and temporal. Marian Bosch-Rekveldt

DOI: 10.4324/9781003274179-6

and her co-authors (2011) suggest three: technical; organizational and environmental. Joana Geraldi and her co-authors (2011) conducted a literature review and identified that understanding of complexity evolved with time. Initially, people focused on structural complexity, but by the time of their paper, they identified five dimensions: structural; uncertainty; dynamic; pace; and socio-political, though we would suggest that uncertainty is a cause of complexity rather than a dimension.

In their PhD, Marcel Hertogh and Eddy Westerweld (2010) developed a model of complexity. They reviewed five large infrastructure projects to determine what contributed to their complexity. They differentiated between a practitioner view and an academic view. The practitioner view had six dimensions of complexity, which include the four dimensions of Remington and Pollack (2007) and the three dimensions of Bosch-Rekveldt et al. (2011), but only three of the dimensions of Geraldi et al. (2011). The six dimensions are:

- Technical.
- Socio-political.
- Organizational.
- Temporal.
- Financial.
- Legal.

Technical complexity

Technical complexity arises from new and unproven technology and from technical uncertainty. Remington and Pollack (2007) say the challenge is supporting the need for discovery and experimentation while maintaining a realistic hold on the schedule. They suggest that on technically complex projects the initiation and design stages are critical. Solutions will be prototyped in the design and then be available for later use. Unproven technology leads to several dilemmas:

1 Proven technology versus new opportunities.
2 Robustness of design versus adaptiveness.
3 Indivisibility versus optimization.
4 Tight coupling versus easier-to-isolate problems.
5 Fallback option versus reduced costs.
6 Fewer functions versus more flexibility.

Socio-political complexity

Projects involve many stakeholders, who interact on many levels (Derakhshan, Turner, & Mancini, 2019). Conflicts of interest between stakeholders can lead to different perceptions, opinions, and attitudes on issues that have a large impact on their business, life, or environment. Managing these conflicts of interest emerges as a core theme in the management of complexity. Remington and Pollack (2007) imply directional complexity arises from poor project definition. They call it directionally complexity because of the large numbers of networks and nodes. Hertogh and Westerweld (2010) suggest there are four areas of socio-political complexity:

- Conflicts of interest: between the large numbers of stakeholders.
- Different meanings and perceptions: people have different interpretations of objects. Engineers focus on the physical project, the modernist view. Others focus on the stakeholder network. However, the primary focus should be on the benefits to the users and the societal benefits, according to the post-modernist view.
- Large impact on the natural environment.
- Path dependency: views from the past dominate the future, which influences the perceived legitimacy of the project and the project sponsor in the eyes of the local stakeholders (Derakhshan, Mancini, & Turner, 2019).

Organizational complexity

The law of requisite variety says an organization's internal diversity must match the variety in the environment, (Hertogh & Westerweld, 2010). Further organizational members will be better able to cope with uncertainty if they possess the requisite variety of skills. Organizational complexity also extends outside the project organization, to local government, and internal and external stakeholders. They need to organize themselves to organize their response to the project. There are several issues associated with organizational complexity.

- Finding and keeping motivated people appropriate to the challenge.
- Making decisions with no clear best solution: We meet bounded rationality and satisficing later.

- The project organization has numerous work processes that interfere with each other.
- Consultants, contractors, and suppliers require numerous contracts.

Temporal complexity

Megaprojects can last many years and so organizations can have difficulties keeping the same team for the duration of the project. Further politicians can have short memories, and in a democracy, the government can change several times during the life of a large project. In the United States, there are two years between elections to the Congress. (Joe Biden cancelled the Keystone XL oil pipeline, which Donald Trump strongly supported.) There are two issues associated with temporal complexity:

- Long time frame with continuous developments: during the long time frame government change, societies change, new technologies appear, and parent organizations change.
- No sequential process of implementation: Complex projects involve a lot of parallel processes and non-linearity. Non-linearity of course is a feature of complexity, which makes it unlikely that time and cost targets will be achieved (Turner & Xue, 2018).

Financial complexity

There are six issues associated with financial complexity:

- Costs, benefits, and burdens are difficult to calculate and not always equally divided: The main burden is felt by the local community, not the users of the new service. But also, the cost and benefits are not always equally divided between the investors.
- The perception of cost developments can differ from calculations.
- Different perceptions about definitions and agreements: some managers operate at a tactical level, some at a strategic level, and some at a policy level. When these different managers are buyers and sellers to each other it can lead to misunderstandings.
- Strategic misinterpretation, optimism, and pessimism bias (Stingl & Geraldi, 2017).

- The cascade of distortion: Send three and fourpence, we are going to a dance.
- As we have just seen, time and cost targets need to be treated as guidelines rather than rigid targets we expect to achieve.

Legal complexity

There are several elements which cause legal complexity:

- Changing, non-existent, and conflicting laws: Projects which cross national boundaries face differing laws in different countries. Projects with several parent organizations can be subject to conflicting rules in the different organizations.
- Extensive legislation and rules have a significant influence on content and process: projects are subject to rules and laws within the parent organization, within project partners, regions, nations, and supranational levels. They all influence project processes, creating potential conflicts. When a change occurs, you cannot guarantee that all the relevant rules and regulations will be tracked down in good time.
- People involved need space to operate: the more rules the greater the tendency to ignore them. Sometimes you have to be naughty and ignore them to make progress.

Relative occurrence

Hertogh and Westerweld (2010) measured the relative occurrence of the different types of complexity. Socio-political complexity was the most common with about a 50% higher impact than technical complexity, which was second. Organizational complexity was closely behind in third. Financial complexity was fourth, temporal complexity fifth, and legal complexity had the smallest impact.

The academic view

Hertogh and Westerweld (2010) suggest the academic literature on complexity implies two types of complexity, which they label detail complexity and dynamic complexity. Geraldi et al. (2011) identified structural complexity and dynamic complexity as two dimensions. Brady and Davies (2014) also identify structural complexity and dynamic complexity as their two main dimensions of complexity, though their precise definitions differ from Hertogh and Westerweld.

Detail complexity

Detail complexity is complexity in the system. Luhman (2017) suggested that a system with more than three nodes is complex. But, as Remington and Pollack (2007) suggested, it is not just the number of nodes, but the interconnection between those nodes.

Dynamic complexity

Dynamic complexity originates in the fields of biology and mathematics; complex adaptive systems evolve with time. Dynamic complexity is related to the butterfly flapping its wings in Brazil causing a tornado in Arkansas. It is dynamic complexity which means a small change in input leads to a large change in output, making it difficult to predict time and cost to completion (Turner & Xue, 2018). The preferences of stakeholders can evolve with time. Dynamic complexity causes uncertainty, bounded rationality, and bounded manageability which we discuss below.

Hertogh and Westerweld (2010) show the six types of complexity described above all contain elements of detail and dynamic complexity. They suggest high detail complexity results in complicatedness whereas dynamic complexity creates true complexity (Table 5.1). They therefore suggest the standard methods of project management can be used to manage high detail complexity, but alternative methods are needed for high dynamic complexity (Table 5.2). High detail complexity requires innovation, and conventional project management cannot do innovation (Keegan & Turner, 2002).

Uncertainty

Frank Knight (1921) and John Maynard Keynes (1936) differentiated between risk and uncertainty. They suggested risk is predictable events with known probability. There is a chance it might rain tomorrow. I can look back at the weather records

Table 5.1 The impact of detail and dynamic complexity

Detail complexity	*Hi*	*Complicated*	*Dragons*
	Lo	*Simple*	*Complex*
		Lo	Hi
		Dynamic complexity	

Table 5.2 Management approaches

Detail complexity	*Hi*	*Systems management* *Traditional PM modernism*	*Dynamic management*
	Lo	*Internal management*	*Interactive management* *Post-modernism*
		Lo	Hi
		Dynamic complexity	

from the past 100 years and see how often it has rained on the 24th of August. Or I can look at the probability based on the current weather systems. The chance it will rain tomorrow is about 20%. I plan to go walking tomorrow morning, and the risk is there is a 20% chance it will be rained off. Uncertainty is things that are not so identifiable or do not have probabilities that can be estimated. Our knowledge is incomplete. Knight suggested that entrepreneurs make profits by being able to work within uncertainty.

Chris Chapman (2020) takes a slightly different approach. He suggests a risk is a predictable event that may have a negative impact on project outcomes. We may or may not know the potential impact of that event, or its likelihood. If we know the potential impact and likelihood, it is an insurable risk; a known known. If we do not know the potential impact and likelihood, it is an uninsurable risk; a known unknown. To complete Donald Rumsfeld's poem, there are also unknown unknowns, which are events we cannot predict. To complete Johari's window there are also unknown knowns, not relevant here. Before I have to scrape people off the ceiling, Chris Chapman says risks are things that have a negative impact. Opportunities are things that have a positive impact. Some people say risks can have a positive or negative impact.

Jay Galbraith (1977) developed a rather simplistic model of uncertainty. He said uncertainty was the difference between the information we have to make a decision and the information we need. He said uncertainty could be reduced by either increasing the amount of information available or reducing the information needed. Too easy. We don't have enough information; our rationality is bounded. Table 5.3 shows six sources of uncertainty, and incomplete information is just one of them.

John Kay and Mervyn King (2020) differentiate between resolvable and radical uncertainty. Resolvable uncertainty is the known-knowns above, or the situation

Table 5.3 Six sources of uncertainty (after Leitjen, 2017)

	Knowledge		*Interaction*
	Present	*Future*	
Known to manager	Things do not behave the same way as last time	Information is incomplete (Galbraith, 1977)	Other agents have more knowledge than the manager, (asymmetry of information), (Müller, 2017).
Unknown to manager	Tacit knowledge of others is not accessible to the manager	Unpredictable and improbable events occur (black swans, Taleb, 2007)	Actors do not behave as expected, (moral hazard), (Müller, 2017).

in the left-hand column of Table 5.1, with low dynamic complexity. Radical uncertainty is the known-unknowns or unknown-unknowns, or the right column in Table 5.1, with high dynamic complexity. They suggest resolvable uncertainty leads to puzzles and radical uncertainty to mysteries. Puzzles are problems with a solution that can be found by deductive reasoning, the modernist approach. Mysteries do not have a solution but can be better understood by inductive or abductive reasoning, the post-modernist approach. We can better understand mysteries by constructing narratives about them. Narratives do not provide a solution but help us construct scenarios. With slight adaptation, Dwight Eisenhower is reputed to have said:

> In cases of high uncertainty, I have always found that plans are useless, but planning is indispensable.

Plans are solutions to puzzles. Planning creates narratives, which help us better understand possible outcomes. Constructing narratives and scenarios can help us understand possible futures. In Chapter 34 we offer scenario planning and future perfect planning as tools that can help construct scenarios to better understand complex projects. Havermans et al. (2015) suggest expressing problems as narratives is a dynamic process that can frame problems in a new light, aid interaction, and shape actions. Kay and King (2020) suggest we should reason in terms of narratives. They can help people interpret complex situations and suggest how to deal with things if they occur.

The traditional approaches to project management assume projects are puzzles, and therefore manageable and use deductive reasoning to find a solution to the problem. Complex projects, which are mysteries, may require alternative approaches using inductive or abductive reasoning to create narratives. Using inductive or abductive reasoning to create narratives to understand mysteries requires innovation. Conventional project management is not good at innovation (Keegan & Turner, 2002).

Bounded rationality

Henry Simon (1956) introduced the concept of bounded rationality. When people make decisions, their ability to make a perfect decision is limited by their cognitive ability, information, and time constraints. Therefore, people have to satisfice and make a decision that works, often based on heuristics (Kahneman, 2012). Voltaire (1764) said, "The perfect is the enemy of the good." People suffer paralysis by analysis as they seek the perfect solution. Jay Galbraith (1977) just said we have to accept the uncertainty.

Bounded manageability

Standard project management procedures assume that processes are monitorable, predictable, and controllable. Monitorability means the manager can keep track of events and measure performance. Predictability means the manager can foresee the consequences of decisions and emerging situations. Controllability means the manager can intervene in the case of deviance. In your dreams. Uncertainty creates bounded manageability.

Planning under uncertainty

In a famous paper, Klein and Meckling (1958) describe planning and making decisions under uncertainty. They describe a weapons systems development project where there is some uncertainty about the configuration of the end product. They describe the actions of two people whom they call the Optimist and the Sceptic. The Optimist guesses what the configuration of the end product will be. If he or she is right, it will lead to the cheapest solution. But Klein and Meckling say there is a high chance the configuration will not be exactly as predicted, and considerable changes will be required adding to the cost. There will be scope creep, and changes are expensive to make. The Sceptic assumes he or she does not know what the exact configuration of the end product looks like and proposes several options or scenarios. As the project progresses and the uncertainty reduces, some of the options can be removed, and in the end, the project moves towards one configuration. Because work will be done on several options, the outcome will be more expensive than if the Optimist is right, and the one configuration he or she proposes is right. However, because changes, rework, and scope creep will be avoided, the outcome will be cheaper than if the Optimist is wide of the mark.

What Klein and Meckling are describing is where the uncertainty lies in the definition of the end product, but not in the definition of the method of achieving the end product. On projects, there are two sources of uncertainty: uncertainty of the end project; and uncertainty of the method of delivering the end product (Turner, 2014). If the uncertainty lies solely in the method of delivering the end product, the Optimist is right. The configuration of the end product can be assumed, and methods, such as future perfect planning are used to resolve the uncertainty of the work methods. On the other hand, if there is uncertainty in the end product, whether or not there is also uncertainty in the work methods, something must be done to deal with the uncertainty of the end product. One way is to use the Sceptic's approach. Propose several options, or scenarios, for the end product, and then as the project progresses, reduce the uncertainty and slowly eliminate all but one of the options.

Brady et al. (2012) review Klein and Meckling's paper from a modern perspective. They say, as we do above, that traditional project management is based on a mechanistic paradigm of control, with the aim of executing projects on time, on budget, and within the customer specifications. They say projects show poor performance because managers fail to understand the complexity and uncertainty of their projects and do not adapt their management style. They say many of the early military projects, such as the Manhattan Project and the Atlas and Polaris ballistic missile projects applied trial and error, and parallel working in sharp contrast to the control-oriented, phased approach that characterizes modern project management. They suggest that Klein and Meckling (1958) represented the former approach. Pich et al. (2002) recommend that in conditions of high uncertainty, an experimental, iterative approach to project management is adopted in which multiple solutions are pursued in parallel, and the final solution is adopted as the outcomes become clearer. However, on the Manhattan, Atlas, and Polaris projects costs were not important, as it was necessary to beat the Germans and then the Soviets. A desire to balance time and cost leads to more traditional project management. When Robert McNamara became secretary of defence in the USA in 1961, he shifted the emphasis to the more control-based approach, and project management's role became to implement clearly defined objectives to time, cost, and quality.

Building on Klein and Meckling's work, Hirschman and Lindblom (1962) suggest that taking the rational approach can lead to worse outcomes. Controversially they suggested that carefully planning a project may hinder rather than help, and it might be easier to solve a problem if it is not fully understood. The development of complex systems are characterized by emergent phenomena and unpredictability. Unexpected events often occur, (as suggested by Dwight Eisenhower), and gaps emerge between what should be and what is. Hirschman and Lindblom (1962) suggested that in conditions of uncertainty and incomplete information sometimes muddling through can be the best way to proceed, and Klein and Meckling (1958) suggested that can lead to faster cheaper solutions. Satisfice because the perfect is the enemy of the good. Nightingale (2004) found that unpredictability is much more pervasive than many people assume. Bounded manageability is common.

Brady et al. (2012) conclude by saying that in conditions of high uncertainty, project management needs to overcome self-imposed constraints and return to its roots in the Manhattan, Atlas, and Polaris projects. On complex projects, a modernist, positivist, rational approach to project management may lead to inferior results, and a more experimental, iterative approach may be needed. Keegan and Turner (2002) showed that project management is poor at innovation because of an overemphasis on control.

In Chapter 34, we now offer scenario planning and future perfect planning as approaches that may offer a more experimental, iterative approach.

Megaprojects

We were going to have a whole chapter on megaprojects, but in the end had very little extra to say. Megaprojects are a special case of complex projects, so we end this chapter with some views on megaprojects. A lot has been written about how and why megaprojects fail (Flyvbjerg, 2017). Recently, Nathalie

Drouin and Rodney Turner (2022) have taken a more positive approach, and suggest megaprojects can be successful if they are carefully managed. Nathalie and Rodney take two slightly controversial positions:

- Megaprojects can be successful, but unfortunately, when projects fail people externalize their problems, and say the failure was not their fault
- Post-modernism suggests achieving social benefit is more important than finishing on cost and time, though the project ought to make a profit

Megaprojects can be successful

Nathalie Drouin and Rodney Turner (2022) give several case studies of megaprojects, almost all of which were successful. The successful projects had five things in common:

1. They adapted project management to deal with complexity as described above.
2. They chose the economically most advantageous contractor rather than the cheapest. The contractor that bids the least is the biggest liar. Unfortunately, it takes time and effort for contractors to produce economically advantageous bids, and it takes time and effort for clients to assess them. Often corners are cut.
3. They used principal-steward contracting rather than principal-agent. It has been known for a quarter of a century that principal-agent contracting only works on simple projects, and on more complex projects you need principal-steward contracting (Davis et al., 1997), but old habits die hard.
4. They worked closely with the internal stakeholders and treated them with respect.
5. They worked closely with the internal stakeholders and treated them with respect.

There are people who consider themselves tough business people, who think that the means they should choose is to hire the cheapest contractor and squeeze them to almost making a loss. They use principal-agent contracting to closely control the contractors, and try to bully them into submission. They also bully the external stakeholders. When the project fails, as it certainly will, it cannot be their fault because they are tough business people. So they search around in what has been written about why megaprojects fail and conclude it must be because of fragility. "Not my fault, I am a successful tough business person."

Nathalie Drouin and Rodney Turner (2022) give the example of the Amsterdam North-South Metro Line. That project was going late and overspent. However, they changed the relationship between the client and contractor from principal-agent to principal-steward, by making the contractor a department within the client organization. They also started treating the people of Amsterdam with much great respect, adopting a policy called BLVC, in Dutch Bereikbaarheid, Leefbaarheid, Veiligheid, and Communiatie, (accessibility, liveability, safety, and communication). The rest of the project was completed to the revised time and cost target. They also give the example of stormwater tunnels built in Sydney in advance of the 2000 Olympic Games. There was a problem with an air vent. If they had been using principal-agent contracting, the contractors would have said to the client we are out of here until you solve the problem, and the project would have failed at that point. Because they were using principal-steward contracting the contractors shared in the solution of the problem. In the event, they exceeded performance on four of their five key performance indicators. The one where they were slightly below performance was the relationship with the local community.

Post-modernism

Turner and Xue (2018) gave a novel interpretation of the success of megaprojects. What is important is megaprojects should produce social benefit, but they should produce that social benefit at a time and a cost that makes it worthwhile. Turner and Xue (2018) said that complex megaprojects are non-linear, which means small changes to inputs can lead to large changes in outputs. So anyone who claims they can precisely predict the time and cost to completion of a megaproject at the start is a fool, a liar, or a fraud. Turner and Xue give many examples of megaprojects that were somewhat late and/or overspent, but still produced a worthwhile social benefit, and based on that social benefit produces positive net present value.

Nathalie Drouin and Rodney Turner (2022) give the example of the Gotthard Base Tunnel, a tunnel through the Swiss Alps connecting Milan to Zurich. Because of severe geological problems, the project was late and overspent. But one completed project produced substantial social benefit, enabling people to travel between Milan and Zurich more quickly and more comfortably. It also transferred substantial amounts of freight from road and air to rail. The project also made positive net present value and so was an investment success.

Nathalie Drouin and Rodney Turner (2022) also say that unfortunately, people have a tendency to anchor early estimates. They give the example of the Betuweroute, a freight railway line between the Port of Rotterdam and Germany. An early guestimate of the cost was made before any design was done. The project was 30% overspent on that guestimate. The project was only 6% overspent on the estimate produced after front front-end design was done. Unfortunately, people anchor the guestimate and say the project failed.

Summary

Megaprojects can be successful if you:

- Adapt project management to deal with complexity.
- Use the economically most advantageous contractor.
- Use principal-steward contracting, not principal-agent.
- Treat the internal and external stakeholders with respect.

If you don't do that, when the project almost certainly fails, admit your contribution to the failure.

Hopefully, the time and cost estimates for a megaproject are worthwhile guidelines. But because of complexity, the project may not achieve them precisely. Judge the project on the social benefit it produces and whether or not it is profitable.

Conclusion

The literature (Dwight Eisnehower; Brady et al., 2012; Hertogh & Westerweld, 2010; Hirschman & Lindblom, 1962; Kay & King, 2020; Klein & Meckling, 1958; Keegan & Turner, 2002; Pich et al., 2002; Nightingale, 2004) shows that rigid control leads to inferior outcomes under conditions of uncertainty. It is necessary to plan in terms of multiple possible outcomes, and multiple ways of delivering those outcomes, and refine the understanding of outcomes and process as more information becomes available. An iterative, experimental approach leads to better outcomes. Scenario planning and future perfect planning create narratives about possible futures, creating an iterative experimental approach. That means it may not be possible to precisely define the time and cost to completion. People have to be much happier with flexible targets. But it has been known for some time, that leaving options open for longer, can often lead to cheaper outcomes, rather than rigidly trying to define the end objectives and means of achieving them at an early stage because it is possible to be more innovative (Keegan & Turner, 2002).

References and further reading

Bosch-Rekveldt, M, Jongkind, Y, Mooi, H, Bakker, H & Verbraeck, A. (2011). Grasping project complexity in large engineering projects: The TOE (technical, organizational and environmental) framework. *International Journal of Project Management*, **29**: 728–739.

Brady, T & Davies, A. (2014). Managing structural and dynamic complexity: A tale of two projects. *Project Management Journal*, **45**(4): 21–38.

Brady, T, Davies, A & Nightingale, P. (2012). Dealing with uncertainty in complex projects: Revisiting Klein and Meckling. *International Journal of Managing Projects in Business*, **5**(4): 718–736.

Chapman, CB. (2020). *Enlightened Planning: Using Systematic Simplicity to Clarify Opportunity, Risk and Uncertainty for Much Better Management Decision Making*. Abingdon and New York: Routledge.

Davis, JH, Schoorman, FD & Donaldson, L. (1997). Towards a stewardship theory of management. *The Academy of Management Review*, **22**(1): 20–47.

Derakhshan, R, Mancini, M & Turner, JR. (2019). Community's evaluation of organizational legitimacy: Formation and reconsideration. *International Journal of Project Management*, **37**(1): 73–86.

Derakhshan, R, Turner, JR & Mancini, M. (2019). Project governance and stakeholders: A literature review. *International Journal of Project Management*, **37**(1): 98–116.

Drouin, N & Turner, JR. (2022). *The Elgar Advanced Introduction to Megaprojects*. Cheltenham, and Northampton, MA: Edward Elgar.

Flyvbjerg, B, (ed). (2017). *The Oxford Handbook of Megaproject Management*. Oxford: Oxford University Press.

Galbraith, JR. (1977). *Organization Design*. Reading, MA: Addison Wesley.

Geraldi, J, Maylor, H & Williams, T. (2011). Now, let's make it really complex (complicated): A systematic review of complexities of projects. *International Journal of Operations & Production Management*, **31**(9): 966–990.

Hertogh, M & Westerweld, E. (2010). *Playing with Complexity: Management and Organization of Large Infrastructure Projects*. PhD thesis, Erasmus University Rotterdam.

Havermans LA, Keegan, AE & Den Hartog, DN. (2015). Choosing your words carefully: leaders' narratives of complex emergent problem resolution. *International Journal of Project Management*, **33**(5): 973–984.

Hirschman, AO & Lindblom, CE. (1962). Economic development, research and development, policy making: Some converging views. *Behavioral Science*, **7**(2): 211–222.

Kahnemann, D. (2012). *Thinking Fast and Slow*. London: Penguin.

Kay, J & King, M. (2020). *Radical Uncertainty: Decision Making for an Unknown Future*. London: The Bridge Street Press.

Keegan, AE & Turner, JR. (2002). The management of innovation in project based firms. *Long Range Planning*, **35**: 367–388.

Keynes, JM. (1936). *The General Theory of Employment, Interest and Money*. London: Palgrave Macmillan.

Klein, B & Meckling, W. (1958). Application of operations research to development decisions. *Operations Research*, **6**(3): 352–363.

Knight, F. (1921). *Risk, Uncertainty and Profit*. Boston, MA and New York: Houghton Miffin Company.

Leitjen, M. (2017). *What Lies Beneath: Bounded Manageability in Complex Underground Infrastructure Projects*. PhD Thesis Technical university of Delft.

Luhman, N. (2017). *Risk: A Sociological Theory (Communication and Social Order)*. Abingdon and New York: Routledge.

Müller, R. (2017). *Governance and Governmentality for Projects: Enablers, Practices and Consequences*. New York and London: Routledge.

Nightingale, P. (2004). Technological capabilities, invisible infrastructure and the un-social construction of predictability: The overlooked fixed costs of useful research. *Research Policy*, **33**(9): 1259–1584.

Pich, MT, Loch, CH & de Mayer, A. (2002). Uncertainty, ambiguity, and complexity in project management. *Management Science*, **48**(8): 1008–1023.

Remington, K & Pollack, J. (2007). *Tools for Complex Projects*. Aldershot: Gower.

Simon, HA. (1956). Rational choice and the structure of the environment. *Psychology Review*, **63**(2): 129–139.

Stingl, V & Geraldi, J. (2017). Errors, lies and misunderstandings: Systematic review on behavioural decision making on projects. *International Journal of Project Management*, **35**: 121–135.

Taleb, (2007). *Black Swan: The Impact of the Highly Improbable*. New York: Random House.

Turner, JR. (2014). *The Handbook of Project-based Management: Leading Strategic Change in Organizations*, 4th edition. New York: McGraw-Hill.

Turner, JR & Xue, Y. (2018). On the success of megaprojects. *International Journal of Managing Projects in Business*, **11**(3): 783–805.

Voltaire, (Arouet, F-M). (1764). *Dictionnaire Philosophique*. Geneva: Gabriel Grasset.

Chapter 6

Auditing projects and programs

Martina Huemann

Introduction

Project-oriented organizations review and audit their projects and programs for many reasons, including compliance, quality assurance, governance purposes, or learning. Auditing is often related to ISO certification or financial auditing. When we ask project managers or program managers about their experience with auditing, most report it has been a stressful, sometimes even hostile, event. Often it is perceived as a formal box-ticking exercise, to ensure all documents and project plans exist. Project managers often find it hard to find added value in this process that could potentially bring them an outside view on the project and could support them in better managing their projects.

Quite often organizations initiate audits when projects are not performing well, or they suspect a project crisis. In some organizations especially without proper governance in place, projects and programs may be considered as unguided missiles, leading to the feeling they are out of the control of senior management. Little learning on managing projects may take place and mistakes may be repeated again. While the audit is the most formal term, we find different terms in practice, such as project health check, quick check, or review. To perceive project management reviewing and auditing as a learning opportunity calls for a reinvention of this quality assurance instrument. This is reflected in the process and in the methods applied as well as in the attitude and the cultural aspects involved.

DOI: 10.4324/9781003274179-7

Project auditing

Purpose of project auditing

ISO 19011 defines auditing as a systematic, independent, and documented process for obtaining audit evidence and evaluating it objectively to determine the extent to which the audit criteria are fulfilled. The audit criteria are a set of policies, procedures, or requirements set externally to the item being audited. Reasons for audits include certification, internal audits, or contract compliance. Auditing is also a method of quality assurance and quality improvement in the context of projects and programs. A project audit is a systematic and independent investigation to check if the project is performing correctly with respect to product, project, and/or project management standards. Different terms are used such as project health checks, quick scans, or most commonly reviews, which are less formal than audits. In many organizations, the term audit tends to be used in the context of certification or financial auditing. In the context of projects or programs the term review is often used instead.

We differentiate controlling from reviews and audits. Project controlling to check and manage the progress of a project is done by the project manager and the project team, while an audit or review is performed by people outside the project. A specific form of review is the peer review. Peer reviews for projects and programs are done, by peer professionals such as peer senior project managers to provide feedback and advice to a project or the program. An audit is always conducted by a party external to the project. Thus, the auditor provides a perspective external to the project.

Types of project auditing

Either processes or results of processes can be audited. Different audit types exist:

- Audits that consider specific project deliverables like for example design reviews or contract reviews.
- Audits that consider (technical) project processes, often in combination with project deliverables, are commonly referred to as project audits or project reviews.
- Audits that concentrate on a specific topic relevant to the project, like risk audit, financial audit, or sustainability audit.

- Audits that solely consider the project management process and its results are referred to as a management audit of a project or program or simply a project management audit.

Project audits to check the (technical) project processes and project deliverables are commonly applied in construction, engineering, Information Technology, and product development projects and programs. They are applied at the end of project phases. The gate model for an integrated solution delivery of an international engineering company shows for instance the phases: concept, design, development, implementation, and benefits delivery. Reviews are carried out to evaluate the deliverables produced during the phases. These reviews are audits of the solution under development, which include the following:

- *Concept phase review:* To assess the completeness of the design concepts, including consideration of alternative designs.
- *Design phase review:* To assess the completeness of design phase work, which includes process design and system requirements, logical design, operations plan, and test plan.
- *Detailed design review*: To do a complete technical assessment of the detailed design before beginning extensive coding or purchasing of software.
- *Pilot readiness review*: To assess whether the solution is ready to pilot.
- *Implementation readiness review*: To assess the readiness of implementing the solution to its planned full extent.
- *Implementation reviews:* To assess the implementation on each site that implements the new solution. It includes verifying implementation measurements, system performance, site adjustments, planning adjustments, logistics implementation, budget, and schedule.

These reviews are linked to stage gates, which are go/no-go decision points. Only successful reviews allow a project to schedule a gate meeting. These quality assurance activities are an inherent part of the technical content processes and are visualized in the work breakdown structure, the bar chart, and the cost plan of such a project. The processes need to be checked early in the project to ensure the project deliverables' quality, as only sound processes lead to good products and solutions.

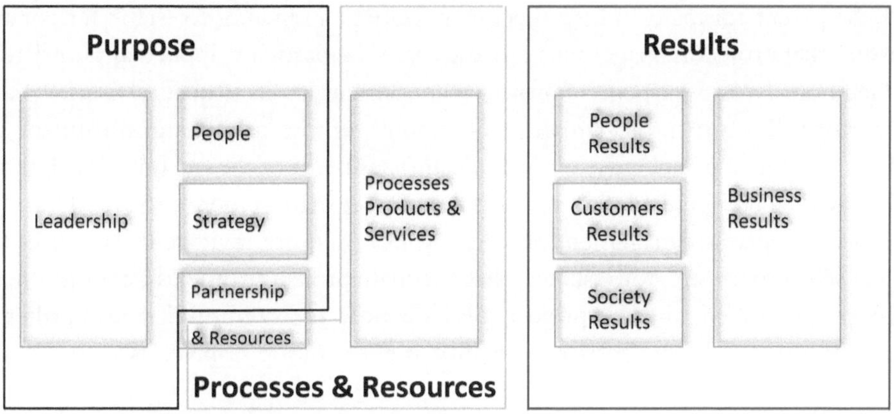

Figure 6.1: Project Excellence Model (IPMA 2018a)

A specific case: IPMA Project Excellence Model

A specific case is the Project Excellence Model, as shown in Figure 6.1. The model was first developed by the German Project Management Association and has been applied as the basis for the assessments regarding the IPMA Project Excellence Awards for many years (IPMA 2018a). We here mention the Project Excellence Model explicitly in the context of project auditing, as it could serve as a baseline for a non-normative model. Project auditing is normative, as it always needs an explicit base to audit against. The IPMA Project Excellence Model offers an audit or assessment questionnaire as a robust enough framework to be the basis for a project audit. If excellent assessors apply the model, the project's strength and development potential can be assessed in a transparent and repeatable way. A major strength of the Project Excellence Model is that it covers project management as well as project results and considers the relationship between process and results. As shown in Figure 6.1, the IPMA Project Excellence Model consists of people and purpose, processes and resources, and project results. Further, it considers social and environmental issues explicitly in some of its criteria, thus it also covers sustainability criteria to a certain extent.

Project management auditing

Management auditing of a project or program is an independent investigation to check if the management processes (project management or program management) are performed according to a specified standard, mostly of the owner organization or of the parent company. The project management audit aims to establish rigor and to assure that project management processes and standards are applied appropriately.

Traditionally, the purpose of project management audits is quality assurance and governance. To turn project management auditing into a learning instrument we add a competence perspective and include an assessment of the organizational, team, and individual competencies to perform the project management process. Thus, the project or program management process and its results are reviewed. Results of the project start process are, for instance, that adequate project plans exist, a project team has been established, and the project roles are clear and communicated. Further in this chapter, we will concentrate on management auditing of projects.

The lenses we put on

The baseline for the project management audit, the management audit criteria, depends on the project management approach used as a basis for the auditing. We can only see what we are looking for. Project management predictive standards (for example Axelos 2020; IPMA 2018b; PMI 2021), project management adaptive standards (for example Axelos 2015; IPMA 2018c; PMI 2017) or company-specific project management guidelines can serve as a baseline, as a pair of lenses the auditor puts on to assess the quality of project management of a particular project. The possible learning is limited by the lenses applied, as we can only see what we are looking for through the filters we use. If our pair of glasses is traditional project management then the audit criteria are limited to the traditional project management objects of consideration like scope, schedule, and costs. Additional project management objects of consideration such as the project organization, the project culture, and the project context only become audit criteria, if a project management approach is used that considers them. If projects are seen as temporary organizations and project management is considered as a business process, the design of the project management process becomes an audit criterion. Only then will the auditor look to see if the project start process, for instance, was designed adequately:

- if there has been a project start workshop and/or a project kick-off presentation.
- if the appropriate persons have been included in the project start.

The auditing forms shown later are based on a systemic-constructivist project management approach that values project organization, context, culture, and process-oriented and considers project management as a business process (Gareis and Gareis 2018).

The project management approach that serves as a base in a project management audit must be agreed on beforehand. In most cases, the audit will be based on the project management standard used in the (project owner) company. In other cases, consultants may be invited to do an audit, explicitly for the purpose of using a different project management approach as auditing criteria. This can increase the added value of the audit for the project as well as for the project-oriented company.

Audits on a regular basis

Project management auditing can be done randomly, regularly, or because of a specific reason. Routine project management audits on a regular basis are rare. They are still often carried out only if the client asks for it or if somebody in the line organization has a bad feeling about the project and suspects a project crisis. Then the method is used for problem identification purposes.

In some project-oriented companies auditing is done on a regular basis. A project needs to build up the project management competencies of its organization and its team. To add most value to the project the ideal point in time to do a project management audit is early in the project – for instance, after the project or program start has been accomplished. This provides feedback and gives the project the chance to further develop its management competence. Further audits later in the project are possible to give further feedback but also to verify if the recommendations agreed on in earlier audits were taken care of by the project.

Structured and transparent process

An audit needs a structured and transparent approach. Before the audit, an assignment is necessary to initialize the audit, appoint the audit owner (which in most cases will be the project owner), appoint the auditors, and provide initial information about the project audit. The result is a project audit assignment that clearly indicates the goals, reason, scope, timing, and methods to be used in the audit. A structured and transparent process supports the acceptance of the results. Depending on the complexity of the project or program and the objectives of the audit, one or more auditors are assigned. A project management audit process should include the following steps:

1 Conducting a situational analysis.
2 Planning the auditing.
3 Preparing the auditing.
4 Performing the analysis.
5 Generating the audit report.
6 Performing the audit presentation.
7 Terminating the auditing.

The objectives of the situational analysis are to clarify the reason for and expectations from the audit. The auditors formulate first hypotheses about the situation the project is in and the quality of its project management process. In the planning step of the auditing, the auditors plan the macro design of the process and the meetings they will have with the audit owner and the project organization, the analysis methods they will apply (like documentation analysis, interviews, observations, etc.) and the presentation methods that will be used. The result of this step is the audit plan as shown in Table 6.1. The audit plan must be agreed on by the audit owner as well as by the project manager representing the project to be audited.

Audit methods

In a project management audit, a multi-method approach is used. Methods to gather information include:

- Document analysis.
- Interview.
- Observation.
- Site visit.
- Presentation.
- Workshop.
- Self-assessment.
- Systemic constellation.

These methods can be used to analyze the project management competence of the project. Which of these methods are applied depends on the specific case and on the audit assignment. An audit should at a minimum include documentation analysis and interviews. The more holistic the picture should be the more different angles on the project or program are necessary, including interviews with

Table 6.1 Example auditing plan

Auditing plan			
Working format	*Participants*	*Date*	*Venue*
Meeting: start-up	Audit owner Auditor	23.02 Duration: 1 hour	Room: 2.22
Meeting: clarification of the auditing	Project manager Auditor	25.02 Duration: 1.5-2 hours	Room: 2.22
Self-assessment: PM competences of the project manager	Project manager	27.02 Duration: 1 hour	
Self-assessment: team PM competence	Project team	27.02 Duration: 3 hours	Room: 2.22
Group interview with the project manager and project team	Project manager Team members Auditor	01.03 Duration: 2 hours	Room: 1.12
Interview with the project owner	Project owner Auditor	01.03 Duration: 1 hour	Room: 1.12
Group interview with client representatives	Client "project manager" Further client representatives Auditor	01.03 Duration: 1.5 hours	At the client's site
Observation: project team meeting	Project team Project manager Auditor	02.03 Duration: about 1.5 hours	Room: 1.22
Presentation: audit results	Audit owner Project manager Project team Client representatives Auditor	03.03 Duration: 2 hours	Room: 1.10
Meeting: close down	Auditor Audit owner	05.03 Duration: 1 hour	Room: 2.22

different representatives of the project and relevant stakeholders such as investors, suppliers, and other parties that are affected by the project. Further to traditional methods, self-assessment methods and systemic working forms can add value. By applying such additional methods, the audit becomes even more of a learning experience for the project.

Methods to present the audit results include:

- Report.
- Presentation.
- Workshop.

The quality of the results of the audit depends very much on the scope of the methods and the professional application of these.

Document analysis

In a document analysis, the project management competence of a project team can be observed. Documents to be considered are project management documents such as the project work breakdown structure, project bar chart, project environmental analysis, project organization chart, project progress reports, and minutes of project meetings. Table 6.1 shows some questions from a questionnaire used in an audit. This questionnaire supports the analysis. To add value to the project team the auditor does not stop with ticking boxes whether a certain project management document is there or not, but the auditor also analyses the quality of the project management plan and provides feedback. Criteria for assessing the quality of the project management plans include completeness, structure and visualization, and consistency between the single project management documents. The quality criteria depend on the project management approach used as a basis for the audit. In the case of a process-oriented project management approach, for instance, the auditor will always look for a process-oriented work breakdown structure.

Interview

Interviews can be conducted to obtain more detailed information based on questions that arose from the documentation analysis. The interviews are conducted with the project manager, the project owner, and representatives of the project team. In the case of a program, interviews with the program owner, the project managers, and the project owners of the different projects are required. To get a holistic perception of the project it is often essential to conduct further interviews with representatives of relevant stakeholders like the client and suppliers. Single and group interviews can be differentiated, while single interviews may allow more concentration on one interview partner and digging into a very specific topic, the group interview has the advantage that the auditors can collect the different perceptions of several interview partners at the same time and see their interaction with each other.

Observation

In an observation, the auditors collect further information about the project management competence based on observation criteria. Project owner meetings, project team meetings, and project sub-team meetings can be observed. For instance, by observing a project team meeting, the auditors gain insight into the project management competence of the team.

Self-assessment

Applying self-assessments can significantly add to the learning perspective of an audit, as the auditees from the project team create for themselves a picture of the situation, which may provide the auditors with additional insights, and at the same time make them understand the situation. Such self-assessments may cover assessments of individual project management competence of players such as the project manager, the project owner, or a project team member. Such self-assessments allow the individuals to reflect on their current project management competencies. In addition to individual self-assessments, self-assessments for the project team may be applied to allow the project team to reflect on whether they have a collective understanding of the project objectives, can develop commitment, use synergies, solve conflicts, or see learning as a value in the project culture.

To make the project team more aware of the status of the project, a project scorecard may be applied to help the project team organize for project control. The assignment to the project team to apply a project scorecard and assess the project status allows the auditors to get a quick insight into the project and the project team to raise awareness as to where they stand.

The auditors may combine the team or project self-assessment with an observation. Both situations provide possibilities for observing the process and gathering further information.

Systemic board

A systemic board is a specific working form in which an individual or a small team uses different objects (for example wooden bricks) to visualize a project situation. For example, we ask a project manager to visualize the current situation of a project by using bricks. Figure 6.2 provides an example of such a systemic board. This working form allows relationship visualization, abstraction, and systemic thinking. The method is increasingly applied in project and program evaluations and allows the generation of a rich picture of the project situation. This is an immediate intervention, the person visualizes and verbalizes the situation, makes their implicit knowledge explicit, and therefore can find or be guided to find solutions for the project situation. The systemic board especially suits well for wicked project situations. If the setting includes finding a solution for example in a crisis or conflict situation, the differentiation to project coaching might get blurred.

Figure 6.2: Example of a systemic board

Presentation and workshop

As part of collecting information on the project as well as for presenting the project management audit findings, presentations and even workshops can be used. Presentation situations can help ease a stressful situation for the project manager, as they usually want to present the project to the auditors. Such project presentations are an adequate method for example early in the audit, in an audit kick-off, when the auditors and the representatives of the project or program meet, and the auditors provide an overview of the auditing plan. The project manager might be given the task to introduce the project briefly in a 15–20-minute presentation. To make an audit a learning experience, an in-depth presentation of the results is needed. The results should at least be presented to the project manager, the project team, and the project owner (who is the audit owner). This leads to a better understanding and more acceptance of the results and enables the project to become a learning organization.

Report

The report's objective is to summarize the audit findings and provide recommendations to further develop the project. Table 6.2 shows the structure of a project audit report. We differentiate between recommendations for the project and those for the parent company if some of the issues are of general concern for all projects or if issues cannot be solved at the project level, but only at the company level.

Table 6.2 Report

Structure: project management audit report
1 Executive summary
2 Situation analysis, context, and description of the auditing process of Project XY
3 Brief description of the Project XY
4 Analysis of the project management of Project XY
5 Analysis of the project start
6 Analysis of the project coordination
7 Analysis of the project controlling
8 Analysis of the project close down
9 Recommendations for Project XY
10 Recommendations for the company
11 Enclosures

To increase acceptance, the project manager should be able to provide feedback on a draft report. The audit report is the basis for the follow-up agreement between the project manager and the project owner/audit owner. The latter is responsible for checking whether the recommendations have been followed.

Clear auditing roles

The auditing system is a temporary communication system in which the audit owner, the auditor(s), representatives of the project, and representatives of relevant environments cooperate. We differentiate between the initiator of the audit and the audit owner. Initiators of the audit can be for example the PM office, a representative of a profit center, or the client.

Audit owner

We recommend the audit owner should be the project owner, whose interest is to ensure the quality of the management of the project, provide a learning opportunity for the project team, and ensure the audit can be performed. The audit owner is responsible for the assignment of the audit and agreements about the scope, and timing of the audit with representatives of the project and the auditor. Further, the audit owner must ensure the (project) resources for the audit.

Auditors

Often the audit is performed by two to three auditors, one of whom takes over the role of lead auditor. The auditors analyze the project management and give recommendations regarding the further development of the management of the project. The auditor is not responsible for following up, to see whether the recommendations are implemented into the project. The auditor needs not only profound project management competencies but also auditing competencies like designing the auditing process or performing an interview professionally. Thus, attitude, social competence, and emotional intelligence are important.

Auditees

The role of the main representative of the project is taken over by the project manager. The objective of this role is to contribute information for the audit and to invest resources. Tasks of the project manager in an audit are for example to contribute to clarification of the situation in the project, give feedback to the audit plan, agree on the scope and methods of the audit, provide documents for the documentation analysis, or be an interview partner. Further representatives of the project and project stakeholders serve as information providers in the audit process.

Rules, values, and communication

The rules for the audit must be agreed on in the auditing system. The communication policy should be agreed on between the auditor and the project manager as the main representative of the project at the beginning of the audit. To provide a learning opportunity for the project, the audit needs to be performed in a cooperative style. That also means that the representatives of the project that is audited should be kept informed by the auditor. Circumstances that should lead to a cancellation of the audit and the consequences of a cancellation should also be agreed on at the start. The quality of the audit depends on the willingness of the project to cooperate and the time and resources available. One major challenge is that the results of the audit are not perceived as personal feedback to the single project manager who then will be blamed for mismanagement. This means also that there is a need for a certain culture of openness in the project-oriented company.

Follow-up of the audit

Often the results of the audit are not implemented by the project. A formal follow-up is necessary. A follow-up agreement signed by the project manager and the project owner ensures the implementation of audit results. After the auditors have provided their feedback and recommendations in the audit presentation and documented them formally in the audit report, they step out. The audit is formally determined in a last meeting with the audit owner. Which of the actions recommended in the audit report need to be implemented in the project is agreed between the project owner and the project manager or project team. Thus, also the follow-up of the audit is the task of the project owner and not the auditor.

Auditing for the governance of projects

So far, we have discussed the methods and process of management auditing of projects and programs, in this section, we reflect the need and benefits.

Need and benefits

The need for management auditing of projects derives from the empowerment of the project and programs, which is an ideal project-oriented organization acts autonomously with a minimum of intervention by the line organization. To assure quality and the application of agreed standards, management auditing is necessary. Therefore, we perceive project and project management auditing as instruments for governance in the project-oriented company. The benefits of audits of projects are twofold. On the one hand, they provide a learning opportunity for the single project to improve its project management competence. On the other hand, by evaluating the results of several management audits, patterns can be found. For instance, if a lot of the projects have a low-quality cost plan or do not apply proper project control, these issues are general subjects for improvement in the parent organization. The results of the audits can further lead to an improvement of the business processes project management or program management.

Responsibility

Empowerment of projects and programs is one of the key values of the project-oriented company. To govern the projects and to ensure the quality of the project management and program management processes, the PMO provides project management guidelines and procedures, standard project plans for repetitive projects, project management infrastructure, management consulting services, and management auditing for projects and programs. Thus, the PM office is responsible for the development of guidelines and procedures for the management auditing of projects. A standardized auditing process ensures the comparability of the auditing results between projects.

Auditors may be recruited externally to the company (such as consulting companies), or internally. Auditing can be considered as job enlargement for senior project managers. The auditors are often organized in a (virtual) pool linked to the PMO. Also, the PMO is responsible for the training of the auditors. Professional auditors not only need to be experienced project managers but also need to know the auditing process and methods.

Conclusion

The chapter shows what a systematic auditing process might look like. We describe widely applied methods such as documentation analysis, interviews, and observations and introduce less traditional ones such as self-assessment and systemic board. We conceptualize the audit as a communication system, which stresses the need for clear roles, and communication policies. Finally, we discuss the responsibility of the PMO and its task to provide auditing guidelines, and forms and ensure the quality of the auditing of projects and programs.

The benefits of management auditing of projects and programs are to provide governance as well as learning to a project or program. However, the evaluation of the results of several project management audits may serve as a basis for the further development of project management in a project-oriented organization.

The chapter advocates that management auditing of projects and programs should be performed to value. The recommendations as shown in this chapter can be summarized as follows:

- *A modern predictive, adaptive, or hybrid project or program management approach* must be the basis for managing auditing of projects and programs (see Chapter 22).
- *Project auditing on a regular base should be considered as part of the governance system* of a project-oriented organization. For example, each project or program with a certain complexity should be checked after its start and significant stages.
- *A certain formalism is required:* Auditing process description and forms like auditing assignment, and auditing follow-up agreement, support the standardization and transparency of the audit.
- *Clear expectations and communication agreements:* Objectives, scope, and consequences of the auditing must be clear. It is not the project manager who is audited but the project. This must be clearly communicated! A communication policy must be agreed on.
- *Assessing the quality of project management:* It is not good enough to tick boxes whether a certain project management document exists or not, but to add value it is necessary to go one step further and assess the quality of project management and provide feedback.

- *Multiple audit methods:* Interviews with the client and suppliers are particularly challenging but add different and significant perspectives to the audit results. An audit based on only one interview with the project manager is extremely limited. Self-assessments and systemic constellations are good instruments for learning. A presentation of the audit results adds to the understanding and supports the acceptance of the results.
- *Clear role and responsibility of the auditor:* The auditor provides his or her feedback on the project and recommends actions. Which of these actions need to be implemented in the project is agreed between the project owner and the project manager or project team. The follow-up of the audit is the task of the project owner and not the auditor.
- *Responsibility for the auditing:* The PMO can provide auditing as a service to projects and programs.
- *Professional auditors:* The auditors need to be experienced project managers, but also need to know the auditing process and methods. Senior project managers, who would like to act as auditors, need special training in auditing methods.

References and further reading

Axelos (2015). *PRINCE2 Agile*, London: The Stationary Office.

Axelos (2020). *An Executive Guide to Prince2 Agile*, London: The Stationary Office.

Gareis, R., Gareis, L. (2018). *Project. Program. Change. A Textbook and Handbook for Intrapreneurs in Project-Oriented Organizations*, 1st Edition, Abingdon: Taylor & Francis Group.

IPMA (2018a). *Project Excellence Baseline for Achieving Excellence in Projects and Programmes*, Zurich: International Project Management Association.

IPMA (2018b). *Individual Competence Baseline for Project Management*, Zurich: International Project Management Association.

IPMA (2018c). *ICB4 in an Agile World*, Zurich: International Project Management Association.

Project Management Institute (2017). *Agile Practice Guide*, Newton Square, PA: Project Management Institute.

Project Management Institute (2021). *A Guide to the Project Management Body of Knowledge PMBOK Guide*, 7th edition, Newtown Square, PA: Project Management Institute.

Part II

Performance

Part II is about the doing of the work of the project, and the delivery of the project results and benefits. We start by describing how to measure performance and manage requirements, scope, and configuration. Then there are two chapters on organization. The first describes the project organization, and the second the role of the owner organization. We explain the business case and benefits realization, return to the owner organization, and consider the delivery of value. Then we explore integrated project delivery. There are two chapters on data management. The first looks at the use of data analytics, and the second at managing digital infrastructure. We then describe the management of risk and the management of project crises. We end this part with a chapter on sustainability in project management.

Chapter 7: Measuring project performance

Ossi Pesämaa introduces principles, issues, and concepts for measuring project performance. The chapter is prepared for an applied audience searching for inspiration to observe performance qualitatively and quantitatively. While the area of measuring performance covers a broad range of principles, issues, and concepts, this chapter can be seen as an overarching umbrella that inspires readers to dig deeper and approach project performance empirically. The chapter offers hands-on qualitative definitions and diagnostics of empirical observations.

Chapter 8: Managing requirements, scope and configuration

Focusing on requirements, scope, and configuration, Hemanta Doloi highlights the elements of the three interrelated dimensions. Keeping stakeholders and customers at the core of decision-making in front-end requirement analysis, the processes of managing and controlling projects with a clear alignment of needs and requirements in the product or services in relation to the operating environment are established. The underlying processes are analyzed and the

DOI: 10.4324/9781003274179-8

extension of knowledge in integrated management is highlighted. It is suggested that the project scope must be defined to include only essential activities to provide the deliverables and meet requirements. However, an important issue in scope planning is the alignment of the requirement and configuration with the activities that result in a product maximization of the business goals. Lack of effective scope planning can lead to different issues such as dissatisfied customers which potentially results in sub-standard operational performance. The project management team must adopt a comprehensive approach to managing requirements and configurations within the processes of scope management meeting or exceeding the strategic and business objectives and ensuring long-term success.

Chapter 9: Project organization

Rodney and Martina describe the development of the project organization. Project organization defines the roles, responsibilities, relationships, and rights of internal project stakeholders. People need to know what is expected of them, and what are the lines of authority. We define relationships, which include communication. People need to know to whom they send information and from whom they receive it. People also need to know where they stand and from whom they will receive help and support. We introduce social representation as a social construct for defining order to enable people to orientate themselves to their work environment and to enable communication. We introduce identity, which is about people feeling they belong to the project, and know their roles, responsibilities, relationships, and rights. We introduce responsibility matrices. Traditionally, people have suggested five types of project organization, which we describe. We finish by considering three contemporary design elements.

Chapter 10: Project owner organizations

Graham Winch explores the role of the project owner organization. The project owner is at the heart of the project process; without an owner identifying the need for a new asset, developing a robust value proposition for it, and then ensuring that the asset resulting from the project is moved into beneficial use for customers, the investment cycle that we know as a project does not work. The owner needs to define clearly the project mission and supporting value proposition and raise the required finance. The owner then designs the arrangements for managing the governance interface with the delivery project and the commercial interface with suppliers. Finally, the owner needs to take the asset delivered by the project and achieve its beneficial use, thereby generating the funding to repay the finance raised.

Chapter 11: Managing business case and benefits realization

A project starts with the development of a business case, which can be modified throughout the execution and implementation of the project. The project ends with the often-difficult task of implementing the project, usually involving the utilization of the project's output by the end-users, to achieve the desired benefits described in the business case. Jack Merideth and Ofer Zwikael discuss the need for a senior manager who will have the overall accountability for a project, oversee project execution by the project manager, and be responsible for achieving the benefits desired from the project by the funding organization, a person we refer to as the project "owner". They describe how the project and its environment play out as the project is executed and implemented to achieve those benefits. The success of the project can be determined by three measures: the success of achieving the project plan, the success of attaining the desired benefits, and the satisfaction of the project's funder with the overall results.

Chapter 12: Managing value in projects

Recent research often considers projects as ways to create value for organizations, instead of devices for reaching momentary goals. The subjective, multidimensional, and evolving nature of value requires consideration of value creation in complex organizational constellations and in uncertain, evolving contexts. Such conditions give rise to project actors' errors in planning and assessing value, most often the overestimation of benefits and underestimation of costs. Miia Martinsuo introduces three main processes of managing value in projects: making the value proposition, planning and managing value streams, and delivering value outcomes. Also, she discusses the manifestations of errors in value-related planning, when the project progresses on its lifecycle. As value concerns both material and immaterial benefits and sacrifices, managing value is equally much a task of managing perceptions and impressions as managing very practical products. The chapter concludes with some suggestions for project managers who aspire to enhance their capabilities for managing value in projects.

Chapter 13: Managing integrated project delivery

The prevailing model for construction delivery has been based on a highly competitive tendering approach based on cost/time bids with the client (and facility operations team) taking a hands-off orientation towards direct project delivery involvement. This traditional approach is increasingly challenged by a radically different integrated and collaborative concept in which the project design, (contractor and often major services subcontractors) delivery team, the facility operations team, and the project owner's representative form a united team to design and deliver the project. This integrated project delivery (IPD) form is governed by a multi-party alliancing contractual contract, binding participating teams into a single functioning entity that is contractually assured to meet a mutually agreed fixed cost/time delivery plan. The contract uses the agreed cost/time target to incentivize participants through a gain-pain sharing mechanism based on the final project cost/time and agreed key result performance measures. IPD performance is governed by the contract form adopted, effective collaborative, and integrative interpersonal participant behaviours, and a systemic focus on innovation and reflexivity action in response to unanticipated events affecting "the delivery plan". Superior performance requires participants to develop and use a specific set of knowledge, skills, attributes, and experience to support effective participant team integration and collaboration. Derek Walker and Beverley Lloyd-Walker explain how this novel project delivery form achieves this challenge.

Chapter 14: Data analytics in managing projects

In today's society, project work gains traction across many industries. As projects are characterized by novelty and uncertainty, emerging digital technologies promise solutions that improve performance and help deliver full benefits. Amidst this digitization, digital technologies such as data analytics and Artificial Intelligence (AI) streamline the large amount of data generated. However, this critical information is only partially leveraged during and after projects to date. Project data are generated, collected, and analyzed across all stages of project management and delivery. Eleni Papadonikolaki and Carlos Galera-Zarco conceptualize the relation between projects, information, and data, and discuss key application areas of data analytics in projects, for instance in scheduling and costing. Next, they present the state-of-the-art applications, means, and tools of data analytics in key areas of project management. Finally, they set out challenges and future opportunities around project data analytics especially with regard to leadership, teamwork, and talent management.

Chapter 15: Managing digital projects infrastructure

Digital infrastructures are increasingly used in project delivery. They are made up of complex and evolving sets of interconnected software packages and applications. Managing digital infrastructures is challenging as they are largely invisible to their users while their functioning is uninterrupted, and as they involve various technical and social boundaries beyond the scope of projects. Especially, the growing global production of generic software implies that although digital infrastructures facilitate complex project work, they also shape and standardize certain work practices and power relations that appear novel to project practitioners. Jennifer Whyte and Ali Eshraghi discuss some practical lessons and considerations for future project managers.

Chapter 16: Managing project risk

Our ability to manage risk is directly proportional to our chances of successfully delivering our project. David Hillson explains why, starting from first principles. Risk is "uncertainty that matters" and we need to understand and manage any uncertainty that can affect our objectives. This includes future events, variability, ambiguity, and emergence. We can address future risk events using a simple and intuitive process based on answering eight basic questions. Variability risk can be modelled, ambiguities can be clarified, and we can become resilient to emergent risks. But processes and models don't manage risk; people manage risk. We need emotional intelligence if we are to understand the effect of underlying risk attitudes for ourselves and others and manage them intentionally. By recognizing the full range of risks faced by our project and addressing them proactively and intentionally, we can give our projects the best chances of success every time.

Chapter 17: Managing project crisis

Projects are conducted in an environment increasingly characterized by volatility, uncertainty, complexity, and ambiguity and are due to their nature susceptible to unexpected events. These unexpected events can create a project crisis if their impact is severe and a threat to the achievement of high-priority project objectives. A successful response to a project crisis requires a responsive and functioning structure, good interpersonal relationships, and competent people. However, there is a tendency that the measures necessary to successfully manage a crisis tend to be absent when they are required the most. Christine Unterhizenberger suggests that enhanced resilience will enable the project to recover better from crisis situations by facilitating desirable structures and behaviours prior to the occurrence of a crisis. She also raises awareness for potential opportunistic aspects in a crisis.

Chapter 18: Sustainable project management

Sustainability is one of the most important challenges of our time. How can prosperity be developed without compromising the lives of future generations? As companies are integrating sustainability in their products, services, and business processes, the concept of sustainability has more recently also been linked to project management. From the emerging sustainability school of project management, two types of relationship between sustainability and project management appeared: the sustainability of the deliverable that the project realizes, and the sustainability of the process of delivering and managing the project. Gilbert Silvius, Ron Schipper, and Martina Huemann identify the areas of impact of sustainability on project management. They also cover examples and instruments for the integration of sustainability into project management and conclude that Sustainable Project Management needs a scope, paradigm, and mind shift in managing projects.

Chapter 7

Measuring project performance

Ossi Pesämaa

Introduction

When I offer workshops and meet students in methods classes, I often use the metaphor of taking pictures. I often use the example of taking pictures of cars. This is not because I am a fan of cars but rather because cars are good examples of being portrayed in a rather similar way for most of us. In short, I say a car is just a theoretical construct. All of us can visualize a car by closing our eyes. This is the "closed eyes" definition of face validity. In practice, this means that if I take 1,000 different pictures of different quality, the clarity of a car may vary. Some pictures may look blurred and unclear, whereas you can specify every little detail in others. For most of us, it is enough to see four wheels and the body of a car to make an assessment. For operationalization and measuring a car, we just need these two items. When we take pictures of project performance, we may need much more detail. Some of us may not be able to visualize project performance by closing our eyes; we need much more detail. Therefore, in order to complete what project performance is, we need a definition that tells us what constitutes project performance in this particular case.

This chapter introduces a framework for measuring and diagnostics for analyzing performance measures. The chapter introduces ideas and means to understand the direction or context for measuring project performance. Upon reading and reflecting on the content of this chapter, the reader should be

DOI: 10.4324/9781003274179-9

prepared to see different options for upcoming situations as well as follow up and improve individual or organizational project management skills.

Project performance is not always linear

Performance is one of the most widely discussed concepts in project management. Although it is tempting to match performance measures to linear predictive models (Brunsson, Rasche, & Seidl, 2012), we notice that the process is often not serial but involves multiple parallel processes that contribute to deviation. The parallel nature of projects tends to result in delays (e.g., time overruns) at any stage of a project. Consequently, such lags in lead time and other processes add to cost overruns and delays in other planned activities. Already, at an early stage, the plan needs to be adjusted to upcoming situations.

While project performance is complex, uncertain, temporal, and evaluated conceptually, Speklé, Verbeeten, and Widener (2021) suggest that there is a need to bridge organizational action with standardized metrics and to document whether activities are certain or uncertain. Such an evaluation may appear to be simple, but it is not. However, this process will tell us what is certain and what is not. Furthermore, this device will also tell us how to assess the risks from all uncertainties. This step is just the beginning of gaining an understanding of a project but yet a critical one.

What is project performance?

To this end, project performance is a relative measure. It is observed in reference to an activity, previous project, other individuals, standards, or some other reference point. Project performance can sometimes be measured directly by direct measures such as financial budgets, the use of materials, or the length of a project. Sometimes a project also involves elements that cannot be measured directly but are measured through a series of indirect measures such as team satisfaction, perceived quality, or the following work processes.

Furthermore, the temporal nature of projects means that activities follow budgeted plans, specifications, and goals. For instance, performance is assessed in relationship to specified goals, expectations, and budgets of time and costs.

Although identifying adequate measures of performance may appear simple, it is not. There are several reasons why measuring performance is not simple. First, many projects tend to be surrounded by many unknowns, uncertainties, and risks that cannot be foreseen. For instance, detailed plans change, key decision makers are replaced, financing is withdrawn, and permissions for the project may be delayed. Therefore, many project managers view projects as creative, problem-solving, and iterative processes. This means that one step forward is often preceded by a step backwards. In addition, plans are complemented and performance aspirations revised. This is also part of project performance.

While investors, administrators, and surrounding stakeholders may expect predictive models, reality tells us that a too-predictive model instead fails to offer true performance. A senior project leader I previously interviewed claimed that

> if you ask individuals in an organization to maximize X activities in order to maximize Y performance and offer rewards for maximizing X. Guess what? The entire organization will maximize X. However, the organization may maximize the predicted model but may not truly maximize performance.

An example here is megaprojects which may take years to complete, and technology X can change during the project. So, the result may well match with defined performance criteria but not with the latest technology at hand. The route moving from defining goals towards ending a project and evaluating the goals is often not (and should not be) as linear as planned.

Conceptual assumptions of project performance

Knowing how to contribute to performance requires conceptual boundaries of performance. In the beginning, I referred to a definition. An adequate definition is the first step to set up boundaries. This is important for practice. If something boils only at 100 degrees, then this is a boundary, and it should be clearly addressed. Yet, a performance measure is often very fine-tuned, and we can say it is almost boiling at 99 degrees, close to boiling at 90 degrees and frozen below zero degrees. To this end, the measurement allows us to measure an activity at a certain point. In practice, such boundaries mean that the organization needs to know and agree on what project performance is. Such elements of performance involve both tangible estimates (e.g., length and weight, or in a construction project, the use of raw materials, use of certain equipment) and intangible estimates (e.g., frequency of cultural background, frequency of interaction within a team, and knowledge).

While tangible elements allow us to almost exactly measure a degree, intangible measures are estimated according to a standard or in relationship to an expected value. Many of the latter measurements are often assessments of some kind.

An assessment or measurement of an exact point is an observable property or point of observation. A point of observation is measurable. If you cannot observe it – you cannot measure it. To this end, certain observations are more tangible and offer correct estimates, whereas other measures are intangible and more difficult to observe exactly. Yet, typically the more you observe, the more you will know how much error or bias comes with an observation.

Measuring project performance quantitatively and qualitatively

In my early research career, I was advised not to collect data quantitatively with open-ended questions but rather to focus on capturing unstandardized answers through interviews or small focus groups. Today, we have indeed developed more structured techniques and advanced programs to code data and structure large datasets with non-standardized data. Nonetheless, there is a long tradition of distinguishing between what we refer to as qualitative and quantitative research traditions. A pragmatic way of defining a quantitative tradition is that it uses measures that quantify a specific economic, engineering, social, or some other specific activity (Pesämaa et al., 2021). The quantitative tradition pushes to standardize a measure, so it repeatedly measures similar activities in the same way. It is a measure that repeatedly captures a phenomenon in the same way with only marginal bias or error and possesses high reliability. We say it measures what it is purported to measure.

For instance, by measuring the same thing in the same way, we can compare lengths, usage, or effectiveness between one project (or organization) and another. Such quantitative measures appear in statistics and use numbers to describe a pattern (e.g., how much gas per mile a specific car is using).

Instead, qualitative research traditions focus on non-standardized measures and rather look for richness to describe a certain activity. Some claim that it is very difficult to standardize certain concepts such as creativity, passion, and enthusiasm. By describing these activities qualitatively, using social properties, we often get rich definitions that vary and may not even be commensurable with other situations than a particular situation. Nevertheless, we still use qualitative measures to learn and build experiences from project work.

Below, I distinguish between quantitative tangible performance measures, intangible quantitative performance measures, and qualitative performance measures. Each section is purported to inspire different research approaches to measure project performance.

Quantitative tangible project performance measures

Tangible performance measures of a project could be budgeted costs, lengths, or distances. It is fairly easy to gain exact metrics if the performance is measured in metres during a given time. However, many performance measures are combined with less certain measures which may involve subjective qualities. For instance, the measures may be of a quality that meets certain criteria such as a level of sustainability, delivery time, use of local suppliers, or some other criteria.

Table 7.1 lists a number of project performance constructs that address a certain dimension of performance. First of all, Table 7.1 suggests that the various dimensions of performance (Table 7.1 column 1) can be measured directly by a number of different items (Table 7.1 column 3).

The second column in Table 7.1 suggests an overall definition of the construct. The third column in Table 7.1 suggests three different observables related to the associated definition. Note that Table 7.1 reflects tangible direct measures, and therefore it is designed to reflect "true" measures in terms of number, size, and use. The accurate "true" point of observation is emphasized here to say that something is measured by a tangible property rather than a self-reported estimation or a self-assessment of a perceived situation.

Quantitative tangible project performance measures

The following section will bring the measurement process closer towards intangible activities. You will find that these activities are based on assessments and therefore not exactly fit a continuous metric system.

Different from Table 7.1, Table 7.2 lists a number of intangible project performance constructs. First, Table 7.1 suggests that the various dimensions of perceived performance (Table 7.2 column 1) can be measured directly by a number of different items (Table 7.2 column 3).

The second column in Table 7.2 suggests an overall definition of the construct. The emphasis here is on "perceived" definitions. The third column in Table 7.2

Table 7.1 Tangible project performance measures

Construct	*Typical definition*	*Example of operationalization (proxy)*
Cost performance	… refers to the use of budgeted resources.	Use of raw materials in $
		Use of equipment in $
		Use of facilities in $
Time performance	… reflect scheduled precision in projects.	Meet budgeted time limits
		Deliver project goals on time
		Respond to inaccuracies quickly
Quality performance	… is limiting the number and size of inaccuracies.	Number of inaccuracies
		Size of inaccuracies
		Delivery as expected
Sustainability performance	… is the degree of environmental, economic, and social inclusion.	Meet budgeted waste of water
		Use of local suppliers
		Above-average support of local unions
Innovation performance	… is the degree of newness in the project outcome.	Number of new raw materials
		Number of new production techniques
		Number of changes to project design
1 Process performance	… is the overall degree of creativity during the project process.	Number of co-created solutions to problems
		Frequency of meetings to discuss upcoming issues
		Average number of issues during a weekly work meeting

Table 7.2 Quantitative intangible project performance measures

Construct	*Typical definition*	*Example of operationalization (proxy)*
Cost performance	… use of budgeted resources in relation to past experiences.	Used raw materials more efficiently than in previous projects. Used equipment more efficiently than previous projects. Used facilities more efficiently than previous projects.
Time performance	… reflect perceived time precision in projects.	I would say that the project was characterized by time efficiency. I would say that the project proceeded as planned. I would say that project inaccuracies were resolved quickly.
Quality performance	… is the perceived work to limit the number of quality issues.	I would say that we had a strong focus on limiting inaccuracies. I would say that overall we met the specified quality. I would say that there were fewer quality issues vis-à-vis other similar projects.
Sustainability performance	… is the perceived environmental, economic, and social inclusion.	I would say that we limit the waste of water at all times. I would say that we tried our utmost to contract local suppliers. We supported local unions more than in previous projects.
Innovation performance	… is the perceived degree of newness in the project outcome.	I would say that we often use new raw materials. I would say that we often questioned past techniques. I would say that we often adopted changes in project design.
Process performance	… perceived degree of creativity during the project process.	I would say that we often co-created solutions to problems. I would say that we often discussed upcoming issues. We allocated sufficient time to discuss project issues.

suggests three different observables related to the associated definition. In this table, the operationalization is an assessment rather than an accurate measure. Note that Table 7.2 reflects intangible direct measures, and therefore it is designed to reflect "perceived" measures (self-assessment). The perceived point of observation here is emphasized to reflect an assessment rather than an exact true value.

Qualitative performance measures

As mentioned earlier, a qualitative measure is herein a non-standardized measure. It describes a certain activity qualitatively. Qualitative measures are extremely important because we often want to know why certain outcomes deviate and to enrich explanations beyond given numbers. A qualitative definition may still benefit from a protocol that systematically scrutinizes every detail in the observed project experience.

Table 7.3 lists the same theoretical constructs as in Tables 7.1 and 7.2. This time, we are looking for open loose ends to the questions and allow the respondent to elaborate on the answers. What, why, and how questions are typical questions to open up for enriching, describing, and understanding a process or outcome (Martinsuo & Huemann, 2021). Table 7.3 suggests definitions to reflect the specific operationalizations suggested in column 3.

Diagnostics of quantitative and qualitative project performance measures

Measuring something is a goal and purpose-oriented activity (Pesämaa, 2017). Measuring in projects means that the project managers place sensors in the temporal organization to follow up on signals. The signals are used to learn, understand, and gain information from one or multiple units in the organization. The sensor is the measurement instrument. A sensitive measurement captures small nuances of a situation or an activity. A less sensitive situation may not grasp every detail but identify an ongoing process and maybe something with a relationship to other processes and activities.

When we set up a system of sensors that measure various activities, we can find commonalities, associations, and relationships between different processes and outcomes. In research, we often study such relationships to determine how much the X-factor may influence the Y-factor. Therefore, a common goal is not just to measure with sensors in a project but to suggest an overall design of various

Table 7.3 Qualitative project performance measures

Construct	*Typical definition*	*Example of operationalization (proxy)*
Cost performance	… the total direct and indirect cost outcome of a project.	What are the properties of financial costs in this project? Describe how costs are related to lead times. Why are most cost outcomes known and expected?
Time performance	… is the use and management of time during a project.	What was the expected outcome in time? How would you describe time management in this project? Why is time allocation critical in this project?
Quality performance	… is the perceived work to limit the number of quality issues.	What are the important quality properties of this project? Describe how you met the expected quality. What was the most typical quality issue?
Sustainability performance	… is the sustainability outcome of a project.	What were the principles for sustainability in this project? How did you involve sustainability in the project work? Why is this a typical sustainability issue?
Innovation performance	… is the process to adopt and replace past processes and outcomes.	What are the known and unknown processes in this project? How did you question the processes and routines? Why did you adopt new routines during the project?
Process performance	… is the means to reach certain outcomes.	What specific processes did you co-create? How did you deal with upcoming issues? Why was it critical to discuss rather than trust past routines?

measurements (i.e., sensors). Each sensor will then send a signal which can be collected into a system of various measures. The commonalities of these measures are the basic inputs of a research model.

Diagnostics of quantitative performance measures

When we consider a standardized quantitative measurement in a system of measurements, we also tend to focus on direction. Some refer to this direction as a sequence, causality, influence, association, or relationship. The idea for a direction is that one specific measurement is designed to pick up a defined activity, for instance, a team process, and then see if variations in the team process have any commonalities with an outcome of performance, e.g., innovation. In practice, what could we figure out from such a model? Is there an association that tells us that when a team process goes up, we also see that innovation performance goes up? The diagnostics of such a model would tell us if we have a positive association (i.e., correlation) and how strong this association is. Herein, such a model is simplified and very deterministic. Yet, in practice, many situations are extremely complex and may require very detailed in which each activity or process is specified in detail. Every model will engender deviation, bias, or error. We cannot explain all variations.

Diagnostics of qualitative unstandardized performance measures

While much of the quantitative tradition typically searches for explanatory predictive models – qualitative measures describe the same measures but rather openly ask for nuances and richness. What, why, and how questions (see Table 7.3) allow the qualitative researcher to understand and gain information from rather untrusted and unstandardized data. This absorption of data means that the data is not pre-defined by standardized answers.

A rather popular research design is to approach data using thematic analysis (Braun & Clarke, 2006). A simplified definition of thematic analysis is that it is a structured process to code unstructured data systematically with pre-defined themes and subsequent codes.

Table 7.4 visualizes a stepwise model to structure unstructured data (unstandardized) into a model. As projects can become rather complex and pre-defined situations are difficult to predict, there is a need to find means to stay closer to

Table 7.4 Thematic process to qualitative data

Transcribe data	Convert data from a recording or situation into text.
Generate codes	Code activities, process, and outcomes according to a model.
Identify a theme	Merge and integrate codes with commonalities into a theme.
Revise themes	Revise themes and suggest hierarchies for different themes.
Define and categorize themes	Revise the theme and suggest a model or a story that can be used for communicating a specific management idea.

the context and categorize situations according to defined rules. Performance measurement in projects involves many such unknowns, and there is a need to try out different work processes to collect evidence.

Implications for project performance measures

A project is a goal-oriented applied practice to organize a set of activities, resources, and individuals towards a set of temporarily defined goals. It has become increasingly popular to use structured means to measure performance qualitatively. This chapter has discussed principles, procedures, and practices for measuring project performance. The paper has shed light on the following questions:

1 What are the principles behind measuring project performance?
2 What are the procedures to set up a plan for measuring project performance?
3 What are the typical practical measures for measuring project performance?
4 What do they entail and what do they tell us?

Principles

A principle is a notion that bundles together assumptions behind a measurement and organizes the thoughts. A principle not only defines the measure but also asks what it is purported to measure. Any performance measure picks up a signal that can be more or less critical for explaining something by itself or together with another measure.

Procedures

A procedure is more or less a systematically defined idea to reach a conclusion. One idea is for management to suggest answers to problems and suggest means to organize a way to reach such answers. This chapter presented a number of assumptions and premises for project management. For instance, project management is applied, temporal, and goal-oriented. Performance measures in such organizations should therefore deliver signals that align with such measures.

Conclusion

This chapter also attempted to inspire the applied side of management. An applied tradition integrates concrete means with practices. While theory helps us align our practices with other reference points, other types of evidence, and other contexts. Practice operationalizes the theoretical notions by suggesting operational definitions. This chapter is anchored with a number of tables (Tables 7.1–7.3) to illustrate how a theoretical concept can be measured.

References and further reading

Braun, V., & Clarke, V. (2006). Using thematic analysis in psychology. *Qualitative Research in Psychology*, *3*(2), 77–101.

Brunsson, N., Rasche, A., & Seidl, D. (2012). The dynamics of standardization: Three perspectives on standards in organization studies. *Organization Studies*, *33*(5–6), 613–632.

Martinsuo, M., & Huemann, M. (2021). Designing case study research. *International Journal of Project Management*, *39*(5), 417–421.

Pesämaa, O. (2017). Personnel and action control in gazelle companies in Sweden. *Journal of Management Control*, *28*(1), 107–132.

Pesämaa, O., Zwikael, O., Hair Jr, J., & Huemann, M. (2021). Publishing quantitative papers with rigor and transparency. *International Journal of Project Management*, *39*(3), 217–222.

Speklé, R. F., Verbeeten, F. H., & Widener, S. K. (2021). Nondyadic control systems and effort direction effectiveness: Evidence from the public sector. *Management Accounting Research*, 100769.

Chapter 8

Managing requirements, scope and configuration

Hemanta Doloi

Introduction

Projects are the strategic tools of organisations which not only support achieving their business goals and objectives but also satisfy the needs and the requirements of the community at large. While projects provide different deliverables comprising products, services, and knowledge, the scope being the functions of requirements and configurations, consideration of purpose-specific scope definition is an important first step in an effective scope management process. Thus, project deliverables are dependent on the requirements of the stakeholders which eventually shape the configuration of the project product, enabling the realisation of the business objectives of the organisations.

In this important juncture of requirements and configuration, project scope must be defined to include only the essential activities that should be performed and coordinated to provide the deliverables and meet the requirements. However, an important issue in scope planning is how we could align the requirement and configuration with the project activities which results in a product that maximises the business goals and objectives. Lack of effective scope planning will lead to different issues such as unsatisfied customers and potentially contribute to project failure. Thus project managers need a comprehensive approach to managing requirements and configurations within the processes of scope management.

DOI: 10.4324/9781003274179-10

Managing requirements in the project

Requirement is a broad term and it may vary from project to project based on the perspectives being applied. In a nutshell, project requirements comprise three key dimensions, business requirements, stakeholder requirements, and product or service requirements.

Business requirements are about how the project is aligned with the business and strategic objectives of an organisation in the long run and how the investments in the project ensure long-term sustainability from a business perspective. Thus, business requirements must be developed by taking into consideration of the current market needs, future market growth, and emerging market forces in such a way that the owning organisation becomes adaptive to changes with necessary provisions of buffers and resilience in relation to the project operating environment. While business requirements are best assessed through traditional financial measures such as Return on Investment (RoI) or Cost-Benefit Ratio (CBR) at the feasibility stage, continuous reviewing, tracking, and monitoring including necessary realignments must be undertaken as per the changes in operating market conditions including supply-demand fluctuations.

Stakeholder management entails the detailed mapping of stakeholders with respect to their requirements focusing on the entire lifecycle phases of the project. In the stakeholder requirement plan, first, a comprehensive list of stakeholders needs to be prepared, and second, identify all the key requirements of each of the stakeholders over each phase of the project from concept, initiation, planning, execution, commissioning, and handover and operation. Due to the involvement of a large number of stakeholders and an overwhelming amount of conflicting requirements especially in large projects, good stakeholder requirement planning requires careful assessment of the relative importance of the stakeholder with respect to the underlying requirements. While there are many different methods available for stakeholder requirement mapping, the research conducted by the author highlighted Social Network Analysis (SNA) as being one of the most sophisticated mapping tools for handling large data and accurate understanding of stake and impact in stakeholder requirement analysis (Doloi 2018).

Product or service requirements are at the intersection point of both business and stakeholder requirements in projects (APM 2012). The product requirement being a function of both business and stakeholder requirements, the plans should clearly reflect the key priorities of business and stakeholder needs ensuring

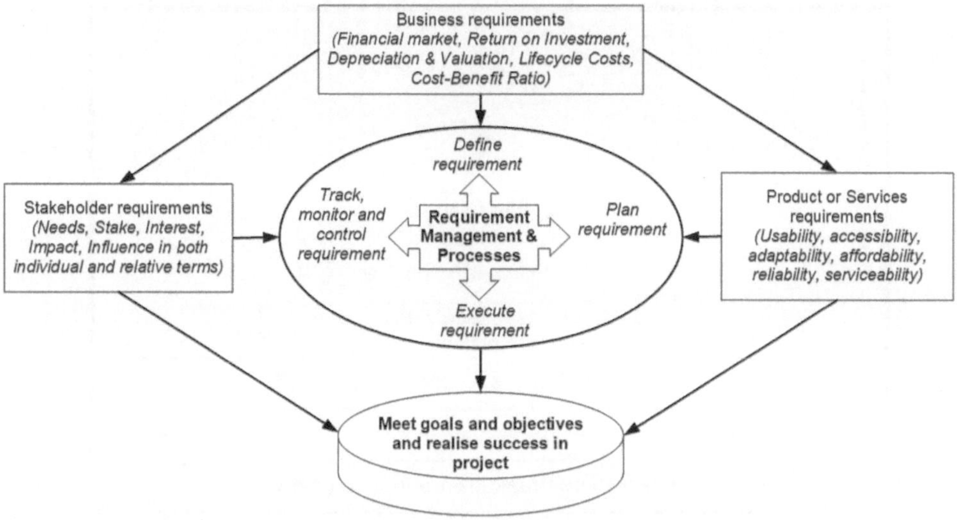

Figure 8.1: Dimensions of requirement management and underlying processes

long-term overall success in the project. Product requirement plans must ensure that project goals and objectives are met from both stakeholder satisfaction and business outcome perspectives. Figure 8.1 shows the integrated requirement management plan in projects. As seen, requirement management entails four key processes namely defining the requirement, planning requirements, executive requirements, and tracking, monitoring, and controlling requirements. These four processes across all three dimensions collectively support the underlying goals and objectives and drive ultimate success in projects.

Scope definition

Having defined the project requirements effectively, the project scope can be defined ensuring organisations' needs and alignment to the operating business environment. Execution of requirement processes along with close vigilance of the operating business environment is required for venturing into new opportunities, flushing out problems and threats, or meeting legislation compliances.

Based on the business environment and requirement analysis, the mission, vision and finally goals and objectives of organisations may need to be revised. The vital point is thus the alignment between business and project goals and objectives as per the requirement analysis.

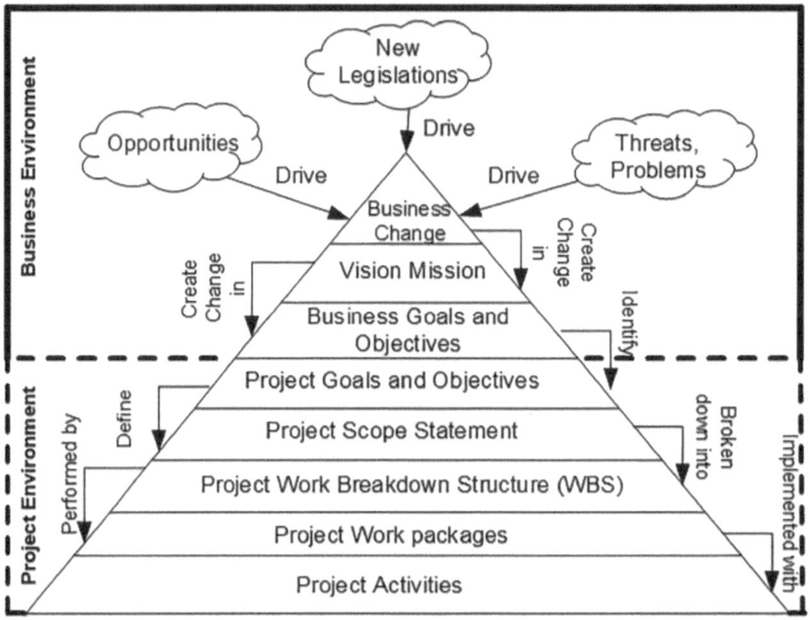

Figure 8.2: Scope definition pyramid

The following diagram shows the scope pyramid encompassing the business environment and project environment in the scope management context.

As seen in Figure 8.2, projects need a sequential top-down evaluation to identify the precise, progressive, and accurate scope.

The scope pyramid helps the project team to harmonise all of the project efforts with the business goals and objectives. Scope definition based on scope pyramid structure will be described in this chapter later.

Detection of errors in scope definition

In the scope definition process, errors and omission of errors (E&OE) are quite obvious and errors are important elements to identify, monitor, and control effectively. Efforts should be made to detect the upfront sources of errors so that precautions can be taken to mitigate or minimise the occurrence of such errors in the downstream execution processes. Following are the five common error types that prevail in a typical project:

- Error type 1: Inconsistency between business and project goals and objectives.
- Error type 2: Inconsistency between project goals and objectives and project scope statement.
- Error type 3: Inconsistency between project scope statement and project Work Breakdown Structure (WBS)/deliverables.
- Error type 4: Inconsistency between project WBS/deliverables and work packages.
- Error type 5: Inconsistency between project work packages and activities.

These errors will be further referenced in the subsequent sections.

Progressive elaboration

As projects create unique products or services at different times, the projects are new experiences. Although experiences could be perceived as similar, due to the virtue of projects being done at different times and locations, there is no similar experience between the two projects in entirety. This characteristic of the project creates some impact on project behaviour. There are always unknown unknowns in every project and often there is a tendency for projects that can be planned without considering them. During the project lifecycle, these unknowns are transformed into known items. Therefore, project scope and consequently time, cost, and other relevant plans should be revised based on them. In a project environment, this phenomenon is called progressive elaboration. It means that during the project lifecycle, more detailed information about the project is being identified.

Scope creep

Changes are inseparable parts of any project. It cannot be possible to prevent changes. Some changes are positive for projects and without them, project goals and objectives cannot be achieved. However, it is important to prevent uncontrolled changes in the project, especially in project scope. Scope creep is an uncontrolled change in the project scope and it is the project manager's responsibility to prevent the scope creep.

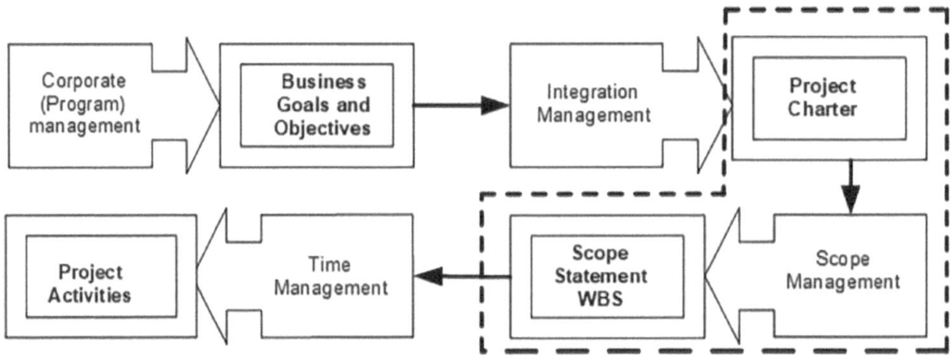

Figure 8.3: Approach to prepare an accurate and comprehensive scope

Scope management scope

As shown in the scope pyramid diagram in Figure 8.1, there are seven important stages in defining accurate and comprehensive scope. However, the layers in the scope pyramid can't be managed in isolation but in conjunction with the multiple core knowledge areas namely corporate management, integration management, and schedule management concurrently. Figure 8.3 shows a clear relationship between corporate, integration, scope, and time management leading to a precise scope definition and associated deliverables.

As can be seen, at first integration management should receive the business goals and objectives and based on its functionalities transform them into the project charter. The project charter is the major input of scope management. Scope management as it will be discussed later evaluates the project charter and defines the project scope with detailed information. The major scope management outputs are the project scope statement and WBS. Finally, time management based on scope management inputs results in detailed project activities ready for logical sequencing and plan for implementation.

Current best practices

Among many available standards in the project management area, two major project standards are the Project Management Body of Knowledge (PMBOK) (PMI 2021) and Project in a Controlled Environment (PRINCE2) (OGC 2017). On the other hand, another two key standards, the Association of PMBOK

(APM 2012) and International Competence Baseline (ICB) of the International Project Management Association (IPMA 2015) present the required body of knowledge in relation to the project manager's competency framework. In fact, most of the location-specific standards have been derived from these key standards across the countries and thus the current review of the best practice is limited to only these key sources in the context of scope management.

PMBOK Seventh Edition (PMI 2021) contains five process groups and ten knowledge areas. Scope management is one of the knowledge areas within the ten key knowledge areas of project management.

PMBOK considers five key processes in order to manage the project scope as discussed below.

1 Collect requirement

Stakeholders are the primary source of identifying project requirements. These requirements are derived from business goals, objectives, and acceptable services or product specifications at completion. In this process, detailed information about project requirements is sought and analysed with respect to the underlying project objectives.

2 Define scope

Based on the gathered information, the project scope should be defined in a detailed manner. The document containing a detailed description of the project is known as a scope statement or Statement of Work (SOW). The scope statement should include detailed information about project deliverables and its products.

3 Create WBS

In order to provide a clear structure for the project, the project should be broken into more manageable components. The most appropriate way to provide this structure is to prepare a WBS.

4 Verify scope

After identifying detailed information about project scope including project scope statement and WBS, project execution is started to provide project deliverables. After completing each deliverable, it should be formally verified that the project customer or sponsor is satisfied with the completed deliverables.

5 Control scope

Changes are considered to be only constants in projects. Any changes in the project usually will have a some impact on project scope, time and cost.

Thus, control scope is one of the key elements to manage any change on project scope during project lifecycle.

In addition to managing scope changes, control scope evaluates the project status in relation to the scope baseline being established before the implementation stage. The control scope processes are the key elements in the scope creep prevention context.

Unlike PMBOK, the PRINCE2 (OGC 2017) does not have a separate part that directly refers to scope management, but it has a clear approach to scope management, and scope management is distributed into plans and quality themes. PRINCE2 consists of Principals, Themes and Processes. Furthermore, "Product focus" is a PRINCE2 principle that states that project scope should be defined based on products. In fact, PRINCE2 uses a technique in planning called "Product based planning".

In Prince2, the following are the key processes used to define the project scope:

1 Write the project product description

   Project product description describes the major project products and customer quality expectations and acceptance criteria.

2 Create the product breakdown structure

   Based on the products that were identified in the project product description, a product breakdown structure will be created. Product breakdown structure is a specific type of WBS that breaks down project scope based on its products.

3 Write the product descriptions

   For each of the products identified in the project product description, a document should be prepared which provides detailed information about them. In other words, a detailed project scope is provided in this stage.

4 After providing a detailed definition of the project scope, project execution will be started and deliverables will be produced in the "Managing product delivery". At the same time "Controlling a stage" reviews the work package status and controls the project progress in terms of time, cost, and scope management. This process prevents scope creep.

5 "Managing a stage boundary" may be a most significant part of PRINCE2. As stated before, progressive elaboration is an important concept in scope management. In the PRINCE2 model, at the end of each stage, different aspects of the project including the business aspect and scope are evaluated and

updated again. At this point, new findings can be added to the project scope by considering business, financial, and social impacts. Therefore, the project manager should be mindful of the progressive elaboration issue.

Scope management process

As stated in the second part of this chapter, the scope management process is launched by receiving a clear project charter from integration management.

The scope management process consists of five major parts namely defining scope, creating WBS, verifying scope, scope review, and scope control.

1 Define scope

Defining scope is the first step in scope management. The main responsibility of scope management is producing a comprehensive statement about the project based on the project charter. In the project charter, the majority of information is of high level including high-level definitions, requirements, and goals and objectives. They are neither measurable nor tangible.

Scope definition should define the project as specific and measurable deliverables and products.

An effective solution for scope clarification is defining project scope as a set of products. If a project is defined as a set of products, the project scope will be product description. If for each product, detailed and clear information including product purpose, product elements, and quality and acceptance criteria is provided, the project scope will be clarified as well. This approach, defining based on the products, is called product-based planning and is a suitable approach for project scope definition.

Designing a product breakdown structure is a helpful approach to illustrating products and their relationship. After defining different products, the provided information will be documented in the project scope statement. The project scope statement includes detailed information about the project scope as follows:

- Project description.
- Project products structure.
- Product detailed information.

- Project assumptions and constraints.
- Project exclusions.

Project exclusion can be helpful, especially in projects wherethe scope is not clear.

Referring to the errors earlier, usually project benefit map is a good basis to prevent such errors effectively. By using a project benefit map, each project's goals and objectives can be assigned to project products. This helps to first analyse whether or not there is a clear product or products for each of the project goals and objectives and secondly, do all of the products relate to one or more project goals and objectives? Figure 8.4 below illustrates a sample project benefit map with estimated benefits shared with respective deliverables.

2 Create a WBS

Although the scope statement includes detailed information about the project scope, further planning needs a suitable scope structure. Project management needs an accurate estimation of cost and time. The most appropriate approach is dividing the project scope into more manageable, measurable, and time-bounded components. WBS is one of the best approaches where work is grouped in a hierarchical structure following a top-down approach. It helps the project team to provide detailed information about work that should be done by the project and what is included and not included in the project.

Furthermore, the hierarchical structure of WBS is the unified and perceptible model between the project team, suppliers, and customers. WBS is an appropriate tool that projects major stakeholders can be linked and the underlying communication protocol can be established.

There are different approaches to defining the WBS. The more common approaches but not limited as listed below:

- Phased-based WBS.
- Deliverable-based WBS.
- Geographical WBS
- Technical process-based WBS

There is a golden rule in preparing WBS which is usually called Rule 100% (Haugan 2003). This Rule states that project WBS should cover 100% of the

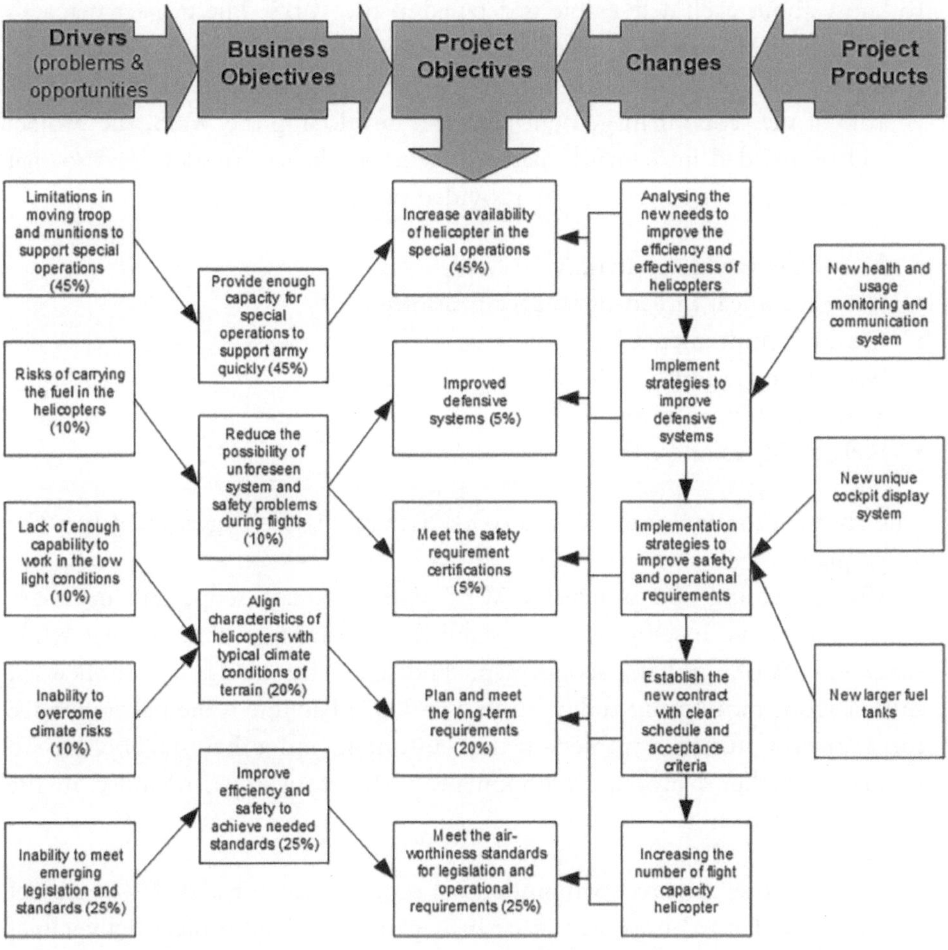

Figure 8.4: Sample benefit map with an estimated share of benefits

work included in the project. This rule is related to Error Type 3 as described earlier. It means that all of the project deliverables that are stated in the project scope statement and contract should be covered in WBS.

The highest level of WBS is called work package. Work packages are further decomposed into project activities for the necessary accuracy required for estimating scope, effort, and resources in the time management module.

An important point in designing WBS is considering the appropriate level of scope and appropriate details. The level of information that the project needs to know about each deliverable is detailed in the WBS. The project manager and the project team are usually responsible for identifying an appropriate scope and level of detail in the context of developing the WBS in the project. As part of the scope management plan and developing the WBS, the project should be divided into smaller parts till work packages are identified so that the following information can be provided on them:

- Needed effort and materials.
- Clear technical agreed-upon specifications.
- Quality requirements.
- Acceptance criteria.
- Verification procedure.
- Related Milestones.

The above information for all the work packages is then aggregated into the scope plan.

After providing comprehensive WBS with adequate scope and necessary details, the scope baseline is then established capturing a clear project scope statement, WBS, and the scope plan. The scope baseline is a reference for further scope monitoring and control. The scope baseline is the best reference for a project manager, project team, customer, and other stakeholders to evaluate whether a product, component, or functionality is included in the project scope or not.

3 Verify scope

Based on the prepared comprehensive scope statement and WBS, project activities are defined in project time management. When project deliverables are completed, the project team should evaluate the deliverables and obtain customer acceptance.

At this stage, the project team should compare the characteristics and functionality of deliverables in comparison with the contract, scope statement, and other documents that describe deliverables.

4 Review scope

As stated before, progressive elaboration is an important issue in the project and one of the project failure sources. Managing progressive elaboration needs an iterative process in scope definition. It means that after a specific point throughout the project lifecycle, the project team should evaluate the scope definition chain. Once a new component including product, functionality, and/or serviceability is found that needs to be in the project scope, the project scope document should be updated provided the new component is accepted by the change control board. The review scope can be done at any time but review at the end of each project phase or stage is effective and efficient.

5 Control scope

One of the key responsibilities in the control scope process is to monitor, track, and prevent the errors arising from upstream processes. As described earlier, there are usually five major errors in the scope definition pyramid, and three of them namely Error types 2, 3, and 4 belong to the control scope process. Scope control always oversees the alignment and consistency between project goals and objectives, scope statements, and the project WBS. On the other hand, scope control ensures that all the works stated in the project scope statement are covered by the WBS and get delivered so that project goals and objectives are met.

Scope Creep is a critical issue in project management and control scope thus ensuring that project scope is not changed without following agreed-upon processes for change management throughout the project lifecycle. The responsibilities of scope control include the preparation of an accurate scope and then integration as a scope baseline. Meaning, accurate scope control practice guides the project team to maintain the workflow following the agreed scope baseline in the project.

Managing scope configuration

Projects facilitate the production of new assets or products. These assets should be managed during the project lifecycle.

Each of the project assets that should be delivered based on the scope baseline is called a Configuration Item (CI). Configuration Items (CIs) have two major relationships, Internal and external relationship. It means that the project team should consider the relationship between project products i.e. CIs and the relationship between project CIs and the external CIs, those assets that project CIs should be integrated with after project completion.

For example, consider an IT project that should deliver project management software that includes different modules including WBS creation, schedule management, cost management, and so on. This software will be installed in the X Company which has other systems such as human resource management, asset

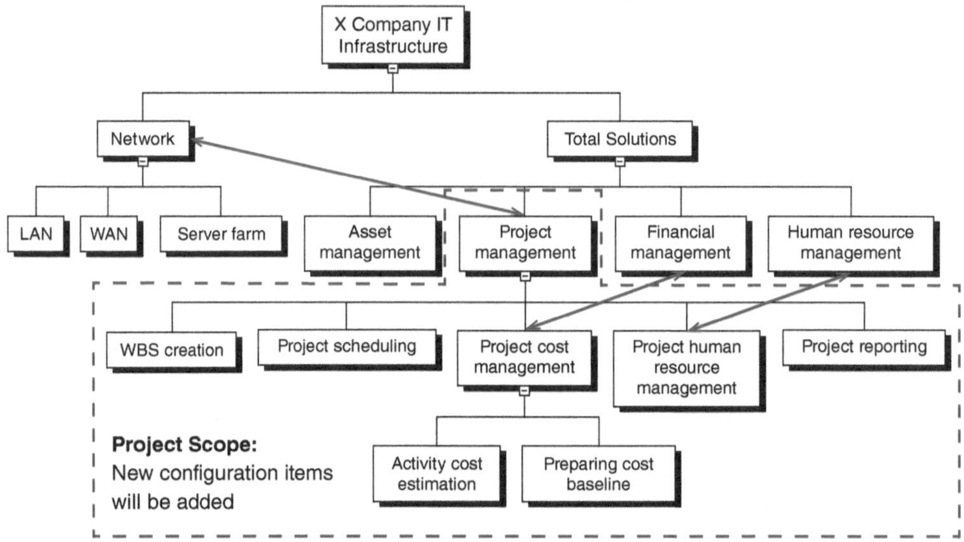

Figure 8.5: Relationship between project CIs and existing customer CIs

management, and financial management. Therefore the final project product (project management software) will be added to the existing systems. The diagram below illustrates this example case highlighting the relational links between various levels of CIs

As can be seen in Figure 8.5, there are three main relationships between project CIs and organisation CIs. The project technical team should consider these relationships during project design and implementation and the project manager should monitor their efforts.

In addition to the external relationships, different project CIs may be logically or physically related to each other. The project technical team should take into account these relationships as well.

Configuration management is responsible for CI identification and controlling their status during project execution and finally verifying them when they are completely provided. The configuration management process is almost similar to the scope management process and should be carried out in parallel. Configuration management is more technical while scope management concentrates on the management aspect. Therefore, providing a clear relationship between scope and configuration management is an appropriate approach to creating a close and effective relationship between management and the technical team.

Figure 8.6 below illustrates the configuration management process and its relationships to requirement and scope management processes.

The configuration management process includes four major activities as follows:

1 Identifying configurations

In this stage, CIs that are included in the project scope should be identified. As can be seen in Figure 8.6, this activity should be carried out at the same time as the defined scope process. It means that when the project team defines the project scope including project products or deliverables, the configuration management team should identify the CIs that are related to those products or deliverables.

2 Create Configuration Management Database (CMDB)

After identifying project CIs, the required information that is needed by the project team should be identified and recorded. Different information can be recorded for different CIs.

The document that the configuration information is recorded is called Configuration Management Database (CMDB). Although CMDB is almost similar to WBS, there are three major differences between them. First, it only

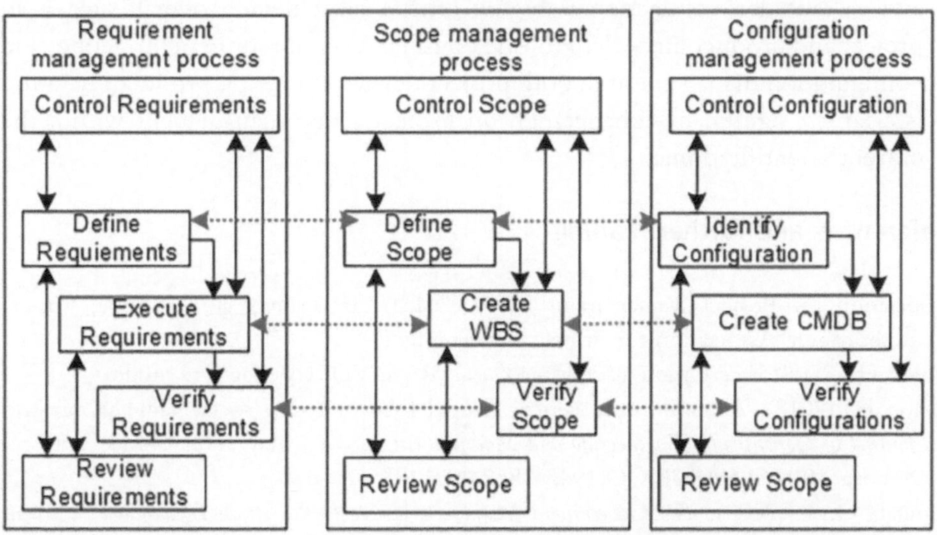

Figure 8.6: Configuration management and its relationship with requirement and scope management processes

includes the final project products and their components. WBS can include different components including project phasing, geographical locations, planning and control, and so on.

Second, CMDB generally includes the technical and logical relationship between different CIs (products or their components).

Third, CMDB includes a more detailed level of information about project products than WBS.

As depicted in the diagram, CMDB should be provided at the same time as WBS.

3 Control configurations

The aim of this activity is to ensure that no CI can be added, deleted, or changed without a clear change management procedure. The nature of control configurations is similar to control scope.

4 Verify configurations

When CIs are provided completely, their functionality should be evaluated in comparison with the information that is recorded in the CMDB. This evaluation should be carried out with verify scope.

In summary, requirement, scope, and configuration management is one the integral knowledge areas in project management. Understanding the project's requirement, scope, and configuration from the long-term business success and stakeholders satisfaction is highly crucial in achieving overall success in project and product lifecycle. Holistic consideration of requirement, scope, and configuration management in both project development and product operation is clearly a significant enhancement in project scope management within the current scientific domain.

References and further reading

Association for Project Management (APM 2012). *APM Body of Knowledge*, Princes Risborough: Association for Project Management.

Doloi, H. (2008). *Life Cycle Project Management*, Riga: VDM Verlag Dr. Muller.

Doloi, H. (2018). A community centric model for evaluating social value in projects, *Journal of Construction Engineering and Management*, ASCE, May, Vol. 144 (5). https://doi.org/10.1061/(ASCE)CO.1943-7862.0001473

Haugan, G. T. (2003). *The Government Manager's Guide to the Work Breakdown Structure.* VA: Management Concepts Press/ Oakland CA: Berrett-Koehler Publishers.

International Project Management Association (IPMA 2015). Individual competence baseline for project, Programme & Portfolio Management, p. 416, International Project Management Association, Zurich, Switzerland.

OGC (2017). *Managing Successful Projects with PRINCE2,* London: Office of Government Commerce.

Project Management Institute (PMI 2021). *A guide to the Project management Body of Knowledge(*PMBOK 7*)*, Newtown Square, PA: Project Management Institute.

Chapter 9

Project organization

Rodney Turner and Martina Huemann

Introduction

The purpose of designing a project organization is to set those elements of governance associated with defining the roles, responsibilities, relationships, and rights of (internal) project stakeholders. We define the roles and responsibilities, so people know who is responsible for delivering which elements of the project's results. In defining roles and responsibilities we also define lines of authority and communication, so people know to whom they are responding, where they will receive information from, and where they need to send it to. Communication is related to relationships, so people know with whom they are interacting and what the basis of those interactions is. Finally, we need to define people's rights so that they know where they stand with respect to the project, that they know what support they can expect to receive to help them deliver the project results for which they are responsible, and suggest how institutional theory can help create cohesion

We introduce social representation as a social construct for defining order to enable people to orientate themselves to their work environment and social context and to enable communication between members of a community. We describe a model for creating social representation and describe cultural assets to enable the project organization to function. We then explore identity, and its contribution to defining people's roles, responsibilities, relationships, and rights. We suggest how institutional theory can help create cohesion.

DOI: 10.4324/9781003274179-11

We introduce responsibility matrices. Traditionally, people have suggested five types of project organization. We describe these five types. We finish the chapter by considering three contemporary design elements.

Social representation

Moscovici (1973) defines social representation as:

> A system of values, ideas and practices with a twofold function: first to establish an order which enables individuals to orientate themselves in their material and social world and to master it; and secondly to enable communication among the members of a community by providing them with a code for social exchange and for naming and classifying unambiguously various aspects of their world.

Moscovici is mainly talking about people in society, but a project can be considered as a society. We need to create order so that internal stakeholders can orientate themselves and create transparency for external stakeholders. We need to facilitate communication, create a common language, and create codes for how people and companies interact. There are two main processes by which the unfamiliar can be made familiar:

1 *Anchoring – discursive abilities:* classifying and naming the new using familiar systems of meaning and integrating new knowledge, values, and objects into existing frameworks, using metaphors as ways of familiarizing people.
2 *Objectification – process facilitators:* the transformation of abstract representations into routines, stories, institutions, and concrete objects gives a concrete reality to ideas, values, and mental models, using the institutions of governance.

Figure 9.1 shows six steps for creating a social representation. We start by designing the organization, including governance and governmentality, which sets the objectives, and defines the roles, responsibilities, and rights of and relationships between stakeholders. The organization also defines the structures within which people work, and the shape of social norms: how people work together and cooperate. Crawford et al. (2005) say it is essential to develop a common language, so you understand what you are saying to each other, and to avoid

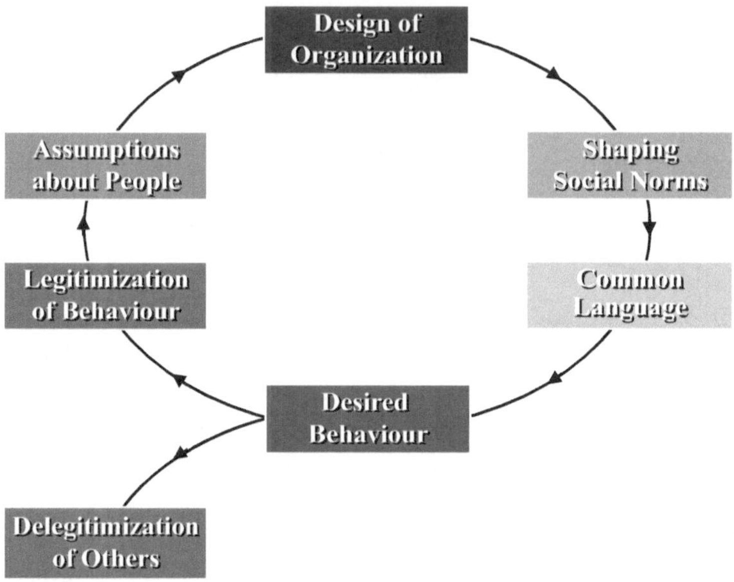

Figure 9.1: Developing social representation

mistakes through miscommunication. Then you define desired and undesired behaviours. Desired behaviours should include friendship, cooperation, and trust.

Pitsis et al. (2003) describe a project to construct stormwater tunnels to clean up Sydney Harbour ahead of the Olympic games in 2020. The project was based on a designer culture with:

- Individual enthusiasm with values of dedication, loyalty, self-sacrifice, and passion for the project.
- Strong customer focus.
- Discourse is characterized by the familial language of team and family.
- Public display of designer culture.

Legitimization of behaviours leads to assumptions that people are playing the game. The Sydney stormwater tunnel was also based on ten cultural commitments:

1 Build and maintain a champion team with champion leadership, integrated across all disciplines and organizations.
2 Commit corporately and individually to openness, integrity, trust, cooperation, mutual support and respect, flexibility, honesty, and loyalty to the project.

3 Honour our commitments to one another.
4 Commit to a no-blame culture.
5 Use breakthroughs and the free flow of ideas to achieve exceptional results.
6 Outstanding results provide outstanding rewards.
7 Deal with and resolve all issues from within the alliance.
8 Act in a way that is best for the project.
9 Challenging BAU (business as usual) behaviours.
10 Spread the Alliance culture to all stakeholders.

The project had the strapline to do what was best for the project. In Chapter 2 we suggested that you get the best project outcomes if everybody does what is best for the project, not themselves individually.

Capability and cultural assets

Chris Chapman (2020) defines 11 capability and cultural assets. There are four capability assets:

1 immediate use of available knowledge and skills.
2 pathways for drawing upon and integrating all requisite knowledge and skills.
3 pathways for feeding back and systematically accumulating requisite knowledge.
4 pathways for all other relevant communication.

He suggests there is knowledge you need but know you do not know. That is a liability. It creates ambiguity and uncertainty. There are four cultural assets:

5 routine encouragement and empathetic governance initiated top-down and bottom-up.
6 fully developed teamwork and cooperation.
7 spirit of continuous improvement.
8 encouragement of innovation.

He suggests that self-serving, inflexible, and unsympathetic project organization is dysfunctional. If managers do what is best for themselves, everyone, at all levels, suffers. The slogan is, "Do what is best for the project". He adds two middle-ground assets, related to the legitimization of behaviour:

9 encourage positive behaviours.

10 discourage negative behaviours.

Then there is a key which ties them all together.

11 promote and protect the good, contest and discourage the bad.

Identity

Identity is our sense of belonging to a group that leads to specific cognitive and behavioural responses. Identity enables people to categorize themselves as a group member, and comparison with other groups leads to positive differentiation between the in-group and outgroup (Haslam, 2004). Identity includes at one level, the social categories people belong to, but at another level, their roles and relationships with others. Identification is the process through which an identity is adopted. There are three components: a cognitive one where somebody recognizes they may be a member of a group; an evaluative one where they decide this is a group they want to belong to; and an emotional one where they like the choice. Identification matters because it enhances an individual's self-esteem as a member of an organization or group. Identification can improve communication and improve group performance because it can improve many of the inputs and processes of team performance mentioned above, including norms, values, team characteristics, communication, leadership and followership, and coordination.

Through identity, governance defines people's roles, responsibilities, and authorities on projects, that is defining their roles and relationships with others (see for instance, DeFillippi & Sydow, 2016; Lappi et al., 2018; McGrath & Whitty, 2015; Sergeeva, 2019). DeFillippi and Sydow (2016) identify four mechanisms which they call the four Rs, roles, relationships, responsibilities, and routines. Roles refer to authority assignments, including hierarchical authority and lines of communication. Relationships are how people interact while doing project work. Qualities include trust and reciprocity. Responsibilities are the requirements or deliverables expected of participants and the consequences of failing. They encompass four Ts, task, team, time, and transition. Routines are related to social representation and culture. They are shared artefacts which reflect established ways of working. Sergeeva (2019) says that the organization should try to ensure that decisions are taken by the right group of people, and that they carefully consider the appropriate information. She suggests that people can be empowered to make decisions, giving them appropriate authority and representation. McGrath and Whitty (2015) identify five elements of organization:

- Structure through how people interrelate.
- Positions through the definition of roles and responsibilities, which we will return to in identity.
- Rules through the definitions of through the definition of policies and procedures, which we will return to in groups and teams.
- Decisions through the delegation and approval processes.
- Reporting through the involvement of stakeholders.

Derakhshan et al. (2019a) consider the importance of defining rights, roles, responsibilities, and relationships to engage both internal and external stakeholders. We found that two themes influenced the assignment of those four factors: success, performance, efficiency, and value; and ethics, transparency, and accountability. The second of these is consistent with the four principles suggested by the OECD: transparency; accountability; responsibility; and fairness (Millstein et al., 1998). Derakhshan et al. (2019b) use attribution theory to show that if this is not done well, it can leave external stakeholders with a negative assessment of the project.

DeFillippi and Sydow (2016) also say tensions can exist between individual identity and team identity. There can also be tension if people from different organizations are working on the same projects. They suggest that a clear definition of roles can reduce these tensions. They also suggest that there can be tensions if somebody has different roles on different projects.

Institutional theory

Müller et al. (2014, 2015) show identity is an organizational enabler for governance and governmentality. They quote Stoker (1998, p. 155):

> Project organization is ultimately concerned with creating the conditions for ordered rule and collective action, which is accomplished through a framework for ethical decision making and managerial actions based on transparency, accountability, and defined roles.

They suggest project organization builds social exchange and cohesion. In the first paper, they consider people's sense of self-responsibility and self-awareness, and their willingness to take on responsibility for results, associated tasks, projects, and other efforts for the benefit of the organization. In the second paper, they invoke institutional theory to investigate regulative, normative, and cultural-cognitive elements to investigate the stability and meaning of social life in organizations. Institutions comprise actors (including both individuals and organizations) that become real through the social behaviour of the actors. Informal norms, values, standards, and formal and informal roles make up the normative elements of governmentality. Shared conceptions about the nature of social reality make up cultural-cognitive elements, and create frameworks of meaning, shared beliefs, symbols, identities, and mental models. Organizational enablers provide for the development of individuals who are mindful of the organization, self-responsible, and self-organizing to a degree that matches the goals of the organization. For companies with a strong project culture, a strong project identity enables governmentality.

Müller et al. (2014) investigate how in bringing knowledge to people, social representation influences project organization. They suggest four steps:

a *Setting the goals – macro antecedents:* project and organizational culture, dynamic learning boundaries, and job characteristics.
b *Providing the means – micro conditions:* beliefs, attitudes, values, and knowledge expectations.
c *Controlling progress – micro behaviours:* knowledge behaviour, communication, and shared decisions.
d *Achieving knowledge-based goals – macro constructs:* dynamic capabilities, competencies, and communities of practice.

Defining responsibility

Projects require a collection of different competencies and need to define their involvement in the project. A very simple tool for defining the project organization is the responsibility matrix. Usually, the rows will show work elements or project results to be delivered, and the columns will represent people or organizational units involved. Symbols are then placed in the cells of the matrix to show the responsibility of the organizational units for delivering the work or results. Develop symbols that suit your project – that is part of social representation. Typical symbols required are for who does the work, who manages the work, who takes decisions, and who needs to give and receive information. You can use matrices at all levels of the project hierarchy, policy, strategic tactical, and operational. At the strategic level, the rows will represent project outputs, and at the operational level work elements. At the strategic level the columns will be departments or contractors involved in the project, and at the operational level named individuals.

Five project organization types

Conventionally people have suggested five project organization types from line to matrix and back to line.

Functional Line. If the project is small enough, it can be organized wholly within one department in the functional line organization, with the resources drawn just from that one group. The manager of the group can then assign people from within their department to the project. If a small number of resources are needed from another department, the departmental manager can negotiate with the other departmental manager. It is his or her responsibility, not the project manager's, and it will rely on the personal relationship between the two departmental managers.

Project Line. Going next to the other extreme we look at the project line. If the project is big enough, or if the parent organization is a project-based organization, such as a construction company or software house doing nothing but projects for external clients, the parent company may create a project function within the company for doing projects. People will work permanently for the project function, and projects will be assigned to the project function for delivery.

For the vast majority of projects, they are not small enough to fit just within one function and not big enough that all the project team members can work within the project hierarchy, and some form of matrix structure is necessary. Under the matrix structure, people from the line organization are given project responsibilities for the duration of their involvement in the project. However, I firmly believe that people should be receiving instructions from just one manager, either the project manager or the line manager, and that is the fundamental difference between the two matrix structures I suggest.

Secondment Matrix. The project team member is seconded onto the project for the duration of his or her involvement in the project. While working on the project, he or she receives instruction from the project manager about what work he or she will do day by day. The project team member may only be working on the project for a limited period, for the duration of the work package only, and may only be working part-time, three days a week, but while working on the project, he or she receives instruction from the project manager. This form of working is necessary if the work package involves the input of more than one type of resource. You cannot have several functional managers trying to coordinate the work of several different resource types on one work package; you must have just one project manager.

Functional Matrix. If the work package involves the input of just one resource type, then it can be assigned to the functional manager resource, and he or she can be made responsible for delivering the milestone by the due date. The resource manager may have work packages from several projects to assign people to, as well as ongoing functional duties, and can balance priorities between those different demands to deliver the project milestones within the requirements of the different projects. This only works if the work package involves the input of one function. It might work if it involves the input of one person from another function and there is a good working relationship between the two functional managers.

Balanced Matrix. People also suggested the balanced matrix. Here the project manager and functional manager share responsibility, and the team member receives instruction from both. We do not think this works well; people can only have one boss. The project team members will try to play the two managers off against each other, and the more charismatic one will win, or the line manager will win because he or she controls the annual bonus. The English king, Henry VIII, declared himself head of the church in England because he realized people could not have split loyalty to him as king and the pope in Rome. The Holy Roman Empire solved that problem by having the emperor crowned by the pope. If you know your history, 1532 is about the time Henry VIII declared himself head of the church of England. Early editions of The Prince appeared about 1515. Machiavelli (1532) said the only stable European state is one where church and state are merged at the top.

You can mix project organization types on a single project. An organization might operate a project hierarchy, but second specialist resources onto projects for short durations, or there may be elements of work requiring very specialist inputs and they are assigned to the function to deliver.

Contemporary design elements

Contemporary elements to designing project organizations include:

- Empowerment.
- Integration.
- Virtual teams.

Empowerment

Empowerment involves project, project team, and project team members and gives increased autonomy and responsibility to them (Huemann, 2015). Galbraith (2001) suggests that new product developments require more decision-making and more information processing than a functional organization can provide. We suggested that a project is an agency for change (see Chapter 2), thus project requires cross-functional collaborations. The decision-making power at lower levels of the organization must be increased without losing the inputs of all affected levels. Turner and Müller (2004) show that better project outcomes are achieved if the project manager and project team have the flexibility to make changes and deal with uncertainty as new information becomes available while leaving the project sponsor and higher levels of governance able to provide guidance as to what is required. Empowerment needs to take place on the project, the team, and the individual level (Huemann, 2015).

Integration

Integration is necessary between the single project and the permanent organization to allow enough alignment as well as enough autonomy for the project. The organizational design of the project takes care of the necessary coupling between the project and the permanent structures of the company. The important role to consider is the project owner also called the project sponsor (Chapters 11 and 25). Turner and Miterev (2019) show how to align project orientation with the culture of the parent organization, project working with organization processes, project culture with behaviours, HRM at the project and organization level, and the fit of the project with the structure of the organization.

Integration as a design element relates to creating "salt and pepper" organizations thus integrating representatives from the owner organization, partner and supplier organization, and representatives of local authorities (Huemann, 2015). The slogan used for this type of organization is "leave your business card on the project door step". This design element leads to integrated project delivery or project alliance when based on contractual arrangements (see Chapter 13).

Virtual teams

People have been researching working in virtual teams on projects for at least 25 years, though people have probably been working on virtual teams for as long as people have been doing projects. Simply defined, a virtual team is one where project team members are not collocated. When Brunel built the Great Western Railway in the mid-19th century, team members were working in London and Bristol, and many places in between. In the UK in the early 19th century, semaphore towers were built. That enabled people working for the Royal Navy in Portsmouth to communicate almost instantaneously with people working in London.

Virtual teams are now defined as a group of skilled individuals who communicate electronically. Clearly, the explosion of the internet and electronic communication has made virtual working more pervasive, even more so than 25 years ago. It is now very rare for all team members to be collocated and can work anywhere in the world. The Covid-19 pandemic, and the resultant working from home, also increased the amount of virtual teamwork. People moved away from cities and now work more remotely from their home office. Project teams will now often involve people working all around the world, but communicating in real time. Most project teams are now also hybrid, with a mixture of people collected and people working remotely.

Virtual teams can provide flexibility and knowledge sharing. But they also offer challenges. Key issues to be considered by project managers are communication planning, leadership style, and goal setting. They also need to consider the impact of virtual working on integration and scope planning. Other issues include:

- Cultural and language barriers, and time differences.
- Differences in perception – people only tend to see what is in front of them, so it may be necessary to keep people fully informed about what is happening on the project.

- Balanced and horizontal leadership – if there are a large number of people working in a remote location, particularly if they are working on a distinct work package, it may be necessary for the project manager to make one of the people their leader for that work.

Conclusion

What becomes evident is that project organizations need to be designed for the purpose. The design of the project or program needs to fit the contractual arrangements. While many organizations still rather apply standard forms, the explicit design of a project or program enriched with modern design elements such as empowerment, integration, and virtuality brings a competitive advantage. The project manager becomes a designer.

References and further reading

Chapman, CB. (2020). *Enlightened planning: using systematic simplicity to clarify opportunity, risk and uncertainty for much better management decision making*. Abingdon and New York: Routledge.

Crawford, LH, Hobbs, JB & Turner, JR. (2005). *Project categorization systems: aligning capability with strategy for better results.* Newtown Square, PA: Project Management Institute.

DeFillippi, R & Sydow, J. (2016). Project networks: governance choices and paradoxical tensions. *Project Management Journal,* **47**(5): 6–17.

Derakhshan, R, Turner, JR & Mancini, M. (2019a). Project governance and stakeholders: a literature review. *International Journal of Project Management,* **37**: 98–116.

Derakhshan, R, Mancini, M & Turner, JR. (2019b). Community's evaluation of organizational legitimacy: formation and reconsideration. *International Journal of Project Management,* **37**(1), 73–86.

Galbraith, JR (2002), *Designing organizations. An executive guide to strategy, structure, and processes*, Revised edition, San Francisco, CA: Jossey-Bass.

Haslam, SA. (2004). *Psychology in organizations: the social identity approach.* London: Sage.

Huemann, M. (2015). *Human resource management in the project-oriented organization: towards a viable project-oriented HRM system for project personnel.* Aldershot: Gower.

Lappi, T, Karvonen, T, Lwakatare, LE, Aaltonen, K & Kuvaja, P. (2018). Toward an Improved Understanding of Agile Project Governance: A Systematic Literature Review. *Project Management Journal,* **49**(6), 39–63.

Machiavelli, N. (1532). *Il principe.* Florence: Antonio Blado d'Asola.

McGrath, SK & Whitty, SJ. (2015). Redefining governance: from confusion to certainty and clarity. *International Journal of Managing Projects in Business,* **8**(4): 755–787.

Millstein, IM, Albert, M, Cadbury, A, Feddersen, D & Tateisi, N. (1998). *Improving competitiveness and access to capital in global markets.* Paris: OECD Publications.

Moscovici, S. (1973). Introduction. In C. Herzlich (ed.). *Health and illness: a social psychological analysis.* London: Academic Press.

Müller, R, Pemsel, S & Shao, J. (2014). Organizational enablers for governance and governmentality of projects: a literature review. *International Journal of Project Management,* **32**(8): 1309–1320.

Müller, R, Pemsel, S & Shao, J. (2015). Organizational enablers for project governance and governmentality in project-based organizations. *International Journal of Project Management,* **33**(4): 839–851.

Pitsis, TS, Clegg, SR, Marosszeky, M & Rura-Polley, T. (2003). Constructing the Olympic dream: a future perfect strategy of project management. *Organizational Science,* **14**(5): 574–590.

Sergeeva, N. (2019). Towards more flexible approach to governance to allow innovation: the case of UK infrastructure, *International Journal of Managing Projects in Business,* **13**(1): 1–19.

Stoker, G. (1998). Governance as theory: five propositions. *International Social Science Journal,* **50**(155): 17–28.

Turner, JR & Miterev, M. (2019). The organizational design of the project-based organization. *Project Management Journal,* **50**(4): 487–498.

Turner, JR & Müller, R. (2004). Communication and cooperation on projects between the project owner as principal and the project manager as agent. *The European Management Journal,* **22**(3): 327–336.

Chapter 10

Project owner organizations

Graham M. Winch

The project "was assembled around a hole like a Polo Mint… [there was] no client driving it forward with a vision of what the operator needed to have".

Introduction

Sir Alistair Morton, the Co-chair of Eurotunnel plc during the delivery phase of the Channel Fixed Link megaproject reflected (*Financial Times*, 19/09/95) on the challenges of delivering that extraordinary asset by likening the project organization to a Polo Mint (Lifesaver for a US audience) with no capable owner at its heart. The aim of this chapter is to lay out how project owners can avoid promoting polo mint projects by ensuring that they are capable owners of filling the hole at the heart of the project organization.

We start by presenting a generic business model for project owners that will show how they have three broad areas of responsibility: (1) to define the project mission and raise the finance required for that investment; (2) to design the arrangements by which the project will be shaped and delivered; and (3) to ensure that the services provided by the asset resulting from the project are achieved thereby meeting the expectations of the business plan. We will discuss each of these areas in turn before presenting data from a recent initiative in the UK infrastructure sector that presents the capable owner as the crucial underpinning of collaborative working for project delivery. One important aspect of project owner organizing that we do not cover here is leadership; this is covered in Chapter [X].

 DOI: 10.4324/9781003274179-12

The generic project owner business model

Figure 10.1 presents a generic business model for the project investment process associated with assets such as a bridge, a complex information system, or a block-buster product. It places the project owner at the heart of that process. We use the term "owner" rather than "client" used by Sir Alistair Morton and many others, because "client" implies a focus on the contractual relationship with suppliers, rather than the broader set of responsibilities that owners have towards their projects. The project owner is a public or private organization that defines the need for the investment project and then sees that investment process through to the beneficial use of the asset created.

However, the business purpose of the owner is not projects – its purpose is to provide services to customers by operating the asset. So, for example, a highways agency provides roads for motorists to drive on; a bank provides information systems for customers to manage their accounts; a manufacturer develops products

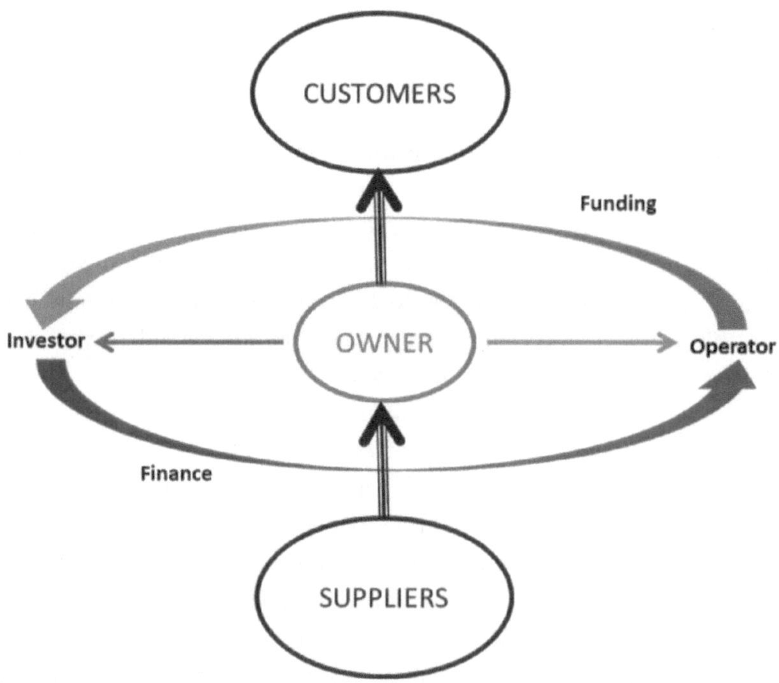

Figure 10.1: The generic owner business model (Winch et al., 2022)

to make and sell to their customers and so on. Assets delivered by projects are merely the enablers of the delivery of goods and services to customers. In order to make the investment, the owner needs to raise finance. This may be from external borrowing or from retained funds (profits or taxes); where the external investment is secured on the asset being created this is known as project finance. Within large organizations – in both the public and private sectors – business units typically bid for funds from the financial centre.

Once the asset has been delivered by the project, it needs to be moved into beneficial use by the owner operating the asset to achieve the outcomes projected in the business case. The revenues from customers thereby generated provide the funding that repays the original finance invested. While this process is clearest in the case of assets such as toll bridges, it underpins all investment in productive assets and is at the heart of investment appraisal tools such as net present value calculations. Where costs and benefits are not directly monetized such as in the provision of public services or benefits such as safety, then cost-benefit analysis techniques are used to provide the simulated funding stream from the operation of the asset.

In order to shape and deliver the asset, the owner needs resources from the project-based firms (PBFs) which form the supply side of investment projects. These PBFs may be various types of consultants, specialist technology suppliers, or general contractors and systems integrators. Their business purpose is projects, and they typically have a very different financial structure from owners. Whereas owners are typically asset-heavy and only intermittently engage in significant projects, PBFs are often asset-light and only exist to do projects. For owners, return on capital employed is a key performance metric; for PBFs, the key performance metric is profit on turnover.

Defining the project mission

The first, and indeed foremost, responsibility of the owner organization is to define the *project mission*. Unless the project mission is clear and achievable, disappointment with the outcome will inevitably result. This definition process is a multilateral and iterative one that may take many months, or even years in the case of megaprojects, but a full commitment to doing a thorough job is vital. During this process, the appetite of financiers for the investment project is tested and often found wanting in which case the project does not go ahead. Inevitably, the project will be shaped by their requirements; in particular, for confidence in the resilience of the funding stream that will repay their investment. It is also during this process that the principal stakeholders need to be engaged in the project (see Chapter 14). These obviously include financiers, but also regulators; holders of key resources that the project may require (e.g. land or intellectual property); and powerful potential opponents.

A helpful framework for defining the project mission is the 5 Business Cases framework. Originally developed by the UK's HM Treasury (HMT, 2020), as adapted in Table 10.1 it provides a framing for the key questions that the owners need to ask themselves for any investment project. At the heart of the framework is the Strategic Case – this is *why* the project is being done and articulates the *project mission* as a reference narrative (Kay & King, 2020) to which all other

Table 10.1 The project mission in 5 Business Cases

1 Strategic case	Addresses the question of *why* the project is being done and the fit of the investment with the purpose of the owner organization. It forms the project mission and is communicated as the project reference narrative.
2 Economic case	Addresses the question of *which* options deliver the project mission while providing acceptable value. No project should go ahead if there is not a supportive Economic Case, but this is a necessary rather than sufficient condition. This forms part of the *value proposition*.
3 Financial case	Addresses the question of *whether* the project is viable by identifying sources of finance and affordable funding streams to repay that finance and to support the asset through life. This forms the other part of the *value proposition*.
4 Commercial case	Addresses the question *of whether* the project is done in terms of the capabilities of the suppliers to deliver the project mission and *whether* an equitable commercial deal be struck with those suppliers.
5 Governance case	Addresses the question of *how* the project is to be delivered including the capabilities of the owner organization for project governance and benefits realization.

Source: Winch et al. (2022: Table 5.1)

project decisions refer back. The relationship between the economic case and the financial case constitutes the *value proposition* for the project, usually calculated using standard investment appraisal tools. The value proposition provides a sense-check against the project mission. Thus, while a particular investment project may be highly desirable in principle, a negative value proposition may argue against it. This is the case for housing retrofit projects, for instance. While investment appraisal tools are valuable for incremental development projects (e.g. which upgrade should we develop next?), they tend to work less well for transformative projects that significantly alter the economic landscape, such as major transportation infrastructure investments or major leaps in information technology, due to the inherent uncertainty of the future. The commercial and governance cases address the question of whether there are suppliers available capable of delivering the asset, and whether the owner has the capability to oversee that delivery. We turn to these two cases next.

Designing the governance and commercial interfaces

The field of project organizing can be broadly divided into three domains: (1) the domain of the owner (which may be a JV or other complex organization); (2) the domain of the suppliers consisting of tiers of PBFs in contract with the owner and in sub-contract with each other; and (3) the domain of the temporary project organization that actually delivers the new asset (Winch et al., 2022). The owner and supplier domains provide the resources that the temporary project organization requires to do its work – the owner provides the financial resources, and the suppliers provide the human and technical resources. Between these three organizational domains, the owner participates in two of them: the *commercial interface* between the owner and its chosen suppliers, and the *governance interface* between the owner and its temporary project organization. The third, resource, interface is between the PBFs and the temporary project organization to which they supply resources, and is not directly of concern to the owner.

While developing the commercial case, questions that need answering include whether there is a competitive market for the resources we need from suppliers in the region where the project is located; if not, do we need to ally with a supplier to ensure a smooth supply of those resources, or even sponsor the innovation of new types of resources? Long lead resource inputs also need to be identified. As the project moves along, the owner's *commercial strategy* matures, addressing questions such as how the delivery of the project should be packaged into deliverables that PBFs can compete to supply; which is the most appropriate contract type for each of these packages (e.g. high uncertainty, reimbursable; low uncertainty, lump sum), and how the owner is going to manage the *interfaces* between each of these packages.

The importance of commercial strategy is well illustrated by the case of COVID-19 vaccine development. The remarkable schedule compression demonstrated was achieved because the project owners (i.e. national governments responsible for health care) took all the liabilities held by suppliers (i.e. the pharmaceutical companies) for the failure of their vaccine project to pass a stage gate (Winch et al., 2021) by pre-purchasing the vaccines before it was known they would work. More generally, the evidence (Merrow, 2023) is that simple contractual arrangements work the best and that repeated transactions with the same suppliers confer considerable performance benefits. This raises the important question of how the focal project fits within the owner's overall investment portfolio.

While developing the governance case, questions need to be answered on how the project is going to be governed through shaping and delivery, and whether the owner has the capability and capacity to ensure effective governance. There are a number of different elements of effective governance interface design. At the heart of effective governance arrangements is a stage-gate procedure (Merrow, 2011) which provides evaluation "gates" at which the project must pause while progress against the business case is evaluated by parties external to the project organization. There are many varieties of stage-gate processes; a generic one is presented in Figure 10.2 showing successive gates from opportunity to outcome

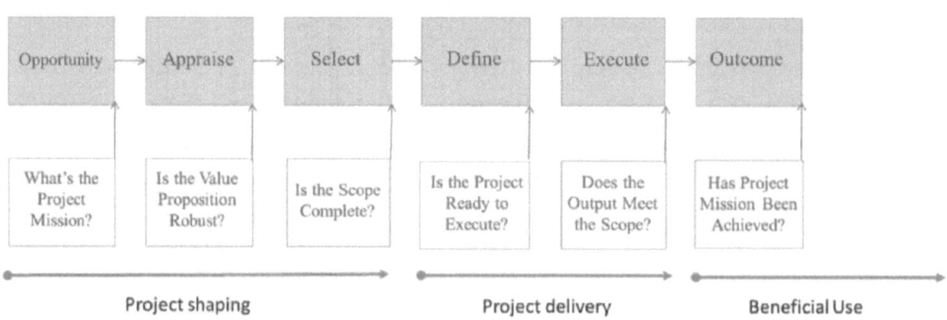

Figure 10.2: Generic gateway process
Source: Winch et al. (2022)

over the project lifecycle. Within this lifecycle, the key gate is at the end of Select which is typically the point at which the Final Investment Decision is made on the basis of a robust project mission case supported by a positive value proposition complemented by a fully specified project scope and Project Development Plan including a P90 budget and schedule. After this point, the project is very difficult to stop as the level of resource commitment grows rapidly.

Progress through this stage-gate process is best supported by a number of other elements (Barshop, 2016). These include the appointment of a project sponsor who is accountable for the performance of the project (see Chapter 2) and reports directly to the owner's senior leadership team; this person usually chairs a Project Board that ideally includes the program manager, the benefits realization manager, and senior representatives of key suppliers. These activities are usually supported by an owner project management office (PMO). To support decision-making at gates, the PMO provides project control data on progress against budget and schedule. These data are typically independently assured through project assurance processes constituting the "three lines of defence" – effectively controlled by the PMO, internal assurance by the PMO reporting to the project sponsor (not the program manager), and internal audit reporting to the owner's senior leadership team. An effective PMO also has a broader set of responsibilities towards the overall portfolio of the owner's investment projects. In addition to acting as (1) a *controller* with respect to project assurance, it acts as (2) a *coordinator* allocating the required resources to each project in the portfolio; (3) a *developer* of those resources ensuring that people have the competencies required to manage projects from an owner perspective; and (4) *supporter* providing peer support and review for project staff.

From outputs to outcomes: achieving the project mission

Owners invest in assets delivered through projects to change and expand their operations. Operating assets enable the provision of services to customers to fulfil their purpose as an organization, and to generate the funding streams that repay the investment finance. The temporary project organization delivers *outputs* in the form of working assets (which may be a form of intellectual property such as a film). That asset then has to be brought into beneficial use in order to achieve the *outcomes* envisaged in the project mission and detailed in the business case. For some assets, this transition from outputs to outcomes is relatively straightforward – a new bridge can be transformed from an output into an outcome by inviting the head of state to cut a tape – but for the vast majority of projects, this is a difficult, and even fraught, challenge.

At one level, there is the challenge of commissioning the asset as a co-learning process between the suppliers and the owner's operational team. This challenge was significantly underestimated on both the Channel Fixed Link and Elizabeth Line major projects. As assets increasingly become cyber-physical systems, the commissioning challenge will only grow and arguably requires new levels of systems thinking across professionals who tend to be siloed in their own professional disciplines (ICE, 2020).

At a broader level, achieving beneficial use encompasses a much wider variety of issues. Delivery of the working asset often involves investment in a further project or program. The incredible international achievement of delivering COVID-19 vaccines in late 2020 launched a large number of nationally based vaccination campaigns with variable outcomes. Similarly, many new assets require marketing campaigns to bring them to customers' awareness and hence achieve the desired sales targets. In the area of complex information systems that underpin organizational transformation projects very significant changes are often required to move from the asset of a functional IT system to an organization that can make the best use of its affordances. These changes include redesigned business processes; training for users; reconfigured reporting relationships and, indeed, broader cultural changes and shifts in power relationships. Resistance to technological change in organizations is often resistance to the associated organizational changes and the uncertainties around one's place in the organization that they generate.

An important lesson of the Private Finance Initiative in the UK is that this transformation from outputs to outcomes and beneficial use of the asset delivery by the project has to be done by the owner. While suppliers can be contracted to sustain asset availability over time, the associate organizational changes to make the best use of the asset's affordances need to be led and delivered by the owner organization. Due to the differences in competencies from the more traditional delivery-oriented project manager, owners often appoint a separate benefits realization manager for this state of the project. The role of the sponsor then includes ensuring that the program manager and benefits realization manager are working closely together to ensure that the asset delivered is the most appropriate for ensuring a smooth transition into beneficial use.

Owner capabilities

We have presented the project owner organization as the key player in organizing projects from shaping through to delivery. All the evidence is that if the owner is not capable, then projects will indeed be over budget and schedule (Merrow, 2011; Barshop, 2016). These capabilities are *dynamic* – that is to say, they are the capabilities required to change and expand the organization's *operational* capabilities. However, they are distinct from those operational capabilities, and organizations that are very good operationally can fail dismally dynamically as Flughafen Berlin Brandenburg GMbH recently demonstrated. These dynamic project capabilities are also very different from the operational project capabilities that PBFs need to have in order to resource the projects on which they work. We now turn to look more closely at those dynamic capabilities.

Recent research under the auspices of Project 13 (www.project13.info) has explored these owner project capabilities in more detail. In the Project 13 model, the capable owner pillar underpins (along with digital transformation) the three principal pillars of collaborative working in the project enterprise: organization (teamwork and behaviours); integration (selecting the most appropriate supplier); and governance (in which value is owner-defined from the outset). Working through a series of workshops in which many of the principal UK infrastructure owners and operators were represented, the research team identified the six owner project capabilities shown in Table 10.2.

Table 10.2 Owner project capabilities

Owner capability	*Description*
Articulating the voice of the customer	The ability of the organization to understand who the customer is, engage with the customer, obtain customer feedback, analyze the feedback, and translate and articulate it into an outcome. This includes the ability to flow the voice of the customer into the front end of the project and sustain that activity, as well as the ability of the organization to balance and align customers' views and expectations with the organization's values and strategic goals for infrastructure investment.

(*Continued*)

Table 10.2 (Continued)

Owner capability	*Description*
Value-driven mindset	Ability to focus on value delivery rather than asset delivery where value is defined in terms of outcomes for customers and hence value to the business rather than the net present value of the investment. Ability to provide and present a broader view of the value in the business case. Ability to manage both the revenue and capital side of the business plan.
Articulating the voice of operations	Ensuring that project managers engage with asset operators and asset maintainers and both have clarity of the business objectives and the service offer to the customer and are able to plan for the operations and maintenance during front end definition of the project.
Relating to the supply chain	The ability of the organization to modify, create, or develop new commercial models that facilitate early engagement of suppliers on the project and alignment between customers' needs and the supply chain.
Creating and managing complex systems	Bringing together the appropriate technology, structures, and processes and infusing a common understanding of what is to be achieved by the investment project and the ability to manage change.
Recruiting, building, and retaining talent	Ability to attract, build, and retain the right 'talent' i.e. individuals who are professionally qualified, knowledgeable, experienced, competent, innovative thinkers, who can challenge, who can deal with ambiguity. This talent is more akin to a business manager profile rather than a project manager, and people who can be advocates of the business case.

Source: Maytorena-Sanchez and Winch (2022: Table 3)

The table shows the importance of integrating the voice of the customer and the voice of operations into the owner project team as well as the more established concerns relating to the supply chain and creating and managing complex systems, all with a value-driven mindset. There is also a pressing concern for recruiting, building, and retaining talent without which none of the other five dynamic capabilities are possible. Infrastructure owners, at least in the UK, a very concerned about the dearth of talent available to them, particularly as those who acquired their competencies working for suppliers are not always the most appropriate for owner roles given their very different emphases (Winch et al., 2022: Table 12.1).

A note on delivery partners

All the evidence is that capable owners need to have the resources they require for managing their projects in-house (Merrow, 2011). However, many owners are only intermittent investors in projects, or particular projects may be very large in relation to their in-house resources. How can they acquire the human resources necessary for being a capable owner? The answer is the *delivery partner,* or integrator in Project 13 terms. This is a temporary organization that has the purpose of acting as the owner's agent for the project. This worked extremely well on the London Olympics where the CLM consortium played this role on behalf of the UK government's designated owner and operator, the Olympic Delivery Authority. It worked less well on the Elizabeth Line project where the delivery partner, Crossrail Ltd, appears to have suppressed the flow of project progress information to the designated owner and operator, Transport for London, resulting in something of a last-minute shock in 2018 when project delivery objectives proved to be unachievable. The asset finally opened in May 2022, but even then, it was not fully operational. Delivery partners themselves need to be carefully governed by project owners!

Conclusion

In this chapter on project owner organizations we have shown how the owner needs to be a capable owner in order to avoid the risk of investing in a polo mint project that exhibits major schedule and budget overruns, and perhaps does not even work properly. A recent example of a polo mint project is Berlin Brandenburg airport, which opened in 2020 nine years late with a spending of more than double the original estimate. This failure was due in large part, in our opinion (Winch et al., 2022), to an incapable owner who was an effective airport operator but lacked the dynamic capabilities required to deliver a (largely) new airport. We have identified the importance of the design of both the owner's commercial interface with its suppliers and its governance interface with its temporary project delivery organization to avoid the polo mint effect. We have also reported on some applied research, which identified what UK infrastructure owners believe are the principal dynamic capabilities they need for their investment projects.

Practice in project management and organization tends to emphasize the project delivery capabilities and competencies required by PBFs and their staff to meet their obligations to owners, rather than the specific project capabilities and competencies required by project owner organizations. More work is required to identify fully the dynamic organizational capabilities and supporting individual competencies required to be a capable owner and thereby avoid polo mint projects.

References and further reading

Barshop, P. (2016). *Capital Projects: What Every Executive Needs to Know to Avoid Costly Mistakes and Make Major Investments Pay Off.* Hoboken, NJ: Wiley.

HMT. (2020). *The Green Book: Central Government Guidance on Appraisal and Evaluation.* London: HM Treasury.

ICE. (2020). *A Systems Approach to Infrastructure Delivery.* London: Institution of Civil Engineers.

Kay, J., & King, M. (2020). *Radical Uncertainty: Decision-Making for an Unknowable Future.* London: Bridge Street Press.

Maytorena-Sanchez, E., & Winch, G. M. (2022). Engaged scholarship in project organizing research: The case of UK infrastructure. *Project Leadership and Society, 3*, 100049.

Merrow, E. W. (2011). *Industrial Megaprojects: Concepts, Strategies, and Practices for Success.* Hoboken, NJ: Wiley.

Merrow, E. W. (2023). *Contract Strategies for Major Projects: Mastering the Most Difficult Element of Project Management.* Hoboken, NJ: Wiley.

Winch, G. M., Cao, D., Maytorena-Sanchez, E., Pinto, J., Sergeeva, N., & Zhang, S. (2021). Operation warp speed: Projects responding to the COVID-19 pandemic. *Project Leadership and Society, 2*, 100019.

Winch, G. M., Maytorena-Sanchez, E., & Sergeeva, N. (2022). *Strategic Project Organizing.* Oxford: Oxford University Press.

Chapter 11

Managing business case and benefits realization

Jack Meredith and Ofer Zwikael

Introduction

The purpose of a project is to deliver benefits for the funder or recipient of the project. The realization of these benefits is what justifies the funds and effort of executing the changes that will be supported by the project. The business case is the key document that describes the benefits the funder wants to achieve from the project, but problems inevitably occur during the project – costs go up, competitors jump in, government regulations change – and plans therefore must be adjusted, including the business case. As the old saying goes: "planning is easy; it is the re-planning that is hard." During project execution, the expected benefits may go down, or the time to their realization may increase. If the problems are too serious, the business case may no longer be viable, and the entire project may need to be cancelled.

One of the early decisions in any project is selecting a project manager to execute the project and deliver the outputs that are intended to achieve the target benefits. This is usually a person who is highly experienced in the area but also very good at motivating the project team to do the necessary work, and more critically, the *rework* that will typically also be encountered. However, just producing the desired output – a tunnel, a software package, or a reorganization – does not

DOI: 10.4324/9781003274179-13

automatically achieve the target benefits because, *remarkably*, sometimes, no one has usually been appointed as responsible for using the output to realize those benefits (Meredith and Zwikael, 2020). Many people think that the project manager should be responsible for realizing benefits, but project managers are experts at delivering an output, not convincing people to actually use it. Being a project manager is enough work; convincing people to *use* something is not their expertise. Besides, as Zwikael et al. (2019) point out: project managers lack the political power typically required for benefit accountability, and project manager appointments are usually transitory so that after the output has been delivered, the project manager is off to a new project. Moreover, the project manager is usually appointed after project approval and unaware of the strategic discussions involved in the project's approval.

In the next section, we discuss the appointment of a suitable person to be responsible for attaining the benefits from the project's output, which is specifically important for longer, larger, internal projects. If a project is small or short, such as within a single function, there may be less need for this role, or it can be performed by a middle manager. In major inter-organizational projects, there is usually a group of people responsible for achieving the benefits, such as the project steering committee. We refer to this person as the "*project owner*" and discuss what their duties are, what their experience should be, and what talents they should have. We should note here that some writers use this same term to refer to the funding organization or a client, rather than an individual in the project funding organization. We refer here to the individual project owner (rather than the organization) to emphasize the important individual accountability of a senior manager steering the project, as opposed to the case where a leadership vacuum allows project managers to make decisions that support their short-term goals (e.g. completing the project on time) rather than the funding organization's long-term benefits.

(In Chapter 2, Rodney and Martina identify the roles of sponsor and business change manager which cover the role of the owner as identified here. Rodney and Martina say that usually, the sponsor and business change manager are the same person, but sometimes they are two people. They give an example where there are two people. In Chapter 27, Graham Winch identifies the owner as an organization, with very much the same concerns as the owner as identified here. The owner as identified here will be a senior manager working for the organization described by Graham Winch, with the responsibilities as described here.)

Following this, we describe in a diagram what a successful project should look like and discuss the many relationships that most large projects involve. Next, we discuss the initiation of the project through its business case and the various elements involved in developing it, emphasizing that the business case needs to be monitored and updated throughout the project. Finally, we describe the final stage of every project that usually involves a group of users: benefits realization. This implementation stage may be even more difficult than the execution stage. We then summarize our major points about the business case and benefits realization in our Conclusion section.

The project owner

Although the project owner may be the individual accountable for attaining the benefits of a project as approved in the business case, he or she cannot simply step in after the project manager is finished with output development to "just implement" the project. First, the project owner needs to set the strategic goals of the project and hence should be involved in the discussions leading up to the approval of the project, as well as the development of the business case that proposed the project. Then, given that there will probably be many changes in the direction of the project and the business case, the project owner needs to oversee and work closely with the PM during the execution of the project. While that is happening, the project owner will want to acquaint the users of the project with the reasons for the upcoming changes due to the project and any education and training the users may need to successfully implement the project's outputs. Last, the project owner will need to oversee the transition of the implementation and respond to any problems that arise before handing the change over to the relevant functional department(s). The high importance and level of work required in the activities above justify the need for an *individual* to perform the role of the project owner, rather than just defining a "project owner organization." Next, we aim to identify who in the organization is a better fit for the role of the project owner.

There are a variety of positions in organizations other than the project manager that might be appropriate (Zwikael and Meredith, 2018) to fill the role of the project owner, such as a program manager, a change manager, an appointed "sponsor," or a functional manager. Due to the intensity of the effort, the project owner role cannot be that of a part-time manager, so a manager with other serious responsibilities unallied with the project, such as a VP, a program manager, the manager of the

Project Management Office, or a general manager should not be considered. Given the responsibility of overseeing the project manager, the project owner should have sufficient technical understanding of the area of the project and as a project manager him- or herself, which a change manager typically would not have.

Two types of candidates hence seem appropriate for the role: a person with experience as a project manager who also has excellent people skills. Alternatively, the project owner could be a line manager of the area where the project is being implemented but again with the same experience and skills noted. Also, the candidate will need to either have prior experience as a project owner or else be trained for the unique responsibilities of a project owner, as illustrated in the case study of Zwikael et al. (2019).

Looking at the larger picture (see Figure 11.1), the project manager will be responsible for the project plan and execution, but the project owner will be responsible for the justification for the project and the strategic benefits expected from it, the business case, the ownership of project itself, its implementation, and the handoff to operations. There will be challenges to the project that the project owner will have to help the project manager overcome, frequently by getting additional resources and people, or by convincing upper management of the importance of the project, and then help re-motivate the project team.

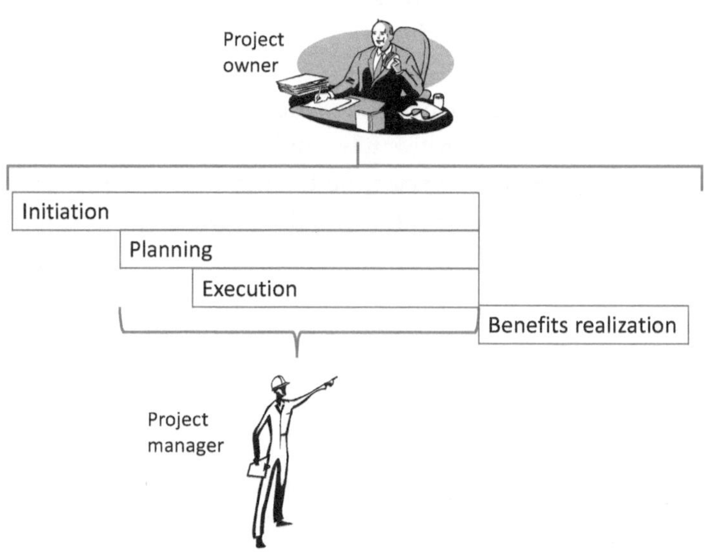

Figure 11.1: The project stages are under the responsibility of the project owner and project manager

Discouraging changes will arise, and the project may even be cancelled. While the project is being executed by the project manager, the project owner will have to prepare for the implementation of the project including any material changes as well as governance and responsibility changes. This may involve both education and training of managers, staff, and workers. Following implementation, the project owner will need to monitor the changes in the organization and measure the realization of any benefits as they arise during implementation. For example, with changes in processes such as implementing advanced technologies, it is typical for productivity to temporarily decrease during implementation, then level out, and then rise back up, hopefully to a higher level than before the change.

What does a successful project look like?

Figure 11.2 illustrates our vision (Meredith and Shafer, 2022; Zwikael and Smyrk, 2019) of the development and execution of a typical successful organizational project. In order to include most of the organizational interplay that might be

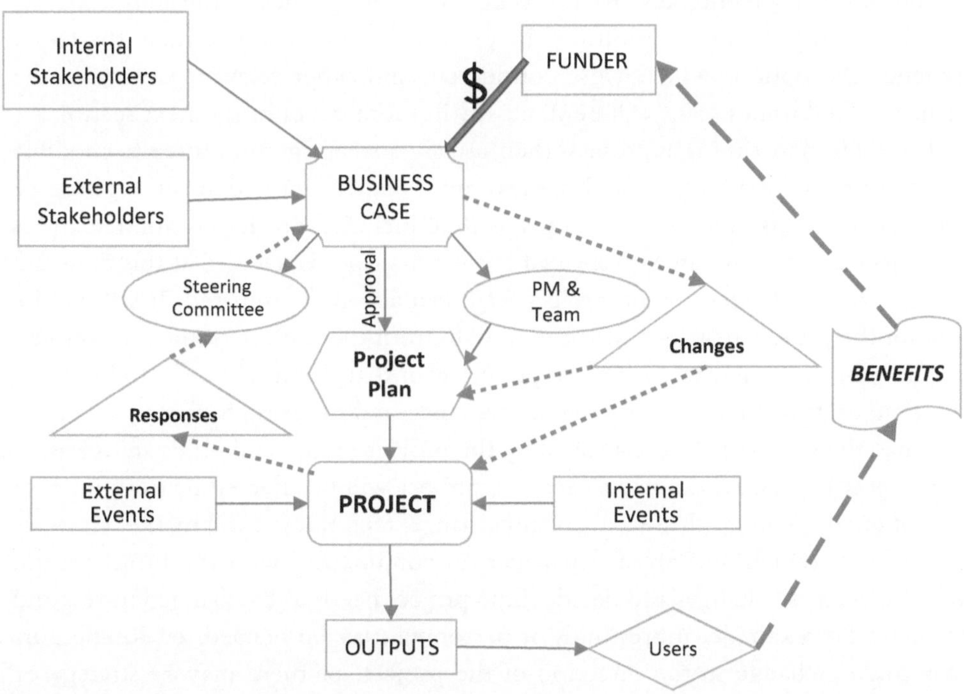

Figure 11.2: The process of executing a successful project

required, this would be appropriate for a large, strategic project. We will discuss changes to this model for other situations later. Thus, for purposes of simplicity, for now, we will assume that the funder is a private organization and then later will discuss the complications that a public sector project can have.

At the top left, internal stakeholders such as the project champion, the relevant functional department head and some key ultimate project users, the project owner, a representative of the funder, and other key stakeholders organize to develop the business case for the proposed project. At the top right is the funder, either a person, group, or organization, who will be approving the project and desires the expected benefits from the project, as well as authorizing the resources (e.g. funding) to be used during the project. Note that a project can have multiple funders, of course, but for the simplicity of discussion, we will refer to a single funder. This funder will also have the major input regarding the evaluation of project success when it is completed. Beneath the group of internal stakeholders are the key external stakeholders who have the power to help, hinder, or even stop the project. The interests of this group may be widely disparate, as compared to the internal stakeholders. At the centre of these groups is the business case, which includes the justification for the project, its costs and schedule, the target benefits, the options which were considered, and other relevant aspects of the project. The business case will be discussed in more detail in the next section.

If the business case is approved, then usually a steering committee to monitor the progress of the project and address any issues is formed from a group of relevant managers. The project owner will be included on this committee and is likely to chair it. Also, an experienced project manager is selected at this time and appropriate candidates for the project team can also be nominated. It will be the duty of the project manager, along with help from the project team and overseen by the project owner, to design the project plan that details the tasks to be done, the time each will take, their precedence, costs, and other such matters.

Once the project plan is approved by the project owner and funds are released, the project begins. As time proceeds, the project will be affected by both internal and external events, such as strategy, governance, technology, and market changes. The project owner and project manager, in conjunction with the project team, will discuss these changes and decide if the project needs to be changed to respond to them. For example, more funds or personnel may be needed, or competitors may force a change in the direction of the project, or there may be strategy or governance changes. These will be evaluated by the steering committee for their thoughts and recommendations, and the final results may then alter the business case and the project's direction and/or timing.

As the project proceeds, there will continue to be more such internal and external events that will affect the project and it is the job of the project owner to monitor these and revise the business case appropriately, or perhaps recommend cancelling the project entirely. If not cancelled, the revised outputs will eventually be delivered and passed on to the users, who have been updated on the progress of the project and trained in the use of the outputs as the project execution has progressed. Modifications to the outputs may be required to ensure the end user is satisfied with them and can utilize them effectively and regularly as required. Following the handover to the project owner and the functional operational area, the project manager and project team will then be released from their duties and move on (usually to their next project). The project owner will work with the users to ensure that the revised benefits in the business case are achieved and will indeed continue. Then there will come a point where the project owner will be satisfied with the results and deem the project to be completed. In the case of new technology projects, accountability is typically transferred to the relevant functional area at the 80% utilization level, though this varies with the technology. Last, the project owner will summarize the events of the project, evaluate its success, and describe the lessons learned, thereby closing the books on the project.

There are dozens of research papers on how to evaluate the success of a project, mentioning everything from meeting the project plan "iron triangle" constraints of cost, schedule, and scope/performance to "contributing to the future of society." For each project with its own purposes, many items specific to the project can be included but a short generic list of critical questions is more useful, such as that mentioned in Zwikael and Meredith (2021):

- How well did the project and project manager meet the project plan requirements of time, cost, and scope?
- How well did the project and project owner meet the business case requirements, as last modified?
- How satisfied was the funder with the outcome of the investment?

These three questions can be used for any project and should, at minimum, be included in the project owner's report on the project.

It was noted earlier that the model in Figure 11.2 had many of the complications that might exist in a large, strategic project. If a project is smaller and less complex, some of these elements might be ignored, such as the need for a steering committee, or the role of external stakeholders. On the other hand, the model ignores the situation of an even larger, inter-organizational project, where coordination among entities can become a major problem. This is especially the case in public projects – national, regional, and local. In addition, with public projects, it is often the case that the beneficiaries are poorly defined. The public can be very fickle about public projects, supporting something at one time and then rejecting it later, or vice-versa. In addition, some parts of the public may be pleased with the outcome while others are enraged. Another issue arises regarding the complication of time. Are the beneficiaries those at the time the project was approved, or the beneficiaries in the future, or for that matter, the province or nation itself? One of the most famous examples is the Sydney, Australia Opera House, extensively over budget and schedule, but yet now a world-famous architectural landmark and a UNESCO World Heritage Site for which its architect received architecture's highest honour (the Pritzker Prize), and Sydney benefited from a major increase in the number of tourists.

The business case

How did we get to the idea of a business case? The business case is kicked off by someone(s) either inside or outside the organization who sees an interesting opportunity for the organization. Hence, they submit a "project proposal" that has a short title to identify it; an objective that justifies the project; some background on the proposal such as how the idea arose, what is known about it, how long might it take, and what is the opportunity to exploit or problem to deal with; and the key players in the business case to follow if the idea is approved. If the proposal is approved, then the key members involved in constructing the business case will have to identify multiple ways that the desired benefits could be attained, analyze them in terms of time, cost, risk, competition, etc., and select one (or occasionally two) best option(s) for recommendation to the funder.

Current research on the use of the business case in practice indicates that it is sometimes used only to justify the funder's investment in the project and then ignored (Einhorn et al., 2019, 2022). This is like setting the steering wheel and speed on a car to drive itself down a highway and expecting it to get to its destination. It might work for a short distance but the longer the destination, the less likely the car will successfully arrive. This is also the major reason why so many projects fail, especially lengthy projects, and why a project owner is needed to monitor and oversee the project and its business case as events and responses occur during execution and then to change the direction of the project as needed, or terminate it entirely if it is no longer justified.

As Einhorn et al. (2019) point out, the business case underpins sound project governance and due to its relevant, timely, and realistic information on which to base decisions, has the greatest overall effect on project success. The purpose of the business case is to set out the rationale for the project investment, justify it, and obtain management's commitment and authorization to proceed. It summarizes the anticipated benefits for all the stakeholders, considers alternative options, and recommends a preferred solution. It also provides not only an overview of the iron triangle elements (the scope of work, the time frame, and the costs), but also the risks and benefits and, importantly, what the organization can expect should the project *not* be approved or successfully implemented. Last, it identifies the responsible project owner for overseeing the project. The advantages of having a business case are that by creating and tracking it, stakeholders get a better understanding of the benefits, costs, and risks of the project; the benefits are measurable and quantifiable, with responsibility assigned; continuing reviews of the business case allow ongoing optimization of the project in response to business and other changes inside or outside the organization, and after the deliverables have been handed over, the business case allows results to be compared with expected benefits, thus ensuring that none are overlooked.

There is growing literature on how to develop a business case (e.g. Keen, 2011; Messner, 2013; Zwikael and Smyrk, 2019). Since the recommended business case contents have also been growing over the years, and our goal is the realization of the project's benefits, we follow the most recent reference, Zwikael and Smyrk (2019), in our description of the business case's contents. Many of the elements of the business case have been discussed earlier but here we lay out the sections in greater detail.

- **Introduction**: this short section should include the name of the project, the purpose of the business case, key stakeholders, and a concise overview of the project.
- **Business context**: the project's general scope and major outputs, what success will look like, the rationale for the project and its tie to strategy, the

sustainability of the project, the organizational impacts in terms of resources and outcomes, the analysis of options, any related projects/programs, and identification of key assumptions and constraints.

- **Project definition**: detailed scope and limits, target outcomes and limits, committed outputs and limits.
- **Project governance**: the set of roles and their definitions that will be employed in the project.
- **External environment**: stakeholders and communications strategy, risks, issues of concern such as environmental impacts, and the likely market and technology environment existing at the time of expected project completion, whether approved or not.
- **Project analysis**: Gantt chart, schedule of milestones, internal resource plan, external resource acquisition plan, project budget, and cash flow.

As noted earlier, many things change as a project progresses: the environment changes, project activities do not turn out as planned, assumptions may turn out to be wrong, top management may change, or the strategic plan may change. These changes may impact the internal or external stakeholders in the project in undesirable ways, which then have to be considered and rectified. Plans and the business case will likely need to be changed or at least adjusted, and the costs and benefits may need to be altered. If these alterations make the project less attractive, top management will have to reconsider the project and perhaps change its direction, or possibly even terminate it. These critical changes should be analyzed during the project by the project owner and steering committee (if one exists) and decisions made by the project owner (and funder, e.g. in the case of project termination). Figure 11.3 illustrates the various stages of the business case across a project's life, starting with its development and approval during initiation, monitoring during project planning and execution, and finally its evaluation during the benefits realization stage.

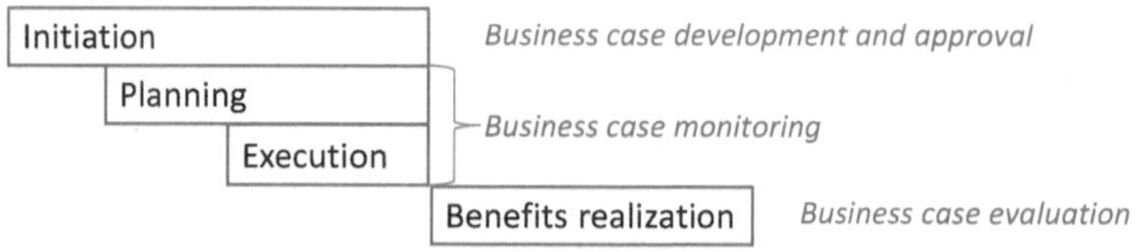

Figure 11.3: The business case stages across a project's life

One last consideration concerning the creation of the business case that justifies the initiation of a project is the fallibility of managers when anticipating the future. One well-recognized behavioural tendency is a natural optimism bias, believing that generally, everything will go as planned. Another similar problem is a pro-innovation bias, which often turns out to be harder than expected. Also, there is the all-too-common assumption that the future will still look like the environment existing when the project was approved. These kinds of assumptions can be dangerous when large or long-term projects are being considered. A separate managerial problem is the difficulty of any managerial response occurring during the "window of opportunity" to respond to external or internal events that threaten the project while it is being executed (Kunisch et al., 2017). Managers need to be on their guard against these kinds of biases and assumptions when building the business case for a project.

Benefits realization

This is the last project stage, which starts with the completion and delivery of the output to be used. Yet, the project owner has a lot of work to do before the project can realize its benefits. In terms of effort, this may well be the most difficult task the project owner faces in the project since the project manager is gone after delivering the outputs and the other staff and managers who helped prepare the business case are now working on other tasks or projects.

Although the project owner will be thinking about how to achieve the benefits desired since the development of the business case, the multiple changes in the direction of the project since then will also mean changes in how the benefits will be achieved, and now they might be even harder, or possibly easier. For instance, there might be changes in the strategic plan for the output, requiring a different approach to achieve different benefits than were originally set. Or there might be changes in the views of top management, or the top managers themselves, and these changed views could well impact both the project and the benefits desired. Hence, the project owner has to stay in touch with such changes and be ready to react when the unexpected happens. This means the project owner should maintain a list of possible threats to the project or strategy, and monitor them continuously, as well as keep alert to unexpected threats.

Perhaps the hardest task the project owner will face in realizing the benefits of the project is getting the users of the output to fully embrace the changes that will be required. People like to stick with a system they have taken the effort to learn and would rather not have to learn a new one, not just because it is more work, but because they might make a mistake and be reprimanded, or they might not understand how this new approach operates and will look stupid. Therefore, the project owner will need to make a major effort to engage with the users early, and not "spring" the change on them at the last minute. This is why it is helpful to have some of them involved in developing the business case right from the start. Then, as the project execution proceeds, the project owner can develop the appropriate training, education, and possibly visits of the employees to other organizations that use this new system or technology, and help them understand what their new roles and responsibilities will be in the changed process, and possibly even reorganized departments and reporting to a new superior.

Although the project owner will need to start all this work with the users ahead of time, the project owner also needs to make sure that it does not start too early while the project execution is still changing substantially. Since changes occur throughout execution, the project owner will need to monitor the changes in terms of number and extent, to pick a time to start the training and engagement and hope that the remaining changes are not too extensive in nature. It is a delicate tradeoff.

As the users begin utilizing the new technology or system, it is common for their productivity, quality, or output to drop as they gain proficiency with the new system. Part of this may be due to problems using the new system, confusion in its operation, or bugs. These take a while to work out. However, if the change is a good one, eventually, these measures should rise again and surpass their previous levels. One common problem that the project owner must guard against is "slippage," where the users revert to old habits and routines and slow down (or stop) the implementation of the new system. At some point, the implementation of the new system becomes routine, and the main task of the project owner is completed. Then, the project owner's final task is to write the amended *business case Closeout Report.* This will include a discussion of the three measures of success detailed earlier as well as any lessons learned from the project that can be useful to the organization and its future projects.

Conclusion

The procedure for running a successful project is more complicated than most managers assume. The role of a project owner is mandatory because projects do not implement themselves and the project manager is not an expert in getting people to change – they are experts in producing project outputs on time, on cost, and to spec. To measure success, only three items are required, though additional items of interest can, of course, be added: the success of the iron triangle, the success of the modified business case, and the satisfaction of the funder with the results. The business case is not only for gaining project approval; it is a document that should be modified and updated as internal and external changes impact the project, and thereby guide the continuing development of the project. Last, the realization of the project's target benefits is the entire purpose of the project, and this typically involves changing the habits and patterns of the users, a task as difficult as producing the project outputs, and sometimes impossible.

References and further reading

Einhorn, F., C. Marnewick, J. Meredith, 2019, Achieving Strategic Benefits from Projects: The Critical Importance of Using the Business Case Over the Entire Project Lifetime, *International Journal of Project Management*, 37(8), 989–1002.

Einhorn, F., J. Meredith, C. Marnewick, 2022, A Model to Guide the Effective Use of a Business Case for IT Projects, *International Journal of Managing Projects in Business*, 15(1), 36–57.

Keen, J. M., 2011, *Making Technology Investments Profitable: ROI Road Map from Business Case to Value Realization*. Hoboken, NJ: Wiley.

Kunisch, S., J. M. Bartunek, J. Mueller, Q. N. Huy, 2017, Time in Strategic Change Research, *Academy of Management Annals*, 11(2), 1005–1064.

Meredith, J. R., S. M. Shafer, 2022, *Project Management: A Strategic Managerial Approach*, 11th ed. New York: Wiley.

Meredith, J. R., O. Zwikael, 2020, Achieving Strategic Benefits from Project Investments, *Business Horizons*, 63, 61–71.

Messner, W., 2013, *Making the Compelling Business Case*. Basingstoke and New York: Palgrave Macmillan.

Zwikael, O., J. R. Meredith, 2018, Who's Who in the Project Zoo? The Ten Core Project Roles, *International Journal of Operations and Production Management*, 38(2), 474–492.

Zwikael, O., J. R. Meredith, 2021, Evaluating the Success of a Project and the Performance of its Leaders, *IEEE Transactions on Engineering Management*, 68(6), 1745–1757.

Zwikael, O., J. R. Meredith, J. Smyrk, 2019, The Responsibilities of the Project Owner in Benefits Realization, *International Journal of Operations and Production Management*, 39(4), 503–524.

Zwikael, O., J. R. Smyrk, 2019, *Project Management: A Benefit Realization Approach*. Cham: Springer.

Chapter 12

Managing value in projects

Miia Martinsuo

Introduction

Projects are increasingly considered processes of value creation for organizations (Laursen & Svejvig, 2016; Winter & Szczepanek, 2008). The value represents the worth of something to someone (Martinsuo, 2020; Martinsuo et al., 2019a); in the context of projects, it is the worth of the project and its outcomes to its key stakeholders. Besides economic worth, value is largely understood as a multidimensional phenomenon (Eskerod & Ang, 2017; Martinsuo, 2020; Martinsuo & Killen, 2014). Perceptions of value are highly subjective (Ahola et al., 2008; Eskerod & Ang, 2017): what is valuable to one stakeholder is not necessarily so for the other stakeholders, so value depends on the stakeholders' unique perspective. A common starting point with any project and for portfolios of projects is the aspired maximization of value for customers (or sponsors, owners).

Value is considered as the aggregation or ratio of achieved benefits and sacrifices made in the project, and it emerges and accrues over time (Ahola et al., 2008; Laursen & Svejvig, 2016). Maximal value would be reached, if benefits were extremely high and sacrifices were extremely low. Yet, implementing projects with high quality requires that all stakeholders somehow invest their resources, time, and materials that represent the necessary sacrifices to achieve any benefits. The sacrifices do not occur equally, and stakeholders tend to negotiate and agree on purposive transactions and exchanges, based on their unique

DOI: 10.4324/9781003274179-14

capabilities. Therefore, the pursuit of value maximization is more often an issue of value optimization, in light of the diverse value expectations expressed by stakeholders, the distribution of capabilities among them, and negotiated transactions between them.

The pursued optimization of value requires skillful management, and this chapter focuses on managing value in projects. Value appears in the constructions, infrastructures, new products, software and services, and new ways of operating beneficial for the organization using them. These valuable outcomes enable future business and operations for firms, and new surroundings and livelihood for the society at large. Some studies emphasize that a significant proportion of the value achieved through projects will appear long after the project is completed when the project outcomes are in use (Ahola et al., 2008; Artto et al., 2016; Fuentes et al., 2019). Yet, the main expectations are directed at the outcomes as such: what the constructions, infrastructures, or new products are and represent when they are completed and transferred to the customer. Due to the plethora of different expectations toward projects, the treatment of value in managing project work is extremely important and often also problematic.

Managing value occurs on the different levels of the organization and among different stakeholders, and here I concentrate on how value should be managed in projects generally. The purpose is to offer a value-driven perspective to managing project operations. I treat value as worth, as an outcome that is initially promised, then purposely created and co-created, and eventually captured in different ways by the project contractor and customer. I acknowledge that value in projects can also be treated as a belief of what is good and right and as culture-bound behavioural guidance (Martinsuo, 2020), but this aspect of values is purposely excluded. There is a need to distinguish between the value that is intended and espoused vs. the value that is actually used and captured (Martinsuo, 2020). If planned with care and implemented well, projects should deliver exactly the value they promised in the beginning. This is a rare reality. More often, the benefits are over-estimated in the beginning, project work is under-budgeted, and outcomes may appear disappointing. Managing value in projects can be challenging as the creation of value is extremely sensitive to uncertainties.

This chapter concentrates on the value that is created and achieved during and at the end of the project, as illustrated in Figure 12.1. Value has to be managed throughout the project lifecycle, from the very early ideas to the final dismantling and disposal of project deliverables even decades after their delivery. However,

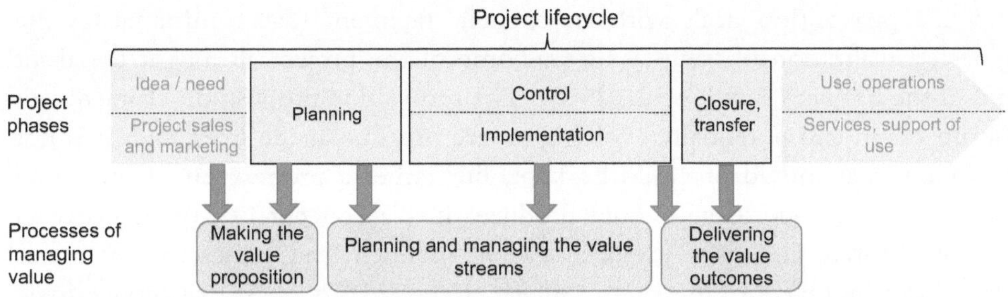

Figure 12.1: Key processes of managing value in projects

I will purposely exclude the consideration of post-project operations where the client and user of the project outcomes create additional value using the project outcomes.

This chapter covers the three processes of managing value, as illustrated in Figure 12.1. I will first discuss how the value proposition is made at the front end of the project. Then, the focus is shifted to planning and managing the value streams in project operations. Also, an outcome view of value is covered, in terms of delivering value. In the end, I will conclude the key tasks in the processes of managing value and propose some ideas for project managers who aspire to enhance their capabilities for managing value in projects.

Making the project value proposition

The most influential strategic decisions are made at the front end of the project, either when responding to a customer's needs or otherwise generating ideas for a new project (Martinsuo et al., 2019b). Martinsuo (forthcoming) emphasizes that the creation of value at the front end of the project concentrates on immaterial processes of sensemaking and negotiation among the stakeholders who have expectations toward the project. Value at this stage emerges through information sharing, relational dialogue, and interaction taking place among the key stakeholders, to come up with the key project decisions (Smyth et al., 2018). Managing value at the project front end centres on identifying and agreeing on such a value proposition that can satisfy the key actors, typically a customer (or sponsor) investing in the project and the main contractor responsible for the project delivery.

Value proposition deals with an explicit statement that communicates the expected realization of value as an outcome of the project already at the front end of the project (Smyth et al., 2018). The term value proposition characterizes the uncertain and potentially evolving nature of value at the front end: it is not a promise that should or could be kept, but rather a proposition of outcomes that the project operations should produce. It is a concept used particularly in service research, and since projects tend to represent the contractor's activities carried out on behalf of the client, Smyth et al. (2018) suggest that service logic and its concepts can be applied in projects, too. Such a value proposition could be stated as part of a project charter or purpose, and it also should be repeated in the project plan.

Managing value at the project front end and coming up with a credible value proposition may be challenging due to the complexity of different expectations. Expectations of value can be identified at the different levels of the system, e.g., local, sectoral, and users (Zerjav et al., 2021), project, region, and portfolio (Martinsuo et al., 2019b), or firm, relationship, and network (Martinsuo, 2019). The question then is: how will the project customer and contractor together navigate among the different expectations and conclude a value proposition that serves the different expectations sufficiently? Any stakeholders may attempt to influence the decision-makers on purpose, to drive their own interests. When negotiating and deciding on the value proposition, different stakeholders may frame their value expectations (Martinsuo et al., 2019b) and argue for their value priorities proactively (Zerjav et al., 2021) to ensure that their perspective is taken into account in the value proposition. It is important that social sessions and meeting arenas are organized, for the stakeholders to share their viewpoints with each other (Liu et al., 2019). The negotiated aspects of creating the value proposition are sometimes referred to as the co-creation of value (Liu et al., 2019; Smyth et al., 2018).

A common error at the front end of the project is when the key project actors decide on an overly optimistic value proposition: overestimate the benefits and underestimate the sacrifices, which is referred to as the planning fallacy (Flyvbjerg, 2021, based on Kahneman & Tversky, 1979). A proportion of this error may stem from the necessity to anticipate and plan both immaterial and material value creation within the project. Immaterial value creation is very often highlighted and emphasized as part of the benefit statements, whereas the cost calculations are dominantly done based on material value creation, only after sufficient estimates and assessments have been completed. When crafting the value proposition for projects, there is a need to acknowledge both aspects of value creation equally carefully.

Managing the value streams in project operations

Value is created in the tasks and processes through which the project is implemented. Mapping the project's activity network or, using terminology from lean operations, value stream, effectively implies identifying the tasks (information and material) and outcomes that add value to the customers. At the same time there is a need to map the consumed resources and monetary investments and identify also non-value-adding necessities during the process, understanding the value stream of operations in the project will be a key step in managing a project's value. In reality, each project is likely to have multiple value streams, some of which are well planned whereas others are not planned. The focus tends to be on the value stream-oriented toward the customer and the main outcome, but the other stakeholders' value streams might be quite different and, yet, equally relevant.

Value streams in projects require good planning of project operations and identifying "who does what and when and with what outcomes". General project management relies on planning tasks, activity networks, resource consumption, schedules, procurements, dependencies, and the critical path required for completing the project product. However, there may be a difference between value accumulating to the project product and value outcomes achieved for the customer and other stakeholders. Many immaterial aspects in the project process are important sources of value for the stakeholders, even if they are not embedded in the measurable outcomes (Chih et al., 2019; Laursen, 2018). When attention is switched from the product only to value more generally, there is a possibility to keep track of value that is missed due to the lack or misuse of resources (Laursen, 2018) and also avoid causing waste both in time and material.

Managing value during project implementation requires designing an operational system for the involved organizations to create value together (Artto et al., 2016). Laursen (2018) refers to the project network conducting the project work as the constellation for value creation. Each of the actors may have their own tasks and processes, but for the purposes of value creation, the entire operational system requires integration and mechanisms of coordinating the network actors' efforts into one coherent entity (Artto et al., 2016). There, value creation occurs through various interactions among the project actors over the duration of the project (Chih et al., 2019; Fuentes et al., 2019). Value is co-created among multiple actors, each consuming their own time, materials, and resources. Research has discussed the co-creation and integration activities in projects (Artto et al., 2016; Fuentes et al., 2019; Laursen, 2018), and shows somewhat different approaches for value co-creation, depending on the needs of each specific project type. The attention in project studies tends to be on the events and episodes where knowledge from multiple actors is integrated, whereas the research on material-related value creation occurs elsewhere.

The problem of planning fallacy may become extremely visible when the possible uncertainties concerning resources, tasks, and materials take shape in project operations. While project management techniques and methods clearly advise that uncertainties must be planned for in project scheduling and budgeting, the reality of projects shows that contingency planning is rare and requires extremely skilled management. If customers and sponsors request a tight budget and schedule, that is what they are likely to get, along with a minefield of uncertainties. In reality, however, value creation in the project operations takes place in the tasks and activities of key project actors and stakeholders in the project's specific circumstances and contexts, facing uncertainties. During project implementation, managing value implies not just implementing the overly optimistic plan, but awareness of uncertainties and diligent and skilled responses to them.

Delivering the value outcomes

Each task and process requires inputs (resources, material, time) and produces outputs (products, services, knowledge, change), so they all create some value. These inputs and outputs together turn into project value outcomes that are eventually assessed and compared with the project's original value proposition. Project management generally emphasizes following and fulfilling the plan, but the delivery of value outcomes is influenced also by all the possible contextual and circumstantial uncertainties that emerge during the project and through stakeholders' responses to them. Project management guidelines tend to acknowledge the need for managing changes during the project and such changes may well be handled at the task level, but it is much less common to change the value proposition, when the project is ongoing.

Value outcomes, thereby, may be partly the same as planned and partly emergent, being shaped only through the project actors' awareness of and spontaneous responses to events and each other's actions. Improvisation is necessary in uncertain projects, as all events and behaviours cannot be anticipated. However, project customers and contractors need to stay alert to what such improvisation might mean for the value outcomes espoused in the original value proposition. Allowing too much flexibility will mean that the value proposition is not going to be achieved. Fuentes et al. (2019) emphasize that the delivery of value outcomes will likely require occasional refinements to the value proposition that was made early in the project, in terms of solving any problems during the project and collaborating during the transfer of project outcomes to the customer. The delivery of value outcomes may continue long after the project is completed, but the use phases are usually a concern of the customer, not the contractor.

Delivering the expected value outcomes is monitored and controlled in various ways in projects (Kivilä et al., 2017), and achieved value may be compared to the original value proposition. Some aspects of value can be easily measured, quantified, and compared to the plans, whereas other aspects of value rest on the perceptions and impressions of stakeholders. Assessing the value outcomes is equally subjective as the expressions of value expectations at the beginning of the project, so the project stakeholders may have very different views on the value outcomes. There is a need to consider both non-monetary and monetary aspects of value outcomes (Chih et al., 2019). Delivering the value outcomes, therefore, concerns both calculating the measurable benefits and sacrifices and managing the impressions and perceptions of involved stakeholders.

At the time of project completion and soon after it, it is customary to assess project success, both in terms of reaching the original goals and achieving stakeholders' satisfaction with the value outcomes. Contrasting the project outcomes with the original value proposition often represents a moment of truth for the customer, the contractor, and other stakeholders. They all want to capture value from the project. With deficient planning and, e.g., planning fallacy, assessment of value outcomes may cause disappointments, especially for the customer, since it is quite likely that some risks have been realized and caused extra costs. Uncertainty, however, may appear also in positive opportunities whereby unplanned benefits are achieved for some stakeholders. When delivering and assessing a project's value outcomes, there is a need to consider achievements realistically but at the same time turn to look toward the future. The sacrifices made to resolve uncertainties and manage risks may well be surpassed by all the benefits accumulating in the future, when the project outcomes are in the customer's use.

Conclusion

This chapter has offered an overview of the key processes of managing value in projects. To complement the earlier concentration on benefits and sacrifices, I have emphasized the necessity to acknowledge both material and immaterial aspects of value and their respective processes. Figure 12.2 summarizes some key tasks in managing value, as covered in the previous chapters. Projects are often carried out in inter-organizational networks, so managing value requires alertness to the stakeholders' different expectations, some of which may be explicitly voiced whereas others remain implicit and invisible. Particularly the difficulty of planning for immaterial value creation and failure to serve some unvoiced stakeholder expectations may explain problems and failures in projects.

Managing value is both a task of managing project work to accomplish very practical products and of managing perceptions, expectations, and impressions. This implies that project managers and owners need to be able to plan and manage both the tangible and intangible aspects of creating value. In ordinary project management, benefits may be negotiated and planned among owners and customers, whereas the project, its resources, and procurements are planned

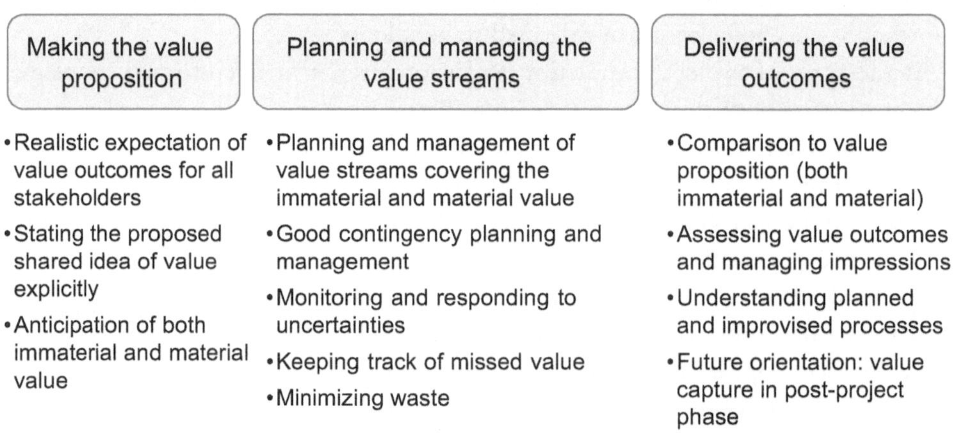

Figure 12.2: Summary of key tasks in the processes of managing value in projects

within the project group. It may imply that some stakeholder expectations are never included in the benefits expectations, as the planned project work covers technical product-related work only, and the immaterial aspects of value are not planned, resourced, scheduled, and budgeted. This is a possible explanation for projects ending over budget and over time.

To avoid such problems, the project owners and managers could manage the different value expectations already at the front end of the project. They could help stakeholders in being realistic about value already in the beginning, to ensure the feasibility of the value proposition. They could make an effort to communicate uncertainties, missed opportunities, and possibilities to avoid waste during the project, and to manage perceptions and impressions before major problems occur. Finally, project managers and owners could help stakeholders in forming a positive, constructive, and future-oriented impression of the project, when assessing value outcomes during project completion. The end of the project is only the beginning for significant additional value potentials, to be captured when the project outcomes are in the customer's use.

References and further reading

Ahola, T., Laitinen, E., Kujala, J. & Wikström, K. (2008). Purchasing strategies and value creation in industrial turnkey projects. *International Journal of Project Management*, 26(1), 87–94.

Artto, K., Ahola, T. & Vartiainen, V. (2016). From the front end of projects to the back end of operations: Managing projects for value creation throughout the system lifecycle. *International Journal of Project Management*, 34(2), 258–270.

Chih, Y-Y., Zwikael, O. & Restubog, S.L.D. (2019). Enhancing value co-creation in professional service projects: The roles of professionals, clients and their effective interactions. *International Journal of Project Management*, 37, 599–615.

Eskerod, P. & Ang, K. (2017). Stakeholder value constructs in megaprojects: A long-term assessment case study. *Project Management Journal*, 48(6), 60–75.

Flyvbjerg, B. (2021). Top ten behavioral biases in project management: An overview. *Project Management Journal*, 52(6), 531–546.

Fuentes, M., Smyth, H. & Davies, A. (2019). Co-creation of value outcomes: A client perspective on service provision in projects. *International Journal of Project Management*, 37(5), 696–715.

Kahneman, D. & Tversky, A. (1979). Intuitive prediction: Biases and corrective procedures. In S. Makridakis & S. C. Wheelwright (Eds.), *Studies in the management sciences: Forecasting* (Vol. 12, pp. 313–327). Amsterdam: North Holland.

Kivilä, J., Martinsuo, M. & Vuorinen, L. (2017). Sustainable project management through project control in infrastructure projects. *International Journal of Project Management*, 35(6), 1167–1183.

Laursen, M. (2018). Project networks as constellations for value creation. *Project Management Journal*, 49(2), 56–70.

Laursen, M. & Svejvig, P. (2016). Taking stock of project value creation: A structured literature review with future directions for research and practice. *International Journal of Project Management*, 34(4), 736–747.

Liu, Y., van Marrewijk, A., Houwing, E.-J. & Hertogh, M. (2019). The co-creation of values-in-use at the front end of infrastructure development programs. *International Journal of Project Management*, 37(5), 684–695.

Martinsuo, M. (2019). Strategic value at the front end of a radical innovation program. *Project Management Journal*, 50(4), 431–446.

Martinsuo, M. (2020). The management of values in project business: Adjusting beliefs to transform project practices and outcomes. *Project Management Journal*, 51(4), 389–399.

Martinsuo, M. (forthcoming). Project value creation: Sensemaking, shaping and monitoring in a project network. In G. Winch, M. Brunet & D. Cao (Eds.), *Research handbook on complex project organizing*. Edward Elgar.

Martinsuo, M. & Killen, C.P. (2014). Value management in project portfolios: Identifying and assessing strategic value. *Project Management Journal*, 45(5), 56–70.

Martinsuo, M., Klakegg, O.J. & van Marrewijk, A. (2019a). Editorial: Delivering value in projects and project-based business. *International Journal of Project Management*, 37(5), 631–630.

Martinsuo, M., Vuorinen, L. & Killen, C. (2019b). Lifecycle-oriented framing of value at the front end of infrastructure projects. *International Journal of Managing Projects in Business*, 12(3), 617–643.

Smyth, H., Lecoeuvre, L. & Vaesken, P. (2018). Co-creation of value and the project context: Towards application on the case of Hinkley Point C Nuclear Power Station. *International Journal of Project Management*, 36(1), 170–183.

Winter, M. & Szczepanek, T. (2008). Projects and programmes as value creation processes: A new perspective and some practical implications. *International Journal of Project Management*, 26(1), 95–103.

Zerjav, V., McArthur, J. & Edkins, A. (2021). The multiplicity of value in the front-end of projects: The case of London transportation infrastructure. *International Journal of Project Management*, 39(5), 507–519.

Chapter 13

Managing integrated project delivery

Derek Walker and Beverley Lloyd-Walker

Introduction

Project Management (PM) integrates teams across interfaces: multiple organisations; supply chains for components; design and delivery teams, and project owner-end users. Traditional PM knowledge has been evolving, for example: re-thinking PM and what new valid PM research should be addressing; the impact of project complexity and complicatedness; PM as a lived experience of practitioners; strategic and leadership considerations, and PM institutional and societal considerations. This has led to calls for project managers to be experts at integrating teams to collaborate in achieving the project owner's anticipated benefit through interface management.

Project delivery team integration takes place across industry contexts, mainly in-house for product or process development but also across organisational cultures and sub-cultures. Internal projects tend to be not as interface-diverse as, for example, construction infrastructure projects – many require multi-billion-dollar cost and multi-year time (mega-project) commitments. Interface management across most types of projects shares similar demands. Therefore, this chapter describes integrated project delivery (IPD) from a mega-project infrastructure perspective. This context offers an interesting extreme, but common perspective. The impact of these projects is experienced by all, in one way or another, as participants or stakeholders.

DOI: 10.4324/9781003274179-15

This chapter provides a basic understanding of IPD and its forms, as an emerging and significant PM innovation. We focus on large construction infrastructure projects because this perspective provides numerous references that readers can explore to gain deeper insights and appreciate how the learning may apply to smaller and more organisation-internal contexts.

Definition

IPD is

> … a project delivery approach that integrates people, systems, business structures and practices into a process that collaboratively harnesses the talents and insights of all participants to optimize project results, increase value to the owner, reduce waste, and maximize efficiency through all phases of design, fabrication, and construction.
>
> (American Institute of Architects – AIA California Council, 2007, p. 1)

IPD principles can be applied to a variety of contractual arrangements and IPD teams may include members well beyond the basic triad of owner, architect, and contractor. IPD projects are uniquely distinguished by the highly effective collaboration between the owner, the prime designer, and the prime constructor, commencing at early design and continuing until project handover. In the USA, IPD spans a spectrum with three identified levels (NASF, COAA, APPA, AGC, & AIA, 2010, p. iii):

1. Collaboration Level One – Typical; collaboration is not contractually required.
2. Collaboration Level Two – Enhanced; some contractual collaboration requirements.
3. Collaboration Level Three – Required; collaboration required by a multi-party contract.

Alliancing is a specific form of IPD that has been used for several decades in Australia. The Victorian State Government's Department of Finance and Treasury (2006, p. 9) – defines Alliancing as

> … delivering major capital assets, where a public sector agency (the Owner) works collaboratively with private sector parties (Non Owner Participants

> or NOPs). All Participants are required to work together in good faith, acting with integrity and making best-for-project decisions. Working as an integrated, collaborative united team, they make unanimous decisions on all key project delivery issues. The alliance structure capitalises on the relationships between the Participants, removes organisational barriers and encourages effective integration with the Owner.

The quoted definition is from a guide that provides additional specific information about required team behaviours and organisational culture and is the approach adopted by the Australian Federal Government.

The IPD and Alliancing definitions illustrate key highest-level collaboration and integration features. The integrated contract form, collaborative and respectful team behaviours, and integration of the design, project owner, and project delivery teams comprise a minimum requirement.

Evolution

The genesis for change stems from widespread dissatisfaction with the performance of traditional forms of project delivery and a sense of crisis about how to effectively meet demanding project time and cost commitments. UK reports during the last century criticise team fragmentation and participants' opportunistic behaviour. Australia's 'No Dispute' report responded to an adversarial construction industry climate marred by opportunistic contractor-client behaviour and a militant industrial relations workplace culture. Earthquake damage impacting health care infrastructure and other social and commercial infrastructure systems in California in the 1990s, could not be rapidly replaced and upgraded using conventional design-bid-build or design and construct delivery approaches. Sutter Health, a private health care operator, championed and developed Level 3 IPD forms with IPD's institutionalisation in North America becoming an effective new project delivery form. IPD did not magically appear. Their historical context helps us to better understand its emergence.

Early Alliancing literature cites British Petroleum's Andrew Alliance hydrocarbon field development when Alliancing was focussed upon by the oil and gas sector. However, Lahdenperä (2012) provides a more comprehensive review of the global history of multi-party contractual project partnering, Alliancing, and IPD arrangements. He maps its 1980s origins from Japan through quality and continuous improvement adaptation emerging, then migrating to the USA and UK followed by partnering, to evolve into the more integrated collaboration form represented by multi-party commercial risk and reward sharing philosophies and incentivisation processes.

Discussion of this evolution by numerous practitioner authors progressed from an early focus on *what* IPD is, to a focus on how practitioners may learn about this new concept. Early literature inferred *somehow* content, but it concentrated more fully on describing characteristics and features than on providing detailed case study data on IPD and Alliancing mechanisms. Ross (2003), an expert practitioner, provided a comprehensive Alliancing overview. Early literature exploring *why to* procure using IPD or Alliancing included industry associations and government auditing agencies.

IPD has been documented as an evolution of the Lean Construction Concept. Lean waste minimisation principles (material, equipment and management, and worker energy) are applied to collaboration and integration through IPD. In Australia, learning through Alliancing as a better way to cope with and address rework in projects has been the focus of much research.

Recently, the context of IPD has received attention, with research exploring the global state of play. An early example of Alliancing used in the Australian Museum has been comprehensively detailed by Walker and Hampson (2003). The UK Heathrow Terminal 5 project (arguably an IPD project) was detailed in Doherty's book (2008) and in numerous academic journal articles. The Amended New Engineering Contract form 3 and 4 projects, following IPD principles, include Crossrail, Thames Tideway Tunnel, and High Speed 2. In-depth case study research has examined these megaprojects, focussing on innovation, learning, and human aspects of these collaborative integrated project delivery (IPD) forms (see, Davies *et al.*, 2014).

In summary, the emerging IPD and Alliancing literature has progressed from asserting that it is often superior to conventional design-bid-build or design and construct delivery approaches to explaining, citing considerable data and evidence, *how* and *why* this approach functions.

Characteristics

Based on literature, including numerous research studies, the main characteristics and mechanisms are identified and discussed, attempting to answer the question: What is it about IPD or Alliancing that makes it substantially new and different?

Collaborative integration

IPD and Alliancing imply and express integration and collaboration as being a core concept. Traditional project delivery teams and individuals are *notionally* integrated through interface management routines and PM practices. It follows that it would be implicitly expected that collaboration between project teams would be required for them to effectively carry out their roles. However, traditional project delivery forms assume that team members respect their *fiduciary duty of care*, being loyal and obedient to their *home-based* organisation. This inhibits prioritising a *best-for-project* mindset and encourages opportunistic behaviours favouring their 'home' organisation. The Integrated Form of Agreement (IFOA) and the Project Alliance Agreement (PAA) remedy this deficiency through a binding multiple-organisational single contract form. These include performance criteria that relate to the finished project output, not focussing on individual organisation's project participants.

Further, it incentivises integration through a gain-pain sharing mechanism where the agreed and contracted Target Outturn Cost (TOC) plan benchmarks performance. Overperformance results in a bonus (gain) and underperformance in a penalty (pain). The TOC is more than a contract price. It is also a delivery time commitment and project strategy plan that includes the design, defining the scope, and plan of action. Alliance participants sign off on the TOC and are accountable and responsible for it. It is in their interest to adhere to TOC achievement and to respond reflexively to unexpected events with resilience.

Front-end and delivery processes

The project Alliance Team is integrated into the development of the TOC. For many construction infrastructure projects, this requires a six to nine-month gestation period. Thus, collaboration and integration are *designed into* this system. The gestation period enables the design scope and detail to be developed collaboratively by the integrated team, enabling multiple perspectives on emergent issues, questions, and quandaries to be resolved. The TOC development process allows not only better risk and uncertainty clarification and resolution, but according to a recent research study, it also improves the consideration around what unexpected events may be reasonably managed through the alliance's TOC contingency budget or the project owner's contingency. This front-end Target

Adjustment Event process strengthens trust and preparedness for the unforeseen. The TOC process helps prepare teams to understand their accountabilities and, through the various risk workshops during the process, prepares them to be resilient.[1]

Technology and people

One significant difference between IPD and traditional approaches is the explicit contract conditions that govern team participant behaviours. The PAA contract comprises three principles (Ross, 2003). The first requires all direct project-related costs to be reimbursed or paid for by the project owner covering the agreed TOC and contingency being auditable through open-book accounting. The second compensates for an agreed profit/fee and delivered expertise. The third incentivises performance, specifying the degree of gain and pain available for performing better or worse than the agreed TOC. Further, PAA terms also explicitly state behavioural norms to design a collaborative workplace culture.

The PAA uses reinforcing language terms framed as 'we' will … and not 'you' … or the 'designer' (or 'contractor') will … Thus, collaborative language explicitly reinforces a positive workplace culture. Requirements of evidence for a no-blame and consensus-based approach to decision-making at the governance level (an Alliance Management Team and Alliance Leadership Team) ensures that when the Alliance Team agrees to something if anything goes wrong, no *individual* can be blamed. This encourages individual honesty, warning signalling, and resilience because it is in everyone's interest to address problems quickly. This approach also encourages innovation and continuous improvement. Alliances and similar forms actively seek innovation with examples from Crossrail in the UK (Davies *et al.*, 2014), and in Australia (Love & Walker, 2020) being explained by the workplace culture. In this way, innovative technology is enhanced by effectively engaging people through a design-shaping organisational architecture process.

Knowledge, skills, attitudes, and experience

What knowledge, skills, attitudes, and experience (KSAEs) need to be marshalled for the above to occur? A significant difference between traditional and IPD procurement is its selection processes. Traditional approaches are often open for all to make a bid screening confined to technical and financial excellence capabilities. Alliancing and IPD require interested syndicates to go through a detailed and *rigorous preselection process to compete* as syndicate teams based on *evidence* presented addressing a required project team characteristics profile. Collaborative and non-opportunistic behaviour conditions require competing syndicates to provide firm evidence of their capabilities. Many project owners also require environmental, social, and well-being standards supported by evidence to justify consideration of a syndicate's case. The National Museum of Australia Alliance project provides an early team selection example.

Key KSAEs are discussed in depth by Walker and Lloyd-Walker (2020a). These support effective integration and collaboration. They argue that open communication capabilities are vital to support strong technical and general PM expertise. Central to collaboration is the ability to engage in dialogue. Dialogue does not advocate a fixed position but explains reasons supporting a tentative position – open to challenge and assumption questioning from different perspectives. More robust outcomes are likely to be developed when the project owner, design team, delivery team, and operational team are represented in dialogue.

Many participants may possess the KSAEs; for others, these may need to be developed. Their development is a continuous process, linked closely to an authentic leadership style that temporarily gives participants with the specific expertise the required leadership of discussions aimed at solving issues. Development also requires an engaging intellectually safe workplace culture, free of power, and with information asymmetry that allows people to effectively interpret the meaningfulness of their work, their responsibility, and feedback, through dialogue.

Figure 13.1 illustrates how the IPD approach motivates the required behaviours and how that makes engaging in dialogue salient to their role. Through work activity crafting, with PAA or IFOA supporting authority, task variety is expanded enabling people to consider multiple perspectives. Task identity and significance are influenced by being 'part of the Alliance Team' that has a greater level of integration and collaboration. This shapes perceptions and interpretations of work. Expertise is valued, and autonomy allows dialogue to legitimise asking questions regarding decision-making and action. This helps people realise their responsibility and accountability as Alliance Team members. Authentic leadership

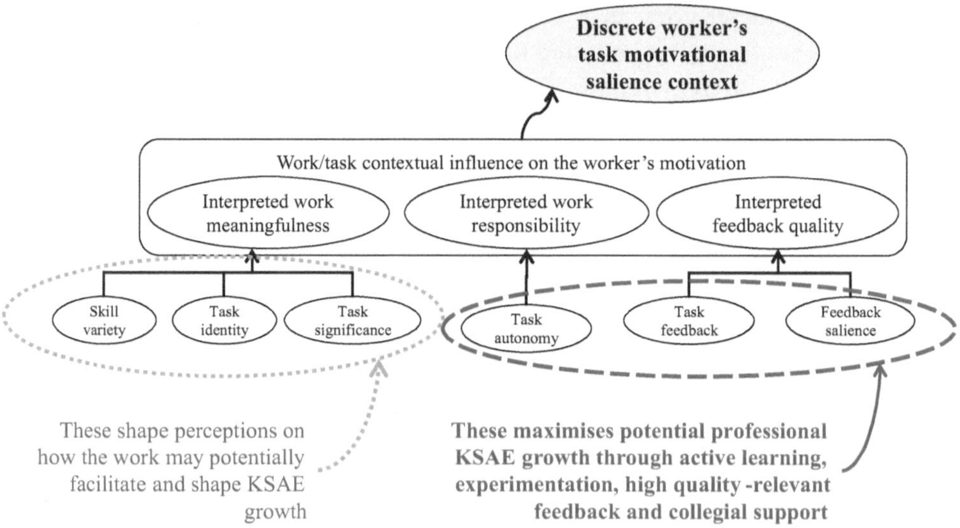

Figure 13.1: KSAE growth
Source: Walker and Lloyd-Walker (2020a, p. 235)

and a fertile organisational learning culture based on experimentation, innovation, and resilience shape task and salience feedback, creating a virtuous learning circle.

Collaboration and team integration is thus supported by behaviours, governance system design, and routines and processes.

Performance frameworks

Project performance has been shown to be consistently high on Alliances completed in Australia between 2008 and 2012 (Walker, Mills, & Harley, 2015). That study investigated how success was measured and assessed. Key Result Areas and key performance indicators include the 'iron triangle' but also social and environmental measures. The projects studied include societal infrastructure projects such as roads, rail, water utility, etc., so the projects' purpose was social benefit delivery.

Project Alliance Agreements and Integrated Form of Agreements also inject another level of project governance. Most projects have project control committees comprising owner, design, and delivery team representatives. Alliancing has an Alliance Management Team, however, a further committee comprising senior alliance participant organisations also forms governance arrangements. Its role is bridging the participating organisational base with project teams. The Alliance Leadership Team acts as an oversight body, monitoring and ensuring Key Result Area performance, and being a resource link to an external stakeholder network. Their members can provide an important additional governance entity for maintaining the project vision.

Additionally, collaboration performance is also important. A Collaboration Framework has been developed and used to assess and measure the extent of collaboration between teams on projects (Walker & Lloyd-Walker, 2020b).

Conclusion

This chapter provides a brief introduction to IPD and especially to Alliancing as a project delivery process innovation. We explain IPD and Alliancing as exemplars of project delivery that enhances the potential of human capital thereby ensures short- and long-term benefits realisation. The context for its emergence is important and specific organisational design and KSAE enabling elements were explained. We encourage interested readers to follow up on cited references.

Where are IPD and Alliancing heading? Why consider it more broadly for future project delivery?

These delivery forms are appropriate for complex projects with expert owners and non-owner participants who have the requisite KSAEs. We have traced its global use for major infrastructure projects. These are getting larger and more complex in their interface with other projects and systems. Thus, in the future we can expect its use to expand increasing the need for more people to develop the requisite and vital KSAEs to generate effective team integration and collaboration.

Smaller in-house and multi-organisational projects are also requiring IPD integration and collaboration characteristics as we enter the greater digitisation and technology-integrated project world of the Fourth Industrial Revolution (Industry 4). This requires significant interdisciplinary collaboration and team integration across many organisational and social interfaces.

IPD is likely to become a traditional default approach globally for an increasing range of projects during the coming decades. However, as was once attributed to

Sheik Yamani in the 1970s Oil Crisis, 'the stone age did not end through lack of stones'. Similarly, projects will continue to be delivered through DBB and D&C, but an increasing number will adopt IPD forms.

We introduced integrated delivery concepts and focussed on supporting contractual, governance, and, most importantly, the KSAEs people required to *effectively* deliver projects through IPD. Three key features are central:

- Collaboration – people actively engaged in sharing perspectives and avoiding an asymmetric power and information workplace culture;
- Dialogue – people open to challenge and questioning to holistically consider issues; and
- Integration – people effectively organisationally designed in unified teams possessing a common project outcome purpose.

Note

1 https://www.researchgate.net/publication/346646354_Investigating_the_Treatment_of_Target_Adjustment_Events_in_Alliance_Projects_FINAL_REPORT.

References and further reading

American Institute of Architects – AIA California Council. (2007). *Integrated Project Delivery: A Guide*. Sacremento, CA: American Institute of Architects.

Auditor-General of the Australian National Audit Office. (2000). *Construction of the National Museum of Australia and the Australian Institute of Aboriginal and Torres Strait Islander Studies* (34, 1999–2000). Retrieved from Canberra, Australia: https://www.anao.gov.au/work/major-projects-report/construction-national-museum-australia-and-australian-institute

Ballard, G., Dilsworth, B., Do, D., Low, W., Mobley, J., Phillips, P., & Wood, N. (2015). How to make shared risk and reward sustainable. *Lean Construction Journal*, 25–33.

Burström, T., & Jacobsson, M. (2013). The informal liaison role of project controllers in new product development projects. *International Journal of Managing Projects in Business, 6*(3), 410–424. https://doi.org/10.1108/IJMPB-10-2011-0069

Davies, A., MacAulay, S., DeBarro, T., & Thurston, M. (2014). Making innovation happen in a megaproject: London's crossrail suburban railway system. *Project Management Journal, 45*(6), 25–37. https://doi.org/10.1002/pmj.21461

Denicol, J., Davies, A., & Pryke, S. (2021). The organisational architecture of megaprojects. *International Journal of Project Management, 39*(4), 339–350. https://doi.org/10.1016/j.ijproman.2021.02.002

Department of Finance and Treasury. (2006). *Project Alliancing Practitioners' Guide*. Retrieved from Melbourne, Australia.

Doherty, S. (2008). *Heathrow's T5 History in the Making*. Chichester: John Wiley & Sons Ltd.

Hodgson, D., & Cicmil, S. (2016). Making projects critical 15 years on: a retrospective reflection (2001–2016). *International Journal of Managing Projects in Business, 9*(4), 744–751. https://doi.org/10.1108/IJMPB-10-2015-0105

Lahdenperä, P. (2012). Making sense of the multi-party contractual arrangements of project partnering, project alliancing and integrated project delivery. *Construction Management and Economics, 30*(1), 57–79. https://doi.org/10.1080/01446193.2011.648947

Lichtig, W. A. (2005). Sutter health: developing a contracting model to support lean project delivery. *Lean Construction Journal, 2*(1), 105–112.

Love, P. E. D., Ackermann, F., Teo, P., & Morrison, J. (2015). From individual to collective learning: a conceptual learning framework for enacting rework prevention. *Journal of Construction Engineering and Management, 141*(11), 05015009. https://doi.org/10.1061/(ASCE)CO.1943-7862.0001013

Love, P. E. D., & Walker, D. H. T. (2020). IPD facilitating innovation diffusion. In D. H. T. Walker & S. Rowlinson (Eds.), *The Routledge Handbook of Integrated Project Delivery* (pp. 393–416). Abingdon: Routledge.

Morris, P. W. G., & Geraldi, J. (2011). Managing the institutional context for projects. *Project Management Journal, 42*(6), 20–32. https://doi.org/10.1002/pmj.20271

NASF, COAA, APPA, AGC, & AIA. (2010). *Integrated Project Delivery for Public and Private Owners*. Retrieved from Lexington, KY.

Ross, J. (2003, 30 April). *Introduction to Project Alliancing*. Paper presented at the Alliance Contracting Conference, Sydney.

Walker, D. H. T., & Hampson, K. D. (2003). *Procurement Strategies: A Relationship Based Approach*. Oxford: Blackwell Publishing.

Walker, D. H. T., & Lloyd-Walker, B. M. (2020a). Knowledge, Skills, Attributes and Experience (KSAE) for IPD Alliancing task motivation. In D. H. T. Walker & S. Rowlinson (Eds.), *The Routledge Handbook of Integrated Project Delivery* (pp. 219–244). Abingdon: Routledge.

Walker, D. H. T., & Lloyd-Walker, B. M. (2020b). Characteristics of IPD: a framework overview. In D. H. T. Walker & S. Rowlinson (Eds.), *The Routledge Handbook of Integrated Project Delivery* (pp. 20–40). Abingdon: Routledge.

Walker, D. H. T., & McCann, A. (2020). IPD and TOC development. In D. H. T. Walker & S. Rowlinson (Eds.), *The Routledge Handbook of Integrated Project Delivery* (pp. 581–604). Abingdon: Routlidge.

Walker, D. H. T., Mills, A., & Harley, J. (2015). Alliance projects in Australasia: a digest of infrastructure development from 2008 to 2013. *Construction Economics and Building, 15*(1), 1–18. https://doi.org/10.5130/ajceb.v15i1.4186

Winter, M., Smith, C., Morris, P., & Cicmil, S. (2006). Directions for future research in project management: the main findings of a UK government-funded research network. *International Journal of Project Management, 24*(8), 638–649. https://doi.org/10.1016/j.ijproman.2006.08.009

Chapter 14

Data analytics in managing projects

Eleni Papadonikolaki and Carlos Galera-Zarco

Introduction

Information is a key part of our everyday lives and it affects each of our decisions and our communication with others. According to early organisational theorists, the information relates to communication. Robbins and Judge (2013) argued that during communication, information plays a key role in structuring a message that is first coded by a sender and subsequently decoded by a receiver. Therefore, the information relates a lot with humans, their perceptions, and interactions. In organisations and projects, where information is the foundation of communications among project team members, the more complex the system, the higher the likelihood of information uncertainty.

Information was linked to organisational processes as early as the 1970s by Galbraith (1974), who focused on internal organisations and how information processing related to tack uncertainty. Galbraith (1974) stated that "the greater the task uncertainty, the greater the amount of information that must be processed among decision makers during task execution in order to achieve a given level of performance". Galbraith (1974) presented the information processing approach as a non-deterministic view of organisations designed "to create mechanisms that permit coordinated action across large numbers of interdependent roles". This was among the first theories to relate task uncertainty and organisational form through information processing.

 DOI: 10.4324/9781003274179-16

Because we rely on good information in order to make decisions, the implication of information is that it governs not only human relations but also business relations. Equally, Williamson's (1985) transaction cost economics theory of interfirm relationships was theoretically compatible with Galbraith's (1974) information processing view linking information processing and uncertainty of economic decision-making. Therefore, information can be defined as being between the 'human things' and 'operational things' of (project) work and bridging them.

The information processing view and its relation to uncertainty shows the criticality of information in communications. For instance, Robbins and Judge (2013) identify various problems with communication depending on how information is filtered by senders, selectively perceived by receivers, mixed with noise, information overload, and various emotional and cultural biases among others. As projects too are intensive information processing organisations, one of the nine dominant views of project management (PM) (Turner et al., 2013), the "decision school: the project as a computer", emphasises the view of projects as information processing systems.

A project organisation can be formulated as an information processing system and project organising as information processing (Winch, 2015). Based on this view, projects are vehicles for processing information and reducing uncertainty in the process, hence linking also with the "process school" of PM. In the "process school", projects are processes for processing information. With the aim to reduce uncertainty through information, the information processing view of the project also relates to the "success school" of PM, according to which, processing information enables us to make better decisions and increase performance in decision-making, sense-making during and reviews to reduce uncertainty, which is a success factor. Thus, the information processing view of projects has strong relations to dominant views of projects, from technocratic approaches to processes and decision-making, success and performance, showing the versatility and applicability of this idea.

According to Whyte and Levitt (2011), "information management has played a central, but under-recognised, role in the history of project management". It relates to better decision-making and generally decision theory in projects. At the same time, information uncertainty increases the difficulty of task coordination and PM (Hobday, 1998). To this end, information flows among project stakeholders and potential information asymmetries are detrimental to project success (Turner and Müller, 2004) where various types of information are exchanged.

In our current digital economy, which is characterised by a proliferation of information artefacts, the information processing view becomes less related to the 'human things' and instead grows increasingly related to 'operational things' due to datafication, digitalisation, and innovative Information Systems (IS). Having established the relation between projects and information, this chapter will focus on projects and data, for which information is foundational. In particular, it aims to discuss key application areas of data analytics in projects, for instance scheduling and costing, present the current industry practice, means, and tools, and outline future challenges around data analytics and PM.

From information to data

In many aspects of our lives, we are experiencing the developments first invented and established in the Information Age, that is also known as the Computer Age, which started in the mid-20th century and is characterised by a rapid shift from traditional industries towards a digital economy, an economy primarily based upon Information and Communication Technology. The birth of the Information Age coincided with the origins of PM and the first efforts in computerised planning and scheduling. This fruitful period after the 1950s is known as the origin of Cybernetics, where interactions among numerous fields such as anthropology, mathematics, neuroscience, psychology, and engineering, led to the establishment of information theory and the emergence of computing, Artificial Intelligence (AI), cognitive science, and robotics.

A key framework developed during Cybernetics is the Data-Information-Knowledge-Wisdom hierarchy by Ackoff (1989). This framework is useful in understanding the relationship between information and data, which are not interchangeable. According to Rowley (2007) in both the Information System and knowledge management literature, "information is defined in terms of data, and is seen to be organised or structured data. This processing lends the data relevance for a specific purpose or context, and thereby makes it meaningful, valuable, useful and relevant" (p. 72). Thus, information and data have a foundational and mutually reinforcing position as data lack context and only after people attribute context to it becomes useful for decision-making.

Lately, there is an increase in *digitalisation* – the operational shift from analogue to digital – and *datafication* – a technological trend shifting many aspects of our life into data that is then transferred into information realised as a new form of value – due to: (i) various pervasive devices, e.g., mobile, headsets, drones, etc., (ii) better internet connectivity, e.g., 4G, 5G, (iii) computer infrastructure with high computing power and (iv) connected technologies.

Data in PM

There are different types of data across a project's lifecycle. During a project, the front end is typically one of the most user-centric phases with little data generated. Project execution and hand-over are the least digitised phases, abound with traditional practices; relying on professionals' experience and skill. Figure 14.1 illustrates the data analytics potential across the project lifecycle. As project-based industries are in a transition, data, and information will be blurred more in the future, and more domain experts will develop mature data expertise. Nevertheless, currently, data and information are still discrete and usually treated in silos.

The importance of data in projects has been highlighted the recent years in practices of managing change in large, complex projects in Airbus, CERN, and Crossrail (Whyte et al., 2016). In delivering these complex projects, large data sets, in the form of 'big data' have significant potential to be used to help configuration management and after-hand-over asset management too, although this could be in hierarchical, asynchronous, and sequential approaches. Different type of data is used in projects, from visual, textual, and numerical as seen in Table 14.1. Additionally, the increasingly pervasive use of digital information

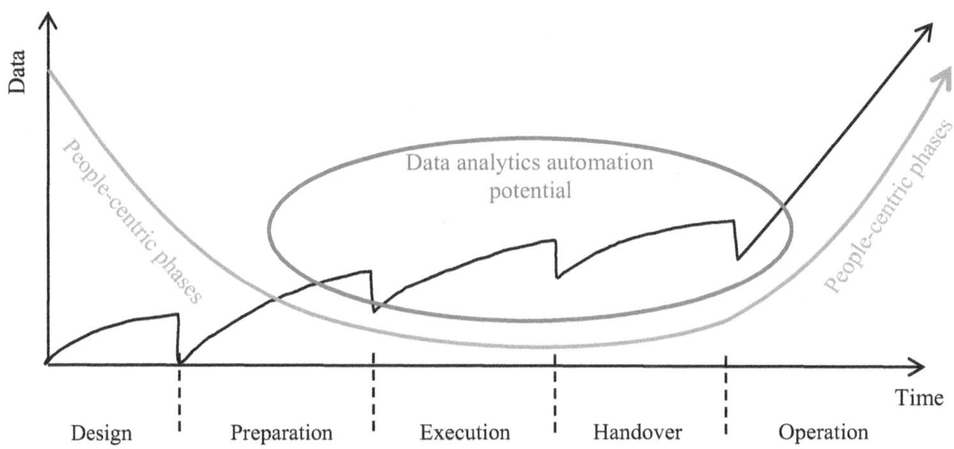

Figure 14.1: Data analytics automation potential across the project lifecycle

Table 14.1 Types of data used in projects

Types of data used in projects (and examples)		
Visual	*Textual*	*Numerical*
• Drawings, photographs • 3-Dimensional (3D) Models • Building Information Models (BIM) • Geographic Information Systems (GIS) • Asset registries	• Emails, chats • Minutes of meetings • Project plans • Progress reports • Contracts • Stakeholder data	• Spreadsheets • Project planning tools • Risk registers • Enterprise Resource Planning (ERP) systems • Metadata

transforms project delivery models as seen across the London megaproject ecology of Heathrow T5, the London 2012 Olympics, Crossrail, and Thames Tideway Tunnel among others (Whyte, 2019). The above shows not only the impact of automation on projects but also implications for PM delivery models, processes, and skills.

Data analytics

Before going deeper into the use of data analysis in projects, it is required to provide some conceptualisations about data and their use in the journey towards wisdom generation. *Data science* is an interdisciplinary field aiming to turn data into value for individuals, organisations, and the whole society (Van Der Aalst, 2016). This field can be seen as an amalgamation of different disciplines including statistics, data mining, programming, visual communication, ethics, and law. The process of data-driven value creation can adopt different forms: automation of operations, predictions, improved models, generative design, or insightful data visualisations. Data science assists organisations in these value-creation processes by answering four main categories of data questions:

- What happened? (Reporting)
- Why did it happen? (Diagnosis)
- What will/might happen? (Prediction)
- What is the best that can happen? (Recommendation)

In recent years, we are witnessing an evolution from explanatory analysis (e.g., determining causes) to exploratory analysis (e.g., what-if questions) in data science. This transformation is enabled by an increased ability to collect bigger amounts of data and more complex data types, together with the evolution in data analytics techniques and tools. Hence, organisations are now able to answer more challenging questions and generate new forms of value. In particular, three main categories of data analytics can be distinguished:

- *Descriptive Analytics*: Consists in processing current and past data to organise information in a way that makes easier the identification of trends and relationships. It is linked with the concept of Business Intelligence (BI) and the development of web dashboards
- *Predictive Analytics*: Consists in the analysis of current and past data to forecast future behaviours
- *Prescriptive Analytics*: Lies in the process of applying heavy mathematical, statistical, and computational methods to achieve actionable insights. By using prescriptive analysis, organisations are able to assess different hypothetical scenarios and optimise solutions

Moreover, it is important to clarify and delimit three popular concepts that interact with data analytics: *Big Data*, *Artificial Intelligence* (AI), and *Machine Learning* (ML). It is well-known that the volume of data created nowadays grows at an ever-increasing rate. Big data is defined as these data whose scale (huge volume), complexity (different data types), and velocity (speed of data generation) require the use of new analytical tools and architectures to unlock business value (Dietrich, 2015). There are many different definitions for AI, but in general terms, AI can be understood as algorithmic systems able to interpret external data, learn from these data, and, by flexible adaptation, develop solutions to problems at near-human level or even exceeding human capabilities. Finally, ML is simply a subset of AI characterised by the development of algorithms that mimic the human cognitive process by learning from experience and improving accuracy gradually. It is important to note that *Deep learning* (DL) is a subtype of ML.

The characterisation of data analytics in project business is known as project data analytics. The nature of projects, characterised by uniqueness, uncertainty, and temporariness, makes their type of data, analytics tools, and areas of application present specific characteristics. The significant amount of data available, together with technological progress to collect, store, and analyse data represent a huge opportunity for the PM discipline in order to improve project performance and better address historical problems to deliver projects on time and within budget. At this time, PM is moving on to leverage data analytics in the way projects, programs, and portfolios are delivered. According to Bodea et al. (2020), PM professionals identified enhanced decision-making, increased productivity, and improved reporting and performance as the key reasons to adopt data analytics in projects. Additionally, time, quality, and transformation/change were the identified issues in PM that could benefit the most from project data analytics.

Scheduling

Scheduling is an essential part of planning projects. In scheduling, logic and different techniques are used to determine where and when project activities will be performed in the most time-efficient way. Scheduling considers the scope, the duration, and the resources demanded for each activity. Traditional methods of scheduling are usually based on experience from similar projects, expert judgement, and performance rates. However, none of these approaches take project uncertainty factors into consideration. Although there are some probabilistic methods for scheduling (e.g., Program Evaluation and Review Technique (PERT)), they mainly consider just a few scenarios (pessimistic, neutral, and optimistic) and do not really appraise either particular uncertainties of the project or changes of behaviour over time.

The use of predictive and prescriptive analysis helps organisations to better manage uncertainty. Therefore, scheduling, which is an activity dealing with high levels of uncertainty, benefits from the use of data analytics. Nonetheless, there are some barriers to unleashing the full potential of data analytics in scheduling; first, the conceptualisation of production in projects, which should adopt a *flow view* instead of presenting the usual hierarchical decompositions of the project scope; second, *digitisation* of projects, being needed a transition from hard-copy to digitised information to achieve machine readability; and third, the *interconnection of information*, that should evolve to allow better coordination in complex project environments (e.g., a construction site in a large project).

Scheduling in projects differs from classic machine scheduling problems from operations research in terms of resource consumption and complexity in precedent constraints. As optimisation problem, project scheduling is defined as

Resource-Constraint Project Scheduling Problem (RCPSP). Within Data analytics, ML is playing a key role in trying to address this extremely complex problem. Among different approaches, *Reinforcement Learning* (RL) emerges as a promising area to improve project scheduling. RL is an area of ML whose objective is to instruct an agent on how to make (sub-)optimal sequential decisions in a deterministic or stochastic environment in order to maximise or minimise a cumulative benefit or penalty that is determined by the environment in which the agent is operating (Vengerov et al., 2005). Reward is a key element in RL problems, as it defines how good the action executed by the agent is, and consequently, influences its future behaviour. In the context of projects, the reward is usually a function of (1) completion of the activity, (2) constraint satisfaction, and (3) resource cost.

Thus, ML frameworks are already showing the way towards automated project scheduling, being particularly effective in look-ahead scheduling (LAS). Nonetheless, in achieving that goal, project data need to be correctly integrated and codified.

Cost management

Data analytics in project cost management aims to generate the best possible information in order to: (1) budget the project, (2) control cost and (3) enhance cost-related decision-making. As with scheduling, because of its inherent uncertainty, the estimation of project cost at the front end of a project is a pretty challenging task. Predictive analytics has the potential to play an important role in the cost estimation stage, for both direct and indirect costs. By combining historical data prices with macroeconomic trends and project scheduling data, it is possible to provide clearer information for cost forecasting. A crucial element in making that process successful is the use of sufficient good-quality data to feed the ML models. It allows organisations to better predict the evolution of prices and create the most accurate cost baseline for the project.

In the execution of a project, the ability to control the cost and avoid deviation is essential to evade budget overrun. In that stage, the use of real-time dashboards (descriptive analytics) is useful to integrate the data available and produce insightful and visual information. Furthermore, when the quality, variety, and volume of cost data are good enough, predictive analysis can be done to anticipate cost deviations and implement the corresponding measures.

Cost is a decisive input in any managerial decision. Consequently, organisations which are able to capture the right cost-related data in each project, and "play" sufficiently with these data, will have the potential to make better cost-informed decisions leading to more efficient projects.

Project monitoring and control

During project execution, the monitoring and control of activities become critical to successfully achieving the objectives within the allocated timeframe and budget. Monitoring encompasses the collection, recording, and reporting of project data, while control activities aim to avoid project deviations by using the collected data. An important aspect of monitoring is to identify what needs to be more carefully controlled in each specific project. Key common aspects across projects are time and cost, but other elements such as physical design, quality, safety, resource usage and changes, risks, or stakeholder expectations can equally determine the future success of a project.

Data collection in project monitoring deals with a variety of data types associated with the diverse project items that need to be monitored. Hence, visual data, numerical data, and even textual data (e.g., sentiment analysis) may be required for a comprehensive monitoring of a project. Additionally, data quality and data reliability are vital in project monitoring since the final objective is to provide the most accurate information to control the project's progress. In traditional practice, monitoring has largely relied on direct observation and measurement, being this a manual and time-consuming work, which is, in nature, error-prone. Thus, the automation of data collection is a first step in enabling data analytics for monitoring and control, and we can already identify a series of data collection technologies investigated for monitoring activities in projects: smart sensor networks, communication networks, audio and sonar, tag identification systems, computer vision, and electronic location and distance measurement (i.e., robots and drones equipped with laser scanning).

Automated data monitoring increases data reliability and improves project control. The key focus of project control is to compare actual performance (i.e., as-built) with planned performance (i.e., as-planned), adopting the corresponding corrective actions. Going a step further, proactive project control requires monitoring data from activities' feeding flows as well as the activities themselves. To leverage project data analytics and drive project control to its next level, we

Figure 14.2: Example of Construction Production Control Room (credits: IUK project ref.: 106169)

need data processing technologies that can combine different data streams and data types to enable data-driven constraints checking and provide more accurate and comprehensive status reports.

Another research stream in this area focuses on the creation of *production control rooms* in large projects, which are aligned with descriptive analytics. An example is shown in Figure 14.2. These NASA-inspired operations rooms are based on visualisation of real-time project information and 4D models to provide instant analysis of various key performance metrics, enabling interoperability and collaboration between stakeholders and facilitating objective comparison between planned and actual performance.

Risk management

Risks are intimately ligated to uncertainty and the probability of occurrence of future events. Therefore, the use of data analytics to enhance risk-related predictions in projects contributes to an improved management of risks. The classic view of risk management includes four main stages: (1) risk identification, (2) risk quantification, (3) response development and (4) risk control. Traditional approaches typically combine both quantitative and qualitative approaches and use historic data and internal/external subjective judgements as main sources of information to perform project risk analyses.

These traditional approaches, deeply based on subjective perceptions from individuals, must evolve towards more objective assessments by embracing data analysis. The involvement of data analytics in risk management should take place throughout the whole process, from identification to risk control. Each stage in project risk management presents opportunities to leverage data analytics:

- *Risk identification*: the root of project risks can be external (e.g., growing inflation rate, adverse weather) and/or internal (e.g., funding problems, stakeholder disagreements,). The global trend to increased digitisation impacts positively risk identification since the availability of big data (e.g., macroeconomics data, data on weather trends) combined with advanced analytics tools allow the identification of incipient external risks. At the internal level, *datafication* of the project environment provides enhanced opportunities to identify internal risks, and ultimately, will enable richer analysis of historical data. Some technological developments such as data ingestion tools, web scrapping, and visualisation platforms are useful in that stage.
- *Risk quantification*: organisations are using data analytics to determine thresholds and cluster risk profiles. The development of analytical models is being used to assess risks by balancing the impact on strategic aspects of the project with the quantification of the mitigation actions that would be required. Likewise, predictive analytics has the potential to better determine probabilities of risk occurrence.
- *Response development*: Prescriptive analytics (i.e., simulations and what-if scenarios) becomes relevant here. This kind of analyses helps in deciding the best alternative to respond to a risk by comparing options, even considering the consequential impacts of each choice. Moreover, prescriptive analytics can assess the implementation effectiveness of different responses.
- *Risk control*: during the control phase, monitoring and visualisation can be deployed to create risk workflows and automate triggers to alert the risk owner about deviations, enabling a quick or even automated implementation of corrective actions.

Lessons learned

The concept of lessons learned refers to gaining knowledge from the process of performing projects. Capturing lessons must be a continuous effort throughout the whole project. For organisations, it takes place at three levels. At the project level, by defining the processes, tools, and techniques to capture lessons. At organisational level, when these processes become part of the organisational culture, the information is shared through the creation of repositories. And at the analytical level, these data are rich enough to be analysed and converted to benchmarks and metrics (Rowe and Sikes, 2006).

In lessons learned, some aspects such as the lack of standard processes, the presence of too much data, the lack of time to perform review activities during the project, and the reluctance to share information (especially relative to errors) are pointed out as main barriers to learning efficiently from past projects. Observing the nature of these barriers, the automation of the processes to capture lessons arises as a solution to overcome them; first, by liberating the project team from these tasks and settling the problem of data volume; and second, by obtaining objective information without the subjective human screening. Likewise, the automation of data collection and storage would improve data quality and standardisation, and consequently, the possibility of aggregating data and performing more insightful analyses. In this area, organisations deal with different types of data (textual, numerical, and visual), so different analysis can take place here: from pattern recognition to sentiment analysis of meeting minutes or stakeholder communications.

Corresponding to Figure 14.1 and the automation potential of data analytics across the project lifecycle, Figure 14.3 illustrates the opportunities of different categories of data analytics (descriptive, predictive, prescriptive) across preparation, execution, and hand-over phases, summarising the data-driven approaches in PM.

Challenges and opportunities

Despite the identified applications of data analytics in PM, there are several barriers that currently hinder its full development. First, more intense digitisation in projects is needed, as this process is crucial to the establishment of digital flows that can jointly benefit different areas of PM. Organisations need to identify better

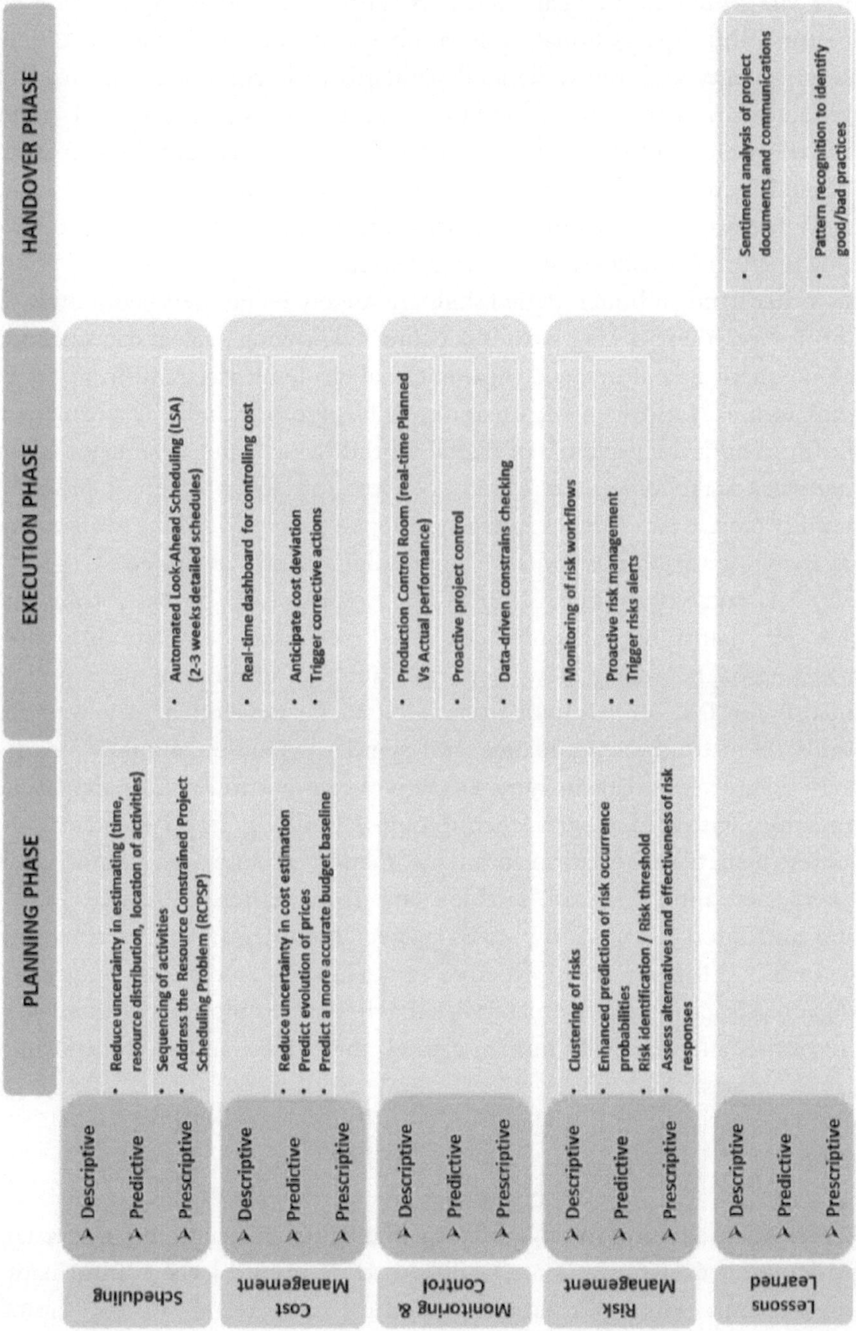

Figure 14.3: Applications of data analytics and their impacts on PM

the type of data which must be gathered in order to be correctly aligned with key project features and organisational business objectives. Likewise, these data must have enough quality and follow defined standards to become machine-readable and enable automation processes. In addition to that, improvements in data sharing in projects are paramount to unlock the potential of data analytics. Project stakeholders should increase collaboration to ensure the creation of centralised digital information platforms (e.g., Common Data Environment (CDE) in construction projects) where project data are stored and shared.

On the other hand, although digital skills are hugely recognised as important in the PM profession, there is still a lack of data literacy slowing project data analytics. To conclude, there are cultural and organisational challenges to transform project-based firms into a data-driven organisation. A change of mindset is required to increase trust in both the potential of digital workflows and the advantages of data sharing between stakeholders. Increased collaboration across different industries could avoid project data analytics being developed in silos, leading to democratised data analytics capabilities and accelerated digitalisation in projects.

Project data analytics offer a variety of approaches, process, tools and techniques for managing schedule, cost, and performance. Naturally, these innovative approaches bring new opportunities for developing new policies and standards for PM, as AI algorithms need to be developed in a way that corresponds to institutional guidance and standard practice. Equally, from a technology side, project data analytics initiatives can link to existing approaches for connecting with linked-data technologies, building upon standard web technologies to share information in an automatic computer-readable manner. The linked-data approach can enable data from different sources to be connected and queried and allow cross-project comparison and performance tracking. Finally, all these transformative opportunities at process, policy, and technology levels can only be materialised when technology is aligned with human resources and especially human capital, their skills, and the social capital of project ecologies.

Conclusion

This chapter focused on data analytics in managing projects. To understand the importance of data on projects, it is key to define projects as information processing systems. The information processing view relates to the 'human things' and 'operational things' of projects affecting not only stakeholders' communications and relations but also decision-making in projects. Currently, due to the intensified datafication, data analytics offer various approaches to increase automation across the project lifecycle (Figure 14.1), especially in the preparation, execution, and hand-over phases. The upsurge in data and the advancement of digital technologies offer an increased ability to collect more complex data types, analyse big data, and follow continuously evolved data analytics techniques and tools from descriptive, to predictive and prescriptive analytics (see Figure 14.3). Key applications of data analytics in projects include scheduling, cost management, monitoring and control, risk management, and lessons learned. Nevertheless, whereas some ongoing technological challenges are addressed through open data science initiatives, future opportunities concern the alignment with processes, policy, and human resources for rising projects digitalisation.

References and further reading

Ackoff, R. L. 1989. From data to wisdom, Presidential address to ISGSR. *Journal of Applied Systems Analysis,* 16, 3–9.

Bodea, C., Ding, R., Stanciu, O. & Mitea, C. 2020. *Artificial intelligence impact in project management.* Nijkerk: International Project Management Association (IPMA).

Dietrich, D. 2015. *Data science & big data analytics: discovering, analyzing, visualizing and presenting data.* Indianapolis, New York, Chichester: John Wiley & Sons.

Galbraith, J. R. 1974. Organization design: An information processing view. *Interfaces,* 4, 28–36.

Hobday, M. 1998. Product complexity, innovation and industrial organisation. *Research Policy,* 26, 689–710.

Robbins, S. P. & Judge, T. A. 2013. *Organizational behavior,* Boston, MA: Pearson Education.

Rowe, S. F. & Sikes, S. 2006. Lessons learned: taking it to the next level. PMI® Global Congress.

Rowley, J. 2007. The wisdom hierarchy: representations of the DIKW hierarchy. *Journal of Information Science,* 33, 163–180.

Turner, J. R., Anbari, F. & Bredillet, C. 2013. Perspectives on research in project management: the nine schools. *Global Business Perspectives,* 1, 3–28.

Turner, J. R. & Müller, R. 2004. Communication and co-operation on projects between the project owner as principal and the project manager as agent. *European Management Journal,* 22, 327–336.

Van Der Aalst, W. 2016. *Process mining: data science in action*. Berlin: Springer.

Vengerov, D., Bambos, N. & Berenji, H. R. 2005. A fuzzy reinforcement learning approach to power control in wireless transmitters. *IEEE Transactions on Systems, Man, and Cybernetics, Part B (Cybernetics),* 35, 768–778.

Whyte, J. 2019. How digital information transforms project delivery models. *Project Management Journal,* 50, 177–194.

Whyte, J. & Levitt, R. 2011. Information management and the management of projects. In P. W. G. Morris, J. Pinto, & J. Söderlund (Eds.), *The Oxford Handbook of Project Management*. Oxford, UK: Oxford University Press, pp. 365–387.

Whyte, J., Stasis, A. & Lindkvist, C. 2016. Managing change in the delivery of complex projects: configuration management, asset information and 'big data'. *International Journal of Project Management,* 34, 339–351.

Williamson, O. E. 1985. *The economic intstitutions of capitalism*. New York: Simon and Schuster.

Winch, G. M. 2015. Project organizing as a problem in information. *Construction Management and Economics,* 33, 106–116.

Chapter 15

Managing digital projects infrastructure

Jennifer Whyte and Ali Eshraghi

Introduction

Projects now use a 'digital infrastructure' for delivery (Whyte and Lobo 2010), made up of interconnected and evolving software packages and applications. This notion of 'digital infrastructure' draws attention to how infrastructure becomes 'taken for granted': infrastructure becomes invisible and usually only becomes noticed by those who use it, when it interrupts their work, either through poor configuration and workflows or through a disruption in service. As digital information becomes pervasive across projects, we argue it is important for managers to pay attention to managing digital infrastructure on projects. Although it is often overlooked and unrecognized, it is through the digital infrastructure on projects that project delivery is mediated and integrated creating new patterns of reliance and risk, and shaping decisions, outcomes, and ultimately project success.

Managing digital infrastructure on projects is challenging due to its under-recognized importance. Digital infrastructure has an inherent anarchic nature (Lyytinen, Yoo, and Boland 2016) that reaches across the boundaries of the social and technical. In some megaprojects, developing the digital infrastructure for delivery is akin to having a complex software development project inside the main project. Although project managers have significant tools and methods

DOI: 10.4324/9781003274179-17

for managing complex projects (e.g. Remington and Pollack 2016), such tools and methods have not always been applied to the management of their digital infrastructure for delivery. Business cases for digital infrastructure on projects can resemble 'fantasy documents' (Clarke 1999), indicating the project's desire to be a leader in the use of some specified digital tools with little or no attention to current capabilities, market capacity, potential technological dynamics, or the associated choices and uncertainties in how to realize the desired future state.

In this short introduction, we provide a theoretical background and context to the idea of digital infrastructure on projects, provide six lessons for managers based on the state of the art, and discuss the points that need further consideration.

Background

An important context is the longstanding interconnections between the development of project management techniques and the development of computer hardware and software. Significant recent innovations using a set of 'Industry 4.0' technologies (Whyte, Farghaly, and Zhou 2022) are enabling projects using new forms of data collection through sensor data, digitally-enabled product platforms (Whyte, Mosca, and Zhou 2022), and analytics. Such a history is set out in a recent review of digital innovation in the context of the built environment (Papadonikolaki, Krystallis, and Morgan 2021).

We argue that framing the interconnected and evolving software packages and applications as digital infrastructure provides a useful way to theorize and understand related phenomena, though it is not the only approach. This perspective is useful in focusing management and scholarly attention on the increasing integration and sedimentation of interconnected and evolving software packages and applications. It also highlights the often under-recognized importance of such a digital infrastructure in organizing, and precipitating technological choices across an ecology of multiple, evolving, and overlapping project practices.

There are various ways to categorize digital infrastructure and its relationship with practice. Shove (2016) draws distinctions between *infrastructure* (necessary but not engaged with directly), *devices* (engaged with and manipulated), and *resources* (consumed and transformed) that support practice. Monteiro et al. (2012) use the idea of infrastructure to draw attention to non-local constraints, and identify four key characteristics:

> *openness* to number and types of users [...] *interconnections* of numerous modules/systems [...] dynamically *evolving* portfolios of [...] systems and shaped by an *installed base* of existing systems and practices
>
> (p. 576)

As organizational life becomes less fit the strict Weberian notion of division of labour, 'IT silo solutions' have been transformed into more platform-based digital infrastructures (Bygstad and Hanseth 2018). Such infrastructures are no longer bounded within the single organizational boundaries, rather, they span both space and time and involve social and technological actors, changing the traditional mechanisms of coordination and control.

In projects, digital infrastructures are "nested sets of objects associated with coordination of knowledge across multiple knowledge boundaries in the delivery of projects" (Whyte and Lobo 2010, p. 564). Thus, in contemporary project delivery, building on Shove's (2016) distinctions we characterize digital infrastructure, devices, and resources, as shown in Table 15.1. Yet, with ever-changing

Table 15.1 Digital infrastructure on projects and associated digital devices and resources (developed from typology in Shove [2016], and literature on projects)

Type	*Description*
Digital infrastructure	Multiple nested sets of global and customized software packages and applications, that interconnect and evolve: and the related structuring objects, such as repositories, standardized forms, workflows and indexes, and global software that coordinate across boundaries. Such a digital infrastructure exhibits openness, interconnections, evolution, and installed base (Monteiro et al. 2012).
Digital devices	The plethora of laptops, routers, screens, phones, and tablets through which project managers and engineers access data about the project. This may be seen as part of a digital infrastructure, but Shove (2016) distinguishes these devices from the underlying, under-recognized infrastructural interconnections.
Digital resources	The content of the digital information used, and the digital objects consumed and transformed across the project in the work of project managers and engineers. Again, while this may be seen as part of a digital infrastructure, Shove (2016) distinguishes these resources from the devices and infrastructure.

boundaries, the distinctions and relationships in such typologies are heuristic in nature. Work on digital infrastructure has sometimes encompassed the broader set of categories of digital objects (e.g., engineering simulations, standardized indexes, and product configuration information) as part of that infrastructure, mobilized and negotiated to enable coordination within and across organizational groups (Lobo and Whyte 2017).

We highlight repositories, standardized processes (through forms, workflows, and indexes), and global software as parts of the digital infrastructure on projects, where "Standardized forms are integral to the use of repositories, which are populated with sets of maps, models and other documents" (Whyte and Lobo 2010). Hence, in this digital infrastructure for delivery: "different kinds of software and content are integrated through repositories and standardized processes" (Jaradat, Whyte, and Luck 2013, p. 53). Utilizing off-the-shelf, standard, global software (Pollock, Williams, and D'Adderio 2007), these digital infrastructures embed generic processes that become standardized across organizations. Such software may also need, where possible and desirable, to be customized to the project by codifying and representing organizational structure, hierarchy, and work processes in the software. There are limits to the individual users' or project organization's ability to adapt to the technology, and the interconnected and evolving software packages and applications that make up a digital infrastructure provide a form of ordering of work that is 'disguised' (Çıdık, Boyd, and Thurairajah 2017) or hidden from view.

The idea of infrastructure suggests an understanding of technology as involving multiple generations of technology overlaying each other and in use at the same time. It implies a configural understanding of evolution (Henfridsson and Bygstad 2013). Innovation in digital infrastructure on projects involves different interconnected packages and applications evolving on different timeframes, potentially leading to new integration challenges. While the initiation of an individual project is an opportunity to set up a digital infrastructure for delivery, projects also become delivered in complex organizational settings, in which asset owners and operators, government regulators, and other stakeholders have their own evolving infrastructures.

Also, problematically, for long-term projects, which may take decades in planning and delivery, the rate at which digital infrastructures and the associated software and applications change is also significantly faster than the rate of delivery of these projects (Lobo and Whyte 2017), requiring consideration of incorporating new digital technologies during the delivery process. Improvement across generations

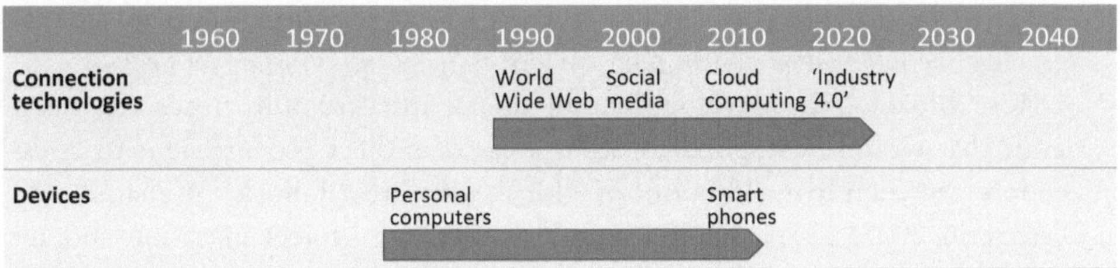

Figure 15.1: Examples to show the rapid developments in connecting technologies and digital devices (see also Lobo and Whyte [2017]).

of individual digital technologies leads to an evolving digital infrastructure on projects. Figure 15.1 gives a couple of examples of connection technologies and devices to illustrate the rapid developments (see also Whyte 2019).

Six lessons for project managers

Drawing on the state of the art, there are some significant lessons for managers. These include:

1 *Treat the digital infrastructure on projects as a strategic rather than technical concern;*

Early project scholars gave a tactical focus to computer systems as well as organizational techniques, neglecting more strategic concerns (Morris 1990). Yet, digital infrastructure is strategically important and inextricably linked with organization, as delivery models are transformed by digital information (Whyte 2019).

2 *Consider not only the desired benefits but also the steps taken to realize those benefits in a business case;*

Many business cases for the set-up of a digital infrastructure that supports project delivery resemble 'fantasy documents' (Clarke 1999). These documents have many indications of the benefits, and little attention to the practical steps necessary to realize those benefits. They have a significant underestimation of the time and resources required for customizing, maintaining, and upgrading the digital infrastructure, ignore the lack of availability of users who know the system, and do not factor in the time and resources required to train users. It is unsurprising that this is a significant area of cost escalation on projects. To address this, there needs to be more scrutiny and independent review of business cases, holding their authors.

3 *Use project management approaches in procuring, customizing, maintaining, and upgrading the information system that provides a digital infrastructure for delivery.*

More broadly, the development of digital infrastructure needs the same rigour that would be applied to other areas of project procurement to assess vendors and suppliers. Vendors of global software (Pollock, Williams, and D'Adderio 2007) play a significant role in advising project initiation and act as the intermediaries of learning between projects. Although not traditionally seen as part of the supply chain for the project, as projects deliver both physical and digital outputs and outcomes, the suppliers of the digital infrastructure for delivery should be given attention and managed using project management tools and techniques. There is a need for attention to the skills needed in the key project management and project sponsorship roles to make strategic decisions in the management and governance of this digital infrastructure for project delivery, and the project management techniques that can support this decision-making as well as the management of associated risks.

4 *Set up information technology, information management, and data science/project analytics teams, and distinguish between these roles;*

Increasing digitalization is changing the traditional structure of information technology functions and departments in projects as well as in firms, requiring attention to both well-understood and new digital tools and methods. We argue that projects, appropriate to their complexity, need appropriate digital leadership that distinguishes between and sets up information technology, information management, and data science/project analytics teams.

5 *Manage change, in the digital infrastructure, and in the engineering data; and*

In complex projects, the use of an innovation program (Davies et al. 2015) enables one to make choices about where to invest in new technology and to experiment with it offline from the critical path of delivery. Such an approach is suitable to the challenge of continuing to upgrade a digital infrastructure for delivery to incorporate new generations of technology, which requires some oversight and governance. This work might consider, and also draw tools and methods from, the management of change in the digital engineering data (Whyte, Stasis, and Lindkvist 2016).

6 *If there are physical, as well as digital deliverables, then implement explicit processes to translate between digital representations and the physical world.*

Project work involves engaging both online and offline. A challenge where futures are designed online is to ensure that the physical deliverables become tested outside of the digital realm, through heterogeneous trials (Whyte 2013), changing medium to test ideas as they are realized (Whyte, Comi, and Mosca 2022).

Conclusion

This chapter provides a short introduction to digital infrastructure on projects, with theoretical context and lessons for project management and leadership. As digital information is shareable, accessible remotely, searchable, and updateable, increasing integration brings projects into new relations with their suppliers and users (Whyte 2019). It is the under-recognized digital infrastructure that makes this possible. Thus, a focus on the digital infrastructure of projects suggests some future research directions for project scholars:

First, be aware of the challenges of managing the digital infrastructure on projects. While digital infrastructures afford significant benefits to many users, they also reveal some tensions, adding to the challenges of their management (Edwards et al. 2007). Data needs to be shared and stored, but who makes decisions and enforces rules? If there is friction between global standards and localized routines needs, how we should resolve this for an effective collaboration? These examples indicate that the boundaries between social and technical within digital infrastructures are flexible and political, making their planning and management problematic. Project leadership requires attention to these boundaries, and political decisions associated with changing technologies (Whyte, Naderpajouh, et al. 2022), and there is a need for a greater base of empirical evidence on the impacts of different configurations and workflows on project success.

Second, digital practices and digital infrastructures. We argue for work on digital practices on projects to consider these interconnections between evolving digital infrastructure and project organizing. As project work becomes more distributed beyond the traditional organisational boundaries, the digital infrastructure supporting this work "appears more tightly coupled, with a centralization and formalization of work methods and objects that reduces discretion" (Whyte and Lobo 2010). This ordering of work is 'disguised' as it is written into the unnoticed digital infrastructure. While infrastructure may require multiple permissions where there is commercially sensitive information, the use of personal devices can bring new challenges (Jarrahi, Reynolds, and Eshraghi 2020). Thus, there are a range of new questions about how digital infrastructure shapes personal, team, and project-wide practices, and the consequences of these changes.

Third, digital infrastructure and the changing structure of project-based industries. While the long- and wide-reaching implications of general-purpose technologies such as information technologies have been anticipated by innovation scholars, there is a need for work to track the implications of new forms of digital infrastructure that are transforming production systems and reconfiguring work across project-based industries, project ecologies, and innovation ecosystems. Work is beginning to bring together infrastructure and platform studies, and to explore these issues in project-based contexts (Whyte, Mosca, and Zhou 2022).

Although there are many claims of efficiencies through the use of novel digital technologies, it is sometimes difficult to understand the relationship between the project's digital infrastructure and its productivity in delivery, for example as it creates new patterns of reliance and risk. There is scope for scholars to develop new empirical studies to explore more deeply, or test the proposed lessons in particular project contexts, to examine new questions around relations with project productivity, the carbon footprint of project digital infrastructures, or to trace new algorithms and developments such as the digital twins and project analytics. We hope this short introduction is useful to managers and scholars as they engage in the needed future work to manage digital infrastructures on projects, and to further examine the interconnected and evolving software packages and their applications, their integration and sedimentation on projects, as they mediate project delivery.

References and further reading

Bygstad, B. and O. Hanseth (2018). "Transforming digital infrastructures through platformization." *26th European Conference on Information Systems: Beyond Digitization - Facets of Socio-Technical Change, ECIS 2018.*

Çıdık, M. S., D. Boyd and N. Thurairajah (2017). "Ordering in disguise: digital integration in built-environment practices." *Building Research & Information* **45**(6): 665–680.

Clarke, L. (1999). *Mission improbable: Using fantasy documents to tame disaster*, Chicago, IL: University of Chicago Press.

Davies, A., S. MacAulay, T. DeBarro and M. Thurston (2015). "Making innovation happen in a megaproject: London's crossrail suburban railway system." *Project Management Journal* **45**(6): 25–37.

Edwards, P. N., S. J. Jackson, G. C. Bowker and C. P. Knobel (2007). Understanding Infrastructure: Dynamics, Tensions, and Design: Report of a Workshop on History & Theory of Infrastructure: Lessons for New Scientific Cyberinfrastructures.

Henfridsson, O. and B. Bygstad (2013). "The generative mechanisms of digital infrastructure evolution." *MIS Quarterly* **37**(3): 907–931.

Jaradat, S., J. Whyte and R. Luck (2013). "Professionalism in digitally mediated project work." *Building Research & Information* **41**(1): 51–59.

Jarrahi, M. H., R. Reynolds and A. Eshraghi (2020). "Personal knowledge management and enactment of personal knowledge infrastructures as shadow IT." *Information and Learning Sciences* **122**(1/2): 17–44.

Lobo, S. and J. Whyte (2017). "Aligning and reconciling: building project capabilities for digital delivery." *Research Policy* **46**(1): 93–107.

Lyytinen, K., Y. Yoo and R. J. Boland Jr (2016). "Digital product innovation within four classes of innovation networks." *Information Systems Journal* **26**(1): 47–75.

Monteiro, E., N. Pollock, O. Hanseth and R. Williams (2012). "From artefacts to infrastructures." *Computer Supported Cooperative Work (CSCW)* **22**(4–6): 575–607.

Morris, P. W. (1990). "The strategic management of projects." *Technology in Society* **12**(2): 197–215.

Papadonikolaki, E., I. Krystallis and B. Morgan (2021). "Digital technologies in built environment projects: review and future directions." *Project Management Journal*: 87569728211070225.

Pollock, N., R. Williams and L. D'Adderio (2007). "Global software and its provenance: generification work in the production of organizational software packages." *Social Studies of Science* **37**(2): 254–280.

Remington, K. and J. Pollack (2016). *Tools for complex projects*, Abingdon: Routledge.

Shove, E. (2016). "Matters of practice." *The nexus of practices*. A. Hui, T. Schatzki, and E. Shove (Eds.), London: Routledge: 155–168.

Whyte, J. (2013). "Beyond the computer: changing medium from digital to physical." *Information and Organization* **23**(1): 41–57.

Whyte, J. (2019). "How digital information transforms project delivery models." *Project Management Journal* **50**(2): 177–194.

Whyte, J., A. Comi and L. Mosca (2022). "Making futures that matter: future making, online working and organizing remotely." *Organization Theory* **3**: 1–20.

Whyte, J., K. Farghaly and A. Zhou (2022). "The digital revolution and complex project organizing: towards Project Management (PM) 4.0?" *Research handbook on complex project organizing*. G. M. Winch, M. Brunet and D. P. Cao, Cheltenham: Elgar, 383–392.

Whyte, J. and S. Lobo (2010). "Coordination and control in project-based work: digital objects and infrastructures for delivery." *Construction Management and Economics* **28**(6): 557–567.

Whyte, J., L. Mosca and A. Zhou (2022). "Digital project capabilities and innovation." *Elgar handbook on innovation and project management*. A. Davies, S. Lenfle, C. Loch and C. Midler. Cheltenham, 408–422.

Whyte, J., N. Naderpajouh, S. Clegg, P. Matous, J. Pollack and L. Crawford (2022). "Project leadership: a research agenda for a changing world." *Project Leadership and Society* **3**: 100044.

Whyte, J., A. Stasis and C. Lindkvist (2016). "Managing change in the delivery of complex projects: configuration management, asset information and 'big data'." *International Journal of Project Management* **34:** 339–351.

Chapter 16

Managing project risk

David Hillson

Introduction

Of all the different elements required for the successful management of projects, risk management is arguably the most important. This rather bold assertion is based on the following factors:

- We plan our projects in order to achieve all objectives in full.
- During the execution of the project, things happened that were not in the plan.
- Many of these unexpected situations, circumstances, and events lead to deviations from the plan that affects our ability to achieve our objectives. These things are called "risks."
- If we had foreseen these risks in advance, we might have been able to prepare for them proactively, thus minimising potential deviations from the plan.
- Our ability to achieve project objectives successfully is therefore directly proportional to our ability to identify and manage risks effectively.

At first sight, the solution to deviations that arise from unexpected situations and events occurring during project execution seems obvious: better planning. But projects are inherently risky due to their uncertain nature (Hillson, 2011):

DOI: 10.4324/9781003274179-18

- *Uniqueness.* Every project involves at least some elements that have not been done before, and naturally, there is uncertainty associated with these elements.
- *Complexity.* Projects are complex in a variety of ways, and they are more than a simple list of tasks to be performed. There are various kinds of complexity in projects, including technical, commercial, interfaces, or relational, each of which brings risk into the project.
- *Assumptions and constraints.* Project scoping involves making a range of guesses about the future, which usually include both assumptions (things we think will or will not happen) and constraints (things we are told to do or not do). Assumptions and constraints may turn out to be wrong, and it is also likely that some will remain hidden or undisclosed, so they are a source of uncertainty in most projects.
- *People.* All projects are performed by people, including project team members and management, clients and customers, suppliers and subcontractors. All of these individuals and groups are unpredictable to some extent, and introduce uncertainty into the projects on which they work.
- *Stakeholders.* These are a particular group of people who impose requirements, expectations, and objectives on the project. Stakeholder requirements can be varying, overlapping, and sometimes conflicting, leading to risks in project execution and acceptance.
- *Change.* Every project is a change agent, moving from the known present into an unknown future, with all the uncertainty associated with such movement.

These risky characteristics are built into the nature of all projects and cannot be removed without changing the project. For example, a "project" which was not unique, had no constraints, involved no people, and did not introduce change would in fact not be a project at all. Trying to remove the risky elements from a project would turn it into something else, but it would not be a project.

In recognition of the inbuilt riskiness of all projects, many standard project management techniques are designed to address common forms of uncertainty. For example:

- A Work Breakdown Structure defines what is included in the project and what is not, dealing with scope uncertainty.
- The project schedule tells us what will be done when tackling time-related uncertainty.

- We develop the project budget or Cost Breakdown Structure to deal with cost uncertainty.
- An Organisational Breakdown Structure or Responsibility Assignment Matrix removes uncertainty about who does what.

If the standard techniques of project management are designed to tackle the common risks that affect projects, why do we need risk management? Even well-managed projects deviate from their plan during execution, and many are challenged or fail outright, which indicates that something more is needed in addition to good project management. The purpose of risk management in projects is to address those uncertainties that are not covered in standard project management disciplines.

What is risk?

If routine project management tackles those risks that are recognised as common to most projects ("known-unknowns"), risk management aims to expose and manage the ones that haven't yet been embodied into standard techniques ("unknown-unknowns"). This requires a clear understanding of what we mean by "risk."

So far, we've used two different words: *uncertainty* and *risk*. Although these are related, they are not the same. All risks are uncertain, but not all uncertainties are risks. There are innumerable uncertainties in the world, but only a few of them need to be identified as risks, then recorded, assessed, prioritised, responded to, and reported on. We need a filter to determine which uncertainties need to be understood and managed as risks. This filter is embodied in a simple proto-definition of risk: "***uncertainty that matters***." The vast majority of uncertainties do not matter and we can safely ignore them.

What matters is defined by our objectives; these describe what is "at risk". We can therefore expand our proto-definition of risk to be a little more specific: "*Risk is* ***uncertainty*** *that, if it occurs, would* ***affect objectives***." This most basic definition of risk is reflected in all current risk management standards and guidelines, from the international standard ISO 31000:2018 *Risk Management – Guidelines* to examples from the world of projects, as shown in Table 16.1.

Table 16.1 Risk defined as "uncertainty that matters"

Source	*"Uncertainty …"*	*"… That matters"*
International Organisation for Standardisation ISO 31000:2018 Risk Management – Guidelines (2018)	"Effect of *uncertainty* …"	"… on objectives."
Project Management Institute The Standard for Risk Management in Portfolios, Programs, and Projects (2019)	"An *uncertain* event or condition …"	"… that, if it occurs, has a positive or negative effect on one or more *objectives*."
Association for Project Management Project Risk Analysis and Management Guide (third edition) (2022)	"An *uncertain* event or set of circumstances …"	"… that, should it or they occur, would have an effect on achievement of one or more of the *project's objectives*."
Association for Project Management *APM Body of Knowledge* (seventh edition) (2019)	"The *potential* of a situation or an event…"	"… to impact on the achievement of specific *objectives*."
Institution of Civil Engineers Risk Analysis and Management for Projects (third edition) (2014)	"A *possible* occurrence …"	"… which could affect (positively or negatively) the achievement of the *objectives* for the investment."

While these definitions capture the two most basic characteristics of risk, there are two important additional features that need to be clarified:

- Risk encompasses *any uncertainty that matters*, not just uncertain future events (Hillson, 2014), including:
  - *Variability*. Certain future events where a range of values are possible for some parameters. Examples include productivity rates, raw material prices, exchange rates, trial durations, ground conditions, weather, amount of rework, etc.

    - *Ambiguity*. Certain future events where some key aspects remain unclear and/or unknown. This includes client or competitor behaviour, developing technology, changes in regulatory requirements, etc.
    - *Emergence*. Future events which are currently unknowable and which appear without warning.
- *Not all risk is bad*. It's common to think that all risks are *threats*, but the term "uncertainty that matters" also includes *opportunities*. These are uncertainties that, if they occurred, would help us achieve our objectives. The modern concept is double-sided, covering both downside threat and upside opportunity, both of which need to be identified and managed proactively (Hillson, 2019). This is also recognised in all the standards listed in Table 16.1, either explicitly in the definition or implicitly in the supporting text.

The simple definition of risk as "uncertainty that matters" covers all forms of uncertainty and recognises that they might matter in positive and/or negative ways. Consequently, our approach to risk management needs to be sufficiently broad to tackle the full range of the risks facing our projects. Unfortunately, this is often not the case.

Typical risk management process

Most organisations rely on a structured process for managing risk as part of their project management approach, recognising that all projects are risky and that risk needs to be managed if we're to give ourselves the best chance of succeeding. The specific details of risk management processes may vary, but in principle, they are (or should be) designed around asking and answering eight basic questions:

1 **What are we trying to achieve?** Risks only exist in relation to defined objectives. This means we cannot start the risk process without first clearly defining its scope by clarifying which objectives are at risk. It is also important to know how much risk key stakeholders are prepared to accept in the project since this provides the target threshold for risk exposure on the project. These factors must be addressed in the first step of any risk process, to ensure that the scope and objectives are well defined and understood.

2 **What might affect our ability to achieve these objectives?** Once the scope and objectives are agreed, it is possible for us to start identifying risks,

which are those uncertainties with the potential to affect the achievement of one or more of our objectives (including both threats and opportunities). We could use a variety of risk identification techniques, each of which has strengths and weaknesses, so it would be wise to use more than one to ensure that as many risks as possible are identified. The aim is to expose and document all currently knowable risks, recognising that some risks will be inherently unknowable and others will emerge later in the project. This is why the risk process needs to be iterative, coming back later to find risks which were not evident earlier on. In addition to considering individual risks within the project, risk identification should also address the overall risk exposure of the project.

3 **Which of these are most important?** Of course, not all the risks we identify are equally important, so we need to filter and prioritise them, to find the worst threats and the best opportunities. This will inform how we respond to risks. When prioritising risks, we could use various characteristics, such as how likely they are to happen, what they might do to project objectives, how easily we can influence them, when they might happen, etc. (Association for Project Management, 2008). We should also consider the degree of risk exposure for the overall project as a whole, either by categorising risks to find out whether there are any significant hot spots, or by using simulation models to analyse the combined effect of risks on the final project outcome.
4 **What can we do about them?** Once we have prioritised individual risks and understood the degree of overall project risk exposure, we can start to think about what actions are appropriate to deal with individual threats and opportunities, as well as consider how to tackle overall project risk. We might consider radical action such as cancelling the project, or decide to do nothing, or attempting to influence the level of risk exposure. We should also consider involving others in responding appropriately to the risks.
5 **Having done what we planned, did it work?** We can make great plans to address the risks in our project, but nothing will change unless we actually do something. Planned responses must be implemented in order to tackle individual risks and change the overall risk exposure of the project, and the results of these responses should be monitored to ensure that they are having the desired effect. Our actions may also introduce new risks for us to address.
6 **Who should we tell?** After completing these various steps, we are in a position where we know what the risks are and how they would affect the project, and we understand which ones are particularly significant. We have

also developed and implemented targeted responses to tackle our risk exposure, with the help of others. It is important to tell people with an interest in the project about the risks we have found and our plans to address them.

7 **What has changed?** We have clarified our objectives and found the risks that could affect them, then prioritised the important ones and developed suitable actions – so have we finished? Actually no, because risk poses a dynamic and changing challenge to our project. As a result, we know that we have to come back and look again at risk on a regular basis, to see whether our planned actions have worked as expected, and to discover new and changed risks that now require our attention.

8 **What should we do differently next time?** When the project ends, should we heave a sigh of relief and move quickly on to the next challenge? As responsible professionals, we wish to take advantage of our experience on this project to benefit future projects. This means we will spend time thinking about what worked well and what needs improvement, and recording our conclusions in a way that can be reused by ourselves and others. Identifying such lessons should not occur only at the end of our project, but it can also usefully be done during the project, to benefit future phases.

These eight questions provide a framework around which a more formal risk management process can be developed, mapping each question to a process step. This is the case for each of the risk management standards in Table 16.1, as well as various proprietary risk methodologies (for example Hillson & Simon, 2020), although the names used for each process step may differ. Table 16.2 shows how the questions map to the names of typical process steps, and Figure 16.1 illustrates this mapping for the risk process in ISO 31000:2018.

Structuring the risk process around these generic questions makes it more intuitive, as each question naturally and logically leads on to the next. It also allows scalability, as each question can be answered at a range of levels, from the simplest to highly detailed. For example:

- An individual could complete the entire process alone in about 30 minutes, thinking through their plans for the coming day or week and answering the questions at the highest level. Alternatively, a major program may employ a team of risk professionals to work with stakeholders over a period of weeks, using multiple techniques to address each question in turn.

Table 16.2 Mapping questions to formal risk process steps

Informal question	*Formal process step*	*Purpose*
1 *What are we trying to achieve?*	Risk process initiation	To define the scope, objectives, and practical parameters of the project risk management process.
2 *What might affect our ability to achieve these objectives?*	Risk identification	To identify all currently knowable risks, including both threats and opportunities.
3 *Which of these are most important?*	Qualitative risk assessment	To evaluate key characteristics of individual risks enabling them to be prioritised for further action, and recognising patterns of risk exposure.
	Quantitative risk analysis	To evaluate the combined effect of risks on the project outcome and assess overall project risk exposure.
4 *What can we do about them?*	Risk response planning	To determine appropriate response strategies and actions for each individual risk.
5 *Having done what we planned, did it work?*	Risk response implementation	To implement agreed actions.
	Risk review	To determine whether actions are working as expected, and identify any resultant secondary risks.
6 *Who shall we tell?*	Risk communication	To inform project stakeholders about the current level of risk exposure and its implications for project success.
7 *What has changed?*	Risk updates	To review changes in identified risks and overall project risk exposure, identify additional actions as required, and assess the effectiveness of the project risk management process.
8 *What should we do differently next time?*	Learning lessons	To identify risk-related lessons to be learned for the remaining phases of this project and for future projects.

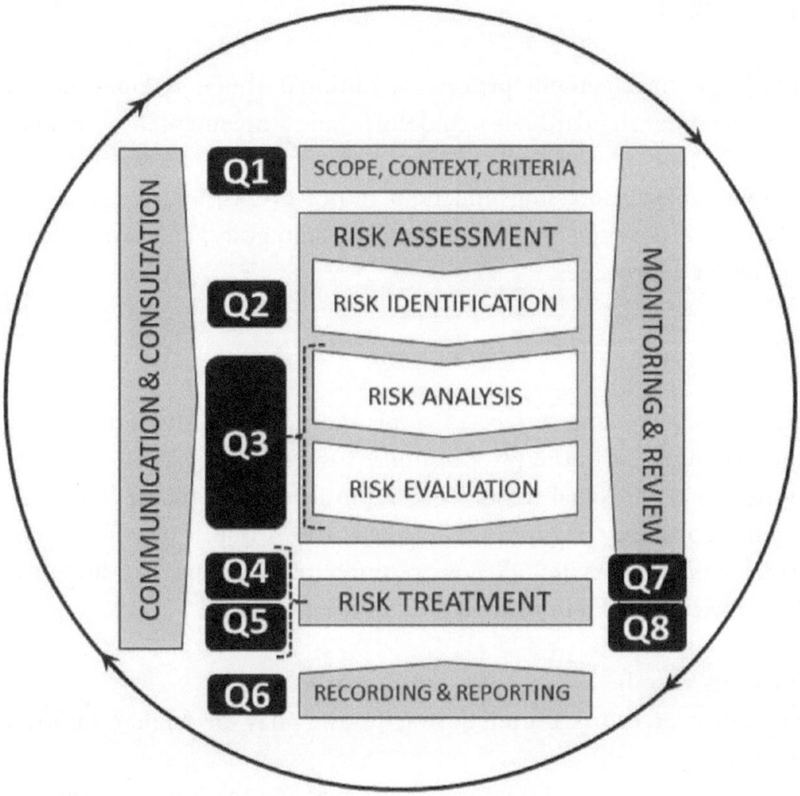

Figure 16.1: Mapping questions to ISO 31000:2018 risk process steps

- A small project might run a short brainstorming session within a project team meeting to identify risks, whereas a complex project might use multiple risk identification techniques with different groups of stakeholders over a series of dedicated facilitated workshops.
- Quantitative risk analysis might not be deemed appropriate for some projects, but mandated for others.
- Reporting of risk results might be done verbally during a routine project progress meeting, or multiple targeted risk communications might be produced for different stakeholders using a range of formats and media.

The level of intensity for each implementation of the risk process should be chosen to match the degree of the risk challenges faced by each particular project.

Other approaches

The typical risk management process as outlined above is embodied in most project management standards and guidelines, and implemented by many organisations as their main way of tackling risk in their projects. However, this process is largely focused on addressing uncertain future events, and it is unable to deal effectively with other types of risk: variability, ambiguity, and emergence. These require different approaches.

Variability risk

Variability is where some aspect of a planned task or situation is uncertain. A common example from the project arena is the situation where we plan to run a 15-day trial, but the actual duration could in fact be anywhere between 10 and 25 days. The probability of running the trial is 100%, but its duration is uncertain. Other variable parameters include cost, resource requirement, productivity, defect rate, performance, etc. Example variability risks include:

- Productivity may be above or below the target.
- The number of errors found during testing may be higher or lower than expected.
- Unseasonal weather conditions may occur during the construction phase.
- Exchange rates could vary beyond the range used to build our quotation.

Variability risks typically result in a potential spread of possible values for some parameter relating to a planned event or activity, covering outcomes that are both higher and lower than expected. This presents a problem if we try to manage variability risks using the standard risk process. How can a range of possible outcomes be represented by a single "risk event"? If the variability includes both upside and downside, is the risk a threat or an opportunity, or both? What do we do if the range of potential impact is very wide (for example a supplier may deliver late, by one day, one week, one month, or one year)? Should the risk be split into several?

The best way to analyse variability risks is in a quantitative risk analysis model using Monte Carlo simulation (Vose, 2008; Hulett, 2011). The standard probability distributions used in these models (triangular, lognormal, beta, gamma,

Weibull, etc.) represent a range of values from a credible minimum to a credible maximum, with various intermediate values such as mean or most-likely. These ranges are specifically designed to reflect the degree of uncertainty in key parameters such as time, cost, resource requirement, productivity, etc., which makes them ideal for describing variability risks.

Typically, quantitative risk analysis models are based on a project baseline such as the schedule or budget, with specific risks and other sources of uncertainty being added into the model. This shows the influence that individual risks or uncertainties might have on outcomes and objectives, allowing us to identify and prioritise those which require attention and action. It's also possible to model risks in isolation, separate from a baseline plan, focusing on finding the worst threats and the best opportunities.

Alternatively, we can represent the entire project (or elements of it) as a system, using simple influence diagrams or more complex system dynamics models, into which risks and uncertainties are added (Williams, 2002). Non-risk versions of these models should operate in steady-state conditions, but including risk will cause instability in the system, leading to unforeseen outcomes. These can arise from previously unidentified feedback or feedforward loops, or from unrecognised dependencies and linkages within the system.

Once variability risks have been identified and their potential impact on project outcomes has been analysed in a risk model, responses can be designed to manage them. Responses to variability risks can address the range of possible variation, seeking to narrow the min-max spread by reducing or avoiding those threats that drive the worst-case values, and by exploiting or enhancing the opportunities that contribute to the best-case outcome. Alternatively, responses can aim to shift the entire range towards the upside, by targeting the risks that influence the expected-value outcome.

Ambiguity risk

Risks relating to ambiguity describe uncertainties arising from a lack of knowledge or understanding. Areas of the project where imperfect knowledge might affect our ability to achieve project objectives include:

- Elements of the requirement or technical solution.
- Use of new technology.

- Market conditions.
- Competitor capability or intentions.
- Future developments in regulatory frameworks.
- Inherent systemic complexity in the project.

Ambiguity risks are addressed through exploration and experimentation, seeking first to define the scope and boundaries of those areas where we have a deficit of knowledge or understanding. The aim is to transform ambiguous risks into "known-unknowns."

Having understood where lack of knowledge might cause a problem, we can then take action to fill the gap, perhaps by obtaining expert external input, or by benchmarking our approach against best practices so that we can learn from the experience of others.

A second strategy to tackle ambiguity risk is through incremental development, prototyping, or simulation. Adaptive or agile methods also offer a useful approach to tackling ambiguity. These allow us to take small steps within the scope of our existing limited knowledge, gradually extending the boundaries of our understanding. It is important with these approaches to ensure clear acceptance criteria for our project deliverables, so that each incremental step is directed towards achieving the overall project goals.

Emergent risk

Risks that appear out of our blind spots are often known as "Black Swans" (Taleb, 2007), although they are more accurately termed "emergent risks." They arise from limitations in our conceptual frameworks or worldview. These are risks which we are unable to see because they are outside our experience or mindset, so we don't know that we should be looking for them.

It is hard to give examples of typical emergent risks in projects since by definition they are things outside of our current mindset or cognisance. In general terms, emergent risks arise from game-changers and paradigm-shifters, such as the release of disruptive inventions or products, or the use of cross-over technology from previously unforeseen sources.

Traditional risk management cannot manage emergent risks, since it only targets uncertainties that can be seen in advance and which we can prepare for or address proactively. At the strategic level, emergent risks are tackled through business continuity management (BCM; see Business Continuity Institute, 2013), which identifies areas of vulnerability and then builds sufficient organisational resilience to cope with the impact of the unexpected, wherever it comes from. BCM also looks for early warning indicators or trigger events to tell us that something is different from normal. Finally, BCM uses environmental scanning to help us discover potential emergent risks before they strike. It is possible to apply the same approaches for projects, which we might call "project continuity management," aiming to develop strong project resilience, through:

- The right level of *contingency* is built into its budget and schedule for currently unknown emergent risks, in addition to a specific *risk budget* for known risks.
- Project *processes* that are flexible enough to cope with emergent risk while maintaining overall direction towards project goals, including strong change management.
- An *empowered project team* with *clear objectives*, who are trusted to get the job done within agreed limits, without needing approval for every small deviation from the original plan.
- Frequently targeted *project reviews* which review early warning signs and triggers in order to identify emergent risks as early as possible and allow proactive action to be taken.

Risk and people

It is a common fallacy to think that risk management is just a process, and all the project team has to do is follow the process and risks will be managed effectively. However, processes do not manage risk. Risk is managed by people making judgements, decisions, and choices in the face of uncertainty as they see it. Different people see the same risk differently, and this influences the way they behave towards it. Some will feel driven to caution, afraid of what might go wrong. Others might react more positively, hoping to exploit the risk to their benefit.

These internal responses to risk are called *risk attitudes*, and they affect every aspect of the risk process, even if people are unaware of it. Risk attitude can be defined as "*a chosen response to uncertainty that matters, influenced by perception*"

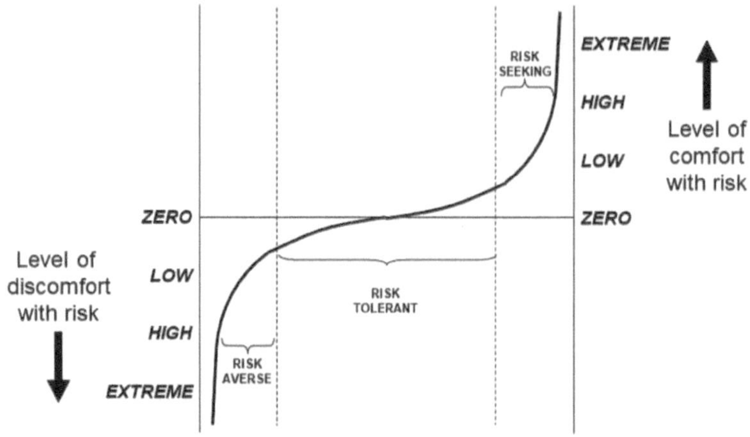

Figure 16.2: Risk attitude spectrum

(Hillson & Murray-Webster, 2007). It exists as a continuous variable, as illustrated in Figure 16.2, although it is commonly referred to using only a few terms such as risk-averse (uncomfortable with uncertainty), risk-tolerant (no strong response), risk-seeking (welcoming uncertainty), and risk-neutral (taking a long-term view). These basic risk attitudes are summarised in Table 16.3.

Risk attitude is important because it determines behaviour towards risk (attitude leads to action). Sometimes the risk attitude initially adopted by an individual or group may not support effective management of risk or may lead to counterproductive or inappropriate behaviour, for example, if a product innovation team is risk-averse, or if a nuclear safety inspector is risk-seeking. In these cases, action may be required to modify risk attitude.

Emotional intelligence and applied emotional literacy provide a means by which attitudinal change can be promoted and managed, for both individuals and groups (Hillson & Murray-Webster, 2007; Murray-Webster & Hillson, 2008, 2021). Project managers and risk practitioners should consider their own risk attitude first as individuals, in order to ensure that they are adopting a risk attitude that is appropriate in light of the uncertainty currently faced by the project and the decisions that need to be taken. They can then assist the project team as a group towards adopting a shared risk attitude that will support the required behaviour. Depending on the circumstances of the project, this may be extended to other project stakeholders, including client and user representatives, project sponsors, project review boards, etc.

Table 16.3 Risk attitude definitions and characteristics

Term	*Definition*
Risk-averse	A *conservative risk attitude with a preference for secure payoffs*. Risk-averse individuals and groups are practical, and accepting, and value common sense. They enjoy facts more than theories, and they support established methods of working. They may feel uncomfortable with uncertainty, with a low tolerance for ambiguity, and be tempted to seek security and resolution in the face of risk. They may also tend to over-react to threats and under-react to opportunities.
Risk-seeking	*A liberal risk attitude with a preference for speculative payoffs*. People who are risk-seeking are adaptable and resourceful, enjoy life, and are not afraid to take action. They may underestimate threats, seeing them simply as a challenge to be overcome. They might also overestimate the importance of possible opportunities, wishing to pursue them aggressively
Risk-tolerant	*A balanced risk attitude with no strong reaction to uncertain situations.* Risk-tolerant individuals and groups are reasonably comfortable with most uncertainty, accepting it as normal, and taking it in their stride with no apparent or significant influence on their behaviour. They may fail to appreciate the importance of threats and opportunities, tending to be reactive rather than proactive. This may lead to more problems from impacted threats, and loss of potential benefits as a result of missed opportunities.
Risk-neutral	*An impartial risk attitude with a preference for future payoffs*. People who are risk-neutral are neither risk-averse nor risk-seeking, but rather they seek strategies and tactics that have high future payoffs. They think abstractly and creatively and envisage the possibilities. They enjoy ideas and are not afraid of change or the unknown. For both threats and opportunities, they focus on the longer term and only take action when it is likely to lead to significant benefit.

Conclusion

It's axiomatic to say that risk management manages risk. In the world of projects, risk management should complement good project management, since routine project processes also address some forms of risk. The specific contribution of risk management is to address those risks not covered by standard project management techniques.

Defining risk as "uncertainty that matters" makes it clear that risk management should tackle any and all uncertainties that could affect our ability to achieve our objectives. This includes both *upside opportunities* as well as *downside threats*. It's also not limited to *uncertain future events* but also covers *variability, ambiguity,* and *emergence*. To be fully effective, we need to adopt an integrated approach to managing all uncertainties that matter within a single risk management process.

But risk management should not only be integrated within itself to address all forms of risk; it also needs to be integrated into the way we manage the project. We need to turn analysis into action, using the results and insights generated by the risk management process to influence and shape other project management activities and project decisions. The project schedule and budget must be risk-informed, applying contingency to high-risk areas, and managing that contingency proactively and responsively. Impact analyses conducted during change management must take account of the effect of the proposed change on risk exposure. Stakeholder reporting should raise awareness of key risks, indicating where support is required.

We began with an assertion that risk management is arguably the most important thing project professionals can do to ensure that their project succeeds in meeting all its objectives in full. Support for this view comes from considering what would happen if we failed to manage the risks facing our project. Unmanaged risk means that some avoidable threats will turn into problems, and some potentially useful opportunities will be missed. The likelihood of achieving project objectives would inevitably be suboptimal. The alternative is clearly preferable. Effectively managing risk means minimising threats, maximising opportunities, and optimising our chances of project success.

References and further reading

Association for Project Management. (2008). *Prioritising Project Risks*. High Wycombe: APM Publishing.

Association for Project Management. (2019). *APM Body of Knowledge* (seventh edition). Princes Risborough: Association for Project Management.

Association for Project Management. (2022). *Project Risk Analysis and Management Guide* (third edition). Princes Risborough: Association for Project Management.

Business Continuity Institute. (2013). *Good Practice Guidelines.* London: The Business Continuity Institute.

Cooper, D.F., Bosnich, P., Grey, S., Purdy, G., Raymond, G., Walker, P., & Wood, M. (2014). *Project Risk Management Guidelines: Managing Risk with ISO 31000 and IEC 62198* (second edition). Chichester: Wiley.

Hillson, D. A. (2011). *Managing Risk in Projects.* Farnham: Gower Publishing.

Hillson, D. A. (2014). *How to Manage the Risks you Didn't Know You Were Taking.* Proceedings of PMI Global Congress North America 2014, Phoenix, AZ, October 2014.

Hillson, D. A. (2019). *Capturing Upside Risk: Finding and Managing Opportunities in Projects.* Boca Raton, FL: Taylor & Francis.

Hillson, D. A., & Murray-Webster, R. (2007). *Understanding and Managing Risk Attitude* (second edition). Aldershot: Routledge/Gower.

Hillson, D. A., & Simon, P. W. (2020). *Practical Project Risk Management: The ATOM Methodology* (third edition). Oakland, CA: Berrett-Koehler.

Hulett, D. T. (2011). *Integrated Cost-Schedule Risk Analysis.* Farnham: Gower Publishing.

Institution of Civil Engineers. (2014). *Risk Analysis and Management for Projects* (third edition). London: Thomas Telford Publishing.

International Organization for Standardization. (2018). *ISO 31000:2018. Risk Management – Guidelines.* Geneva: International Organization for Standardization.

Kendrick, T. (2018). *Identifying and Managing Project Risk: Essential Tools for Failure-Proofing Your Project* (third edition). New York: AMACOM.

Murray-Webster, R., & Hillson, D. A. (2008). *Managing Group Risk Attitude.* Aldershot: Routledge/Gower.

Murray-Webster, R., & Hillson, D. A. (2021). *Making Risky and Important Decisions: A Leader's Guide.* Boca Raton, FL: Taylor & Francis.

Project Management Institute. (2019). *The Standard for Risk Management in Portfolios, Programs, and Projects.* Newtown Square, PA: Project Management Institute.

Taleb, N. N. (2007). *The Black Swan: The Impact of the Highly Improbable.* London: Allen Lane/Penguin.

Vose, D. (2008). *Risk Analysis – A Quantitative Guide* (third edition). Chichester: Wiley.

Williams, T. (2002). *Modelling Complex Projects.* Chichester: Wiley.

Chapter 17

Managing project crisis

Christine Unterhitzenberger

> When written in Chinese, the word crisis is composed of two characters. One represents danger and the other represents opportunity.
>
> John F. Kennedy

Introduction

Due to their nature projects regularly experience unexpected events. These events might occur due to the inherent uncertainty and complexity of many projects or due to the increasingly volatile, uncertain, complex, and ambiguous environment within which they operate. Unexpected events might (or might not) have been identified, but it was not expected that these events would happen (Geraldi et al., 2010). They are unexpected due to their low probability and high impact in combination with low topicality and sudden occurrence. Conventional planning techniques have only limited ability to predict unexpected events and their interactions and even the most comprehensive risk management cannot de-risk a project. Therefore, these unexpected events can cause crisis situations in projects and pose an existential threat to high-priority objectives such as time, quality or cost. This chapter considers the concept of project crisis, how crises develop, their impact, and potential measures for dealing with them. This chapter will also consider the role of resilience in dealing with crises.

DOI: 10.4324/9781003274179-19

A project crisis

A crisis is not a permanent state, but a critical and decisive stage, which potentially comprises an existential threat to a project and which requires a timely response (Unterhitzenberger et al., 2021). A crisis is not considered to be an acceptable state a project should be in, but a situation that needs to be resolved due to the potential harm it can do to the project and its environment. If a crisis occurs, the project's survival may be at risk as it can lead to the early closure of the project (Simard and Laberge, 2018). The impact of a crisis can also go far beyond the project organisation itself and affect any component of its social system from individuals to teams and other organisations involved to the industry or even society level. It is often impossible to prevent crisis situations as crises tend to be unanticipated, unforeseeable, and unknowable.

An unexpected event does not need to be of huge magnitude to instigate a crisis. Whilst this can be the case, the conglomeration of smaller events (or stressors) which ultimately erupt can also lead to a crisis (Hällgren and Wilson, 2008). Hence, the cause of a crisis can be differentiated as follows: (1) a sudden change through an unexpected event which triggers a crisis (event approach) or (2) a slow accumulation of deficits or stressors which expose an underlying weakness through a trigger event (process approach). In both cases a trigger is involved, however, the speed of the development of the crisis varies significantly. A recent example causing a crisis in many projects is the policy interventions introduced as a response to the Covid-19 pandemic. This unexpected event was a sudden trigger which came into effect with very little notice and is therefore associated with the event approach. An example of the process approach leading to a crisis in a project is Crossrail[1] which suffered from a combination of delays, challenges with the signalling systems, budget overruns, and technical difficulties leading to a major crisis in 2018 with the opening being delayed by more than four years. There was not one unexpected event which caused this crisis, but the slow and steady accumulation of a variety of stressors erupted when it became evident that the opening date could not be achieved resulting in a whole new leadership team being installed.

It is also important to note that a crisis is not necessarily perceived in the same way by all actors involved. It is a cognitive phenomenon which is interpreted differently by different actors meaning what one person might perceive to be a crisis another person might not. It alters how individuals see the world and themselves (Simard and Laberge, 2018) and undermines assumptions many people adhere to. This includes the assumptions that individuals suppose that bad things don't happen to them, that by doing the right things good things will follow and that they have a sense of worth and control. However, with these assumptions challenged during crisis situations, there is a need for psychic reorganisation and reconstruction of the individual's worldview.

The origins and nature of crises in projects

The acknowledgement that a crisis is a cognitive phenomenon means that the nature of a crisis can depend on how its occurrence is perceived by the project manager (Wang and Pitsis, 2020). If a project manager has an increased crisis orientation and awareness it is more likely that more resources are dedicated to mitigating crisis situations and that crisis preparedness is enhanced and therefore the likelihood of a crisis is reduced. Wang and Pitsis (2020) conceptualise crisis orientation (or rather its absence) through five factors: (1) lack of project management skills of project manager, planners, and contractors; (2) clash of interest between and within project participants due to a lack of stakeholder engagement; (3) lack of responsibility leading to normalisation of anomalies and opportunistic behaviour; (4) red tape and centralisation leading to excessive bureaucracy and authoritarianism and (5) lack of ability to forecast due to underestimation of complexity, risk, and uncertainty. This crisis orientation together with the project manager's awareness of how a crisis is characterised are antecedents of megaproject crises, i.e. they impact the origins and nature of crises in projects.

However, there are also other factors that influence the origin and nature of crises in projects. Projects are particularly vulnerable to crises due to the interactions and interdependencies that characterise them (Wang, 2019). Looking at a project from a network perspective, the number and relationship of the project components play an important role in how susceptible a project is to a crisis. The project components, which make up the network are of human, technical, organisational and management nature and include project tasks, changes, and stakeholders. Small events can lead to a project crisis if they are at a centrally located or highly connected node in the network due to the cascade effect. The interdependencies and interactions between project components are often insufficiently considered in regard to potential crisis vulnerability when designing the network topology. Further factors potentially contributing to project crises, especially in the context of megaprojects, are outlined in Table 17.1

Table 17.1 Potential factors contributing to megaproject crises (adapted from Wang and Pitsis, 2020)

Feature	*Crisis factor*
Strategic importance	Excessive intervention by top management
	Irresponsible decision maker
	Irrational decision-making process
Dynamic complexity	Conflict of interest among internal project participants
	Substantial change in project execution
	Contractual change
	Market forecast failure
Adaptability	Ineffective oversight mechanisms
	Centralised management without flexibility
	Lack of managerial leadership
	Unqualified project manager
	Unqualified contractor
	Inadequate risk assessment
	Irresponsible team member
Extensive impacts	Conflict among external project participants
	Inadequate stakeholder engagement

(Wang and Pitsis, 2020). They relate to four high-level features namely the strategic importance of the project, its dynamic complexity, its adaptability and extensive impacts.

In the context of construction projects, a broad variety of events was identified which can lead to a crisis (Hällgren and Wilson, 2008): this reaches from the discovery of an underestimate or dilemma in negotiations to factory shutdowns and engine accidents to non-compliance and unwillingness to accept transfers, with the majority being related to contract disputes. The change of leadership appears to be a particular challenge for IT projects with the potential to lead to a project crisis due to organisational changes and reframing of project scope (Simard and Laberge, 2018). In summary, there is a multitude of factors which influence if and how crises in projects are perceived and occur. They range from external factors which are beyond the control of the project to internal challenges which significantly disrupt the project.

Managing a project crisis

Once a crisis occurs in a project and is recognised as such its management is often of existential importance to the project. Geraldi et al. (2010) determined three pillars which characterise successful responses to unexpected events and hence, crises as shown in Figure 17.1. First, on the organisational level, a responsive and functioning structure is required. This means that organisations need to be able to respond to a change, i.e. the crisis, adequately and rapidly. A high degree of freedom facilitates empowerment and fast decision-making. Project managers need to be able to decide what response is appropriate, what resources are required, and how to implement the decision. Micromanagement leads to unsuccessful crisis management outcomes. Second, on the group level good interpersonal relationships are necessary. During a crisis situation, it is imperative to engage with stakeholders and negotiate with them to develop suitable solutions. Information needs to be shared with the right parties and communication needs to take place. Third, on the individual level, competent people are essential. This is not only the case for the project manager but also for team members. The general ability to trust others' judgements and capabilities is crucial in this context. For the project manager as leader, it is also important to be able to manage their emotions, i.e. recognise them through self-awareness and then act upon this through self-management. In the event of a crisis, a leader with high emotional intelligence is beneficial.

However, it has also been recognised that in crisis situations, when the responses in line with the three pillars are needed the most it is less likely that they are actually present. Loosemore (1998, p. 139) termed this the three ironies of crisis management

Successful Response to Unexpected Events		
Organisational level **Responsive and functioning structure** • High degree of freedom • Pace to make and implement decisions	**Group level** **Good interpersonal relationship** • Engagement with stakeholders, including ability to negotiate solutions • Communication, including availability of information as well as its communication	**Individual level** **Competent people** • Competence of leader and team • Behaviour, including self-awareness and ability to deal with stressful situation

Figure 17.1: Three pillars to a successful response to unexpected events (Geraldi et al., 2010)

> at a time when effective communication is important it is less likely; at a time when mutual sensitivity between project members is important it is less likely; at a time when collective responsibility and teamwork are important they are less likely.

As mentioned above communication and information flow are key elements of a successful response to a crisis. They facilitate the significant change required to manage the crisis and mitigate the perceived uncertainty. However, information is power, and individuals and groups tend to use information to protect their own interests and positions. In crisis situations, it can also be the case that a huge amount of information is generated and requires processing. This can lead to either very formal or very informal approaches on how to deal with information and its communication. Both approaches have been found to be unsuccessful. What is required is a balanced and flexible approach, which allows open communication but also some control. Interpersonal relationships, the second pillar, also relate to mutual sensitivity. A crisis situation is prone to create conflicts of interest amongst project team members who are responsible for protecting different project objectives, e.g. adherence to schedule vs adherence to budget. Individuals exclude others from decision-making or do not share information with them in order to protect their own goal and therefore, display insensitivity towards others and their interests. Finally, collective responsibility and teamwork, which are related to pillars one and two, have been found to be challenging in crisis situations. A crisis typically requires extra resources in some shape or form and the responsibility for providing these resources is usually established through contractual arrangements. Responsibilities tend to be uniquely allocated to one party rather than shared, which leads to little collective responsibility, the emergence of losers and winners, and a dominance of contractual documents including differences in interpretation. Due to the financial impact of a crisis relationships are at risk of experiencing fundamental change with every party trying to maximise their own gain and exploit the situation in their favour.

Other strategies for managing a project crisis include raising of awareness of the social responsibility of the project, the strengthening of stakeholder management, and the implementation of mandatory third-party evaluation (Wang and Pitsis, 2020). These strategies aim to systematically reduce interactions between critical crisis factors. Overall, the relationships with stakeholders, communication and the way project team members collaborate appear to be critical to managing a project crisis successfully.

The role of resilience in managing a project crisis

A concept often addressed in the context of crisis management, and sometimes used interchangeably with it, is resilience. Resilience refers to the ability of a project to perform even if conditions change for example due to disruptions or a crisis (Naderpajouh et al., 2020). It is about a project's ability to survive and thrive in light of changes and modifications such as a crisis. In simple terms, resilience enables a project to "bounce back" to its original performance after it has experienced a crisis. Therefore, whilst crisis takes an external exogenous view looking at crisis antecedents, management, and consequences, resilience takes an internal endogenous view looking at the project itself and its ability to absorb, adjust, and transform (Unterhitzenberger et al., 2021). Resilience relates to the characteristics of a project which enable it to deal with unexpected events more successfully; it becomes decisive for a project when facing a crisis. Therefore, crisis and resilience are two different, but related concepts which should not be used interchangeably.

The discussion on the three ironies of crisis management above showed that often certain behaviours and structures are not in place when they are needed most and therefore lead to unsuccessful crisis responses. The absence of the required behaviours and structures suggests that the project is not resilient – it cannot survive the crisis. To enable the project and the project team to better deal with a crisis and its impact and hence, to avoid the three ironies of crisis management, measures need to be taken before a crisis occurs by creating a more resilient project in regard to crisis response. Measures can be for example project governance which fosters collaboration, long-term and high-value commitment as well as trust as is the case in a stewardship approach to governance. Research has shown that if such an approach is adopted the response in a crisis situation creates opportunities for connection, harmony and efficiency rather than leading to a lack of communication, sensitivity and teamwork (Loosemore, 1998). Also, leadership based on principles of organisational justice (Unterhitzenberger and Lawrence, 2022) can contribute to a fairer treatment of all parties involved in managing the response to a crisis and therefore potentially avoid the three ironies of crisis management.

If resilience is present in a project it can also shape the response to future crises through a resilience feedback loop after a crisis is successfully overcome (Williams et al., 2017). These resilience feedback loops rely on the individual's interpretations and experiences. How an individual, in this case the project manager, interprets tasks and relationships depends on their past exposure to crises and may even hamper resilience. An individual's experience with crises can improve resilience, however, the learning required for this improvement is dynamic and depends on goal emphasis and the environment. In summary, the resilience of a project develops and changes over time as the project and its project manager interact with the environment. Resilience as the project's ability to adapt, improvise and recover is crucial for a project facing a crisis.

Conclusion

As outlined earlier, a project crisis is an existential threat to a project which requires a timely response. It can be triggered by a single unexpected event or through the accumulation of stressors which expose underlying weaknesses. Being aware and oriented towards crises shapes – amongst other factors – the nature and origin of the crisis itself. The management of the response to a project crisis is most likely to be successful if it involves the three pillars of responsive and functioning structure (organisational level), good interpersonal relationships (group level) and competent people (individual level). However, the three ironies of crisis management suggest that such elements are less likely to be present in crisis situations when they are needed most. Resilience as a project's ability to perform even if conditions change is crucial when experiencing a crisis. Hence, a project crisis is conceptualised as a critical and decisive stage with the potential to threaten the existence of the project.

However, the quote by John F. Kennedy at the beginning of this chapter suggests that every crisis has threatening and opportunistic aspects: "When written in Chinese, the word crisis is composed of two characters. One represents danger and the other represents opportunity." Loosemore (1998) has also found that a crisis created opportunities for increased connection, harmony and efficiency. If an environment of commitment to project success and sensitivity towards each other is created, cohesion within the team increases and unexpected events are managed collectively with a common goal in mind rather than adversely with only the best self-interest in mind. Seeking to exploit the opportunistic aspects in a project crisis requires awareness of their potential presence and the courage to embrace them.

Note

1 Crossrail is a new railway line under central London, UK with estimated cost of £18.8 billion and expected to be fully operational in May 2023 as Elizabeth Line.

References and further reading

Geraldi, J.G., Lee-Kelley, L. and Kutsch, E. 2010. The Titanic sunk, so what? Project manager response to unexpected events. *International Journal of Project Management,* **28**(6): pp. 547–558.

Hällgren, M. and Wilson, T.L. 2008. The nature and management of crises in construction projects: Projects-as-practice observations. *International Journal of Project Management,* **26**(8): pp. 830–838.

Loosemore, M. 1998. The three ironies of crisis management in construction projects. *International Journal of Project Management,* **16**(3): pp. 139–144.

Naderpajouh, N., Matinheikki, J., Keeys, L.A., Aldrich, D.P. and Linkov, I. 2020. Resilience and projects: An interdisciplinary crossroad. *Project Leadership and Society,* **1**: p. 100001.

Simard, M. and Laberge, D. 2018. Development of a crisis in a project: A process perspective. *International Journal of Managing Projects in Business,* **11**(3): pp. 806–826.

Unterhitzenberger, C. and Lawrence, K. 2022. *Fairness and Unfairness in Projects.* Princes Risborough: Association for Project Management.

Unterhitzenberger, C., Naderpajouh, N., Hällgren, M. and Huemann, M. 2021. Call for papers: Temporary organising and crisis. *International Journal of Project Management,* **39**(2): pp. 209–212.

Wang, A. 2019. A framework for assessing project vulnerability to crises. *International Journal of Managing Projects in Business,* **12**(4): pp. 1079–1096.

Wang, A. and Pitsis, T.S. 2020. Identifying the antecedents of megaproject crises in China. *International Journal of Project Management,* **38**(6): pp. 327–339.

Williams, T.A., Gruber, D.A., Sutcliffe, K.M., Shepherd, D.A. and Zhao, E.Y. 2017. Organizational response to adversity: Fusing crisis management and resilience research streams. *Academy of Management Annals,* **11**(2): pp. 733–769.

Chapter 18

Sustainable project management

Gilbert Silvius, Ron Schipper and Martina Huemann

Introduction

The awareness that our current use of Earth's natural resources is not sustainable has entered the boardrooms of many organisations. It is a fact that the consumption of resources exceeds the natural regenerative capacity of our planet, with mankind using up resources of around 1.7 piles of earth per year. In 2023, "Earth Overshoot Day", which marks the day when all resources Earth can provide in an entire year are exhausted, is calculated to be on August 2nd. An urgent change is therefore required, and this change will affect organisations, companies and individuals, as actors within societies. While the conversation on the limits of our Earth´s natural resources, as well as the issues of climate change, have entered many board rooms, we argue that projects play and important role in the changes that organisations and societies will need to implement to develop towards sustainability (Huemann, 2022).

In this chapter we distinguish "*Sustainability by the project*": the sustainability of the project's output and outcome, from "*Sustainability of the project*": the sustainability of the project's delivery and management processes (Huemann and Silvius, 2017). Sustainability *by* the project is well studied and addressed, for example in the fields of eco-design and 'green' construction. The sustainability *of* the project is less established in literature but is one of the most important global project management trends today. Silvius (2017) concludes

 DOI: 10.4324/9781003274179-20

that sustainability should be considered a new "*school of thought*" in project management. It is this integration of the concepts of sustainability into project management that this chapter addresses.

To discuss how sustainability can be integrated into project management, we start this chapter with an overview of the main concepts of sustainability.

Sustainability and responsibility

The most broadly used definition of sustainable development is based on the Brundtland report which states it as "*development that meets the needs of the present without compromising the ability of future generations to meet their own needs*" (World Commission on Environment and Development, 1987). This definition reflects several core principles. First, it stresses the aspect of transition and positions sustainability as a process: sustainable development. Second, the definition outlines concepts based on values such as equality and future orientation. Sustainability is inherently a normative and value-based concept, often also associated with fairness, ethics, transparency, accountability and responsibility. The Brundtland report also describes that sustainability requires a social and an environmental perspective on development and performance, next to the commonly applied economic perspective. The vision that economic growth, social well-being, and a wise use of natural resources, are interrelated was widely accepted as the 'Triple Bottom Line' or People – Planet – Profit, concept of sustainability (Elkington, 1997).

Sustainability therefore refers to more concepts than 'green', which highlights mainly the environmental perspective. A broader understanding of sustainability refers also to the concepts of (social) responsibility and can be summarised in the following four concepts.

Balancing people, planet and profit

The Triple Bottom Line (Elkington, 1997) offers a set of perspectives for assessing, reporting or communicating the impact of actions and policies on nature and society, forming the foundation of many sets or frameworks of sustainable development indicators that aim to measure, communicate or evaluate an organisation's societal impact or performance. And although the operationalisation of sustainability in measurable indicators is practical, and probably also necessary, it introduces the risk that the interrelations between the perspectives are overlooked and that social, environmental and economic impacts are each considered in isolation. A holistic understanding of the integration of economic, environmental and social perspectives is therefore one of the key-concepts of sustainability.

Life-cycle orientation

Sustainability is about consuming income and not capital (Silvius et al., 2012). In other words, organisations should not 'consume' the capacity to produce and create value in the future. Sustainability requires that "the natural capital remains intact" and that therefore the extraction of natural resources "should not exceed the rate at which they are renewed, and the absorptive capacity of the environment to assimilate waste, should not be exceeded" (Gilbert et al., 1996). From the introduction to this chapter, it should be clear that this is at the moment not the case. The sustainability equilibrium, where extraction of natural resources equals their renewal, was passed in the 1970s of last century. This means that for the past 50 years, mankind has been depleting Earth's resources. The impact of this depletion and the resulting waste, however, was not always visible in the short term. In order not to compromise "*the ability of future generations to meet their needs*", as stated in the World Commission on Environment and Development (1987) definition, sustainability requires a balance between both short and long term. This balance requires the consideration of the complete life-cycle and/or value chain of a product or service. A promising strategy to prevent the depletion of natural resources, is that of the 'circular economy' that aims to realise resource minimisation and the adoption of cleaner technologies by promoting the benefits of recycling residual waste materials and by-products. Raw materials and resources are processed from used products, thereby minimising waste, and the need for extraction of 'virgin' resources. Although there may be technical and economic challenges to the development of completely circular products, the concept of the circular economy is at the moment the most promising concept that combines sustainable development with economic performance.

(Corporate) social responsibility

The concept of the circular economy highlights the 'systems change' that development towards sustainability (sustainable development) needs. Sustainable development is a shared responsibility between authorities, companies and consumers, which can only be realised in cooperation. In the 1990s, the concept of sustainable development therefore also got applied to businesses and organisations, thereby creating a link between sustainable development and (Corporate) Social Responsibility (CSR). Organisations are more and more expected to take responsibility for the societal impacts of their decisions and actions. They are asked to contribute with their behaviour to sustainable development and to take care of their stakeholders (International Organisation for Standardisation, 2010).

The social responsibility of organisations is defined as the

> responsibility of an organisation for the impacts of its decisions and activities on society and the environment, through transparent and ethical behaviour that: contributes to sustainable development, including health and the welfare of society; takes into account the expectations of stakeholders; is in compliance with applicable law and consistent with international norms of behaviour; is integrated throughout the organisation and practiced in its relationships.
>
> (International Organisation for Standardisation, 2010)

Central to this responsibility is the orientation on stakeholder's interests. The interests of all stakeholders should be embraced by the organisation and win-win situations should be sought (Eskerod and Huemann, 2024). Stakeholder orientation is therefore also an inevitable concept of an organisation's role in, and responsibility for, sustainable development.

The ISO 26000 definition of (C)SR also highlights the responsibility and accountability that an organisation has for the societal impact of its decisions and actions, and the transparency and ethicality of its behaviour. This ethical dimension is an inseparable aspect of CSR and emphasises the normative, values based, nature of sustainability and CSR. Sustainability is a value-based concept, reflecting values and ethical considerations of society, and its integration into business decisions and actions should go beyond being compliant with legal obligations.

Integrating sustainability in project management

A broadened scope

Considering Sustainability implies a scope shift in project management: from focusing on managing the iron triangle (time, budget and scope), to managing social, environmental and economic value creation (Huemann, 2022; Silvius et al., 2012). This scope shift inevitably requires a broader consideration of the project and its context. Both the time and the spatial boundaries of the context are stretched when considering sustainability. Silvius (2017) illustrates this recognition of the broader context of 'Sustainable Project Management', compared to 'Traditional Project Management' or 'Modern Project Management', through the context dimensions of stakeholder orientation and time orientation (Figure 18.1).

While one can argue that the integration of sustainability increases the complexity of a project (Sabini and Silvius, 2022), one can also argue that the broadened scope of consideration makes the already existing complexity that a project is in, explicit. As its social and time related context are comprehensively considered and not ignored. Often projects still fail, because the management is primarily focused on delivering the project's output fast, thereby simplifying tasks and underestimating the social complexity that results from diverse interests of stakeholders. Many projects get simplified too much and fail to adequately handle the actual complexity, especially in scope, stakeholder engagement and project organisation, to deliver sustainable outcomes. Project managers are often focused on reducing complexity and getting outputs delivered. However, we argue that

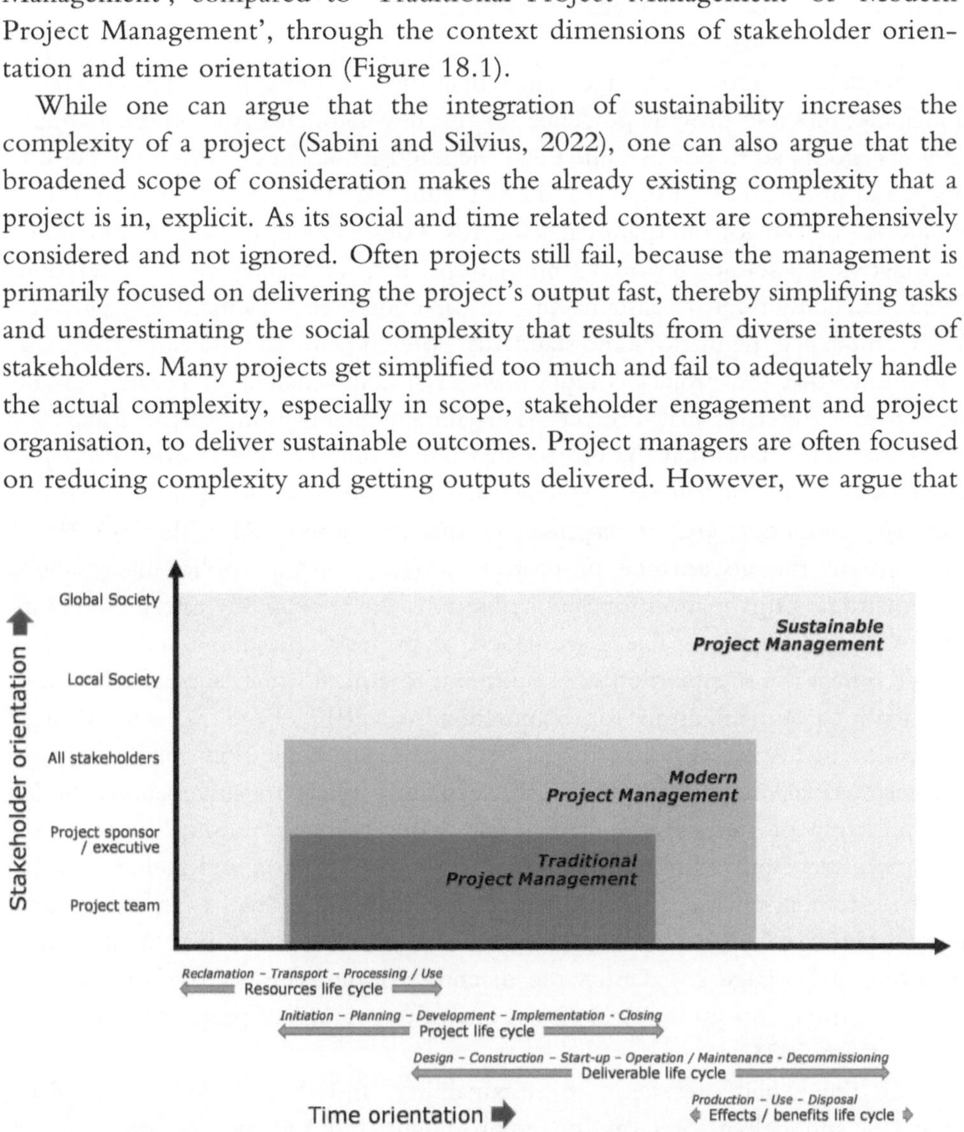

Figure 18.1: The broadened scope of sustainable project management (Silvius, 2017)

a better understanding of the project's impacts and context, and embracing the resulting complexity, leads to the potential of achieving more sustainable project outcomes.

Sustainability in project management standards

The standards of project management reflect the development of the profession, and sometimes also provide guidance for this development. And where a couple of years ago it had to be concluded that the standards failed to address the consideration of sustainability (Eskerod and Huemann, 2013; Silvius, 2015a), this is now included in all major international standards. For example, the IPMA Individual Competence Baseline version 4 (International Project Management Association, 2015), explicitly refers to sustainability in the competence element 'Perspective'. In "Compliance, regulations and standards", they include the indicator "Identify, and ensure that the project complies with relevant sustainability principles and objectives" (International Project Management Association, 2015, Page 52). Thus the ICB4 states that the project manager should be able to *assess the impact of the project on the environment and society* and that they need to *research, recommend and apply measures to limit or compensate negative consequences*. Also, the ISO 21505 standard on the governance of project, program and portfolio management (International Organisation for Standardisation, 2017) explicitly refers to sustainability and states that "The governance of projects, programs and portfolios should reflect the organisation's commitment to ethical values and sustainability" (International Organisation for Standardisation, 2017, Page 5). The Project Management Institute's Guide to the Project Management Body of Knowledge (Project Management Institute, 2021), explicitly refers to sustainability under the principle of stewardship. The guide states that stewardship encompasses responsibilities both within and external to the organisation and includes in the external responsibilities "Environmental sustainability", "use of materials and natural resources", as well as impact on social communities (Project Management Institute, 2021, Page 25). Lastly, the recently released version 7 of the Prince2 standard now mentions sustainability as one of the aspects of project performance (PeopleCert, 2023).

With the explicit reference to sustainability, and the effects of a project's processes and deliverables on the environment and society, the standards of project management now acknowledge the relation between projects and sustainability and establish a role for the project manager in this relationship. How this role changes the practices of project management is not addressed in the above-mentioned standards. It is this practical guidance that is much needed for the implementation of sustainability in project management. Nevertheless, some guidance can be found in academic studies on the impact of sustainability on project management.

Sustainability in project management practices

Several publications have identified a large number of 'impact areas' of the earlier mentioned concepts of sustainability and responsibility, and project management. The focus thereby is on the sustainability *of* the project, in other words, considering sustainability in the processes and practices of project management. However, when considering sustainability in the management and governance of a project, inevitably the content of the project is touched upon, thereby also considering the sustainability of the project's deliverables and effects. In the next section, we discuss what the integration of sustainability consideration means for selected project management practices.

Benefits management and business case

Based on the perspective that projects are about enabling or realising beneficial change, the planned or aspired benefits, which represent the goal and thereby the justification of the project, should get adequate attention. These benefits will also need to reflect the concepts of sustainability discussed earlier. The identification of not only benefits but also costs, will need to be expanded to include non-financial factors that refer to for example social or environmental aspects (Silvius, 2015b).

Next to the content of identified benefits and costs, the consideration of sustainability influences the process of valuing these in a business case that provides a justification for the project. A financial return on investment calculation by definition does not comply with the concepts of sustainability, as it focuses solely on the economic perspective. Efforts to financially value social and environmental benefits, do not respect the essence of the Triple Botton Line concept. Considering sustainability in the business case of a project needs a multi-criteria approach to investment evaluation, with consideration of both financial and non-financial criteria, as well as benefits and disbenefits (Zwikael and Huemann, 2023).

Stakeholder engagement

Considering sustainability increases the number of stakeholders to be identified in the project. Typical 'sustainability stakeholders' maybe environmental protection pressure groups, human rights groups, non-governmental organisations, etc., which may provide new perspectives on the project work and objectives. According to the ISO 26000 guideline, proactive stakeholder engagement is one of the basic principles of sustainability (International Organisation for Standardisation, 2010) that requires dialogue, and considering stakeholders as partners to define problems, design possible solutions, collaborate to implement them, and monitor and evaluate the outcome, Integrating a sustainability perspective in project management, therefore implies a more holistic view of project stakeholder management (Huemann et al., 2016) and suggests a more open and proactive engagement of stakeholders. We advocate the importance of stakeholder *participation* in projects and in project management. This principle logically impacts the stakeholder engagement and the communication processes in project management, however, the intention behind 'participation' goes beyond the process of stakeholder management and communication.

Risk management

One of the project management practices in which proactive stakeholder participation can be practiced is the risk management process of a project. The assessment of potential risks will need to further evolve and lead to a broader project risk identification. Many new questions evolve

> Are we, next to the economic risks, considering also environmental risks, impacts and effects?, Are we considering also social risks, impacts and effects?, Are we considering long term risks, impacts and effects?, Are we considering risks related with the disposal phase?, Are we considering risks also in our 'sphere of influence'?, Are we considering risks, impacts and effects also for other/all stakeholders?, Are the/all stakeholders also involved

in the risk management process?, Is the risk management process transparent and performed in an ethical way?

(Silvius, 2016)

Risk assessments are project-centric, however, we can also change the perspective as to what risks arise for different stakeholders during a project and after the project has been completed. (Huemann et al 2016).

The UN Global Compact principles ask organisations to apply a precautionary approach to environmental and social challenges. The precautionary principle is based on the understanding that in environment-society system interactions, the complexity, indeterminacy, irreversibility and nonlinearity have reached a level in which it is more efficient to prevent damage, rather than ameliorate it. The Deepwater Horizon oil-spill disaster of 2010, may be an illustration that the economically oriented project risk management methods and techniques are less suitable for the management of societal and environmental risks.

Planning and controlling

Integrating sustainability into project management suggests that the intended outputs and outcomes follow a holistic view. The planning should explicitly include a Triple Botton Line perspective balancing economic, environmental and social impacts. Considering sustainability will therefore influence the specifications and requirements of the project's deliverables (output), and the criteria for the quality of the project. Next to these content-related aspects of the project, sustainability may also influence the approach to planning and controlling a project. As argued earlier, the broadened scope of consideration that sustainability implies, together with the consideration of potentially conflicting economic, environmental and social aspects of a project, inevitably increases the uncertainty and resulting complexity of a project (Sabini and Silvius, 2022). Or, reveals the complex reality of a project, that remains hidden in the traditional deterministic planning methods in project management that assume that performing a project by a large part can be predicted. Handling uncertainty and complexity requires a more dynamic and non-deterministic perspective on the planning and controlling of a project. In other words, considering sustainability in a project requires an approach to planning and controlling that addresses the variability in project phenomena and employs appropriate methods and techniques to handle this variability. In project planning, this implies an increased focus on the goal and the value of the project, instead of the deliverables and objectives. So, a more out*come*-oriented approach, instead of an out*put*-oriented approach. It is expected that an adaptive approach to project planning, based on agile principles, is more suitable for this, than a predictive approach.

Resources management and project organisation

An obvious impact area for sustainability in project management is the selection of materials used in the project. Logical considerations should address the use of hazardous substances, pollution and energy use, both in the production process as in the use in the project and remaining life-cycle. An important sustainability concept regarding the materials used in the project is therefore the application of a life-cycle perspective. This implies considering not only the materials' price/quality relationship and sustainability impact for use in the project's deliverable but also the impact of their production supply chain and aspects such as reusability and recyclability at the decommissioning stage of the project's deliverable.

Another area of impact of sustainability is the project organisation and management of the project team. Social considerations, such as equal opportunity, non-discrimination and personal development, can be put into practice in the management of the project team. Also, aspects such as commuting distance, digital/hybrid working opportunities and work-life balance may be considered in the organisation and management of the team.

Reporting

The impact of the concepts of sustainability on project reporting elaborates on what was already argued in the communication management of the project. Sustainability implies proactive and open communication about the project, which also applies to the status and progress of the project. As the project progress reports logically result from the agreed project objectives, scope of work, milestones, business case, etc. the content of the project's status and progress reports will be influenced by the inclusion of sustainability aspects in the objectives and processes of the project.

Lessons learned

As sustainability in projects and project management is still a developing topic, extracting learnings from practice is extremely important. Both in the process of considering sustainability in the execution and management of the project, as on the solutions for making the project's deliverable more sustainable, new knowledge needs to develop. Logically, the project's objectives and quality requirements build upon the available knowledge, but as sustainability is considered a 'wicked' problem, solutions to sustainability challenges will also develop bottom-up from practice. It is therefore crucial that the knowledge of these solutions is effectively captured during the project and made available for future use. Organisational learning is therefore another impact area of sustainability in project management. Organisations should learn from their projects in order to not 'waste' energy, resources and materials on their mistakes in projects.

Instruments for assessing project sustainability

With the consideration of sustainability now being addressed in standards and literature, the question remains, what practical instruments and tools are available to enable the project manager to assess a project's environmental, economic and social impact? Good intentions do not automatically lead to a change in behaviour. To assess sustainability in a project, the project manager can logically choose to use an unstructured method to assess the sustainability impact of the project, for example brainstorming together with members of the project team, or a structured method. In the last years, a number of structured 'project sustainability impact analysis' instruments have been published, of which 16 were discussed by Silvius and Schipper (2020). Based on this review, they make a number of observations.

The consideration of the Triple Botton Line is a recurring element in most instruments, however, the operationalisation of the different perspectives in criteria or indicators differs. Consensus on how to measure and assess sustainability has not emerged yet and many specialists actually question whether or not a universal list is even possible, given the wide variety of conditions and the differences in values in different contexts. The criteria for assessing sustainability in projects should therefore be configured to the context and specifics of the project

(Silvius and Schipper, 2015). The materiality or relevance of a specific criterion will depend on the industry and strategy of the organisations involved, as well as the type of the project.

A second observation is that most project sustainability impact analysis instruments recognise the different levels of impact of a project: impacts related to the project's delivery, management and governance processes (Sustainability *of* the project) and impacts related to the project's deliverables, impacts and benefits (Sustainability *by* the project). In their nature, most instruments are assessment models, with some earlier ones being simple checklists, and two others being developed as maturity models. Some are developed with a focus on a specific industry, whereas others have a more generic orientation. Silvius and Schipper (2020) categorised the project sustainability impact assessments into three groups, which include

- **Rudimentary checklists,** that provided indicators for the assessment of the sustainability impact of projects, based on the Triple Botton Line perspectives of social impacts, environmental impact and economic impact.
- **Incidental study-based project sustainability impact analysis instruments**, which are academically published instruments or methodologies, developed in empirical case studies with no further applications of or experiences with these instruments have been documented, beyond their initial development study.
- **Further developed project sustainability impact assessment instruments,** of which multiple applications and studies are published. These were the Wa-Pa-Su Project Sustainability rating system (Poveda and Lipsett, 2012), the **Sustainable Project Management Maturity Model (SPM3)** (Silvius and Schipper, 2015) and the **P5 Standard for Sustainability in Project Management** (GPM Global, 2019).

Next to these generic project sustainability impact assessment instruments, the more construction-focused Building Research Establishment Environmental Assessment Method (BREEAM) and Leadership in Energy and Environmental Design (LEED), should not go unmentioned. These instruments are explicitly developed for the built environment and focus mainly on project outputs, with limited coverage of the project management processes.

Conclusion

This chapter describes the *scope shift* that considers sustainability in the content and the process of planning, organising, managing and governing a project implies and offers practical implications. However, the impact of sustainability on project management is more than adding a new perspective or aspect to processes and formats of the current project management standards. Adding new perspectives to the way projects are considered also adds complexity. Project management therefore needs to adopt a holistic, adaptive and less predictive approach.

The traditional task-oriented project management paradigm of controlling the 'iron triangle' performance criteria of time, budget and quality suggests a level of predictability and control, that does not fit the 'wicked' character of sustainability challenges and solutions. The integration of sustainability therefore requires a *paradigm shift* (Silvius et al., 2012). From a task-oriented 'predict & control' paradigm to a change-oriented 'prepare & commit' paradigm, that is characterised by uncertainty, flexibility, complexity and opportunity.

Figure 18.2 summarises the three shifts that sustainable project management implies.

The basis for the scope shift and the paradigm shift described above is the way the project management professional see their role. Project managers are well-positioned to play a significant role in the implementation of the concepts of sustainability in organisations and businesses. However, project managers are

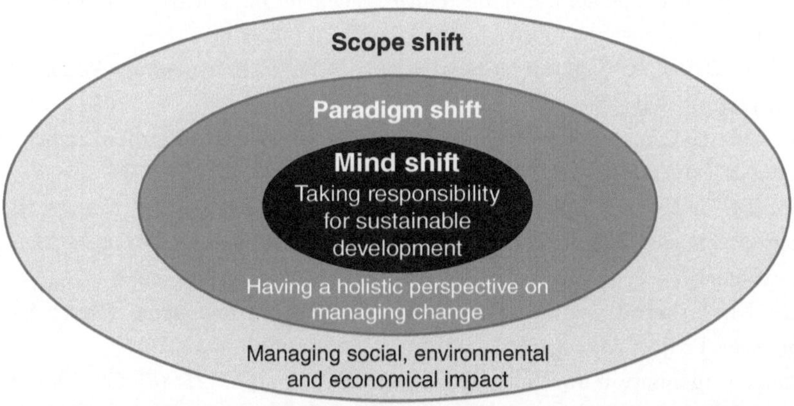

Figure 18.2: The three shifts of sustainable project management (Silvius and Schipper, 2014)

observed to be reluctant to use the influence they have on the sustainability of the project, as they are uncertain about how this would influence their relationship with the project owner (Silvius and De Graaf, 2019). Integrating sustainability requires that project managers take up a responsibility for the sustainability of their projects, and act as partner of and peer to stakeholders. This requires a *mind shift* of the project manager (Silvius and Schipper, 2014). In this mind shift, the change a project realises is no longer the exclusive responsibility of the project sponsor, but also the responsibility of the project manager with ethics and transparency as a basic touchstone. Sustainable project management requires that the role of the project manager evolves from that of a planning and control-oriented manager to a co-creating and shaping leader.

References and further reading

Elkington, J. (1997), *Cannibals with Forks: The Triple Bottom Line of 21st Century Business.* Capstone Publishing Ltc, Oxford.

Eskerod, P. and Huemann, M. (2013), "Sustainable development and project stakeholder management: What standards say", *International Journal of Managing Projects in Business*, 6(1): 36–50.

Eskerod, P. and Huemann, M. (2024), "Project stakeholder orientation principles for managing projects sustainably", in Silvius, G. and Huemann, M. (eds.), *Research Handbook of Sustainable Project Management.* Edward Elgar Publishing, in press.

Gilbert, R., Stevenson, D., Girardet H. and Stern, R. (Eds.), (1996), *Making Cities Work: The Role of Local Authorities in the Urban Environment*, Earthscan Publications Ltd, Milton Park.

GPM Global. (2019), *P5 Standard for Sustainability in Project Management Version 2.0.* GPM Global, Detroit, MI.

Huemann, M. (2022), "Celebrating the power of projects and their management", *International Journal of Project Management*, 40(1): 1–3.

Huemann, M. and Silvius, A.J.G. (2017), "Projects to create the future: Managing projects meets sustainable development", *International Journal of Project Management*, 35(6): 1066–1070.

Huemann, M., Eskerod, P. and Ringhofer, C. (2016), *Rethinking Project Stakeholder Management.* Project Management Institute, Newtown Square, PA.

International Organisation for Standardisation. (2010), *ISO 26000 Guidance on Social Responsibility.* International Organisation for Standardisation, Geneva.

International Organisation for Standardisation. (2017), *ISO 21505:2017, Guidance on Governance of Project.* Programme and Portfolio Management, Geneva.

International Project Management Association. (2015), *Individual Competence Baseline Version 4*. International Project Management Association, Nijkerk.

PeopleCert. (2023), *Managing Successful Projects with PRINCE2*, 7th edition. PeopleCert, London.

Poveda, C. and Lipsett, M. (2012), "Wa-Pa-Su project sustainability rating system: Assessing sustainability in oil sands and heavy oil projects", in Brebbia, C. A. and Chon, T.-S. (eds.), *Environmental Impact*, 115–128. WIT Press, Southampton.

Project Management Institute. (2021), *A Guide to Project Management Body of Knowledge' (PMBOK Guide)*, 7th edition. Project Management Institute, Newtown Square, PA.

Sabini, L. and Silvius, A.J.G. (2022), "Embracing Complexity in Sustainable Project Management", in Winch, G. (ed.), *Research Handbook on Complex Project Organizing*. Cheltenham and Northampton, MA: Edward Elgar Publishing.

Silvius, A.J.G. (2015a), "Considering Sustainability in Project Management Processes", in Thomas, K. (ed.), *Handbook of Research on Sustainable Development and Economics*, Ch. 14, 311–334, IGI Global, Hershey, PA.

Silvius, A.J.G. (2015b), "Sustainability evaluation of IT/IS projects", *International Journal of Green Computing*, 6(2): 1–15.

Silvius, A.J.G. (2016), "Integrating sustainability into project risk management", in Bodea, S., Purnus, A., Huemann, M. and Hajdu, M. (eds.), *Managing Project Risks for Competitive Advantage in Changing Business Environments*, 23–44. IGI Global, Hershey, PA.

Silvius, A.J.G. (2017), "Sustainability as a new school of thought in project management", *Journal of Cleaner Production*, 166: 1479–1493.

Silvius, A.J.G. and Graaf, M. de. (2019), "Exploring the project manager's intention to address sustainability in the project board", *Journal of Cleaner Production*, 208: 1226–1240.

Silvius, A.J.G. and Schipper, R. (2014), "Sustainability in project management: A literature review and impact analysis", *Social Business*, 4(1): 63–96.

Silvius, A.J.G. and Schipper, R. (2015), "Developing a maturity model for assessing sustainable project management", *Journal of Modern Project Management*, 3(1): 16–27.

Silvius, A.J.G. and Schipper, R. (2020), "Sustainability impact assessment on the project level; A review of available instruments", *The Journal of Modern Project Management*, 8(1): 240–277.

Silvius, A.J.G., Schipper, R., Planko, J., Brink, J. van der and Köhler, A. (2012), *Sustainability in Project Management*. Gower Publishing, Farnham.

World Commission on Environment and Development. (1987), *Our Common Future*. Oxford University Press, Great Britain.

Zwikael, O. and Huemann, M. (2023) "Rethinking project benefits management: making an impact on organizations and society through projects and program", *International Journal of Project Management*, 41(8), Elsevier. https://doi.org/10.1016/j.ijproman.2023.102538

Part III

Process

Part III considers the project process. We start by describing a process perspective on projects. We differentiate three sets of processes, the investment process, the delivery process and the project management process. We then consider feasibility and planning and design thinking. We explain predictive, adaptive and hybrid project approaches and end by describing scenario planning. We don't have a chapter on project start-up. We felt we had said everything we wished to say about start-ups in the chapter on project organisation. In this part, there are chapters on feasibility and planning, and design thinking, and the chapter on teams also considers start-up.

Chapter 19: Managing the process

Martina and Rodney describe the processes of projects. There are three types of processes, which are the investment process, the project delivery process, and the project management process to manage the project. The investment process delivers the outcome of the project or program, and often encompasses a sequence of projects. It takes a more long-term perspective and that is what delivers value. The project delivery processes create the output. How these processes are designed depends on the project approaches taken. They can be predictive, adaptive or combine elements from both approaches, then called hybrid. The project management processes are processes such as project starting, project coordinating, project controlling, and project closing down. It is the management process of the project and ensures that the project is delivered.

Chapter 20: Feasibility and planning

Early project phases are crucial for the chance of project success, yet uncertainties stemming from the dynamic context of projects are difficult to manage in a pure waterfall approach. Marian Bosch-Rekveldt, Hans Bakker and Marcel Hertogh explore how the feasibility and planning phases could benefit from a more flexible

DOI: 10.4324/9781003274179-21

approach, specifically focusing on interaction, collaboration and adopting a change mindset. The real-life example of the complex Zuidasdok project illustrates that uncertainties are part of the project manager's job and these uncertainties have to be dealt with, rather than reduced. This implies additional requirements for individual and team competencies. In addition to affinity with the content and more flexible project management tools, collaborative skills are becoming more and more crucial as 'People are Key'. These skills create a pole position for the later stages of the project and allow us to act upon any changes in the context.

Chapter 21: Design thinking in projects

Today´s projects need to solve wicked problems. The solution is often unclear to the project owner which makes it hard to explain to the project manager what the project outcome should be, a reason why agile project approaches have become more and more applied in practice. Ruth Lechler, Martina Huemann and Patrick Lehner introduce design thinking as an agile project approach to develop products and services in co-creation with end users. The approach best fits projects when the solution or even the problem is not well known yet and innovation desired. This chapter discusses design thinking as a process, toolbox and mindset and encourages its application in projects. Benefits and challenges of design thinking are provided.

Chapter 22: Predictive, adaptive and hybrid project approaches

Today, the majority of projects are managed with a combination of agile and traditional approaches and methods, identified as 'hybrid'. However, many questions about what defines a hybrid approach, when it can be applied, which different types of hybrid can be identified, and what the implications of hybrid are, are still unanswered. Dagmar Silvius-Zuchi and Gilbert Silvius discuss the characteristics of the predictive, adaptive and hybrid approaches to projects, and develop a set of criteria to assess the suitability of an approach for a given project within an organisational context. In the final sections, they identify different types of the hybrid approach and discuss the implications for selected project management methods and the project organisation. They aim to support project managers and project owners in designing an effective approach and organisation for their projects.

Chapter 23: Scenario planning

Conventional project management is a deductive construct that is good at solving the puzzles we meet under resolvable uncertainty. It assumes we are managing known-knowns, and emphasises control. It assumes project management processes are monitorable, predictable and controllable. Complex projects require a different approach. We need an inductive or abductive approach that creates narratives. We need to envisage different scenarios, start by planning for them all, and then eliminate scenarios as more information becomes available. Rodney and Martina describe scenario planning and future planning as ways of taking a more experimental, descriptive and innovative approach to managing projects.

Chapter 19

Managing the process

Martina Huemann and Rodney Turner

Introduction

In this chapter, we describe a process perspective on projects. Rodney Turner (2014) suggests the purpose of project management is to convert vision into reality. We start with a vision that there is a change we can make to give a beneficial outcome. The delivery of that beneficial outcome is an investment. When we start, we may not be sure that the solution exists or is achievable, but we work through the stages of the process to improve our understanding of what the solution may be and how it can be achieved until we actually achieve the desired outcome. Graham Winch (2002) has similarly talked about converting desire to memory. We start with the desire to achieve a beneficial outcome, and when we finish, we have a memory of what the outcome is and how it was achieved. Graham Winch (after Galbraith, 1977) also talks about the project as a computer. The project gathers and processes information, to give us the information and knowledge we need to convert desire to memory. This is related to Jay Galbraith's (1977) definition of uncertainty (Figure 19.1). When we want to decide, we may not have all the information we need to make the decision. The information we are missing is a level of uncertainty. We may not even know how much information we are missing. On a project at the start, we have very little information. We must use what we have to make the best decisions we can. This is satisficing (Drouin & Turner, 2022,

DOI: 10.4324/9781003274179-22

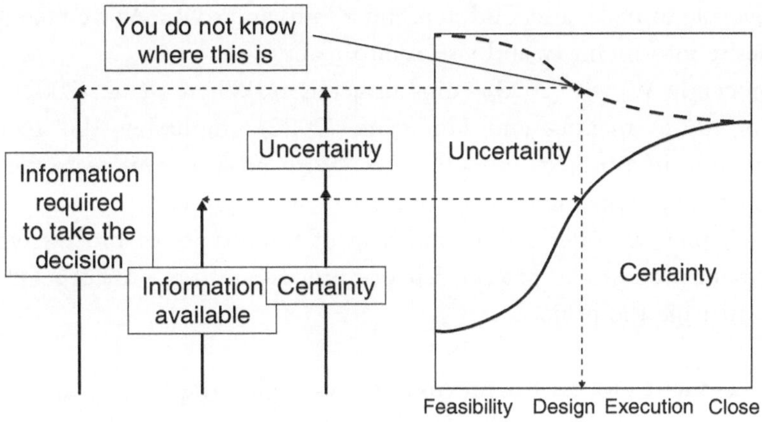

Figure 19.1: Uncertainty is the information you don't have

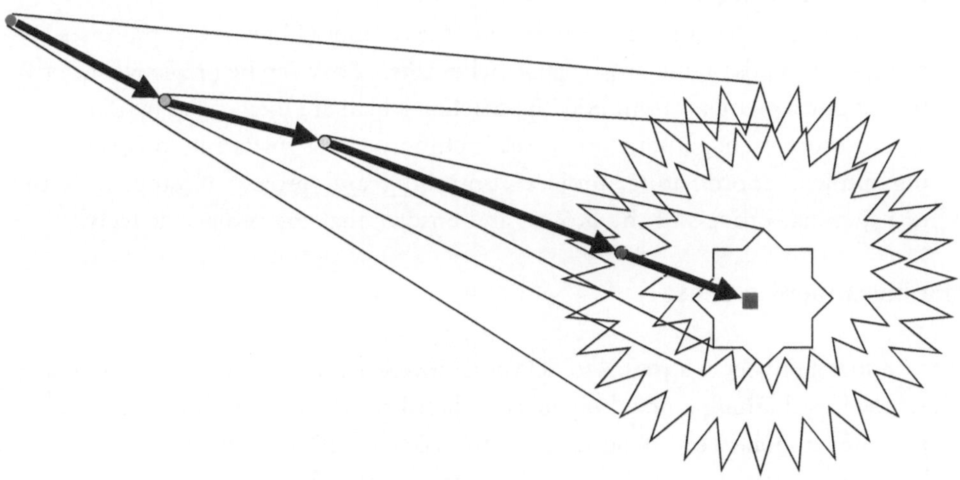

Figure 19.2: The project as an algorithm

Chapter 2). The project is a computer where we gather and process information to improve our understanding.

The process is also an algorithm, to help us find the solution (Figure 19.2). When we start, the definition of the outcome and output may be poorly defined, as is the method of achieving it. However, the process provides a rule to make a step towards the output. As we take that step, the definition of the output and outcome is improved, as is the understanding of the method to achieve them. We then have a rule to make a second step, and a third and so on. As we take steps, we convert desire into memory, and vision into reality.

More recently Winch (2023) coins projectivity, Whyte et al. (2002) use the concept of future making and Huemann (2022) emphasises the co-creation process inherent in a project and advocates "With projects, we create the future." They all share and empathise with a process view on projects.

In this chapter, we offer a differentiation of three types of process which are the investment process, the project delivery process and the project management process to manage the project.

- The investment process has previously been called the project life cycle. The investment process delivers the outcome of the project or program, and often encompasses a sequence of projects. It takes a more long-term perspective and that is what delivers value.
- The project execution processes create the output. How these processes are designed depends on the project approaches taken. They can be predictive, adaptive or combined elements from both approaches, which are then called hybrid.
- The project management processes include project initiating, project starting, project coordinating, project controlling and project closing. It is the management process of the project and ensures that the project delivers.

The investment process

We consider a project as a means to deliver an investment, this can be a new building, a new road, establishing a new hospital or a digital transformation of an organisation. Projects are temporary organisations to deliver all types of investments.

While it is common to talk about the project life cycle, we argue that it is not a cycle, as it does not go back to the beginning. Living things go through a life cycle. Young are germinated and they grow into adults. They germinate new young and then themselves die. The project germinates, but the output is commissioned, and it metamorphoses into the outcome. The project usually dies at some point, but usually doesn't germinate new young. Further, this process is not really a life or life cycle for a project; it is the process that delivers the investment that the project makes, and indeed may consist of several projects.

We also argue that it often needs a project sequence or a program to deliver a comprehensive investment for example in infrastructure, but also changes in

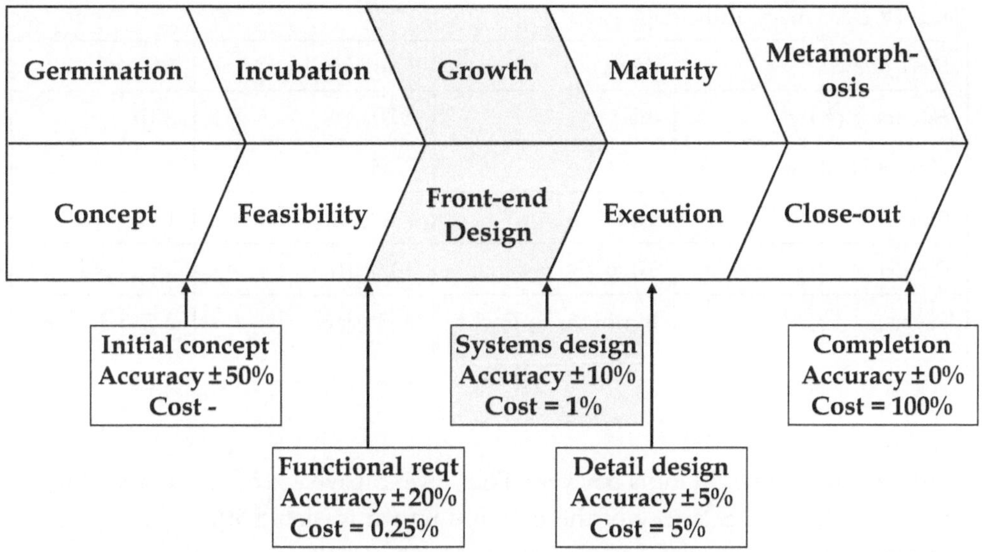

Figure 19.3: A five-stage project investment process (after Turner, 2014)

organisations are rather organised by a series of projects or programs. The basis is the decision to do the investment and perform the investment process. The basis is the business case or a cost-benefit analysis of the investment. The investment represents the long-term perspective.

Figure 19.3 is a five-stage process (Turner, 2014). In this process, it is common for people to describe the first step as birth and the last as death. We use germination and metamorphosis. The word birth implies there is a fixed period of gestation and at the end of that the project will start and nothing will stop it. Germination suggests the seed can sit in the ground and it will only germinate when the conditions are right, and grow if the conditions will remain right. In the South Australian desert, the conditions may only be right once every ten years. There is also an element of the parable of the seeds from St. Matthew's Gospel. Some seeds will fall on the path and not germinate. Some will fall amongst the rocks and not grow well. Some will fall amongst the weeds and be strangled by the weeds. And some will fall onto fertile soil and grow well. Also, the project does not die, it metamorphoses into a successful operation.

The accuracy of the estimates at the end of each stage shows it is dangerous to go from concept to execution in one step. Table 19.1 shows a simple example. At the end of the concept, we estimate the cost of the investment will be 100

Table 19.1 Accuracy at the stage gates

Stage gate	*Concept*	*Feasibility*	*Design*
Accuracy (%)	±50	±20	±10
Cost as % of investment		0.25	1
Cost	100 ± 50	120 ± 20	120 ± 10
Return	50 ± 25	40 ± 10	40 ± 5
Payback	8 months to 6 years	2–5 years	2.5–3.5 years

units and the return 50 units per year. That gives a payback of two years which is wonderful. But the accuracy of the cost and return is each ±50%, so the payback can range from eight months to six years. Eight months is fantastic, but six years is unacceptable. So following the algorithm, we move to feasibility. That costs us 0.25% of the cost of the investment, not much if we lose it. The cost of the investment is now looking like 120 units and the return 40 units per year. That gives a payback of three years with a range from two to five years. Again three years is acceptable, two years is great, but five years is unacceptable. But we can proceed to front-end design. Front-end design costs us 1% of the cost of the investment. More, but still better than doing a project with a payback of five years. The front-end design confirms the 120 and the 40, but the accuracy is now ±10%. So the payback ranges from 2.5 years to 3.5 years. Three and a half years is borderline but acceptable, so we can proceed to detail design and execution. Detail design will cost us 5% of the cost of the investment, and take the accuracy of the estimates to ±5%, but to spend 5% of the cost of the investment, we want to be fairly confident the investment is worthwhile. This is the algorithm.

There are many different versions of the investment process. Figure 19.4 is a version due to Stephen Wearne (1973). This is for the investment through operation and maintenance. It does show something of a cycle because what we learn from one investment can be used in the preparation for the next. But it is the operation that leads to the new project, not the original project.

If we follow the differentiation between investment process and project, we can now zoom in and argue that most of the different phases warrant projects on their own and we end up with a project sequence or a combination between projects and programs or even with program sequences. By that, we offer an alternative view on mega projects with durations of 20–50 years or even longer. For example, in an infrastructure investment, we may have a concept project, a feasibility study organised as a project, and a design project, before we go into the delivery program of the infrastructure. During the use of the infrastructure, there will be maintenance projects and at the end of the life of the infrastructure, the demolition may be considered as a project of its own.

While Figure 19.4 relates to infrastructure investment there are of course different types of investments. Figure 19.5 is a product investment from the marketing literature.

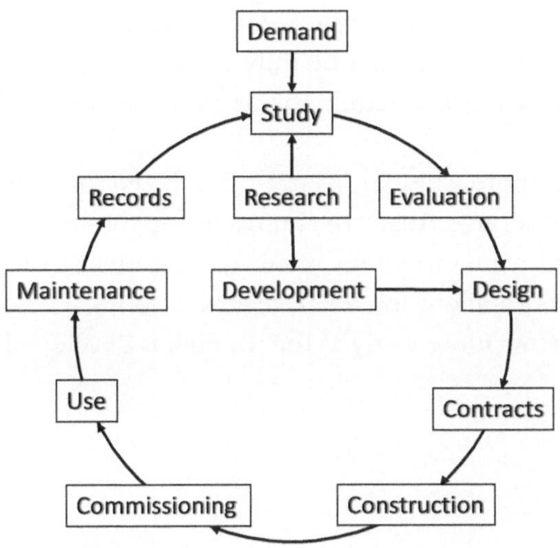

Figure 19.4: The life of the investment (after Wearne, 1973)

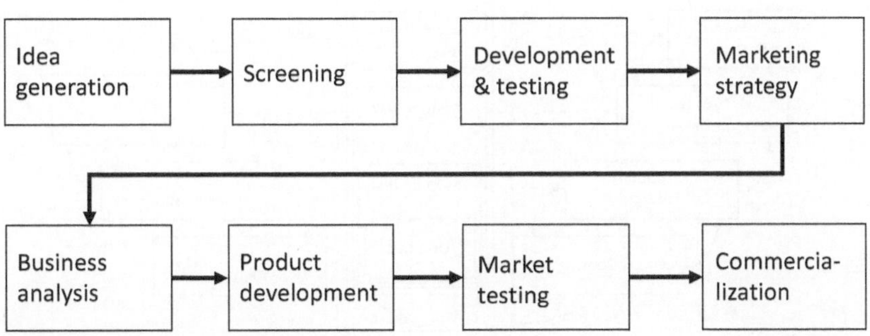

Figure 19.5: New product investment

The delivery process

On a single project, we create outcomes, the outcome of a feasibility project is a feasibility study. There are many types of projects, thus the work will be structured related to the project type. In this chapter we will not discuss how work breakdown structures or project road maps can be structured, but we would like to stay on a higher level and refer to different project approaches, which can be predictive, adaptive or a combination of both. We here provide only a brief overview as Chapter 22 by Dagmar Silivius and Gilbert Silvius is dedicated to this topic.

Predictive project approaches lead to phases that build up on each other. Figure 19.6 is for example a waterfall model for IT projects. The requirements need to be specified before the system is developed. This is a rather linear approach and is based on the notion that phases can be fully completed before the project moves into the next phase. Changes in requirements are therefore challenging and costly in later stages.

Adaptive project approaches in contrast are based on iterative processes to create the product or service. Adaptive approaches apply short development cycles. For example, in scrum methodology, these development cycles have a duration of a couple of weeks to allow for quick feedback loops. These approaches allow changes in requirements more easily as the product is developed in an incremental manner.

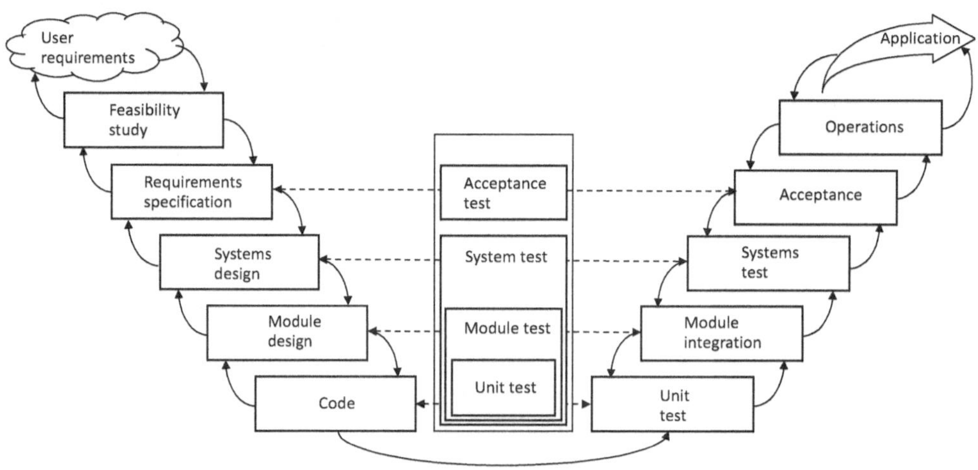

Figure 19.6: The waterfall model

The project management process

The project management process suggests how the project is actually managed. For many years, Rodney (Turner, 2014) has suggested the process in Figure 19.7. You need to plan the work, organise the resources, implement it by assigning work to the resources and control progress. In the middle, you need to manage and lead. It is the management process of the project which ensures that the project delivers.

Another perception of the project management process based on business process management includes processes such as project starting, project coordinating, project controlling, project marketing and project closing.

Rodney (2014) offers a problem-solving cycle as a version of the management process, as shown in Figure 19.8.You identify you have a problem, gather data and define the problem.Then generate a solution, evaluate the solutions and select one for implementation. Rodney suggests evaluating the solutions is decision-making, but selecting it is decision-taking. However, most people just want to use the phrase decision-making.

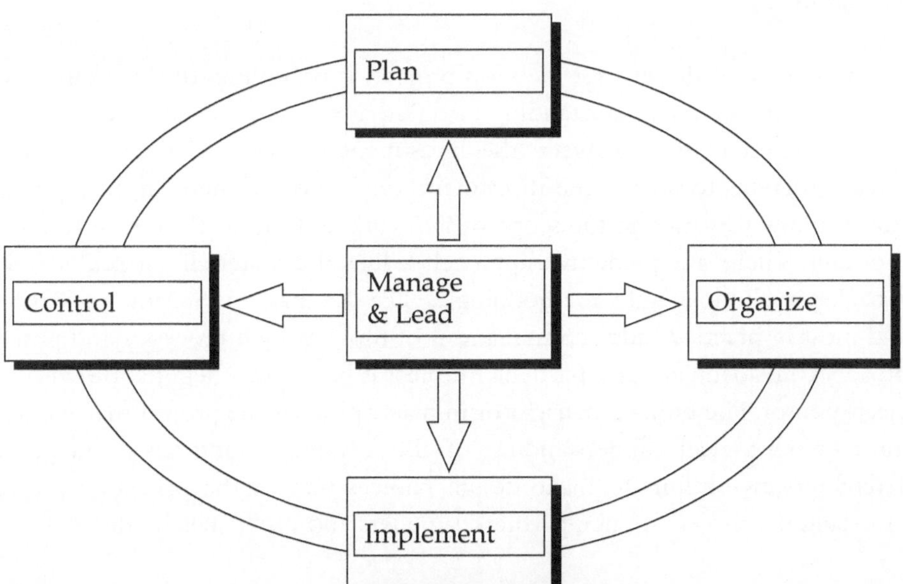

Figure 19.7: The project management process (after Turner, 2014)

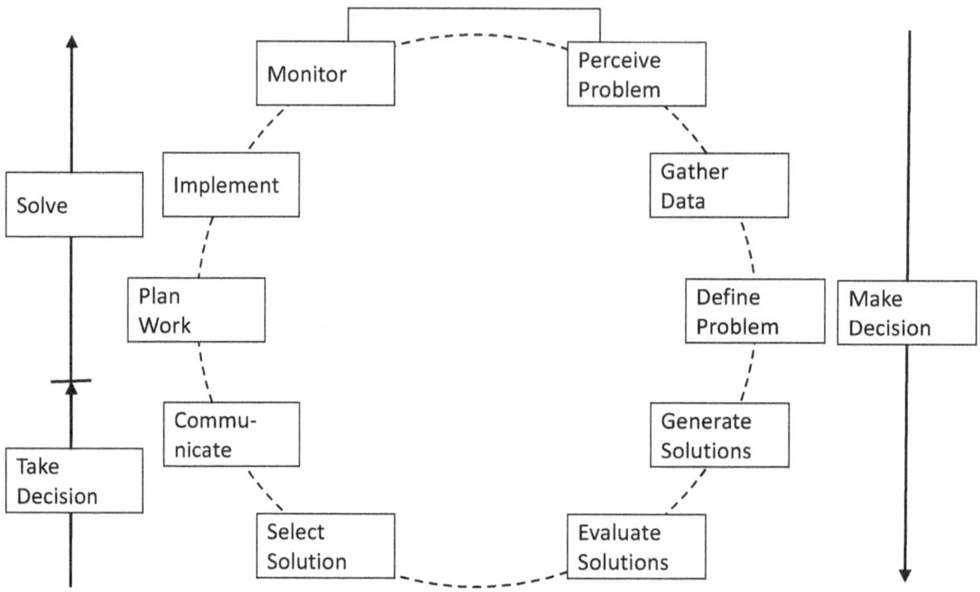

Figure 19.8: The problem-solving process, (after Turner, 2014)

Conclusion

The importance of the process view on projects is prevailing. In this chapter, we contributed to a better understanding of different sets of processes and especially made the differentiation between the investment process and the sequence of projects, programs to deliver the investment. On a project, there are many possibilities for how to structure the scope of the work and the work process to create the output. There are predictive approaches like the waterfall model, adaptive approaches including agile methodologies like Kanban or Scrum, or what is found most in practice today combinations of those. Which processes and project approaches are adequate for a particular project is based on a negotiation with the project sponsor. The project manager or in major projects the project management team requires a deep understanding of the advantages and disadvantages of different process options to make design choices that fit the particular project, considering the project owner, partners, suppliers and other stakeholders.

References and further reading

Drouin, N & Turner, JR. (2022). *The Elgar Advanced Introduction to Megaprojects.* Cheltenham, and Northampton, MA: Edward Elgar.

Galbraith, JR. (1977). *Organization Design.* Reading, MA: Addison Wesley.

Huemann, M. (2022). Celebrating the power of projects and their management, *International Journal of Project Management*, 40(1), 1–3.

Turner, JR. (2014). *The Handbook of Project-Based Management: Leading Strategic Change in Organizations,* 4th edition. New York: McGraw-Hill.

Turner, JR, Huemann, M, Anbari, FT & Bredillet, CN. (2010). *Perspectives on Projects.* London and New York: Routledge.

Wearne, SH. (1973). *Principles of Engineering Organization.* London: Edward Arnold.

Whyte, J, Comi, A & Mosca, L. (2022) Making futures that matter: Future making, online working and organizing remotely, *Organization Theory,* 3(1), 1–20.

Winch, GM. (2002). *Managing Construction Projects.* Oxford: Blackwell Science.

Winch, GM. (2023). Projectivity. In Winch, GM, Brunet M, & Cao, D (Eds.), *Research Handbook on Complex Project Organizing* (pp. 26–43). Cheltenham: Edward Elgar.

Chapter 20

Feasibility and planning

Marian Bosch-Rekveldt, Hans Bakker and Marcel Hertogh

Introduction

Feasibility and planning are part of the so-called Front End Development (FED) phase of a traditional project life cycle (Bosch-Rekveldt, 2014). The aim of the FED phase is to gather as much information as possible to prepare for the final investment decision (FID) and hence the next phases of the project in case a positive decision is taken. Further down in the project life cycle, the activities are performed with an increasing level of detail and accuracy.

The traditional project life cycle (generally subdivided into stages like initiation or concept development/feasibility/plan, define or design/execution or construction/handover or operation) has been a rather linear one: following a waterfall approach, stage gates mark the transition between the different phases. If the feasibility study provides a promising business case, the project is likely to proceed. At each stage gate, the Go/No Go of a project can be decided; however, the overall idea of the waterfall approach provides limited possibilities for changing the scope. What if the context changes? We might go back a phase, but can't we develop something more flexible?

As opposed to waterfall, agile approaches do allow for iteration. Stemming from the ICT industry, agile is characterised by a short cyclic, iterative approach,

DOI: 10.4324/9781003274179-23

in which different parties work closely together. The agile developments started with the agile manifesto in 2001, defining four core ideas (Beck et al., 2001):

- Individuals and interactions over processes and tools,
- Working software over comprehensive documentation,
- Customer collaboration over contract negotiation,
- Responding to changes over following a plan.

It doesn't mean that processes, tools, comprehensive documentation, contract negotiation and following a plan are without value, however, the other items are prioritised stressing the importance of individuals, interactions, a working product, collaboration, and a change in mindset.

Earlier studies have investigated how agile thoughts can be used in engineering projects in a broad sense (Jalali Sohi, 2018). In this chapter, we will explore how the feasibility and planning phases could benefit from a more flexible approach, specifically focusing on interaction, collaboration and adopting a change in mindset. Using some real-world examples, we will illustrate the need for and potential of a more flexible approach.

Illustrating the problem

Large infrastructure projects have a very long lead time. From idea generation to realisation takes easily up to decades. This also means that once the FID is taken, assumptions on which the initial project feasibility was based, are likely to be outdated. Even after the FID, it could take years (in some cases decades) before the project is delivered and taken into operation. What kind of complexities could play a role? (see also Chapter 22).

Controlling complexity?

The case of Zuidasdok presents one of the largest infrastructure projects of the Netherlands. The project aims to improve the accessibility of the Amsterdam business district called 'Zuidas' and the northern part of Randstad by road and public transport. After an intensive tendering process, the Dutch Zuidasdok project was awarded to a contractor consortium in February 2017. Part of the agreement was that the project would start with a so-called 're-baseline' or recalibration phase, which aimed to develop the integral preliminary design and corresponding planning of the construction phase before May 2018. The re-baseline phase was defined as a control measure to manage the expected complexities in the project.

Indeed, the Zuidasdok project was characterised by complexity. The project location faces a lot of dynamism and construction works will have to be done 'while the shop is open' including highways, roads, trains, metros, pedestrians, cyclists and ships, at a prime location in Amsterdam. Following the TOE model to grasp project complexity (Bosch-Rekveldt et al., 2011) all types of complexity were present and interrelated, surrounded by uncertainties.

The technical complexity was observed in the integral character of the project: there were many factors with mutual dependencies, for example, due to the limited space of the construction site. This has implications for both the design and the construction planning. Construction logistics were challenging as different infrastructure modalities should continue their operation while construction was ongoing. The overall size of the project enhanced this complexity although the integral character theoretically also enables optimisations within the scope of the project.

In terms of organisational complexity, finding the right resources was a challenge in this multi-actor project. This is partly due to the fact that there was little experience with the integrated contract and that expertise in the market was scarce in general. The project required input from various disciplines: tunnels, roads, structures, public transport, area development, etc. There were several involved parent organisations and funding streams. On the contractor side, work was done in a consortium consisting of three parties, with an unequal distribution of interests. All this created complexity at the organisational level.

In terms of external complexity, a major factor was the uncertainty in the market. At the time of the tender, the economy was in recession, but that changed in the years thereafter. This had consequences for, for example, the availability of employees with the right experience. The specific environment – Zuidas – also played a role with numerous prestigious companies and law firms who adopted a critical attitude towards the project.

Despite the control measure of implementing a re-baseline phase, the project could not overcome the challenges in the early project stages. On the one hand, the complexity of the Zuidasdok project seems largely underestimated, although it was recognised to some extent. On the other hand, the project organisation seemed unable to act upon changing circumstances: controlling complexity was not feasible.

The role of too rigid early project phases

In the case of Zuidasdok, the tender request concerned an optimisation of one specific future and the contractor optimised their design completely to that future, resulting in a winning bid. During the tender procedure, the clients decided on an important change in the scope, but the change was not reported to the bidders at that time, because the clients didn't want to disturb the tender process. This change hindered the start-up phase of the project. Also, some parameters needed to be adjusted (e.g. concerning the underground) in the calculations of the contractor. For these developments, a re-baseline phase was foreseen in the contract. As a result of these changes and the further developed insights in the context (e.g. underground), however, the invented, over-optimised construction phasing and end-solution from the bid seemed less robust and not feasible anymore. The expected cost overruns due to these changes and new insights were extreme, leading to the termination of the contract.

Towards a more flexible approach

What can be done to overcome this? There is not a single solution, but in Figure 20.1, we present a broad approach that covers:

- Awareness of what is happening, particularly regarding the second-order effects of change,
- Scenario building with a longer horizon, repeated periodically, in combination with adaptive measures,
- Flexible project management (agile) for short-run cycles,
- A more phased approach, such as a two-phase project delivery model and a collaborative attitude,
- A more flexible way of planning.

In all of these aspects, a collaborative approach is a prerequisite.

Thinking in scenarios in combination with adaptive measures

In future projects, we suggest including various options in a feasibility phase, that would allow us to anticipate changes in the context. An example of such

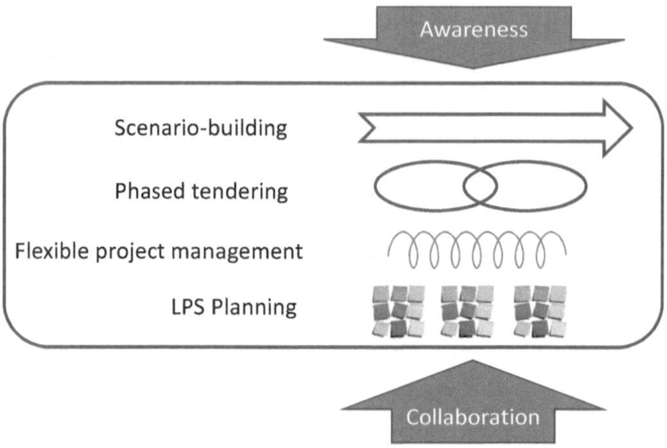

Figure 20.1: Flexibility in feasibility and planning

an approach is found in the Dutch Room for the River program (Rijke et al., 2014), where different scenarios were included, enabling anticipation within certain margins. It is more important to take different scenarios into account than to optimise towards a perfect solution for one scenario, as seen at Zuidasdok in a vibrant environment.

To develop scenarios, a broad view could be adopted, aiming for synergy with other initiatives. A short cyclic approach would allow to adjust scenarios depending on the context, providing flexibility. Flexibility can also be sought in spatial flexibility. In some cases, local space can be reserved for possible future expansions. Even in the highly dense area of the Zuidasdok, this was done by preparing the train station for future track expansion. The use of innovative 3D tools could help to take into account the potential of the subsurface. Also, a network approach could be adopted. For instance, in the scenario of a considerable traffic increase at Zuidasdok, it could be investigated if the capacity of other highways in the network could be used, for instance, the nearby highway A9, south of Zuidasdok.

To develop more robust projects, we need to combine creative solutions with realistic analyses, while working with scenarios. Basically, we need to play with the complexity of the projects. In some instances, we need to expand complexity to create more value or better fit the context. In other instances, we rather split the project into smaller pieces in an attempt to decompose complexity (Hertogh & Westerveld, 2010).

Overall, the Zuidasdok project took place in a very dynamic environment. In an attempt to control complexity, the re-baseline phase was invented, aiming to decompose complexity. Given the immense changes, however, this didn't work out. Awareness of the effects of such changes in an early stage is crucial.

Changing the scope – second-order effects?

In general, additional scope or changes within a project could be expected to lead to higher complexity, with complexity being expressed as a combination of elements and relationships between these elements, with uncertainty in both the elements and the relationships (Williams, 2002). A scope change can affect the number of elements (e.g. scope extension) as well as the relationships between the elements (e.g. scope extension can change the interfaces).

Following an agile change mindset, particularly in the early project phases, embracing scope changes could be considered as long as the consequences are evident and carefully assessed. To avoid premature convergence in scope definition, including multiple stakeholders and seeking interaction is a recommended approach (Hertogh, 2014).

In later project phases, the consequences of such a change need to be carefully addressed. For assessing the consequences of scope changes, it is important to also look at the second-order effects of a scope change. First-order effects of scope changes mainly cover the tangible, visible costs of the changes such as additional scope, delays, and design uncertainties (Bakker, 2020). The second-order effects are the impacts and consequences of the work induced by that change, such as material procurement, increase in equipment cost, increase in overhead, lower productivity, decreased morale, disruption in project progress and scheduling conflicts (Cheng et al., 2015). These second-order effects could largely influence the project and reach a factor of three to four times the direct change costs (Bakker, 2020; Ford & Lyneis, 2019), but these are easily underestimated. This was also the case at Zuidadok, with the scope change that was initiated during the tender process and was reported to the contractor after awarding the project. So, embracing scope changes needs a careful consideration of its effects; first and second order. Another measure would be to contractually split the design phase from the execution phase, as is done in the two-phase delivery model.

Two-phase project delivery model and a collaborative attitude

To avoid problematic project delivery, a more collaborative early project phase is recommended, in which the client and contractor work closely together, even with other actors like local initiatives, stakeholders, specialists, etc. (Hertogh et al., 2008). The expertise of the contractor is included in the project design phase already. The price of the construction phase can be jointly developed during the design phase, but only be fixed after that phase. By delaying the FID, the idea is to have more certainty about the outcomes of the project and the remaining risks. Although development costs might rise, the predictability of the final performance might increase. Still, attention should be paid to a fair risk allocation: the party who is best able to control and bear the risk should take it, which is not always the contractor.

Regardless of the specific project delivery model, from earlier research, we know that a collaborative attitude between client and contractor in an integral, joint project team seems a necessary condition for success (Molaei, 2021). A two-phase delivery model would allow for such an integral and collaborative approach under the conditions of a fair risk allocation and a collaborative attitude of the people involved. Potentially, a two-phase delivery model aligns well with the agile thoughts about collaboration and interaction. Could project planning benefit from a more collaborative and interactive approach as well?

More flexible ways in planning

The famous quote of Eisenhower summarises the essence of project planning: 'Plans are useless, but planning is indispensable' (Garcia et al., 2017). So the process of planning is more important than the actual plan developed with all details, as the process helps in shaping thoughts and rethinking the project planning in case something unexpected happens. With projects taking place in more dynamic environments, this emphasis on the process supports the idea of working with multilevel project planning, which is how even 'traditional' project management methods look like. Following, for example, Prince2, a high-level planning should be available for the whole project. Only at the stage gates, a detailed planning for the subsequent phase is required. Using the Work Breakdown Structure (WBS) as a base, detailed plans are developed on the different WBS levels only in later stages. Overall, the planning should be seen as supportive of realising the project goals, not as a goal on its own.

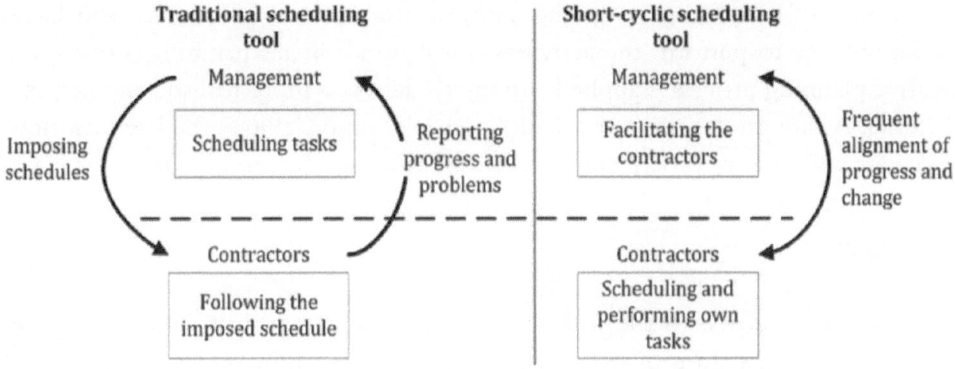

Figure 20.2: Traditional scheduling vs iterative scheduling (after Ballard, 2000)

Figure 20.2 illustrates some differences between traditional project planning and more iterative forms of project planning. In the iterative forms of project planning (right part of the figure), the contractors play a more proactive role as opposed to more traditional forms of planning where management would even impose the project schedule.

The idea of multilevel planning is also adopted in the Last Planner System®, one of the most common Lean Construction approaches (Babalola et al., 2019; Poudel et al., 2020). In traditional project planning, the planning task is seen as an individual task, but with the Last Planner System, this individual task transforms into a collective task. All parties involved in that part of the project have a say in planning those tasks through the presence of the so-called Last Planners, who are the last persons in the value chain. Basically, those who perform the work have a say in planning the work: in an interactive session, the Last Planners discuss the timing and the feasibility of the different activities. A facilitator guides this process of creating the planning, consisting of sticky notes on a schedule. In retrospectives, the earlier activities are reviewed and if needed, the detailed schedule is updated. Reasons for delays are jointly discussed to learn from earlier mistakes and improve future processes.

Implementing Last Planner System (LPS) would lead to a smooth workflow, reduced costs, reduced time of project delivery, improved productivity, collaboration, transparency and mutual understanding between the participating individuals (Lühr, 2021). In practice, cases adopting the LPS suffer from partial implementation, the lack of top management commitment or project practitioners who have difficulties adopting the new ways of working, specifically in transparency between different parties.

The idea of LPS facilitates giving authority to the level of people who have the knowledge to perform the activities. Instead of a linear planning process, an iterative planning process is applied, aiming to deliver a more realistic and flexible planning. Although the iterative scheduling tools could facilitate the late inclusion of changes, still their consequences should be thoroughly considered.

Conclusion

Again, it comes down to the role of the people in the project, and also in the early project phases. In project management literature, more and more attention is being paid towards uncertainties and how to deal with them. In this chapter, we focused on the FED phase which is the phase where projects take shape. FED phase will strongly influence the next phases of a project.

Current developments show that uncertainties will further increase. Think of the uncertain impact of climate change, the shortage of raw materials, changing living patterns, consequences of the ageing of people, new technologies (ICT, blockchain, BIM, new materials, 3D printing), and society will face more unforeseen disruptions such as caused by COVID-19, and large-scale flooding. Also, the extra attention to inclusiveness and biodiversity will increase the importance of the FED. Because of ageing of infrastructures, the focus of project management will shift from newly developed projects to maintenance, upgrade and renewal. Existing structures have additional uncertainties about the state of maintenance, and structural reliability, as well as while adjusting, the operation must continue.

These uncertainties create extra challenges and put additional pressure on the FED. This means that waterfall approaches will be less and less suitable. In this chapter, we presented some more flexible approaches. Agile is a way of working in which a short cyclic and iterative approach is applied, with a focus on collaboration between partners, allowing them to act more flexibly. The Last Planner System can be viewed as an elaboration of a joint planning process. To cope with increasing uncertainties, scenario building is more and more needed. It is essential to discuss for which scenarios the client should be prepared, which will result in more resilient solutions than the optimisation of a single solution. A more phased tendering process could further facilitate such a scenario approach.

Traditional project management theories try to take away uncertainties, but uncertainties are part of the job of a project manager, and cannot always be removed. Crucial is to deal with these uncertainties, to make these explicit for the client and partners, and to manage these.

All in all, project managers and their teams of clients, contractors and other stakeholders have to deal with an increase in complexity, as we have illustrated with the Zuidasdok example. This implies additional requirements for their individual and team competencies. In addition to affinity with the content and with the basics of project management tools, collaborative skills are becoming more and more crucial. In earlier research on the future needs of project management, leadership and corporate culture were considered as 'a basic requirement or even boundary condition for the development of any future model', or to say it shortly: 'People are Key' (Bakker et al., 2018). These human skills are also required in the early project phases, to create a pole position for the later stages of the project and to allow to act upon any changes in context. And these changes will surely happen in the timeframe of current infrastructure projects.

References and further reading

Babalola, O., Eziyi, O.I., & Isidore, C.E. (2019). Implementation of lean practices in the construction industry: A systematic review, *Building and Environment*, 148: 34–43.

Bakker, H. (2020). 2nd Order Effects. White paper Hans Bakker.

Bakker, H.L.M. & de Kleijn, J.P. (Eds.). (2018). *Projects and People: Mastering Success, NAP Network, Nijkerk, The Netherlands* (pp. 3–15). Nijkerk: NAP Proces Industry Network.

Ballard, H.G. (2000). The Last Planner System of Production Control. Retrieved from http://etheses.bham.ac.uk/4789/1/Ballard00PhD.pdf.

Beck, K., Beedle, M., Bennekum, A.V., Cockburn, A., Cunningham, W., Fowler, M., Grenning, J., Highsmith, J., Hunt, A., Jeffries, R., Kern, J., Marick, B., Martin, R.C., Mellor, S., Schwaber, K., Sutherland, J., & Thomas, D. (2001). www.agilemanifesto.org.

Bosch-Rekveldt, M.G.C. (2014). Front-end development. In: Bakker, H.L.M. & de Kleijn, J. (eds.), *Management of Engineering Projects – People are Key*. Nijkerk: NAP Network.

Bosch-Rekveldt, M.G.C., Jongkind, Y., Mooi, H., Bakker, H., & Verbraeck, A. (2011). Grasping project complexity in large engineering projects: The TOE (Technical, Organizational and Environmental) framework, *International Journal of Project Management*, 29(6): 728–739.

Cheng, M.Y., Wibowo, D.K., Prayogo, D., & Roy, A.F. (2015). Predicting productivity loss caused by change orders using the evolutionary fuzzy support vector machine inference model, *Journal of Civil Engineering and Management*, 21(7): 881–892.

Ford, D.N., & Lyneis, J.M. (2019). System dynamics applied to project management: A survey, assessment, and directions for future research. In: Meyers, R. (eds.), *Encyclopedia of Complexity and Systems Science*. Berlin, Heidelberg: Springer. https://doi.org/10.1007/978-3-642-27737-5_658-1.

Garcia Contreras, A.F., Ceberio, M., & Kreinovich, V. (2017). 'Plans are worthless but planning is everything: A theoretical explanation of eisenhower's observation', Departmental Technical Reports (CS). 1102.

Hertogh, M.J.C.M. (2014). Opportunity framing. In: Bakker, H.L.M., & de Kleijn, J. (eds.), *Management of Engineering Projects – People Are Key*. Nijkerk: NAP Network.

Hertogh, M.J.C.M., Baker, S.K., Staal, P.L., & Westerveld, E. (2008). *Managing Large Infrastructure Projects*, Utrecht: NETLIPSE.

Hertogh, M.J.C.M., & Westerveld, E. (2010). Playing with complexity. Management and organisation of large infrastructural projects. PhD thesis, Erasmus School of Social and Behavioural Sciences. Erasmus University of Rotterdam, Rotterdam.

Jalali Sohi, A. (2018). *Flexibility in Project Management*. PhD thesis, Delft University of Technology, Delft.

Lühr, G.J. (2021). *The Impact of the Last-Planner System on Project Culture*. PhD thesis, Alma Mater Europaea.

Molaei, M.M. (2021). *In Pursuit of Success*. PhD thesis, Delft University of Technology, Delft.

Poudel, R.S., de Soto, B.G., & Martinez, E. (2020). Last planner system and scrum: Comparative analysis and suggestions for adjustments, *Frontiers of Engineering Management*, 7(3): 359–372.

Projectorganisatie Zuidasdok, Halfjaarlijkse rapportage Zuidasdok, 1 juli t/m 31 december 2018, 6-3-2019, status definitief, https://zuidasbibliotheek.nl.

Rijke, J., van Herk, S., Zevenbergen, C., Ashley, R., Hertogh, M., & ten Heuvelhof, E. (2014). Adaptive programme management through a balanced performance/strategy oriented focus, *International Journal of Project Management*, 32(7): 1197–1209, ISSN 0263-7863, https://doi.org/10.1016/j.ijproman.2014.01.003.

Williams, T.M. (2002). *Modelling Complex Projects*. London: John Wiley & Sons.

Chapter 21

Design Thinking in projects

Ruth Christine Lechler, Martina Huemann, and Patrick Lehner

Introduction

Clients have become rather vague on what outcomes they are expecting from a project. Today's problems are rather wicked and solutions are often not straightforward. Especially in the front end of projects, project managers find themselves in a situation where they need to support the project owner in better understanding and defining the problem and the purpose a project should solve. While adaptive project approaches like Scrum and Kanban support iterations and the creation of a product or service that fits the needs of the project owner, Design Thinking adds the possibility of creating a better understanding of a problem, the behaviour, and the needs of the end users (Uebernickel et al., 2020). It provides a human-centred approach to solving problems regarding the creation of products, processes, or services. Human-centric means adapting the solution to the target group (or users) based on their needs and pains. Design Thinking enables to solving poorly defined problems by understanding human needs and aligning the project to those needs, with the aim of creating valuable solutions (Brown, 2008). This chapter offers Design Thinking as a project approach to better solve complex problems systematically and enables project teams to create a solution or service that adds value for the end users and thus brings success to the project owner. We provide an overview of the Design Thinking process, mindset, and toolbox and discuss challenges and potentials.

 DOI: 10.4324/9781003274179-24

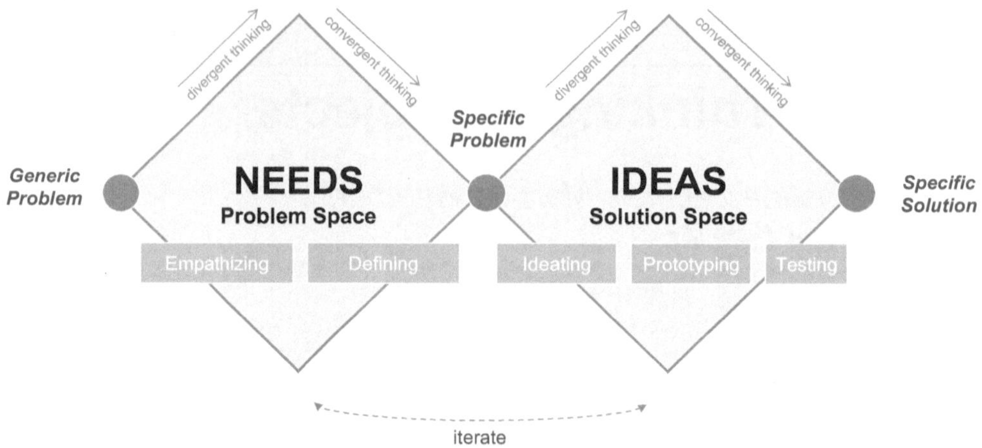

Figure 21.1: The Design Thinking process

A process

The Design Thinking process proposed by the Hasso Plattner Institute of Design at Stanford University provides a five-step approach. This approach is referred to as the "Double Diamond" model as shown in Figure 21.1. It consists of a problem space and a solution space between which the project team iterates. These spaces are represented as diamonds to express that the project team uses both divergent and convergent thinking:

- **Problem space:** This space includes divergent thinking, in which thinking is open, unsystematic, and experimental about user needs and ideas for solving the problem (phases *Empathizing and Ideation*).
- **Solution space:** Convergent thinking, in which linear and strictly rational-logical thinking is used for the definition of the problem and the implementation of the ideas (phases *Defining, Prototyping, and Testing*).

Empathizing: understanding the users and their problems

Empathizing aims to understand the needs of the users and stakeholders and explore the problem in more detail. This can come from observations or engagement through interviews and role-playing. Observation enriches empathy by capturing insights and reflecting behaviours of users who are being observed.

Engagement through interview or role-playing is an effective way to develop empathy. It gives you deeper insights into users' beliefs and values, their behaviours, and their needs through direct interaction with them. This leads to first-hand knowledge of who the target audience is and what their needs and problems are.

Defining: specifying the project goals and the specific problem

Defining aims to synthesize the findings from the empathy phase, and summarize users' needs, pains, and understanding of their environment to draw a user perspective. These findings are then transformed into a project goal. This project goal includes an actionable problem statement, also called a point of view. The process of elaborating insights into a problem statement is the process of reframing a general problem into a specific problem that synthesizes the key insights and findings from the empathy phase to their essence.

Ideating: developing ideas

Ideation aims to develop a variety of possible ideas to solve the defined problem, going beyond obvious solution ideas and trying to come up with new, unanticipated ideas. It is characterized by the collective perspective of a diverse project team. First, as many ideas as possible are collected using creativity techniques (e.g. brain writing, brainstorming), not yet paying attention to the quality or feasibility of the ideas (quantity over quality). Important is a trusting, open interaction in the project team, where no idea is deemed bad. In the second step, the ideas are sorted, discussed in the group, and prioritized. Attention should be paid to the compatibility of feasibility, viability, and desirability of the idea to ensure that the ideas can be implemented later.

Prototyping: implementing the ideas

Prototyping aims to quickly try out the selected ideas using prototypes, which are also called Minimum Viable Products. Prototypes can take many different forms: from a paper model to a role-play to a digital mock-up. Prototyping happens in multiple iterations so that an idea can evolve through different prototype stages (from a paper model to a clickable mock-up) and through different prototypes (variant A to X).

Testing: receiving feedback on the prototypes

Testing aims to determine whether the idea meets the needs of the users and where the implementation of the idea has weaknesses. This feedback early in the project saves the team energy, time, and money. With this feedback, unexpected findings can be made through surprising or unexpected insights that were not thought of in the ideation phase. In addition, close contact with key stakeholders can increase their satisfaction throughout the project.

A mindset

Design Thinking requires a specific mindset to support this project approach. The Design Thinking mindset is visualized in Figure 21.2 and briefly described in the following paragraphs.

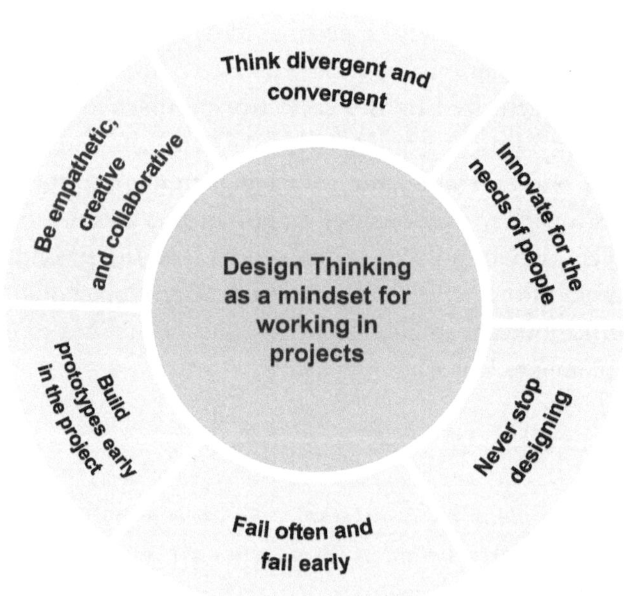

Figure 21.2: Design Thinking project mindset

Think divergent and convergent

Innovative solutions are developed by taking unconventional paths, which is called divergent thinking. Divergent thinking means dealing with a topic or problem in an open, unsystematic, and experimental way. This opens up the space for innovative, surprising ideas. Convergent thinking on the other hand describes linear, strictly rational-logical thinking. This helps to focus on the solution space, prototyping, and testing.

Innovate for the needs of people

At the root of every innovation are human needs. Human-centredness is characterized by a deep empathy for people and the development of ideas based on their needs. As a consequence of Design Thinking's human-centredness, various steps are handled differently than in traditional project approaches. This includes in particular the interaction with the user through empathizing and testing.

Never stop designing

Design Thinking is an iterative process. After testing a solution, the project team reflects on whether it contributes to solving the original problem and whether the original problem definition was valid. This means going back to the beginning of the process and questioning the hypotheses and basic concepts on which the product strategy was built. Through this iterative process, the project team builds knowledge and experience about the problem and the evident and hidden needs of the target audience. This knowledge enables further development of solution ideas that are highly user-centric.

Fail often and fail early

Design Thinking is based on experimenting with many new ideas. In some projects, more than 100 solution ideas are developed, many of which fail. By testing possible solutions with end users and key stakeholders early on, the project team learns from stakeholder feedback early to optimize their solutions.

Build prototypes early in the project

Quickly created and easily understandable prototypes are built to test new ideas. A distinction is made between prototypes with different resolutions, sketches, paper models, or programmable interfaces. The faster a new idea can be tested with users, the sooner the project team knows which aspects of an idea are suitable. Design Thinking forces the project team to be in constant and direct contact with end users. Through that, hypotheses on needs or user behaviour, assumed by the project team, can be tested and reframed.

Be empathetic and collaborative

Project teams need to be empathetic and ready for interdisciplinary collaboration to support co-creation.

An adaptive project approach

Design Thinking can be integrated into projects based on three strategies (see Figure 21.3):

- **Upfront Design Thinking**: at the beginning of the project as a mini-preparatory project
- **Infused Design Thinking:** during the project by selecting specific methods to facilitate certain processes during the project

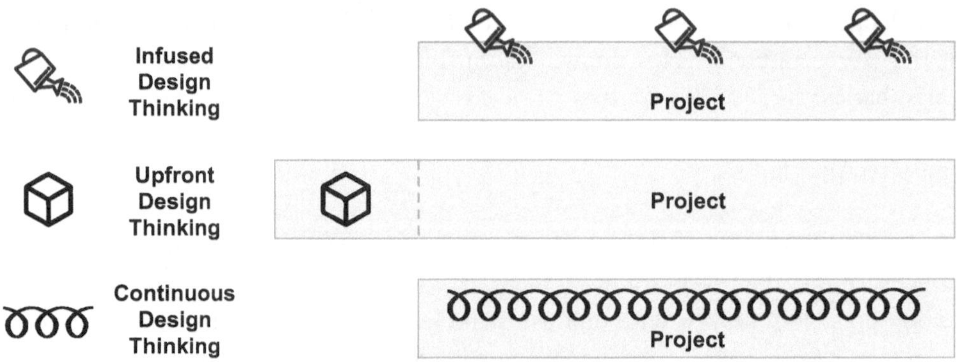

Figure 21.3: Strategies to use Design Thinking as agile project approach (after Hehn et al., 2019)

- **Continuous Design Thinking**: as the guiding method of work in the entire project

Upfront Design Thinking

Upfront Design Thinking is used at the beginning of the project or in the project initiation phase to better understand the context and needs of the users more deeply. Design Thinking is used as a guiding principle in the front end to find a suitable solution, which is then developed and implemented with Scrum, Kanban, or any other agile or predictive project approach. Upfront Design Thinking helps the project team to develop a clear vision in the project initiation. However, the upfront approach is resource and time-intensive, and there is a risk that tacit knowledge is lost when the prototype is handed over to the project team to implement the solution.

Infused Design Thinking

Design Thinking is infused into a project, which means that Design Thinking methods are applied when needed. It is used specifically to support specific challenges, for example, if the project team already has a solution idea but needs to sharpen it or if fuzzy requirements need further clarification. The advantage of this approach is that only minimal changes to existing project practices are required, and individual Design Thinking methods can be used in a resource- and time-saving manner. The danger, however, is that certain issues, for example, the problem context, are not considered enough and the solution developed does not fit well with the end users' expectations.

Continuous Design Thinking

Design Thinking is integrated into the entire project as a comprehensive and continuous project approach reflected in all project routines. Design Thinking is applied comprehensively and constantly throughout the project to support identifying the problem, creating prototypes, testing, and finally delivery of the solution in an iterative process. The requirements can be gathered accurately and comprehensibly through continuous identification of new requirements and tests. Development-critical prototypes are implemented seamlessly. Continuous Design

Thinking is a resource- and time-intensive process that depends heavily on the project team.

A toolbox

Comprehensive Design Thinking methods lists are available. The following selected methods are presented in relation to the problem space and the solution space. Table 21.1 provides an overview of possible methods related to the Design Thinking process.

Methods for the problem space

Methods in the problem space are designed to analyze and understand the problem and to formulate the problem as tangibly as possible. Such methods include:

- **Stakeholder analysis**: Empathizing with and gathering information about stakeholders who will be affected or impacted by the project. This helps to develop assumptions about specific stakeholders in the project.
- **Interviews (5-Whys)**: Iterative interrogative technique used to explore the underlying problem. It encourages the project team to ask why five times to deepen the understanding of the user and also to identify unconscious needs. This helps to make cause-and-effect relationships more transparent.
- **Customer Journey Map**: Visualization of a customer's experience from the first interaction to a long-term relationship, from the users' point of view. It can be used to create a common understanding of the user experience and identify user needs and pains. This can be used to identify touch points and gaps in the customer journey.
- **Personas**: Illustration of typical representatives of a target group with their specific expectations, values, and desires. The goals and needs of a typical user are thus visualized. This enables a consistent understanding of the target group.
- **Empathy Map:** A collaborative tool that is used to gain deeper insight into the target group. Insights from observations or interviews with the target group are documented and recorded from different perspectives. The goal is to better understand emotions and feelings related to potential needs and pain.
- **Point of view (problem statement):** Formulating an actionable problem statement that allows ideas to be developed in a goal-oriented manner.

Table 21.1 Design Thinking as project toolbox

	Process steps	*Focus*	*Methods*
Problem Space	Empathizing	**How to understand the challenge and the user?** • Reflect on the setup (organization, competition, environment) • Observe real users • Conduct studies in users' natural environments • Engage with extreme users	• **Empathize with the environment:** Stakeholder Analysis • **Empathize with the user:** Interviews (5-Whys), Empathy Maps, Customer Journey Maps, Personas
	Defining	**What makes a good problem statement?** • Human-centred and needs-based • Broad enough for creative freedom and narrow enough for manageability	• Personas • Point of View
Solution Space	Ideating	**How relevant and innovative ideas are developed?** • Quantity over Quality • There is no such thing as a bad idea • "Yes and" instead of "Yes, but"	• **Collecting ideas:** How might we Questions, Brainstorming, Mind Mapping, brainwriting • **Refining ideas:** Sketching, Storyboards
	Prototyping	**How are actionable prototypes created that bring ideas to life?** • The right method • Fast and minimal • Rough is good enough	• Low-Fidelity Prototyping • High-Fidelity Prototyping
	Testing	**How can prototypes and their orientation towards needs be evaluated?** • Show don't tell • Ask users to talk through the experience • Observe • Ask follow-up questions	• Concept testing • Usability testing • First-click testing

This involves defining the nature of the specific user about whom the problem statement is being written, identifying the key needs and goals, and summarizing the key information gathered. The better the insights gained are combined and the more specific and actionable the problem statement is formulated, the easier it is to develop ideas that build on the identified problems.

Methods for the solution space

Methods in the solution space are used to develop ideas on how to solve the problem defined in the problem space and to develop initial instantiations to solutions in order to test them at an early stage of the project. Such methods include:

- **How-could-we-ask questions:** Short questions that spur the creative flow of ideas and provide a starting point for idea generation. These questions start from an observation or problem (e.g., "TV stations don't have young viewers") and try to ask questions whose answers might contain an idea for a solution (e.g., "How could we make TV more interesting so that it appeals to young people").
- **Brainstorming:** Idea generation method in which project members contribute ideas in an unorganized and unfiltered manner. Ideas are developed collaboratively, and an attempt is made to build on each other's ideas.
- **Brainwriting:** Written version of brainstorming in which each project member writes down their ideas and shares them with the team for others to add.
- **Mind mapping:** Graphic visualization is used to connect ideas to the most and least important features of problems. This can be used to explain complex thoughts, ideas, and associations.
- **Storyboarding:** A series of drawings that visually explain ideas like a script and give the project team a clear idea of how the story is implemented and is particularly useful for fleshing out ideas.
- **Low-fidelity prototypes:** Prototypes are simply models, specific functions, or special features of the solution. Here it is sufficient to sketch the prototype on paper or Post-Its or roughly depict a process on a storyboard. The project team can get an overview of the proposed solution with minimal time and effort, and gradually focus on the finer details to get closer to the best solution.

- **High-fidelity prototypes**: Prototypes that are closer in appearance and function to the final solution. This type of prototype is used in the advanced stages of the project. The closer the prototype is to the finished solution, the more valid the feedback will be in terms of validity and applicability.
- **Concept testing**: Testing in the very early stages of the design process, initial concepts are tested before they are actually designed further. The purpose is to get the idea across to the target users. This involves interviewing the user to find out what they think about the concept in order to evaluate the potential of the idea.
- **Usability testing**: Testing to determine how easy the design is to use. This involves observing how certain tasks are completed and aspects of the prototype are understandable, and which are unintelligible to the user. In this way, usability issues can be identified to be fixed in the next iteration.
- **First-click testing:** Testing whether the user performs the intended action when landing on a particular digital page or screen. This can be used to determine which visual elements and content should take priority, and where buttons and menu items should be located.

Benefits and challenges

Design Thinking is a problem-solving approach that focuses on breaking out of traditional project patterns that manifest in habitual business behaviour and decision-making based on accumulated knowledge. It is used to solve complex problems and co-create sustainable solutions with end users. However, to adopt a Design Thinking approach, project teams must not only make a cognitive shift but also overcome organizational and cultural challenges (Clark & Smith, 2008; Martin, 2009). The main benefits and challenges of Design Thinking as agile project management approach are listed in the following (see Table 21.2).

Challenges of Design Thinking include:

- **Lack of a human-centric mindset**: Design Thinking requires organizations to reframe the way they think about value and how it is derived. They are encouraged to put people and their needs at the centre of a project.
- **Human-centric outputs without human inputs**: Understanding human challenges takes time. Unfortunately, many Design Thinking teams get asked to

Table 21.2 Challenges and benefits of Design Thinking

Benefits of Design Thinking	*Challenges of Design Thinking*
• Tackling "wicked problems" • Facilitating strong value proposition • Providing sustainability and cost stability • Catalyzing innovation and transformation • Enabling continuous knowledge expansion • Cultivating emotional, integral, and experiential intelligence	• Lack of human-centric mindset • Human-centric outputs without human inputs • Scaling • Excessive expectations • Lack of a design culture

take shortcuts and reduce critical empathizing work to phone interviews and limit the creative period for day workshops.

- **Scaling**: It can be a difficult task to scale Design Thinking in terms of human, business, and technical desirability.
- **Excessive expectations**: Risk of disappointment if (radical) innovation fails to materialize and only a clear problem definition is created.
- **Lack of a design culture**: Organizations should not limit the design mindset to product development and design departments, but rather embed the Design Thinking mindset across all functions.

Benefits of Design Thinking include:

- **Tackling "wicked problems":** Design Thinking reveals the missing parts of a problem and allows for possible solutions; thus it helps to understand problems which are not defined clearly.
- **Facilitating strong value proposition**: Focusing on the needs of the target group, combined with the iterative approach, allows for constant testing and re-testing to find optimal solutions that deliver a robust value proposition which leads to high user satisfaction.
- **Providing sustainability and cost stability**: With a value proposition which is deeply rooted in the needs of the target group and the iterative testing of the solution, products are created that are sustainable. Through that, certainty about future costs can be ensured.
- **Catalyzing innovation and transformation**: Design Thinking encourages collaboration between teams to create a space for the productive exchange of

ideas, out-of-the-box thinking, and the development of innovative solutions. This promotes change and acceptance of new processes or products in the organization.

- **Enabling continuous knowledge expansion**: Co-creation creates a broader and more diverse range of ideas and solutions, enabling an expansion of knowledge as interdisciplinary teams work together to develop, complement, and combine ideas.
- **Cultivating emotional, integral, and experiential intelligence**: Co-creation in ideation and prototyping supports integral and experimental ways of thinking that aim to satisfy the needs of the target group with as much empathy as possible which involves emotional thinking.

Conclusion

Design Thinking enriches managing projects as it facilitates solving complex problems and co-creating needs-oriented, sustainable solutions. The method can be used for two areas of application: First, processing novel problems for which no solution is immediately apparent or completely unknown. Second, the development of implementation possibilities for innovative ideas that cannot be realized with traditional project set-ups. Design Thinking enables solutions to those problems that are feasible, desirable to the user, and viable, hence cost-effective to the business.

It is characterized by a focus on prototypes for solving the problem at different levels of maturity. It also leads to increased team and conflict skills (there is no bad idea), a positive culture of failures (fail often and early), and improved process discipline (follow the process). The focus on needs and the iterative feedback rounds lead to an improved customer-supplier relationship. The consistent involvement of users in the transparent development process with all intermediate results, namely the prototypes, increases the understanding of the target groups' needs and pains.

The advantages of using Design Thinking on projects are manifold. On the one hand, Design Thinking as a process is easy to understand. Project teams and other stakeholders can easily understand the progress and follow its development through the evolution of increasingly viable prototypes. Users are heavily involved in the development of the solution, on the one hand through empathizing through observation and interviewing, personas, and on the other hand through testing specially developed prototypes. Design Thinking promotes an understanding of a positive culture of failure through the open, iterative ideation and prototyping process. Both the problem space and the solution space are considered in an integrated, holistic way. The transparency, openness, and promotion of creativity of the method give room for new ideas as well as previously unknown and unfamiliar approaches to solving relevant problems. This enables companies to face the increasing pressure of change and to deal with the growing complexity of the environment.

References and further reading

Brown, T. (2008). Design Thinking. *Harvard Business Review*, 86(6), 84–92.

Clark, K. & Smith, R. (2008). Unleashing the power of Design Thinking. *Design Management Review*, 19(3), 7–15.

Hehn, J., Mendez, D., Uebernickel, F., Brenner, W., & Broy, M. (2019). On integrating Design Thinking for human-centered requirements engineering. *IEEE Software*, 37(2), 25–31.

Martin, R. (2009). *The Design of Business: Why Design Thinking Is the Next Competitive Advantage*. Cambridge, MA: Harvard Business Press.

Uebernickel, F., Jiang, L., Brenner, W., Pukall, B., Naef, T., & Schindlholzer, B. (2020). *Design Thinking: The Handbook*. Singapore: World Scientific.

Chapter 22

Predictive, adaptive and hybrid project approaches

Dagmar Silvius-Zuchi and Gilbert Silvius

Introduction

A recent study into agile and traditional approaches in projects (Gemino et al., 2021) found that a combination of these approaches, identified as "hybrid", was applied in most projects in the sample of the study. Also Serrador and Pinto (2015) concluded that the hybrid approach was found in "by far, the majority of projects" and that this approach "should be further investigated" (1050). Hybrid project management is an emerging approach in project management practice and literature (Gemino et al., 2021), however, many questions about *what defines a hybrid approach, when it can be applied, which different types of hybrid* can be identified, and *what the implications of hybrid are*, are still unanswered. This chapter discusses these questions and aims to provide support to project managers and project owners/sponsors in their choice of a fitting approach for their projects.

Before we discuss the characteristics of different potential approaches to projects, it is good to first make clear what we consider an approach. An approach is the highest level of concept used "when describing how a project will be designed and governed" (Gemino et al., 2021). It suggests "a set of principles and guidelines which define the way a specific project is managed" (Špundak, 2014).

 DOI: 10.4324/9781003274179-25

An example of an approach is agile. An approach should not be confused with a specific methodology, such as Scrum, or a method/technique, such as a Kanban board or planning poker. An approach provides directions for methodologies that can be developed to fit within the principles of the approach. A methodology is "a comprehensive set of best practices, tools and techniques that are dynamic, flexible, adaptive and customizable to suit different projects within a specific environment" (Chin and Spowage, 2010). When an approach is the highest level of concepts, a methodology is the second level. To follow up on the earlier mentioned example, Scrum is an example of a methodology that is developed within the principles of the agile approach.

A third level of concept is formed by the methods and/or techniques that are used within methodologies, to perform, manage or govern a project. These methods and techniques are manifold, and range from structuring methods (such as a work breakdown structure) to estimation techniques (such as planning poker), to scheduling methods (such as a Gantt chart and critical path analysis), to project justification techniques (such as net present value), to team coordination methods (such as daily stand-ups and Kanban boards), etc. The relationship between methodologies and methods is a many-to-many relationship, with methodologies sometimes prescribing the use of specific methods; however, these methods are normally not exclusive to a specific methodology. We consider methods and techniques as parts of the "body of knowledge" that a project manager should master and apply when appropriate. Although the characteristics of specific methods fit a certain approach more than others, for example, a work breakdown structure and critical path analysis typically fit a plan-driven approach to a project, whereas daily stand-up meetings and a Kanban board are often used in agile approaches, and the mere application of a method or technique does not define the approach to the project. A Kanban board can also be applied in a plan-driven approach, just as a Gantt chart may also be a useful method in an agile project. In practice the different levels of concepts, *approaches – methodologies – methods and techniques*, may all be addressed as 'methodology' (Gemino et al., 2021), and this may lead to confusion. It is important to distinguish the different levels of concepts.

In this chapter, we will be addressing approaches to projects, without discussing specific methodologies. In paragraph 5, implications, we will touch upon some frequently used methods in order to clarify how a hybrid approach affects these methods.

Characteristics of predictive and adaptive project approaches

Early 21st century, agile emerged as a novel and more adaptive approach to development activities that projects, by nature, include. And although the ideas, processes, tools, and techniques that underpin agile trace back to the 1930s (Whiteley et al., 2021), its popularization took off with the publication of the Agile Manifesto in 2001 (Beck et al., 2001). The background of the Agile Manifesto rests in software development and information technology projects, and its contributors tried to identify characteristics the methodologies they used had in common (Lockard and Gifford, 2017), thereby not focusing on processes, but on values and principles (Hohl et al., 2018). The contributors were driven by "the need for an alternative to documentation driven, heavyweight software development processes" (Beck et al., 2001) and aimed to put emphasis on the communication among those involved in the project, and on the handling of changes of requirements and features of the product.

The Agile Manifesto provides values and principles that help to optimize the development process. The values and principles provide no rules but rather represent an approach to development. In the manifesto, this approach is described in four statements, in which the "agile values" are contrasted with common practices of software development projects at that moment in time. Although the contributors of the manifesto recognize that these practices are up to a certain level necessary, they make clear that these practices should not overshadow the values with which each statement starts. So, the agile values at the beginning of each statement are considered more important than the practices at the end of each statement.

The statements of the Agile Manifesto (Beck et al., 2001):

I Individuals and interactions over processes and tools
II Working software over comprehensive documentation
III Customer collaboration over contract negotiation
IV Responding to change over following a plan

Based on these values and related principles, agile became an umbrella term for a highly adaptive approach to product development activities, either within or without the context of a project. Despite its original focus on software development, the perceived success of the agile approach carried its fame over to other domains and types of projects, where agile quickly became a synonym for a more modern approach to projects and development.

In order to characterize agile, for which we will use the term *adaptive* approach to development (Project Management Institute, 2021: 38), we need to contrast it with a less-adaptive approach. This less-adaptive approach is often referred to as "traditional" (Gemino et al., 2021), "plan-driven" or "waterfall" (Turner, 2014). However, we prefer to comply with the terminology used in the latest edition of the PMBoK Guide, which talks about the *predictive* approach (Project Management Institute, 2021: 35).

Characteristic 1. Single versus iterative development cycles

In the adaptive approach, the logical development cycle of sequential activities, for example, *analyze – design – build – test – deploy*, is applied to parts of the product, the so-called increments, and not to the whole product all at once. The breakdown of the product into parts, which will be developed incrementally, needs to be such that each increment already provides functionality and therefore value to the users. As a result, the adaptive approach creates an iterative development process of short development cycles of product increments, instead of a single development cycle for the whole product, as is common practice in the predictive approach. Figure 22.1 illustrates this difference.

In adaptive methodologies, such as Scrum, the development cycles often get time-boxed to a maximum of just a couple of weeks in order to create quick feedback loops on the developed product (increment). The adaptive approach combines short incremental development cycles with just-in-time feature planning and dynamic prioritization (Cohen et al., 2003), therefore absorbing changes in requirements and features of the product, as these only need to be defined shortly before the development cycle of these features starts.

Contrasting this just-in-time feature planning, the single development cycle of the predictive approach, requires a complete and detailed overview of all requirements of the product at the start of the development cycle (Steven et al., 2013), making the development process more vulnerable to changes in requirements or priorities.

It can also be argued that with a predictive approach, the development of a product can be organized with separate development cycles for parts of the product. For example, when an information system is developed in separately usable modules. However, these sub-projects normally do not have the short durations that the iterations of the adaptive approach have.

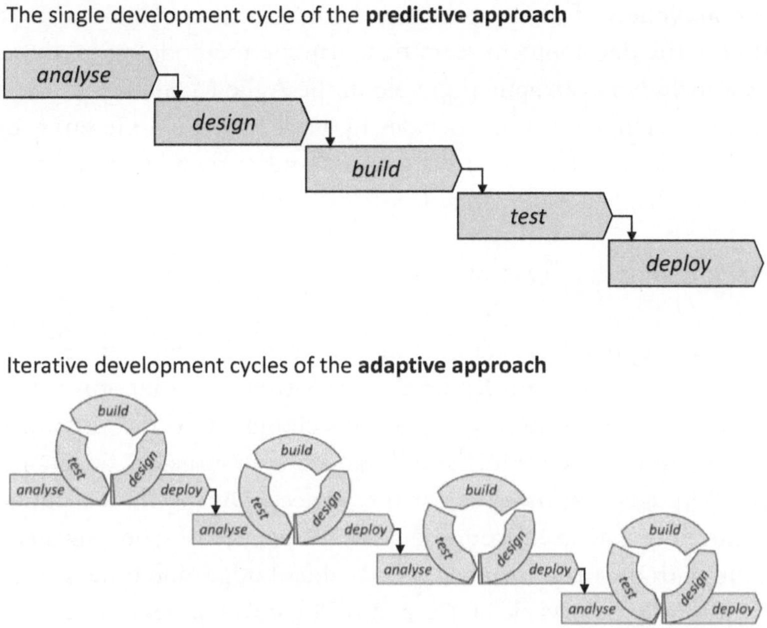

Figure 22.1: Single cycle development in the predictive approach versus incremental development in iterative cycles in the adaptive approach

Characteristic 2. Responsiveness to change

Von Rosing et al. (2014) describe responsiveness and flexibility as two of the defining characteristics of the adaptive approach. As the adaptive approach prescribes that the development process is organized in iterative development cycles of product increments, instead of a single development cycle for the full product, it is much more suitable to accommodate expected and unexpected changes to the requirements and features of the desired product and the priorities with which these are developed. The adaptive approach is therefore more capable of scanning and sensing external and internal opportunities; and forming an appropriate response according to the situation at hand (Van Rosing et al., 2014).

The predictive approach is also capable of handling changes, through a change management process, however, the changes in this case create a disturbance of the plan, whereas in the adaptive approach, changes are not disturbing much, as planning the development activities is only done just-in-time before the relevant development cycle.

The responsiveness of the adaptive approach is further supported by the self-organization of the development team that adaptive methodologies advocate, and that also was included as an agile principle in the Agile Manifesto. In the adaptive approach, the development team decides by itself how the different activities in an iterative development cycle are organized and is thereby stimulated to find solutions to the challenges they may face.

Characteristic 3. Focus of control

In the predictive approach, the desired output of the development project (called deliverables, requirements, or features) is the starting point for the planning of the project. In the resulting plan, the development of the output, required activities are listed and their effort and durations are estimated, which adds up to a "predicted" budget and timeline for the project. During the execution of the project, controlling is centred around the "iron triangle" of scope/quality, budget, and time, but with the main focus on the variables budget and time, as the variable quality often is only observable at the end of the development cycle.

In the adaptive approach, the desired output is logically also the starting point for the planning, however, this output is defined in much less precise features and requirements, often referred to as a "product vision". This high-over description of the product gets detailed during the project through the just-in-time feature planning in the incremental development cycles. And as the variables budget and time are determined by the organization of the development project, through time-boxed iterations and defined use of resources, the focus of control in the adaptive approach is on the output of the development process: the quality or value of the product. This focus is reflected in specific methods and techniques, such as a product burndown chart, that are frequently used in adaptive projects and in specific roles in the project organization, such as the product owner, that adaptive methodologies such as Scrum prescribe (Figure 22.2).

Characteristic 4. Leanness

A third characteristic of the adaptive approach is its leanness (Von Rosing et al., 2014). The adaptive approach focuses on shortening time frames and costs and on improving quality (Qumer and Henderson-Sellers, 2008), through the reduction of resource-intensive intermediate artefacts (Cohen et al., 2003). Documentation

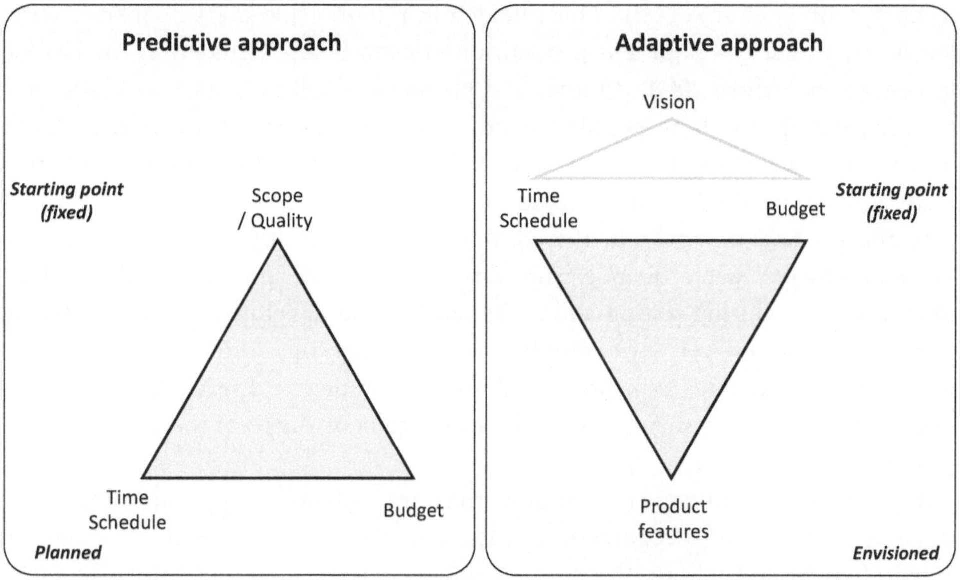

Figure 22.2: The difference in focus of control of the predictive and adaptive approach

is developed only as needed and is often tailored for the project (Steven et al., 2013). Whereas the predictive approach documents each step of the development cycle extensively (Steven et al., 2013), the adaptive approach aims to produce functional product increments rapidly, thereby reducing the need for extensive process documentation. The adaptive approach relies more on tacit knowledge, which is communicated in human interaction, than on explicit knowledge in formal documentation (Špundak, 2014).

This characteristic is sometimes misunderstood in the way that it is suggested that agile development methodologies do not require any documentation. That is of course a misunderstanding, as any product requires documentation about its construction and architecture in order to be maintainable. The leanness of the adaptive approach is oriented at minimizing the documentation about the development *process*, but not the documentation about the resulting *product*.

Characteristic 5. Inclusion and interaction

The reduction of intermediate documentation in the adaptive approach is enabled by a more intensive interaction between developers and (future) users of the product (Cohen et al., 2003). This interaction requires that users cooperate with developers in the development process, often even being included in the development team (Smith, 2008). Qumer and Henderson-Sellers (2008) conclude that the adaptive approach is people-focused and communications-oriented. User interaction and participation are required during each iteration and to make the decision to proceed to the next iteration.

In the predictive approach, the (future) users are mostly involved in setting the requirements, while disappearing during analysis, design, and building. The users re-emerge during testing and acceptance of the developed product (Steven et al., 2013). However, one should mention, that this also depends on the overall attitude towards stakeholders. Also in a predictive approach, applying a more systemic view, a strong stakeholder engagement supports the development approach.

The intensive human interaction that the adaptive approach requires, together with the self-organization of the development team that the adaptive approach advocates, limit the size at which a development team can effectively and efficiently function. Although the effectiveness of teamwork is a relevant success factor in all approaches, the adaptive approach links this more explicitly to the size of a team, with adaptive methodologies such as Scrum suggesting "human sized" teams of two to nine developers. In practice, an effective team size will also depend on the context and the competencies of the team members.

Characteristic 6. Transparency and learning

A final characteristic of the adaptive approach is its support of reflection and learning, by focusing on continuous improvement during the development cycle (Qumer and Henderson-Sellers, 2008). Adaptive methodologies typically prescribe inspection and reflection moments at each iteration. Learning through the adaptive approaches is enabled by high levels of transparency, such as efforts, achievements, performances, and issues. Again, this limits an effective team size, as more team members limit transparency.

Also, the predictive approach facilitates learning, for example by documenting lessons learned after controlling loops and at the closing of a project or by reflecting on the project's progress during project controlling. However, the learning is often less formally embedded in the methodologies.

While in the predictive approach, the execution of the basic project plan (initial plan plus/minus approved changes) is the backbone of the project work, in the adaptive approach it is the working process with transparent communication, short and frequent feedback cycles from the customer or user, and a high level of flexibility (Thesing et al., 2021).

Applicability of predictive and adaptive project approaches

Given the different characteristics of the adaptive and predictive approaches, it can be debated that they are not equally suitable for all projects and all situations. Selecting the right approach therefore has become a decision that may influence the success of a development project (Chin and Spowage, 2010; Špundak, 2014). It is therefore important that project managers and owners/sponsors understand that what kind of situations and which kind of approaches are most suitable.

Product-related criteria

The adaptive approach is mainly targeted at the development of complex products (Scrum Guide, 2020), and projects with dynamic, un-deterministic, and nonlinear characteristics, in which accurate estimates, stable plans, and predictions are often hard to get in early stages (Von Rosing et al., 2014). The flexibility and responsiveness to change that is embedded in the adaptive approach, have most value when the requirements and features of the desired product are either not completely known yet at the start of the development cycle, or uncertain and therefore likely to change during the development process. In the "goals and methods" matrix of Turner and Cochrane (1993) (Figure 22.3), this relates to project types 3 and 4, which are both defined by the fact that the goals are not well defined.

The predictive approach seems to fit best to the type 1 projects (both goals and methods well defined), as the single development cycle of this approach relies on the premise that a complete overview of all requirements of the product is available at the start of the project (Steven et al., 2013). For the remaining project type, type 2 (goals well defined, but methods not), the predictive approach is not very fitting, as this approach also assumes that the development process can be planned and estimated, which requires an understanding of the methods in this process. It can be argued that for this

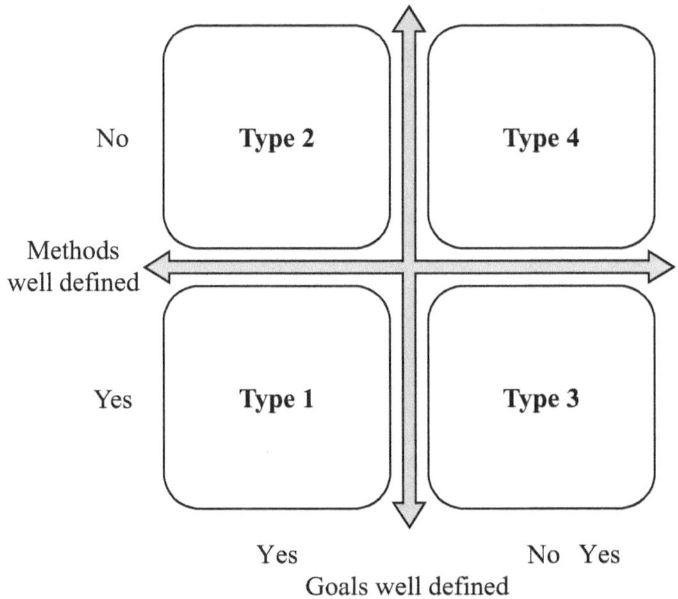

Figure 22.3: Typology of projects based on their clarity of goals and methods (based on Turner and Cochrane, 1993)

type, the adaptive approach is more suitable, as the learning characteristic of this approach supports the development of effective methods.

Based on the goals and methods matrix, it can be concluded that the clarity of goals and the clarity of methods are relevant criteria that should be considered when selecting a suitable approach for the development activities in a project.

A related criterion is provided by the stability of goals and/or methods. As the predictive approach relies on the freezing of requirements and specifications, Ganis concludes that this approach is less suitable if requirements are likely to change in the course of the project. As already described in the previous paragraph, the short incremental development cycles of the adaptive approach, are better suited in case of uncertain and changing requirements.

An additional criterion is provided by Thesing et al. (2020), where it is stated that an adaptive approach is not suitable in case of a "lack of decomposability of the overall result into separate deliverables" (Thesing et al., 2020). In other words, when the product cannot be incrementally designed and developed, for example, because of its (technical) coherence/architecture or because of its legal requirements, a predictive approach is more fitting. This may be the case in construction projects, where an integral design is required before construction can start, but also in non-technical projects where a complete design may be required. For example, when shooting a movie, the order of filming the different scenes is optimized from a logistic and economic perspective and therefore differs from the chronology of the final film. This is only possible if the complete storyline of the movie is already developed and the script is available.

Organization-related criteria

Next to the requirements and features of the product and the methods to develop the project, organizational factors influence the applicability of the approaches. For example in projects where the project sponsor, or the management and governance of the sponsoring organization, cannot or do not want to accept the characteristics of the adaptive approach. This is not unthinkable, because the flexibility of the adaptive approach comes at the price of uncertainty: Uncertainty about the exact features of the product that will be developed in the project. As this uncertainty about the product creates uncertainty about the costs and benefits, and thereby also about the underlying business case of the project, it is not surprising that this may cause a conflict with the logical governance requirement that investments in projects are justified and based on a solid business case (International Organization for Standardization, 2015). In "high-governance" environments or cultures, therefore, a predictive approach may be more fitting. However, this approach also comes with uncertainty about the budget and time conditions with which the project will be performed, although this uncertainty is more hidden. In fact, the value of transparency in an organizational culture also provides a criterion for the fit of an approach. The adaptive approach stimulates a high level of transparency in the project.

Next to the culture of the organization, also the personal attitude of the project owner/sponsor towards uncertainty affects the applicability of the approach. Is he or she willing to accept uncertainty when assigning the project? The control instruments that the adaptive methodologies introduce to handle this uncertainty, for example, the role of a product owner, provide both a solution and a challenge for this issue. In the adaptive approach, the project owner needs to be able to nominate a product owner for the project who is competent, committed, empowered, and respected by all stakeholders. Practice learns that many organizations struggle with filling this role adequately.

Team-related criteria

Thesing et al. (2020) suggest that also project team characteristics provide criteria for the applicability of an approach. The intensive communication and interaction within the development team, that the adaptive approach characterizes, does not always fit the culture of the organization and/or the personalities of the team members. For example, not all team members may like the transparency of their individual work performance, through the daily stand-up meetings and a Kanban board.

The required participation of (future) users in the team, may influence the applicability of the adaptive approach. For example, when future users are not known yet, or when competent users are not available. Or when the user organization cannot spare the effort of the participation of their employees in the development team.

A related consideration is the empowerment of the participating future users. For example, a situation where finding consensus among the users about the features and requirements of the product has been a lengthy and tiresome process, it may be more suitable for a predictive approach, as the adaptive approach suggests that the participating users in the development team can make choices and decision on behalf of all (future) users.

A final team-related consideration is that of its self-organization. Self-organization of teams requires a high level of competence, commitment, respect, and trust of and among the team members. It would be naive to assume that teams can have this self-organization competence without going through a team development process. Adaptive methodologies therefore introduced a coaching and facilitating role, for example, a Scrum master or an agile coach, who supports the team in its development. Nevertheless, teams that are on a low level of self-organization may not be ready to apply an adaptive approach and may be more suitable for a predictive approach.

Figure 22.4 summarizes the considerations discussed above in a compact "criteria catalogue". With these criteria, a project manager, or a project owner/sponsor, can assess the suitability or applicability of the approaches, and design the most fitting approach for his/her project, whereby a combination of approaches is also possible.

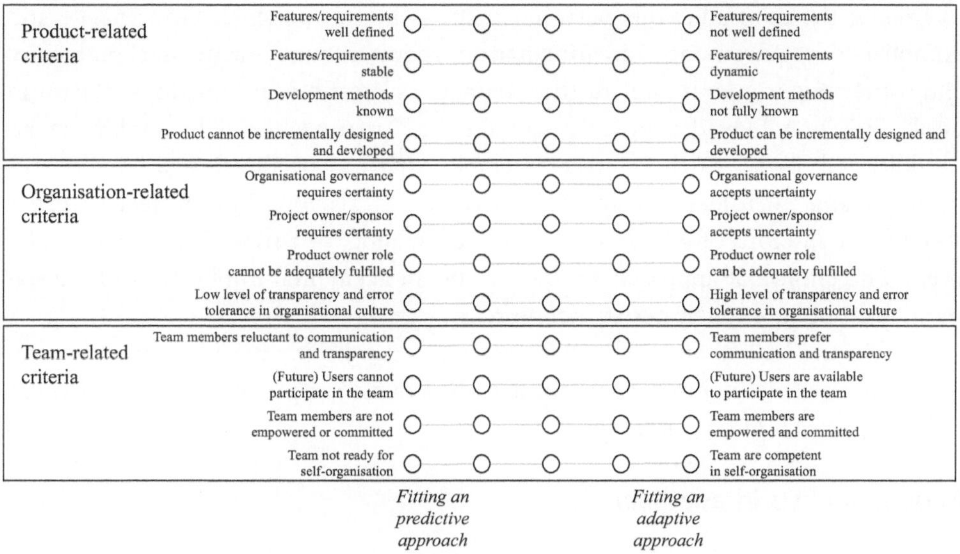

Figure 22.4: Overview of criteria for assessing the applicability of the predictive and adaptive approaches

Characteristics of hybrid project approaches

Based on the criteria explained above, in many projects neither a fully predictive nor a fully adaptive approach is the right choice. Studies, for example by the Hochschule Koblenz in 2020, show that by now a high number of projects use a hybrid approach, and it is concluded that "hybrid is a leading project management approach" (Gemino et al., 2021). But what is a hybrid? Whenever two or more approaches are combined, it may be called a hybrid approach (Timinger, 2017: 241). In the described context, a hybrid approach is "a combination of adaptive and predictive approaches. This means that some elements from a predictive approach are used and some from an adaptive approach are used" (Project Management Institute, 2021: 36).

The reasons for choosing a hybrid approach can be manifold. For example, some of those criteria are discussed in paragraph 3. However, often the choice for a hybrid is not an explicit choice, but the implication of applying different methods of whatever serves the purpose. One motivation for choosing a hybrid approach is the wish to combine the advantages of both approaches and to overcome the contradictions between them as best as possible. Governance and compliance requirements, documentation requirements, or pre-set budgetary and time requirements are further named as possible motivations (Gemino et al., 2021). A hybrid approach may also be "useful when deliverables can be modularized, or when there are deliverables that can be developed by different project teams" (Project Management Institute, 2021: 36). The project manager should be conscious of whether a predictive, an agile, or a hybrid approach can be used. The choice of approach should not be an accidental implication of chosen methods, but an explicit design decision.

Within the hybrid approach, different types can be identified. Below we will discuss a *sequential* hybrid approach, a *parallel* hybrid approach, and an *integrated* hybrid approach (after Timinger, 2017).

Sequential hybrid approach

In a sequential hybrid approach, one or more phases in the project are performed in an adaptive approach, while the other phases are performed with a predictive one. A comprehensive project plan shows sequential phases, of which one or more phases are performed in iterations, each iteration delivering valuable products (Figure 22.5).

In an analysis phase of a software development project, for example, the business case, an overall project plan, and a project organization for the execution can be well elaborated. Methods and techniques from the adaptive approach can be used in this phase to describe desired features and requirements on a high level, for example using "user stories", and estimating effort and cost in ranges. The following design – build – test phases may be performed in adaptive, in iterative development cycles for definable "packages' of features of the product. Prioritization of these packages can be done dynamically, in close co-operation

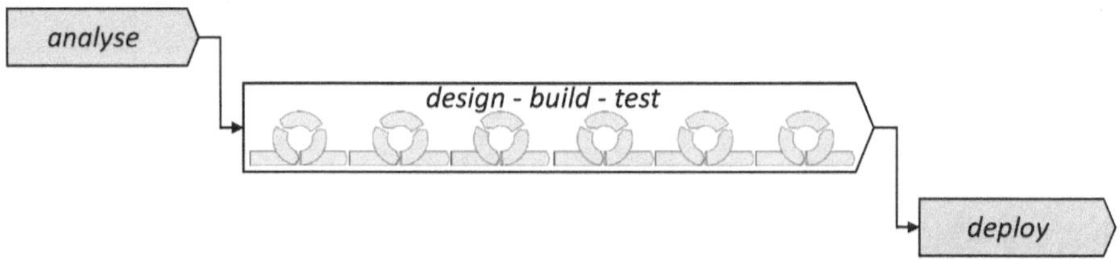

Figure 22.5: Example of a sequential hybrid approach

with the (future) users. The typical characteristics of the adaptive approach, such as the absorption of continuous changes, intensive communications with the main stakeholders, and a high self-responsibility of the team can in this way be integrated. The concluding phase on the other hand, the training of the users, deployment of the product, and handover, probably including the finalization of the product documentation and the adaptations of the business processes within the user organization might then again be organized in a more predictive way as the concluding phases of the overall project.

The sequential hybrid approach can be seen as a response to the demand of most organizations to have a clear 'big picture' of the project and a well-developed project assignment at the beginning of a project. With a sequential hybrid approach, this desire for predictability and controllability enables, for example, by first performing an analysis or conceptualization phase, before entering into an adaptively organized design and development phase. This may be especially relevant when external resources need to be contracted for the development. The sequential hybrid approach can also be applied to other project types than software development. For example in a construction project, the planning phase could be performed in an adaptive way, whereas the actual construction phases are performed in a predictive way (Timinger, 2017).

The main challenge in this hybrid approach is to integrate the different ways of thinking and acting. The interfaces and transitions between the different phases must be well defined (Timinger, 2017). What are the exact rules and values in which phase? Who takes over which role in which phase? How do project management and agile roles relate? For example, the project manager and the product owner? Or the project manager and an agile coach? Is the project manager at all needed during the adaptively organized phases? These are questions that need to be clarified and communicated in the planning of the project. Also, the level of detail in which features and requirements are described provides a challenge when combining approaches. In a hybrid approach, users and developers will need to reach a shared understanding and an agreement on this.

Parallel hybrid approach

In a parallel hybrid approach, some of the project's deliverables are developed with a predictive approach, and in parallel other parts are developed with an adaptive approach (Timinger, 2017) A possible situation could be a reorganization

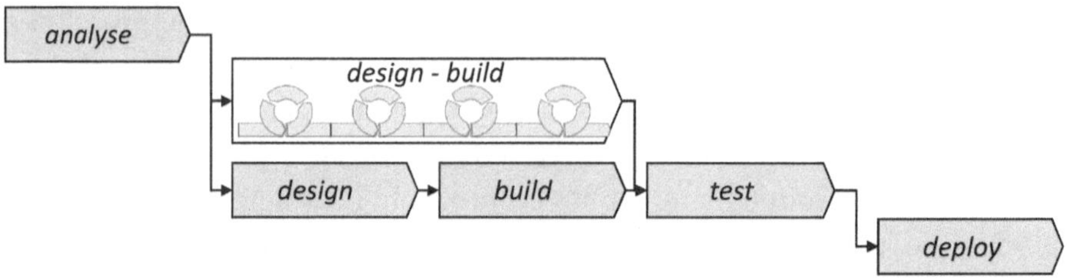

Figure 22.6: Example of a parallel hybrid approach, combined with also two sequential phases

project, where strengths and weaknesses are analyzed, a new strategic orientation developed, and in consequence a new orientation of the company developed and implemented. Whenever there is a software development involved in such a reorganization, that is demanded right from the beginning of the project, the team taking over the responsibility of developing it, might work in an adaptive manner. So, in parallel to the overall predictive approach in the project, one sub-team works adaptively (Figure 22.6).

A parallel hybrid approach is challenging, as there is a fundamental difference in the planning of both approaches, and these different planning approaches are now applied to different parts of a single project. For the part to which the predictive approach is applied, a comprehensive top-down planning is developed with interdependent and scheduled activities which are all sensible and necessary. For the parts to which the adaptive approach is applied, there is no comprehensive planning at the beginning, but more precise requirements are developed during the project according to the prioritization of the product owner. The deliverables that are developed in this way are delivered as early as possible during the project.

As a result of these parallel approaches, synchronization issues may arise when the different parts of the deliverable in the end need to be integrated into a single product. If there are dependencies between the different parts of the deliverables, which in most projects will be the case, these dependencies need to be managed and ways must be found to overcome possible discrepancies. Dealing with deadlines must be agreed on. It will also be a challenge to deal with the uncertainty in the project, as one or more team(s) will not commit to concrete outputs, but may only commit to a (relatively vague) product vision.

Furthermore, change requests exist only in one part of the project; for the adaptively developed part, there are no changes, but for changes in priorities of the product backlog, all are managed and decided by the product owner. So, different cultures arise within the project, which may cause cultural clashes within the team. The project manager but moreover also the project owner should understand and accept these differences.

The perception of roles and the way of co-operation within the same project organization may also differ fundamentally. For the adaptively organized part, there is a very active operational product owner who makes final decisions on what should be done and what should not be done, and that prioritizes in accordance with the interests of the stakeholders. For the predictively organized part, there will be a project owner with a more strategic perception of his/her role. The wish of self-organizing its tasks is achieved by the team itself, which may be supported by a facilitating agile coach, and might contradict the leadership role once a project manager takes over. The role of understanding and leadership style might be challenged.

Integrated hybrid approach

A third type of hybrid is the integrated hybrid approach. Integration of the predictive and adaptive approaches may appear in different forms. For example, when methods of one approach are applied in projects that apply the other approach, it could be called an integrated hybrid approach. So could a project that is approached and managed in a predictive way, apply a Kanban board or a daily stand-up meeting for team coordination purposes? However, this would merely be an integration of methods and not an integration of approaches.

A deeper integration of approaches would combine the characteristics of both approaches. An example of such an integrated hybrid approach would be one in which the development team works in an adaptive way, but with defined results that need to be realized on scheduled milestones in predictive planning. These milestones may for example describe the features that the team needs to have developed after the sixth iteration, and again after the 12th iteration, and after the 18th iteration, etc. Figure 22.7 illustrates such an integrated hybrid approach.

This way of integrating approaches aims to combine the benefits of the development team working in an adaptive way while satisfying also the need for certainty of output, timeline, and budget, which the governing organization has.

A challenge in this integrated approach is the commitment that a development team that is working in an adaptive way, can give to the delivery of a

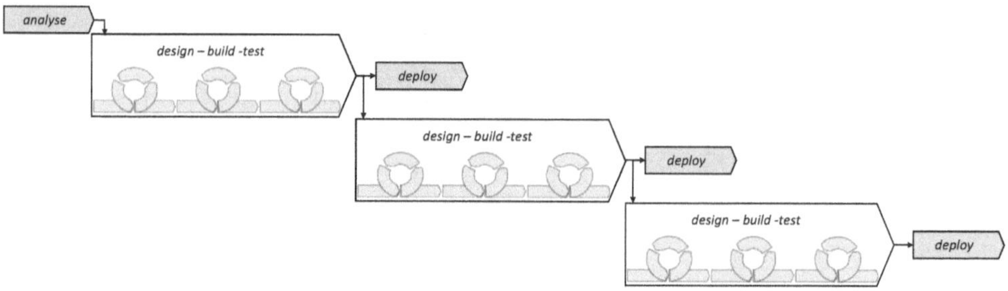

Figure 22.7: Example of an integrated hybrid approach

defined output on a defined date. A solution to this challenge may be to define the scheduled output in a bandwidth of functionality, instead of an exact set of features. Another challenge may be the integration of agile roles in the project organization, as was also discussed for the parallel hybrid approach.

Implications of hybrid project approaches

Implications for project roles, values, and teamwork

When defining roles in a project organization that follows a hybrid approach, the definition of roles and the corresponding perception of these roles, as well as the integration of new roles, will be a crucial step. Roles that are typically associated with a predictive approach, such as project owner, project manager, and project team members, and roles that are typically associated with an adaptive approach, such as product owner, agile coach, and developers, must be evaluated for its necessity, and agreement must be reached about which roles, and to which extent, are needed in the different phases of the project.

The overall responsibility in hybrid projects may still lay with the project manager, who assures efficient communication between all involved parties and maintains an overview. However, although having a leadership function and being the main decision-maker, the team has to be strongly integrated, most necessarily the adaptively working team. In addition, the team, the product owner, and the project manager need to accept each other's role. The project manager needs to understand the dynamics of a self-organizing team and the operational decision-making role of the product owner. When the team works self-organized, the project manager may need to hold back on his/her traditional leading role. Thus, the interrelationships of all roles during the phases or activities that are approached adaptively have to be clarified and made visible in the project organization.

Not only roles, but also leadership styles and teamwork differs in the different approaches. In the adaptive approach, teams work self-organized. Is for these teams a project manager needed at all? What impact does self-organization have on the leadership style of the project manager? How is the leadership style, be it something between participative to authoritarian or even situational corresponding at all with the idea of self-organization?

When working sequentially hybrid, the project manager might take over an interface role between the team and the product owner during the agile phase(s), or at least a triangle construct might arise. Maybe a "project coordinator" might be the better definition for a project manager when taking over this interface role – not acting in a leadership function, and also not being solely responsible for all the project success, but acting as an interface, considering a holistic view on the project. When the project manager is also a content expert, highly integrated into the user organization, can the project manager take over the role of the product owner and thus use his/her presence in the adaptive phase(s) to steer decisions?

When working in a parallel hybrid, where in the project organization chart is the product owner positioned? Is he/she part of the project core team and at the same time of the adaptively working sub-team? And/or do we see the product owner more as an addition to the project owner (team), referring to a "senior user" role as we know it from Prince2?

How in general do the product owner and the project owner relate? Are they directly communicating with each other, or is communication between them only steered over the project manager? And what about the agile coach? Is the project manager familiar with the methodology of the project, which the adaptive working team has chosen, and could therefore take over the role of a scrum master or agile coach? Helping the team with self-organization and applying the adaptive approach according to the agreed methodology?

On many of these questions, there are absolutely no answers. However, they illustrate the necessity to explicitly clarify the mutual role expectations and make relations and co-operations visible in organization charts, responsibility matrices, and communications plans, right from the start of the project, to avoid overlaps, to avoid disappointments.

Implications for project planning

When working with hybrid, it must be considered which methods and techniques are most appropriate for project planning. Methods coming from predictive approaches will quite likely be relevant but may need to be adapted.

When initiating a project, the questions of whether the investment will pay off and whether the investment contributes to the company's strategy must be answered. And also the question of whether the project is the appropriate organization form at all. If so, the project must be designed, its boundaries decided, and its context analyzed. All of this is necessary to have a good basis for assigning the project and to have a good understanding between the project owner/sponsor and the project manager of their responsibilities. In project initiation, it should also be considered whether a project, as an organizational choice, is the most appropriate organizational form to realize the project objectives, and whether the project is of low or high complexity. Building upon what this chapter describes, the approach of the project should be considered in this phase. The criteria we summarized in Figure 22.3 may thereby act as a "checklist" to assess whether a predictive, adaptive or hybrid approach is most suitable. As elaborated in paragraph 3, such a checklist should not only consider the product itself but also other aspects, such as the readiness of the organization to deal with agility for example. Therefore, new steps must be integrated into the initiation process, and new fields must be integrated into a project assignment template (such as "working approach").

When working hybrid, the applications of methods change. When working adaptive or hybrid, uncertainties must be made visible respectively when defining the business case and in elaborating the boundaries and the context of a project. In the business case, the methods of calculating the costs and the benefits might not change, but a higher risk might be allocated as a result of the uncertainty that comes along with the adaptive approach. At the same time, benefits might be generated, which are already available earlier in the process. In the project assignment, the project objectives might not be as SMART anymore but might be replaced or complemented by a (less precise formulated) product vision, as detailed features and functionalities are decided while being developed.

When considering the stakeholders of the project, during the initiation and planning phase, the method itself is important in a predictive, agile, or hybrid approach. Only the responsibilities of engaging with stakeholders might change. In a hybrid approach, we don't only have the project team, the project manager, and the project owner, that are involved in stakeholder engagement activities, but we have new roles, that are in agile approaches strongly associated with stakeholder management, such as the product owner. The product owner decides on what is to be taken into product backlogs, and with what priority, in communication and agreement with the stakeholders. So, in hybrid approaches, responsibilities for stakeholder communications and engagement actions must be clarified, and overlaps to be avoided.

One main instrument to plan the work that has to be done in a project is the work breakdown structure, which is strongly linked with scheduling, and resource and cost planning. The work breakdown structure and the product backlog are two main instruments for planning and steering the scope of the project. In a parallel hybrid approach, the purpose of a work breakdown structure during the agile phase(s) has to be challenged. Shall the iterations be made visible as work packages – as placeholders so to say? If so, the controlling aspect is of limited relevance, still the scheduling aspect is behind, in showing how many iterations are planned, and how long each iteration shall be, and the corresponding timeframe for the agile phase(s) is given. So, the purpose of the work breakdown structure mainly lies with a "placeholder" function. However, the link to the product backlog must be clearly communicated (Figure 22.8).

In a sequential hybrid approach, iterations might be built in, as dependencies between the results of some of the iterations with other work packages can be made visible in the correspondent schedule. Milestones are a valid instrument respectively the main synchronization point (Timinger, 2017) for hybrid projects to show the overall schedule, so not the networked bar chart, and not the sprint plans.

For the resource and cost plan, the demanded resources for the agile work might be relatively stable, as soon as the number of iterations and the size of the development team is fixed. Still, when looking closer to it, in predictive approaches person days are estimated and tracked, in agile approaches, the size of a task in relation to a reference is estimated, and units are often not person days but for example story points. So also new estimation techniques are used. To get a budget, the number of iterations and the amount of resources that are available for one iteration are given, but there is no clear commitment of how much to develop with this budget. Story points will lead to prioritization of what from the product backlog will be realized within the given time and cost frame. So the task of planning resources and costs might be implemented differently by team members of the same team, with conflict being inevitable. Maybe some

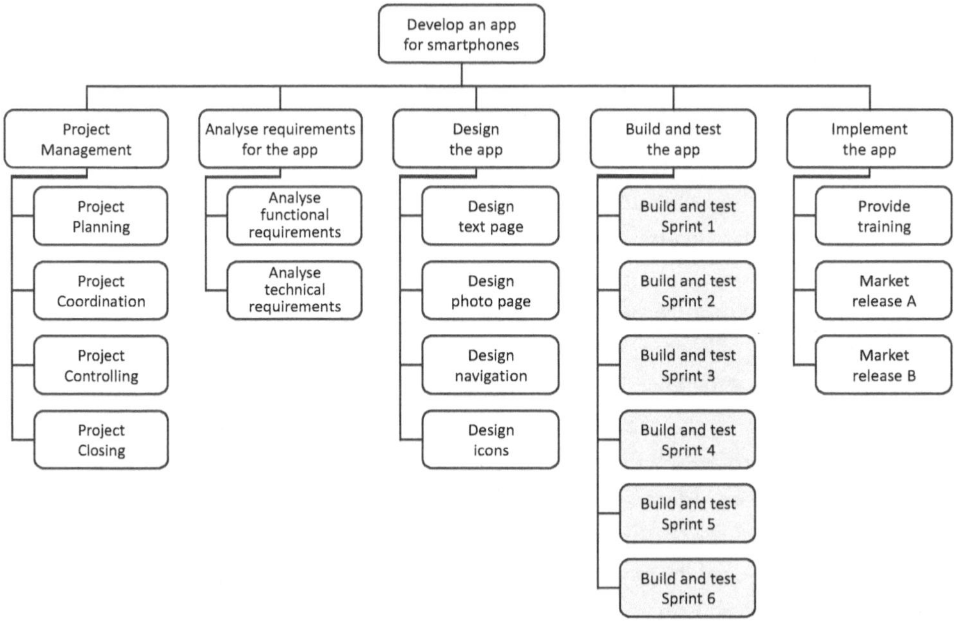

Figure 22.8: Example of a WBS showing a sequential hybrid approach

translations might help (Timinger, 2017), such as that one story point might be two person days for example. Important it is to clarify which estimation technique is based on which assumption.

The main implications of project planning are on the project assignment, the project stakeholder analysis, the scope plan and scheduling, and the building of the project organization, as new roles arise. Uncertainties need to be considered, and new methods (for example, the product backlog) and roles (for example, the product owner) integrated. The claim of being "complete" in understanding and planning details will not be fulfilled in hybrid approaches, all involved parties, especially the project owner but also other relevant stakeholders must be resilient enough to act accordingly.

Implications for project controlling

There is a fundamental difference regarding planning and in consequence controlling in a predictive or an adaptive approach (see characteristics described earlier in this chapter). This has implications for project controlling in a hybrid project.

When working adaptive in one or more phases of the project, a new "hybrid" element is added to the controlling of the gained results. In a project with a sequential hybrid approach, sprint reviews are performed in the adaptive phase(s) to review the actual sprint and hand over the value-creating products to the customers. In addition, on a meta-level, the project manager needs to keep the overview of the complete project and needs to consider the consequences of the results of one iteration to the overall project plan. The project manager needs to check how much budget on the project level is still available and if the actual status of the project has any consequences on stakeholders or risks. A project manager might not interfere in the operational iterations of the developers, the agile coach, and the product owner, but checks at the end of iterations' overall consequences on the project level (Patzak and Rattay, 2018: 672).

The same is valid for a parallel hybrid approach, thus here both worlds exist in parallel. It must be clearly defined how controlling is done for the predictively planned work packages and phases, and how the results from the sprint reviews and retrospectives are integrated into an overall project control. Different controlling methods and techniques exist in parallel and need to be combined. The work breakdown structure on the one side, the product backlog on the other side, where focusing on the progress of scope, schedule, and costs on the one side, and on newly defined and prioritized features for the next iteration on the other side, having the continuous delivery of value-creating results in focus.

An important method that is included in many adaptive methodologies, such as Scrum, is the performance of sprint reviews and sprint retrospectives. The timing of these reviews and retrospectives, and therefore the cycle of the iterations, will have to be synchronized with the project controlling cycles in the overall project. Is the review/retrospective done shortly before the overall project controlling is happening and the representative of the development team presents the result to the overall project team? What if the project controlling is set according to milestones and not according to fixed "iteration" durations – how is the synchronization managed? When performing an integrative controlling meeting with all core team members, the different foci in controlling, the different controlling methods and techniques, and the different controlling schedules must be integrated and accepted by all involved parties.

Furthermore controlling usually leads to the necessity of making decisions. How are decisions on changes taken in hybrid projects? If for example, the number of iterations has to change, the development team needs for example two more iterations, the project owner might need to decide on whether this is possible or not, as the overall project milestone plan is affected, and more budget is needed. If the development team decides in a retrospective, that the duration of its iterations shall not be four weeks but for example two weeks, the project manager needs to be asked, as there might be dependencies on other work packages, correlations to stakeholders, and risks. The product owner decides on which requirements may be taken on the product backlog, and with which priorities. In an adaptive approach, this is not considered to be a change, but this way of planning is an element of how adaptive working is happening. In a hybrid approach though, changes in the product backlog and/or its priorities may affect others in the project team, and again must be agreed on with others but the product owner and the development team. Also, in case the project owner has an overall interest in the product under development, is the last decision-maker on the product backlog and its priorities really solely rest on the product owner or is it not more a combined responsibility of the product and the project owner? Change processes and decision-making must be clearly defined.

Concerning progress reporting, a question is how the progress shown in a work breakdown structure or a Gantt chart, can be integrated into a single report with the progress shown in a product backlog and/or a burndown chart. Often there is an existing template for a project report in a company, historically developed in a predictive environment. Same as with the templates for project assignments, where for example a product vision might be integrated into the project assignment template for the projects, also the project progress report must be altered, to show the actual status of the product backlog and/or the results from the last respectively upcoming sprint plan together with the overall project status.

Conclusion

This chapter aimed to provide support to project managers and project owners/sponsors in their choice of a fitting approach for their projects. We discussed the characteristics of the predictive and the adaptive approaches and their applicability. Based on a deeper understanding of the approaches, it is understandable that the majority of projects today combine elements of both approaches into a hybrid approach. However, this should not be an accidental consequence, but a deliberate design decision by the project manager and project owner. We distinguished three types of hybrid: sequential, parallel, and integrated, and discussed their implications for project management methods.

With this chapter, we hope that we have disarmed the myth that the predictive approach is outdated. Both the predictive and the adaptive approaches have their qualities and their applicability. However, quite often a combination of both is the optimal design for a project. It is therefore up to the project manager to make an informed decision about how a project should be approached.

References and further reading

Beck, K., Beedle, M., van Bennekum, A., Cockburn, A., Cunningham, W., Fowler, M., Grenning, J., Highsmith, J., Hunt, A., Jeffries, R., Kern, J., Marick, B., Martin, R. C., Mellor, S., Schwaber, K., Sutherland, J. and Thomas, D. (2001). History: The Agile Manifesto. Retrieved from http://agilemanifesto.org/history.html

Chin, C. M. M. and Spowage, A. C. (2010). Defining & classifying project management methodologies. *PM World Today*, 12(5), 1–9.

Cohen, D., Lindvall, M. and Costa, P. (2003). Agile software development. *DACS SOAR Report*, 11.

Gemino, A., Horner Reich, B. and Serrador, P. M. (2021). Agile, traditional, and hybrid approaches to project success: is hybrid a poor second choice? *Project Management Journal*, 52(2), 161–175.

Hohl, P., Klünder, J., van Bennekum, A., Lockard, R., Gifford, J., Münch, J., Stupperich, M. and Schneider, K. (2018). Back to the future: Origins and directions of the "Agile Manifesto" – views of the originators. *Journal of Software Engineering Research and Development*, 6(1), 1–27.

International Organization for Standardization (2015) *ISO/IEC 38500:2015: Information technology - Governance of IT for the organization*. International Organization for Standardization, Geneva.

Lockard, R. and Gifford, J. (2017). Agile Uprising Podcast: Manifesto Co-Author Interview: Jim Highsmith. Agile Uprising Coalition. Retrieved from https://agileuprising.libsyn.com/manifesto-co-author-interview-jim-highsmith

Project Management Institute (2021). *A guide to project management body of knowledge' (PMBOK Guide)*, Seventh edition. Project Management Institute, Newtown Square, PA.

Qumer, A. and Henderson-Sellers, B. (2008). A framework to support the evaluation, adoption and improvement of agile methods in practice. *Journal of Systems and Software*, 81(11), 1899–1919.

Serrador, P. and Pinto, J. K. (2015). Does agile work?—A quantitative analysis of agile project success. *International Journal of Project Management*, 33(5), 1040–1051.

Smith, P. G. (2008). CHANGE: EMBRACE IT, DON'T DENY IT Tools and techniques inspired by software development can introduce the flexibility needed to make changes during product development with minimal disruption. *Research Technology Management*, 51(4), 34–40.

Špundak, M. (2014). Mixed agile/traditional project management methodology – reality or illusion? *Procedia - Social and Behavioral Sciences*, 119(2014), 939–948.

Steven, M., Mary, P., Lapham, A., Miller, S., Chick, T. and Ozkaya, I. (2013). Parallel Worlds: Agile and Waterfall Differences and Similarities. Retrieved from http://www.sei.cmu.edu

Thesing, T., Feldmann, C. and Burchardt, M. (2021). Agile versus Waterfall Project Management: Decision model for selecting the appropriate approach to a project. *Procedia Computer Science*, 181, 746–756.

Timinger, H. (2017). *Modernes Projektmanagement, 1. Auflage*. Berlin: Wiley Verlag

Turner, JR. (2014). *The Handbook of Project-Based Management: Leading Strategic Change in Organizations,* 4th Edition. New York: McGraw-Hill.

Turner, J. R. and Cochrane, R. A. (1993). Goals-and-methods matrix: Coping with projects with ill defined goals and/or methods of achieving them. *International Journal of Project Management*, 11(2), 93–102.

Von Rosing, M., Von Scheel, J. and Gill, A. Q. (2014). Applying agile principles to BPM. *The Complete Business Process Handbook: Body of Knowledge from Process Modeling to BPM*, 1, 553–577.

Whiteley, A., Pollack, J. and Matous, P. (2021). The origins of... agile and iterative methods. *Journal of Modern Project Management*, 8(3), 20–29.

Chapter 23

Scenario planning

Rodney Turner

Introduction

In Chapter 5, we described the complexity of projects. We saw that conventional project management is not good at managing complex projects. The management of complexity requires innovation and experimentation, while conventional project management emphasizes control, Keegan and Turner (2002). On defence projects during the 1940s and 1950s, experimentation, discovery, and innovation were the norm. On those projects, time was critical to be ahead of the enemy, but cost was not so important. When he became the US Secretary of Defence in 1961, Robert McNamara required the achievement of cost and time targets, which pushed project management down the current conventional approach emphasizing much greater control. John Kay and Mervyn King (2020) talk about resolvable and radical uncertainty. Resolvable uncertainty is known-knowns, what Frank Knight (1921) and John Maynard Keynes (1936) called risk. Radical uncertainty is known-unknowns or unknown-unknowns. Resolvable uncertainty creates puzzles, which can be solved by deductive means. Conventional project management is good at solving puzzles. Radical uncertainty creates mysteries, which cannot be solved, but can be better understood by inductive or abductive means. John Kay and Mervyn King suggest the creation of narratives. Narratives create scenarios which help us better understand what might happen, and deal with what does happen. Dwight Eisenhower is reputed to have said:

DOI: 10.4324/9781003274179-26

> In preparing for battle, I have found plans are useless, but planning is indispensable.

Plans are solutions to puzzles. But warfare is radical uncertainty, so plans are useless. But through planning, we create narratives, of how the battle might evolve. We expound on different scenarios, and though the battle may not evolve exactly as any of the scenarios, but having pictures of what might happen we can better respond to what does happen.

In Chapter 33, we described the paper by Barry Klein and William Meckling (1958) in which they describe the management of a complex defence project. They describe the actions of two people whom they call the optimist and the sceptic. The optimist assumes they know what the end configuration looks like and works towards that. If they are correct, that will lead to the cheapest outcome. However, it is likely they will not be correct, and there will be a considerable amount of change and rework, adding to the cost. The sceptic assumes they do not know what the exact final configuration will look like and envisages several scenarios. They develop them in parallel, eliminating some as more information becomes available. They do the experimentation, discovery, and innovation suggested above. Because they work on several scenarios, their cost will be greater than if the optimist is right about their one scenario. But because change and rework will be avoided, the cost will be less than if the optimist is wrong. The sceptic is basically doing scenario planning, and creating narratives. Below we describe scenario planning, and a related construct, future perfect planning.

Scenario planning

Scenario planning is primarily used by organizations to plan organizational strategy (Chermack, 2011; Heffernan, 2020). It is also widely used in urban and land planning (Chakraborty & McMillan, 2015; Goodspeed, 2019). In these two areas, it is used to plan what the end product will look like, rather than to plan how to achieve the end product, but that is what the name suggests; it is used to plan scenarios. Scenario planning in an organizational context was first used at Shell in the early 1970s (Heffernan, 2020). Their strategic planning had been a heavily bureaucratic exercise. An idiosyncratic executive, Pierre Wack, regarded these forecasts as a dangerous substitute for real thinking, and it was too easy to mistake financial models for reality. They decided the world was going to change, so they developed stories for what the changed world might look like, many of which challenged conventional wisdom. As a result, they restructured and were better able to respond to changing events than other oil companies. Some people credit the US military or the Manhattan Project in the 1940s with first scenario planning. However, Machiavelli (1532) describes scenario planning and credits a Greek general from about 200 BC with using it. Dwight Eisenhower suggested that in battle, you cannot know the outcome, but planning helps you envisage scenarios, and better respond to what does happen.

Method

The left-hand column of Figure 23.1, shows a model for scenario planning, combining and adapting models by Goodspeed (2019) and Chermack (2011).

Preparation

You need to identify the problem the project is intended to solve, and carefully define its purpose. Develop the expected outcomes. Following Klein and Meckling (1958),

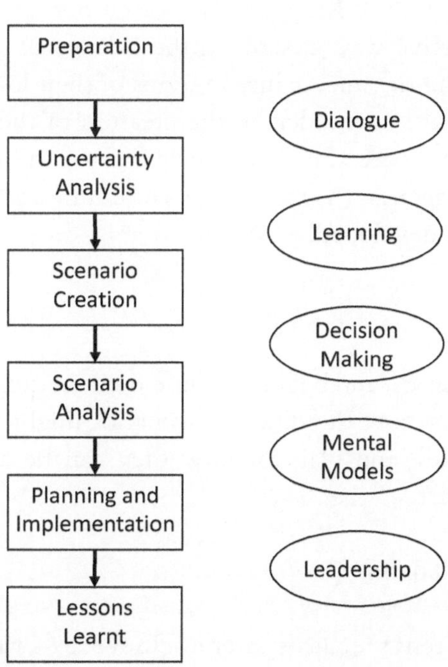

Figure 23.1: Scenario planning

there should be several different possible versions. Also develop the expected scope of the project, and the timeframe. Identify the stakeholders and their needs, build the scenario team, and define roles. It can also be useful for understanding the organizational context, history and culture. Construct a project proposal.

Uncertainty analysis

The team needs to understand what is creating the uncertainty. The definition of the project's end product is not well defined. Why not? What internal and external forces create that uncertainty? Forces include forces from the context, PESTLE (political. economic, social, technical, legal and environmental), and competitive forces from the industry. A SWOT analysis can help define the business concept. Conduct interviews with stakeholders and other people who may be able to help.

Scenario creation

Write scenario stories (Kay & King, 2020). Sketch out alternative outcomes for the project in a qualitative way, describing the balance of competing outcomes. Rank the forces creating the uncertainty in terms of their level of uncertainty and impact. Involve relevant stakeholders in the creation of the stories, and develop a communication strategy. Research may help reduce the uncertainty, so begin to develop a research agenda. A strategy for communicating with and engaging stakeholders should be developed.

Scenario analysis

Further refine the scenarios, and begin to define them in quantitative terms. Begin to develop strategies for how the different scenarios might be achieved. Identify any undesired outcomes, and plan for how they can be avoided. Identify and pursue the future perfect.

Implementation and planning

Plan for how the different scenarios can be achieved. As the project progresses, information will become available (and reduce uncertainty), which says some scenarios are more likely and more realistic than others, and so the range of options can be reduced. As work progresses, it is important to revisit the original, problem and purpose, and ensure work is being done to achieve those. The team should constantly question, question, question, and watch for and interpret signals. Strategies should be revisited. Opportunities for building resilience and robustness should be identified. It is the sceptic approach or attitudes that apply here.

Lessons learnt

Once finished lessons learnt should be recorded. Was the project purpose achieved, and how satisfied are the stakeholders? How well does the final solution satisfy the original project's purpose, the business objectives, and the project management objectives of scope, cost and time? What lessons are there for avoiding similar uncertainty on future projects? What can the organization learn, and what can future projects learn?

Future perfect planning

We now consider future perfect planning, which is based on the concept of the future perfect tense, what will have been. We place ourselves in the future and try to imagine what the past will have been like. We know what objectives we want to achieve, so envisage what work needs to be done to achieve them. It is believed that planning with a future perspective leads to better results. Fuglsang and Mattson (2011) describe the use of future perfect planning on a small but complex innovation project. Pitsis et al. (2003) describe the planning and management of a project to build storm water tunnels in Sydney in advance of the Olympic Games using a future perfect lens. The project was not overtly planned and managed using future perfect planning, but Pitsis et al. suggest it can be analyzed from that perspective.

Pitsis et al. (2003) suggest that future perfect planning is different from scenario planning. If it is different, it is because it comes with a different mindset. Scenario planning was first developed by practitioners. They developed something that worked for them. It worked; so there was no need for theory. Future perfect planning was developed by academics, and academics must support their new theories by reference to existing theories. So the theory behind future perfect planning builds on the work of Schütz (1967) and Weick (1979, 1995), and the concepts of sense-making and sense-giving promoted by Weick. Scenario planning and future perfect planning had different starting points, but we will end up in the same place. We will recommend the process in Figure 23.1 as a process to follow for future perfect planning, with the word "scenario" replaced by "method". Thus, *Scenario creation* becomes *Method creation* and *Scenario analysis* is replaced by *Method analysis*.

There is uncertainty behind the goals and means of achieving some future end state. Goals are not abstract and are not neutral; they are together a construct to achieve some uncertain future. The future is approached through a heuristic trick. It is perceived as if it has already happened. We try to make sense of what the future will be, and it is then easier to imagine a series of events to reach the desired future. At some point the future "will have been" (future perfect), and we imagine what we need to do to reach that will have been state. The sense-making approach needs to be distinguished from the idea that we can have objective knowledge of the future. Our ideas about the future derive from belief (Weick, 1995). People need to engage in dialogue (Pitsis et al., 2003), to model goals, share mental models and metaphors, and select activities and resources to achieve the desired goals.

Fuglsang and Mattson (2011) develop a three-step process for conducting future perfect planning on an innovation project. The three steps are:

1 Gather data about the current situation, which they say is sense-making – this is preparation.
2 Analyse the data to create mental models of possible futures, which they say is sense-giving – this is uncertainty analysis.
3 Construct future states. They suggest many small ideas can be constructed from which a whole will emerge – this is method creation.

This is in fact the first three steps in Figure 23.1, so we also suggest it for future perfect planning, with the word "scenario" replaced by "method". Thus we propose that the process can be used to create narratives for megaprojects with both uncertain objectives and uncertain methods of achieving those objectives. Following the process can create mental models for what the project will achieve and how it will be delivered.

Influencing factors

The right-hand column of Figure 23.1 shows factors which Chermack (2011) suggests influence scenario planning. Pitsis et al. (2003) conducted an ethnographic study of the Sydney storm water project by attending meetings and interviewing people. They describe the five influencing factors.

Dialogue

Dialogue and conversation are essential to scenario planning. The purpose is to create stories, share mental models, and engage stakeholders. There needs to be a shared understanding of how the forces influence the scenarios. It is necessary to communicate and engage with stakeholders. However, the overall aim is to create narratives, and that will be achieved by the project team talking amongst themselves. Havermans et al. (2015) suggest narratives can frame problems in a new light, and shape actions.

The storm water tunnel project was conducted as an alliance, and that required all the parties to share the same values. They needed to be well communicated between the alliance members. A project culture was established based on shared behaviours. They had a slogan, "Do what is best for the project". Turner (2014) suggests that the best outcomes are achieved if the parties to a project do what is best for the project, and not themselves individually, and that was the shared value of this project. Project team members were encouraged to conduct strange conversations (Weick, 1979). Meetings were held where the agenda was unclear, the process emergent and the outcomes unknown. Attendees were encouraged to express anxieties and make suggestions. This might lead to tensions, but hidden problems emerged and were solved.

Learning

Learning is a key driver of scenario planning. Planning is essentially a learning activity, as suggested by Dwight Eisenhower. It is important to understand how the project fits within its context, and the impact of the internal and external forces, and that may require readaptation of beliefs and the creation of new meaning. New meaning is required as scenario stories are constructed, and as they influence project decision-making. The narratives and dialogue will help construct meaning, which adds to learning. Above, we also emphasized the need for lessons learnt after the project. What worked, what didn't work, which one of the scenarios turned out to be the end result and why? Understanding the lessons learnt might help with future projects.

The excitement of the storm water tunnel project created a focus on creativity with constant envisioning and revisioning in a future perfect way of thinking, as suggested by Fuglsang and Mattson (2011); sense-making and sense-giving. This led people to solve problems not previously encountered. Considerable innovation was required, which not have been achieved if the project had been planned in a conventional way. Innovations were needed in design, drilling methods and maintaining safe working conditions. The belief was that learning should be accelerated and focused. Strategizing should be linked to the future vision.

Decision-making

Decision-making is critical to understanding scenario planning and how it works. Scenarios provide a venue for testing decisions and manipulating forces. Scenario planning helps the organization make decisions about expected futures. Decision-makers can test the impact of different policies and examine their effects. By creating shared mental models and strategic conversations, different scenarios can undergo constant scrutiny and modification, to ensure they provide and informed perspective of future uncertainty. We saw in the introduction how bounded rationality and bounded manageability can influence decision-making, and lead to satisficing. The team must make the best decision with the information available, and be ready to modify the decision as more information becomes available. That is the approach adopted by the sceptic in Klein and Meckling's (1958) paper.

On the storm water tunnel project, team members were expected to think creatively and laterally, doing what this project needed, rather than applying tired solutions from previous projects. This they thought would instil future perfect thinking on the life of the project. This linked back to learning; they had to learn new methods. End games reinforced the future perfect thinking. One project leader is reported as saying:

> We know where we want to be, where we want to go, and where we want to finish up. We need to plan the end and work out each step to get there so everything is synchronised.

Mental models

Mental models further help learning and decision-making, and help people navigate unfamiliar terrain. Mental models are people's assumptions and beliefs, based on their experience. Mental models must be constantly questioned during the scenario planning process, but they provide cognitive maps to help people, deal with uncertainty and explore options. Sense-making (Weick, 1995), which we will revisit below, is a process of creating a mental model. A mental model is generally considered a memory representation, with a salient mental-imagery component, depicting states of affairs but linked to or expressed in terms of concepts, principles, and knowledge (Klein et al., 2006).

The storm water tunnel project did things to reinforce the alliance culture and the objectives of the project. Banners were hung in the open plan offices declaring the alliance principles, emphasizing the best for the project and a no-blame culture. In the HQ office there was a fish tank with clear water to emphasize the goal of the project to clean up the water of Sydney harbour (After the project whales returned to Sydney harbour). In the kitchen, the walls were decorated with press clippings describing the project. And there were charts displaying achievement against the five Key Performance Indicators. Staff members displayed considerable awareness of the alliance culture.

Leadership

Leadership is a key component of organizational change. If the leadership is not supportive, the project is likely to fail. For further information on leadership, we suggest Müller and Turner (2010) and Drouin et al. (2021).

On the storm water tunnel project, there was a Project Alliance leadership team (PALT) consisting of senior managers from the client and the three main contractors. On the agenda of each PALT team meeting was an agenda item, "Projecting feelings, concerns and issue". If an issue was raised it remained on the agenda until it was resolved, maintaining future perfect thinking and acting as a reality check. The emphasis was that leadership should be entrepreneurial, that is it should be collaborative and collective, and not individual and hierarchical. Negotiation and compromise were also important. Power should be shared, and risks and rewards shared.

In Chapter 33, we described bounded rationality, and the need to make decisions with limited information. The Australian culture of "She'll be right, mate", led to satisficing to do something and make it work.

Conclusion

Conventional project management is a deductive construct that is good at solving the puzzles we meet under resolvable uncertainty. It assumes we are managing known-knowns, and emphasises control. Risk management as it is taught assumes risks have known probabilities and known outcomes. Complex projects require a different approach to their management. We need an inductive or abductive approach that creates narratives. We need to envisage different scenarios, start by planning for them all, and then eliminate scenarios as more information becomes available. In this chapter, we described scenario planning and future planning as ways of taking a more experimental, descriptive and innovative approach to managing projects.

References and further reading

Chakraborty, A & McMillan, A. (2015). Scenario planning for urban planners: toward a practitioner's guide. *Journal of the American Planning Association*. **81**(1): 18–29.

Chermack, TJ. (2011). *Scenario planning in organizations: How to create, use and assess scenarios*. San Francisco, CA: Berrett-Koehler Publishers.

Drouin, N, Sankaran, S, Van Marrewijk, A & Müller, R, (eds.). (2021). *Megaproject leaders: Reflections on personal life stories*. Cheltenham, UK, and Northampton, MA: Edward Elgar Publishing

Fuglsang, L & Mattson, J. (2011). Making sense of innovation: a future perfect approach. *Journal of Management & Organization*, **17**(4): 448–458.

Goodspeed, R. (2019). Scenario planning: embracing uncertainty to make better decision. *JSTOR and Lincoln Institute of Land Policy* (Downloaded, 20 December 2020).

Havermans LA, Keegan, AE & Den Hartog, DN. (2015). Choosing your words carefully: leaders' narratives of complex emergent problem resolution. *International Journal of Project Management*, **33**(5): 973–984.

Heffernan, M. (2020). *Unchartered: How to map the future together*. London, New York, Sydney, Toronto and New Delhi: Simon & Schuster.

Kay, J & King, M. (2020). *Radical uncertainty: Decision making for an unknown future.* London: The Bridge Street Press.

Keegan, AE & Turner, JR. (2002). The management of innovation in project based firms. *Long Range Planning,* **35**: 367–388.

Keynes, JM. (1936). *The general theory of employment, interest and money.* London: Palgrave Macmillan.

Klein, B & Meckling, W. (1958). Application of operations research to development decisions. *Operations Research,* **6**(3): 352–363.

Knight, F. (1921) *Risk, uncertainty and profit.* Boston, MA and New York: Houghton Miffin Company.

Müller, R & Turner, JR., (2010). *Project-oriented Leadership.* Aldershott: Gower.

Pitsis, TS, Clegg, SR, Marosszeky, M & Rura-Polley, T. (2003). Constructing the Olympic dream: a future perfect strategy of project management. *Organizational Science,* **14**(5): 574–590.

Schütz, A. (1967). *The phenomenology of the social world.* Evanston, IL: Northwestern Press.

Turner, JR. (2014). *The handbook of project-based management: Leading strategic change in organizations,* 4th Edition. New York: McGraw-Hill.

Weick, KE. (1979). *The social psychology of organizing. Topics in social psychology.* Reading, MA: Addison-Wesley.

Weick, KE. (1995). *Sensemaking in organizations, Foundations for organizational science.* Thousand Oaks, CA: Sage.

Part IV
People

Part IV explores people working on projects. We start with the basics, the project manager, the project sponsor, the project team and engaging stakeholders. There are then two chapters on leadership. We describe a new model of leadership and then consider balanced leadership. There is a chapter on motivating Generation Y to work on projects. We then describe diversity, behavioural biases and ethics.

Chapter 24: The project manager

Projects vary considerably in scale, complexity and context and so do the roles, responsibilities, and profiles of those who manage them. The primary role of the project manager is to meet goals and deliver value on behalf of the project owner and there are things that need to be done on all projects to achieve this. What project managers actually do and the way that they do must be tailored to the needs of each project and will reflect the style and experience of the project manager. Lynn Crawford identifies what project managers do, how they become project managers and develop their competence, the personal characteristics they bring to the role and how this interacts with the many different contexts within which they operate.

Chapter 25: The project sponsor

Lynn Crawford describes the role of the project sponsor. Project sponsors provide a critical link between the project owner or owning organisation and the projects that are undertaken to deliver desired value and benefits. Effective project sponsorship and top management support have consistently been shown to be key to successful project delivery. Yet the sponsor role is most often a part-time role, with a limited number of people with sufficient authority and seniority available to meet the governance requirement of taking accountability for the project. Those who are asked to take on the role are usually over-committed

 DOI: 10.4324/9781003274179-27

and time-poor. The role is not well understood, there is often little guidance provided and little appetite or time for training and development. This chapter aims to provide greater clarity on the nature of the sponsor role, the governance and support responsibilities, what they do, what it takes to develop the skills to be effective and tailor actions and behaviours to suit the needs of each project.

Chapter 26: The project team

Projects are performed by people. Nevertheless, the literature is relatively silent when it comes to people in projects, their needs and capabilities, and the dynamics of team development. Reinhard Wagner reveals why projects are a suitable organisational form for people to fulfil their basic needs, namely autonomy, competence and relatedness. Because without the intrinsic motivation of those involved, not much can be achieved in projects. So even when selecting team members for a project, attention should be paid to their motivation and fit. Team development begins early in the project, often even before the first substantive work has been prepared. Since the composition of teams often changes over the course of the project, team development is an ongoing task. Leadership plays an essential role in establishing a viable team. Currently, leadership in numerous projects is changing from something that one person performs to a self-organised, balanced effort within the team.

Chapter 27: Engaging project stakeholders

Pernille Eskerod and Martina Huemann offer a comprehensive understanding of stakeholder engagement, which is defined as the purposeful stakeholder-related practices to support value creation by the project. In contemporary projects, stakeholder engagement is rather considered a must to provide fertile grounds for co-creating better futures. Different perspectives on stakeholder engagement are taken. These include project stakeholder engagement as mindset, process, toolbox and roles. The basis for stakeholder engagement is a mindset that supports stakeholder orientation. Principles of such a mindset include inclusiveness, value transparency, perceived fairness, future orientation, co-creation, and multiple engagement forms. Stakeholder engagement processes a cyclic and comprise (1) identifying and empathising with project stakeholders, (2) building a relationship, interacting and co-creating with project stakeholders, and (3) disengaging project stakeholders.

Additionally, the authors offer a toolbox to support stakeholder engagements and summarise the roles on projects for stakeholder engagement.

Chapter 28: Project leadership model

Natalya Sergeeva, Graham Winch, and Eunice Maytorena-Sanchez present a new model, called the Project Leadership Model, which focuses on what leaders how leaders make sense of their project, and thereby create narratives to build knowledge and understanding of the project. The model encompasses sense-making, relating, projecting, creating and judging. The origins of the model can be traced back to the concept of incomplete leadership. The authors provide examples of the model in practice. They further discuss the nature, role and types of project narratives and counter-narratives, and investigate the process of narrating as fundamental to leading projects. The practical implications of project narratives and narrating are outlined.

Chapter 29: Balanced leadership

Ralf Müller addresses balanced leadership in projects. More specifically, leadership approaches, their particularities in a project context, and the need to balance different leadership approaches in situational contingency over time. He starts with a brief overview of leadership, definition, positioning against management, and the differences between leadership styles and approaches. Sections about horizontal, shared, distributed, and balanced leadership follow. Finally, the coordination needed for shifting leadership approaches over time is explained through the concept of the socio-cognitive space. Practical examples support the discussions of related models and processes. In addition to understanding the differences and particularities of the approaches, the reader will benefit from the chapter's guidance in choosing a 'best fit' leadership approach in different project situations.

Chapter 30: Motivation of young project professionals

Martina Huemann and Ruth Lechler examine what motivates young project professionals from Generation Y to work on projects. Generation Y has unique preferences when it comes to work, highly valuing flexibility, growth opportunities, and engaging in meaningful tasks. They argue that projects provide an appealing work environment that aligns with the career aspirations of these professionals. Drawing upon self-determination theory, they share their research findings and introduce the Model of Young Project Professionals' Motivation. Within this model, four sets of motivators are identified: learning and development, creating and delivering, relating and connecting, and working autonomously. Closing the chapter, we provide practical recommendations for organisations to attract and retain young project professionals, focusing on creating an environment that supports these motivators.

Chapter 31: Managing diversity

The individuals working together on a project differ in personality, gender, age, management status, work experience, seniority, cultural background, etc. In any social system such as a project, diversity is inherent and cannot be prevented. Anna Khodijah describes how diversity, in particular cultural diversity, influences the project and how the project manager (and project team) should deal with the effect of diversity to reach high performance. Several practices to manage diversity in the project are proposed.

Chapter 32: Behavioural bias

Behavioural science has witnessed an explosion in the number of biases identified by behavioural scientists, to more than two hundred at present. Bent Flyvbjerg identifies the most important behavioural biases for project management, including political and cognitive bias. Specifically, the chapter focuses on strategic misrepresentation, optimism bias, uniqueness bias, the planning fallacy, overconfidence bias, and the base-rate fallacy. Each bias is defined and its impacts on project management are explained, with examples. Base-rate neglect is identified as a primary reason that projects underperform. This is supported by the presentation of the most comprehensive set of base rates that exists in project management scholarship, from 2,062 projects. Finally, reference class forecasting, premortems, and decision hygiene are recommended as cures to bias.

Chapter 33: Ethics

In an increasingly uncertain and contested world, ethics plays a crucial role in enabling professionals to conduct their affairs, make decisions and interact with others. Darren Dalcher provides managers with the vocabulary, practical tools and frameworks needed to addresses ethical and moral challenges. He identifies the importance of ethics, before providing a snapshot of ethical challenges and attitudes and presenting some of the key pressures on professionals. He introduces ethics as a clash of value systems leading to ethical dilemmas and offers frameworks and tools for considering and utilising ethics at the personal, collective and professional levels. The concept of responsibility is introduced as a lens for developing professional practice, before highlighting a multiplicity of types of responsibility and presenting a professional code of ethics that can be applied in organisations seeking to develop moral and ethical capability. The approach thus positions ethics as a critical ingredient in avoiding moral hazards and securing enduring success and sustainability.

Chapter 24

The project manager

Lynn Crawford

Introduction

People are central to projects and their management. In the words of Peter Morris, "projects are done by people, for people, through people" (Morris, 2016, p. 368). Of the many people involved in the doing of projects, the project manager plays a key role, responsible for the planning and day-to-day management of the project and the project team in order to achieve goals set by the project owner. This may sound straightforward but will vary considerably according to the nature of the project and its context. This chapter will address some of the key aspects of the project manager role and how it may vary in different contexts. This will include authority and accountability, what the project manager does and the personal characteristics, knowledge, skills, qualifications and experience that are associated with successful performance of the role.

Authority and accountability

The role of the project manager was first recognised around the middle of the 20th century in large-scale engineering, construction, defence and aerospace projects. In this context, where projects were well defined, with largely physical end products generally driven through contracts, it was possible for the project manager to be given authority commensurate with accountability,

DOI: 10.4324/9781003274179-28

and this was considered a pre-requisite for the role. As societal expectations have changed and the types of endeavours identified as projects have increased and evolved, this expectation has become a rarity. As early as 1959, in a paper considered to be one of the first describing the project manager role, Gaddis (1959) acknowledged that the project manager may not have full or any direct authority over those performing the work of the project. There are a number of reasons for this.

Often, this is because project team members are employed by other organisations, report to functional managers in the performing organisation or are subject matter experts contributing to the project but reporting to the business unit or line managers. Many projects, particularly in the not-for-profit sector, involve volunteers whose contribution needs to be guided and nurtured. Where those doing the work are professional specialists, they will be responsible for and have the freedom to determine the details of their own work. In such cases, the project manager will be responsible for ensuring that project team members understand what is expected of them and what they should expect from one another. Finally, through forces of social change and multi-level communication, formal authority is largely a thing of the past outside the military. Project managers are increasingly required to meet accountability requirements through influence and effective relationships rather than the exercise of authority.

What project managers do

Essentially, project managers do whatever is required to achieve project goals which will often include reviewing, refining or defining the goals. What is required will vary according to the nature, size and complexity of the project and what it aims to achieve. A good generic overview of what this involves is provided by the Global Alliance for the Project Professions (GAPPS) in their Getting Stuff Done Framework.[1] This framework was developed by groups of globally representative and experienced practitioners who were asked to identify what really needs to be done on projects in order to achieve desired outcomes in a volatile, uncertain, complex and ambiguous environment. Terms and jargon specific to project management were avoided wherever possible so that the framework would be readily understood and broadly applicable. The resulting framework provides a useful summary of what project managers do. It does not directly reference any specific tools or techniques. The intention is that the

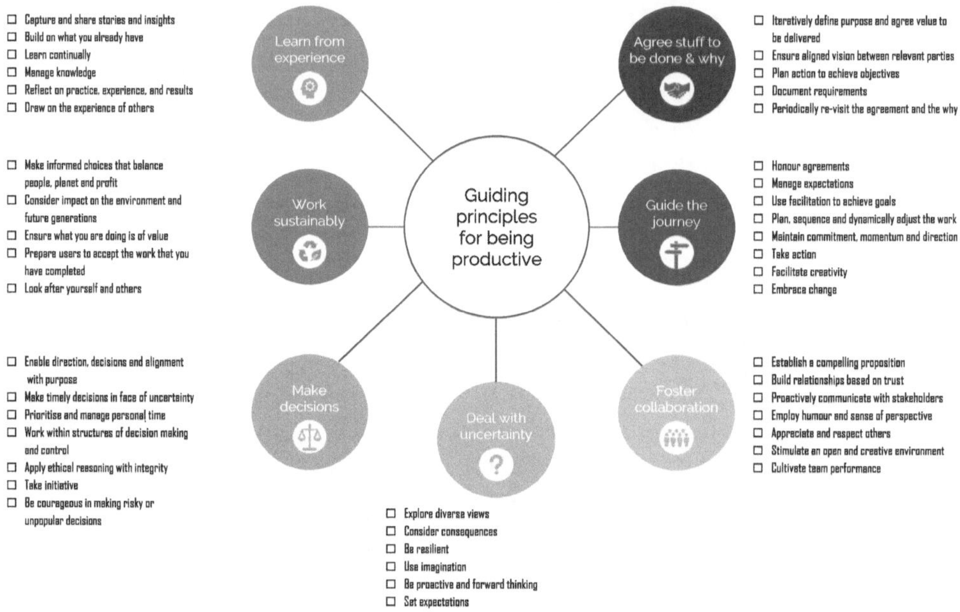

Figure 24.1: GAPPS getting stuff done framework V1.0

framework will provide a basis for deciding which methods, tools and techniques will be best suited to the specific project and its context (Figure 24.1).

The detail of what project managers are expected or required to do in their role is documented in many standards and guides. Like the GAPPS Getting Stuff Done Framework, most of these are generic, intended to be applicable to project managers of a wide range of endeavours including major infrastructure, organisational change, digital transformation, product and software development projects and any other time and resource-constrained endeavour "regardless of purpose, delivery approaches, life cycle model used, complexity, size, cost or duration" (ISO, 2022). These standards and guides have primarily been developed by practitioners drawing on their experience. Examples are ISO 21502:2020 Project, programme and portfolio management – guidance on project management (ISO, 2022), the International Project Management Association's Competence Baseline (ICB) and the knowledge and practice guides of major project management professional associations such as the Project Management Institute (2021) and the Association for Project Management (2019).

Early versions of these guides (1990s to pre-2020) focused on the knowledge, tools and techniques specific to project management and largely assumed that project goals would be set by the project owner. The project manager would then steer the project following a linear life cycle of phases such as initiation, planning, execution, and project close. This approach is still followed for many projects, particularly those involving capital investment in the production of physical end products typical of the construction and engineering sectors. Increasing social, economic and technological change and demand for customer responsiveness and faster delivery have led to the incorporation of more iterative or evolutionary life cycle approaches and adaptive delivery methods such as those referred to as agile. These different approaches have been incorporated into the more recent versions of standards and guides and project managers are now expected to be able to selectively apply a range of different approaches, tailored to the specific needs of their project and its context. Figure 24.2 illustrates the work of the project manager that reflects a project life cycle-based management of project approach (Morris, 2013) and agile iterations.

There are ample resources that the project manager can draw upon to guide them in their role. The challenge is to decide what needs to be done and how for their project. In a rapidly changing environment, they need to act flexibly, focusing on the delivery of value and developing the relationships necessary to enable the achievement of project goals through people. The basics of the project manager role remain much the same but the emphasis has changed over time as the application of project management approaches have been applied to an increasing range and type of endeavours in an increasingly fast-paced and complex world. Projects were initially conceptualised as largely self-contained defined temporary endeavours that could be planned in advance and controlled using well-defined processes, tools and techniques to deliver specific outputs. Over time there has been a realisation that projects are systems within systems that cannot be isolated from their environment, and that the delivery of value is dependent upon looking beyond specific project outputs to the outcomes and benefits they enable.

An illustration of this change in perspective is the move away from processes and knowledge areas towards project management principles in the seventh edition of the Project Management Institute's influential PMBOK®Guide (PMI, 2021). Twelve project management principles (Table 24.1) are intended to guide the behaviour of people involved in projects as they coordinate a collective effort, and facilitate, support and orchestrate the work required to deliver value through projects.

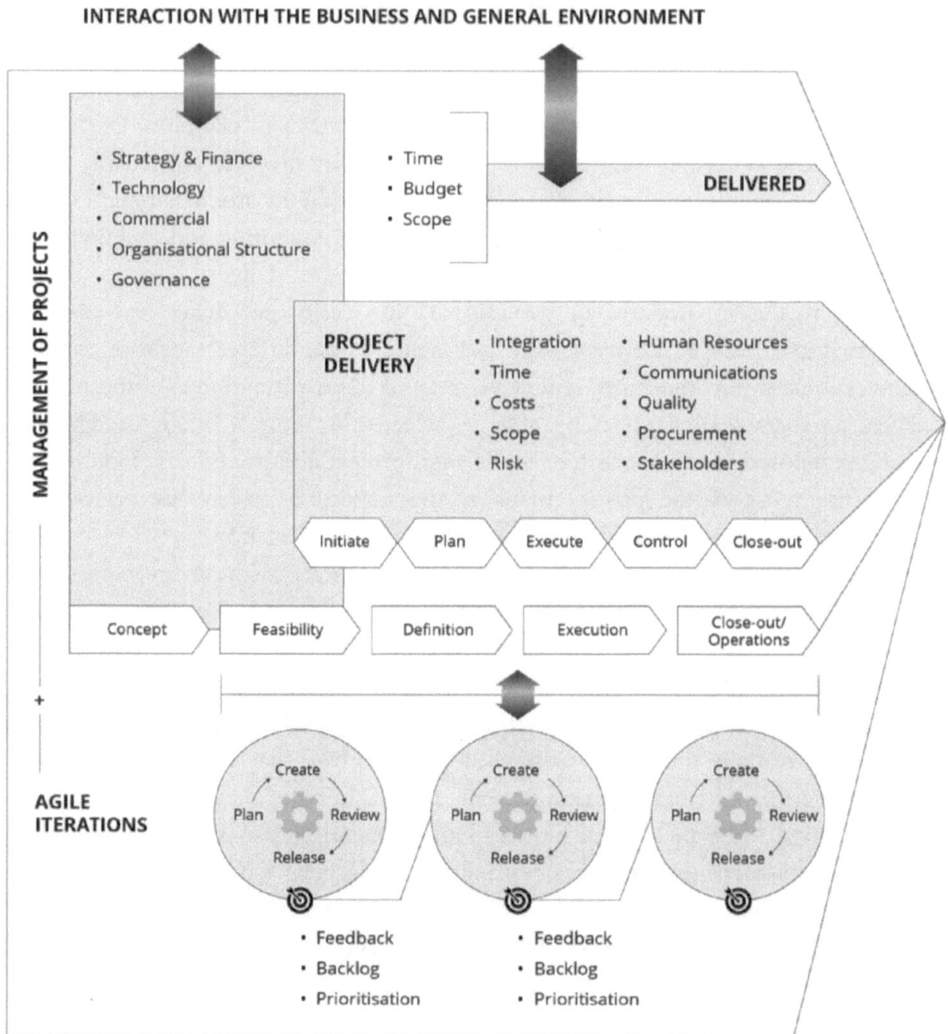

Figure 24.2: Combination of management of projects phases (Morris, 2013) and agile iterations

Considering the role of the project manager as that of a steward highlights the importance of acting ethically and responsibly, and taking care of the interests of others. It ties into the idea of working sustainably as proposed in the GAPPS GSD framework. As noted earlier, the era of command and control has passed, and the project manager must now achieve results through influence, collaboration

Table 24.1 Principles guiding project management (PMI, 2021)

Principles
1 Be a diligent, respectful and caring steward
2 Create a collaborative project team environment
3 Effectively engage with stakeholders
4 Focus on value
5 Recognise, evaluate and respond to system interactions
6 Demonstrate leadership behaviours
7 Tailor based on context
8 Build quality into processes and deliverables
9 Navigate complexity
10 Optimise risk responses
11 Embrace adaptability and resiliency
12 Enable change to achieve the envisioned future state

and effective engagement with a wide range of stakeholders. Focus on delivery of value including outcomes and benefits, rather than pre-defined outputs, has already been mentioned. To do this in a fast-paced and uncertain environment requires resilience and the ability to adapt to changing circumstances and needs. Project managers also need to be systems thinkers, taking a holistic approach and understanding the potential consequences of decisions and actions within and beyond the increasingly permeable and often arbitrary boundaries of their projects.

A particularly important part of the project manager's role, which is instinctively understood by many, is the need for action to achieve behavioural and organisational change to enable realisation of benefits. The primary purpose of some projects is organisational change and such projects may be led by a project, program, or change manager. Even projects which may not be conceptualised as organisational change projects will cause some degree of change to the environment, and to the way people do things. Often, behavioural, process and system changes are required in order to achieve the intended outcomes of the project. Where the focus is on the delivery of value from the project, the project manager's role must integrate project and organisational change management (Crawford et al., 2014; Hornstein, 2015).

Becoming a project manager

The majority of people who find themselves in project manager roles have qualifications and experience in a specific discipline such as engineering, architecture, information technology, computer science, business studies, marketing, communications, education or any number of other fields although it is now possible to take a first degree in project management. Becoming a project manager may be a specific career choice but is often a matter of opportunity or career progression from a specialist field to a more general and managerial role. In many cases, it begins with being asked to take over responsibility for a particular initiative. Those who enjoy being a project manager and choose to continue in the role tend to be those who thrive on challenges and have confidence in their ability to successfully tackle new and different tasks (Lloyd-Walker et al., 2018).

There are many postgraduate degrees available for those interested in academic qualifications to support the transition into or progression in a project manager role. They offer either industry-specific (eg construction, engineering) or generic coverage applicable to a wide range of project types and contexts. The Global Accreditation Center for Project Management Academic Programs (GAC)[2] provides assurance of the relevance and quality of education provided by bachelor, master and doctorate level degrees they accredit. This level of education is beneficial in developing the critical and systems thinking skills needed to tailor project management approaches and exercise the flexibility and interpersonal abilities required for projects in complex and uncertain environments.

For those seeking to develop their skills in project management, there are many opportunities for training in fundamentals and more advanced tools, techniques and approaches that are offered by private training organisations and professional associations. Recognition is available in the form of membership and certifications offered by professional associations such as the Project Management Institute (PMI), the International Project Management Association (IPMA) and the Association for Project Management (APM) which offers Chartered Project Professional (ChPP) status. In addition to project management certifications, project managers extend their capability and add to their career profiles by undertaking training and certification in specific areas such as earned value, risk, change management, and agile approaches and methodologies. Most of these certifications involve a short-duration training program and some form of exam. Professional association certifications such as those offered by IPMA and APM require evidence of practical experience at the level relevant to the certification being sought.

The primary path for developing as a project manager is through experience and the projects they manage. The GAPPS, in developing a performance-based competency framework for project managers, used seven factors to assess the management complexity of projects on which a project manager had worked as a basis for determining their level of competence (Table 24.2). According to the GAPPS CIFTER, using information technology project examples, the entry-level may be the implementation of a software package upgrade in a single business functional area; the next level may be the design of a new corporate website for a multinational manufacturing company and beyond that would be implementation of an enterprise resource planning or similar application across business areas in an environment where implementation has significant legal implications (GAPPS, 2007). In order to learn through experience, project managers need to be reflective practitioners who learn through failure as well as success.

Table 24.2 GAPPS CIFTER table for evaluating management complexity of projects (GAPPS, 2007)

Project management complexity factor	*Descriptor and points*			
1 Stability of the overall project context	Very high (1)	High (2)	Moderate (3)	Low or very low (4)
2 Number of distinct disciplines, methods, or approaches involved in performing the project	Low or very low (1)	Moderate (2)	High (3)	Very high (4)
3 Magnitude of legal, social, or environmental implications from performing the project	Low or very low (1)	Moderate (2)	High (3)	Very high (4)

(*Continued*)

Table 24.2 continued.

4 Overall expected financial impact (positive or negative) on the proiect's stakeholders	Low or very low (1)	Moderate (2)	High (3)	Very high (4)
5 Strategic importance of the project to the organisation or orqanisations involved	Very low (1)	Low (2)	Moderate (3)	High or very high (4)
6 Stakeholder cohesion regarding the characteristics of the product of the proiect	High or very high (1)	Moderate (2)	Low (3)	Very low (4)
7 Number and variety of interfaces between the project and other oroanisational entities	Very low (1)	Low (2)	Moderate (3)	High or very high (4)

Characteristics of effective project managers

Some people make a conscious choice to become a project manager but many find themselves managing projects through necessity or opportunity. Those who tend to enjoy managing projects are those who enjoy challenges and have confidence in their own ability to meet them. A considerable amount of research has been done to identify the characteristics of effective project managers. A worldwide study of leadership competency profiles of successful project managers found evidence of the importance of critical thinking, influence, motivation and conscientiousness across all project types (Müller & Turner, 2010). They also identified variations in the importance of leadership competencies according to application area, level of complexity, contract type and whether the project is mandatory, for renewal or repositioning.

A subsequent study (Moradi et al., 2020) comparing research and industry views on project managers' competencies, confirmed differences in the importance of

Table 24.3 Personal, perspective and interpersonal competencies of project managers considered most important (after Moradi et al., 2020)

Personal	(1) Leadership (2) Goal orientation (3) Creativity (4) Problem-solving (5) Teamwork and cooperation (6) Initiative (7) Analytical thinking (8) Decision-making (9) Flexibility (10) Self-confidence (11) Conceptual thinking (12) Information seeking (13) Ethics (14) Proactivity (15) Self-assessment (16) Self-control (17) Conscientiousness (18) Sensitivity (19) Directiveness (20) Experience (21) Assertiveness (22) Emotional resilience (23) Diagnostic of concepts (24) Perceptual objectivity (25) Trustworthiness (26) Stress management (27) Cognitive capability
Perspective	(1) Strategic direction (2) Developing others (3) Customer focus (4) Continuous improvement (5) Team selection (6) Efficiency orientation (7) Vision (8) Organisational awareness
Interpersonal	(1) Communication (2) Conflict management (3) Problem-solving (4) Negotiation (5) Teamwork and cooperation (6) Impact and Influence (7) Motivation (8) Cultural skills (9) Stakeholder management (10) Team management (11) Interpersonal understanding

competencies in organisational change, construction, engineering, information technology, metallurgical, international NGO and public sector projects. Overall, drawing on both research, standards and practitioner views, they identified the following personal, perspective and interpersonal competencies considered to be important for the effective project manager (Table 24.3).

In practice, supported by findings from research, the balance of importance of these competencies will vary according to the nature of the specific project management role and context.

Different project contexts

Project managers can be found in many different contexts, requiring vastly different levels of experience, disciplinary knowledge and expertise, and personal and interpersonal characteristics. Achievement of project goals remains central to the role and there are transferable skills and qualities but the scale and context may vary considerably.

Specialist or generalist

One question that is often asked and for which there is no definitive answer is whether the project manager needs to be experienced or qualified in the discipline, technology or business of the project they are managing. To some extent, the answer to this question lies in the size of the project and the project team. For small projects where the project manager is required to do a considerable amount of the work of the project, then they will need to have the skills and disciplinary expertise required to do that work. At the other end of the scale, where the project involves many different skills and technologies, the project manager cannot be qualified or experienced in all aspects, so their broader management and leadership skills become more important. It may also be important to put aside disciplinary expertise to avoid becoming too involved in the finer details of the project and focus on facilitating the integration of different disciplines and inputs, collaborating and working together to achieve the project goals.

Permanent or temporary

Projects are temporary and the project manager will therefore move from one project to another throughout their career. Some project managers are employed by organisations that have an ongoing pipeline of projects that provide continuous employment for project managers. Such organisations include large industrial and financial organisations where projects are used to maintain, renew and deliver new products, technology, infrastructure and services. Project managers in these organisations are well supported, are able to develop their skills and experience on diverse and increasingly complex projects and in many cases gain general management experience through postings to operational parts of the business. Where these organisations operate globally there is an opportunity to manage projects in other countries and across borders.

Organisations that do their business through projects, often referred to as project-based organisations such as consulting firms, engineering procurement, construction and commissioning organisations (EPCC) and general contractors also provide continuity of employment for project managers, with a diversity of project opportunities. Employment however may be affected by market demand and the effectiveness of business development to maintain a project pipeline. Such organisations are limited in their ability to predict demand for project resourcing as they are dependent upon market demand and the effectiveness of business development to fill their project pipeline, and this may affect the continuity of employment.

Project management consulting firms, that provide project managers and other project management personnel and services to client organisations, may employ project managers to work on one or more client projects at the same time or in succession providing an ongoing stream of work. Such work will however be affected by market demand and business development activity.

Some project management consulting firms and project owners with intermittent or varying project load will employ project managers on a contract basis. In such cases, the temporary or finite nature of projects can result in periods of unemployment. There is often a premium paid to project managers working on a contract basis and some project managers enjoy the ability to pick and choose their project, seeking challenge and variety. Project managers in research and development and community projects may also be employed on a contract basis that is dependent upon grant funding. Project managers working under such circumstances accept a level of uncertainty that may be offset by their enjoyment of a degree of personal control over their project management career.

Others, particularly those in the early to middle stages of their project management career, with personal and financial responsibilities, do not appreciate the level of uncertainty involved. In any case, project managers without clarity and confidence about their next project will, towards the end of the project, be looking for their next project opportunity.

Conclusion

Project managers are responsible for planning, managing and leading projects and the project team to achieve goals and deliver value on behalf of the project owner. The context in which this is done, the scale of the project, its level of interconnectivity with other projects and activities and the nature of the project owner and their expectations vary considerably from single resource initiatives to megaprojects. Therefore, although many people may be given the title of project manager, the variation in their skills, characteristics, and experience of what they are required to do will be significant. For those looking for project managers and for those wishing to take on or progress in the role there are ample resources to draw upon for guidance. What project manager actually do, and the way in which they do it will be influenced by their experience, learning and personal characteristics applied in context.

Notes

1 www.pmprofessions.net.
2 https://www.pmi.org/global-accreditation-center.

References and further reading

Association of Project Management. (2019). *APM Body of Knowledge*, 7th Edition. Princes Risborough: Association for Project Management.

Crawford, L. H., Aitken, A., & Hassner-Nahmias, A. (2014). *Project Management and Organizational Change*. Newtown Square, PA: Project Management Institute.

Gaddis, P. O. (1959). The project manager. *Harvard Business Review, 37*(3), 89–97.

GAPPS. (2007). *A Framework for Performance Based Competency Standards for Global Level 1 and 2 Project Managers*. Global Alliance for Project Performance Standards. http://www.globalPMstandards.org

Hornstein, H. A. (2015). The integration of project management and organizational change management is now a necessity. *International Journal of Project Management, 33*(2), 291–298.

ISO. (2022). *ISO 21502:2020 Project, Programme and Portfolio Management—Guidance on Project Management*. Geneva: International Organization for Standardization.

Lloyd-Walker, B., Crawford, L. H., & French, E. L. (2018). Uncertainty as opportunity: The challenge of project based careers. *International Journal of Managing Projects in Business, 11*(4), 886–900.

Moradi, S., Kähkönen, K., & Aaltonen, K. (2020). Comparison of research and industry views on project managers' competencies. *International Journal of Managing Projects in Business, 13*(3), 543–572.

Morris, P. W. G. (2013). *Reconstructing Project Management*. Chichester, New York: John Wiley & Sons, Ltd.

Morris, P. W. G. (2016). Reflections. *International Journal of Project Management, 34*(2), 365–370.

Müller, R., & Turner, R. (2010). Leadership competency profiles of successful project managers. *International Journal of Project Management, 28*(5), 437–448.

Project Management Institute. (2021). *A Guide to the Project Management Body of Knowledge (PMBOK® Guide)*, 7th Edition. Newtown Square, PA: Project Management Institute.

Chapter 25

The project sponsor

Lynn Crawford

Introduction

The sponsor is central to the governance and success of projects (Breese et al., 2020; Franke et al., 2022) but this is rarely their full-time or primary role. They may be the project owner but are most often an executive or senior managers with an interest in the results of the project and sufficient decision-making authority to represent the project owner. As a sponsor, they are expected to take responsibility for shaping, overseeing and advocating for the project and are ultimately accountable for realizing value and benefits from the investment (APM, 2019; GAPPS, 2015). This requires a certain level of authority and seniority and such people will usually have many other responsibilities and very little time available to perform a demanding and pivotal role. In practice, very few sponsors receive any preparation or training for the role and while the accountability and responsibility remain essentially the same, they need to be able to understand and respond to the needs of different projects. This chapter will provide an overview of the governance and support roles of the sponsor, some characteristics of effective sponsorship and how this may vary according to the needs of the project, the important relationship between the project sponsor and project manager and the challenge of developing project sponsor capability. A clear understanding of the project sponsor role and how it can be most effective in achieving successful outcomes is useful to sponsors who are asked to take on the role and to the project and program managers who rely upon their sponsors for decision-making and support.

DOI: 10.4324/9781003274179-29

Governance

Over the past three decades, corporate governance and its regulation have become a key concern for both organizations and projects. Government, companies and shareholders alike have actively advocated for the adoption of more robust governance practices to enhance political, board and management accountability to stakeholders. This has been accompanied by public and investor demand for transparency and sustainability evidenced by evolving requirements for environmental, social and governance (ESG) reporting.

Against this background, the project sponsor role has been recognized as central to the governance of projects providing the critical link between the permanent organization and temporary project, and between the project owner (Meredith and Zwikael, Ch. 11), investor, project owner organization (Winch, Ch. 10), board or executive team or client, and the project or program. The sponsor, representing the interests of the project owner, provides the connection between the governance of the organization and the governance of the project.

In terms of governance, the sponsor may act alone or may be supported by a steering committee. The sponsor and the steering committee have similar accountabilities and responsibilities although this may vary from project to project. The sponsor is effectively the governor and is usually the ultimate decision-maker for a project but this responsibility may be devolved to a steering committee which will usually, but not always, be chaired by the sponsor. It is rare for a project to have a steering body but no sponsor (Rudischer, 2020). Results from research by a special interest group of the German-speaking member organizations of the International Project Management Association (IPMA) indicated that over 80% of projects and programs had some form of sponsorship. Of these, 30% of projects had only a sponsor and 52% had both a sponsor and steering committee, These results support the findings of Müller, Shao, and Pemsel (2016), who reported that the majority of projects and programs are likely to have both a sponsor and steering committee. Steering committees are most effective where multiple organizational units or organizations are involved in ownership, provision of resources, operation and realization of benefits over time. Ideally, there will only be one sponsor for a project, providing clarity of accountability and responsibility, but where there are multiple business units or organizational entities providing resources and responsible for the realization of benefits, they may each have a sponsor representing their interests and these sponsors may form or be part of a steering committee that holds ultimate authority.

Where an organization has many projects, they may have a limited number of executives with the necessary level of authority to act as sponsors. These executives are often required, from a governance perspective, to take on the sponsorship of multiple projects beyond their ability to provide sufficient time and attention. Research by the Project Management Institute found that sponsors reported responsibility for an average of three projects or programs at a time, 'spending an average of 13 hours per week on each project or program they sponsor – in addition to their regular jobs' (PMI, 2014, p. 2). The author is aware of one organization where executive sponsors are simultaneously responsible for far more than three projects or programs. In such cases, it may be necessary for the executive sponsor to delegate responsibility and appropriate levels of authority to a project sponsor who will act on their behalf. A good and clearly documented example of this is the well-established role in the UK Government, of a Senior Responsible Owner (SRO), who may be full or part-time and is accountable to a sponsoring body (an individual or steering group) for a project or program 'meeting its objectives, delivering the required outcomes, and realizing the required benefits' (IPA, 2023, p. 45). They are considered to be the owners of the business case and accountable for all aspects of governance.

Table 25.1 below provides brief descriptions of the governance roles and responsibilities for projects, showing the relationship of the sponsoring individuals and groups relative to the project owner and the project manager or director.

Shaping the endeavour, ensuring alignment with strategy, making decisions, overseeing delivery, and taking accountability for the realization of value and benefits from the investment are clear governance responsibilities, but this is only part of the role of the sponsor. An equally important aspect of the role is providing support to the endeavour to ensure conditions that will enable the successful achievement of desired outcomes (Crawford et al., 2008).

Support

Important aspects of the sponsor role are support for the project and for the project manager or director. As a member or delegated representative of the executive, the sponsor is able to address issues and provide support for the project in ways that are above or outside the control of the project manager or

Table 25.1 Key project governance roles

Role	*Responsibilities*
Project Owner	Individual, organizational units and organizations on behalf of whom the project or program is undertaken • ultimate accountability for the endeavour
Steering Group/ Project Board	Represents the owner; most effective where multiple organizational units or organizations are involved in ownership, provision of resources, operation and realization of benefits over time • the principal institution for project governance • promoting, advocating, shaping and overseeing the endeavour • approving, facilitating, guiding, supporting and constructively challenging • accountability for realisation of value and specified benefits over time
Executive Sponsor	Represents the owner; is a senior member of the executive representing those who provide the resources, financial or otherwise – same responsibilities as and may chair steering group or act without a steering group
Project Sponsor	The executive sponsor retains ultimate accountability for the project and the business case but may delegate responsibilities to a less senior and heavily committed project sponsor
Project Manager/ Director	• setting and managing project work to achieve defined objectives • monitoring and reporting on project progress

director (Breese et al., 2020). Operating, as they do, at the interface between the permanent or owning organization and the project, the sponsor is able to promote and advocate for the project at senior levels, provide political support for the project, secure funding, negotiate for and maintain resource commitments, remove roadblocks, cultivate stakeholder engagement and commitment, deal with disruptions and disruptors who may be opposed to the project, and drive change. The sponsor is well positioned to hold uncertainty and to scan the environment to identify organizational, environmental and systemic risks and opportunities that may affect the project.

The sponsor will often be responsible for the appointment of the project manager or director, and in some cases, all or part of the project team and in doing so will have a role in ensuring that those appointed have the skills and capabilities required for the project as it evolves. They will be expected to review the performance of the project manager and provide constructive feedback. Action may need to be taken if the project manager or team is found to lack the necessary skills. Such action may include recommended training and development, addition of team members or replacement of personnel. In any case, the sponsor is expected to coach and mentor the project manager and work with them to assist in assuring they have the human and other resources required for the project.

Support includes showing commitment and clearly taking an interest in the project. Most important is being available to the project manager, sharing information, responding to requests and making decisions in a timely manner.

What project sponsors do

Both governance and support are reflected in the Guiding Framework for Project Sponsors developed by the Global Alliance for the Project Professions (GAPPS, 2015). This framework, developed by practitioners drawing on both research and experience provides minimum performance criteria for what competent project sponsors should do. The units and elements are shown in the table below. The full document is available on the GAPPS website (www.pmprofessions.org) (Figure 25.1).

Effective project sponsorship

The ideal sponsor is one who has a direct interest in the project either because they are likely to benefit from or be affected by it, as they will be motivated to provide support for the project (Kloppenborg et al., 2014). Unfortunately, this ideal is rarely met and there is much discussion about elusive and missing sponsors. Attitude is an important factor in effective sponsorship and Kloppenborg and colleagues (Kloppenborg & Tesch, 2015; Kloppenborg et al., 2009, 2014) have conducted research that provides useful guidance on effective sponsor behaviours. In their research they found three sponsor behaviours that were significant predictors of project success: (1) defining performance/success; (2) mentoring the project manager, and (3) setting priorities. On the other hand, establishing change control was found to have a negative impact, highlighting the need for sponsors

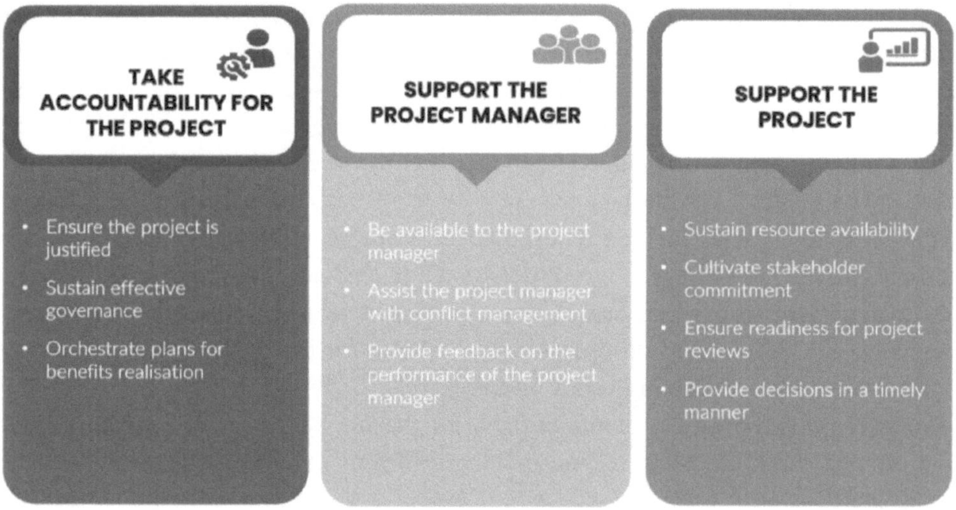

Figure 25.1: GAPPS guiding framework for project sponsors (Unit and Element level only, GAPPS, 2015)

to act as leaders providing oversight and direction and leaving the project manager to manage.

A simple guide to key sponsor behaviours at different stages of the life cycle is provided by Kloppenborg and Tesch (2015) (Table 25.2).

The Project Management Institute found that projects were more likely to achieve desired outcomes and be delivered on time, on budget, with less scope creep if sponsors had five key skills and frequently performed five particular actions:

In many ways, a good sponsor is like a good parent, but parenting is difficult and so is effective sponsorship, especially if you have a large and complex family of projects to nurture to success.

There are many lists that tell us what to do to be more effective parents and if you look at those lists you will find very useful guidance for the sponsor role. The following is drawn from a number of these lists and adapted for the project sponsor:

1 Make yourself available.
2 Be a good role model.
3 Provide feedback.

Table 25.2 Key sponsor behaviours for each stage of the project life cycle (Kloppenborg & Tesch, 2015)

Project stage	*Key sponsor behaviour*
Initiating stage	Set performance goals Select and mentor the project manager Establish priorities
Planning stage	Ensure planning Develop relationships with stakeholders
Executing stage	Ensure adequate and effective communication Maintain relationships with stakeholders Ensure quality
Closing stage	Identify and capture lessons learned Ensure capabilities and benefits are realized

4 Celebrate success.
5 Make communication a priority.
6 Set limits and be consistent.
7 Be flexible and willing to adjust your style.
8 Show your commitment.
9 Know your own needs and limitations.

Situational sponsorship

One characteristic of effective sponsorship, as noted in the list above, is being flexible and willing to adjust your style. Each project will present different challenges and as research has shown (Crawford et al., 2008), some projects will need more governance and support than others. Crawford et al. (2008) developed a simple model that can be used to as a basis for tailoring style and guiding the assignment of sponsors to different projects (see Figure 25.2 below). Understanding this can provide a useful guide to sponsors and to their assignment to particular projects.

An example of a project requiring a 'Guardian' sponsor may be one that is relatively straightforward, with good organizational support, and a competent

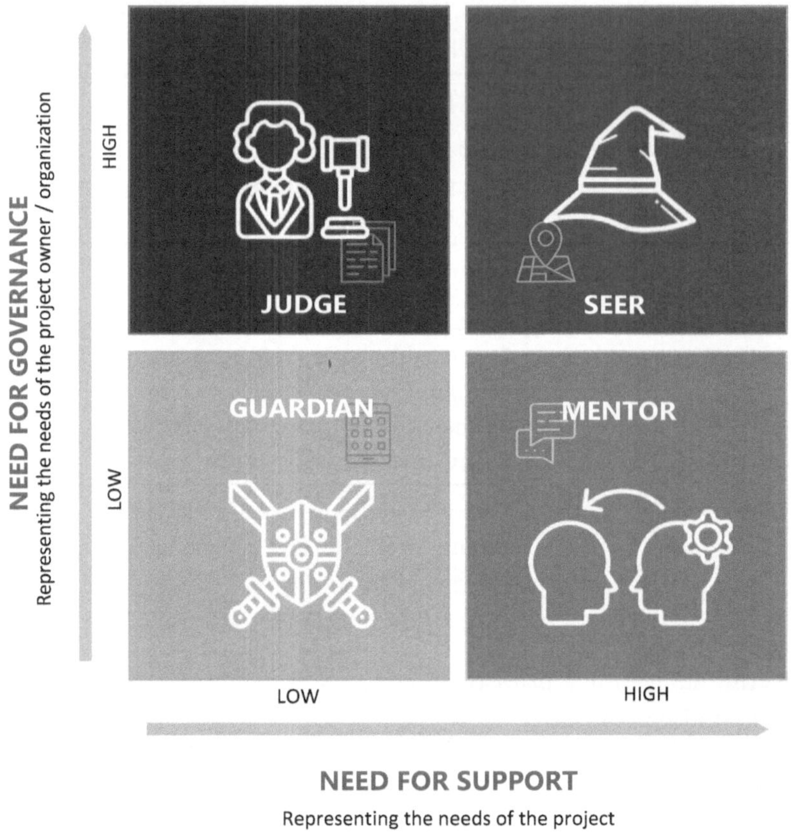

Figure 25.2: Situational sponsorship of projects and programs (based on Crawford et al., 2008, p. 550)

project manager who may have done a similar project in the past. This may not place too much demand on the sponsor. For those new to sponsorship, this may be a good place for them to start. A single sponsor may be able to handle several projects with these characteristics.

A project with a high need for governance may be one that is of critical significance to the project owner, pose a strategic risk or may be subject to shareholder or media scrutiny. A project with a high need for support may be one with a less experienced project manager, resource constraints, or stakeholder resistance. Where the need for governance and support are both high, the sponsor should be experienced and carefully selected and briefed for the role. If the need for governance or support or both are high, then it should be understood that significant time and commitment will be required on the part of the sponsor and the person appointed should have significant experience and a demonstrated track record in successful sponsorship.

The project sponsor and the project manager

Comparing the role of the project sponsor with that of the project manager helps to clarify the project sponsor role as shown in Table 25.3 (Huemann, 2015). While the project manager represents the project interests, the sponsor represents the project-related interests of the permanent organization. While the project manager is responsible for the operational management of the project, the sponsor has a strategic focus. The sponsor only engages with the project from time to time, while the manager is continuously engaged. When the two meet, the sponsor provides context information, while the manager provides project-specific information, such as the status of the project.

Rodney Turner and Ralf Müller (2004) related the success of the project to the nature of the relationship between the sponsor and the project manager. They need a highly cooperative working relationship with clearly defined project objectives. Trust is important. The second dimension they considered was the extent to which the sponsor tries to control the project manager's behaviour. Too much control and the project manager has no flexibility to deal with unexpected risks or find innovative work methods or solutions for

Table 25.3 Key sponsor skills and actions (PMI, 2014)

Key skills	*Key actions*
Ability to influence stakeholders	Removing roadblocks
Ability to work across different stakeholder groups to find win-win solutions	Helping the project team understand the alignment of the project or program to the organization's strategy
Leadership	Championing the project or program
Decision-making	Adding resources when appropriate
Effective communications	Acting quickly to resolve issues

Table 25.4 A comparison of the project sponsor and project manager (Huemann, 2015)

Project sponsor	*Project manager*
Realization of company-related project interests Strategic management of the project Engage with the project from time to time Provision of context information	Realization of Project Interests Operational management of the project Engage with the project continuously Ensuring project information

achieving the project objectives (see Chapter 44). But if the sponsor abdicates all responsibility, they will run the risk of failing their governance accountability and undermining the ability of the project to deliver as required. The sponsor needs to provide direction, but not be a control freak or micromanager, a finding supported by the research of Kloppenborg et al. (2009) (Table 25.4).

Developing project sponsors

Projects and programs with effective and engaged sponsors are demonstrably more likely to deliver value and desired benefits (PMI, 2014) and yet the majority of sponsors receive no training for the role. Some consider it just part of their 'day job' or substantive role, may not have received any preparation for the sponsor role and may view training as unnecessary, while those who distinguish between the two roles are more likely to see the benefit of training (Breese et al., 2020). Experience suggests that even when organizations recognize the need for more effective sponsorship and institute training, and it is strongly promoted by the senior leadership, it is difficult to get senior executives to spend more than half a day at the most in a 'master class'. Often much of the benefit is in raising awareness and providing an opportunity for sponsors to share their experiences. The benefit is not likely to last for long in the face of workplace pressures and career mobility. The GAPPS Guiding Framework for Project Sponsors (GAPPS, 2015) is deliberately brief as it was recognized that this was necessary to attract the attention of and be of use to sponsors.

On-the-job learning and mentoring from other executive sponsors in the organization are seen as the most effective form of development (PMI, 2014).

Conclusion

The project sponsor is potentially the least understood, the least defined and least prepared role in project and program management, yet it has the greatest potential for increasing the performance of projects and their ability to deliver value, benefits and change. It is rarely a full-time commitment and the pool of available sponsors is largely limited to those with sufficient levels of authority and seniority to meet the governance demands of the role. As a result, many sponsors are asked to take on the role of multiple projects, making the challenge of effective sponsorship even greater. Those sponsors who understand the importance of the role, who establish good relationships with their project and program managers and directors, make time for them, make timely and informed decisions and tailor their sponsorship style and actions to the governance and support needs of the project, are most likely to be able to fulfil their own governance commitments of realizing value and benefits on behalf of the project owner. Those who wish to perform more effectively in the role, improving the outcomes of their projects, should seek training and mentorship from peers.

References and further reading

APM. (2019). *APM body of knowledge* (7th ed.). Association for Project Management. https://ebookcentral.proquest.com/lib/westminster/detail.action?docID=6348558

Breese, R., Couch, O., & Turner, D. (2020). The Project Sponsor Role and Benefits Realisation: More Than 'Just Doing the Day Job.' *International Journal of Project Management*, *38*(1), 17–26. https://doi.org/10.1016/j.ijproman.2019.09.009

Crawford, L., Cooke-Davies, T., Hobbs, B., Labuschagne, L., Remington, K., & Chen, P. (2008). Governance and Support in the Sponsoring of Projects and Programs. *Project Management Journal*, *39*(1_suppl), S43–S55. https://doi.org/10.1002/pmj.20059

Franke, H., Wynstra, F., Nullmeier, F., & Nullmeier, C. (2022). Project Managers' Reactions to Project Disruption: Sponsor Actions Versus Environmental Uncertainty. *International Journal of Operations & Production Management*, *42*(13), 335–357. https://doi.org/10.1108/IJOPM-02-2022-0103

GAPPS. (2015). *A guiding framework for project sponsors*. Global Alliance for the Project Professions. http://www.globalPMstandards.org

Huemann, M. (2015). *Human resource management in the project-oriented organization: Towards a viable project-oriented HRM system for project personnel*. Gower, Aldershot.

IPA. (2023). *The role of the senior responsible owner* (Version 2.0). Infrastructure and Projects Authority, HM Government. https://assets.publishing.service.gov.uk/government/uploads/system/uploads/attachment_data/file/1002673/1195-APS-CCS0521656700-001-Project-Delivery-standard_Web.pdf

Kloppenborg, T. J., Manolis, C., & Tesch, D. (2009). Successful Project Sponsor Behaviors during Project Initiation: An Empirical Investigation. *Journal of Managerial Issues: JMI, 21*(1), 140–159.

Kloppenborg, T. J., & Tesch, D. (2015). How Executive Sponsors Influence Project Success. *MIT Sloan Management Review, 56*(3), 27–30.

Kloppenborg, T. J., Tesch, D., & Manolis, C. (2014). Project Success and Executive Sponsor Behaviors: Empirical Life Cycle Stage Investigations. *Project Management Journal, 45*(1), 9–20. https://doi.org/10.1002/pmj.21396

Müller, R., Shao, J., & Pemsel, S. (2016). *Organizational enablers for project governance* (1st ed.). Newtown Square, PA: Project Management Institute.

PMI. (2014). *Executive sponsor engagement: Top driver of project and program success* (PMI's Pulse of the Profession). Newtown Square, PA: Project Management Institute.

Rudischer, C. (2020). *Governance structures in projects and programmes, PM goes boardroom*. GPM/pma/spm special interest group/Rudischer Management Consulting e.U. https://www.dropbox.com/s/avox2nkyqqehoey/Final_Report_Governance_Structures.pdf?dl=0

Turner, J.R., & Müller, R. (2004). Communication and Cooperation on Projects Between the Project Owner as Principal and the Project Manager as Agent. *The European Management Journal, 22*(3), 327–336.

Chapter 26

The project team

Reinhard Wagner

Introduction

Projects enjoy great popularity nowadays, as they are used to accomplish demanding tasks within a limited period of time. In an industrial context, this could be the delivery of self-driving vehicles, in a societal context the design of smart cities, or in a private context the organization of a street festival. However, what has not been given the same attention for so long is that people implement projects for people and that social processes are at the heart of project implementation. Projects unfold as an ever-changing flux of events that involve individuals, teams, and social networks pursuing their interests and agendas. When looking at the performance of projects, it is crucial to understand what really drives team members in a project and how this drive can be orchestrated in a given socio-cognitive space (Drouin et al., 2021) and be directed towards achieving the desired outcomes.

The starting point is the basic needs of people and how these work as a central prerequisite for team development in the context of projects towards high performance and successful project execution. It's basically an intrinsic need of people to perform ambitious tasks together with others. Projects are ideal for this, as they require a joint effort of the team members involved from the start of the project to the defined end to achieve the desired outcomes. Teams go through an intensive development process that commences before the actual implementation of the

DOI: 10.4324/9781003274179-30

project and ends after its delivery. It requires suitable framework conditions. One of these framework conditions is the question of how leadership is exercised. Closely related to this is how much freedom the team is actually given to organize itself and thus react flexibly to changing environmental conditions.

Therefore, this chapter first looks at what drives people at the core to get involved in projects and teams, what distinguishes teams in the context of projects, and how teams develop over time. In the end, it addresses leadership in the context of projects and the self-organization of teams, which modern approaches to delivering projects nowadays cannot do without.

What drives people to work in project teams

As early as 1960, management thought leader Douglas McGregor pointed out that every management decision or action is shaped by basic assumptions about human nature and distinguished two different forms, Theory X and Theory Y (McGregor, 1960). The first form describes people as unwilling to do work. To get them to do it requires the use of power, coercion, and – if necessary – punishment. The description culminates in the statement that the average human brings little drive to work and prefers to be directed. In contrast, the second form, Theory Y, sees the human as being interested in putting physical and mental effort into work, committing to outcomes, and taking responsibility for his or her actions. This serves one's own development and self-realization based on the inner drive.

Building on this distinction, later scientific research has continued to look at what drives people at work and what conditions organizations and management can create so that performance on the one hand, and the well-being of employees on the other hand can be enhanced. One of these theories is the Self-Determination Theory (SDT), which has looked at people's basic psychological needs underlying their motivation in different circumstances (Ryan and Deci, 2017). The theory draws on McGregor's Theory Y and assumes that people are inherently curious, physically active, and socially engaging. SDT describes three basic psychological needs, namely 'autonomy', 'competence', and 'relatedness', which influence our behaviour. Autonomy describes the need for individuals to act in a self-determined way and to assume responsibility for their actions. In acting out, people want to both feel efficacious and be recognized for what they do and how competent they do it. Relatedness means feeling a sense of belonging to others and being able to do and achieve things connected to others that would not be feasible on one's

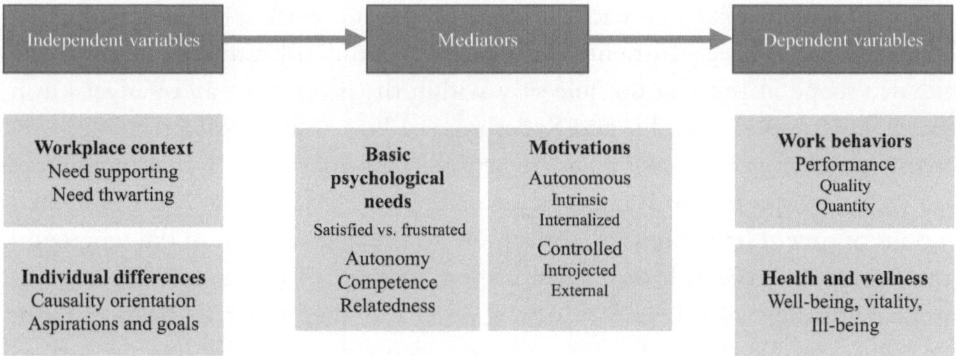

Figure 26.1: The basic SDT model in the workplace (Deci et al., 2017: 23)

own. It certainly depends on the workplace context whether these needs are either supported or thwarted. Projects seem fertile ground for meeting these needs.

Another mediator for work behaviour and well-being is motivation, whether it be autonomous (intrinsic or internalized) or controlled (introjected or external). Figure 26.1 provides an overview of the basic SDT model in the workplace.

In the context of this chapter, the basic need for relatedness, or as it is often called 'social need', is of particular interest. People need other people in what they do. According to Schutz (1998), inclusion, control, and affection are the guiding motives for interpersonal behaviour. So people are primarily concerned with building good or satisfying relationships with other people to feel a sense of belonging to each other and be able to carry out joint activities on this basis. Depending on their individual needs, people may feel the need to exert more or less influence on other people and thus experience the need for competence in a relationship outlined above. Finally, people are not only concerned with the rational level of the interpersonal relationship but also with the affective level of trust, love, and closeness. In summary, it can be said that it is an intrinsic need of people to perform ambitious tasks together with others and that they need suitable framework conditions for this in order to achieve performance and health or well-being in equal measure.

The role of teams in realizing projects

With the introduction of project management in the USA's aerospace and defence industry during the early 1950s, the notion of a project was applied primarily to complex engineering challenges, and their management was accomplished using abstract, mathematical approaches, such as the network planning technique (Morris, 2013). The plan-oriented approach was primarily aimed at reaching the intended scope in the best possible way within the given time and budget ('iron triangle'). However, Lundin and Söderholm (1995) made the case in the early 1990s for a change in thinking and an action-based approach. A challenging task is solved by a team transforming an actual state into a desired state within a limited amount of time. Here, attention shifts more to the demarcation of the temporary organization (a project) from the permanent context of the embedding organization. Ultimately, this comes at a time when the questions raised earlier about the role of people in and for projects were being asked, and questions such as "how to motivate, communicate and build commitment, as it is obvious that the individual's beliefs, attitudes, and expectations will influence teamwork" (Lundin and Söderholm, 1995: 441). Figure 26.2 shows the basic concept of project organizing with the four determinants, or four "Ts", namely 'task', 'time', 'team', and 'transition'. The concept highlights the distinction between temporary and permanent organizations and better integrates the social dimension. This has been called the "Scandinavian Turn" in project management (Jacobsson et al., 2016).

It is essential to mention that teams in projects are assembled with a unique task in mind, and they work together only temporarily, from the start to the end of the project. The team is selected and deployed by a project owner.

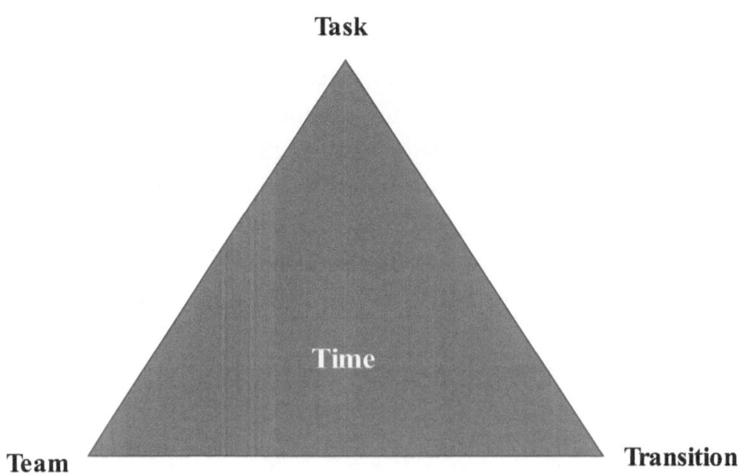

Figure 26.2: Basic concepts in the theory of temporary organizations (Lundin and Söderholm, 1995: 451)

Due to the temporary nature of the task in a project, team members typically are drawn from the permanent organization, possibly remain subordinate to it over the course of the project, and return to their original positions when the project is completed. The more complex the tasks in the context of the project, the more diverse the team should be orchestrated, and the development of the team, or several teams, will dynamically take place, from a small core team at the beginning and the end to the full scale of the team during the execution of the project. Nowadays, project teams are often geographically dispersed, work together using virtual collaboration tools, and involve diverse mindsets and cultural traits in the team. Extended teams may also include external partners. Team members are ultimately aligned by the mission they share for the project, working together in order to meet the requirements (Gareis and Gareis, 2018).

Team development in projects

For the description of the development of a team in projects, the classic model of Tuckman (1965) is often used, which runs from a forming phase through storming and norming finally to the performing. A few years later, this model was extended to include an adjourning phase (see Figure 26.3).

The model describes a sequential progression of activities, from the first meeting of the team, through stormy encounters during role clarification, which eventually transitions into an ordering that allows the team to perform. Changes in the team cause it to go through this sequence again and again until, at the end of the project, the team disbands. However, the model has been criticized, especially for the sequential order of the phases and the fact that the team dynamics are given little consideration in the model. For example, some project teams get stuck in storming and do not even reach the performance phase, or

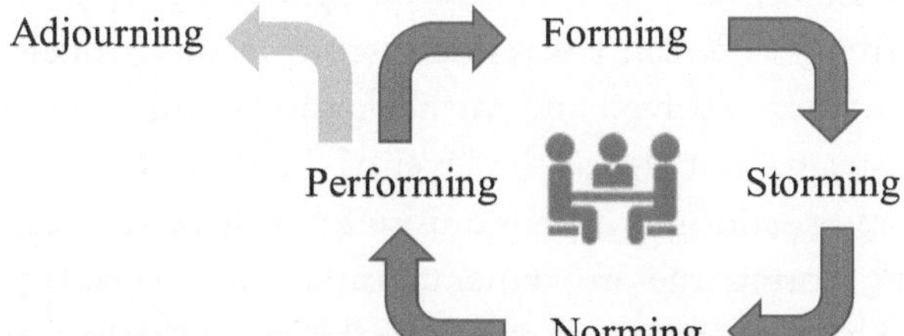

Figure 26.3: Team development stages (Tuckman, 1965)

teams skip individual phases in their development or even fall behind. Other models of team development therefore focus on three stages: beginning, working together, and ending (Robb, 2022).

When the team comes together for the first time, many facets of the overall project are unclear. The team members need information and clarity about their tasks, the framework conditions, and many other matters. In the beginning, there is also a lack of trust among the team and towards leadership. This may also be accompanied by uncertainty, and possibly anxiety, about what the project will entail. Another difficulty in projects is that there is often not just one team, but a multitude of (sub-)teams that take care of specific tasks, sub-projects, or work packages (Skelton and Pais, 2019). A linear model of team development, focused on a single team therefore does little justice to this situation.

In the beginning, it is therefore important that the project leadership provides essential information about the project, describing its purpose and mission and thus attracting the motivation of the team members to get involved. Further information on the intended way of working, the organizational set-up, and the roles or teams involved helps those involved to orient and develop a perspective for their own role in the project. This is comparable to a symphonic orchestra that meets once during the summer break to perform a symphony concert and then returns to their normal activities. The alignment between the conductor and the orchestra includes but is not limited to the particular symphony that will be performed, how it will be interpreted, how the orchestra is supposed to interact, and how individual instrumental groups, such as the strings and the percussion will prepare for the performance. The ultimate goal is to unleash individual competencies and foster team cohesion in a relatively short time. This requires targeted interventions, such as training and team building, "aimed at improving requisite team competencies, processes, and overall effectiveness" (Lacerenza et al., 2018: 518). How long this will take depends on whether the team members have worked together in this constellation before or how complex the project is in technical and organizational terms. There can always be discord in this process, indicating that not everything has been resolved and further intervention is needed. This can be in one of the sub-teams, but also at the level of the overall team. Resolving these discords before the execution is a prerequisite for a successful team performance.

The teamwork during the implementation of a project is typically a very intensive effort. The team or the teams fulfil the agreed tasks and work together as arranged. However, it is common for projects to be subject to unforeseen changes (e.g. the unavailability of a soloist at the symphony concert due to severe health problems). Ideally, this has already been considered in the preparation and the team can respond quickly. It is important that the team members are as well coordinated as possible and able to respond quickly and in a self-organized manner to any critical moment. In general, little outside-in influence or leadership is required in this phase (the conductor of the symphony orchestra just needs to set the pace and "hold threads together"). Nevertheless, interventions such as regular feedback or assistance to the team or individual members in critical situations can be useful (e.g., the conductor provides the cue for critical passages). From time to time, it is also useful to introduce continuous improvements with regard to the process, the methods and tools used, or the team collaboration.

Towards the end of the project, shortly before the team's collaboration ends and the team disbands, it would be useful to conduct a systematic review of the team's work in the sense of a retrospective. This should emphasize the accomplishments of the entire team or individual members, document the shared lessons learned for subsequent projects, and celebrate the dissolution of the team in a dignified manner. This is an emotional moment, especially for longer-lasting projects. A team should also take time to do this because otherwise, it will be difficult to motivate the team to collaborate again.

There are several influencing factors to consider in team development (Jordan, 2013). For example, when external team members are involved, it may be necessary to invest more time and provide targeted interventions at the beginning of the collaboration. The same is required when team members come together with diverse personalities, experiences, skills, or cultural backgrounds. Time is needed to understand each other, build trust, and establish mutual complementarity in the project. It is always important for the project manager or coach of the team, to keep an open eye on the team, to provide feedback on where the team(s) stand, and to foster self-reflection.

Leadership and self-organization

When dealing with teams in the context of projects, inevitably the question arises as to how and by whom leadership is exercised. In the classic conception of project management, leadership was clearly assigned; assuming the role of a project manager, leadership is more or less automatically transferred to that individual. Nevertheless, leadership in the context of a project as a temporary organizational form is different from leadership in the rest of the organization. Leadership in projects builds on an understanding of the purpose and involves team members more in shaping the project. It delegates tasks to fit the capabilities of team members, helping to bring intrinsic motivation, skills, experience, and abilities to bear.

Belbin (2010) showed that successful teams are made up of a diverse mix of behaviours and described nine specific roles: 'Resource Investigator', 'Teamworker' and 'Co-ordinator' (mainly social roles); 'Plant', 'Monitor Evaluator and Specialist' (mainly thinking roles), and 'Shaper', 'Implementer', and 'Completer Finisher' (mainly action roles). In particular, the role of the 'Co-ordinator' (the conductor, to remain in the metaphor of our symphony orchestra) is focused on the team's overall objectives, engages team members, and delegates work packages appropriately in the project. In agile software development methods, such as Scrum, there is no explicit leadership role assigned. The role of the 'Scrum Master' is instead to support the team in a moderating or coaching capacity. Depending on the project phase, different strengths may also be required in leading a team. In a creative project phase, the Belbin role of the 'Plant' is needed, who is creative and can solve problems with unconventional approaches. In contrast, shortly before the end of the project, a 'Completer Finisher' is required to focus the entire team on the completion of the deliverables. Contemporary leadership theories, therefore, focus on 'balanced leadership', the "dynamic and timely shift of leadership authority between project managers and team members to ensure the best possible leader at any point in time in the project." (Müller et al., 2022: 1).

There is also no clear-cut answer to the question of which leadership style should be adopted. The team member responsible for leadership should choose from an extensive repertoire of leadership styles depending on the situation, from a 'laissez-faire' leadership style in the implementation phase of a project, in which the team should be left alone as much as possible, to a more 'directive' leadership style in the beginning stage, in which the team is still looking for orientation, has little competence of its own concerning the project task and needs clear announcements.

In addition to the question of what demands the respective project phase places on leadership, it is also about the team and its stage of development. Ken Blanchard (2018) has defined four leadership styles appropriate for situational leadership, which depend on the competence of the team members and their commitment, a combination of an individual's motivation and confidence in the project. The more developed the competence and commitment of the team is, the less directive leadership has to be but instead giving room for self-organization, own decision-making, and development. Along the way, however, leadership should support the team in its development, e.g., through tailor-made coaching, feedback, and shared learning.

Self-organization in particular is popular as an approach in projects that take place in a dynamic, uncertain, and complex environment.

> Self-organisation in projects is self-determined and creative action of several individuals interacting with themselves and the project environment. In doing so, the procedural models of cooperation are agreed to fulfill a common purpose. Prerequisites for self-organisation in projects are corresponding degrees of freedom from the surrounding environment, e.g. for the distribution of tasks or the design of roles and responsibilities.
>
> (Armatowski et al., 2021: 14)

Self-organization in teams is created not only by the absence of directive leadership. It is achieved by consciously seizing development opportunities within the team, by achieving synergies on the basis of different personalities, strengths, and experiences, and by developing a team's own purpose, mindset, and atmosphere.

The purpose gives the team important orientation during the project work and answers the question of "what for" and thus usually goes beyond the actual project objectives. The clarification of the purpose at the beginning of the project also helps to inquire about the expectations of each team member and to check them for congruency. See Chapter 26, where the purpose is explicitly integrated into a motivation model for young project professionals. The collective mind only emerges during the course of the project through a multitude of interactions, an exchange about the values and beliefs that underlie the actions, and not through the instructions of the project manager. Especially in agile projects, it is often said that team members only need the 'right' mindset to achieve good performance. However, it is much more critical that the entire team shares a collective mindset because this is the basis for effective performance even in dynamic and changing project conditions. The atmosphere in a team expresses the extent to which the perception of the team members of the cooperation, the culture lived and the behaviours shown fit the joint commitment. If these things fit together, then the atmosphere is perceived as positive; if not, then the atmosphere in the team changes, and conflicts unload somewhere along the line.

Conclusion

Working on projects fulfills people's intrinsic drives for autonomy, competence, and relatedness. A challenging task is realized in a limited period of time with a project. A team is formed to accomplish the transition from a given initial situation to the desired target state of the project. It consciously (or unconsciously) goes through a team development process, from the team building through the implementation to the closure of the project. On the one hand, this process is influenced by the team members and their different personalities, skills, and experiences. On the other hand, influencing factors such as leadership, the space to manoeuvre for decision-making and self-organization, the prevailing culture, collective mind, and atmosphere in the project team plays an essential role in success. An increasingly volatile environment and with rising demands of the younger generation with respect to the content of work and its conditions, as well as the refusal of an overly hierarchical leadership, necessitate a rethinking of projects. More attention needs to be paid to team development and to filling team roles. At the same time, modern leadership, self-organization, and the design of the social surroundings in projects must be reconsidered.

References and further reading

Armatowski, S., Herrmann, P., Müller, M., Schaffitzel, N. and Wagner, R., 2021, *The Importance of Mindset, Culture and Atmosphere for Self-Organisation in Projects,* Amsterdam: International Project Management Association (IPMA).

Belbin, R.M., 2010, *Team Roles at Work*, Milton Park: Routledge.

Blanchard, K., 2018, *Leading at a Higher Level: Blanchard on Leadership and Creating High Performing Organizations,* 3rd Edition, London: Pearson Education.

Deci, E.L., Olafsen, A.H. and Ryan, R.M., 2017, Self-determination theory in work organizations: The state of a science, *Annual Review of Organizational Psychology and Organizational Behavior*, 4: 19–43.

Drouin, N., Müller, R., Sankaran, S. and Vaagaasar, A.L., 2021, Balancing leadership in projects: Role of the socio-cognitive space, *Project Leadership and Society,* 2: 1–12.

Gareis, R. and Gareis, L., 2018, *Project. Program. Change. A Textbook and Handbook for Intrapreneurs in Project-Oriented Organizations,* Boca Raton, FL: CRC Press.

Jacobsson, M., Lundin, R.A. and Söderholm, A., 2016, Towards a multi-perspective research program on projects and temporary organizations: Analyzing the Scandinavian turn and the rethinking effort, *International Journal of Managing Projects in Business*, 9(4): 752–766.

Jordan, A., 2013, Creating and changing a project team, In: Lock, D. and Scott, L., *Gower Handbook of People in Project Management*, 243–250, Farnham: Gower.

Lacerenza, C.N., Marlow, S.L., Tannenbaum, S.I. and Salas, E., 2018, Team development interventions: Evidence-based approaches for improving teamwork, *American Psychologist*, 73(4): 517–531.

Lundin, R.A. and Söderholm, A., 1995, A theory of the temporary organization, *Scandinavian Journal of Management*, 11(4): 437–455.

McGregor, D., 1960, *The Human Side of Enterprise,* New York: Mc Graw-Hill.

Morris, P.W.G., 2013, *Reconstructing Project Management,* Chichester: John Wiley & Sons.

Müller, R., Drouin, N. and Sankaran, S., 2022, *Balanced Leadership. Making the Best Use of Personal and Team Leadership in Projects,* Oxford: Oxford University Press.

Robb, M., 2022, *Group Art Therapy. Practice and Research,* Abingdon: Routledge.

Ryan, R.M. and Deci, E.L., 2017, *Self-Determination Theory. Basic Psychological Needs in Motivation, Development and Wellness,* New York: The Guilford Press.

Schutz, W., 1998, *FIRO. A Three-Dimensional Theory of Interpersonal Behavior,* 3rd Edition, Mill Valley, CA: Will Schutz Associates.

Skelton, M. and Pais, M., 2019, *Team Topologies. Organizing Business and Technology Teams for Fast Flow,* Portland, OR: IT Revolution.

Tuckman, B.W., 1965, Developmental sequence in small groups, *Psychological Bulletin,* 63(4): 384–399.

Chapter 27

Engaging project stakeholders

Pernille Eskerod and Martina Huemann

Introduction

Every project needs financial and non-financial contributions from individuals, groups, and entities in order to create value. The non-financial contributions may be approvals from decision-makers, work efforts from project team members, deliveries of the right quality from suppliers, and inputs on expectations from end users. At the same time, each project will affect individuals, groups, and entities, for example positively by creating future income and learning opportunities, and negatively by creating side effects like pollution and stressful working conditions.

All individuals, groups, and entities able to affect or in a position of being affected by the project are called the project stakeholders. Even though stakeholder engagement has been a core activity within project management for many years (Eskerod, 2020), still numerous projects fail because of unsatisfied stakeholders. It may for example be that the project outcomes do not meet the stakeholders' needs, or that the project process does not reflect the expectations of the stakeholders. As we are observing a paradigm shift in project managers towards the creation of value and benefits, engaging with stakeholders, become essential for project success.

Project stakeholders are all individuals, groups, or entities who can affect or are affected by the project outcomes or the process (Eskerod & Jepsen, 2013; Freeman, 1984). Perceiving that they are affected themselves is enough to turn them into stakeholders (Loch, 2011). Some examples of project stakeholders are the project

DOI: 10.4324/9781003274179-31

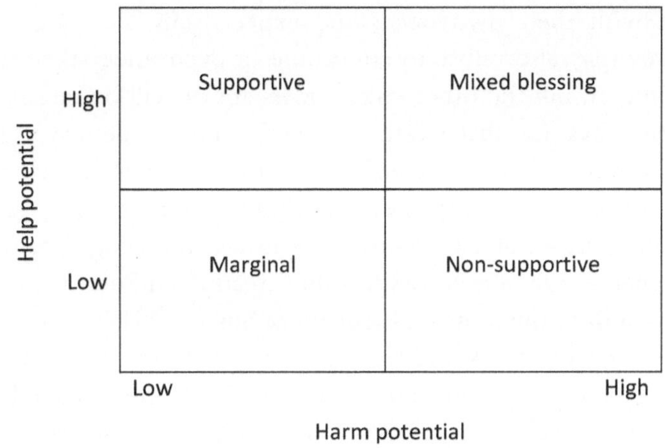

Figure 27.1: Help versus harm potentials (after Savage et al., 1991, p. 65)

investor, project client, employees, users, suppliers, partners, authorities, competitors, communities, and media. Due to their capacity and opportunity to contribute or threaten the project's success, each stakeholder has a help potential and a harm potential (see Figure 27.1). A high help potential implies that the stakeholder can provide significant contributions to the project whether these are financial or non-financial. A high harm potential implies that the needed contributions from this stakeholder are difficult or impossible to replace or that the stakeholder can affect other stakeholders' contributions or perceptions of the project. The stakeholders with high potential to help and/or harm the project's success are the key stakeholders and thereby differentiated from the whole group of stakeholders. Be aware that the status as a key stakeholder may change during a project.

All project stakeholders make their own subjective assessments of (potential) benefits and costs relevant to them that will arise because of a project. These assessments take place prior to the project start, during the project as well as afterwards. They are concerned whether the process and the stipulated outcomes are expected to meet the stakeholders' needs and expectations. If the stakeholders don't believe that the project outcomes or process have the potential to meet or exceed their needs and expectations, i.e. create value for them, they may refuse to contribute to the project. If they assess the project to be unsuccessful after it has been finalized, they may refuse to contribute to future related projects.

Project stakeholders may even influence other stakeholders to perceive the project as unsuccessful. Further on, the project stakeholders may not only be concerned with their own needs and expectations, i.e. value creation for themselves, they may also refuse to contribute or even undertake actions against the project if they think the other stakeholders are or will be negatively affected in unacceptable ways, i.e. that existing value for them is destroyed (Harrison & Wicks, 2021). A contemporary societal request for sustainable development places new demands on how to treat project stakeholders, for example by considering long-term ecological, social, and economic impacts and being conscious, responsible, and transparent when it comes to value creation and destruction due to the project process and/or outcomes (Huemann & Silvius, 2017).

The purpose of project stakeholder engagement is to increase the likelihood of project success by procuring contributions needed by the project and by enhancing that (key) project stakeholders perceive the project as a success. Building on Eskerod and Jepsen (2013) who define project stakeholder engagement as *all purposeful stakeholder-related activities carried out in order to enhance project success*, we take it one step further as our understanding of project success has evolved over time. Thus, we define stakeholder engagement as *the purposeful stakeholder-related practices to support value creation by the project.*

However, defining project success depends on what value and thus benefits and costs the project creates for the various stakeholders, and how they perceive the process. Thus, what is project success is in the eye of the particular stakeholder.

Several challenges in project stakeholder engagement exist:

- First, it may be difficult to identify the (key) stakeholders – as many individuals, groups, and entities may potentially affect or be affected by the project.
- Second, it may be difficult to get proper knowledge about the stakeholders' requirements, wishes, concerns, and success criteria as the stakeholders may not be sufficiently conscious of them or able to express them. Further, for each stakeholder they may be in conflict, as well as they may change over the project course.
- Third, the various stakeholders may have conflicting requirements, wishes, concerns, and success criteria, implying that negotiations and trade-offs acceptable for the stakeholders must take place.
- Fourth, the members of the project organization do not have unlimited resources for engaging with the stakeholders. In order to enhance project success, they must figure out how to spend their scarce resources for stakeholder engagement in efficient ways.

To better tackle these challenges, we need a more comprehensive understanding of project stakeholder engagement. In this chapter, we offer a comprehensive view of contemporary project stakeholder engagement. We take different perspectives, including

- Mindset,
- Processes,
- Methods, and
- Roles.

Mindset

Stakeholder theory

Stakeholder theory within general management literature offers a distinction between two strategic approaches, a management of stakeholders (or managing stakeholders) approach and a management for stakeholders approach (Freeman et al., 2007, 2010). The two approaches reflect different mindsets.

- *Managing Stakeholders* reflects a mindset that is rather rational and instrumental. The perception of stakeholders is limited to their help and harm potentials. The purpose of stakeholder communication limits itself to procuring contributions needed for the project and to 'sell' them the project outcomes. Stakeholders are means to obtain project success for the project investor and the members of the project organization – and project stakeholder management is about making stakeholders comply with the needs of the project. When two or more stakeholders have conflicting demands and wishes, trade-offs between the stakeholders are based on their help and harm potentials, i.e. the more important you are for the project's success, the more likely it is that your interests will be given the highest priority. Stakeholders who are not perceived as very important for the project's success will not receive much attention or be objects for any ethical considerations.
- *Management for Stakeholders* reflects a mindset in which the core thought is that all the stakeholders are valuable in their own right – and that they are entitled to receive management attention regardless of their help and harm potentials. When the demands and wishes of two or more stakeholders are conflicting, an important part of stakeholder management is to search for win-win situations.

If this is impossible to reach, the project aims to minimize the negative effects for each stakeholder and to keep the decision-making process transparent so that the stakeholders understand decisions and actions related to the project. Fairness, transparency, and participation are examples of underpinning values of the management for stakeholders' approach.

Comparing the approaches

The two approaches are extreme positions on a spectrum, both with their limitations. The management of stakeholders, on the first hand, suffers from its manipulative orientation, lack of ethical consideration, and narrow focus on the interests of the project (i.e. the project investor). As the perception of project success is influenced by the stakeholders' subjective assessments; the project investor and project organization typically need to interact with the stakeholders in the future; and a societal request for fair treatment of current and future generations, a narrow and selfish orientation may give very short-sighted benefits if any at all. The management for stakeholders' approach, on the other hand, suffers from its lack of focus on the most important stakeholders due to the request for inclusiveness and equal treatment of stakeholders. Long-lasting negotiations for win-win situations lead to delays or even stopping the project. If this happens, the project does not create value for the beneficiary project stakeholders, (which typically are not only the investor and the project owner organization). By not accepting conflicts and by denying a potential need for unpleasant trade-offs, the management for stakeholders' approach may lead to non-ambitious solutions – and by that put a hindrance to innovation and increased prosperity in society.

A way to take advantage of the strengths of both approaches is to combine them. That is, using the instrumental focus of the management of stakeholders approach to enhance project progress, i.e. by giving most attention to the key stakeholders so that they will help and not harm the project; while at the same time using the ethical focus of the management for stakeholders' approach to ensure that the requirements, wishes, concerns, and success criteria for a broad range of stakeholders are determined and incorporated in the project plan. We can visualize the relationship between the two approaches as a spectrum. It is up to the project to design an adequate strategic approach towards stakeholders. However, the contemporary society's request for sustainable development as fair treatment of all stakeholders leads to a general shift towards the management for project stakeholders approach as the underpinning values of this approach are in line with the underpinning values of sustainable development.

Principles of stakeholder orientation

We advocate the engagement of stakeholders in projects to support the creation of better futures. To consider sustainability in project stakeholder engagement we summarize the following six principles of stakeholder orientation (Eskerod & Huemann, 2024):

Principle 1. Inclusive stakeholder definition: An inclusive stakeholder definition reflects not only current but also future individuals and groups that are affected by the project process or the outcomes. This consideration is regardless of the power of the stakeholder at hand, to protect especially vulnerable groups that are less represented. For example, the children that will need to take a different way to school because of a building site; or the future patients of a hospital to reflect the growing age in our society.

Principle 2. Value transparency: The project explicitly considers and communicates value creation, value destruction, and value distribution due to the project process and outcomes. Objective and subjective value is acknowledged, while simultaneously accepting that all particular project stakeholders assess their subjective value based on their perception.

Principle 3. Perceived fairness: The project aims to be fair to stakeholders. This perceived fairness is subjective, and the stakeholder perspective is taken. It includes several dimensions such as distributional (incl. compensation for value destruction), procedural, interpersonal, and informational dimensions.

Principle 4. Future orientation: The project considers the present as well as the future, as they contribute with their project outcomes to the creation of futures. Future orientation is considered in the process as well as in the consequences created by the outcomes in the form of short-term, mid-term, and long-term consequences for the project stakeholders.

Principle 5. Co-creation: The project strives to create suitable solutions with project distinct stakeholder groups both when it comes to the project process and the project outcomes. The project uses concepts like future-making (Whyte et al., 2022) or projecting (Winch & Sergeeva, 2022) with the project stakeholders, i.e. they aim to manifest better futures. The project is explicitly considered a co-creation process (Huemann, 2022).

Principle 6. Multiple engagement forms: To support inclusiveness, the project engages with various project stakeholders in adequate formats, e.g. consulting them, training them, and informing them, and using accessible media, digital and analogue forms.

Processes

Project stakeholder engagement consists of three processes:

1 Identifying and empathizing with project stakeholders.
2 Building a relationship, interacting, and co-creating with project stakeholders.
3 Disengaging project stakeholders.

These processes are not linear, but circular. To create a solid foundation for stakeholder interactions, the project should identify stakeholders and empathize with them continuously throughout the project course. Ideally, the first *identification and empathizing* happens even before the project starts to find out whether there are powerful stakeholders who will want or be able to hinder the project (Andersen, 2008). *Stakeholder identification and empathizing* as well as *relationship-building, interacting, and co-creating* should be carried out repeatedly in the course of a project. As the project evolves, more detailed information on stakeholders becomes available and new stakeholders may pop up. Stakeholder expectations and relations are dynamic; representatives of stakeholders and project team members will change over time. Thus, the project will constantly need to work on *relationship-building, interacting, and co-creating* with project stakeholders. The process of *disengaging project stakeholders* takes place when an active relationship between the project and the project stakeholder is not of relevance anymore. Following we describe the processes in more detail.

Identifying and empathizing

In order to be able to determine who to target in project stakeholder engagement, we need to find out who can affect or be affected by the project – and identify the stakeholders. When we have identified the project stakeholders, we have to assess how they need to contribute to secure project success, and whether and why they can be expected to contribute as needed – *assess* needed contributions, help and harm potentials as well as the stakeholders' needs, expectations, benefits/costs and success criteria. Core questions may include:

- What do the stakeholders gain/lose from the project?
- How can each stakeholder contribute to creating project success?
- What will constitute satisfaction for each?
- How can we emphasize the needs of a particular stakeholder group?

Based on the former activities in the stakeholder analysis you must *plan how and when to engage and disengage* each stakeholder. You may want to address more stakeholders simultaneously by inviting them for a project event or by providing them with mass-produced info materials about the project, or you may plan to engage with them on an individual basis – and even ask the project owner to be their contact person. In the same way, you may plan to disengage the stakeholder in a way that encourages the stakeholder to work with you again in a future project. Part of planning stakeholder engagement and disengagement is to figure out how to spend resources for stakeholder management in efficient ways.

Building relationships, interacting, and co-creating

In this process, the purpose is to create awareness of the project; to create relationships with the stakeholders; to negotiate aimed-for benefits, scope, and constraints as well as mutual expectations for the project outcomes and the project process with the stakeholders; and to sustain relationships as long as they are relevant for the project. The interactions with the (key) stakeholders typically begin in the pre-project phase and in the project formation phase in order to incorporate the stakeholders' ideas and interests at an early stage. The interactions continue until it is relevant to disengage the particular project stakeholder. For some stakeholders, interactions may last for the whole project process, while for others, e.g. suppliers, the interactions relate to specific parts of the project.

Disengaging

When the project or part of the project has been accomplished, and the relevant stakeholders need to be disengaged, close-down activities with the particular stakeholder are performed, which enhance the possibility that the stakeholders will perceive the project as successful – also when they think back on it in the future. Further, the activities may include reflections on experiences and learning from the project; as well as to release the members of the project organization from their roles.

Methods

Current literature offers plenty of methods for project stakeholder engagement. Following the principle introduced earlier in this chapter that *multiple engagement forms* support inclusiveness and co-creation, we advocate the explicit consideration of a range of methods and design the applications for the purpose of stakeholder engagement. In this section, we, therefore, present selected methods for engaging stakeholders. Table 27.1 offers a toolbox in the form of an overview of selected methods related to the project stakeholder engagement processes. Please notice that the selection of methods should be considered as a catalogue to choose from

Table 27.1 Project stakeholder engagement toolbox

Identifying and empathizing	*Interacting and co-creating*	*Disengaging*
Inclusive stakeholder definition	Info materials	'Thank you'
In the stakeholder's shoes imagination (e.g. local community members)	Town hall meetings	Satisfaction survey
Stakeholder-in-action observations (e.g. users)	Social media interactions	Lessons learned (session or write-up)
Analysis workshops	Engaging dialogue	Celebration event
Explicit mutual expectations	Stakeholder workshops (in person and virtually)	Future-oriented evaluations
Stakeholder reflections	Proto-typing, simulations	
Scenario developments	Integrated project organization	
Systemic board		
Systemic constellation		

based on the characteristics and complexity of the project and the stakeholder engagement issue. It may not be necessary to apply all methods in the same project. Considerations should include the accessibility of different stakeholder groups, for example, digital platforms and social media are quite suitable to reach younger stakeholders, while elderly ones may rather feel excluded.

Inclusive stakeholder definition

This tool strongly relates to the first principle of stakeholder orientation (Eskerod & Huemann, 2024). An inclusive stakeholder definition contains stakeholders with power as well as those without power, those who are vulnerable or not yet presented such as future generations. The project's process and outcomes may affect them, but these stakeholders are not necessarily able to affect the project. A way to operationalize the definition is to incorporate dimensions relevant to sustainable development when identifying stakeholders such as (Silvius & Huemann, in press)

- considering economic, ecological, and social dimensions,
- as well as to broaden the temporal scales including short, medium, and long-term,
- and spatial scales including local, regional, and global orientation.

In the stakeholder's shoes imagination

Taking the position of a given stakeholder or a stakeholder type, e.g. users, suppliers, local community, employees, or managers we coin 'In the stakeholder's shoes imagination'. This can be done by the project team in a workshop or by someone appointed, even the project manager in a small project. Vivid and detailed imagination of the stakeholder's world and situation may help the project take the stakeholder's perspective into account.

Stakeholder-in-action observations

Inspired by practices from the field of innovation, the project can organize observations of a stakeholder conducting a relevant action related to the project process or project outcome. If for example, the project concerns the development of a new product or service, intended users, whether customers or end-consumers, can be invited to try out a prototype of the product or service while being observed or asked for feedback. Hereby, important information can be collected for the benefit of the development of the final deliverable. Another example of the usage of this tool could be to observe coming users in action in their current environment. This could be relevant if the project is supposed to develop a concept for renewing existing work processes, for example at a large hospital aiming for efficiency gains.

Analysis workshops

Stakeholder engagement implies that the project understands the stakeholders' needs, interests, wishes, concerns, and expectations properly. In a workshop, it may be more likely that different perspectives and more knowledge lead to a comprehensive analysis and a better understanding. The workshop participants may be project team members, members of the project owner organization, selected stakeholders, and further experts.

Explicit mutual expectations

For understanding project stakeholders, it is important to make expectations from the project's point of view as well as from the stakeholder's point of view explicit in order to be able to align them. Questions to ask can include:

- What does the particular stakeholder expect regarding the project (outcomes/process)?
- What does the Project expect from the particular stakeholder (contributions to outcomes and process)?
- Are there synergies or conflicts in this relationship?
- Which actions can the project take to better design the relationship with the particular stakeholder?

Stakeholder reflections

Even with the best intentions, it may be difficult to make stakeholders reveal their needs, interests, expectations, and concerns. A classical method to enhance this is to ask the stakeholders to reflect on their relevant previous experiences

(Eskerod & Jepsen, 2013). This is especially valuable when it comes to discussing and planning the project process. Examples of reflection questions:

- Mention three good and three bad experiences you have had in former projects – and that you find relevant for this project.
- What did you especially like or dislike concerning communication in your former projects?

By discussing their personal experiences stakeholders may find it easier to identify and articulate their requirements, wishes, and concerns - and the members of the project organization may find it easier to understand what they mean. It may be advantageous to ask for the reflections in a workshop so that the other participants will be able to benefit from the reflections and build a comprehensive understanding of a particular stakeholder as well as reflect on their own answers to the reflection questions.

Scenario developments

While stakeholder reflections rather draw on the stakeholder's past experiences, scenario developments make the stakeholder's image of the future explicit (Freeman et al., 2007). The underlying idea is to invite the stakeholders to tell how they expect the project to create value for them. This may include how the stakeholder will make use of the project deliverables, for example, the end users of a new IT system or the consumers of a new product – or ask the stakeholder give feedback on a mock-up or prototype. Scenario developments may also use role plays to emphasize with stakeholders. As in the case of stakeholder reflections, the purpose is to create a more comprehensive understanding of the particular stakeholder's situation relevant to the project at hand.

Systemic board

A systemic board can help visualize relations between project stakeholders and between stakeholders and relevant elements in a project, like the project itself, project roles, certain interests, conflicts, and project success. Blocks or figures of different shapes (and sometimes colours) represent stakeholders and the elements as named and positioned by the individual or team applying the method. A facilitator helps the individual in charge to reflect on the board by asking questions. A relevant audience, for example, other project team members are present so that they also can benefit from seeing the board and listening to the dialogue between the facilitator and the individuals. A variation is that more individuals such as the project manager and the team work together on the constellation and construct together a shared picture and understanding of the stakeholder landscape.

The method helps to abstract a situation and simulate possible solutions. The systemic board is well-suited for dealing with the increased complexity that the management for stakeholders' approach adds to the project stakeholder management. Thus the systemic board is especially suitable for development or change projects, or other projects with an extremely varied stakeholder landscape. Figure 27.2 provides an example of a systemic board applied for an infrastructure project (Huemann et al., 2016).

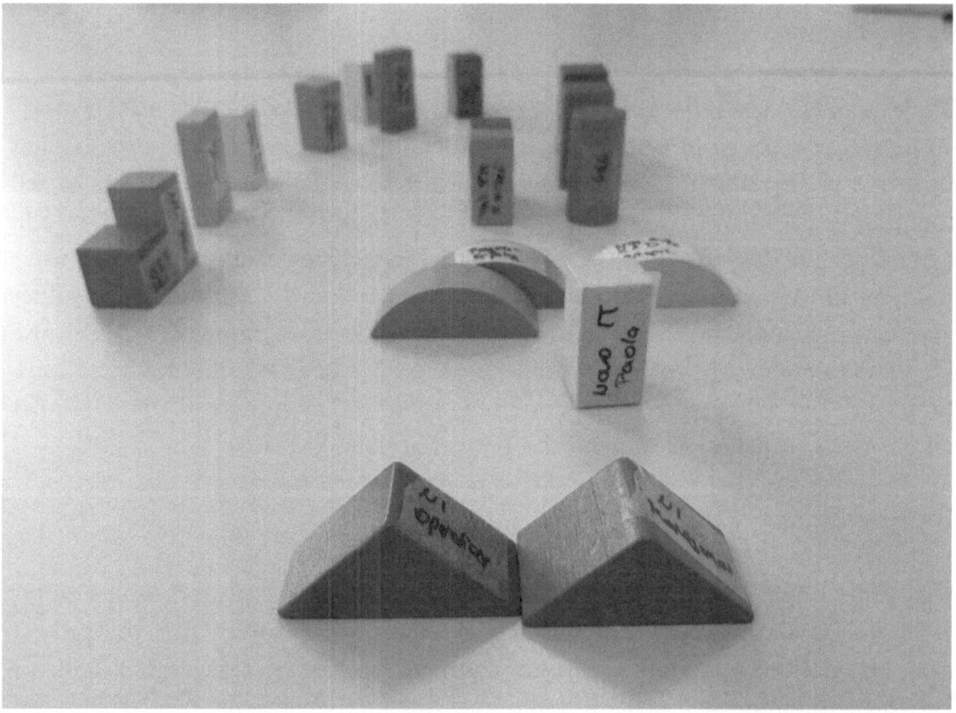

Figure 27.2: Example of a systemic board

Systemic constellation

A systemic constellation resembles a systemic board; however, individuals represent stakeholders and other elements instead of blocks. Representatives take on the position of particular stakeholders or elements – and speak on their behalf. Further, the individual doing the constellation can try out various positions – and feel how this stakeholder is in the particular position. This gives a deeper understanding of the relations between the stakeholders and the selected elements, as well as opportunities to try out various solutions.

This method requires an experienced facilitator as well as a number of people to undertake the representations. Figure 27.3 shows an example of a systemic

Figure 27.3: Example of a systemic constellation

constellation applied for the stakeholder analysis of a development project of a municipality in Denmark. (Huemann et al., 2016).

The man on the table represents the vision of the project. He placed himself on the table so that the vision could be visible to all stakeholders. The woman on the right is the facilitator. She asks well-thought-out questions to make all the participants reflect on the situation at hand. The systemic constellation is especially suitable for analyzing, empathizing, and simulating different approaches to the stakeholders in complex stakeholder settings such as change projects or public investment projects.

Info materials

A classical way to engage project stakeholders is to provide them with info materials, like project brochures, project newsletters, and a project website. Info materials may be a cost-effective way to inform the project stakeholders about the project. This is very much in line with active project marketing and selling of the project to the stakeholders. However, two-way communication with the stakeholders is typically more suitable for a management for stakeholders' approach as it may be difficult to take on their perspective without direct communication with them. Info materials should therefore be seen as a method to supplement other engagement activities, but might be rather essential to explain the how and why of a project. The application of info material is especially useful if the project needs to deal with large and diverse groups of stakeholders, such as the people living in the community in which a new tunnel is built.

Town hall meetings

A town hall meeting is a public meeting in which everyone interested in the project can show up to be informed and to voice their opinion. Town hall meetings are typically supplemented with online materials before and after the meeting. Opportunities to voice opinions can be given in more ways. For example, in real time at the meeting itself, and also after the meeting through online opportunities, e.g. on social media. The town hall meeting may be physical or virtual. It can also take place as a physical meeting that is simultaneously streamed via the internet.

Social media interactions

Social media platforms offer a broad range of opportunities for stakeholder interactions with the project, both when it comes to proactive strategies (e.g. applying a push strategy by posting information about the project, Eskerod & Jepsen, 2013) and response strategies (i.e. responding to stakeholder requests). The social media context implies that stakeholder identification and assessment cannot take place in the classical way as the information about the stakeholders is too sparse. However, issue-based responses as well as 'always respond' and 'acknowledge' strategies are recommended (Chung et al., 2023).

Engaging dialogue

To enhance a trustful and flourishing relationship with a stakeholder the project organization members may apply specific communication styles, e.g. active listening and empathizing. The Appreciative Inquiry method (Cooperrider & Whitney, 2001) which guides positive questions to be asked is another relevant way to create an engaging dialogue with the stakeholder.

Stakeholder workshops

Stakeholder workshops (whether in person or virtually) are well-suited for engaging the project stakeholders in a management for stakeholders' approach because they give the possibility for project representatives and stakeholders to interact on a real-time face-to-face basis. Thereby it is more likely that they can get a better understanding of each other's situations, interests, and expectations – and search for or develop (innovative) win-win solutions. If this is not possible it may be easier to work on trade-offs that are less harmful than if the project organization came up with trade-offs without involving the stakeholders. A stakeholder workshop may address one project stakeholder (group) only, or it may be an arena for more stakeholders to meet.

Proto-typing, simulations

As described for the 'Stakeholder-in-action observations' tool, practices from the field of innovation, like for example proto-typing of project deliverables and simulation of service processes may be a valuable way to get insights about the stakeholders.

Integrated project organization

Another method to engage the project stakeholders is to integrate them into the project organization. By giving them a formal project role they will be involved in decision-making in the project as well and they will get a legitimate arena to voice their points of view at a continuous basis. Further, accepting a formal role is also a way for the project stakeholder to show commitment and willingness to take on responsibilities for the project outcomes.

'Thank you'

When continuous interactions between the project and the project stakeholder are not relevant any longer the members of the project organization must find a way to thank the stakeholder for the project contributions provided. Various means of communication are available for example a personal letter, a telephone call, and acknowledgement statements in reports, books, or on websites. This method may be combined with the next method presented, a celebration event. A management for stakeholders' approach would imply that all (or at least many) stakeholders are thanked – not only the ones who are relevant for future projects.

Satisfaction survey

A satisfaction survey can be conducted to selected stakeholders. The survey may consist of closed or open questions, or a mixture. Closed questions combined with a Likert scale (measuring the satisfaction on a scale from for example 1 to 5) can allow the project to do statistical analyses and thereby get an objective measure of the stakeholders' satisfaction. Even though we have placed this tool in the last stakeholder engagement process, it can be used throughout the course of the project.

Lessons learned

Reflections on lessons learned together with the stakeholders can be done in a real-time session, whether physical or virtual, or it can be done in a write-up carried out by the project or even by the stakeholder, e.g. a supplier. The lessons learned tool can be applied in a structured way, e.g. supported by a bullet point list, or in an unstructured way, letting the participant(s) provide top-of-mind impressions.

Celebration event

To arrange a celebration event is another way of showing the project stakeholders' appreciation of their contributions to the project. Such an event may vary in magnitude, participants, and costs. Varying from having coffee and cake when a project team member leaves the team to breath-taking events at special locations – with fancy project presentations, celebrity guests, gala dinners, shows, media coverage, etc. Sometimes big events solely serve marketing purposes and do not show appreciation to the stakeholders. As an engagement activity, such events should reflect stakeholder-oriented principles and be organized in a way well-suited for the stakeholders.

Future-oriented evaluation

In the management for project stakeholders approach it is acknowledged that a broader time perspective than the project duration should be applied in order to take care of the project stakeholders' long-term interests. This means that it may be relevant to evaluate the project process and outcomes in relation to the future, such as to discuss lessons learned relevant for the stakeholder as well as the members of the project organization.

Roles

It is important to notice that project stakeholder engagement both has a strategic and an operative side, and that it may be individuals in different roles that take care of them. The strategic project stakeholder engagement concerns overall decisions on how to relate to each stakeholder, that is whether the stakeholder should be involved in the project by giving them a formal project role in the project organization or by inviting the stakeholder to project events or a distribution list for a project newsletter. The operative project stakeholder engagement concerns the continuous interactions with the project stakeholder.

Engaging with stakeholders implies that a comprehensive understanding of the project stakeholder's needs, interests, and expectations should be developed and those continuous interactions should take place in order to sustain the understanding and take care of eventual changes. This implies that it may be a good idea to involve a number of project roles in both strategic and operative project stakeholder management, like the project manager, the project owner, and project team members. In big public infrastructure projects in The Netherlands, the stakeholders' interests are even more in focus as the law asks to appoint a specific project stakeholder manager to take on this role explicitly. Thus, the challenge lay in coordinating the tasks and the consistency of the behaviour of the different roles involved in a stakeholder engagement on a project to provide a coherent message to a particular stakeholder.

Conclusion

The chapter offers a comprehensive perspective on project stakeholder engagement by describing mindset, processes, methods, and roles. While we acknowledge the challenges and the comprehensive resource requirements needed for stakeholder engagement, we suggest that especially in large infrastructure projects these activities should be enclosed as a proportion of the entire budget, as they may make a big difference for the communities affected by the project. We advocate that stakeholder engagement is a must today to ensure that projects can provide fertile grounds for co-creating better futures.

References and further reading

Andersen, E.S., 2008, *Rethinking Project Management. An Organisational Perspective*, Harlow: Prentice Hall/Financial Times.

Chung, K.S.K., Eskerod, P., Jepsen, A.L. & Zhang, J., 2023, Response strategies for community stakeholder engagement on social media: A case study of a large infrastructure project. *International Journal of Project Management*, 41(5), 102495.

Cooperrider, D.L. & Whitney, D., 2001, A positive revolution in change: Appreciative inquiry. *Public Administration and Public Policy*, 87, 611–630.

Eskerod, P., 2020, A stakeholder perspective: Origins and core concepts, in Berg D.D. (ed.), *Oxford Research Encyclopedia of Business and Management*, Oxford, New York: Oxford University Press.

Eskerod, P. & Huemann, M., 2013, Sustainable development and project stakeholder management: What standards say. *International Journal of Managing Projects in Business,* 6(1), 36–50.

Eskerod, P. & Huemann, M., 2024, Principles of project stakeholder orientation for managing projects sustainably, in Silvius, G. & Huemann, M. (eds.), *Research Handbook on Sustainable Project Management*, Cheltenham: Edward Elgar Publishing Ltd.

Eskerod, P. & Jepsen, A.L., 2013, *Project stakeholder management*, in, *Fundamentals of Project Management Series*, Dalcher, D. (ed.). Aldershot: Gower.

Freeman, R.E., 1984, *Strategic Management: A Stakeholder Approach*, Boston, MA: Pitman/Ballinger.

Freeman, R.E., Harrison, J.S. & Wicks, A.C., 2007, *Managing for Stakeholders: Survival, Reputation, and Success*, New Haven, CT: Yale University Press.

Freeman, R.E., Harrison, J.S., Wicks, A.C., Parmar, B.L. & De Colle, S., 2010, *Stakeholder Theory: The State of the Art*, Cambridge: Cambridge University Press.

Harrison, J.S. & Wicks, A.C., 2021, Harmful stakeholder strategies. *Journal of Business Ethics*, 169, 405–419.

Huemann, M., 2022, Celebrating the power of projects and their management. *International Journal of Project Management*, 40(1), 1–3.

Huemann, M., Eskerod, P. & Ringhofer, C., 2016, *RETHINK! Project Stakeholder Management, PMI,* Newtown Square, PA: Project Management Institute.

Huemann, M. & Silvius, G., 2017, Projects to create the future: Managing projects meets sustainable development. *International Journal of Project Management,* 35(6), 1066–1070.

Loch, C. & Kavadias, S., 2011, Implementing strategy through projects, in Morris, P.W.G., Pinto, J.K. & Söderlund, J. (eds.), *The Oxford Handbook of Project Management*, Oxford: Oxford University Press, 224–251.

Savage, G.T., Nix, T.W., Whitehead, C.J. & Blair, J.D., 1991, Strategies for assessing and managing organizational stakeholders. *Executive (19389779)*, 5(2), 61–75.

Silvius, G. & Huemann, M., (eds.), in press, Research Handbook on Sustainable Project Management, Cheltenham: Edward Elgar Publishing Ltd.

Whyte, J., Comi, A. & Mosca, L., 2022, Making futures that matter: Future making, online working and organizing remotely. *Organization Theory,* 3(1), 1–20.

Winch, G.M. & Sergeeva, N., 2022, Temporal structuring in project organizing: A narrative perspective. *International Journal of Project Management*, 40(1), 40–51.

Chapter 28

Project leadership model

Natalya Sergeeva, Graham M, Winch, and Eunice Maytorena-Sanchez

Introduction

Previous research on project leadership has focused on who leaders are, investigating their competencies (including traits and behaviours) (Müller & Turner, 2010), their biographies (Drouin et al., 2021), or both (Merrow & Nandurdikar, 2018). We offer an alternative functional model (Edmondson & Harvey, 2017), the Project Leadership Model, that focuses on how leaders make sense of their environment and build relationships, thereby creating narratives about the project and designing how the project mission is delivered. It was developed in collaboration with industry and delegates from the oil and gas and defence material sectors on project leadership executive education programs. The chapter will provide examples of the model in practice. We also discuss the role of narratives and narrating as an important process in project organizing.

The Project Leadership Model

The Project Leadership Model comprises five processes: sensemaking, relating, projecting, creating, and judging as shown in Figure 28.1. The origins of the Project Leadership Model can be traced back to the work of Ancona et al. (2007) and the notion of an incomplete leader. No one person can be equally good at

DOI: 10.4324/9781003274179-32

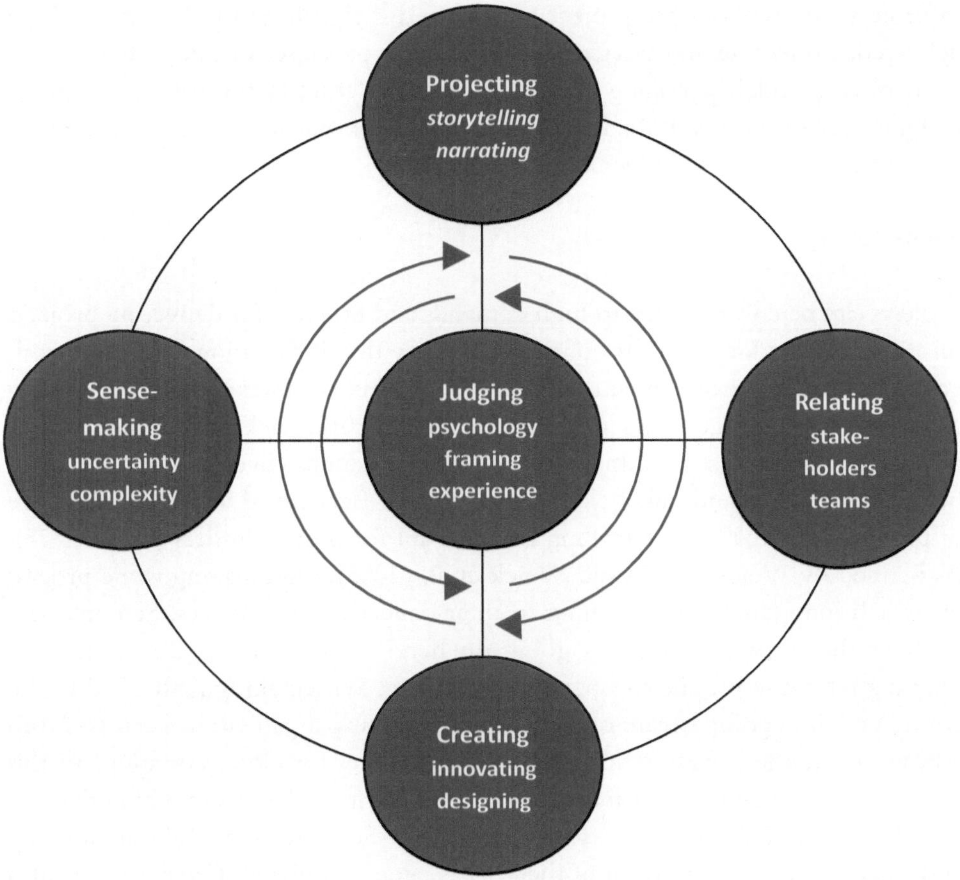

Figure 28.1: The Project Leadership Model (Winch et al., 2022)

all five processes, so the project leader will need to work with others in the team to ensure that all processes are effectively addressed. The next chapter, Chapter 30, deals with balanced leadership and how the leader shares their leadership role. No leader is perfect. The best ones don't try to be – they concentrate on honing their strengths and find others who can make up for their limitations (Ancona et al., 2007).

The Project Leadership Model incorporates five processes which are connected and overlapping but can be viewed as distinctive processes. Relating and sense-making are the *enabling* processes because they are how the leader garners information about what is happening. The project leader then uses this information to project stories about the project mission and design how that mission will be delivered. Projecting and designing are the *acting* processes of the model. At the heart of the model is judging which captures the combination of the decision-making frames, the psychological traits, and the consolidated experience that are the foundations of wise judgement.

Sensemaking

Projects can be complex due to high demands and urgency for delivering projects on time, to budget, and to quality along with globalisation, technological, economic, and environmental requirements. Project complexity could be understood through ambiguity (as projects are idiosyncratic, lacking routine, norms, and predictability) and multiplicity (interdependency, diversity, and tensions between structures and stakeholders) (Chapter 6). Because of the dynamic nature of project complexity, sensemaking is important for project leaders (Chapter 25). As defined by Weick (1995) and Weick et al. (2005), sensemaking is the process by which individuals give meaning to their collective experiences. Sensemaking is about the question: 'What is going on here?' (Kay & King, 2020). It is an ongoing retrospective and prospective processing. Sensemaking is attached to the context of an ongoing stream of activities surrounding organisational actors. From a flow of activities, organisational actors extract cues for closer attention. In this context, sensemaking means interpreting and making sense of something that has already occurred during the organising process. Sensemaking is about noticing and labelling, which follows after the act has been completed. Over time, leaders label organisational activities extracted from the flow.

For example, sensemaking offers an explanation of how individual narratives of innovation are mobilised as part of the means through which leaders construct their own self-identities. This perspective offers insights into how localised narratives of innovation are shaped and constrained by formal narratives of improvement. Sensemaking incorporates an acceptance that identity at different levels (organisation, individual) is socially constructed. From a sensemaking perspective, identity is a dynamic process characterised by ongoing struggles and conflicts around the construction of a sense of self. In portraying identity as fluid and fragmented, it is frequently argued that ambiguity and conflict are central to its social construction. From the perspective of sensemaking, it is self-identity that shapes how individuals act and how they interpret organisational phenomena.

The sensemaking perspective takes seriously subjective beliefs and opinions (individual), and inter-subjective (social) judging as essential contributions towards a reasonable explanation of narratives mobilised by project leaders. Sensemaking is a social process not just concerned with leaders but shaped by other employees and events (discussions, interactions). Communication is a central component of sensemaking and is described as an ongoing process of making sense of the situations in which actors collectively find themselves and their activities. Sensemaking is an active process throughout the project lifecycle. There is a continuous process of making sense of a project's progress, team arrangements, identities, activities, etc.

Relating

One of the most important activities of the project leader is relating both internally with project and functional teams and externally with various stakeholders. Relating is both formal through structured communication and informal through social networking which is probably the most important in the contemporary world of project organising. Relating is about building and maintaining relationships within and outside the project organisation. For project leaders relating is critical in delivering projects, as they constantly need to find opportunities, and search for new projects to work on. In the era of networks, being able to build trusting and long-lasting relationships is fundamental.

According to Ancona et al. (2007), there are three ways to do this: inquiring, advocating, and connecting. The concepts of inquiring and advocating come from the work of Argyris (1994) and Schön (1983). Inquiring is about listening with the intention of understanding the thoughts and feelings of the speaker. The listener tries to understand and comprehend how and why the speaker makes sense and interprets experiences and situations. In the context of project leadership, inquiring is also about asking perceptive questions at the earlier phases of the project process. Advocating is about explaining one's own perspective; it is how project leaders make clear to others how they reached their interpretations and conclusions. Project leaders make judgements and explain the reasoning. They are using clear and coherent narratives to communicate with project teams and external stakeholders. Connecting involves a network of people who can help a leader to accomplish a wide range of goals. Building positive relationships and connections with key stakeholders is important for achieving project outputs and outcomes.

The related dimension of sensemaking is sensegiving (Chapter 25), as directed at external parties whose perceptions are held to be important, and hence worth influencing (Weick et al., 2005). Sensegiving is a process by which individuals attempt to shape the sensemaking processes of others. Leaders make sense of the environment (sensemaking) and then communicate with others to gain support (sensegiving). Thus, sensemaking is connected to sensegiving: sensemakers are shaped by "saying" oriented towards a specific audience. Sensemaking is incomplete without sensegiving: target audiences may affect sensemakers. Both sensemaking and sensegiving are important processes of relating.

Projecting

Sensemaking and relating are the enabling processes of the Project Leadership Model; we now turn to the action processes which are about getting something done. An important part of leading is the process of projecting (Defoe, 1697) – imagining how a project will be developed, progressed, and delivered, and how private and public benefit will be realised into future value. It is at the earlier phases of the project process when project leaders with others are projecting the desired future of a project. Project leaders tend to think strategically and have a vision for the completion of a project. Projecting involves creating compelling images of the future; it produces a map of what could be done, and what a leader wants the future to be. It is an ongoing process. Project leaders skilled in projecting use stories and narratives to project the desired future. Projecting is about narrating a future. Narratives can be understood as a discursive construction that project leaders use to shape their own individual (sensemaking) and others' understanding (sensegiving), and an outcome of the collective construction of meaning (Havermans et al., 2015). For projecting our future, the standard tools of investment appraisal are necessary but not sufficient to mobilise the resources required. Leaders need to craft a project narrative that convinces themselves, convinces the team, and convinces stakeholders to allow the project to go ahead by providing resources and giving permissions (Sergeeva & Winch, 2021). Once mobilised, the narrative needs to become delivery-orientated to incentivise all the suppliers and their employees to give their best for the project. Project leaders are motivating and inspiring the team to help implement the project. Creating a shared vision with a project team is key to achieving the goals of a project. It helps the team to work towards the desired goals. Projecting in the context of projects is a purposeful process that aims at achieving set goals.

Creating

Project leaders use the outputs of sensemaking and relating as the enablers for projecting the project mission and then creating how that mission will be delivered. A project narrative therefore ties together the projecting and creating processes of the Project Leadership Model. Creating has two considerations: designing and innovating. Designing how the project organisation will deliver the outputs and innovate which is increasingly recognised as an important activity which project leaders and their teams do. Designing is the process of developing a temporary project organisation (e.g. project team, project DNA and project identity) which is then communicated internally with the team with the aim of creating a common vision for delivering the owner's mission. Creating is about forming a project identity and image. Organisational identity is defined as an organisation's members' understanding of the features presumed to be central and relatively permanent, which distinguish the organisation from other organisations. Organisational image is the perception of the organisational purpose, aims, and values, resulting in the general impression in the mind of all stakeholders. Project identity and image are formed through narratives. A project identity narrative is conveyed internally, whereas a project image narrative is projected to external stakeholders as project branding (for financiers, policy makers, potential objectors, environmentalists, etc.) (Sergeeva & Winch, 2021). Innovating is about problem-solving whether by setting out to advance technology or by combining existing technologies in a novel way to deliver the owner's project mission. Innovating is a step change in best practice that could be a product, process, and service new to the specific context, not necessarily to the world that could be economic, environmental, or societal benefits for the owner and its stakeholders. Innovating is usually achieved collaboratively across organisations by the people within them, and orchestrating such collaboration is one of the great challenges and opportunities of project organising. Collaborating between various individuals, teams, organisations (owners, supply chain, and others) is the way to innovate.

Judging

The Project Leadership Model focuses on the four processes, but who they are and how they think impacts how and what leaders do. Judging is at the heart of the model and broadly speaking is about psychology, framing, and experience

(Winch et al., 2022). Project leaders are judging on many aspects of the project throughout the project process based on their sensemaking and related activities. Project leaders are judging what to do and how to do and their decisions and actions have important implications for future decision-making processes. Project leaders' judging impacts the project's DNA and the image of the project. Judging is hence also connected with projecting and creating aspects of the model.

Arriving at the right judgements in projects is fundamental because it has important implications for the health, safety, and well-being of workers for instance. This relates to the training necessary to be obtained by workers and leaders, everyday instructions for performing the work, monitoring the workers and their performance, and other psychological judgements.

The Project Leadership Model provides an understanding of the leading process in project organising and the key processes associated with it: sensemaking, relating, projecting, creating, and judging. Understanding project leadership in processual terms enables an understanding of the nature of the leading process and its dynamics. This generates a large research agenda, of which we will focus on two aspects here.

Narratives and narrating as fundamental in leading projects

One area in which the Project Leadership Model identifies as a fruitful area for project organising research is in projecting – or what Defoe (1697) calls the mystery of projecting. Core to projecting is, we suggest, narrating (Havermans et al., 2015; Winch & Sergeeva, 2021). Narratives play an enormously important role in projecting by connecting the present with the future and are the essential means for maintaining or reproducing stability and promoting or resisting change in and around organisations and are essential for decision-making under uncertainty (Kay & King, 2020). Havermans et al. (2015) suggest expressing problems as narratives is a dynamic process that can frame problems in a new light, aid interaction, and shape actions. Narratives are persuasive in nature and are used by project leaders to convince stakeholders during project shaping and mobilisation of resources during project delivery. In this section, we outline the role of narratives, their types, and the process of narrating in project organising.

Project leaders craft and communicate a project shaping narrative that inspires employees, excites partners, attracts customers, and engages influencers and, perhaps most importantly, investors (Sergeeva & Winch, 2021). The project shaping narrative is used to explain why the project exists and what makes it unique, the value and relationships it creates and communicates these to both internal project team members and external stakeholders – in sum an *image* for the project. The image-shaping narrative generates a project mission as a compelling *why* statement for the project. To develop that mission into a compelling narrative for the project that will motivate staff and suppliers and commit stakeholders, it is usually complemented with other materials that communicate the principles underpinning *how* the project will be done. These include ethical principles, expectations of suppliers, and benefits for stakeholders. This creates a project *identity* narrative that persists for the project process This helps to create a shared purpose for the team and a projection for its purposeful and successful delivery.

For example, the Tideway megaproject mission statement is

> The 25km super sewer is a vital infrastructure project that will modernise London's ageing sewage system and dramatically improve the environment by preventing millions of tonnes of sewerage overflowing into the river each year. But for Tideway, it's more than just clearing up the river.
>
> (https://www.tideway.london/news/press-releases/2018/september/tideway-unveils-vision-for-new-public-space-along-the-river-thames/)

The image narrative of Tideway was always strong as an environmental improvement project to (1) protect the Thames Tideway ecosystem; (2) to reduce pollution from sewage-derived litter; and (3) to protect the health of recreational river users. However, the identity narrative was missing. Tideway therefore launched the "Our Space" initiative and asked employees to reflect on what they were doing on this megaproject in that open meeting space. This included a whiteboard wall map of the River Thames on which to brainstorm ideas. This generated many keywords and a strong theme emerged as "reconnecting Londoners with the River Thames". This identity narrative was captured in a cartoon of all the activities enabled by Londoners on the Thames. The CEO of Tideway spent 50% of his time on this crafting during the early months of project delivery, playing a crucial role in forming the megaproject's identity narrative. He has also delivered a number of presentations about Tideway and its identity at various external industry and academic events.

The CEO was also keen to encourage early career professionals to be heavily engaged with the innovation program at Tideway. Tideway is the first megaproject to use the UK industry-wide i3P (infrastructure industry innovation partnership) platform. The approach to innovation in Tideway is to encourage and stimulate innovation across the supplier domain. The reasons for encouraging innovation in the program are multiple. Firstly, the research for novel ideas aims to increase project performance in terms of schedule and budget savings. Second, it aims to create beneficial effects for stakeholder communities making construction works safer, shorter, and less disruptive. Thirdly, innovation is seen as a catalyst to create a world-class workforce which benefits not only Tideway but also the sector overall. Finally, by proving its capability to deliver projects more quickly and effectively through innovation, Tideway aims to attract future investments.

The way in which project narratives are communicated is important. A project narrative is commonly communicated in spoken (talks and presentations), written (reports and business cases), and visual (videos, pictures, and slide packs) forms to various internal and external stakeholders. All these are evident on Tideway's megaproject website, there are a number of video materials from the employees sharing their everyday stories and experiences of managing the work. Such videos capture people's experiences of their everyday work in the project environment. It is also (re)iterated and restated in many different ways throughout the project process to serve various purposes and audiences.

There are always counter-narratives, often mobilised by external stakeholders, to the dominant project narrative and ongoing interactions between them. The distinctive characteristics of counter-narratives are oppositional to the dominant project narrative. As demonstrated by Ninan and Sergeeva (2021), in the case of High Speed 2, there are narratives of the need for a project, and there are also counter-narratives that the project is not needed. The promoters are interested in supporting the completion of the megaproject, whilst protesters are interested in derailing the megaproject. The authors explored the role of labels in the sensemaking process and the process through which these labels are maintained and contested in megaproject settings. The promoters labelled the HS2 megaproject as "fast" and "low-carbon", the protesters labelled it as a "vanity project" and as a project "for the rich". Focusing on counter-narratives enables us to capture some of the political, economic, social, and/or cultural complexities and tensions in projecting and capturing the diversity of stakeholder positions in relation to the project narrative. The dynamic interaction between dominant and counter-narratives is part of the power game around project shaping.

Narratives and the process of narrating have important implications for internal and external perceptions of a project. Project identity is conveyed internally to the project team and the supply chain whereas project image is projected to external stakeholders such as investors, campaigners, and policymakers. Project identity narratives are about what project leaders tell the team to achieve shared understanding and vision; they are about a sense of what the delivery project organisation's purpose is that creates its identity (Ninan et al., 2019; Sergeeva & Winch, 2021). Project leaders communicate a narrative about project identity to the project team. This commitment is based on the connection of the group combined with the emotional value that is attributed to this connection. Project image narratives stimulate stakeholders to commit themselves to the project. Crafting a favourable image is important for gaining legitimacy and support from external stakeholders which in turn affects the delivery of project outputs. Projects require convincing narratives to build strong brand attributes and loyalty. This is why it is important to brand the project with a well-crafted external image from the start and hence crafting a project image narrative as part of project shaping is essential for the successful delivery of projects from an external stakeholder management perspective.

Project leaders craft and maintain project narratives (about the mission, scope, identity, image, innovation, sustainability, health, safety and well-being, and value) throughout the project lifecycle and their work-life experience. They communicate and share their project narratives internally with the team and externally with people outside (through social media, Facebook, LinkedIn, and Twitter). Sharing project narratives may have an impact on winning new projects, feeling proud of the work completed, and making new connections and contacts. There is an ongoing process of narrating and storytelling in different forms in project organising.

Conclusion

This chapter offers an important foundation for understanding the process of leading complex projects. We present the Project Leadership Model that inspires project leaders to think about their own and their team members' competencies.

Sensemaking, relating, projecting, creating, and judging are key processes that project leaders and their teams need to engage with when leading complex projects. Project leaders share their experiences through narratives and stories to receive pride and recognition for their completed projects. This is usually done through social media channels and communication. The pride and recognition provide a motivation for doing other interesting and exciting construction projects in the future.

References and further reading

Ancona, D., Malone., T.W., Orlikowski, W.J. & Senge, P.M. (2007). In praise of the incomplete leader. *Harvard Business Review*, February 2007, 92–100.

Argyris, C. (1994). Good communication that blocks learning. *Harvard Business Review*, July–August.

Defoe, D. (1697). *An Essay on Projects*. London: Cockerill.

Drouin, N., Sankaran, S., van Marrewijk, A. & Müller, R. (2021). *Megaproject Leaders: Reflections on Personal Life Stories*. Cheltenham: Edward Elgar.

Edmondson, A.C. & Harvey, J.-F. (2017). *Extreme Teaming: Lessons In Complex, Cross-Sector Leadership*. Bingley: Emerald.

Havermans, L.A., Keegan, A.E. & Den Hartog, D.N. (2015). Choosing your words carefully: Leaders' narratives of complex emergent problem resolution. *International Journal of Project Management, 33*(5), 973–984.

Kahneman, D., Sibony, O. & Sunstein, C.R. (2021). *Noise: A Flaw In Human Judgment*. London: William Collins.

Kay, J. & King, M. (2020). *Radical Uncertainty: Decision Making For an Unknowable Future*. London: The Bridge Street Press.

Merrow, E.W. & Nandurdikar, N. (2018). *Leading Complex Projects: A Data-Driven Approach to Mastering the Human Side of Project Management*. Wiley.

Müller, R. & Turner, J.R. (2010). *Project-Oriented Leadership*. Farnham, WA: Gower.

Ninan, J., Clegg, S. & Mahalingam, A. (2019). Branding and governmentality for infrastructure megaprojects: The role of social media. *International Journal of Project Management, 37*(1), 59–72.

Ninan, J. & Sergeeva, N. (2021). Labyrinths of labels: Promoters' and protesters' narrative constructions in mega projects. *International Journal of Project Management* (in press).

Schön, D. (1983). *The Reflective Practitioner: How Professionals Think in Action*. New York: Basic Books.

Sergeeva, N. & Winch, G.M. (2021). Project narratives that potentially perform and change the future. *Project Management Journal, 18*(4), 312–326.

Weick, K.E. (1995). *Sensemaking of Organizations*. Thousand Oaks, CA: Sage Publications.

Weick, K.E., Sutcliffe, K.M. & Obstfield, D. (2005). Organizing and the process of sensemaking. *Organization Science, 16*(4), 409–421.

Winch, G.M., Maytorena-Sanchez, E. & Sergeeva, N. (2022). *Strategic Project Organizing*. Oxford: Oxford University Press.

Chapter 29

Balanced leadership

Ralf Müller

Introduction

The phenomenon of leadership is a classic theme in, for example, management, psychology, or politics. It is also an umbrella term that covers various perceptions of the phenomenon, like the behaviour of politicians, the 'vibration' between musicians and their audience, or the visions of so-called technology leaders. The present chapter looks at the locus of leadership within projects. Most obviously, this is the project manager. However, this is not always the case, as we will see later. The complexity of projects and the many different specializations and skills needed in these projects often challenge project managers. They become uncomfortable making decisions and leading the team in areas they are not specialized in. A typical example is airport construction, where the project manager cannot be the expert in all questions related to innovation, construction work, IT, training, local politics, etc. In cases of problems that require skills outside his or her specialization, the project manager often relies on team members to lead the project successfully through the issue at hand. Therefore, the authority to exercise leadership alternates between team members and project managers dynamically over time in projects. This alternation is called *balanced leadership* and aims to find the most suitable leader for any situation in the project. To execute balanced leadership, the project manager has several options at his or her disposal. These options are called leadership approaches, of which four are addressed here, namely vertical, shared, distributed, and horizontal leadership.

DOI: 10.4324/9781003274179-33

Before entering into the discussion about leadership approaches, a definition and positioning of leadership are indicated. In this chapter, leadership is defined as an interpersonal, person-oriented, social influence that guides direction, course, action, and opinion (Bennis & Nanus, 1985; Endres & Weibler, 2017). Hence, this chapter is written from the perspective of leadership as an interpersonal process between individuals in a project.

Leadership's personal orientation makes it different from management, which is a task-oriented activity. Examples include the classic management tasks of planning, controlling, and reporting. Or, as Bennis and Nanus (1985) said, it is bringing about or accomplishing something, being responsible for, or conducting something.

Both leadership and management are needed in projects. However, the balance thereof is highly dependent on the project manager's personality and the situational requirements.

In this chapter, only the leadership is addressed.

Leadership in projects

Historically, little or no difference was perceived between leadership in temporary organizations like projects and the more permanent or functional organizational settings from which existing leadership theories derived. These theories fall into two categories: (a) vertical leadership by formally appointed leaders, such as project managers, and their particular leadership styles and personalities; and (b) team leadership, where one or several team members are granted leadership authority and the emergence of related processes for identification and execution of this type of leadership. A deeply rooted assumption in these theories was that teams must work together for a long time in order to be performant (Tuckman, 1965). However, this is not the case in projects where team members frequently change, sometimes almost daily. Team members show up to fulfill their particular tasks and then move on to other projects. That leads to the question of how project teams (and their projects) can be performant without a long collaboration experience.

A series of empirical investigations into the relationship between vertical leadership by the project manager and team-based leadership revealed several particularities only found in projects. These include horizontal and balanced leadership. The studies showed that practicing balanced leadership compensates for the team's lack of collaboration experience. Hence, rather than having one leader and team members that get acquainted with each other over time, as in functional organizations, temporary organizations become performant by deliberately looking for and using the best suitable leader at any time in the project. This insight reveals the critical role of the leadership approach for team and project performance (Müller, Drouin, & Sankaran, 2022).

Leadership approaches and leadership styles

Leadership approaches are different from leadership styles. The leadership approach refers to the locus where leadership occurs, such as vertical (from project manager to team member), shared or distributed within the team, or horizontal by an appointed temporary horizontal leader for the project. These four approaches are described further in the chapter.

Leadership styles describe the particular way of interaction chosen by the leader when dealing with the follower(s). A wide variety of these styles exists and these styles are popular themes in the literature. Examples include servant leadership, transactional and transformational leadership, or autocratic, democratic, and laisses-faire leadership styles (see Northouse [2014] for an overview), and many studies addressed the 'fit' between project type and leadership style (e.g., Nauman, Bhatti, Imam, & Khan, 2021).

Leadership approaches and styles are active at different levels. Approaches describe the locus from which leadership originates and styles the particular ways leaders interact with their followers in exercising their leadership. Within each leadership approach, all leadership styles are possible. While leadership styles are similar in projects and functional organizations, approaches can be project-specific and are addressed throughout this chapter. Table 29.1 summarizes their key definitions.

Leadership approaches

Vertical leadership

Vertical leadership is the traditional top-down leadership of a formally appointed leader in an organizational hierarchy or network, such as a project manager in a project. This leadership is crucial for enabling any of the other

Table 29.1 Leadership approaches

Leadership approach	*Definition*	*Source*
Vertical	Top-down leadership by an appointed formal leader	Müller et al. (2022. p. 10)
Horizontal	The temporarily granted authority of a team member to execute vertical leadership on behalf of the project manager	
Shared	A collaborative, emergent process of group interaction in which members engage in peer leadership while working together	Cox, Pearce and Perry (2003, p. 53)
Distributed	A collective social process emerging through the interactions of multiple actors	Bolden (2011, p. 251)
Balanced	The dynamic, temporary, and alternating transitions between vertical, shared, distributed, and horizontal leadership for the accomplishment of desired states in, for example, a task outcome, or the entire project	Müller et al. (2022, p. 10)

leadership approaches. Some project managers do not like the idea of temporarily giving up their leadership authority. They like to have uncompromised control over the project and its team. In these cases, project managers do not empower others to lead temporarily. None of the other leadership approaches will happen. However, this behaviour is not frequently found. In their book about life stories of successful megaproject leaders, Drouin et al. (2021a) show that one of the commonalities of the interviewed leaders was their trust in, reliance on, and frequent interaction with their teams. For them, team involvement was a success factor.

Other reasons for only allowing vertical leadership in projects might stem from the interaction of national and industry cultures. Studies have shown that in some industries and countries, like the construction industry in Canada, it is perceived as a 'face loss' or weakness of the project manager when he or she empowers someone from the team to lead the project temporarily. In these cases, it is often found that the project manager, in need of good advice, consults the related specialist and then announces the specialist's opinion as his or her own decision. Hence there are overt and covert ways to foster vertical leadership.

Horizontal leadership

Horizontal leadership is the temporarily granted authority of a team member to execute vertical leadership on behalf of the project manager. The locus of horizontal leadership is between pure vertical and pure team leadership. In horizontal leadership, the project manager empowers a team member to lead the project temporarily, and then the project manager subordinates to the horizontal leader for the time of empowerment. The latter makes it different from simply delegating leadership, where the project manager would delegate the leadership task but not follow the leadership of the empowered leader. Rather than that, the project manager would fulfill only a supervisor role without engaging in the project tasks. This also happens in projects but is not of interest to this chapter because it is mainly a management function.

Horizontal leaders are typically appointed for their specific skills, such as technical skills the project manager does not possess or their acquaintance with a particular group of stakeholders and their profession, language, or culture. Examples of the former include the database specialist, whose design work is crucial for turning around a project in a crisis situation with unhappy customers due to delays and lack of visible outcomes. Examples of the latter include the industry specialist of a supplier organization who is required to talk to the business managers of the buyer organization about the adjustment of the project to new market requirements and the related business implications to prevent the customer from stopping the project due to budget constraints.

Despite the subordination to the leadership of the horizontal leader, the project manager retains accountability for the project and its outcome. Hence, simultaneously with the subordination, the project manager governs the actions of the empowered leader to ensure they are in the project's best interest. For the horizontal leader, the project manager is both a team resource and a governance institution, which needs leadership with political and situational sensitivity.

Shared leadership

Shared leadership is a collaborative, emergent process of group interaction in which members engage in peer leadership while working together (Cox, Pearce & Perry, 2003, p. 53). The locus in shared leadership is the team and their joint efforts in leading each other to successful outcomes. Its underlying premise is that teams are more effective when several members are involved in their leadership. Team members exercising shared leadership must possess the required authority, which is granted through empowerment by the project manager, and self-management capabilities to gain the respect of the team.

This approach fits especially well in situations of high task interdependence and complexity. In other words, several interdependent skill sets need to be synchronized and coordinated over time for a successful collaborative outcome. Such as in new product development (NPD) projects or for innovative problem-solving.

The project manager's role in shared leadership is often one of 'social architect' in charge of anticipating and identifying the project's needs in terms of skills and personalities, assembling a team with complementary skills and temperaments, plus developing existing team members' skills and their self-leadership capabilities (Cox, Pearce, & Perry, 2003; O'Toole, Galbraith, & Lawler, 2003).

Distributed leadership

Distributed leadership is *a collective social process emerging through the interactions of multiple actors* (Bolden, 2011, p. 251), such as team members. The locus in distributed leadership is the interaction between individuals within and possibly outside the project team. It is related to shared leadership but different in its focus on leadership through interaction. Instead of leadership stemming from a team member, such as in shared leadership, distributed leadership proposes that the interaction between team members as well as possibly individuals outside the team, create new perspectives and insights, which lead the team in creating their intended outcomes. To that end, distributed leadership builds on diversity of perspectives and inclusiveness and emphasizes democratic leadership styles.

Distributed leadership not only fits well in situations similar to those mentioned under shared leadership but is also characterized by even higher levels of complexity or newness. This includes projects requiring the project team to involve universities, research, or other institutions external to the project team to develop their outcomes through interaction and mutual learning.

As in shared leadership, the project manager's role in distributed leadership is mainly that of a social architect in charge of identifying and assembling the required resources and skills and granting the leadership authority to the right team at the right time.

Balanced leadership

Balanced leadership is the *dynamic, temporary, and alternating transition between vertical, shared, distributed, and horizontal leadership for the accomplishment of desired states in, for example, a task outcome or the entire project* (Müller et al., 2022, p. 10). Leadership in projects is dynamic—different stages in the project life-cycle demand different leadership results, which require different leadership approaches. For example, a project's concept stage typically requires leadership that fosters creativity, innovation, and conceptualization skills to define the project's deliverables. Leadership approaches supporting this make use of the combined creativity of the team members, like shared and distributed leadership. This is different in the implementation stage, when the project manager, as the vertical leader, handles scope, time, and budget decisions. However, sudden issues emerging at this stage might require the project manager to revert to the innovation skills of the team and apply horizontal or team-based (shared or distributed) leadership. Figure 29.1 depicts these dynamics over time and shows the most often used and other frequently used leadership approaches at different stages in the project.

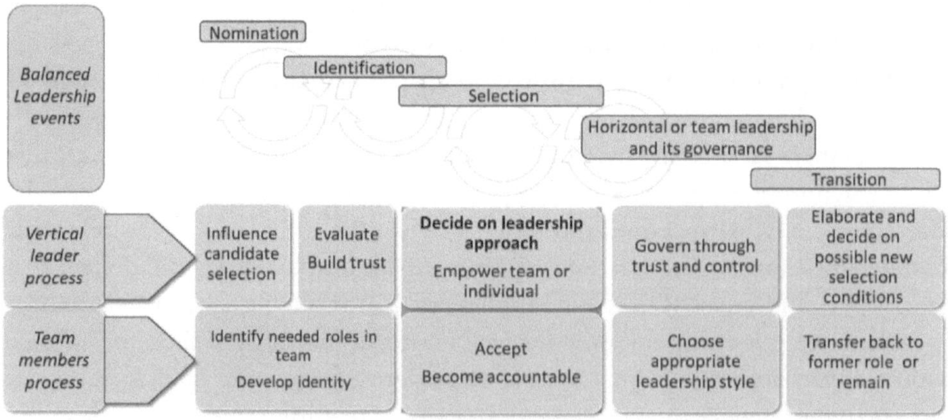

Figure 29.1: Balanced leadership events and associated processes (after Müller et al., 2022)

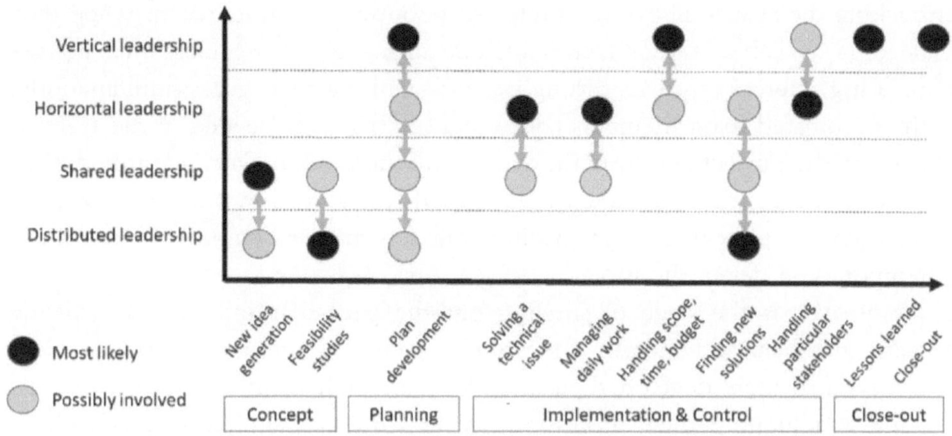

Figure 29.2: The dynamic of shifting leadership approaches (after Müller et al., 2019)

Balanced leadership aims to find the most appropriate leadership approach at any time in the project. As such, it is a form of leadership exercised or enabled by the project manager. It consists of five events and two parallel processes, as shown in Figure 29.2.

The balanced leadership events are depicted in the upper part of Figure 29.2. They may appear in sequential order as shown but more often revert to earlier stages or are nested in each other. For balanced leadership to happen, the five events must have been completed. These events start long before the first decision on shifting leadership authority to others or team members is made.

Within these events, two parallel processes take place. One is executed by the project manager as a vertical leader, while the other is executed by the team members.

The events and related process steps are:

- *Nomination* is the appointment of individuals as team members, which happens at the beginning and during the project. In this stage, the project manager anticipates some of the expected issues and the skills needed to solve them. Because of that, the project manager likes to influence candidate selection for the benefit of the project. However, project managers often do not have the authority to appoint individuals and therefore pursue various tactics to influence the decisions of the nominating (typically functional) manager. These tactics include using social relations with these managers or tracking the availability of the preferred resources to request them when they become available. Other tactics include engaging in organizational politics or using reference power through a high-ranking manager. Simultaneously, the nominated team members try to identify the roles needed in the team to execute the project and how they might fill these roles. Once identified, they develop an identity that suits the identified role and show this to the project manager, emphasizing their specific skill sets and willingness to become a temporary leader in the project.

- *Identification* is the stage of singling out the particular skills of the existing team members and judging their ability to act as temporary leaders. Here project managers develop their trust level in each team member by evaluating and judging their professionality in particular skill sets, personalities, fit to leadership situations, and the leadership ambitions the individuals have shown. Occasionally project managers motivate team members at this point to train specific skills that can be of benefit at later stages in the project. Team members continue refining the development of their role identity to be ready for empowerment when the situation arises.
- *Selection* is the point in time when the project manager decides whether an individual or a team becomes empowered to lead the project. Reasons for the empowerment of individuals as horizontal leaders can be manifold. These can range from requiring a specialist in an area that the project manager is not an expert in but currently causes an issue or crisis in the project to allowing junior managers to train their leadership skills for future roles. Teams are typically empowered to solve issues requiring new thinking or work in teams to generate solutions using shared or distributed leadership. In all these cases, the empowered leader(s) are asked to accept their assignment and assume accountability for their temporary role.
- *Horizontal or team leadership and its governance* mark the duration of the empowerment of the individual or team as the temporary leader(s). When empowering an individual as a horizontal leader, the project manager subordinates to the empowered leader for the time of the empowerment. However, the project manager simultaneously governs the appointed leader during their empowerment to ensure no detrimental effects emerge from the appointment, such as a mismatch of the empowered leader(s) leadership style with the team's expectations. The project manager balances trust and control as governance mechanisms depending on the trust level developed during the identification event. In the case of lower trust levels, control prevails in governance,

often through behaviour control, for example, by enforcing methodology compliance or frequent project reviews. In higher trust levels, freedom is given to the empowered leader, and governance merely looks for results and deliverables generated during the assignment. The empowered leader(s) have to choose the appropriate leadership style for their assignment based on many factors, including their personal leadership preferences and the expectations of the team members they lead. For example, a mismatch between a team of senior specialists who expect democratic leadership and an empowered leader's authoritarian style might threaten the project's progress.

- *Transition* indicates the end of empowerment. Here, the project manager and the empowered leader(s) evaluate the situation. This includes discussions on the extent the expectations for the assignment were accomplished, difficulties that came up, lessons learned, and possible consequences for the future. This typically leads to decisions on the possible re-empowering of the same leader in similar situations in the future; and the re-use or change of the existing leader selection criteria for a better leader-situation fit in the future. The empowered leaders are then typically transferred back to their earlier role in the project or occasionally are re-empowered to solve the next issue or crisis.

This concludes the discussion of the leadership approaches and their shift over time through balanced leadership.

Coordination through the socio-cognitive space

The above discussion on different leadership approaches and their dynamic application through balanced leadership leads to the question of how all these approaches are coordinated.

Studies by Drouin et al. (2021b) showed that for leadership approaches to shift back and forth dynamically, a set of social and cognitive structures must be in place to allow project managers and team members to synchronize their understanding of the presence and the future of the leadership situation in the project. These structures include shared knowledge about:

- *Empowerment*: An unambiguous, shared understanding of who is empowered to lead. This requires decision-making and transparency by the project manager, as well as appropriate meeting and communication structures to communicate these decisions.

- *Self-management*: The empowered person's skills in self-administering the tasks they are empowered to. Empowerment can have very different causes; the team needs to understand them to behave appropriately. For example, a senior professional, known as a specialist, is empowered to solve a technical issue. As a specialist, the person is perceived as high on his or her self-management capabilities to fulfill the task. In this case, the team will typically naturally follow the leadership of the specialist. In another project, a junior project manager might be empowered to lead in order to build up his or her leadership skills. In these cases, the self-management capabilities of the person will be perceived as relatively low. Here the team will be supportive and help the person solve issues and struggles. Hence, knowledge about self-management capabilities influences the way the team reacts to and interacts with the empowered leader.
- *Shared mental models*: The shared knowledge about the project's skill and resource requirements now and in the future. Knowing this allows team members to foresee when shifts in leadership approaches will occur and who the likely candidates for empowerment are.

Synchronizing the knowledge in these three structures allows for transparency and expectation setting. This, in turn, influences the team's behaviour and reduces confusion, competition, and frustration during times of changing leadership authority.

Conclusion

This chapter described the four leadership approaches of vertical, horizontal, shared, and distributed leadership and their dynamics in shifting over time through balanced leadership. For that, the chapter introduced each approach, its 'best fit' situations, and the role of team members and project managers therein. The five events of balanced leadership were presented together with the processes the project managers and team members go through in these events. Finally, the chapter discussed the socio-cognitive space as a structure to synchronize and manage team and manager activities in balanced leadership.

References and further reading

Bennis, W., & Nanus, B. (1985). *Leaders: The Strategies for Taking Charge*. New-York: Harper and Row.

Bolden, R. (2011). Distributed leadership in organizations: A review of theory and research. *International Journal of Management Reviews*, *13*(3), 251–269.

Cox, J. F., Pearce, C. L., & Perry, M. L. (2003). Toward a model of shared leadership and distributed influence in the innovation process: How shared leadership can enhance new product development team dynamics and effectiveness. In C. L. Pearce & J. A. Conger (Eds.), *Shared Leadership* (pp. 48–76). Thousand Oaks, CA: SAGE Publications Inc, USA.

Drouin, N., Müller, R., Sankaran, S., & Vaagaasar, A. L. (2021a). Balancing leadership in projects: Role of the socio-cognitive space. *Project Leadership and Society*, *2*(December 2021). https://doi.org/10.1016/j.plas.2021.100031

Drouin, N., Sankaran, S., van Marrewijk, A., & Müller, R. (2021b). *Megaproject Leaders: Reflections on Personal Life Stories*. (N. Drouin, S. Sankaran, A. van Marrewijk, & R. Müller, Eds.). Cheltenham: Edward Elgar Publishing Limited. Retrieved from https://www.e-elgar.com/shop/gbp/megaproject-leaders-9781789902969.html

Endres, S., & Weibler, J. (2017). Towards a three-component model of relational social constructionist leadership: A systematic review and critical interpretive synthesis. *International Journal of Management Reviews*, *19*(2), 214–236. https://doi.org/10.1111/ijmr.12095

Müller, R., Drouin, N., & Sankaran, S. (2019). *Organizational Project Management: Theory and Implementation*. Cheltenham: Edward Elgar Publishing Ltd.

Müller, R., Drouin, N., & Sankaran, S. (2022). *Balanced Leadership*. New York: Oxford University Press.

Nauman, S., Bhatti, S. H., Imam, H., & Khan, M. S. (2021). How servant leadership drives project team performance through collaborative culture and knowledge sharing. *Project Management Journal*, *53*(1), 17–32.

Northouse, P. G. (2014). *Leadership: Theory and Practice* (4th edition). Thousand Oaks, CA: SAGE Publications Inc.

O'Toole, J., Galbraith, J., & Lawler, E. E. (2003). The promise and pitfalls of shared leadership: When two (or more) heads are better than one. In C. L. Pearce & J. A. Conger (Eds.), *Shared Leadership* (pp. 250–268). Thousand Oaks, CA: SAGE Publications Inc, USA.

Tuckman, B. W. (1965). Developmental sequence in small groups 1. *Psychological Bulletin*, *63*(6), 384–399.

Chapter 30

Motivation of young project professionals

Martina Huemann and Ruth Christine Lechler

Introduction

The need for skilled project professionals is growing rapidly. This is true for both traditional industries such as engineering and construction, as well as newer fields like banking and healthcare. A significant proportion of the workforce today consists of Generation Y, or millennials, individuals born between the early 1980s and mid-1990s (Barford & Hester, 2011). These young professionals have a unique set of expectations for their work. They seek opportunities for personal growth, continuous learning, and work-life balance. They are inclined to work for employers who value social responsibility. The nature of project work seems to align well with their aspirations. Projects are goal-oriented and teamwork-based, and often lead to tangible, meaningful outcomes. As such, project careers are an attractive proposition for young professionals. Projects represent the future of work.

As millennials constitute a significant proportion of today's workforce, their skills, values, and perspectives are likely to influence the nature of work. However, our understanding of what motivates these young professionals to work on projects. A better understanding of these motivators will help project-oriented organizations establish effective strategies for attracting and retaining young talent in project careers.

DOI: 10.4324/9781003274179-34

Motivation

Motivation drives behaviours. It moves us to take or not take action (Guay et al., 2010). We take a self-determination theory perspective on motivation, which states that people are naturally driven towards growth, learning, mastery, and social connection (Deci et al., 2017). Self-determination theory suggests satisfying individuals' basic psychological needs for autonomy, competence, and relatedness fosters their motivation (Deci et al., 2017).

- **Need for autonomy** suggests that individuals desire control over their own actions and objectives. In other words, it is the inherent urge to organize one's experiences and actions so that they align with a coherent sense of self.
- **Need for competence** relates to feeling capable and effective in one's interactions with the surrounding social environment and having opportunities to demonstrate one's abilities.
- **Need for relatedness** speaks to the fundamental human desire for connection with others and the sense of belonging. It includes the need to establish meaningful relationships with others and to give and receive affection.

Why young professionals work on projects

Figure 30.1 visualizes the motivation of young project professionals (Lechler & Huemann, 2023). The model shows the relationship between the young project professionals' motivation to work on projects and their basic psychological needs. In the projects we identify in addition to the three needs outlined by self-determination theory, the need for purpose.

Need for autonomy

Working autonomously is a fundamental need for young project professionals. It manifests as a desire to work independently, have authority over one's tasks, and make self-determined decisions. To work autonomously resonates strongly with young professionals as they appreciate the chance to take full responsibility and accountability for their professional performance. Self-determination fuels

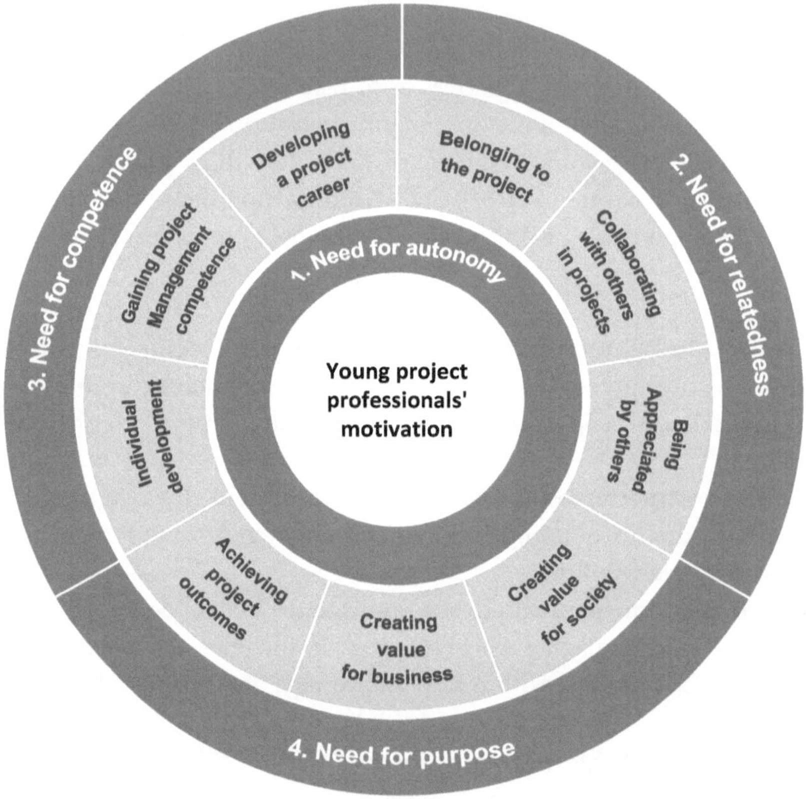

Figure 30.1: Motivators of Young Project Professionals (after Lechler & Huemann, 2023)

their need to direct and manage their tasks on their own. Young professionals are keen on taking ownership of their work and making impactful decisions, which amplifies their sense of empowerment.

Need for relatedness

The need for relatedness shows the significance of creating connections and fostering a sense of belonging to the project team. This corresponds with the need to build relationships and establish connections with others. Young professionals seek acknowledgement and the chance to collaborate with others. This includes exchanging ideas and collaboratively crafting innovative solutions in a shared creative environment. They want to be part of a successful team. Nurturing the sense of relatedness is based on feeling appreciated. Teambuilding, empathetic, and respectful communication, with recognition and praise, can satisfy this need.

Need for competence

The need for competence is driven by the desire to acquire mastery and expand expertise and competencies. It closely relates to the motivation to learn and develop as young professionals, seek to enhance skills and knowledge. When young professionals recognize that their competencies contribute to creating project value and achieving project success, they feel confident in overcoming challenges. This recognition encourages them to seek learning opportunities and embrace new challenges, leading to continuous personal development. This fosters not only their personal development but also enhances their project careers.

Need for purpose

The need for purpose includes the desire to create and deliver results. Young professionals seek the opportunity to contribute to something meaningful that creates value. They strive to align their actions with their core beliefs, which increases their need for purpose. Having a sense of purpose and connection to the project, their team, and the organization enhances their motivation to generate outcomes that benefit businesses by addressing the needs of customers and stakeholders. Simultaneously, they aim to create a positive societal impact, contributing to the betterment of society.

Motivation in context

In practice, we can observe that the nature of different project types and organizational contexts impact the prevalence of the four dimensions of motivation to work on projects.

Motivation in high-tech projects

In high-tech contexts, young professionals find learning and development to be most motivating. These project contexts are known for their fast-paced and changing nature, driven by the implementation of new technologies, innovation, and adaptability. Working on these projects, young professionals learn skills and knowledge to navigate dynamic environments and deal with uncertainty. These projects encourage them to stay up to date with the latest technologies and methodologies, creating a pathway for continuous learning and personal growth. By embracing opportunities and striving for competence, they can stay ahead of emerging trends and technologies and are especially supported in lifelong learning. They especially invest in their employability.

Motivation in engineering projects

Projects in building construction, civil engineering, transport construction like road and rail networks, and hydraulic engineering like water supply and disposal create concrete and publicly visible outcomes. In these contexts, often the need for purpose emerges as a dominant motivating force. This motivation arises from the visible and tangible nature of the projects, like building a new hospital, rebuilding a bridge, or contributing infrastructure to a city development. Engineers' innovative solutions are instrumental in meeting business requirements and addressing societal needs, leading to positive transformations within local communities. Therefore, these projects not only provide value to the businesses themselves but also offer young professionals to contribute to a broader societal impact. This purpose-driven motivation suggests that young professionals like to contribute to creating a better world and making a meaningful difference.

Motivation in transformation projects

In transformational contexts, learning and individual development are particularly motivating for young project professionals. These contexts mainly revolve around internal projects about digital transformation, organizational restructuring, or business development. The value placed on learning and personal growth is deeply connected to the abundant learning opportunities inherent in transformation projects. These projects often focus on enhancing internal processes and systems, providing motivation for young professionals' intent on improving their work's efficiency and effectiveness. These opportunities enable them to acquire new skills and expand their knowledge, fostering personal growth and professional development.

Motivation in business consulting projects

In business consulting, management and IT consulting projects play a significant role, serving primarily external clients. Such consulting environments are classified by their problem-solving focus, tasking young professionals with identifying and resolving issues for a variety of clients. In business consulting contexts, we often find that motivation is based on combining the need for competence and the need for purpose. Given the nature of the projects to deliver valuable insights and solutions to clients, professionals are driven by their desire to showcase their expertise and capabilities. The complex and challenging nature of the work demands a high level of competence, motivating individuals to continuously improve their skills and knowledge. Furthermore, the purpose-driven aspect emerges from the understanding that the outcomes of their efforts can have a significant impact on clients' businesses and success. This sense of purpose fuels their motivation and drives them to achieve meaningful results for their clients.

Practical implications

To motivate young professionals effectively, project-oriented organizations should create an environment that nurtures continuous learning, personal growth, collaboration, and the opportunity to make a purposeful impact. Organizations can do this by considering specific strategies.

Project-related incentive systems

Many organizations lack project-related incentive systems. However, it is crucial to meet the needs of young professionals to establish motivation by providing incentives that are not based solely on money, like bonuses. Incentives, that do meet the needs of young professionals, may include flexible working hours, mentoring programs, team activities, and recognition through praise and increased responsibilities.

Career systems and community of practice

Some organizations explicitly offer and communicate career paths. These include a distinct Project Management career track, especially young professionals' orientation, and support them in their career aspirations (Huemann, 2015). Belonging to an important profession within an organization and a community of practice creates a relatedness, and supports autonomy, as well as competence development beyond the single project. Competence. By outlining clear developmental and career paths, and offering network opportunities professionals can form meaningful connections with others. Career systems serve as a roadmap, providing a clear trajectory that aligns personal goals with organizational goals, fostering motivation and a sense of direction for these young project professionals.

Mentoring

Mentoring is vital for supporting young professionals' careers. Experienced professionals provide guidance and support, helping them grow. Organizations should make this kind of career support easily accessible and tailored to the needs of young project professionals. Excellent mentoring programs offer valuable guidance, knowledge sharing, and personal development opportunities (Huemann et al., 2019). Mentoring transfers expertise, builds relationships, and boosts confidence, motivating young professionals to work on projects and build up a satisfying career.

Meaningful projects

Being able to offer interesting and meaningful projects enables organizations to attract and retain talented project professionals. Projects – with their limited time frames – enable young professionals to explore their interests, develop their skills, and accomplish something challenging. By showcasing the potential of the impact young professionals can make by achieving the project goals and creating value for the organization and even the society, the organization fulfils the need for young project professionals to thrive. Many organizations today offer young professionals to engage in projects and frame these projects as explicit learning opportunities for young professionals. Projects especially offer an early possibility to lead small teams and early in a career gain leadership experience.

Conclusion

Projects provide an appealing work environment that aligns with the career aspirations of Generation Y professionals. Drawing upon self-determination theory, we introduce autonomy, competence development, relatedness, and purpose as central motivators to work on projects. Projects offer autonomy by empowering young professionals to make decisions and control their actions. Projects provide rich learning opportunities, satisfying their thirst for knowledge. Projects also serve as social hubs, fostering connections, and a sense of belonging. Moreover, projects foster creation, enabling young professionals to generate value for businesses and society. This emphasis on purpose adds a new dimension to motivation through the lens of project work.

References and further reading

Barford, I. N., & Hester, P. T. (2011). Analysis of generation Y workforce motivation using 19 utility theory. *Defense Acquisition Research Journal: A Publication of the Defense Acquisition University* 18(1), 63–80.

Deci, E. L., Olafsen, A. H., & Ryan, R. M. (2017). Self-determination theory in work organizations: The state of a science. *Annual Review of Organizational Psychology and Organizational Behavior, 4*, 19–43.

Deci, E. L., & Ryan, R. M. (2000). The "what" and "why" of goal pursuits: Human needs and the self-determination of behavior. *Psychological Inquiry, 11*(4), 227–268.

Guay, F., Chanal, J., Ratelle, C. F., Marsh, H. W., Larose, S., & Boivin, M. (2010). Intrinsic, identified, and controlled types of motivation for school subjects in young elementary school children. *British Journal of Educational Psychology, 80*(4), 711–735.

Huemann, M. (2015). *Human Resource Management in the Project-Oriented Organization: Towards a Viable Project-Oriented HRM System for Project Personnel.* Gower, Aldershot.

Huemann, M., Ringhofer, C., & Keegan, A. (2019). Who supports project careers? Leveraging the compensatory roles of line managers. *Project Management Journal, 50*(4), 476–486.

Lechler, R., & Huemann, M. (2023). Motivation of young project professionals: Their need for autonomy, competence, relatedness and purpose. *Project Management Journal, 0*(0).

Ryan, R. M., & Deci, E. L. (2002). Overview of self-determination theory: An organismic-dialectical perspective. In E. L. Deci & R. M. Ryan (Eds.), *Handbook of Self-Determination Research* (pp. 3–33). Rochester, NY: University of Rochester Press.

Chapter 31

Managing diversity

Anna Y. Khodijah

Introduction

When managing a project, the project manager must deal with various stakeholders, such as the project sponsor, project team, customer/end users, and other relevant parties. These stakeholders differ in terms of their characteristics, such as age, gender, national/cultural background, work experience, personality traits, etc., known as diversity. These differences, if not understood and managed properly, will create some challenges and issues in the project. For example, when the project manager asks project members' opinions in the project meeting, people from certain cultural backgrounds might feel disturbed and confused because they expect the project manager to decide without consulting them. Another example, an introverted project member might not be willing to speak out voluntarily and if the project manager does not understand this person's personality (of being introverted), the project manager might think that the project member does not want to contribute to the discussion. Understanding the stakeholders' expectations and needs will help the project manager not just to communicate with each of them but also reduce the friction or negative aspects that diversity might cause.

DOI: 10.4324/9781003274179-35

Diversity in projects

Diversity refers to "the differences among members of some particular collectivity ... most often been used to refer to demographic differences" (McGrath et al., 1995, p. 22). Some types of diversity can be easily observable, such as age, gender, and cultural background. But other types of diversity are not based on physical appearances, such as education, functional background, organizational tenure, personality traits (Milliken & Martins, 1996), attitudes, beliefs, and values (Harrison et al., 1998). Meanwhile, Lee Gardenswartz et al. (2010) propose that diversity consists of four dimensions (see Figure 31.1) as follows:

1 Personality dimension, which is invisible to others.
2 Internal dimension, partly visible to others, such as age, gender, etc.
3 External dimension, such as work experience, educational background, etc.
4 Organizational dimension within an organization, such as functional level, seniority, etc.

The model provides guidance on the criteria we can consider when we discuss or analyze diversity in projects. Individuals are diverse in the sense that the different dimensions have different meanings and different parameters emerging from individual biographies as well as cultural backgrounds influencing those aspects.

Diversity comprises two sides, differences, and commonalities. In some criteria, two individuals may have commonalities or similarities, and in other criteria, they may have differences. That implies that diversity is inherent in any group, team, project, or project-oriented organization.

Diversity is also often portrayed as a "double-edged sword" (Milliken & Martins, 1996) due to its positive and negative impacts on the team. On the one hand, it fosters a positive effect as a result of the variety of knowledge, perspectives, and experiences (Pieterse et al., 2013). On the other hand, the dissimilarities between team members can lead to intergroup biases, which then result in people closing their minds to ideas that are based on different backgrounds (Pieterse et al., 2013).

Martina Huemann et al. (2007) suggest that diversity can be perceived as a deficit or as a potential for a project. Table 31.1 provides a summary of the two perceptions of diversity.

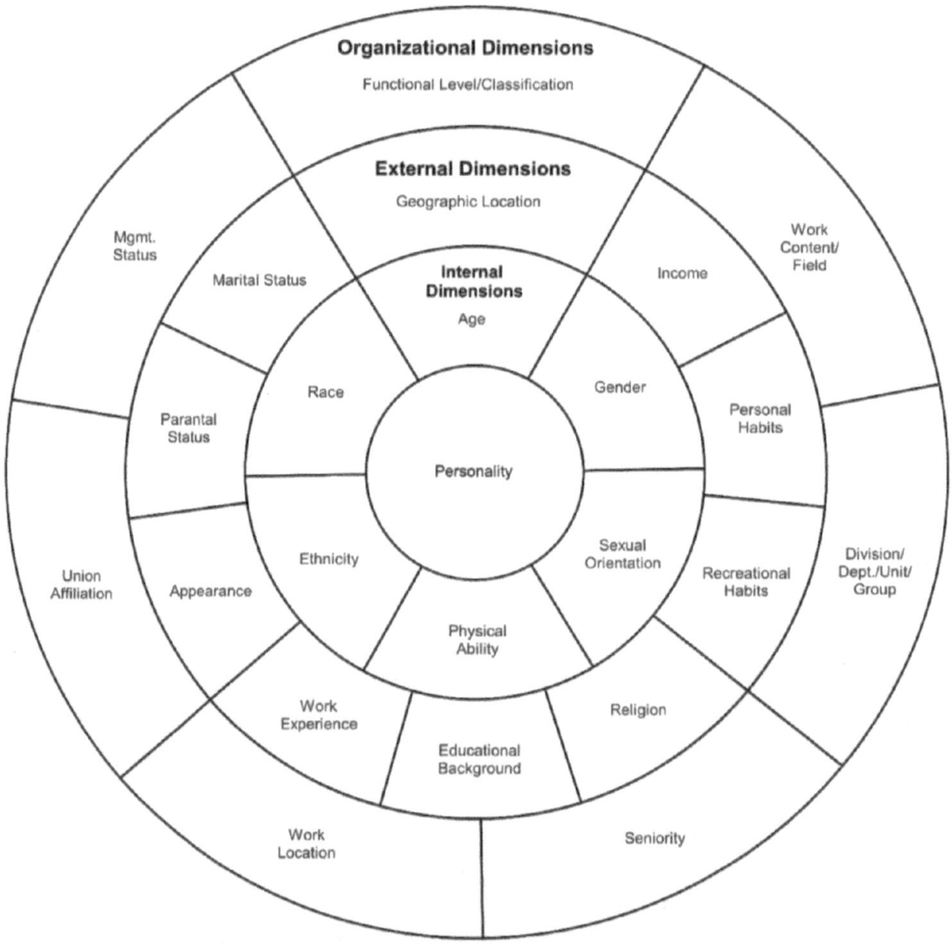

Figure 31.1: Dimensions of diversity (after Gardenswartz et al., 2010, p. 77)

Cultural diversity in projects

From all of these types/dimensions, cultural diversity has a stronger effect on the project team (Stahl et al., 2010). Cultural diversity encompasses national and linguistic variations between members, as well as variations across wider cultural dimensions (Hofstede et al., 1991).

Quite often, if not managed properly, cultural diversity will bring numerous negative effects to the project. One very obvious thing is that it creates communication

Table 31.1 Diversity as deficit versus potential in projects (Turner et al., 2010, p. 164)

Diversity in projects as deficit	*Diversity in projects as potential*
Diversity is perceived only as differences Being different is perceived as a deficit in comparison to the norm Diversity brings conflicts in projects thus diversity should be ignored Diversity in projects is a threat to the effectiveness Values and norms of the organization are not to be questioned Equal treatment means treating people equally Project managers and team members need social competencies to deal with diversity They must change, not the organizational structures Diversity management is an extra in projects, considered a nice-to-have	Diversity is perceived as differences and commonalities Being different is perceived as potential which allows for different contributions Diversity in projects must be analyzed and managed Diversity in projects brings business benefits Values and norms of the organization are subjects to be questioned Equal treatment means providing equal opportunities considering diversity Organizational structures must support diversity management; not only social competencies required by project owners, project managers, and project team members Diversity management is an integral part of project management

barriers among the project members/stakeholders. People from different cultural backgrounds tend to choose and structure words differently according to their mother language. In addition, they will also use different metaphors when trying to explain a complex problem or scenario. When English is not their first language, they will speak English with some degree of accent, which makes it harder for others to comprehend.

Another aspect of communication that is also impacted by cultural background would be communication style. People from high-context cultures (Hall, 1989), such as Japan, India, China, and many Asian countries, tend to speak indirectly (soften the talk) to avoid conflicts or uneasy situations. A situation that I observed when I was in Japan, on one of the hot summer days in Tokyo, a project team, consisting of all Japanese, gathered to discuss the project's progress. Since many office rooms are not equipped with air-conditioning, one senior manager grabbed a document booklet and started to use it as a fan. Immediately, two junior members jumped out of their seats and opened the windows, even though none of them talked to each other.

I was told, many times, by my Japanese colleague, that when you are in Japan, and deal with Japanese, either in business or daily situations, you need to do "Kuuki wo yomu" – which literally means "read the air" – that you have to be sensitive to the situation, read the other person's expression or gesture, and figure out (without talking) how to deal with the situation appropriately and timely.

On the contrary, people from low-context cultures (Hall, 1989), such as Germany, the US, and Scandinavian countries, tend to speak rather directly. For Germans, communication is among the most direct in the world following the ideal of being "honest, even if it hurts" ("Country Comparison," n.d.). During my first few months in Germany, I struggled to get used to this kind of style. For people from low-context cultures, direct speaking can be considered rude and will impair the trust and willingness to communicate/collaborate further.

Cultural dimension

Another aspect to be considered is the cultural dimension. Hofstede (2011) categorizes the cultural dimensions as (1) power distance, (2) uncertainty avoidance, (3) individualism versus collectivism, (4) masculinity versus femininity, (5) long-term versus short-term orientation, and (6) indulgence versus restraint (see Figure 31.2). We will discuss two dimensions that bring the most impact to the project team, which are power distance and uncertainty avoidance.

Power distance

Power distance can be characterized as where members with less power within organizations tolerate and put up with the power distribution being unequal (Hofstede, 2011). Asian, African, Latin, and Eastern European countries tend to be more power distance orientated than Western and English-speaking countries (Hofstede, 2011). Centralization is common, subordinates expect to be told what to do, leaders must be directive (and somewhat autocratic), and any challenges to the leader will be not well-received. We need to be careful and use polite tones when raising questions, e.g., in the meeting to avoid others' misperceptions that we challenge the superior. I remember the time when I started my early career as a junior project manager, I had to wait until the meeting ended and immediately followed the senior manager to his desk to ask a delicate question – just to avoid such an uneasy situation in the meeting or other word, "saving the face." A few

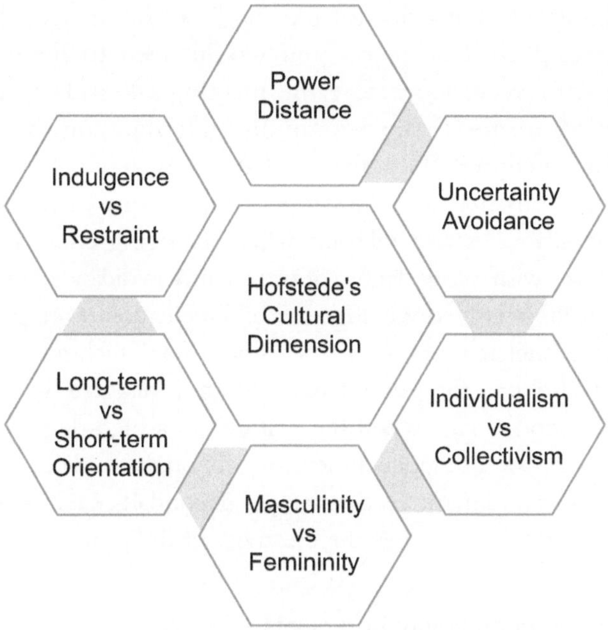

Figure 31.2: The six dimensions of national culture (after Hofstede, 2011)

countries might have different degrees of power distance, depending on the regions. For example, in Switzerland, the German-speaking region scores higher than the French-speaking one. This means that people in the German-speaking region tend to be more direct and informal than those in the French-speaking region.

Uncertainty avoidance

Uncertainty avoidance is another dimension that is highly relevant for conflict management in the project. It characterizes how people in certain cultures behave or feel in uncertain, unknown, and uncomfortable situations (Hofstede, 2011). Cultures with a high degree of uncertainty avoidance will try their best to avoid situations that give them uncertainty or insecure feeling as this will cause them stress and anxiety. Countries that belong to this category are Japan, Germany, Austria, and Switzerland (Hofstede, 2011). During my observation of projects involving members from these countries, they would like to develop a profound plan, stick to it, and work on the tasks in a very structured manner. Any deviations from rules or plans would need to be properly analyzed and discussed. They do not like surprises or unclear situations. One example, if working with Japanese, you would need to discuss the content of the meeting with everyone before the meeting takes place (this practice is called "nemawasi"), to foster their common understanding so that when they participate in the meeting, they already have "one-voice" and nobody will have different opinions that will "destroy" the harmony of the meeting.

Uncertainty avoidance is also relevant when managing conflict in the project. People from cultures with a low degree of uncertainty avoidance tend to choose the soft approach in dealing with conflict. Instead of directly confronting their opponent, they will soften the language, or choose the "smoothing" technique, quite common that they would also opt for "withdrawal" if they disagree with their leaders/ superiors. This situation occurs when the culture has a high degree of both uncertainty avoidance and power distance dimensions. Though conflict is inevitable in any project, not all conflicts are negative. Some types of conflicts, such as task conflict, can help generate ideas and thus increase the creativity of the project team (Jehn, 1997).

Diversity as a source of creativity in projects

Cultural diversity fosters creativity in generating ideas and solving problems, and this is a positive aspect of cultural diversity for the project team (Stahl et al., 2010, p. 698). When project members/stakeholders discuss ideas or solutions, they will bring their different perspectives and problem-solving styles to each situation.

Another positive aspect of cultural diversity is that it potentially enhances teamwork over time. Though in the early stage of the project members still face misunderstandings and disagreements, when they finally come to know each other and understand each other's expectations and working style, they will finally come to effective teamwork, if the negative effect of diversity is well managed. Besides teamwork, the project manager would also want to foster a positive working climate by fostering trust and respect among team members, while these aspects will increase the member's commitment to the project.

Unmanaged diversity decreases project performance

If the project team size is large, and the degree of diversity is low, the project members will potentially group with others who have similar attributes thus splitting the project team into two or more subgroups, also known as faultlines (Figure 31.3).

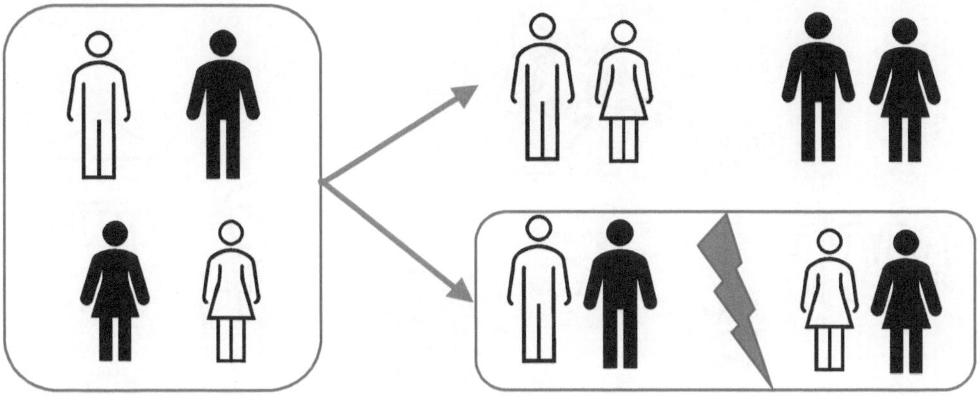

Figure 31.3: Faultlines in the team

This situation will also lead to in-/out-groups in which members tend to evaluate the behaviour/actions of their group much more favourably/positively than those of outgroup members. Not only it will decrease the ability of the project team to achieve teamwork, but it will also impair the trust and ultimately satisfaction and commitment to the project. Stereotypes, favouritism, and other political behaviour will become "diseases" to the project that need to be resolved quickly before it harms the entire project.

Practices to manage diversity in projects

Nevertheless, there are a few practices that can be applied to minimize the negative and optimize the positive effect of diversity. These are project member selection, common goals and clear objectives, organizational climate, leadership style, and cultural awareness (see Figure 31.4).

Project member selection

If the project manager can select project members before the project starts, they should pick the members who like to learn something new and have a stronger focus on building their knowledge and competence. These members would likely endure the challenges and obstacles caused by diversity throughout the project. Another aspect is that the member should be open-minded and more willing to consider different views, opinions, and ideas from others. A personality test

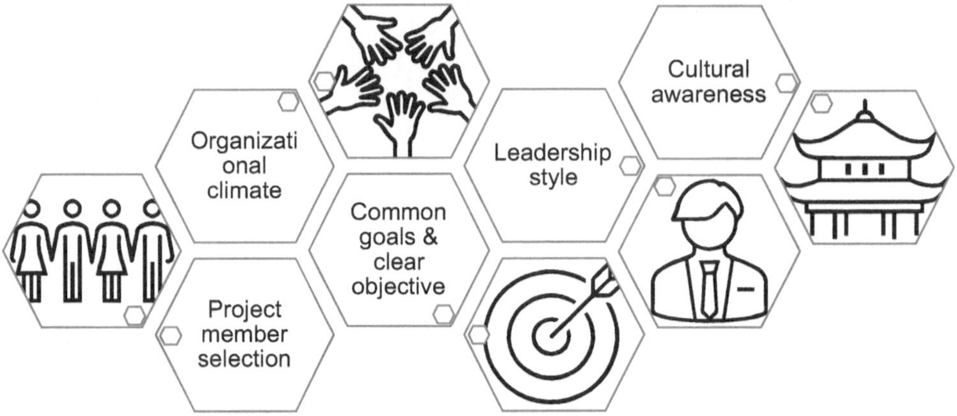

Figure 31.4: Practices to manage diversity in the project

(if feasible) should be carried out to select members with a high degree of learning orientation and openness to experience.

Common goals and clear objective

The project manager (or those who hold the senior position of the project) should actively communicate the common goals so everyone is aware of the project objectives and that they are focused on fulfilling those, regardless of the differences. The project manager should also establish a shared agreement on clear, transparent, and fairly distributed task-related goals among members. This will help not only avoid overlapping tasks but also to increase trust and collaboration/teamwork.

Organizational climate

Organizations should encourage a climate that allows employees to feel assured that they will not receive any negative consequences if they make mistakes, whereas mistakes are considered part of the organizational learning process (Pieterse et al., 2013, p. 798). In particular, the project demands a high degree of innovation, such as product development, or agile projects.

Leadership style

It is well known that the leadership style of a project manager highly influences project team performance. Thus, appointing a project manager with a proper leadership style, such as a transformational leadership style, can help the project team to go through difficult situations caused by diversity. The project manager can also adjust his/her leadership style to meet the situation in the project.

Cultural awareness

The project manager, together with project members and other key stakeholders should be aware before starting the project that they will be working with people from different cultural backgrounds. They would need to be emphatic and sensitive towards others. Organizations can provide training or workshops (the best is before the project starts) to give an overview of everyone's cultural traits and practices, aiming to increase the cultural awareness of the training/workshop participants. Another method is to run a small pre-project partnering program so that the project members can get to know each other before the "real" project starts. This practice is extremely useful when the project team size is large, and they work in a different location.

Conclusion

By understanding the effects of diversity, the project manager and project team would be able to alleviate the negative effects of diversity. Taking into account this double-edged sword effect of diversity, we shed light – to a certain extent – for the project manager on how to manage diversity in the project. Regardless of how effectively the project manager manages the project, the project's success is still highly dependent on the project stakeholders' cooperation, including their abilities to manage and resolve conflicts.

References and further reading

Country Comparison. (n.d.). *Hofstede insights*. Retrieved August 21, 2022, from https://www.hofstede-insights.com/country-comparison/

Gardenswartz, L., Cherbosque, J., & Rowe, A. (2010). Emotional intelligence and diversity: A model for differences in the workplace. *Journal of Psychological Issues in Organizational Culture*, *1*(1), 74–84.

Hall, E. T. (1989). *Beyond culture*. Harlow: Anchor.

Harrison, D. A., Price, K. H., & Bell, M. P. (1998). Beyond relational demography: Time and the effects of surface-and deep-level diversity on work group cohesion. *Academy of Management Journal*, *41*(1), 96–107.

Hofstede, G. (2011). Dimensionalizing cultures: The Hofstede model in context. *Online Readings in Psychology and Culture*, *2*(1), 2307–0919.

Hofstede, G., Hofstede, G. J., & Minkov, M. (1991). *Cultures and organizations: Intercultural cooperation and its importance for survival. Software of the mind*. London: McGraw-Hill.

Huemann, M., Keegan, A., & Turner, J. R. (2007). Human resource management in the project-oriented company: A review. *International Journal of Project Management*, *25*(3), 315–323.

Jehn, K. A. (1997). A qualitative analysis of conflict types and dimensions in organizational groups. *Administrative Science Quarterly*, *42*(3), 530–557.

McGrath, J. E., Berdahl, J. L., & Arrow, H. (1995). Traits, expectations, culture, and clout: The dynamics of diversity in work groups. In *Diversity in work teams: Research paradigms for a changing workplace* (pp. 17–45). American Psychological Association. https://doi.org/10.1037/10189-001

Milliken, F. J., & Martins, L. L. (1996). Searching for common threads: Understanding the multiple effects of diversity in organizational groups. *Academy of Management Review*, *21*(2), 402–433.

Pieterse, A. N., van Knippenberg, D., & van Dierendonck, D. (2013). Cultural diversity and team performance: The role of team member goal orientation. *Academy of Management Journal*, *56*(3), 782–804. https://doi.org/10.5465/amj.2010.0992

Stahl, G. K., Maznevski, M. L., Voigt, A., & Jonsen, K. (2010). Unraveling the effects of cultural diversity in teams: A meta-analysis of research on multicultural work groups. *Journal of International Business Studies*, *41*(4), 690–709.

Turner, R. J., Huemann, M., Anbari, F. T., & Bredillet, C. N. (2010). *Perspectives on projects*. London and New York: Routledge.

Chapter 32

Behavioral bias

Bent Flyvbjerg

Introduction

Psychologists Amos Tversky and Daniel Kahneman pioneered the study of behavioral bias. Since they did their original, Nobel Prize-winning work, the number of biases identified by behavioral scientists has exploded in what has been termed a behavioral revolution in economics, management, and across the social sciences. Today, Wikipedia's list of cognitive biases contains more than 200 items. The present paper gives an overview of the most important behavioral biases in project management, summarized in Table 32.1 (for more biases and more detail, see Flyvbjerg 2021). They are the biases most likely to trip up project managers and negatively impact project outcomes if left unmitigated.

Many would agree with Kahneman (2011: 255) that optimism bias "may well be the most significant of the cognitive biases." However, behavioral bias is not limited to cognitive bias. Political bias is the other half of the story. Political bias – understood as deliberate strategic distortions – arises from power relations, instead of from cognition. In this chapter, we cover both political and cognitive bias because both significantly impact project management. This is especially the case when projects are big and consequential, with high political-organizational pressures. In fact, for very large projects – so-called megaprojects – the most significant behavioral bias is arguably political bias, more specifically strategic misrepresentation. Cognitive bias may account well for outcomes in the simple lab

DOI: 10.4324/9781003274179-36

Table 32.1 Six key behavioral biases in project management

Name of bias	*Description*
1 Strategic misrepresentation	The tendency to deliberately and systematically distort or misstate information for strategic purposes. A.k.a. political bias, strategic bias, or power bias.
2 Optimism bias	The tendency to be overly optimistic about the outcome of planned actions, including overestimation of the frequency and size of positive events and underestimation of the frequency and size of negative ones.
3 Uniqueness bias	The tendency to see one's project as more singular than it actually is.
4 Planning fallacy	The tendency to underestimate costs, schedule, and risk and overestimate benefits and opportunities.
5 Overconfidence bias	The tendency to have excessive confidence in one's own answers to questions.
6 Base-rate fallacy	The tendency to ignore generic base-rate information and focus on specific information pertaining to a certain case or small sample.

experiments done by behavioral scientists. But for real-world decision-making – in big hierarchical organizations, with office politics, salesmanship, jockeying for position, and millions, sometimes billions, of dollars at stake – political bias is pervasive and must be taken into account. Below I describe some of the most important behavioral biases in project management, starting with political bias, followed by several cognitive biases. We will also see how political bias and cognitive bias interact and amplify each other.

Strategic misrepresentation

Strategic misrepresentation is the tendency to deliberately and systematically distort or misstate information for strategic purposes. This bias is sometimes also called political bias, strategic bias, power bias, or the Machiavelli factor. The bias is a rationalization for which the ends justify the means. The strategy (e.g., get funded) dictates the bias (e.g., make projects look good on paper).

Strategic misrepresentation can be traced to agency problems and political-organizational pressures, for instance, competition for scarce funds or jockeying for position. Strategic misrepresentation is deliberate deception, and as such it is lying, per definition.

Here, a senior Big-Four consultant explains how strategic misrepresentation works in practice:

> In the early days of building my transport economics and policy group at [name of company omitted], I carried out a lot of feasibility studies in a subcontractor role to engineers. In virtually all cases it was clear that *the engineers simply wanted to justify the project and were looking to the traffic forecasts to help in the process*… I once asked an engineer why their cost estimates were invariably underestimated and he simply answered, '*if we gave the true expected outcome costs nothing would be built*'
>
> (personal communication, author's archives, italics added)

Signature architecture is notorious for large cost overruns. A leading signature architect, France's Jean Nouvel, winner of the Pritzker Prize, explains how it works:

> I don't know of buildings that cost less when they were completed than they did at the outset. In France, there is often a theoretical budget that is given because it is the sum that politically has been released to do something. In three out of four cases this sum does not correspond to anything in technical terms. *This is a budget that was made because it could be accepted politically. The real price comes later.* The politicians make the real price public where they want and when they want.
>
> (Nouvel 2009: 4, italics added)

This is a strategic misrepresentation. Following its playbook, a strategic cost or schedule estimate will be low because it is more easily accepted, leading to cost and schedule overrun. Similarly, a strategic benefit estimate will be high, leading to benefit shortfalls. Strategic misrepresentation therefore produces a systematic bias in outcomes. And this is precisely what the data show (see Table 32.2). We see that the theory of strategic misrepresentation fits the data. Project planners clearly do not get base rates right. The data show strong biases for (a) cost underestimation

Table 32.2 Base rates for cost and benefit overrun in 2,062 capital investment projects across eight types

Investment type	*Cost overrun (A/E)*			*Benefit overrun (A/E)*		
	N	*Average*	*p**	*N*	*Average*	*p**
Dams	243	1.96	<0.0001	84	0.89	<0.0001
BRT[a]	6	1.41	0.031	4	0.42	0.12
Rail	264	1.40	<0.0001	74	0.66	<0.0001
Tunnels	48	1.36	<0.0001	23	0.81	0.03
Power plants	100	1.36	0.0076	23	0.94	0.11
Buildings	24	1.36	0.00087	20	0.99	0.77
Bridges	49	1.32	0.00012	26	0.96	0.099
Roads	869	1.24	<0.0001	532	0.96	<0.0001
Total	**1,603**	**1.39/1.43**[b]	**<0.0001**	**786**	**0.94/0.83**[b]	**<0.0001**

Source: Author's database; see Flyvbjerg (2016: 181–182) for a description of the data.

* The p-value of the Wilcoxon test with the null hypothesis that the distribution is symmetrically centered around one; the thesis is overwhelmingly rejected.

[a] Bus rapid transit.

[b] Weighted and unweighted average, respectively.

and overrun and (b) benefit overestimation and shortfall. Overrun is measured as actual divided by estimated costs and benefits (A/E), respectively, in real terms, baselined at the final investment decision.

Professor Martin Wachs of UC Berkeley and UCLA, who pioneered research on strategic misrepresentation in transportation infrastructure forecasting, recently looked back at more than 25 years of scholarship in the area. After carefully weighing the evidence for and against different types of explanations of forecasting inaccuracy, Wachs summarized his findings in the following manner:

> While some scholars believe this [misleading forecasting] is a simple technical matter involving the tools and techniques of cost estimation and patronage forecasting, there is growing evidence that the gaps between forecasts and outcomes are the results of deliberate misrepresentation and thus amount

> to a collective failure of professional ethics... Often... firms making the forecasts stand to benefit if a decision is made to proceed with the project.
>
> (Wachs 2013: 112)

Wachs found a general incentive to misrepresent forecasts for infrastructure projects and that this incentive drives forecasting outcomes. Wachs's review together with other studies falsifies the notion that optimism and other cognitive biases may serve as a stand-alone explanation of cost underestimation and benefit overestimation, which has been the common view in behavioral science. Explanations in terms of cognitive bias are especially needed in situations with high political and organizational pressures. In such situations forecasters, planners, and decision-makers intentionally use the following Machiavellian formula to make their projects look good on paper, with a view to securing approval and funding:

Underestimated costs + Overestimated benefits = Funding

Finally, recent research has found that not only do political and cognitive biases compound each other. Experimental psychologists have shown that political bias directly amplifies cognitive bias in the sense that people who are powerful are affected more strongly by various cognitive biases – e.g., availability bias and recency bias – than people who are not. A heightened sense of power also increases individuals' optimism in viewing risks and their propensity to engage in risky behavior. This is because people in power tend to disregard the rigors of deliberate rationality, which are too slow and cumbersome for their purposes. They prefer – consciously or not – subjective experience and intuitive judgment as the basis for their decisions. For instance, people in power will deliberately exclude experts from meetings when much is at stake, to avoid clashes in high-level negotiations between power's intuitive decisions and experts' deliberative rationality. Experimental psychologists similarly found that people in power rely on ease of retrieval more than people without power. In consequence, total bias – political plus cognitive – escalates, but not in a simple linear manner where total bias equals the sum of political and cognitive biases, but instead in a complex, convex way where political bias amplifies cognitive bias, leading to amplified risk. This, undoubtedly, is one reason we find strong convexities (non-linearities) in the planning and management of big projects. Decisions about big projects are typically made by highly powerful people, and such individuals are convexity generators, with political bias driving their cognitive biases, which are larger for powerful individuals than for non-powerful ones.

Optimism bias

Optimism bias is a cognitive bias. It is the tendency for individuals to be overly positive about the outcomes of planned actions. Sharot (2011: xv) calls it "one of the greatest deceptions of which the human mind is capable." Where strategic misrepresentation is deliberate, optimism bias is non-deliberate. In the grip of optimism, people – including experts – are unaware they are optimistic. They make decisions based on an ideal vision of the future rather than on a rational weighting of gains, losses, and probabilities. They overestimate benefits and underestimate costs. They involuntarily spin scenarios of success and overlook the potential for mistakes and miscalculations. As a result, plans are unlikely to deliver as expected in terms of benefits and costs.

In project management, an optimistic cost or schedule estimate will be low, leading to cost and schedule overrun. An optimistic benefit estimate will be high, leading to benefit shortfalls. Optimism therefore produces a systematic bias in project outcomes, which is what the data show (see Table 32.2). The theory of optimism bias fits the data, which lends support to its validity.

Interestingly, however, when researchers ask forecasters about causes of inaccuracies in their forecasts, they do not mention optimism bias as a main cause, whereas they do mention strategic misrepresentation and the usual suspects: scope changes, complexity, price changes, unexpected underground conditions, bad weather, etc. Psychologists would argue this is because optimism bias is a true cognitive bias. As such it is unreflected by forecasters, including when they participate in surveys about causes of forecasting inaccuracy. Psychologists would further argue there is a large body of experimental evidence for the existence of optimism bias. However, the experimental data are mostly from simple laboratory experiments with students. This is a problem because it's an open question to what extent the results apply outside the laboratory, in real-life situations like project management.

Optimism bias can be both a blessing and a curse. Optimism and a "can-do" attitude are obviously necessary to get projects done. Kahneman (2011: 255) calls optimism "the engine of capitalism." But optimism can seriously trip us up if we are unaware of its pitfalls and therefore take on risks we would have avoided had we known the real, non-optimistic, odds.

During the Apollo program (1961–1972), the NASA administration criticized its cost engineers for being optimistic with their initial US$10 billion estimate for the program (approximately US$90 billion in 2021 dollars). The engineers assumed "that everything's going to work" and the administration pointed out it was a false assumption (Bizony 2006: 41). The engineers then increased their estimate to US$13 billion, which the administration adjusted to US$20 billion and got approved by Congress, to the shock of the cost engineers. Today, the NASA administration's US$7 billion increase has a technical name: "optimism bias uplift." NASA jokingly called it an "administrator's discount." But they were serious when they advised that all senior executives in charge of large, complex projects must apply such a discount to make allowance for the unknown. Whatever the name, it is the single most important reason Apollo has gone down in history as that rare species of multi-billion-dollar project: one delivered on budget. The NASA administration "knew exactly what [it] was doing" with Apollo, as rightly observed by space historian Piers Bizony (ibid.).

Above we saw that strategic project planners and managers sometimes underestimate cost and overestimate benefits to achieve approval for their projects. Optimistic planners and managers do this, too, albeit non-intentionally. The result is the same, however, namely cost overruns and benefit shortfalls. Thus, optimism bias and strategic misrepresentation reinforce each other when both are present in a project.

Uniqueness bias

Uniqueness bias was originally identified by psychologists as the tendency of individuals to see themselves as more singular than they actually are, e.g., singularly healthy, clever, or attractive. In project management, the term was first used by Flyvbjerg (2014: 9), who defined uniqueness bias as the tendency of planners and managers to see their projects as singular. It is a general bias, but it turns out to be particularly rewarding as an object of study in project management because project planners and managers are systematically primed to see their projects as unique.

The standard definition of a project, according to the biggest professional organization in the field, the US-based Project Management Institute (PMI 2017: 4), directly emphasizes uniqueness as one of two defining features of what a project is: "A project is a temporary endeavor undertaken to create a *unique* product, service, or result" (italics added). Similarly, the UK-based Association for Project Management (APM 2012) stresses uniqueness as the very first characteristic of what a project is in their official definition: "A project is a *unique*, transient endeavor, undertaken to achieve planned objectives" (italics added). Academics, too, define projects in terms of uniqueness, here Turner and Müller (2003: 7, italics added): "A project is a temporary organization to which resources are assigned to undertake a *unique*, novel and transient endeavor managing the inherent uncertainty and need for integration in order to deliver beneficial objectives of change."

The understanding of projects as unique is unfortunate because it contributes to uniqueness bias among project planners and managers. In the grip of uniqueness bias, project managers see their projects as more singular than they actually are. This is reinforced by the fact that new projects often use non-standard technologies and designs.

Uniqueness bias tends to impede managers' learning because they think they have little to learn from other projects as their own project is unique. Uniqueness bias may also feed overconfidence bias (see below) and optimism bias (see above), because planners subject to uniqueness bias tend to underestimate risks. This interpretation is supported by my team's research on IT project management, where we found that managers who see their projects as unique perform significantly worse than other managers. If you are a project leader and you overhear team members speak of your project as unique, you therefore need to react.

It is self-evidently true, of course, that a project may be unique in its own specific geography and time. For instance, California has never built a high-speed rail line before, so in this sense, the California High-Speed Rail Authority is managing a unique project. But the project is only unique to California, and therefore not truly unique. Dozens of similar projects have been built around the world, with data and lessons learned that would be highly valuable to California.

Uniqueness bias feeds what behavioral scientists call the "inside view." Seeing things from this perspective, planners focus on the specific circumstances of the project they are planning and seek evidence from their own experience. Estimates of budget, schedule, etc. are based on this information, typically built "from the inside and out," or bottom-up, as in conventional cost engineering. The alternative is the "outside view," which consists of viewing the project you are planning from the perspective of similar projects that have already been completed, basing your estimates for the planned project on the actual outcomes of these projects. But if your project is truly unique then similar projects clearly do not exist, and the outside view becomes irrelevant and impossible. This leaves you with the inside view as the only option for planning your project. Even if a project is not truly unique, if the project team thinks it is then the outside view will be left by the wayside and the inside view will reign supreme, which is typical. "In the competition with the inside view, the outside view does not stand a chance," as pithily observed by Kahneman (2011: 249). The inside view is the perspective people spontaneously adopt when they plan, reinforced by the uniqueness bias for project managers. The inside view is therefore typical of project management. The consequences are dire because only the outside view effectively considers all risks, including the so-called "unknown unknowns." These are impossible to predict from the inside because there are too many ways a project can go wrong. However, the unknown unknowns are included in the outside view because anything that went wrong with the completed projects that constitute the outside view is included in their outcome data. Using these data for planning and managing a new project therefore leaves you with a measure of all risks, including unknown unknowns. Uniqueness bias makes you blind to unknown unknowns. The outside view is an antidote to uniqueness bias.

Project managers, in addition to being predisposed, like everyone else, to the inside view and uniqueness, they have been indoctrinated by their professional organizations to believe projects are unique, as we saw above. Thus, it's no surprise it takes substantial experience to cut loose from the conventional view. The NASA administration, mentioned above, balked when people insisted the Apollo program, with its aim of landing the first humans on the moon, was unique. How could it not be, as putting people on the moon had never been done before, people argued. The administration would have none of it. They deplored those who saw the program "as so special – as so exceptional," because such people did not understand the reality of the project and therefore placed it at risk. The administration insisted, in contrast, that "the basic knowledge and technology and the human and material resources necessary for the job already existed," so there was no reason to reinvent the wheel (Webb 1969: 11, 61). The NASA-Apollo view of uniqueness bias saw this bias for what it is: a fallacy.

In sum, uniqueness bias feeds the inside view and optimism, which feeds underestimation of risk, which makes project teams take on risks they would likely not have accepted had they known the real odds. Good project leaders do not let themselves be fooled like this. They know PMI and APM are wrong when they say projects are unique. Projects are often unique locally, yes. But to be locally unique is an oxymoron. This, however, is typically the meaning of the term "unique," when used in project management. It is a misnomer that undermines project performance. Truly unique projects are rare. We have lots to learn from other projects, always. And if we don't learn, we will not succeed with our projects.

The planning fallacy

The planning fallacy is a subcategory of optimism bias that arises from individuals producing plans and estimates that are unrealistically close to best-case scenarios. The term was originally coined by Kahneman and Tversky to describe the tendency for people to underestimate task completion times. Psychologist Roger Buehler continued work following this definition. Later, the concept was broadened to cover the tendency for people to, on the one hand, underestimate costs, schedules, and risks for planned actions and, on the other, overestimate benefits and opportunities for those actions. Because the original narrow and later broader concepts are so fundamentally different in the scope they cover, with Cass Sunstein I suggested the term "planning fallacy writ large" for the broader concept, to avoid confusing the two.

The tendency to plan according to best-case scenarios has been called the "EGAP-principle," for Everything Goes According to Plan. The planning fallacy and the EGAP principle are similar in the sense that both result in a lack of realism, because of their overreliance on best-case scenarios, as with the NASA cost engineers above. Both lead to base-rate neglect, the illusion of control, and overconfidence. In this manner, both feed into optimism bias.

At the most fundamental level, Kahneman and Tversky identified the planning fallacy as arising from a tendency of people to neglect distributional information when they plan. People who plan would adopt what Kahneman and Tversky (1979: 315) first called an "internal approach to prediction," and later renamed the "inside view," under the influence of which people would focus on "the constituents of the specific problem rather than on the distribution of outcomes in similar cases." Kahneman and Tversky (ibid.) emphasized that "The internal approach to the evaluation of plans is likely to produce underestimation [of schedules]." For the planning fallacy writ large, such underestimation applies to costs, schedules, and risk, whereas overestimation applies to benefits and opportunities.

Interestingly, experimental psychologists found that subjects who had been made to feel in power were more likely to underestimate the time needed to complete a task than those not in power, demonstrating a higher degree of planning fallacy for people in power. Again, this is an example of how power bias and cognitive bias interact, resulting in amplification and convexity.

The planning fallacy's combination of underestimated costs and overestimated benefits generates risks to the second degree. Instead of cost risk and benefit-risk canceling out one another – as some theories predict, e.g., Albert Hirschman's principle of the Hiding Hand – under the planning fallacy the two types of risk reinforce each other, creating convex (accelerated) risks for projects from the outset. The data support the planning fallacy, which goes a long way in explaining the Iron Law of project management: "Over budget, over time, under benefits, over and over again." As a project leader, you want to avoid convex risks because such risks are particularly destructive. You want to avoid committing the planning fallacy, especially for people in power.

Overconfidence bias

Overconfidence bias is the tendency to have excessive confidence in one's own answers to questions and to not fully recognize the uncertainty of the world and one's ignorance of it. People have been shown to be prone to what is called the "illusion of certainty" in (a) overestimating how much they understand and (b) underestimating the role of chance events and lack of knowledge, in effect underestimating the variability of events they are exposed to in their lives. Overconfidence bias is found in both laypeople and experts, including project managers.

Overconfidence bias is fed by illusions of certainty, which are fed by hindsight bias, also known as the "I-knew-it-all-along effect." Availability bias – the tendency to overweigh whatever comes to mind – similarly feeds overconfidence bias. Availability is influenced by the recency of memories and by how unusual or emotionally charged they may be, with more recent, more unusual, and more emotional memories being more easily recalled. Overconfidence bias is a type of optimism, and it feeds overall optimism bias.

A simple way to illustrate overconfidence bias is to ask people to estimate confidence intervals for statistical outcomes. In one experiment, the Chief Financial Officers (CFOs) of large US corporations were asked to estimate the return next year on shares in the relevant Standard & Poor's index. In addition, the CFOs were asked to give their best guess of the 80% confidence interval for the estimated returns by estimating a value for returns they were 90% sure would be too low (the lower decile, or P10) and a second value they were 90% sure would be too high (the upper decile, or P90), with 80% of returns estimated to fall between these two values (and 20% outside). Comparing actual returns with the estimated confidence interval, it was found that 67% of actual returns fell outside the estimated 80% confidence interval, or 3.35 times as many as estimated. The actual variance of outcomes was grossly underestimated by these financial experts, which is the same as saying they grossly underestimated risk. It is a typical finding. The human brain, including the brains of experts, spontaneously underestimates variance. For whatever reason, humans seem hardwired for this.

In project management, overconfidence bias is unfortunately built into the very tools experts use for quantitative risk management. The tools, which are typically based on computer models using so-called Monte-Carlo simulations, or similar, look scientific and objective, but are anything but. Again, this is easy to document. You simply compare estimated variance in a specific, planned project with actual, historic variance for its project type, and you find the same result as for the CFOs above. The bias is generated by experts assuming thin-tailed distributions of risk (normal or near-normal) when the real distributions are fat-tailed (lognormal, power law, or similar). The error is not with Monte-Carlo models as such but with erroneous input into the models. Garbage in, garbage out, as always. To eliminate overconfidence bias you want a more objective method that takes all distributional information into account, not just the distributional information experts can think of, which is subject to availability bias. The method needs to run on historical data from projects that have actually been completed. Flyvbjerg (2006) describes such a method.

Finally, regarding the relationship between power bias and cognitive bias mentioned above, powerful individuals have been shown to be more susceptible to overconfidence bias and availability bias than individuals who are not powerful. The causal mechanism seems to be that powerful individuals are affected more strongly by ease of retrieval than by the content they retrieve because they are more likely to "go with the flow" and trust their intuition than individuals who are not powerful. This finding has been largely ignored by behavioral economists, which is unfortunate because it documents convexity to the second degree for situations with power. By overlooking this, behavioral economists in fact make the same mistake they criticize conventional economists for, namely overlooking and underestimating variance and risk. Conventional economists make the mistake of disregarding cognitive bias; behavioral economists by ignoring power bias and its effect on cognitive bias. Underestimating convexity is a very human mistake, to be sure. We all do it. But it needs to be accounted for if we want to understand all relevant risks and protect ourselves against them in our projects.

The base-rate fallacy

The base-rate fallacy – sometimes also called base-rate bias or base-rate neglect – is the tendency to ignore base-rate information (general data pertaining to a statistical population or a large sample, e.g., its average) and focus on specific information (data only pertaining to a certain case or a small number of cases). If you play poker and assume different odds than those that apply, you are subject to the base-rate fallacy and likely to lose. The objective odds are the base rates.

People often think the information they have is more relevant than it is, or they are blind to all the relevant information they do not have. Both situations result in the base-rate fallacy. The base-rate fallacy is fed by other biases, for instance, uniqueness bias, described above, which results in extreme base-rate neglect, because the case at hand is believed to be unique, wherefore information about other cases is deemed irrelevant. The inside view, hindsight bias, availability bias, recency bias, overconfidence bias, and framing bias also feed the base-rate fallacy. Base-rate neglect is particularly pronounced when there is a good, strong story. Big, monumental projects typically have such a story, contributing to extra base-rate neglect for those. Finally, we saw above that people, including experts, underestimate variance. In the typical project, base-rate neglect therefore combines with variation neglect, along the following formula:

$$\text{Base-rate neglect} + \text{variation neglect} = \text{strong convexity}$$

Preliminary results from our research indicate that variation neglect receives less attention in project management than base-rate neglect, which is unfortunate because the research also indicates that variation neglect is typically larger and has an even more drastic impact on project outcomes than base-rate neglect.

The base-rate fallacy runs rampant in project planning and management. Table 32.2 shows the most comprehensive overview that exists of base rates for costs and benefits in project management, based on data from 2,062 projects covering eight project types. Most projects do not get base rates right – not even close, as documented by averages that are different from one (1.0 ≈ correct base rate) at a level of statistical significance so high ($p < 0.0001$) that it is rarely found in studies of human behavior. The base-rate fallacy is deeply entrenched in project management, the data show. Base-rate neglect results in a behavioral bias called the "cost-benefit fallacy," which routinely derails cost-benefit analyses of projects to a degree where such analyses cannot be trusted for the simple reason that estimates of costs and benefits are highly unreliable and biased.

As pointed out by Kahneman (2011: 150), "anyone who ignores base rates and the quality of evidence in probability assessments will certainly make mistakes." The cure to the base-rate fallacy, in and out of project management, is to get the base rate right by taking an outside view, for instance through reference class forecasting, carrying out premortems, or doing decision hygiene (Flyvbjerg 2006; Klein 2007; Kahneman 2011; Kahneman et al. 2021).

If you're a project planner or manager, the easiest and most effective way to get started with curbing behavioral biases in your work is getting your base rates right, for the projects you're working on. Hopefully, most can see that if you don't understand the real odds of a game, you're unlikely to succeed at it. But that's the situation for most project managers: they don't get the odds right for the game they are playing: project management. Table 32.2 documents this beyond reasonable doubt and establishes realistic base rates for a number of important areas in project management that planners can use as a starting point for getting their projects right. Data for other project types were not included for reasons of space but showed similar results.

Conclusion

Scientific revolutions rarely happen without friction. So, too, for the behavioral revolution. It has been met with skepticism, including from parts of the project management community. Some members prefer to stick with conventional explanations of project underperformance in terms of errors of scope, complexity, labor and materials prices, archaeology, geology, bad weather, ramp-up problems, demand fluctuations, etc.

Behavioral scientists would agree with the skeptics that scope changes, complexity, etc. are relevant for understanding what goes on in projects but would not see them as root causes of outcomes. According to behavioral science, the root cause of, say, cost overrun, is the well-documented fact that project planners and managers keep underestimating scope changes, complexity, etc. in project after project.

From the point of view of behavioral science, the mechanisms of scope changes, complex interfaces, price changes, archaeology, geology, bad weather, business cycles, etc. are not unknown to project planners and managers, just as it is not unknown that such mechanisms may be mitigated. However, project planners and managers often underestimate these mechanisms and mitigation measures, due to optimism bias, overconfidence bias, the planning fallacy, strategic misrepresentation, etc. In behavioral terms, unaccounted-for scope changes, etc. are manifestations of such underestimation on the part of project planners and managers, and it is in this sense that bias and underestimation are *root causes* and scope changes, etc. are just *causes*. But because scope changes etc. are more visible than the underlying root causes, they are often mistaken for the cause of outcomes, e.g., cost overrun.

In behavioral terms, the causal chain starts with human bias (political and cognitive) which leads to underestimation of scope during planning which leads to unaccounted-for scope changes during delivery which leads to cost overrun. Scope changes are an intermediate stage in this causal chain through which the root causes manifest themselves. Behavioral science tells project planners and managers, "*Your biggest risk is you.*" It is not scope changes, complexity, etc. in themselves that are the main problem; it is how human beings misconceive and underestimate these phenomena, through optimism bias, overconfidence bias, strategic misrepresentation, etc. This is a profound and proven insight that behavioral science brings to project management. You can disregard it, of course. But if you do, project performance would likely suffer. You would be the gambler not knowing the odds of their game.

References and further reading

APM, Association of Project Management, 2012, *APM Body of Knowledge*, 6th Edition (High Wycombe: Association for Project Management), https://www.apm.org.uk/body-of-knowledge/context/governance/project-management/, accessed May 1, 2021.

Bizony, Piers, 2006, *The Man Who Ran the Moon: James Webb, JFK, and the Secret History of Project Apollo* (Cambridge: Icon Books).

Flyvbjerg, Bent, 2006, "From Nobel Prize to Project Management: Getting Risks Right," *Project Management Journal*, vol. 37, no. 3, August, pp. 5–15.

Flyvbjerg, Bent, 2014, "What You Should Know about Megaprojects and Why: An Overview," *Project Management Journal*, vol. 45, no. 2, April–May, pp. 6–19.

Flyvbjerg, Bent, 2016, "The Fallacy of Beneficial Ignorance: A Test of Hirschman's Hiding Hand," *World Development*, vol. 84, May, pp. 176–189.

Flyvbjerg, Bent, 2021, "Top Ten Behavioral Biases in Project Management: An Overview," *Project Management Journal*, vol. 52, no. 6, pp. 531–546.

Kahneman, Daniel, 2011, *Thinking, Fast and Slow* (New York: Farrar, Straus and Giroux).

Kahneman, Daniel, Olivier Sibony, and Cass R. Sunstein, 2021, *Noise: A Flaw in Human Judgment* (London: William Collins).

Kahneman, Daniel and Amos Tversky, 1979, "Intuitive Prediction: Biases and Corrective Procedures," in S. Makridakis and S.C. Wheelwright, eds., *Studies in the Management Sciences: Forecasting*, vol. 12 (Amsterdam: North Holland), pp. 313–327.

Klein, Gary, 2007, "Performing a Project Premortem," *Harvard Business Review*, September, pp. 1–2.

Nouvel, Jean, 2009, "Interview in Weekendavisen," *Copenhagen*, January 16, p. 4.

PMI, Project Management Institute, 2017, *A Guide to the Project Management Body of Knowledge (PMBOK® Guide)*, 6th Edition (Newtown Square, PA: Project Management Institute).

Sharot, Tali, 2011, *The Optimism Bias: A Tour of the Irrationally Positive Brain* (New York: Pantheon).

Turner, J. Rodney and Ralf Müller, 2003, "On the Nature of the Project as a Temporary Organization," *International Journal of Project Management*, vol. 21, pp. 1–8.

Wachs, Martin, 2013, "The Past, Present, and Future of Professional Ethics in Planning," in Naomi Carmon and Susan S. Fainstein, eds., *Policy, Planning, and People: Promoting Justice in Urban Development* (Philadelphia: University of Pennsylvania Press), pp. 101–119.

Webb, James, 1969, *Space-Age Management: The Large-Scale Approach* (New York: McGraw-Hill).

Chapter 33

Ethics

Darren Dalcher

Introduction

The area of ethics is assuming greater importance in project management with most professional associations establishing their own codes of conduct. Indeed, in an era of professionalisation and reflection, there is an implicit expectation that project managers will behave in an ethical way and discharge their duties in a moral and responsible fashion. Many of the codes stipulate that potential breaches may result in exclusion or further sanctions, suggesting that there is a clear position that can be evaluated and judged by an external agency. In reality, with the exception of the most obvious and unprofessional practices, this is likely to prove challenging as will be shown in this chapter.

Published codes of ethics require individuals to follow standards of professional ethics and behave "appropriately". They broadly explain that project managers need to act in equity, good faith and good conscious with due regard for the interests of the organisation or client. Ethical requirements form an integral part of professional behaviour and require a fundamental understanding of expectations, moral values and legal boundaries, thereby necessitating managers to display morally, legally and socially appropriate manners of behaving and working. Other professional standards such as the IPMA Competence Baseline (ICB4) clearly place ethics amongst the required behavioural competencies of a project manager.

DOI: 10.4324/9781003274179-37

The implication is that practitioners require both knowledge and competence related to ethics and its application within the project context.

Ethics is considered to be essential to free enterprise, democracy and the functioning of a fair society. Yet, despite the good intentions, the establishment of ethical thinking and reflection in practice seems a long way off. In particular, there are a number of primary challenges that impinge on the application of ethics in practice:

Practicality: Establishing ethics as a valid practical concern that extends beyond theoretical moralising. Professionals require practical tools, approaches, thinking frames and ways of applying them to their own contexts rather than generalised philosophical positioning and preaching.

Complexity: Recognising the complexity of ethical settings. Overly simplistic depictions of ethics as a choice between *right vs wrong* need to be replaced by more nuanced understanding of multidimensional dilemmas and conflicting sets of choices.

Pressure: Acknowledging and addressing organisational realities and politics. Individual decision makers do not operate in a vacuum. Even in situations where the right course of action is somewhat obvious, constraints related to business competitiveness, institutional pressures, political concerns, internal priorities, conflicts of interests and even personal gains and future promotions and remuneration may be applied and promoted by various parties.

Courage: Developing moral courage and conviction. Against the backdrop of a moral decline and a series of ethical and financial scandals (including Enron, Bernard Madoff, VW emissions scandal), it might prove essential to develop personal moral courage as a way of combatting the so-called *ethics recession* and overcoming organisational and urgent project-related pressures.

Guidance: Moral action is not automatic. Knowing that a situation is not right does not offer an obvious course of resolution. Guidance and practical tools and frameworks are needed to support deliberation, resolution and action.

The following sections offer the vocabulary and thinking tools required to address the challenges, reason about ethical dilemmas and develop a professional responsibility and the practical tools to address ethical concerns in projects.

What is ethics?

Ethics is increasingly viewed as essential to how we conduct our affairs, make decisions and interact with others. The Oxford English Dictionary defines ethics as the moral principles that govern a person's behaviour or the conducting of an activity. The Cambridge English Dictionary describes ethics as a system of accepted beliefs that control behaviour, which is often predicated on morals. Ethics is derived from the Greek word ethos, which means a way of living and typically encompasses the customs of a particular group. Moral systems and principles can be viewed as the surrounding climate of ideas which dictate how we view the world and guide our actions and the harm that they may cause to others. Ethics can therefore help in making moral and professional judgements about how we ought to live and guide and manage our actions. For a more detailed coverage of different types of systems of moral principles and values based on virtues, duties, outcomes, utility or pragmatism and their specific implications, please consult (Dalcher, 2022; Jónasson, & Ingason, 2013).

Peter Drucker (1999) offered a simple definition of management as the art of getting things done through people. Managers and leaders act to achieve certain effects. Action is therefore carried out by people, for people, and is also likely to service and harm those who receive the effects of that human action. The role of managers is to consider the action and its effects, as well as what they believe to be the desired impacts. Management ethics is thus concerned with the moral and professional systems, judgement, choices and behaviours of managers in conducting their work, including the products, artefacts, deliverables, systems and structures that they design and the consultancy and advice that they provide. In short, ethics forms an important guiding principle which should be utilised to govern important professional and personal decisions.

Do we have a problem with ethics?

A 2018 survey conducted by the Institute of Business Ethics in eight European countries reveals that 78% of employees say that their organisation always or frequently acts with honesty. The values range from 69% in Germany to 88% in Ireland. Employees seem more likely to speak up about misconduct with 54% recorded overall, ranging from 67% in the UK to 49% in Portugal. However, one in three employees has been aware of misconduct at work, with 46% recognising that people have been treated unethically, 35% misrepresenting hours worked, and 30% reporting safety violations. Pressure on workers is also intensifying: 16% of respondents across Europe have felt some form of pressure to compromise their organisation's ethical standard, with the figure rising in every country. Conversely, just under a quarter of participants (23%) are feeling incentivised to act ethically. Moreover, a 2021 survey with 10,000 respondents indicates that 43% of people who spoke about ethics lapses and misconduct at work experienced retaliation as a result.

The 2020 Global Business Ethics survey reports similar trends and insights for the US and globally. The pressure to compromise ethical standards is the highest it has ever been throughout 20 years of surveys, with 29% of respondents reporting pressure. Observed incidents of misconduct are on the rise. In the US 80% of respondents reported observed misconduct or unethical behaviour. However, 79% of US employees and 61% of global employees also reported experiencing retaliation for raising ethical concerns. In 2016 the greatest pressure to compromise standards was reported by respondents from Brazil, India and Russia.

The main reasons given for the pressure to act unethically in 2018 across all European countries will feel familiar to many project managers (listed in order):

- Time pressure
- I was following my boss's orders
- We were under-resourced
- I had to meet unrealistic business objectives/deadlines
- I was being asked to take shortcuts
- I felt peer pressure to be a team player
- I was trying to save my job
- There were financial/budgeting pressures at the company

Indeed, the pressure of delivering to a strict deadline on a short-term intensive project with unrealistic objectives and deadlines in an intense team setting may resonate with many imperatives observed within the specific context of projects and programs. If ethics is concerned with making good decisions regarding people, resources, objectives and the environment, attention to ethics is particularly important in times of change and transformation, which is when the temptation to rush and cut corners may be at its highest.

Ethics raises interesting questions regarding priorities, pressure and power. Explaining the host of reasons for pressure as listed above and the concerns regarding speaking about misconduct and ethical lapses invokes the need to introduce a further *prudential* dimension concerned with self-interest. Prudential reasons relate to the personal interest of the decision maker that could be described in terms of personal financial gains, or some other pertinent values such as fairness, justice, loyalty, honesty, openness, integrity, accountability, kindness, charity, friendliness or trustworthiness. Prudential considerations would necessitate balancing issues, trading off values and reaching difficult compromises between competing personal priorities and unethical concerns, which may result in increased pressure and anxiety for managers, leaders, and other participants. Many ethical dilemmas embody such prudential elements making the ethical vs. prudential trade-offs both personal and problematic. Ironically, even the decision to speak up about unethical concerns and lapses involves a balancing between ethical considerations and recognition of potential prudential harm to the informant, their interests or their community.

Ethics as a clash of systems

Many books and commentators position ethics as the choice between right and wrong, often relating it to fairness or to some kind of acceptable standards for human behaviour and conduct. Indeed, it would be reassuring to be able to reduce ethical conflict and professional decisions to rights and wrongs; however, this is an overly simplistic representation of ethics offering the wrong starting point. Right versus wrong situations imply a relatively straightforward resolution, a choice between black and white. Ethics becomes more arduous when we encounter grey areas, where managers have to choose between right and right as conflicting perspectives and different shades of grey come into play. Ethics is also invoked in situations where the right course of action is somewhat obvious, but constraints related to business competitiveness, institutional pressures, political concerns, internal priorities, conflicts of interests and even personal gains and promotions may be applied by various parties.

The basis for ethics is the focus on values held by different individuals and groups and the ability to reconcile different sets. Values emerge from fundamental beliefs. Managers will have different sets of beliefs derived from their personal background, upbringing, education, training and experiences. They can thus accumulate personal, team, organisational, professional, sector-related, national, societal and human values. They will also be expected to gain an understanding of the values relevant to their clients, users, and stakeholder communities, which may originate from a variety of backgrounds. More complex trade-offs, such as the triple bottom line where financial, environmental and social perspectives are combined, require even more sensitive ways of balancing values and preferences.

Ethical dilemmas are problematic because they represent a clash between right and right (or sometimes between wrong and wrong), implying a direct conflict between competing moral requirements. For instance, how do we choose between being a good parent and a good employee? The existence of moral pluralism is problematic precisely because it eliminates the judgement between right and wrong as the deciding criterion, introducing a need for demarcating different aspects and shades of goodness, developing grading structures for determining preferential or better fits, or establishing who should suffer more and over what time.

Ethical decision-making is about grappling with conflicting values from different thinking systems and perspectives rather than undisputable scientific facts. Dilemmas imply that neither of the propositions is unambiguously and universally preferable, mandating a new capability for dealing with competing and even opposing moral positions, rules, and criteria.

The objective is to make informed, good-enough decisions. Ethical responsibility is therefore concerned with how we behave and how things are done within our personal, collective and professional realms, freedoms and limits. In the course of taking action we strive not to compromise the interests of the project, the interested parties, the organisations involved, society and the environment, whilst upholding our own personal values, addressing our innate sense of fairness and considering the common good.

Personal ethics

Ethical behaviour does not simply emerge from having a professional code of conduct, a series of workshops, a neat form or a departmental ethics committee. Ethical behaviour starts with individuals who are willing to engage and grapple with their personal values, social or communal assumptions, choices and decisions. Individuals endeavour to balance their own levels of discomfort in a given situation, with their internal values, whilst taking into consideration the prudential dimension and the potential for personal impact. Not surprisingly, unpacking the set of questions required to make sense of a situation can be difficult and many managers lament the lack of concrete suggestions to explore whilst engaging with ethical dilemmas. The following set offers a simplified framework for engaging with ethical concerns and developing moral and ethical competence:

i Is it legal?
The first question is occasionally positioned by some organisations as the lowest bar, established by focusing on what the law requires, expects or permits. The aim of the question is to consider the existing standards as ethics and the law are often intertwined, but they can also be used to augment, refresh and strengthen legislative and governance scrutiny. The ethical features of a situation are frequently contrasted with legal aspects, representing a minimal standard. However, the law creates structures within which rules and codes are intended to operate. Murder, assault and drug taking may be illegal in most jurisdictions, whilst paying tax is an obligation in most, albeit not all, domains. Legislation is unlikely to be sufficiently comprehensive to address all potential circumstances and conceivable human actions. Moreover, legal standards are reactive, often induced by significant ethical lapses and may take years to catch up and become enshrined as statutes, laws and legislative standards as exemplified by slavery and bribery. This is particularly applicable in the case of new technologies and novel applications that may raise ethical concerns long before they mature into fully formed legislative criteria. What is legal is not necessarily ethical; whilst, what is not illegal is not necessarily moral. Ethics generally extends beyond the regulatory dictates of the legal system into the discretionary world of fairness, honesty, trust, responsibility and choice, thereby enabling additional tests and enhanced standards of behaviour to be introduced.

ii Is it fair?
The second question probes the integrity and fairness aspects by addressing concerns through sub-questions such as: Is it right? Is it balanced? Am I hurting anyone? Who will be affected by it? Is it fair to all concerned parties?

The set of questions looks at who might be favoured by the action (or lack thereof) immediately and over the long term. It identifies affected parties and potential stakeholders and looks at the implications of taking action, as well as leaving things as they are. Win-win scenarios may be difficult to construct, but understanding the potential winners and losers amongst stakeholders helps to clarify levels of power, resistance, and resentment and map potential future conflicts. Imbalances tend to hamper future relationships and hinder the potential for sustainable success and prosperity.

iii How will I feel afterwards?
Ethics is personal. The third question returns to the ethical dilemma and the feelings and emotions it engenders. It examines the position and role of the decision maker, encouraging scrutiny of their ethical values and priorities, their sense of morality, their emotions, their standards, their prudential concerns, their willingness to engage, their readiness to take remedial action or potentially to report an injustice. It encourages decision-makers to take ownership of the decisions they make or fail to make. It can also give managers the courage to ask brave questions, seek answers, raise concerns and report ethical breaches. Additional sub-questions may include:

- Can I live with this situation?
- Can I look at myself in the mirror afterwards?
- Will it make me feel proud?
- Can I afford to ignore it?
- Will it keep me awake at night?

iv Can I really justify it?
Some deliberations are tougher than others. The final set of heavy-duty questions and considerations requires deeper engagement with the scenario through the use of more sophisticated and emotional questions.

- First of all, put yourself, in the other person's shoes – will the affected person also think that the decision is ethical?
- How would I like it if it happened to my daughter, partner, father, or grandmother?
- How would I explain the decision to my (future) children?
- How would my mother feel about my decision, if she were to hear about it in the shop or read about it in a newspaper?

Collective ethics

Groups, teams and communities play an ever-increasing role in the workplace. Projects bring together temporary groups of engineers, developers and managers, collections of stakeholders and specific interest groups, whilst creating new communities of users. Such endeavours rely on professionals to apply their own moral and ethical codes. Organisations often seek to engender an ethical culture; yet, whilst they may establish a moral identity, recruit individuals with moral sensitivity and awareness and provide support and encouragement for ethical scrutiny, it is ultimately up to the individuals to choose to think ethically and act responsibly.

But what happens when many individuals only consider their own interests? Individualism seems to be a prevalent feature of modern life. The legal system specifies unacceptable behaviour in society for the good of all. Yet, well-intended individual acts of freedom can accumulate and strain the entrained community. Dalcher (2022) explores the implications of community life that require cooperative co-existence and implied adherence to group patterns that focus on the long-term sustainability of a cherished resource and the community it supports. Moreover, even an individualistic and seemingly harmless action, such as hanging a lovelock on a bridge to signify an eternal commitment to a beloved partner, multiplied thousands of times over can lead to the collapse of a highly prized common resource or the destruction of a landmark when individual freedoms and moral expectations clash. The ethics and realities of living and working in a community are bound together through the actions, infractions, priorities and morals of individual members.

Collective working requires long-term consideration of impacts and actions across and between groups. Yet, it also carries the benefit of enabling multiple independent ethical agents to collaborate, share and support one another. Organisations can play a part in motivating and encouraging communal ethical behaviour. Morality is developed and fine-tuned over time and can be encouraged to grow and develop. The main influencing behaviours in organisations stem from the establishment of culture, values, standards of behaviour and practices that support community co-existence, ethical behaviour and moral decision-making. Blanchard and Peale (1988) formalised a 5Ps framework as the basis for developing an ethics policy and attitude offering a way of structuring an underpinning ethical perspective and an enduring matching attitude (re-labelled and paraphrased below):

Purpose: a high calling. A combination of vision, values and shared meaning that helps to mould the expectations of acceptable and unacceptable behaviours.

Pride: Healthy self-esteem. A healthy balance of dignity, self-respect and humility play a part in encouraging employees to act in an ethical manner. Pride also enables actors to resist the temptation to behave unethically.

Patience: A question of faith. Patience requires commitment, long-term dedication and capacity to accept setbacks and having faith and belief that things will work out in the long run. Belief in long-term success encourages resilience in the face of obstacles and bad news, whilst sustaining a positive disposition and a long-term perspective.

Persistence: Afull-time commitment. Perseverance and commitment to staying the course.

Perspective: Seeing what is really important. The ability to step back, pause, reflect, take stock, see the big picture and understand what matters most in order to support the making of short-term as well as long-term decisions.

Ethical decisions are made by individuals. Nonetheless, the organisation, department or unit may also wish to review project-related dilemmas to evaluate their potential for harm and the impact on stakeholders, especially if the issues have been raised by employees, formally or informally. Specific new questions can build on the individual questions described above:

- Does the action/decision fit our values?
- Will it build goodwill?
- How would it look in the newspapers?
- Will it reflect poorly on our company?
- Will it cause long-term damage?

Professional ethics and the role of responsibility

Projects aim to solve problems or improve on a status quo, yet, their very emergence and their rushed implementation schedule open the potential for doing harm as well as good. Ethics is an important source of guidance for decision-making. Indeed, ethics as a set of values is expressed and given meaning through commitments, responsibilities and obligations. The values come into play when the boundaries between correct and incorrect behaviour are not clear, especially when multiple viewpoints and perspectives co-exist. According to the Institute for Business Ethics, business ethics is the application of ethical values to business behaviour. Project management ethics could therefore be defined as the application of ethical values to project management behaviour but can be more usefully defined as the application of ethical values and principles to the management of projects, their outcomes and implications, whilst considering all involved parties and stakeholders.

Given that the responsibility for deploying projects and overseeing their outcomes resides with project managers and project sponsors, their ability to act independently and make decisions and their professional responsibility is crucial to understanding the role and impact of morality and ethics in this area. The Oxford Dictionary defines "responsible" as either "liable to be called to account" or "morally accountable for one's actions" thus encompassing two rather different interpretations. Nonetheless, the increasing focus on the certification of project managers and the development of a chartered status standard for the profession in the UK carry significant implications in terms of assumed responsibility. Employing a professional represents the transfer of risk and decision-making obligations to a better-qualified agency, also known as transcendent responsibility. It carries within it the implicit assumptions of:

- trust in their ability;
- security in the knowledge that a qualified expert is employed; and,
- the comfort and peace of mind that comes from this knowledge.

Employing a professional expert is akin to buying additional insurance (through a risk transfer). In return for the trust exhibited by the client, the professional project manager takes responsibility for the deployment of the agreed function, capability, or quality for the process and the product itself. This aspect of responsibility is subject to professionalism, morality, and ethics.

Whilst responsibility entails owning up to acts, effects and consequences, one can identify distinctly different types of responsibility (Dalcher, 2007), as shown in Table 33.1.

Moral responsibility implies being answerable for one's actions and decisions and typically assumes some degree of causal responsibility. Therefore, a professional can also be held morally responsible for failing to act (i.e. re-setting the focus and scope of responsibility from harming to not aiding). Guilds, associations and professional bodies often look after the role responsibility aspect, thereby helping to enforce a more professional practice. Professional codes, introduced by such bodies, allow us to appreciate the standard, evaluate what could be expected from a member of the profession, and provide an implicit definition, at the very least, of acceptable professional behaviour. Indeed, with professional accreditation and certification, apportioning responsibilities may become a key activity in failure investigations.

Table 33.1 Different types of responsibility

Causal responsibility	associated with bringing something about either directly or indirectly (e.g. by ordering someone else).
Legal responsibility	associated with fulfilling the requirements for accountability under the law.
Moral responsibility	associated with having a moral obligation or fulfilling the criteria for deserving blame or praise for a morally significant act, or omission, and the resulting consequences.
Role responsibility	associated with performing duties that are attached to particular professional, or societal, (or even biological) roles. Failure to fulfil such duties can expose the role-holder to moral, legal or constitutional censure.

Developing your code of ethics

Project managers have a responsibility to their profession and to the wider society, in addition to their clients and company. Developing a code for resolving dilemmas and making moral decisions by building on the preceding discussion can be useful in supporting the development of communal ethical reasoning and deliberation. A code of ethics comprises a set of ethical principles. It would therefore place several essential normative requirements on professional engineers and project managers, including, as a minimum:

- an obligation to technical, managerial, leadership and moral competence, which may also entail personal and organisational recognition of gaps, shortfalls, limitations and lack of expertise, knowledge, capability or experience;
- an obligation to present and review evidence, theory and interpretation honestly, accurately and without bias and quantify all risks;
- an obligation and wider responsibility for timely communication of both positive and negative results;
- an obligation to voice concerns and speak truth to power in moral dilemmas;
- an acceptance of responsibility (causal, legal and moral) for actions, impacts and consequences;

- an obligation to limit the harms and ensure the safety of products, systems and outcomes and their effects on the environment; and
- an obligation to guard the interests of multiple participants and stakeholder groups.

Responsibility thus encompasses constant awareness, total autonomy and explicit accountability. The focus on accountability for consequences and outcomes of actions (or lack thereof) is essential in projects, programs, portfolios and initiatives, and can point to the potential for severe impact following deployment, during usage, and beyond, extending into decommissioning and disposal and possibly supporting recycling and reuse options. It also recognises the impacts on others, including human, societal and environmental effects.

The penultimate clause encourages managers to ensure the public's safety and limit the potential harm to others. This is particularly important considering the experimental nature of every project and undertaking, the residual uncertainty that accompanies them, and the inability to predict and forecast all potential side effects and consequences (Martin & Schinzinger, 2010). If projects represent the ambition and the experiments of society, project managers thus become the responsible experimenters embracing a conscientious commitment to live by moral and ethical values required to safeguard society, the environment and all participants and stakeholders.

Conclusion

Invoking codes of ethics is not a new endeavour. Ancient societies have practiced various ways of introducing such principles. One example is provided by Hammurabi, King of Babylon, who recognised the perils of design and project management over 3,775 years ago and enacted a building code that clarified the "responsibilities" of designers: "If a builder has built a house for a man and his work is not strong, and if the house he has built falls and kills the householder, that builder shall be slain" – Code of Hammurabi, 1755 BC.

Professional societies are unlikely to introduce similar censure in the foreseeable future. They do however encourage members to consider the ethical and enduring implications of their decisions and actions. This should entail looking at the concerns, assumptions and impacts across different groups and making decisions that are informed by the different concerns and preferences. Adopting a reflective practice that questions the assumptions and limitations of our approaches should be used by all practitioners interested in improving project success rates, delivering business value, and maintaining stakeholder relationships whilst preserving and sustaining the environment.

Moral codes give individuals and communities the courage to act ethically. Professionals are duty-bound to update their knowledge, skills and attitudes. This may well include making sense of personal uncertainties and conflicts of opinion. Ethical issues become a concern when there are no written rules, when they raise moral problems for a member of the team when they make managers reflect on what is right, when you are forced to consider where your obligations and duties lie (and probably when you are told that "this is what you are being paid to do"). The role of ethical thinking is to safeguard practitioners, the profession and the stakeholders. The outcomes of our projects determine our progress towards a better and more comfortable future. Clients, users, stakeholders, employees and colleagues rely on the professionalism, responsibility and ethics of managers and developers in delivering that future responsibly. Who better to remind us of the need for professionalism than Astronaut Alan B. Shepard, who whilst awaiting blast-off atop the space shuttle Columbia, commented that it was a humbling experience knowing that his fate depended on a vehicle built by the lowest bidder!

A humbling food for thought for project managers, and another indication of the true complexity of responsibility, ethics and professionalism in projects.

Historically, ethics would only come to the forefront in the wake of significant disasters or scandals, raising questions regarding the use of flammable cladding materials in residential high-rise buildings, insufficient testing and lax governance in the space shuttle program or the manipulation of emissions controls during car testing. Indeed, the combination of temporary setting, constant pressure, short deadlines, impending handover, multiple contractors, diverse participants and competitive pricing all add to the complexity and potential ethical vulnerabilities. However, there is a crucial need to use ethics as a force for identifying concerns, resolving issues and avoiding accidents, scandals or disasters. Professionals thus play an important part in raising awareness of impending moral hazards and in mitigating their potential effects, thereby adding to the risk, governance and assurance aspects of the project structure whilst contributing to the enduring success and sustainability of the endeavour.

The social, political, environmental and moral impacts of projects and their outcomes will continue to rise to match accelerating societal ambitions. To gain and retain trust, and enable communities to realise the benefits of these remarkable endeavours, managers will need to cultivate an ethical and professional dimension. Creating a fairer future for all would thus depend on our ability to confidently apply ethical tools, approaches and attitudes, such as the ones explored throughout this chapter, and to develop the determination to continue to ask courageous questions and speak truth to power, especially during the most trying and challenging times.

References and further reading

Blanchard, K., & Peale, N. V. (1988). *The power of ethical management*. New York: William Morrow and Company.

Dalcher, D. (2007). Why the pilot cannot be blamed: a cautionary note about excessive reliance on technology. *International Journal of Risk Assessment and Management*, 7(3), 350–366.

Dalcher, D. (2022). Morality and spirituality, in, Pasian B. & Williams, N. (Eds.). *Handbook of responsible project management*, 11–52. Berlin: De Gruyter.

Drucker, P. (1999). *Management challenges for the 21st century*. London: Harper Collins.

Jónasson, H. I., & Ingason, H. T. (2013). *Project ethics*. Farnham: Gower.

Martin, M. W., & Schinzinger, R. (2010). *Introduction to engineering ethics* (2nd ed.). New York: McGraw-Hill.

Part V

Portfolio

Part V explores elements of multi-project management. We start with the management of three types of groups of projects, programs, portfolios and sequences. There is a chapter on the application of machine learning to portfolio selection. Then there are two chapters on organisations undertaking multiple projects. We describe organisational project management and then the project-oriented organisation. There is a chapter on the governance of projects, and one element of governance is the project management office.

Chapter 34: Managing programs

Is this piece of work a project or a program? This question has been asked for many years and in many contexts with varying answers. The definition is important, but some pieces of work benefit from being called a program, and some do not. Harvey Maylor and Ruth Murray-Webster describe an alternative pragmatism. Indeed there are programmatic aspects to most managerial and leadership tasks, and considerable overlap with technical project management, change management and strategy. They consider 'managing programs' to be an expression of this diversity of influences. They frame the challenge of managing programs in systems terms, with managers as designers of systems of work. The challenge is the creation of 'holism' in the delivery of the purpose of the program. It must meet the organisational requirement: providing a layer of coordination to achieve benefits that could not be achieved, where individual aspects of that program are managed separately.

Chapter 35: Managing project portfolios

Companies use projects as temporary organisations to develop innovative solutions and transform themselves. Concurrently running many interdependent projects requires the dedicated management of project portfolios. Project portfolio management (PPM) means selecting the most beneficial projects and coordinating

DOI: 10.4324/9781003274179-38

their successful realisation. Hans Georg Gemünden and Alexander Kock describe PPM's main objectives, highlighting its essential role for organisations as the central link between strategy and projects. They then illustrate the major challenges associated with PPM, which are rooted in projects' uncertainty and interdependency, and stakeholders' diverging interests and biases. Based on a review of empirical work, they then discuss how companies can address these challenges by providing strategic and operational transparency. After reviewing the main portfolio practices, they finally focus on empirically-derived best practices of how organisations can enhance innovation and deal with risk in their PPM.

Chapter 36: Managing project sequences

Hans Georg Gemünden and Alexander Kock address the issue of managing sequences of projects that build on each other, and create, develop, or terminate paths of innovation development and innovation exploitation or paths of organisational transformation. They first describe the nature of project sequences and why it is useful to manage project sequences. We then present the goals of project sequence management. After illustrating the main challenges of project sequence management, they derive, based on empirical work and theoretical foundations, five principles for good project sequence management.

Chapter 37: Machine learning in project portfolio selection

In a world of limited resources, the ability to achieve one's desired outcomes by selecting and managing the most appropriate projects is an increasingly fundamental skill. An ability to forecast and prioritise successful options from a bucket of candidate projects has become a source of sustainable competitive advantage for businesses and firms. Machine learning allows companies to exploit knowledge gained from past projects and to use this knowledge to make better decisions about new projects. However, some major challenges persist, such as the difficulty of creating a consistent and sufficiently large dataset and the computational burden of the algorithms. Costanza Mariani and Mauro Mancini provide an overview of the methods currently used to select projects, thus highlighting how supervised and unsupervised machine learning can be applied to different phases of project portfolio selection to forecast the outcomes of projects, classifying and clustering upcoming projects in a predictive way.

Chapter 38: Organisational project management

Shankar Sankaran explains the Organisational Project Management (OPM) model, which can help organisations integrate all project management-related activities in an organisational hierarchy or network to ensure that projects create value for stakeholders. The model has seven layers and 22 elements derived through the literature. It includes some novel concepts that have not been used in previous conceptions of OPM, namely, organisational philosophy, projectification and governmentality, which have become important in managing projects. The OPM model has practical value to practitioners and organisations delivering projects as an assessment tool to evaluate their OPM capability. The model has been validated through theory and its application in organisations.

Chapter 39: The project-oriented organisation

Martina describes the model of the project-oriented organisation and its specific features expressed in its strategy, structure and culture. The model offers a theoretical perspective applicable to any organisation that performs projects. The project-oriented organisation is based on organisational fit theory combined with a business process perception, which allows one to assess how well organisations are equipped to perform their projects. The organisational design of a project-oriented organisation includes permanent and temporary structures, which follow different management logics causing tensions and contradictions. The chapter then focuses on Human Resource Management in Project-oriented Organisations and provides an overview of challenges and potentials.

Chapter 40: The governance of projects

Ralf Müller addresses the governance of projects from an intra-organisational and inter-organisational perspective. Governance – the framework for managers to execute their management task – needs to be set up in contextual contingency and synchronized between the organisation's project, program, portfolio, corporate, and inter-organisational layers to accomplish its benefits. The present chapter starts by looking at project governance for a single project in a company and then widens the perspective for the governance of programs and portfolios and its links to corporate governance, followed by a discussion on the governance of inter-organisational networks for project delivery. Throughout the text, models are provided to visualise and explain the particular governance functions at each layer. Through that, the chapter provides insights and implementation hints for the different governance tasks at different layers in corporate hierarchies, or nodes in corporate networks, and across inter-organisational networks.

Chapter 41: The PMO

Monique Aubry offers a PMO toolbox for those who are designing a new project management office (PMO) or wish to update or modify existing PMO. The toolbox approach makes it possible to design a PMO specific to an organisational context. This chapter is the result of a multi-year research program dedicated to the study of PMOs. The toolbox contains four basic elements from which to build a PMO: organisational context, characteristics of projects, PMO structural characteristics, and PMO activities. The chapter also offers five fundamentals on PMOs which inform PMO design with the use of the toolbox: the toolbox approach, thinking globally, working with frequent changes, understanding and managing chaos versus order, and building performance. Together, the PMO toolbox and fundamentals form a reference framework which can be transferred to the professional world.

Chapter 34

Managing programs

Harvey Maylor and Ruth Murray-Webster

Introduction

Programs are temporary organisations set up for the purpose of delivering benefits at scale and over time. They are complex, socio-technical systems, characterised by a high degree of dynamics and systems interactions, with incremental delivery of benefits. In addition, they have high sub-system diversity. 'Managing' in this context requires those charged with the design and delivery of program, to 'go beyond' the management of projects, to work with ambiguity, emergence and dynamism, and yet retain the defining purpose of the organisation by considering holistically the delivery of benefits.

In this chapter, we begin with narrating the emergence of the concept of 'program' and its expansion into many aspects of organisational life. There have been enduring aspects of this history, notably the vital role that programs play in the delivery of organisational strategy. There has been a growing toolkit and pragmatism in its application, and there are aspects of this development, notably the search for exclusive definitions of program, that have been less productive. Looking forward, there are also warnings about the longevity of the concept.

We then move from consideration of the concept to the notion of programs as systems of work. This thinking has evolved considerably and is where the most challenging notion for practice – that of *holism* – is described. We then consider the task of managing and three interdependent aspects of program work: strategic,

DOI: 10.4324/9781003274179-39

managerial and relational tasks. Finally, we focus on the program manager and their requirements for the role.

What is a program and does it matter?

NASA's Apollo Space Program is a classic example of a program that is used in many sources. This began in 1961 and ran until 1975. The early flights tested the technology to be able to launch people and equipment into space, to return them safely to Earth and then to push the boundaries still further, culminating in the moon landings from 1968 to 1972. It was one program, comprising many projects and requiring that as a minimum the learning from each launch was passed on to the next. Benefits were realised with each launch, most important given the highly politicised nature of the program in the context of the cold war. Moreover, this gradual and highly publicised realisation of benefits was essential for such a long program of work, which existed in a fiscal environment which favoured annual budget rounds and continually had to demonstrate that this justified being a national priority.

Whilst the Apollo Program was 'business as usual' for NASA, elsewhere, there was a growing realisation that "organising by program" might be beneficial. Accompanying this, we find that from the late 1970s onwards, there were efforts to define programs and program management, as distinct from projects and project management. This effort continues today in both academic and practitioner literatures.

Through the 1990s, the conversation was largely focused on establishing the role of programs in providing the *"bridge between strategy and projects"* (Murray-Webster and Thiry, 2000) and in attempts to identify types of program distinct from projects. This included Pellegrinelli's work (1997) focused on the role of programs in pursuing common goals (for instance a program of business expansion), common themes (e.g. an employee welfare improvement program), or continuous development of common systems/platforms (e.g. Apollo or in Formula 1 where cars are subject to ongoing development during each season).

By the turn of the century, the dominant conversation in academic and practitioner literature was to conceptualise programs and projects as different vehicles for delivering planned change with projects focused on planning and controlling and executing a plan, and programs focused on discovery and adjustment.[1] This was accompanied by more widespread adoption of the term 'program' (Maylor and Turkulainen, 2019) and the development of standards and guides (e.g., MSP latest version Axelos, 2021; PMI, 2006).

With the general agreement that projects and programs are both temporary organisational forms, this "quest for definition" focused on drawing distinctions. Rather than bringing clarity to the practice, the early 2000s saw the different labels being used for similar jobs and (often) grade or rate card inflation.[2] This was exacerbated by a wide variety of labels being used by those making decisions to invest in and deliver beneficial change, including the addition of prefixes such as major, mega, complex or strategic to both projects and programs and associated aims to define what makes a project, or program 'major' or 'mega' or 'complex' or 'strategic'.

Whilst is it undoubtedly the case that some project-based endeavours are larger (consuming more resources) and more complex (with many multiple interfaces and expectations) than others, by the late 2010s we see a pragmatism emerging where prefixes of major/mega/complex/strategic are offered as descriptors rather than definitions, and with the conversation switching to a more conditional space exploring different knowledge sets and a focus on 'what works where' in response to particular challenges faced, regardless of the label attached.

One such development is to move from a (maybe always pointless) aim to define projects as 'delivering outputs' and programs 'creating outcomes, realising benefits and developing legacy to an accepted position that all investments in change are reliant on a return on that investment in line with financial, social, environmental or public value objectives' (APM, 2019).

Another development is the shift away from a position where projects are concerned with technical work and technical deliverables, and programs with organisational and cultural change. The evolution of modern project management from roots in defence, nuclear and the built environment through IT-based change, led to professional bodies adopting a predominantly rational-technical stance. Projects were vehicles for delivering technical outputs and project managers as technical experts with project management skills bolted on. In parallel, organisational and cultural change was seen as central to different professional bodies (e.g. those interested in human resources) with change managers as 'people' experts with project management skills bolted on. Again, the reality for organisations has always been more nuanced and it is now mainstream for investing organisations to embrace a whole-life approach to the development and use of physical and organisational assets to achieve strategic objectives.

In line with this blurring of the attempted exclusivity of program and project management definitions, the lead editor of the fifth edition of Managing Successful Programs (MSP) noted that "much planned change work that could benefit from a programmatic approach is not called a program, strategic projects and major projects being two examples" (Axelos, 2021: xii). Accordingly, this guidance, reflecting practice, acknowledges the different reasons for using a programmatic approach to:

- configure and coordinate multiple projects to achieve the desired goals, and
- provide a set of principles to guide the work.

Three examples from our own recent experience illustrate different reasons for adopting a programmatic approach:

a Decommissioning a nuclear facility – in reality, a 100+ year endeavour organised into five-year investment periods to progress multiple projects. Annualised budget cycles make the work of **prioritisation** across the program of projects a key focus.
b Delivering a new military capability – a large number of projects that are too big and risky to stand on their own. A **coordinating layer** is vital to ensure unintended consequences from decisions in one project do not affect the whole.
c Divesting a part of a business – where the initial agreement to sell assets may be a single project, the work to 'carve-out' different processes, technologies, people and the collective capabilities they represent is messy and requires an **incremental approach** to ensure the continued functioning and viability of both the divested element and the main business.

These three activities: differential prioritisation between projects and other activities, coordination between various streams of work being carried out and executing activities in an incremental manner are then responses to organisational requirements and are shaped very differently. It is this lack of homogeneity in the use of programs,that to our minds renders any ongoing attempt at the development of mutually exclusive definition, nugatory. What is valuable to organisations (and in line with the definition of a program in MSP 2021[3]), is the capability to:

- Design temporary structures, to
- Lead multiple inter-related projects and other work (often across a high diversity of organisational units and with projects using different delivery modes), to
- Achieve measurable benefits for one or more investing organisations over time.

This approach accords with our experience from working with large numbers of practitioners in the public, private and third sectors. We frame managing programs as experiencing the combined challenges of designing and integrating multiple projects, each a system in its own right, usually in the context of a dynamic operating environment. Whilst we situate the discussion in the context of a Handbook of Project Management, the endeavour of interest in this chapter may not be called "a program" or contain anyone with the title of 'program manager'. Indeed, we see that there are programmatic aspects of the roles of most leaders involved in change, regardless of title. These would benefit from both sensemaking and sensegiving approaches that come from considering the requirements that have been recognised and developed and today constitute 'program management'.

Before leaving this section on definitions, it is useful to consider that there are lower limits, at which the terminology of 'programs' may be less than helpful, but there are also upper limits. For instance, if one considers NEOM, the visionary new city being designed in the north of Saudi Arabia, the program layer of coordination is certainly not at the top of the hierarchy of the organisation. Indeed, such a 'giga project' includes many mega projects and programs, and the challenges for the 'giga' level are unlike anything attempted in this generation. Similarly, whilst there is a notion that global de-carbonisation could usefully be considered as a program, the scale and reach of that task are way beyond anything that current approaches to program management were conceived to deal with.

In addition, whilst 'programmification' (the increased use of the program form of organising work) has been observed over four decades or more, we are seeing organisations shift away from this approach. One major European bank, for instance, has shifted in favour of organising by 'product'. Their concern was with the realisation of benefits, and how teams that developed financial products would "hand them over to operations" at various stages, leaving the operations teams accountable for benefits realisation in which they had a little stake. The same narrative has emerged in a number of UK government departments.

The next section explores programs using a systems perspective. We then continue to consider the notion of the task of the program manager and then as the guiding mind for the program.

Programs as systems of work

Programs are temporary organisations and socio-technical systems. We find the application of systems thinking to be most helpful in providing sensemaking of their inherent complexities. Systems Thinking is "...a set of synergistic analytical skills used to improve the capability of identifying and understanding systems, predicting their behaviours, and devising modifications to them in order to produce desired effects. These skills [themselves] work together as a system" (Arnold and Wade, 2015).

The evolution of programs as an organisational construct was in part due to project management traditionally being 'hard systems' and 'deconstructionist' (e.g. as discussed by Winter et al, 2006). In systems terms, this is too limited a consideration. For our consideration here, we take a number of steps. First, to be broader, incorporate soft systems into our analysis of the work that comprises programs. Second, we recognise the multiple systemic levels at which activities take place. Last, we promote the notion of systemic holism.

Hard and soft systems

Project management can be viewed as taking a "rational systems perspective" on the organisation of work. This is an important and accepted element of program work today. However, recognising programs as social and well as technical systems and that they are socially constructed as means of organising, requires the addition of soft systems to our analysis. As with other ways of breaking down systems, often the most interesting aspects lie not in either hard or soft systems, but at the *interfaces* between the two. For instance, the interface of the human system containing *optimism bias* with the rational system for project and program costing and evaluation creates a problem with performance. This inclusion of soft systems thinking has profound implications for systems design.

Systemic levels

Programs have multiple levels at which systems of work can be viewed. A breakdown is helpful here so that any discussion can be made specific to the level of interest. Table 34.1 shows level 1 to be that of the program which has a high degree of uniqueness. In contrast, work carried out at level 3 is predominantly repetitive. As for hard and soft systems, defining systemic levels in this way creates interfaces. For instance, how projects report progress into a program represents an interface.

Holism

In dealing with the complexities of programs, there is a requirement for deconstruction. Breaking tasks down into manageable units of work means that, for instance, a project can be given to a group or contractor to deliver. Given the scale of some programs, there is an imperative to do this because potentially the balance sheets of individual contractors could not sustain a failure if they took on the whole program, or the locus of capabilities required for a program is dispersed over many firms. Once deconstructed, however, a major task for

Table 34.1 Systemic levels in programs

	Description	*Characteristics*
Level 1	Major Program: comprises many projects operating together as *systems of systems*	Main governance layer Ownership of systems and associated problems and solutions. Unique ($n = 1$)
Level 2	Projects: each project is a system with interfaces to other projects	A mixture of functional and other activities undertaken. Work usually dependent on other projects in the program Predominantly a *batch* process
Level 3	Operational: tasks and work packages carried out at this level	Generally small functionally-centred activities. Predominantly *repetitive* tasks

leadership as noted above is the coordination or integration of those parts. This can be achieved via what has become known as the 'systems of systems' approach.

However, as we have seen in numerous highly problematic major programs (London's Crossrail is a classic case), this integration must not simply focus on the bottom-up joining of those parts. Instead, achieving good outcomes requires both bottom-up and top-down, keeping the overall function of the system in mind. As Jackson notes:

> Holism considers systems to be more than the sum of their parts. It is of course interested in the parts and particularly the networks of relationships between the parts, but primarily how they give rise to and sustain in existence the new entity that is the whole....
>
> (Jackson, 2016: p. 4)

The 'new entity' or 'whole' is level 1 as shown above. The program then defines (the classic approach), but also is defined by its constituent activities (holism). Ensuring that this second is maintained is a crucial role for managers.

The roles of program managers cannot be specified in the detail that may be appropriate for more contained projects; the level of complexity and dynamism usually precludes that. There are, however, some generic tasks that will present with differing importance, as the program progresses.

What are program managers concerned with?

At Level 1 in the system, the work of managers is *strategic, managerial* and/or *relational*. A common characteristic of many programs is uncertainty and change, and this is where the work is strategic in nature. Managerial work is a set of tasks are predominantly focused on hard systems aspects – organising, planning and control. Last, working with complex stakeholder arrangements is not unusual and this is where the 'relational' aspects of the task are most relevant.

The aspects of the task are illustrated in Figure 34.1.

The three aspects of work are interdependent. For instance, a change in strategy as the result of a threat, will knock onto planning and stakeholder engagement. This reflects a characteristic of programs, that they require a dynamic approach to their management and one that is integrative.

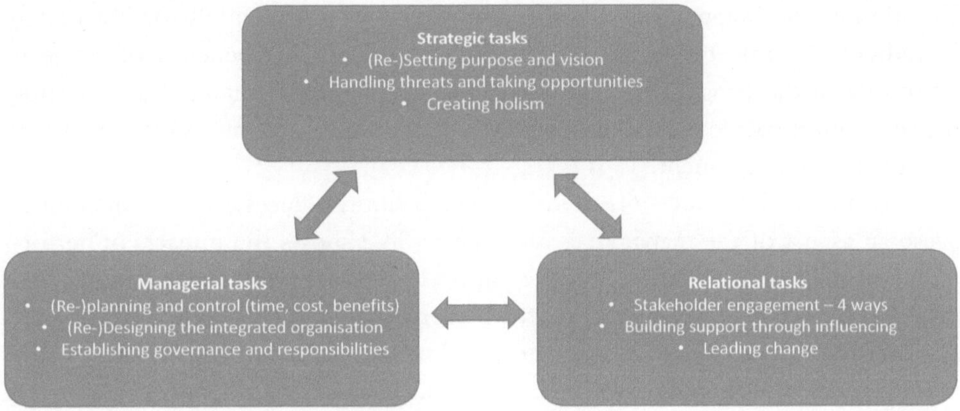

Figure 34.1: The tasks of managing programs

Strategic tasks

The strategic tasks begin with the creation of purpose: the 'north star' or guiding rationale for the program. For change programs, this is often termed the 'target operating model' or what will the organisation function like, once the change is achieved. This is not only a 'fire and forget' but also an ongoing process. Threats to the program will abound and require careful scanning, as many programs are caught out by 'surprises' that had already been anticipated, but with no action to respond. A significant area for development though, lies in the exploitation of opportunities. For instance, a program developing new wearable technologies for use in healthcare, was incredibly innovative. They generated many potentially useful side-products, but were unable to exploit any of them, due to lack of time, funding or a process to do so. This capturing of opportunities is a crucial role for the program manager. Last, holism has been described above, and creating this forms part of the strategic tasks and demonstrates that they are both top-down (setting purpose and vision) AND ground-up (creating holism).

Managerial tasks

Program work, like project work, should be forward-looking. Planning and control for key program objectives is needed at multiple systemic levels and a non-trivial challenge is the integration of these plans. Decisions include the allocation of contingency and whether this should be held centrally or distributed to individual projects. Aggregating costs, ensuring the benefits of projects contribute to the program purpose (e.g. through benefits mapping) and putting in place appropriate controls, balancing leading and lagging measures are part of this aspect of management.

Designing an integrated organisation which has the necessary accountabilities is also an aspect of the managerial task. Figure 34.2 shows the impacts of performance of the systemic design and the nature of *shadows* (yesterday's designs) and *projections* (future systems designs) on the performance of the systems. Performance lags the design activity, so it may not be known for some time what are the consequences of design decisions. In addition, there is a gap between "intended future designs" and "realised future designs" due to practical "of the moment" constraints.

The topic of organisational design is covered elsewhere in this Handbook, and we will not attempt to reprise it here. Like every other aspect considered here, it is repeated over the program life cycle. There is no single 'optimised design'; as soon as it settles it is time to move on. In addition, 'human-centred design' has to sit alongside 'the wiring diagram' or organisational hierarchy. For instance, at

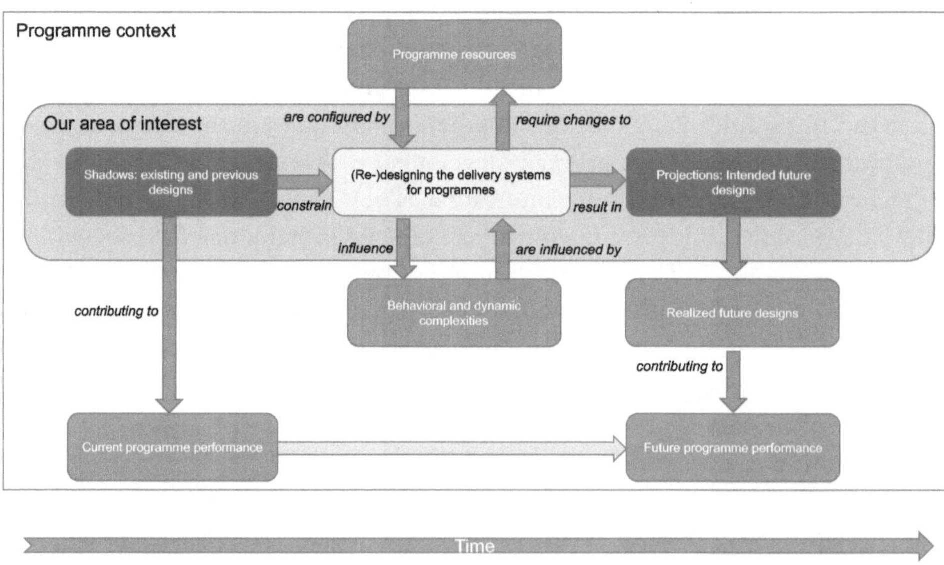

Figure 34.2: (Re)designing the integrated organisation

London's 2012 Olympic and Paralympic Games, the design had to be managed very carefully as firms wanted their staff focused on successful delivery rather than worrying about what they were going to be doing for a job when it was over. Redeployment plans were put in place to allay any worries individuals quite understandably would have had. Finally, a recent visit to a major defence program was instructive. During the visit, discussions were held with many individuals about leading and the nature of leadership in that program. It was notable that no less than five people identified themselves as the leader and were ultimately accountable for that program. This is an extreme example and evidence of a problematic structure for that program. However, it is generally true of programs that leadership is not enacted by a single superhero style leader, but instead is shared; it is a collective endeavour often widely distributed horizontally and vertically within systems and organisations. The locus therefore is wide and the notion of *program management* by necessity incorporates a correspondingly wide range of expressions.

Relational tasks

In programs, the relational tasks will often be dominated by stakeholder engagement. The program managers who are most effective can operate "up and out" as well as "down and in". 'Up and out' refers to interactions with those who are in senior positions in their organisations, but also with key stakeholders, be they individuals or groups. "Down and in" refers to interactions with those delivering the program, including the managers of the constituent projects. Consistent with such interaction, are aspects including the narrative (communicating purpose and why should anyone buy into it?), trust (of the manager and the program) and networks (what is the level of equity that managers have with stakeholders?). 'Up' and 'down' are two of our four ways of engagement. The other two involve the work of managers with suppliers and 'customers'. Narrative, trust and networks are likewise central to these tasks, and "winning hearts and minds".

Programs usually involve significant aspects of change. This is often done 'to' people rather than 'with' people, which slows or stops progress towards benefits being realised. Whilst we noted earlier that this is a significant topic of study and practice in its own right, it is central to the task of managing programs.

We now turn to consider the requirements of those charged with managing programs.

Program managers

There are a number of characteristics to be considered in selecting and developing program managers. Firstly, they should be SQEP – Suitably Qualified and Experienced Personnel. Qualifications are necessary for many technical roles, but this is only part of what constitutes 'knowledge' or 'Human Knowledge Capital'. Experience likewise is essential for many but needs to be qualified by the level of reflection that has been applied to that experience, and the range of contexts in which that experience has been gained. To think of knowledge in terms of individuals also misses a large aspect particularly relevant to programs: knowledge networks. People usually have networks of professionals with whom, for instance, they have worked or studied in the past. With suitable recognition, these can be usefully considered as a knowledge asset. In addition are they motivated? Will they bring the discretionary effort to their work, over and above simply turning up? Lastly, the idea of the superhero leader is outdated, and instead, we prefer the notion of "incomplete leader, complete team" (Ancona et al, 2007), where the program manager recognises their own shortcomings and builds a team around them with complementary knowledge, experience, networks, attitudes and skills.

There is one more relevant dimension to consider. This is the 'conceptual level' of individuals. The work of Partington, Pelleginelli and Young (2006) demonstrated that people have varying levels of conception of their work, with the lowest being concerned with immediacy and narrowness. Higher-level conceptions were associated with the requirements placed on program managers and the ability to see broader implications of decisions and issues, both positive and negative. This links well to the idea of holism, and its achievement but program managers with the right (higher) level of conception are needed to achieve it.

Conclusion

We began our discussion with a description of attempts over a number of decades to define 'program' as if establishing the genus of a plant. Whilst specificity is helpful, and indeed considered crucial for the progress of the scientific enquiry, there are some broad characteristics that have been established. We concluded that further attempts to provide hard boundaries and categoric exclusivity for temporary endeavours, are unlikely to be helpful.

Instead, we have looked at managing in the context where there are programmatic aspects – many projects, benefits to be delivered over time, considerable dynamism, and resulting emergent complexity. We framed the purpose of managing programs as an organisational response to the challenge of achieving holism in the program, integrating diverse projects and related efforts. Further, the act of managing is carried out by a dispersed group, with our focus on systemic design, being undertaken at multiple levels in the system. This is an ongoing process throughout the life of the program.

The requirement for managers as designers of program systems is to achieve the twin objectives of:

1 Focus, control, efficiency and effectiveness of delivery for component projects, and
2 Flexibility, accommodation and staged benefit realization for the overall program.

They will do this through the tasks they carry out, described as being strategic, managerial or relational. It helps to have the right person in the role as program manager. As we have shown, this is a complex task, requiring many skills, knowledge and experience, but also the right networks and ability to function at the right level.

Lastly, a program manager has to "hold the tensions" within and between ever-changing elements of their program, in both hard and soft systems. And these elements when combined will define what is "the program" as much as the intent that started the program design in the first place.

Notes

1 For a good discussion of the bibliometric foundations of 'program management' see Artto et al (2009).
2 This was notable in IT services in particular, where service providers could charge higher fees for 'program managers/management' than 'project managers/management.'
3 "A temporary structure designed to lead multiple interrelated projects and other work in order to progressively achieve outcomes of benefit for one or more organisations." (Axelos, 2021: p. 3).
4 This was the original standard, latest currently the fourth edition, 2017.

References and further reading

Ancona, D., Malone, T. W., Orlikowski, W. J., & Senge, P. M. (2007). In praise of the incomplete leader. *Harvard Business Review*, *85*(2), 92-100.

APM (2019). *Body of Knowledge*, 7th ed. High Wycombe: Association for Project Management.

Arnold, R. D., & Wade, J. P. (2015). A definition of systems thinking: A systems approach. *Procedia Computer Science*, *44*, 669–678.

Artto, K., Martinsuo, M., Gemünden, H. G., & Murtoaro, J. (2009). Foundations of program management: A bibliometric view. *International Journal of Project Management*, *27*(1), 1–18.

Axelos (2021). *Managing Successful Programmes (MSP ®)*, 5th ed. Norwich: Stationery Office.

Jackson, M. C. (2016). *Systems Thinking: Creative Holism for Managers*. New York, Chichester and Indianapolis, IN: John Wiley & Sons, Inc.

Maylor, H., & Turkulainen, V. (2019). The concept of organisational projectification: Past, present and beyond? *International Journal of Managing Projects in Business*, *12*(3), 565–577.

Murray-Webster, R., & Thiry, M. (2000). Managing programmes of projects. *Gower Handbook of Project Management*, *3*, 47–64.

Partington, D., Pellegrinelli, S., & Young, M. (2005). Attributes and levels of programme management competence: An interpretive study. *International Journal of Project Management*, *23*(2), 87–95.

Pellegrinelli, S. (1997). Programme management: Organising project-based change. *International Journal of Project Management*, *15*(3), 141–149.

PMI (2006). *The Standard for Program Management*. Newtown Square, PA: Project Management Institute.[4]

Winter, M., Smith, C., Cooke-Davies, T., & Cicmil, S. (2006). The importance of 'process' in rethinking project management: The story of a UK government-funded research network. *International Journal of Project Management*, *24*(8), 650–662.

Chapter 35

Managing project portfolios

Hans Georg Gemünden and Alexander Kock

Introduction

In today's dynamic environment, organizing by projects has become the rule rather than the exception, and companies use projects as temporary organizations to develop innovative solutions and transform themselves. Typically, they run many projects concurrently, and generally, the share of project work increases compared to operational work (Schoper et al., 2018). Especially when implementing complex innovations, it is not enough for organizations to focus on successfully managing individual innovation projects; they must also manage a large number of interdependent projects from a portfolio perspective.

A project portfolio is a set of projects executed by a particular organization that is managed as a group to achieve strategic objectives and in which projects compete for limited resources in terms of budget, personnel, and time. The project portfolio represents the organization's strategy as it is a collection of projects and programs that embody strategy realization (Meskendahl, 2010). Therefore, the dedicated management of a project portfolio is responsible for the prioritization of projects and the respective allocation of scarce resources in order to realize the most favourable selection of projects for an organization. In addition, PPM refers to the continuous and overarching coordination and steering of the project portfolio. In that regard, managing a portfolio can provide benefits (e.g., exploitation of synergies between projects and management of portfolio risks)

DOI: 10.4324/9781003274179-40

that would not occur in the case of independently managed projects (Teller and Kock, 2013).

PPM is a dynamic decision-making process to select the most beneficial projects and coordinate their successful realization. It thus helps exploit the potential of a portfolio of projects and mitigate risk accumulation. Its main tasks are to lead the organization properly so that it carries out the right projects, staff these projects with competent project managers and teams, use the project results sustainably, and achieve all stakeholders' value-creating objectives.

In the following, we will discuss PPM's main objectives, challenges, and practices. We then review empirical findings on how to appropriately organize PPM with a special focus on innovation and risk.

Objectives

Project portfolio management (PPM) pursues several goals (Cooper et al., 2001; Kaufmann et al., 2020; Kester et al., 2014; Kopmann et al., 2017):

1 Portfolio managers should strive to maximize the *overall value* across the portfolio's projects by ensuring that projects achieve their individual objectives and deliver benefits for the organization.
2 Portfolio Managers should aim for a *balanced portfolio* that minimizes risk, given a certain value creation. Specifically, Project Portfolio Managers should ensure a good *balance of exploration and exploitation.* This means simultaneously performing sufficient projects that hone and improve existing products and competencies (i.e., exploitation) and sufficient projects that develop new competencies and create new options (i.e., exploration).
3 Portfolio Managers should ensure that all projects support the overall strategy. Strategic implementation success describes the extent to which a portfolio's projects align with the overall business strategy.
4 Portfolio Managers should ensure a project portfolio high in *future preparedness.* Such a project portfolio is one that, in the present, builds new skills, competencies, products, and technologies that open up long-term future opportunities for shaping the organization's market and gaining a competitive edge.

Since there may be some trade-offs between these objectives, we need to assess the success of project portfolios multi-dimensionally. Firms achieving success in these different dimensions have higher customer satisfaction, market effectiveness, and

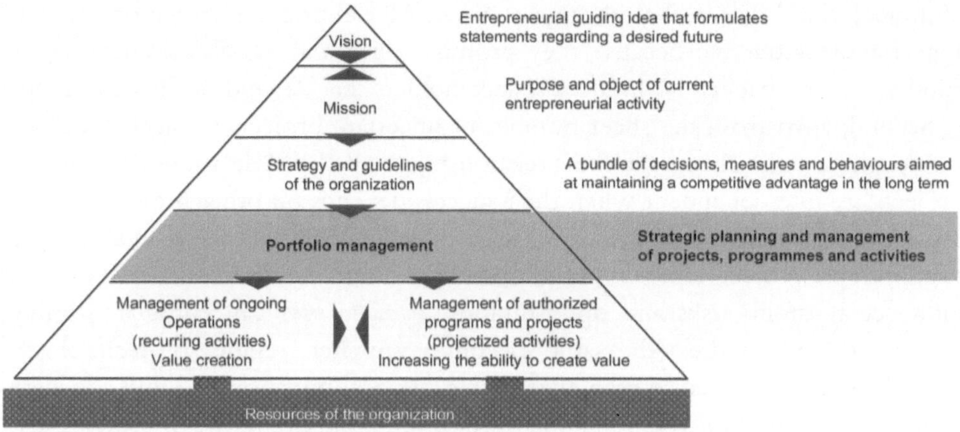

Figure 35.1: Portfolio Management links strategy with projects and operations (PMI, 2017)

profit (Kester et al., 2014). The success dimensions highlight PPM's essential role for organizations as the central link between strategy and projects (Meskendahl, 2010), as shown in Figure 35.1.

Challenges

Project management is useful for solving single complex problems in a limited time using a temporary organizational design that fosters cross-functional and cross-disciplinary teamwork. However, the usefulness of this approach, and the increasing problem complexity, led to an exponential growth of project work. This created *new problems*: the high workload and their project landscape's lack of transparency stress many organizations. Resource spending does not reflect strategic goals, projects are delayed because of a lack of resources, and the allocation of bottleneck resources becomes a highly conflict-loaded process. Overall, we see three major challenges that PPM needs to face.

First, the projects themselves are often uncertain, difficult to predict, and complex, especially when they apply new technologies or address new user needs. Managing a collection of projects which are individually difficult to predict makes portfolio decisions even more challenging. Organisations need to make conscious decisions about the degree of innovativeness of their projects and the overall portfolio. Balancing projects from different innovation horizons (e.g., exploration and exploitation) is challenging because with increasing proficiency in one type of project, the ability in the other type wanes. All too often, exploitation projects appear more attractive because they promise quicker gains, face lower uncertainties, and are backed by influential stakeholders that depend on their funding.

Second, apart from the sheer number of uncertain projects, projects' interdependencies and the changes in these relationships make PPM decisions demanding. Projects are interdependent when their success depends on other projects, which can relate to benefits, resources, risk, or knowledge. PPM needs to address these relationships: projects do not only compete for scarce resources, but they also influence portfolio risks and opportunities. *Portfolio risks* can cumulate rapidly if many projects address the same customer, supplier, region, or technology. Portfolio managers need to recognize such a risk accumulation and find adequate coping measures. *Portfolio opportunities* come from synergies between projects that should be recognized and pursued. It might be wise to launch projects that deliver platforms and then set up projects that deliver derivative solutions based on the platforms. It is also possible to save money and time by bundling the development of critical components in specific projects instead of allowing every project to develop its own project-specific version. Recognizing and exploiting such opportunities are typical portfolio management tasks. It requires a deep understanding of how the projects are related and how the timing of the projects that build on each other should occur. Making holistic portfolio decisions – instead of isolated project decisions – is therefore essential. However, decision-makers struggle with understanding interdependencies, which can overload their mental capacity to analyze the high number of combinations and the variety of information (Killen et al., 2020).

In addition, most PPM approaches deal with interdependencies between projects that occur *concurrently* (i.e., within a typical budgeting period). However, portfolio managers should be aware that they are managing innovation and transformation *paths*. Successful new products usually build on successful and unsuccessful *previous* products and improve, for example, their functionality, usability, reliability, or safety. Therefore, firms develop sequences of projects that describe successful innovation paths. In a similar vein, not only the products of the future but also the *competencies* of the future are created by the learnings in *current* projects. Therefore, decision-makers need to be aware of how their choices impact both path-dependency risks and path-creation opportunities. They should use road-mapping and scenario techniques, which possible project portfolios will develop based on their current strategic choices.

The third major challenge is that portfolio decision-making can be very political and subject to bias. Deciding which project gets more resources is often more a power game than a rational strategic choice. This is understandable because the stakes are high when deciding to initiate or terminate projects that determine the organization's future and viability. In addition, many different and influential stakeholders need to be involved in the decision process. This constellation invariably leads to negotiation and bargaining (Martinsuo, 2013). For example, influence, persuasion, and negotiation can allow more powerful groups or individuals to make decisions that reflect their personal interests. Connected to that, portfolio decisions about project initiation, continuation, or termination are often subject to cognitive biases (Killen et al., 2020). For example, portfolio decision-makers tend to prefer less novel project proposals, especially when their cognitive load is high.

Structures

Addressing these challenges requires that PPM establishes strategic and operational transparency. This transparency is established (a) if processes and structures for PPM are well organized, (b) if planning and control instruments are established professionally, and (c) if information systems with a high utility and usability support both functions.

Organization: The formalization of project portfolio processes into different stages has been shown repeatedly to increase project portfolio performance (Teller et al., 2012). Establishing clear rules and guiding principles at the decision points leads to data integrity and facilitates the comparison of divergent projects ensuring that processes are comprehensive and responsibilities well defined. Portfolio process formalization improves information and coordination quality by supporting interactions between different functional groups and projects and facilitating inter-project learning. A clearer formalization of roles also increases performance. In particular, the roles of the project portfolio manager, the mid-level line managers, and the project owners should be clearly defined.

Planning and controlling: A future-oriented organization requires that the organization develops a well-founded long-term viable strategy, which is broken down to the project portfolio level because a company's strategy is realized by the entirety of its projects (Kopmann et al., 2017). This means that operational criteria are developed, which allows aligning the project portfolio with the organizational strategy. *Strategic clarity* of deliberate strategies is the first condition for successfully planning and controlling project portfolios. *Operational clarity* about the projects, their expected benefits, risks, and resource requirements; the resources and their quality and availability are the second condition for successfully planning and controlling project portfolios. Operational clarity and a better decision-making quality of project portfolio decisions, and higher agility of project portfolio decisions, can be improved by (1) *formalized PPM processes*; (2) *controlling intensity*, the frequency, and thoroughness of assessing goal attainments, and (3) *business case control* (Kock and Gemünden, 2016). Kopmann et al. (2015) show that the significant positive effect of business case control on project portfolio success increases when the project and line managers are accountable and incentivized for project portfolio success.

ICT systems to support planning, controlling, coordinating, and decision-making for single projects and project portfolios increase performance. Whereas ICT systems are used for the vast majority of single projects, ICT systems for PPM are used less often. Kock et al. (2020) find a positive impact of PPM information systems' usage on project portfolio success. This effect only materializes when organizations reach a sufficient maturity of their project management processes.

Practices

Several process models have been proposed for PPM. Such process models typically highlight the role of project prioritization and selection and the ongoing coordination of the portfolio of projects. The PMI standard for portfolio management differentiates initiation and planning, as well as execution and optimization (PMI, 2017). Kock and Gemünden (2021) refer to portfolio structuring and portfolio steering. In the following, we refer to the process defined in the OGC/Axelos standard (see Figure 35.2), which differentiates two cycles of practices: portfolio definition and portfolio delivery (AXELOS, 2011).

The purpose of the **definition cycle** is to generate an understanding of what the portfolio should deliver, i.e. decisions on the scope, contents, and results anticipated from delivering the portfolio. The main task of this cycle is to define a portfolio of project investments that, in its entirety, optimally reflects the strategic objectives while also considering the constraints of the funding organization. The definition cycle thus focuses on "doing the right things" by aggregating information to provide decision-makers clarity about which initiatives should be undertaken and how they will deliver the greatest contribution to strategic

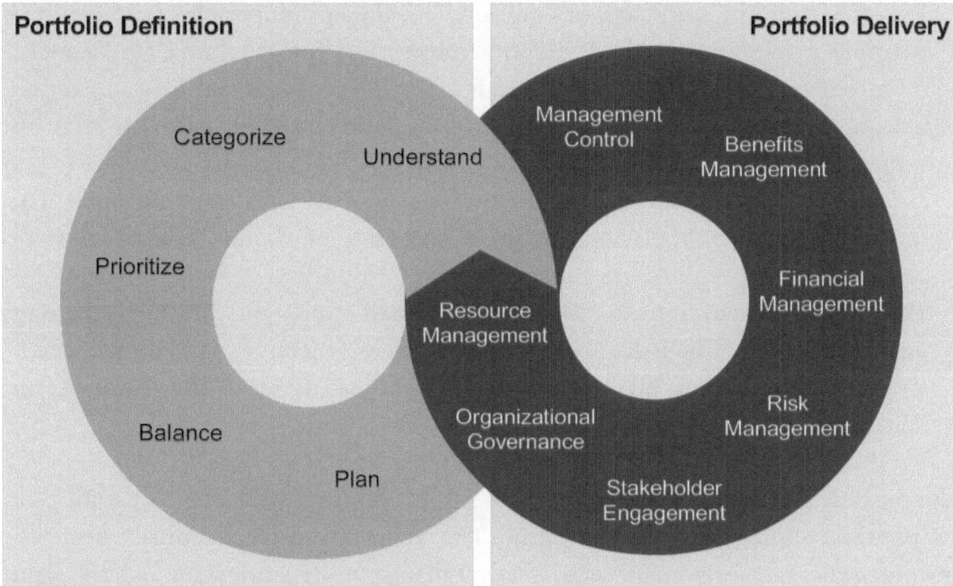

Figure 35.2: Portfolio Management Cycles (AXELOS, 2011)

objectives. The definition cycle typically contains the following practices understand, categorize, prioritize, balance, and plan.

- *Understand:* The purpose is to gain an initial understanding of the portfolio scope, including the existing and required initiatives. So this includes obtaining a transparent view of what is in the current portfolio and project development pipeline, getting a clear understanding of the corporate objectives, and translating the organization's strategic goals into portfolio objectives. Techniques such as Objectives-Key-Results (OKR) may be helpful here. Consequently, the gap between the portfolio pipeline and the objectives is identified, and project ideas are identified.
- *Categorize:* This practice entails grouping project ideas into categories or strategic buckets to create transparency, helping decision-makers to better understand the make-up of their portfolio and to make balanced and strategically aligned decisions.
- *Prioritize:* Initiatives are ranked within the portfolio based on several agreed measures. Typically, companies use some form of multi-criteria analysis. The criteria may be different for different strategic buckets to ensure an appropriate

assessment within each category and prevent direct competition between, for example, exploration and exploitation projects. Typical criteria are financial metrics (Net Present Value, Internal Rate of Return), strategic fit or contribution, risk, risk of not doing the project, innovativeness, and the time of value generation.

- *Balance:* Under consideration of the previous practices, balancing ensures that the resulting portfolio is well balanced in terms of timing, contribution to strategic objectives, business impact, risk, and resources.
- *Plan:* Based on the information of the defined cycle, this practice creates a portfolio strategy (high-level overview of how objectives will be achieved) and portfolio delivery plan (more detailed understanding of the shorter-term delivery schedule).

The purpose of the **delivery cycle** is to ensure the successful implementation of the portfolio strategy and delivery plan. The main task is to coordinate projects, promote synergies, reduce project issues by managing dependencies and risk, and ensure that the portfolio adapts to changes and that the benefits are realized. Accordingly, it comprises the following practices that are continuously executed:

- *Management Control:* Both individual and portfolio-level decisions are made regarding progress against the portfolio delivery strategy and plan.
- *Benefits Management:* Clearly identify and manage the benefits being realized from the portfolio, the contribution to operational performance, and strategic objectives.
- *Financial Management:* Ensure that the portfolio management processes and decisions are aligned with the financial management cycle and that financial considerations form a key element in all decisions.
- *Risk Management:* Ensure consistent and effective management of the portfolio's exposure to risk at both individual and collective levels.
- *Stakeholder Engagement:* Ensure the needs of the portfolio's customers (both internal and external stakeholders) are identified and managed appropriately.
- *Organizational Governance:* Ensure portfolio management governance is aligned with the wider organizational governance structure enabling a clear understanding of all decisions.
- *Resource Management:* Put in place mechanisms to understand and manage the amount of resources required to deliver the projects.

In the following, we focus on empirically derived best practices to enhance innovation (mainly an issue in the definition phase) and to deal with risk (mainly an issue in the delivery phase).

Enhancing innovation

Reaching higher innovation success for the offered products and services and for process innovations of their business functions is a strategic goal of most organizations. This is justified because all of the authors' nine benchmarking studies on PPM show a significant positive relationship between the innovation success of the projects in the portfolio and the project portfolio success, which in turn positively influences business success. *Which factors drive the innovation success of the project portfolio?*

First, the ideation pipeline matters. Portfolio management does not just start with the prioritization of project proposals. In fact, the right ideas have to be generated and further processed much earlier to become such a project proposal. If there are no good candidates, then the "winners", which are picked, will probably deliver only a modest innovation success. Thus, the goal of an ideation initiative is to develop ideas and concepts with a higher value creation potential and a sufficiently high chance that the selected candidate will deliver such solutions. To reach this goal, many firms have implemented an ideation program and process. The ideation program is driven by a strong encouragement of employees, a formalized and transparent selection and support process, and guidance by an ideation strategy informing which strategic goals and ideas should be strengthened. The study from Kock et al. (2015) uses a measure for front-end success comprising three components: effectiveness (value potential) of the developed concepts and speed and cost-efficiency of the concept development. It turns out that encouragement is the major driver, but with an increasing number of ideas, process quality, and strategic clarity become more important and leverage the creative energy of the employees. The study also shows that front-end success is an important driver of the later project portfolio success. Project-related homework is, therefore, not only important on an individual project level but also on the *portfolio* level. Interestingly, the impact of front-end success on portfolio success depends on several contingencies (Kock et al., 2016): If the project portfolios are more complex (i.e. if there are more projects in the portfolio and/or if the projects have a higher interdependence), then it matters more to be to select project candidates that may create more value. Also interesting: if the company that owns the project portfolio is not afraid of taking risks when making fundamental project decisions, and/or if it frequently supports projects when the expected return is still uncertain, and/or if the company accepts a high degree of risk within its strategic limits, then a good front end also exerts a stronger influence on project portfolio success. The latter characteristics describe the willingness of a company's executive decision-makers to accept risks if high returns can be realized.

Second, the innovativeness of the decision-makers matters. Innovativeness is the willingness to introduce newness and novelty through experimentation and creative processes aimed at developing new products and services, as well as new processes. It is one of the components of entrepreneurial orientation. The other two are pro-activeness and risk-taking. Innovativeness has a significant positive effect on PPM success – even when controlling for several other success factors like stakeholder involvement, strategic clarity, business case monitoring, and agility (Kock and Gemünden, 2021). Moreover, it further *increases* the positive effect of three of these success factors. This means that with increasing innovativeness, the positive impacts of stakeholder integration, business case monitoring, and agility at the project portfolio level will become even stronger.

Third, the innovation climate matters. Innovation climate relates to the support, autonomy, and creative feedback employees receive from management, encouraging them to pursue innovative tasks (Kock et al., 2015). Innovation climate has a strong influence on project portfolio innovativeness, which in turn has a positive influence on project portfolio success (Kaufmann et al., 2021). Innovation climate also has a positive influence on decision-making quality, even when holding constant several other antecedents (Kock and Gemünden 2016).

Coping with risk

Risk management has always been a central theme in project management and in portfolio management. Whereas Markowitz (1952) focused on the composition of a portfolio of financial entities, modern PPM has gone beyond his basic article.

First, the risk of a *single* project is sometimes more difficult to assess than the risk of a firm because projects are temporary endeavours, their business cases may be unique, and their expected revenues will realize later than in the case of mass-customized offers. Irrespective of their sometimes very high volume, projects are not listed on a stock exchange.

Second, the risk of a *project portfolio* can differ very much from the sum of the risks of its projects. This may come from a *systematic accumulation of risks* because projects tend to cluster around certain technologies, regions, industries, suppliers, or customers. However, there are *reasons* for this clustering: The firms that own and/or contribute to these projects focus on certain technologies, regions, industries, suppliers, and customers because they have *specialized* in them and gained *specific competencies* or *specific preferences* from their market and technology partners. Balancing the regions, industries, suppliers, or customers in a different way in order to reduce the systematic risk would also mean that the firm would have to find other ways to exploit its resources and competencies or to gain preferences from other partners. It may even lose some of its competitive advantages. Thus, there are frictions to change the structure of a project portfolio, there is a cost of changing project portfolios, and it will take more time than simply selling or buying a financial security. *What can be done to avoid negative developments of the systematic risks and to avoid path dependencies?*

The empirical study by Teller and Kock (2013) tests how the measures taken to cope with project portfolio risks will affect two main components of risk management quality: (1) Risk transparency and (2) Risk Coping Capacity. They also test to which extent these two components of risk management quality influence project portfolio success.

Risk transparency: Their results show that the risk management factors (1) portfolio risk identification, (2) formalization of the risk management process, and (3) risk management culture increase risk transparency. However, these three factors differ in their strength. Risk management culture has the strongest effect, followed by portfolio risk identification and then formalization of the risk management process. A strong risk management culture means that individual risk managers communicate risks openly and honestly and that they feel responsible for the risks and the associated measurements for their resolution. In addition, employees at all levels of the portfolio regard risk management as a part of their everyday business activities and are conscious of the necessity of risk management.

Risk Coping Capacity: The results show that the risk management factors (1) risk prevention, (2) risk monitoring, and (3) integration of risk management into PPM positively influence risk coping capacity. All three measures exert a significant and moderate influence. The two components of risk management quality positively influence project portfolio success.

Using a new data set, Kock and Gemünden (2016) show that *risk management culture* exerts a significant positive impact on decision-making quality of project portfolio decisions, even when controlling for five other influence factors (strategic clarity, formality of the project portfolio process, controlling intensity of the projects in the portfolio, and innovation climate).

Thus, the behavioural side of risk management appears to be very critical in gaining the right information and taking measures for avoiding or mitigating high risks. For a classification of ex-ante and ex-post measures and their etiological or palliative nature, see Teller (2013, p. 43, Figure 35.2).

The study by Teller et al. (2014) documents that project portfolio risk management is more than the management of the risks of all single projects in a project portfolio. Isolating two components, (1) the formalized risk management activities for single projects and (2) the integration of their informational inputs into PPM, the authors can show that both components exert a positive influence on project portfolio success. However, the effect of the integration is much stronger than the influence of risk management at the level of single projects. The effect of the integration increases in dynamic portfolios and with external turbulences.

This means if systematic risks in a project portfolio should be recognized and strategic shifts of a project portfolio are intended or required in order to adapt to external shocks, then an integrative assessment of project portfolio risks is indispensable.

Conclusion

PPM is essential to coordinate and strategically align project work in today's organizations. Facing the challenges rooted in uncertainty, interdependency, and stakeholders' diverging interests and biases, PPM needs to provide strategic and operational transparency through adequate processes, structures, and culture. We argued that – beyond well-defined practices supporting a portfolio's definition and delivery – PPM requires practices supporting innovation, such as a good idea pipeline fuelled by a climate for innovation, and practices increasing risk transparency and risk coping capacity to enable long-term organizational success and viability.

References and further reading

AXELOS. (2011). *Management of Portfolios (Managing Successful Portfolios)*. London: TSO, The Stationery Office.

Cooper, R. G., Edgett, S. J., & Kleinschmidt, E. J. (2001). *Portfolio Management for New Products* (Vol. 2nd). Cambridge, MA: Perseus Pub.

Kaufmann, C., Kock, A., & Gemünden, H. G. (2021). Strategic and cultural contexts of real options reasoning in innovation portfolios. *Journal of Product Innovation Management, 38*(3), 334–354.

Kaufmann, C., Kock, A., & Gemünden, H. G. (2020). Emerging strategy recognition in agile portfolios. *International Journal of Project Management, 38*(7), 429–440.

Kester, L., Hultink, E. J., & Griffin, A. (2014). An empirical investigation of the antecedents and outcomes of NPD portfolio success. *Journal of Product Innovation Management, 31*(6), 1199–1213.

Killen, C. P., Geraldi, J., & Kock, A. (2020). The role of decision makers' use of visualizations in project portfolio decision making. *International Journal of Project Management, 38*(5), 267–277.

Kock, A., & Gemünden, H. G. (2021). How entrepreneurial orientation can leverage innovation project portfolio management. *R & D Management, 51*(1), 40–56.

Kock, A., & Gemünden, H. G. (2016). Antecedents to decision-making quality and agility in innovation portfolio management. *Journal of Product Innovation Management, 33*(6), 670–686.

Kock, A., Heising, W., & Gemünden, H. G. (2016). A contingency approach on the impact of front-end success on project portfolio success. *Project Management Journal, 47*(2), 115–129.

Kock, A., Heising, W., & Gemünden, H. G. (2015). How ideation portfolio management influences front-end success: Ideation portfolio management. *Journal of Product Innovation Management, 32*(4), 539–555.

Kock, A., Schulz, B., Kopmann, J., & Gemünden, H. G. (2020). Project portfolio management information systems' positive influence on performance – The importance of process maturity. *International Journal of Project Management, 38*(4), 229–241.

Kopmann, J., Kock, A., Killen, C. P., & Gemünden, H. G. (2017). The role of project portfolio management in fostering both deliberate and emergent strategy. *International Journal of Project Management, 35*(4), 557–570.

Kopmann, J., Kock, A., Killen, C. P., & Gemünden, H. G. (2015). Business case control in project portfolios – An empirical investigation of performance consequences and moderating effects. *IEEE Transactions on Engineering Management, 62*(4), 529–543.

Markowitz, H. (1952). Portfolio selection. *Journal of Finance,* 7(1), 77–92.

Martinsuo, M. (2013). Project portfolio management in practice and in context. *International Journal of Project Management, 31*(6), 794–803.

Meskendahl, S. (2010). The influence of business strategy on project portfolio management and its success – A conceptual framework. *International Journal of Project Management, 28*(8), 807–817.

PMI. (2017). *The Standard for Portfolio Management.* Newton Square, PA: Project Management Institute.

Schoper, Y.-G., Wald, A., Ingason, H. T., & Fridgeirsson, T. V. (2018). Projectification in Western economies: A comparative study of Germany, Norway and Iceland. *International Journal of Project Management, 36*(1), 71–82.

Teller, J. (2013). Portfolio risk management and its contribution to project portfolio success: An investigation of organisation, process, and culture. *Project Management Journal, 44*(2), 36–51.

Teller, J., & Kock, A. (2013). An empirical investigation on how portfolio risk management influences project portfolio success. *International Journal of Project Management, 31*(6), 817–829.

Teller, J., Kock, A., & Gemünden, H. G. (2014). Risk management in project portfolios is more than managing project risks: A contingency perspective on risk management. *Project Management Journal, 45*(4), 67–80.

Teller, J., Unger, B. N., Kock, A., & Gemünden, H. G. (2012). Formalization of project portfolio management: The moderating role of project portfolio complexity. *International Journal of Project Management, 30*(5), 596–607.

Chapter 36

Managing project sequences

Hans Georg Gemünden and Alexander Kock

Introduction

Rome was not built in a day: Important changes do not come about through a single project or program but through a *sequence* of projects that build on each other. Projects are important elements that contribute to an *innovation path* of new product, service, or infrastructure, or to a *developmental path* that transforms an organization or an inter-organizational network.

Different terms have been used to describe and analyse project sequences.

1 *Roland Gareis* (2006, pp. 489–490) coined the term "Projektkette", which means "*project chain*". Two or more consecutive projects are linked together in a "project chain" if they belong to the same investment activity (Gareis and Gareis 2017, p. 600). For example, a project that offers a solution to a client and a consecutive project that is contracted with the same client to develop and deliver that solution build on each other and are both elements of the same investment activity.
2 *Christophe Midler* (2013) introduced the term "*project lineage*" to the project management literature. He did not look at sequences of projects belonging to the same investment activity but at different successive generations of projects belonging to different investment activities. Using the Logan Case from Renault's Daccia division, Midler's case study frames project lineage

DOI: 10.4324/9781003274179-41

management as a way to expand the initial move of building a new low-cost car into a diversified range of products and a multi-continent deployment, while keeping the key specificities of the pilot project. His case study does not only cover the development of a single product's different generations, such as the different product generations of the famous Volkswagen Golf. Rather, it analyses the strategic process of developing a completely new low-cost product family that created a completely new high-volume brand within the Renault and Nissan car family. Thus, Midler's case study does not only analyze the impacts of a project sequence, but it also analyses how a new *portfolio* of projects unfolds over time.

The two seminal contributions from Roland Gareis and Christophe Midler and their co-authors analyze project sequences, but they have different foci, which both contribute to a better understanding and more effective project management.

Gareis and Gareis (2017) concentrate more on the operational issues of two or more projects that follow each other in a chain of value creation and value exploitation. They are more tightly connected through the inherent logic of the project business to which they belong than the project sequences that Midler and co-authors address. *However, this business logic does not guarantee that the different projects of a chain are seamlessly integrated.* If two projects in a project chain have different project leaders and project teams, or if they have different project owners, and fulfil different goals, useful knowledge likely get lost and interface problems occur. Therefore, Gareis and Gareis (2017) are right to emphasize that organizational and human resource measures are necessary to establish strong links between the projects in such a chain. The logic from Gareis and Gareis (2017) is very clear: project management of a single project is a concept that *integrates different stakeholders* to achieve a common goal within a given time and given resources. If two different projects of an investment activity form a project chain, then the links in this chain need to be strengthened in order to integrate these two projects. This needs to be planned and organized, and a continuity of team members in both projects and principles for knowledge transfer is necessary to support the intertemporal integration task. Such project chains occur very often, and it is therefore useful that an organization recognizes their importance and develops practices to overcome their challenges.

Midler and his co-authors concentrate more on the *strategic aspects* of more *loosely* connected project sequences. If a firm introduces a new product or service in a market, the market participants usually assume that this firm will also develop a follow-up product, particularly, if the current new product is successful. Midler (2013) reports that the *profitability* of products that are developed in sequences may increase during such a sequel. For example, for the Renault Logan and the following product family, profitability was only 8% in the first generation, 23% in the second generation, and then over 100%. Other very successful project sequels with similar patterns exist, such as the Toyota Prius, the "Star Wars" movies, or the iPhone sequels, which made Apple the first trillion-dollar company.

Why does such a rise in profitability occur when follow-up generations of a new product are developed and marketed? First of all, it usually takes time for a technological innovation to demonstrate its positive impact, to improve it or add new functionalities, to make it cheaper, safer, more reliable, and more convenient. It also takes time to develop variants that are tailored better to different target groups possessing different requirements and preferences. The organization offering the new product must learn new capabilities, integrate new suppliers, address new customers, etc. Changes in the environment may also impede success in the first product generation: for example, electric vehicles require a new infrastructure to provide them with electricity, hydrogen vehicles need a supply of hydrogen, and autonomous cars need new regulations to get them approved as safe enough. Therefore, Kock et al. (2011) found a net effect of zero on performance for the first generation of radically new products. There was a significant value creation of the radically new product and its new functionalities, but the sum of negative influences attached to the still imperfect and developing new product reached the same effect size.

Changes in the market have also to be considered. The case study of Midler (2013) on the Logan car describes how aggressive penetration price marketing started first in low-income peripheral markets and then moved to higher-income central markets. It is important for a low-cost car, and even more for the later low-cost car family, that a high volume of sold products can be reached. The goal of Renault for Daccia in Rumania was to offer a new car that was able to compete against the used cars coming from the West-European countries, in order to create permanent new jobs in an underdeveloped low-wage country. Once the diffusion has reached a certain threshold of many satisfied users, word-of-mouth will help to increase the diffusion speed, and profitability will rise.

Apple had a different strategy for its sequence of iPhone products. The idea was to make them a high-valued fashioned product that was sold at a high price.

While there was an increase in the number and quality of the iPhone's newly offered Apps (a unique novel functionality). they also witnessed an increase in speed, storage space, and, last but not least, the quickly increasing functionality and performance of the cameras increased the demand for these products so strongly that the number of sold products increased quickly despite high prices, and the profitability and market value of Apple increased even more quickly.

Thus, increasing the profitability of subsequent product generations is not a simple law that you always earn more with the projects for your next product generations. Rather, it can be attributed to the fact that the firms offering the innovation have implemented strategies that offer a better value-cost relationship for their products. While even the diffusion process has not yet reached its maturity stage, the firms have overcome their internal barriers and developed better capabilities and more efficient processes, and the barriers in the environment have also been lower with the new products' ongoing diffusion. External barriers occur because radical products often require newly built critical infrastructure or new regulations that make the products sufficiently safe and convenient. Overall, these processes occur with developing business ecosystems that interact with stakeholders from states and regulatory institutions, and from financial institutions that act as investors in new infrastructures.

Goals

As explained in the introduction, the management of project sequences can have different meanings. In the remaining parts of this chapter, we will address the management of project sequences that belong to different investment activities. This means that we focus on strategic issues. We take the view of the strategic goals of a single organization, which is of course, embedded in a network of organizational and individual actors. There are parallels to project portfolio management (see also the corresponding chapter in this handbook). However, while project portfolio management typically considers selecting, coordinating, and steering *concurrent* projects (i.e., a cross-sectional perspective), project sequence management considers the dynamic sequence over time (i.e., a longitudinal perspective).

An organization's long-term goals comprise its survival, the attainment of economic, ecological, and humanistic goals, as well as cultural, technological, and scientific goals. The management of a project sequence is a means to attain high levels of these goals. Usually, projects consume financial, human, technical, and social resources, but they also deliver economic, ecological, social, cultural, technical, or scientific benefits. The goal is to provide more benefits of different kinds than resource consumption of different kinds.

We suggest three goals for project sequence management:

The *first* goal is to maximize the overall value across the sequences of projects by ensuring that the project sequences achieve their individual objectives and deliver benefits for the organization. The question is how we measure *"overall value"* measured and which stakeholder group's preferences this "*overall value*" reflects. It is probably not sufficient to address only the goals of the shareholders and to consider only monetary goals. There is no convincing answer to this question, but it has become clear that a multitude of competing goals need to be achieved in a balanced way, particularly in times of climate and social challenges.

Second, the impacts of a project do not only depend on its own deliveries and consumptions but also on its contributing or inhibiting effects to other projects and from other projects that occur concurrently or subsequently. Synergies and risk accumulations between *concurrent* projects are in the scope of traditional project portfolio management approaches, whereas synergies and risk accumulations with *subsequent* projects that occur in the future are often neglected. The goal of project sequence management is to balance both kinds of synergies and risk accumulations, concurrent and intertemporal ones.

Third, managers of project sequences should ensure that all projects eventually support the overall strategy. Strategic implementation success describes the extent to which the project sequence aligns with the overall business strategy. Does the "overall business strategy" reflect all stakeholders' goals or is it mainly a strategy to deliver monetary business success – and other success criteria describing ecological, social, or cultural success are only considered as long as they increase monetary business success? Again, there is no clear answer to such a question. Recognizing that climate change may accelerate and reach tipping points, the need to lay more stress on ecological impacts in the current state, and not postpone these priorities has become evident. In addition, new strategies have to be developed to attain such goals. Similar arguments can be made to avoid a further increase in social inequality.

We raise these kinds of questions because the sequences of major projects affect longer time horizons. Projects shape our future. However, the projects that we undertake *today* will influence our knowledge, infrastructure, social and cultural life, the careers that we make, and the solution spaces that we will have tomorrow. If we do not incorporate pressing ecological, social, cultural, and political demands in our *current* projects, we may not to be able to cope with them in the future. We need to reduce consumption and waste of resources as soon as possible and to use the savings for investments in effective projects that are realized and delivering value in a comparatively short time. Thus, we make a plea to reflect the content of the strategic goals, and their relative value and prioritization in order to master our long-term challenges. The focus should be not only on implementing already existing strategies but also on developing new emerging strategies that fit better to the changed requirements. *It is important to create new development paths that give us new strategic options.*

Challenges

Managing a sequence of projects poses fundamental challenges to the basic assumptions of a project's nature.

First, envisioning a sequence of projects does not imply that the corresponding business activity has a determined time horizon because it is not decided ex ante *how many elements* the sequence will have. Single projects are the only endeavours with a determined time horizon. Thus, project sequence management is not a predetermined temporary activity. For example, Volkswagen currently considers whether to build a ninth generation of its very successful Golf model, but it appears that this will not be the case because the business environment has changed. Consumers were asked which car they would buy in five years and their preference for a new ID-electric car was much higher.

Second, it is not necessarily determined ex ante *how big the step should be* in each of the consecutive projects. For example, only a few development projects in the car industry create a significantly changed new product generation. But there are also more incremental changes – face-lifts – that are also organized as projects. Such intermediate projects in a project sequence are also used to make face-lifts or to adapt a car's IT infrastructure in between the longer normal development circles. In software development project sequences, we encounter different types of releases that may vary in the number of changes. Product changes of prototypes in agile development may use sprints of a fixed length so that the boundaries between pure project management and the management development processes increasingly resemble operational processes. The more the projects built on already existing projects or platforms, the less unique will be the result of each single project. The project delivers a new product or service that is customized to specific wishes. The term mass customization expresses this trend well, and the boundaries between unique customizations and automated adaptations blur.

If we look at the more significant changes, then the question arises: Should the firm make a very big step, or is it better to make a significant step that delivers considerably more customer value, but can be managed with lower risk and shorter time, so that follow-up projects can still keep the company an innovation leader? The study from Schultz et al. (2013) shows that when all positive and negative effects of innovations are captured in one scale of innovativeness, the relationship between new products' innovativeness and innovation success is inverted U-shaped, meaning a too high level of innovativeness should be avoided. A sequence of projects that each have a high but still manageable level of innovativeness and are performed with sufficient speed could thus outperform a single breakthrough project. Empirical evidence further shows that a sequence of comparatively short but highly interactive projects can deliver substantial performance increases. This increase is much higher than the existing industry standard and can reposition an underperformer into a top-in-class performer (Berggren 2019).

The *third* challenge is that a sequence of very successful projects, which even created increasing returns, may lay the foundation for *path dependencies,* resulting in costly and inefficient lock-in situations. In their seminal paper, Sydow, Schreyögg, and Koch (2009) offer a theoretical foundation for how very successful processes may end up in inefficient path-dependent constellations. While such processes are very open in the *preformation stage,* it becomes progressively more difficult to reverse the course of action. The *formation stage*

> starts at the critical juncture when a new regime takes over: the dynamics of self-reinforcing processes. (…) The notions of increasing returns and positive feedback describe self-reinforcing processes by which benefits grow when a specific pattern of action or routine is repeated. There is a push for doing more of the same.
>
> (Sydow, Schreyögg and Koch 2020, p. 718)

The transition to the third stage, *the lock-in stage*, delivers an additional constriction. "A lock-in implies that the path has led the organization into irreversibility;

alternative solutions are no longer within reach (or have even disappeared)" (Sydow, Schreyögg, and Koch 2020, p. 719). The challenge for the managers of project sequences is to recognize potential path dependencies and avoid them, and to build up new development trajectories by sequences of projects that allow to create new paths that are successful for a sufficiently long time.

A concept that shares striking similarities with organizational path dependence is *escalating commitment* (Sleesman et al. 2018). It prevents organizational decision-makers from changing their course of action, despite continued negative feedback on the outcome. Instead of stopping, the agents replicate the inefficient solution and throw good money after bad. There is, however, a major difference: path dependence has a longer phase of success; it is only in the *final stage* that the persistent course of action shifts into inefficiency. In contrast, escalating commitment captures situations where the course of action *fails from the very beginning*. Since there are no increasing returns or similar enhancing effects, it highlights another problem area – namely, pathological decision behaviour based on the dynamics of self-justification and fears of losing face (Sydow, Schreyögg, and Koch 2009). Escalating commitment is based on the abuse of power. Very often the power holders who suffer from this behaviour have been successful in previous projects, and are not willing to step back and give up their power. They also often formed a strong coalition of power holders that was able to implement a very ambitious but also very risky project, and they neglected good planning and put controlling mechanisms out of order. Hubris can also play a major role.

A solution to this processual challenge is better governance and independent and competent control. Using a project sequence can avoid too big innovation steps, and feasibility tests can be run with smaller projects. The Berlin Airport project BER is surely an often-cited example of escalating commitment. Testing the smoke-detection systems with a smaller building might have been necessary but there were many severe faults that together produced a remarkable failure. The buildings for the German re-unification (i.e., the Chancellor's office, the buildings for the members of parliament, and the restoration of the German Reichstag parliament building) were all done on time, on budget, and within specifications. An independent and competent steering committee, in which politics plays a minor role, and professional general contractors are two governance features that differ from the Berlin government buildings and the BER.

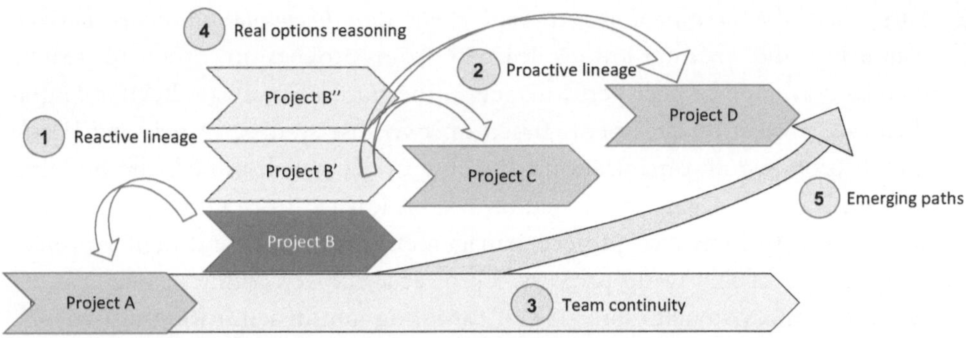

Figure 36.1: Five principles of project sequence management

Principles

Managing project sequences instead of individual projects offers the following advantages: You can choose smaller innovation steps but complete them faster and more cost-effectively and reap the project benefits sooner, gather usage experience from early application, and finance the follow-up project. The Airport in Tirana in Albania was built by its owner HochTief AG through a sequence of three projects and was, in contrast to the BER Berlin Airport project, very successful.

We identify five principles that characterize successful project sequence management (also shown in Figure 36.1):

1 *Proactively roadmap where the journey should go. Proactive lineage* means recognizing options for follow-up projects by planning generations of projects in advance, using tools like road mapping or scenario analysis (Kock and Gemünden 2019). The study from Rohrbeck and Kum (2018) shows that firms that had a high future preparedness in 2008 significantly outperformed firms in 2015 that had a low future preparedness in 2008. Their seminal study applies a wide range of foresight practices to measure how firms perceive, prospect, and probe future options. Proactive lineage helps assess a project's strategic contributions by not only assessing their direct expected outcome but also valuing of future projects they may enable. It thus supports projects that detect and seize future opportunities.

2 *Save knowledge in current projects and apply such knowledge in future projects.* Capturing and sharing lessons learned from projects in order to realize increased average project performance in the future has always been a central theme in project management. Based on two case studies, Davies and Brady (2000) proposed an organizational learning cycle, which models the building of organizational capabilities based on lessons learned from initial projects and which leads to improved project management procedures and higher project performance of follow-up projects. Ekrot et al. (2016) define lessons-learned systems as the systematic practice of capturing and disseminating knowledge gained during projects. They show that lessons-learned systems increase competence levels of project managers and project portfolio performance. This *reactive lineage* helps exploit past experiences and seize opportunities created in previous projects. Together, proactive and reactive lineage thus support balancing exploration and exploitation, helping firms become more ambidextrous—i.e., increasing competence to cope with future opportunities and risks, while at the same time building on past experiences and exploiting positions built by past investments (Kock and Gemünden 2019).
3 *Ensure that a high proportion of people work together again in the follow-up project.* Kaufmann et al. (2021) found that *team continuity* positively affects the commercial success of movie projects but with decreasing returns. Buengeler et al. (2021) derive and find in a study of 5,370 video games development projects, several inverted U-shaped relationships between team continuity and different market-related measures of the business success. Overall, team continuity pays back in project sequences, but its effects decrease with increasing team continuity and can even become negative. Thus, there is a positive influence of team continuity regarding shared tacit knowledge and better mutual understanding, but there is also a flip side to losing creativity. The inverted U-shaped relationship comes from this duality, suggesting an optimal level of team continuity.
4 *Understand projects and project portfolios as real options and manage them accordingly.* High performing companies incorporate *real options reasoning* in their decision-making. Instead of deciding whether or not to fully finance an option at a certain point in time, decision-makers distribute the investment sequentially over a period of time. Such distribution enables the option owner to decide on further investment, depending on the asset's development. When applying real options reasoning, only a low investment is initially made in selected options,

increasing the autonomy of future decisions. All available options, independent of their current phase, compete against one another for further investment. Investments can, therefore, efficiently shift from low-potential options to more promising ones. Kaufmann et al. (2021) show that ROR positively relates to a project portfolio's innovativeness and success, especially when executives have a mindset favouring risk-taking, pro-activeness, and innovativeness and when the environment is turbulent.

5 *Support emerging innovation paths.* Managers of project sequences should recognize, develop, and use emergent strategies. High performing companies achieve strategic adaptiveness better implement deliberate strategies *and* create emergent strategies because they scrutinise their portfolio strategy through strategic monitoring. Developing new emerging strategies is also fostered by using agile practices in projects and by listening to the voice behaviour of project managers (Kaufmann et al. 2020).

Conclusion

Project sequence management is essential to develop and implement strategic goals and strategies that meet the challenges of the present and the future. It has its own challenges, goals, and instruments. Compared to the management of single projects or project portfolios, project sequence management is less often used, less elaborated, and empirically much less often researched. Therefore, this chapter intends to be a door opener for a new way of understanding and managing in the realm of projects, innovation, and entrepreneurship, rather than a final taking stock of what we know. Feedback from our readers is very much welcome for this promising new field of practice and research.

References and further reading

Berggren, C. (2019): The cumulative power of incremental innovation and the role of project sequence management. *International Journal of Project Management,* 37(3), 461–472.

Buengeler, C., Situmeang, F. B. I., van Eerde, W., Wijnberg, N. M. (2021): Fluidity in project management teams across projects. *International Journal of Project Management,* 39(3), 282–294.

Davies, A., Brady, T., (2000): Organisational capabilities and learning in complex product systems: towards repeatable solutions. *Research Policy,* 29, 931–953.

Ekrot, B., Kock, A., Gemünden, H. G. (2016): Retaining project management competence – antecedents and consequences. *International Journal of Project Management,* 34(2), 145–157.

Gareis, R. (2006): *Happy Projects!* 3. Auflage. Wien: Manz.

Gareis, R., Gareis, L. (2017): *Projekt.Programm.Change.* Lehr- und Handbuch für Intrapreneure projektorientierter Organisationen. Wien: Manz.

Kaufmann, C., Kock, A., Gemünden, H. G. (2020): Emerging strategy recognition in agile portfolios. *International Journal of Project Management,* 38(7), 429–440.

Kaufmann, C., Kock, A., Gemünden, H. G. (2021): Strategic and cultural contexts of real options reasoning in innovation portfolios. *Journal of Product Innovation Management,* 38(3), 334–354.

Kock, A., Gemünden, H. G. (2019): Project lineage management and project portfolio success. *Project Management Journal, 50*(5), 587–601.

Kock, A. Gemünden, H. G., Salomo, S., Schultz, C. (2011): The mixed blessings of technological innovativeness for the commercial success of new products. *Journal of Product Innovation Management,* 28(S1), 28–43.

Midler, C. (2013): Implementing a low-end disruption strategy through multiproject lineage management: the Logan case. *Project Management Journal,* 44(5), 24–35.

Rohrbeck, R., Kum, M. E. (2018): Corporate foresight and its impact on firm performance: a longitudinal analysis. *Technological Forecasting & Social Change*, 129, 105–116.

Schultz, C., Salomo, S., Talke, K. (2013): Measuring new product portfolio innovativeness: how differences in scale width and evaluator perspectives affect its relationship with performance. *Journal of Product Innovation Management,* 30(S1), 93–109.

Sleesman, D. J., Lennard, G., McNamara, G., Conlon, D. E. (2018): Putting escalation of commitment in context: a multilevel review and analysis. *Academy of Management Annals,* 12(1), 178–207.

Sydow, J., Schreyögg, G., Koch, J. (2009): Organizational path dependence: opening the black box. *Academy of Management Review,* 34(4), 689–709.

Sydow, J., Schreyögg, G., Koch, J. (2020): On the theory of organizational path dependence: clarifications, replies to objections, and extensions. *Academy of Management Review,* 45(4), 717–734.

Chapter 37

Machine learning in project portfolio selection

Costanza Mariani and Mauro Mancini

Introduction

In a world undergoing digitalization, in which technological innovation is an increasingly significant source of competitive advantage, practitioners and researchers working in the project management field are more and more interested in understanding the potential benefits of new systems capable of handling vast amounts of data.

Machine learning techniques offer exciting new ways to handle vast amounts of data from different industries and business sectors. In particular, machine learning allows us to make efficient predictions based on historical data. Among many possible implementations, project management seems to finally be ready to take advantage of the benefits of machine learning, including a general increase in efficiency, such as cost and risk reduction, increased profits, and better resource management, particularly in processes where human interaction does not predominate. In addition, project portfolio management seems to be a field suited for machine learning. Project portfolio management aims to generate an optimal project selection under a complex multi-constrained problem and then coordinate its successful implementation. The selection and setup of a balanced portfolio allow companies to pursue strategic goals and maximize value creation

DOI: 10.4324/9781003274179-42

by leveraging possible synergies among projects and minimizing risk exposure by diversification of selected projects. However, this highly strategic selection process often faces several challenges: (i) multiple and conflicting strategic objectives may exist, making it difficult to create a common set of evaluation parameters for portfolio selection; (ii) some objectives may be qualitative (i.e. consistency of the projects with strategic objectives, level of innovation), thus implying a certain level of subjectivity in the evaluation of parameters; (iii) uncertainty and information scarcity can affect the evaluation process; and (iv) interdependence among some projects could mean that the effects of the projects' interrelations also need to be evaluated. The literature analyses several methods for optimizing portfolio selection, ranging from simple score models to mathematical programming. This paper aims to propose supervised and unsupervised machine learning as a valid and reliable alternative for selecting the optimal project portfolio. The predictive capability of machine learning and the possibility it offers for using companies' data on ongoing or completed projects to select and prioritize future projects can be exploited by portfolio managers for anticipating and improving strategic decisions. The paper is organized as follows: the first section outlines the project portfolio selection phase, highlighting its objectives, the extant selection methods, and the main challenges that can be faced in this stage; the second section describes the possible applications of supervised and unsupervised machine learning to the project portfolio selection process (i.e. the analysis of each individual project, the screening phase, and the optimization of the portfolio); finally, the last section presents an application of a supervised classification algorithm for project selection prioritization in a business context, illustrating both the main benefits such an algorithm can provide to a consulting firm and the possible barriers to implementation.

Project portfolio selection

Project portfolios are defined as collections of single projects that run concurrently (Archer and Ghasemzadeh, 1999), thus a multi-project setting is constituted by an organizational unit that executes a substantial part of its operations as projects. Such a setting can result from an explicit company strategy or from a scenario where many different projects with independent existence and individual goals happen to run simultaneously (Engwall and Jerbrant, 2003). However, most frequently, companies apply project portfolio management to manage different projects holistically and strategically. Project portfolio management as a discipline is grounded in the financial theory of investment portfolio management, which is largely based on Markoviz's Nobel Prize-winning work (Markowitz, 1959). In this work, portfolios are defined as a coordinated set of entities or investments managed together with the aim of leveraging synergies and controlling the overall risk exposure. The most relevant insight of Markoviz's work is that well-established portfolio management increases business value by aligning projects with the organization's strategic direction, allowing an effective use of the limited resources at its disposal. The extant literature on project portfolio management focuses on specific topics that consider the phases of selection, governance, and management of a portfolio (Hansen and Svejvig, 2022); although the authors consider the study of governance and ongoing portfolio management relevant, this paper aims to emphasize the criticality of the setup and selection phase. First, it is increasingly important for companies' processes to be optimized, and made more efficient and so an ability to select and prioritize the right project in which to invest limited resources can be a source of sustainable competitive advantage for companies. Second, being able to quickly set up a balanced portfolio allows the time between the '*business idea*' and the '*ongoing implementation*' to be reduced, ensuring faster time to market for product-based projects. In addition, anticipating Go-No-Go decisions very often means avoiding sunk costs of projects on which time and resources have already been spent but which have been in the decisional phase for too long. However, the selection phase is often challenged by factors external to the organization. In fact, the increased instability and volatility of the current economic environment have led to a continuous need for target re-alignment and re-planning. As a consequence, for an effective selection, the decision-maker should have at his disposal (i) a large set of data and information concerning the projects, the markets, and the company's strategic objectives and operationally, and (ii) a set of possible methods that can support in accurately evaluating and prioritizing projects by considering a set of defined evaluation parameters. The scientific literature over the last decade has reviewed and analyzed the methods most used by practitioners for selecting and evaluating project portfolios. Table 37.1 aims to classify the currently available methods by highlighting each of the main strengths and weaknesses and the type of portfolio for which they are most suitable.

In addition to the methods presented in Table 37.1, some authors have begun to study the potential that machine learning can have in project portfolio selection for

Table 37.1 Comparison of portfolio selection methods

Method	*Strength*	*Weakness*	*Type of portfolio*
Scoring models	Simple method adaptable to different portfolios; flexible selection of criteria to be scored (may also be strategic, concerning time and cost); simple to understand and communicate; sensitivity analyses can be performed straightforwardly, evaluating trade-offs between different criteria.	The score is a relative measure, it does not represent the utility associated with the execution of a project; criteria must be weighted otherwise they will all have the same relative importance; the simplicity of the tool leads often to the addition of many criteria, diminishing the holistic view of relative evaluation between projects.	Relatively simple and small portfolios where there is a need to systematize the decision-making process with cross-project scoring criteria
Decision analysis (decision tree, expected value)	Useful for a clear analysis of the payoffs of undertaking a project; simple to understand and easy to modify considering different scenarios and evaluation criteria.	Decision Analysis is an unstable instrument, as a small variation in one of the inputs can cause the output to vary significantly; the inputs must be precise to guarantee a sufficiently accurate result.	Portfolios require an assessment of the possible impacts of different and considerably variable scenarios

(Continued)

Table 37.1 (Continued)

Method	*Strength*	*Weakness*	*Type of portfolio*
Economic models (net present value, real options)	Consider the time value of the investment; quantitative evaluation that considers the cost of capital; a simple way to compare the value generated by different projects.	The degree of uncertainty profoundly influences the outcome of these indexes (due to the possible variance in the inputs); the measures do not incorporate qualitative factors (e.g. the connection to the strategy); the size of the evaluated projects must be homogeneous.	Portfolios in which the value of the initial investment and future returns are stable from the pre-project stage allowing for reliable quantitative evaluation. Expected stability of the project's financial return conditions
Mathematical programming	Good quantitative optimization of a function considering defined constraint as resource utilization, strategy, and project planning; promising results in comparing projects in respect to fixed constraints.	High computational effort is required; the complexity of implementing this method in companies results in the need for expert support; the input variables must be as stable as possible to ensure accurate results.	portfolios characterized by scarcity of resources where it is necessary to select the portfolio that maximises the efficiency of resource utilisation given certain constraints

evaluating and prioritizing projects (Magaña Martínez and Fernandez-Rodriguez, 2015). Even if in the literature the examples of machine learning applications in this field are limited to specific cases (Costantino, Di Gravio, and Nonino, 2015), the authors consider the possible adoption of machine learning relevant for the following reasons:

The method increases the reliability of the selection, as it extracts implicit knowledge from past data without involving managers in subjective and fallible judgements. This also enables us to exploit the predictive potential of company data of past or ongoing portfolios.

The dynamic learning capability of machine learning allows revisions of the portfolio evaluation throughout its life cycle. This enables the quick implementation of corrective actions during the portfolio management phase.

This method can easily be applied to any type of industry and portfolio because it is customizable to different types of evaluation parameters. In addition, since the learning of the algorithm is based on individual company data, the obtained evaluation results are highly tailored to the company.

The method can be iterative: data gathered from completed projects can become part of the algorithm's training set. This allows new predictions on project performance to be aligned with the results of new projects and with the relative know-how acquired by the company.

Machine learning

Machine learning is a subset of artificial intelligence that deals with creating systems that learn or improve performance based on the data they use. The definition provided by (Samuel, 1969), states that "machine learning is the field of study that gives computers the ability to learn without being explicitly programmed". This definition highlights the algorithms' capability to learn autonomously from a provided dataset, using the lessons it learns to generate predictions on new data. Statistics and computational informatics are key to developing an effective machine learning model; in particular, inductive statistics is the very basis of how machine learning works. This means, as highlighted by learning theory, the machine can generalize from its own experience and thus carry out inductive reasoning. In order to succeed in learning, the algorithm needs to analyze a series of training examples from a probability distribution, and the distribution must be representative of the space of occurrences that could effectively describe the response the machine should give. From the processing of these examples, the algorithm will build up a probabilistic model of the space of occurrences so that when new cases are submitted for analysis, it will be able to generate realistic and accurate classification predictions. In principle, machine learning works based on two distinct learning approaches, identified by Arthur Samuel at the end of the 1950s: in supervised learning, the analyst gives the computer complete examples to be used as instructions for performing the required task, while in unsupervised learning, the machine works without any labelled example and autonomously recognizes patterns in the dataset provided. Thus, in supervised learning, the machine is instructed to automatically make predictions about the output variables of a system based on a set of ideal examples (which consist of input and output pairs) initially provided by the analyst. On the contrary, in unsupervised learning, the machine is provided with unlabelled data with the aim of identifying hidden patterns or logical structures in the dataset provided. Considering the project portfolio selection framework proposed by (Archer and Ghasemzadeh, 1999), the predictive capability of machine learning can be exploited by applying both types of learning to different phases of the selection process (Figure 37.1).

> At the project level, during the *Individual Project Analysis*, an initial assessment of projects is carried out in preparation for the subsequent screening phase. A common set of parameters for the evaluation of individual projects is defined, which are then used in the second screening phase to decide which project to include in an extant portfolio. Thus, project risk, net present value, return on investment (ROI), and other parameters are calculated for each project, and a set of cross-cutting parameters is established for the subsequent decision phase. Note that projects already ongoing in the portfolio that have reached a certain milestone or are not performing in line with the baseline may also be re-evaluated at this time. The application of machine learning in this phase can be either supervised or unsupervised. From the point of view of supervised learning, it is indeed possible to identify a target parameter (such as the ROI) and train the algorithm on data from past projects to obtain an accurate prediction of the level of ROI that a new group of projects can achieve. Unsupervised machine learning, on the other hand, can be used to identify clusters of projects that present similar parameter values. For example, clusters

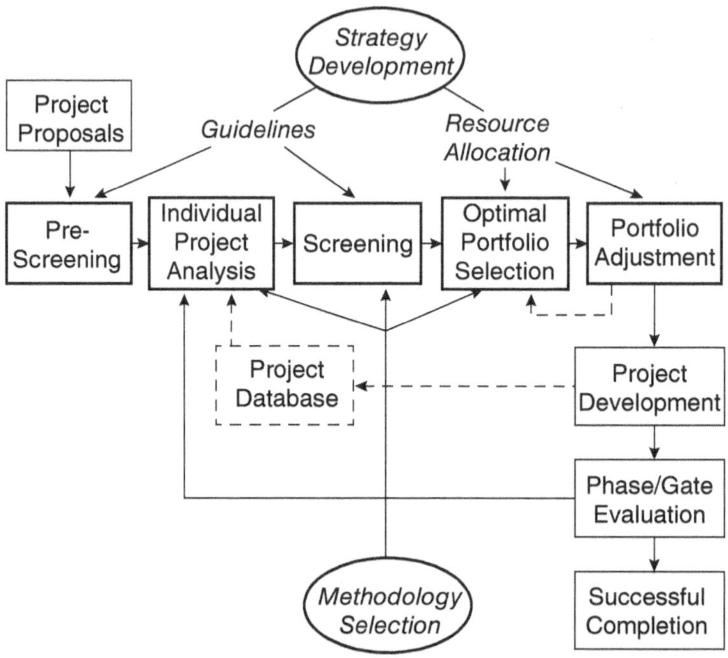

Figure 37.1: The project portfolio selection framework (reprinted from Archer and Ghasemzadeh [1999], An integrated framework for project portfolio selection', *International Journal of Project Management*, 17(4), p. 211)

of projects with a high level of innovation but high risk, standard low-risk projects, and projects with a high ROI can be autonomously grouped by the machine. This allows different types of projects that need to be evaluated and managed according to common parameters to be identified in advance. The main benefit of unsupervised clustering is that in the screening phase, it will be possible to make an overall assessment by cluster and not by individual project, allowing one to start setting the balance between different groups of projects in the portfolio. Moreover, in addition to speeding up the screening process, this anticipates what type of management approaches and processes will be needed for the different groups of similar projects included in the same portfolio.

During the *Screening phase*, the objective is to eliminate projects or clusters of projects that do not meet the predetermined parameters, such as the level of ROI or the net present value of the project. Thus, this phase aims to eliminate any non-starters by reducing the number of projects to be considered simultaneously in the subsequent portfolio selection phase. Therefore, it is necessary to set thresholds for the predefined parameters that determine the elimination or inclusion of projects. Care should be taken to avoid setting thresholds that are too arbitrary, leading to the elimination of projects that may actually be very promising. At this stage, supervised machine learning can be implemented in two different ways: (i) the target variable can be dichotomous and provide a simple "include/not include" classification as the project evaluation result. In this case, the classification algorithm learns from a database of past projects and identifies whether an upcoming project belongs to the "include" or "not include" category. This method provides an initial general assessment of the performance of future projects; however, in principle, it discriminates rather harshly between inclusion and non-inclusion. In fact, a simple 'yes-no' classification does not capture all the possible nuances of a potential project's performance and the presence of outliers in the training set can cause serious classification problems and lead to the elimination of potentially promising projects; (ii) the target variable can be expressed by selecting one of the evaluation parameters such as ROI and categorizing the values it assumed in past projects on a scale ranging from "Very Low" to "Very High". Note that the definition of the scale point numbers is up to the company, which can choose the granularity desired for the analysis. At this point, the classification algorithm can be trained on past projects' ROI scales and provide a prediction of the classification of future projects. This method allows the projects to be ranked in each of the identified classes of values, thus obtaining a scale from the best to the worst in terms of predicted performance. This allows for a prioritization of the projects under screening that is less radical than the above-mentioned dichotomous method; also, the ranking can be useful for anticipating some subsequent decisions. For example, projects with a predicted ROI level between high and very high can be immediately included in the portfolio and aggregated to groups of other high-performing projects, while those with an average ROI value can be kept in the observation phase for longer so that their progress and potential can be assessed.

In the *Optimal Portfolio Selection* phase, the level of analysis switches from the single project level to the entire portfolio optimization. This means that the interactions between different project variables, including organizational interdependencies, competition for resources, and timing, are considered. Selecting the optimal portfolio, considering the interrelationship between projects and a set of constraints such as the maximum acceptable level of risk and resource availability will mean solving a multi-constraints optimization problem that is usually addressed in companies by using methods such as the analytical hierarchy process, scoring models, and portfolio matrices. The most suitable technique for this task is Deep learning, which is a branch of machine learning that autonomously generates the features of a model by performing the prediction task on the provided dataset without any intervention from the analyst (Dahrouj *et al.*, 2021), is. However, the application of clustering algorithms may be useful in this phase. In fact, although clustering cannot be used to solve optimization problems, it can support the identification of interrelationships between projects, leading to the recognition of possible connections, for example, in terms of resource utilization or shared risks. This can be a starting point for solving the optimization problem, as well as a useful means for management to understand the existing interrelationships between projects.

Applying machine learning for project prioritization

In this section, an application of supervised machine learning in a company in the project prioritization phase is presented. The company is a multinational group operating globally with a total of more than 340,000 employees across multiple sectors, with a particular focus on the engineering and construction industries. Our research focused exclusively on the Italian subsidiary, which, having been recently established, is currently developing an overall project portfolio selection strategy (Figure 37.2).

In particular, referring to the framework of (Archer and Ghasemzadeh, 1999), the project portfolio selection phase for which a decision support system was developed was the project screening phase. The level of analysis was therefore the individual project level, and the objective was to obtain a ranking of optimal projects so that the management could choose which of these to include in a portfolio of newly started projects. This is, therefore, a prioritization task that can be solved by means of a supervised classification algorithm. During an initial workshop with the team of portfolio managers, the ROI was identified as the target variable to be classified by the algorithm. Also, a list of thirteen project evaluation parameters was selected, relying on a combination of parameters extracted from the extant literature and the judgement of managers:

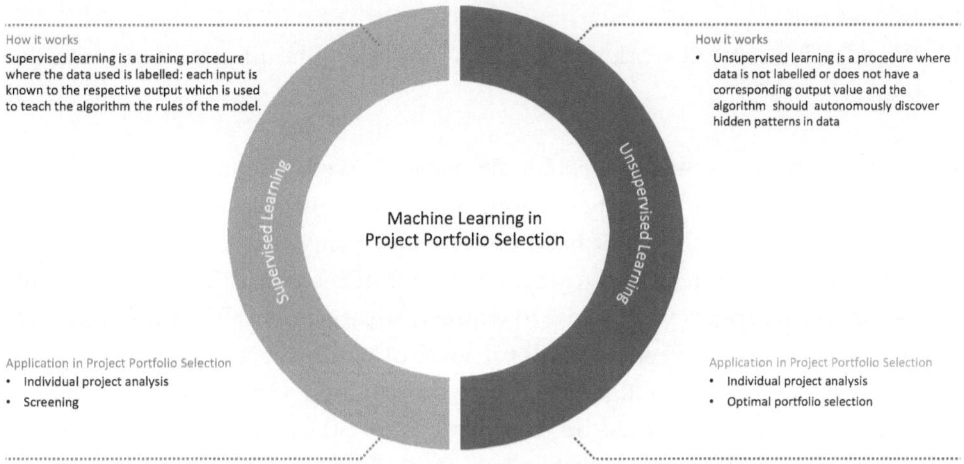

Figure 37.2: Supervised and unsupervised machine learning in project portfolio selection

1 Strategic alliance: alignment of the projects with the organizational mission, vision, and values (Martinsuo and Lehtonen, 2007).
2 Financial risk: investment risk level considered as the probability or likelihood of occurrence of losses relative to the expected return of a project.
3 Project innovation: level of potential for innovation of the project.
4 Expected impact for clients: role of new project in achieving a client's goals.
5 Clarity of scope and intermediate objectives (Elonen and Artto, 2003; Pinto and Covin, 1989).
6 Organizational readiness: previous and common experiences of the organization in the same field.
7 Multidisciplinary (marketing, R & D, production) of the project team.
8 Standardization of project management (Artto and Dietrich, 2007; Payne and Turner, 1999).
9 Technical complexity: it is associated with operational tasks, technology, and related risks of the project.
10 Organizational complexity: it is linked to the size of a project, availability of resources for the project, and related risks.
11 Environmental complexity: it is influenced by the stakeholders involved, the location of the project, market conditions, and associated risks.

12 Budget size.
13 Workload: expected workload in terms of working hours associated with the project.

Once the parameters were selected, 28 projects were identified for use as a knowledge base for building the dataset. Since the numerical reference value in the company's database had not been collected for many of the identified parameters, it was necessary to resort to the assessment of managers. Thus, in a second workshop, the managers were asked to express an assessment of the impact of each of the identified parameters on the ROI level of past projects using a five-point scale of linguistic variables ranging from very low to high. One issue with machine learning algorithms that should be considered is that they cannot directly process linguistic evaluations because they work through mathematical structures and relations, which requires the input data to be in numerical form. As such, since the management expressed linguistic evaluation, a data transformation procedure was required. Fuzzy Logic, which allows for passing from linguistic evaluations to a range of crisp values that enable the imprecision in the original information to be accounted for, was implemented to obtain a numerical and consistent dataset for use in the training and test phase. A significant amount of data is required to achieve a good level of accuracy in the prediction of results, and so the relatively small number of 28 past projects limited the potential for achieving significant results. For this reason, a valid data augmentation procedure was implemented to significantly increase the amount of data available to train and test the algorithm in project classification.

At this point, seven different classification algorithms were trained on a split part of the dataset (equal to 80% of the data available) randomly shuffled. The results were then tested on the remaining 20% of the dataset to assess performance in terms of capacity for predicting project success, making use of some predefined performance measures. After performance assessment and comparison, a test with a new project was performed to help visualize and interpret the results of the algorithm and to analyze its capacity for assisting managers in the project prioritization phase. The results obtained are promising: the algorithm showed good levels of accuracy in predicting the expected ROI classification on the test set, resulting in an almost unitary accuracy level on the training set and on the test.

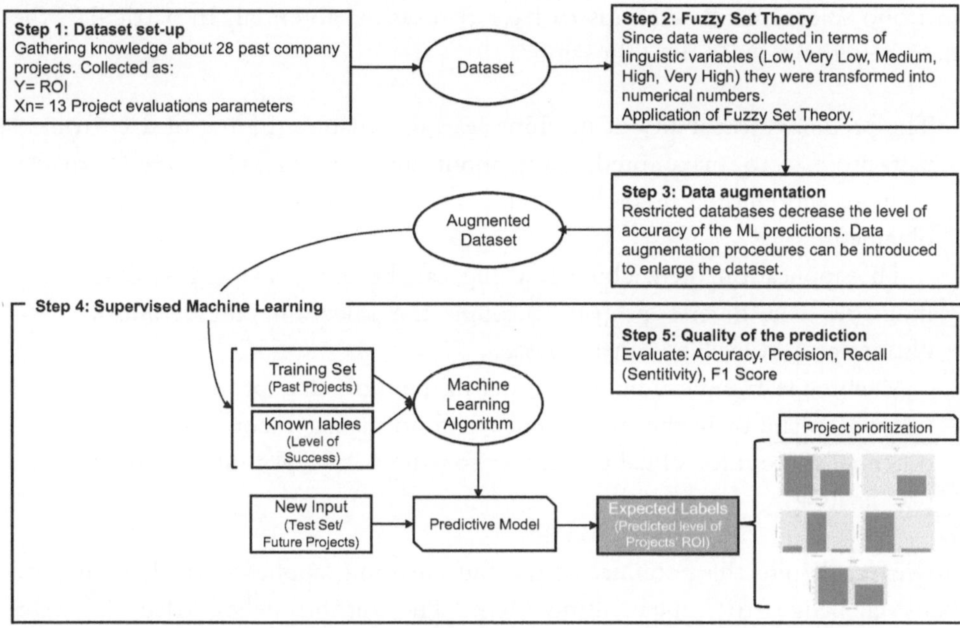

Figure 37.3: Supervised machine learning applied in an Italian consulting group

The company portfolio managers involved expressed a positive evaluation of the proposed prioritization method and are considering integrating it as a company decision support system for the project screening phase (Figure 37.3).

Conclusion

This paper presents machine learning as a possible alternative method for performing project portfolio selection. For each of the project portfolio selection phases outlined by (Archer and Ghasemzadeh, 1999), the possible applications of supervised or unsupervised machine learning were presented, highlighting the potential benefits in terms of prediction of performance results. Furthermore, a case of an application of supervised machine learning in a consulting group was presented and the satisfactorily accurate results obtained from this application were highlighted. Considering the positive feedback obtained from the project portfolio managers of the company where the case was developed, the adoption of supervised machine learning in the project portfolio selection phase seems to have promising potential. In particular, the main benefits include the following:

> The predictive capability of machine learning enables the use of data from past projects to make predictions about future ones. This ensures that accurate and tailored predictions built on the knowledge of companies are obtained.
>
> The application of machine learning can be easily adapted to different industries and diverse projects through the selection and definition of distinct project evaluation parameters.
>
> Machine learning can be used either in the individual project analysis and selection phase or in the subsequent portfolio management phase, and so it potentially provides valuable support for alternative planning or recovery plan analysis.

However, despite the potential of machine learning applications, there are still many challenges to implementing them. The authors believe that the main issues can be divided into two distinct categories. The first concerns the limitations of the adoption of the machine learning algorithm process per se, while the second concerns the lack of organizational and data management competence in companies. From a technical point of view, the main weaknesses of the procedure presented are (i) that extensive and consistent databases are needed for obtaining accurate results, while companies' raw data often tend to be corrupted by missing values, outliers, noise, non-consistent observations, or unexpected trends and patterns. Consequently, to be processed by an algorithm, the databases typically need to be first prepared, explored, and understood so that the relevant information can eventually be extracted. This process is quite cumbersome and typically requires significant knowledge, time, and effort; (ii) the computational burden and the processing time are two other critical factors that may prevent the practical adoption of machine learning in companies. From an organizational perspective, a possible factor that may limit the adoption of machine learning as a decision support system is the lack of data management skills that prevails in companies. While the application of classification algorithms is a well-known process, the preparation of datasets is frequently a long and delicate process that requires the skills of a good data scientist, especially when the number of projects to be analyzed is high. In conclusion, the application of machine learning to project portfolio selection has high potential for both the individual project assessment phase and the overall portfolio assessment phase. However, computational complexity, the need to structure a consistent and valid dataset, and the lack of established data management skills in companies remain key barriers to the adoption of machine learning in this field.

References and further reading

Archer, N. P. and Ghasemzadeh, F. (1999) 'An integrated framework for project portfolio selection', *International Journal of Project Management*, 17(4), pp. 207–216. doi: 10.1016/S0263-7863(98)00032-5.

Artto, K. A. and Dietrich, P. H. (2007) 'Strategic business management through multiple projects', *The Wiley Guide to Managing Projects*, pp. 144–176. doi: 10.1002/9780470172391.CH7.

Costantino, F., Di Gravio, G. and Nonino, F. (2015) 'Project selection in project portfolio management: An artificial neural network model based on critical success factors', *International Journal of Project Management*, 33(8), pp. 1744–1754. doi: 10.1016/j.ijproman.2015.07.003.

Dahrouj, H. *et al.* (2021) 'An overview of machine learning-based techniques for solving optimization problems in communications and signal processing', 9. doi: 10.1109/ACCESS.2021.3079639.

Elonen, S. and Artto, K. A. (2003) 'Problems in managing internal development projects in multi-project environments', *International Journal of Project Management*, 21(6), pp. 395–402. doi: 10.1016/S0263-7863(02)00097-2.

Engwall, M. and Jerbrant, A. (2003) 'The resource allocation syndrome: The prime challenge of multi-project management?', *International Journal of Project Management*, 21(6), pp. 403–409. doi: 10.1016/S0263-7863(02)00113-8.

Hansen, L. K. and Svejvig, P. (2022) 'Seven decades of project portfolio management research (1950–2019) and perspectives for the future', *Project Management Journal*, 53(3), pp. 277–294. doi: 10.1177/87569728221089537.

Magaña Martínez, D. and Fernandez-Rodriguez, J. C. (2015) 'Artificial intelligence applied to project success: A literature review', *International Journal of Interactive Multimedia and Artificial Intelligence*, 3(5), p. 77. doi: 10.9781/ijimai.2015.3510.

Markowitz, H. M. (1959) *Portfolio Selection*. Yale: Yale University Press.

Martinsuo, M. and Lehtonen, P. (2007) 'Role of single-project management in achieving portfolio management efficiency', *International Journal of Project Management*, 25(1), pp. 56–65. doi: 10.1016/J.IJPROMAN.2006.04.002.

Payne, J. H and Turner, J. R. (1999) 'Company-wide project management: The planning and control of programmes of projects of different type', *International Journal of Project Management*, 17(1), pp. 55–59. doi: 10.1016/S0263-7863(98)00005-2.

Pinto, J. K. and Covin, J. G. (1989) 'Critical factors in project implementation: A comparison of construction and R&D projects', *Technovation*, 9(1), pp. 49–62. doi: 10.1016/0166-4972(89)90040-0.

Samuel, A. L. (1969) 'Some studies in machine learning using the game of checkers. II—Recent progress', *Annual Review in Automatic Programming*, 6(PART 1), pp. 1–36. doi: 10.1016/0066-4138(69)90004-4.

Chapter 38

Organizational project management

Shankar Sankaran

Introduction

How an organization can achieve its strategy effectively through projects has been a matter of concern for both project management researchers and practitioners over the years. One way proposed to address this is to link an organization's strategy to projects systematically by managing the 3Ps – portfolios, programs, and projects – hierarchically. It also became clear that strategic execution through the 3Ps had to be governed well, in line with corporate governance. To develop this integrated capability by combining the 3Ps and their governance Drouin, Müller, and Sankaran (2017, p. 13) proposed Organizational Project Management (OPM) as an organizational capability to integrate 'the structures, processes and practices of all project management-related activities throughout the organizational hierarchy or network in an effective manner'. However, a more comprehensive model of OPM linking both practice and theory was needed. This was achieved through the development of a seven-layer model for OPM (Müller et al. 2019a), which is the focus of this chapter.

DOI: 10.4324/9781003274179-43

The seven-layer model

The seven-layer OPM model is represented as layers of an onion with 22 elements as shown in Figure 38.1 (Müller et al. 2019b, p. 9). One of the practical uses of this model is that it helps organizations examine their processes and practices and evaluate their capability to use projects and programs to achieve their strategy.

The seven layers of the OPM model are:

Organizational philosophy: How does an organization present itself to the marketplace to legitimize its actions towards customers, partners, and suppliers?

OPM approach: What strategies does an organization adopt to carry out its business through projects?

OPM governance: How are projects governed and controlled across an organization?

Business integration: How does an organization identify, select, prioritize, and authorize projects that can contribute to its strategy?

Organizational integration: How does the organization then integrate opportunities identified at the business integration layer into its workflow?

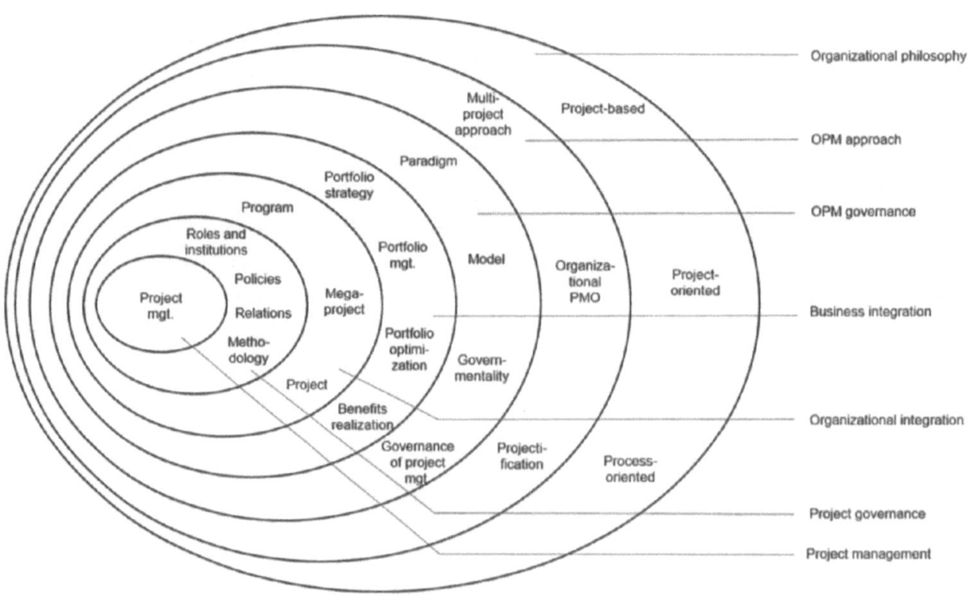

Figure 38.1: The onion model of OPM

Project governance: How does an organization set up governance structures and processes to achieve consistent delivery of projects?

Project management: How does an organization conduct projects to deliver the transformation opportunities it has identified into products or services that result in beneficial change?

In developing the model, Müller et al. (2019a) analyzed mainstream project management journals to identify 22 elements that could be placed in the various layers of the onion model to cover the concept of OPM comprehensively.

The 22 elements have been ordered in the seven layers using two principles – *cohesion* and *adhesion*. Elements that had a strong mutual relationship (adhesion) and collectively a strong relationship (adhesion) with the next inner layer were placed in one layer. Thus, the elements in the higher layer had a governing relationship with the elements of the layer below.

The main aim of developing this model was to present a more integrative version of OPM. The benefits expected from this integrated model are twofold. For practitioners, it serves as a guide to the OPM design adopted by an organization to enhance its capability. For example, organizations delivering several complex projects may consider a design that encompasses all the layers whereas a small organization delivering simple projects may only concern itself with the elements at the bottom layers of the model. For academics, it is a way to further theorize on the role, importance, and functions of OPM.

Next, we will look at each layer of the model.

Layer 1: Organizational philosophy

The way in which projects are carried out and the importance paid to them may result in three types of organizations: process-oriented, project-oriented, and project-based.

Process-oriented organizations run a few projects under the responsibility of functional organizations. Such organizations are found in stable markets and rely on mass production and economies of scale. An example is the production of stationery used in offices or schools and sold in outlets like Officeworks.

Project-oriented organizations are often found in dynamic markets where the management recognizes the importance of projects to deliver strategies. A supermarket such as Walmart relying on effective management of its supply chain may adopt such an orientation.

Project-based organizations are those whose units of production are projects, such as construction firms which carry out projects to meet a client's specifications.

Layer 2: OPM approach

The OPM approach is the overall approach of an organization towards multi-project management (Blomquist & Müller 2006). An organization may decide to implement its projects using four different strategies:

Multi-project approach when it decides to take on as many projects as it can secure. It is not concerned about resources to deliver projects nor whether the objectives of projects undertaken are aligned. It hires external resources or subcontracts projects as needed.

Program strategy when projects in programs contribute to higher level objectives than individual projects. Here, resources are not critical but sharing of objectives is important.

Portfolio strategy when resources are shared with effective use of skill sets. The objectives of projects may not be shared.

Hybrid strategy when both objectives and resources are important, and when a balance of program or portfolio strategy is adopted.

An *organizational project management office (OPMO)* is set up at a strategic level servicing portfolio, programs, and/or projects.

The degree of *projectification* adopted by the organization is dependent upon the significance it attaches to projects being carried out. The projectification of an organization is gauged by: the status of project management in the organization; a clear career path for project managers; the extent to which employees recognize projects as part and parcel of the business principles; the extent to which business is carried out by projects; and the project mindset and culture that pervades the organization.

Layer 3: OPM governance

OPM governance refers to how projects and groups of projects (in programs or portfolios) are governed; that is, how they are directed, controlled and resourced, and how managers are held accountable for their results. Governance of projects, programs and portfolios are discussed in more detail in Chapter 40 of this handbook.

Therefore, it is only discussed briefly here. Paradigms refer to the basis on which the governance is carried out. This is based on whether the governance is designed based on stakeholder or shareholder orientation and whether control over people delivering projects is based on their behaviour or the outcome expected from projects.

Governance models used could be rule-based (strict adherence to rules) or principles-based (where explanations are required only if there is a breach of compliance to rules. In practice, these governance models address both structural and human aspects of governance. Models can be nested focusing on relationships and processes or layered taking into consideration interfaces between 3Ps.

Governmentality explains ways in which governance is implemented in organizations (Clegg 2019). An authoritarian view would rely on compliance specifying a rigid governance structure. A liberal view of governmentality would be based on outcome control with flexible governance structures. A neo-liberal view of governmentality would be based on self-control exhibited by actors.

At Layer 3, an organization would also consider a professional view of how governance is empowered in organizations. The organization would consider 'How much is project management relevant to what we do here?' or 'What is the capability required of our project managers?' and set up measures for training and education to meet the demand from management of portfolio, program and project managers and address the perceived pressure on these managers to deliver results. Based on such an evaluation, an organization could address three important concerns– education, management demand, or perceived pressure – as shown in Table 38.1.

Table 38.1 Governance of project management (adapted from Müller et al. 2019b, p. 56)

Step	*Basic*	*Intermediate*	*Advanced*
Education	Basic project management training; Project management methodologies	Certification/ accreditation of project managers	More advanced training/education; Internal accreditation
Management demand	Steering groups; project boards	Set up an appropriate project management office (strategic/tactical)	Benchmarking performance against competitors or with organizations overseas
Perceived pressure	Audits; Reviews; Stage gates	Establish mentoring and coaching	Establish maturity models or profiles

Layer 4: Business integration

This layer is the interface between OPM governance discussed in the previous section and the organization integration layer to be discussed in the next section.

The business integration layer is concerned with how projects or programs are identified, selected, and prioritized, how the benefits expected are defined, and how these projects or programs are authorized.

Management of Portfolios standard (MoP 2011) defines a *portfolio* as 'the totality of its investment (or segment thereof in the changes required to achieve its strategic objectives' (p. 11). To implement project portfolio management (PPM) to meet its strategic objectives, an organization needs to balance investments that lead to desired change and the maintenance of business as usual (BAU). PPM can help in realizing such a balance.

Before portfolio management can be planned, a portfolio strategy needs to be developed to align with the business strategy.

Project Portfolio Management 'deals with the coordination and control of multiple projects pursuing the same strategic goals and competing for the same resources, whereby managers prioritize among projects to achieve strategic benefits' (Martinsuo 2013, p. 794). Some portfolio management standards expect organizations to consider both the activities needed for BAU along projects delivered through PPM to achieve desired changes. This implies that an organization must decide what is covered by PPM – just projects and programs or the wider organizational activities.

Once the initiatives to be included in PPM are identified, they need to be divided into categories such as strategic (e.g., new markets), high potential (e.g., innovative technologies), operational necessities (e.g., new government regulations) and support processes (e.g., replacing obsolete equipment), so that investments can be allocated to what are often called 'buckets' of investments to pursue. Next, the organization needs to prioritize initiatives based on what it can afford using methods such as return on investment, scoring and ranking, or visual methods such as bubble maps portraying risk vs returns. While prioritization helps to rank projects in a portfolio, balancing, or *portfolio optimization*, aims to decide on the right mix of projects and initiatives based on factors such as timing, stage of development, available resources, and impact across the organization. Balancing can also utilize visual methods, providing a holistic picture of the initiatives for comparison (Killen et al. 2020).

Once decisions on what to include in portfolios are made, organizations need to decide how these will be delivered, by paying attention to the establishment of management controls, benefits management, financial, risk and resource management, stakeholder engagement, and organizational governance.

Benefits management or *benefits realization* is gaining attention in project management as outcomes from projects and programs are emphasized more. Bradley (2016) provides a comprehensive guideline on benefits realization, starting with engaging stakeholders early to establish a vision owned by them to help set realistic benefits to be achieved. A benefit map is often constructed to set up milestones and track benefits.

Layer 5: Organizational integration

The organizational integration layer helps integrate the opportunities determined at the business integration layer into the workflow of the organization using programs, projects, or a megaproject.

Projects can be delivered sequentially (using) a waterfall model or iteratively using agile methods. While waterfall methods are used where the specifications are well known at the start of the project, such as a construction project or building a power station, agile methods are more useful for projects in which the requirements are closely discussed with the customer and tested more frequently to deliver intermediate outcomes such as in IT projects.

Often, the project management office in an organization advocates the type of methodology best suited to the projects carried out. Some organizations develop their own methodology as a combination of waterfall and agile methods.

When it is more efficient and effective to manage jointly several projects that contribute to a common objective, they can be managed as a program of projects. For example, building a hospital can be considered a program as it involves several projects that need to be coordinated such as the building, facilities, laboratories, training, etc. Large defence endeavours are set up as programs to develop capability. An example is the Apollo space program, which needed several projects to achieve the mission of the program. A program can be vision-led, with all the projects in the program combined with a common goal or vision, or an organization may decide to combine a group of projects being managed independently to be brought together to be managed as a program as they are found to be working towards the same goal. Often, programs include change management to deliver benefits from outputs created by projects.

Megaprojects are 'large scale, complex investments that typically cost a billion dollars and up, take many years to develop and build, involve multiple public and private stakeholders, are transformational, and impact millions of people' (Flyvbjerg 2014, p. 6). Examples of megaprojects are the Oresund Bridge that links Sweden and Denmark and the High-Speed Rail project in the United Kingdom, Megaprojects are complex undertakings that involve several agencies working together and face technical, structural, temporal, directional, sociocultural and socio-political complexity. Megaproject leaders usually require additional skills and traits than managers who manage regular projects (Drouin et al. 2021).

Layer 6: Project governance

Project governance deals with the application of principles of good governance to projects to ensure consistent and predictable delivery of projects (Müller 2017).

Project governance involves:

- Establishment of *roles and institutions* such as steering groups or committees, a project sponsor, and tactical PMOs
- Setting up *policies* that govern project management execution.
- Establishing *relations* between parties using mechanisms like formal or relational contracts depending on the circumstances in which projects are carried out.
- Establishing *methodologies* (discussed earlier) that suit the project context.

Project governance is dealt with in more detail is Chapter 40 in this handbook.

Layer 7: Project management

The innermost layer is *project management.*

The purpose of a project is to deliver beneficial change. Managing projects requires management of scope, time, cost, and quality as well as relationships with stakeholders including the functional organizations. Risks arising from projects also need to be analyzed and managed (mitigated/accepted or transferred). Several tools such as Gantt charts and precedence diagrams, work breakdown structures, responsibility charts, earned value calculations, quality assurance and review processes, and configuration management are available to guide project managers and their teams. Human resource management, especially management of teams, and leadership attributes are also important as people management skills are needed by project managers for managing project performance.

Assessing OPM capability

A questionnaire has been developed by Müller et al. (2019b), which can guide organizations on how to assess their OPM capability. A survey tool has also been developed based on the questionnaire, and it can help organizations to carry out such an assessment. A typical report from this web-based survey tool outputs the results as a dashboard showing how the organization fared and in the assessment, and can help it to consider improvements.

Conclusion

OPM capability is important to organizations to deliver value through projects. The developers of the OPM model explained in this study have validated the model through organizational theories such as institutional theory, resource-based view, and systems theories. They have also used assessment tools to validate the usefulness of the OPM model with practitioners and through case studies. The model is also being used to teach postgraduate students at universities in Europe, North America, Asia, and Australia, who use it to assess the OPM capability of their own organizations.

Acknowledgements

The OPM model was developed collaboratively with Professor Ralf Müller, BI Norwegian Business School, Oslo, Norway, and Professor Nathalie Drouin, University of Quebec in Montreal (UQAM), Canada.

References and further reading

Blomquist, T., & Müller, R. (2006). Practices, roles, and responsibilities of middle managers in program and portfolio management. *Project Management Journal*, *37*(1), 52–66.

Bradley, G. (2016). *Benefit realisation management: A practical guide to achieving benefits through change*. Hampshire: Gower.

Clegg, S. (2019). Governmentality. *Project Management Journal*, *50*(3), 266–270.

Drouin, N., Müller, R., & Sankaran, S. (2017). The nature of organizational project management through the lens of integration (pp. 9–18), in Drouin, N., Müller, R., & Sankaran, S. (eds.), *Cambridge handbook of organizational project management*. Cambridge: Cambridge University Press.

Drouin, N., Sankaran, S., van Marrewijk, A., & Müller, R. (Eds.). (2021). *Megaproject leaders: Reflections on personal life stories*. Edward Elgar Publishing.

Flyvbjerg, B. (2014). What you should know about megaprojects and why: An overview. *Project Management Journal*, *45*(2), 6–19.

Killen, C. P., Geraldi, J., & Kock, A. (2020). The role of decision makers' use of visualizations in project portfolio decision making. *International Journal of Project Management*, *38*(5), 267–277.

Martinsuo, M. (2013). Project portfolio management in practice and in context. *International Journal of Project Management*, *31*(6), 794–803.

MoP (2011). *Management of portfolios*. TSO.

Müller, R. (2017). *Project governance*. Routledge.

Müller, R., Drouin, N., & Sankaran, S. (2019a). Modeling organizational project management. *Project Management Journal*, *50*(4), 1–15.

Müller, R., Drouin, N., & Sankaran, S. (2019b). *Organizational project management: Theory and implementation*. Edward Elgar Publishing.

Chapter 39

The project-oriented organization

Martina Huemann

Introduction

The project-oriented organization is a contemporary organization form with increasing importance. In addition to traditional industries such as construction and engineering, which traditionally perform large contracting projects, internal projects such as strategic planning, marketing, personnel development, and organizational development are increasingly performed in organizations. Projectification of organizations (Midler, 1995) can be considered as an answer to the demand for managing uncertainty, agility, and flexibility has been spreading into all kinds of industries including service industries and the public sector. In the public sector, for example, projects and programs are especially applied for organizing digital transformation and change. This is why I explicitly use the term project-oriented organization to include public and non-profit organizations.

The objective of this chapter is to describe the project-oriented organization and indicate the challenges and potentials that projects and programs bring to any organization from the perspective of Human Resource Management.

This chapter is organized as follows. I start by clarifying the model of the project-oriented organization and describe its specific strategy, structures, and culture.

After having introduced the project-oriented organization, I describe the tension between temporary projects and the permanent organization which both follow different management logics. This can explain some of the frictions project

DOI: 10.4324/9781003274179-44

managers may experience in project-oriented organizations. I then focus on the HRM system as a functional sub-system and summarize a viable HRM system for the project-oriented organization to fit its specific context.

Project-based or project-oriented?

Labels vary; organizations that carry out projects may be called project-based, projectified project-led, or project-oriented. Often these labels are used synonymously. But there are differences. Traditionally a project-based organization is an organization that carries out contract projects for external customers, which is in line with management theory which says that the production process determines the form of the organization (Woodward, 1965). The project-based organization is project-based *perforce* because of the customized nature of the demand from its customers (Turner & Keegan, 2001). On the other hand, a project-oriented organization is such by *strategic choice*, based on the organizational strategy of *Management by Projects* (Gareis, 1989; Huemann, 2015). It carries out projects or programs for performing business processes, whenever adequate. These projects may be external contract projects or internal projects such as product development, organizational development, or change. There is also a difference in the understanding of projects and project management. Table 39.1 summarizes the main differences between the project-based and the project-oriented organization. The project-oriented organization is explicitly framed as a construct and therefore also describes how a project-oriented organization can be equipped to be capable of performing projects and programs. This is reflected in the definition of the project-oriented organization (Gareis, 2005), as an organization which:

- defines *Management by Projects* as its organizational strategy,
- applies for projects and programs as temporary organizations,
- manages a project portfolio of different internal and external project types,
- project management, program management, and portfolio management are specific business processes,
- has specific permanent organizations like a project portfolio group or a project management office to provide integrative functions,
- applies a management paradigm which reflects the ability to deal with uncertainty, contradiction, change, collaboration,
- and views itself as being project-oriented.

Table 39.1 Project-based versus project-oriented (after Huemann, 2015)

	Project-based organization	*Project-oriented organization*
Reason for projects	Projects are performed *perforce*, because of the customized nature of the project	Projects are *strategic choices* Project is one option for the organizational design
Relation	Production process	Business processes
Type of projects	Mainly external projects	External and internal projects
Understanding of project	Project is considered a complex task or system	Project is considered a temporary organization
Understanding of project management	Mainly operational capability	Operational and strategic capability
Paradigm	Different paradigms Prevailing mechanistic planning paradigm	Systemic-constructivist explicitly farmed as construction

To provide a clearer picture of a mature project-oriented organization, Gareis and Stummer (2008) describe the characteristics of an immature project-oriented organization, which are:

- The term project is used to describe many different things, including temporary tasks that are unworthy of a project. There is an inflationary use of the term project. As a consequence, every temporary task is labelled a project, there is not enough management attention paid to projects.
- The wheel is repeatedly reinvented. The way a project is performed varies because it depends on the competencies of individuals. There are no organizational standards. Professional project management methods are not applied. As a result, the projects lack transparency and efficient communication. Creativity declines rather than increases.
- The objectives and the tasks are always agreed upon from one project meeting to the next. There is no "Big Project Picture", so the project team members lack orientation.

- Projects are defined within division or department boundaries. As a result, there are too many small projects, which lead to sub-optimization. Projects are not holistically defined, thus cooperation across department boundaries is not pursued.
- Nobody knows which projects or how many projects are conducted at any given time. There is no overview of the projects concurrently performed and thus no information about the project portfolio. Thus meaningful decisions on starting new projects and adequate resource allocation are not possible.
- Projects are initiated informally; projects with the same objectives are implemented concurrently and the allocation of project resources cannot be adequately managed.

A project-oriented organization is perceived as an organization with specific permanent and temporary structures and specific cultural values. The project-oriented company can be described by its strategy, structure, and culture.

Managing by projects

Organization theory and management studies have from early on searched for adequate organizational structures to support the production process of an organization (Woodward, 1965). The project-oriented organization applies the organizational strategy Management by Projects as a strategic choice to organize business processes, not just production processes. Not everything is a project, but the essence of *Management by Projects* is that the organization applies a project or a program for the performance of a business process, when adequate.

Some organizations only apply projects for their internal processes and not for their primary processes with customer processes because these are routine and a project would not be appropriate. To illustrate with an example: if you go to the bank to open up a bank account, you hope that the organization will not make a project for this repetitive routine process of short duration and small scope. You will expect the bank to have a defined process supported by an adequate IT infrastructure to deliver quickly and effectively. You will get your new bank card within a couple of days in your mail. But if the same bank changes the account management system for all their branch offices and online customers you will hope that they take it more seriously strategically and that they organize it as a project and professionally manage it, because if the new account management system fails, the organization will be in trouble. As a consequence, organizations require a sound understanding of their business processes to apply the strategy of Managing by Projects adequately. Only if the organization understands its business processes, can it explicitly choose which of these are better performed as projects and which should be taken over by the routine permanent organization. By that, projects and programs are considered strategic options for the organizational design.

Many organizations perform their primary business with clients as projects but do not consider that they may need professional project management for internal projects. However, these organizations may still be considered to be project-oriented, but they have some development potential. In practice, they perform projects when confronted with the customer demand to develop bespoke products. But as a consequence, these organizations may not be project-oriented enough. They may not have adequate and corresponding structural and cultural prerequisites to perform projects and manage a project portfolio professionally. In these organizations project management is often considered from an operational perspective for delivering projects, but the strategic perspective of managing projects and thus the specific organizational structures and a specific culture to support project orientation is not created. These organizations have the potential to develop further by applying the organizational strategy of *Managing by Projects* explicitly.

Temporary and permanent structures

Project-oriented organizations apply permanent and temporary structures in their organizational design. Permanent structures are for example functional departments or expert pools and profit centres. Temporary organizations are projects and programs. Project-oriented organizations perform a number of different internal and external, small and large projects at the same time. The size and number of the temporary part of the organization can change considerably, especially if the organization uses projects for organizing customer contracts. The basic assumption is that this flexible organization form allows for better innovation. Further, the projects allow more organizational differentiation, which helps to deal with the increasing complexity of the environment.

However, to cope with this organizational differentiation, integration and specific alignment are required to keep the organization streamlined, and ensure synergies and strategic alignment. There is a need for integration between projects and between the projects and the permanent organization. Forms of integration between projects are for example to cluster projects into chains of projects, project portfolios, and networks of projects. Specific governance forms are required, like the provision of guidelines and rules for the projects in the form of project and project management standards. Specific integrative structures include the project management office, project portfolio group, or expert pools.

Project portfolio group

The project portfolio group is a specific, permanent communication structure to steer the project portfolio. Services offered by this group include (Huemann, 2015):

- Assigning a project or program: aligning project objectives with company strategy; deciding on the organization form for initializing an investment, and nominating the project owner.
- Project portfolio coordination such as coordinating (human) resources used in projects; determining project priorities, stopping and interrupting projects and programs, and determining strategies for designing relations with relevant project or program stakeholders.
- Networking of projects such as organizing learning of and between projects, using synergies.

Project management office

In contrast to project offices, which are set up to support single large projects, the PMO is set up to be a permanent structure in the project-oriented organization. The objective of the PMO is to ensure professional project, program, and project portfolio management in the project-oriented organization. PMOs are a central means of integrating an organization's strategic priorities, permanent structures, and temporary projects. Although the PMO has a kind of chameleon function and often needs to take on additional services to justify its existence, core services offered by the PMO include (Huemann, 2015):

- services for project and program management such as providing project management guidelines, standards, forms, etc.; organizing management auditing and consulting to ensure management quality in projects and programs,

- services for project portfolio management such as providing project portfolio guidelines, standards, forms, etc.; maintaining a project portfolio database, developing project portfolio reports; initializing project networking,
- services for project management personnel: organizing training and coaching, exchange of experience for project management personnel, further developing and marketing of the profession of project management; support in recruiting, selecting, evaluating, and determining salaries for project managers.

On how to design a PMO see Chapter 41.

Expert pool

In a project-oriented organization, the project personnel can be organized in expert pools, Table 39.2. Responsibilities of the expert pool comprise competency development of the personnel managed, process management, and knowledge management. Depending on the industry and business, different expert pools exist in an organization. In an engineering construction company technical expert pools such as mechanical engineering, electrical engineering, and project management can be differentiated (Huemann, 2015).

Table 39.2 Traditional department versus expert pool (after Huemann, 2015)

	Traditional department	*Expert pool*
Empowerment	Employees are not necessarily empowered to take on responsibility for the quality of their work	Pool members are empowered to take on responsibility for their work in projects and programs
Perception of the manager role	Manager is a content expert and is responsible for the quality of the work of the experts	Pool manager is not necessarily a content expert Pool manager has HRM and managerial responsibilities; Pool manager is not responsible for the work quality of pool members

Different management logics

Nevertheless, tension and different management logics exist in temporary structures in comparison to the permanent line structures. Above I have described several specific structures such as the project portfolio group, the PMO, and expert pools to allow for integration between projects and between projects and permanent line organization. However, there exist structural tensions between the temporary and permanent line parts of the organization which make it necessary to live with two management logics. Table 39.3 contrasts these two logics.

Project-oriented culture

Classical project management considers a project as a complex technical system. While classical project management is based on a mechanistic and linear planning paradigm, the project-oriented organization understands projects as temporary

Table 39.3 Management logics of projects in contrast to permanent organizations (after Huemann, 2015)

	Temporary project	*Permanent line organization*
Time	Temporary, duration is planned at the beginning of the project, end is inherent in the project start Short to medium-term orientation Temporality creates urgency, rhythm is driven by the project end date and milestones	Permanent organization is planned unlimited in time Short, medium, and long-term orientation Time is cyclic, driven by the rhythm of the annual budgeting cycle, and related to quarterly reports
Business process	Relatively unique, short to medium term, strategically important, medium or large scope High result orientation to achieve project objectives, as this is the raison d'etre for the existence of the project.	Routine, short term, not strategically important, small scope Result orientation may vary considerably

(Continued)

Table 39.3 (Continued)

	Temporary project	*Permanent line organization*
Personnel	Personnel are put together on a project based on a project requirement Personnel may even be integrated from external organizations for example partners, suppliers, customer Contribution to project result (even when intangible as a feasibility study) is visible for the project personnel	Personnel with same competencies is organized in functional departments or in expert pools The relation between own contribution and company results may not be so clear for the single employee
Team	Team structures are central to a project Different teams within one project are possible Temporary teams	Team structures possible Teams then have the character of permanent teams
Change	Dynamic, as projects organize change. Change object is the project itself and the organization(s) for whom the project is delivered	Often also increasingly dynamic, as change is common in the contemporary organization Change for the permanent organization is often organized by projects
Identity	Temporary, needs to be created for the specific project Relatively autonomous but embedded in the context May be influenced by several organizations	Is created and shaped over time, embedded in its context

organizations. Traditional project management methods like scheduling, scope, and cost planning remain important but are set in a different context. The project management plans are not expected to steer reality, but they are considered as means of making sense of reality. Their purpose is to give orientation and allow for agreements in the project and with the project stakeholders.

A project-oriented organization requires a culture which is able to deal with uncertainty, contradictions, and change. Values and cultural elements that support project orientation are empowerment of personnel and projects, team orientation, stakeholder orientation, process orientation, diversity, innovation, and change orientation. Table 39.4. outlines values to support Managing by Projects. However, as the organization acts in its industry and national contexts, any organization has its own blend of values deeply depending on its own contexts.

Human resource management

Because of the specific features of a project-oriented organization all functions in the organization need to adapt when an organization becomes project-oriented.

Table 39.4 Project-oriented culture (after Huemann, 2015)

Empowerment	Increasing the autonomy and responsibility of the personnel. Empowerment comprises the project, the project team project team members.
Team orientation	Projects require teamwork. Problem-solving through teams and projects instead of excessive functional differentiation.
Stakeholder orientation	Projects meet the customers´ expectations. Projects create value for the customer and further project stakeholders.
Process orientation	Processes as the basis for project work. Project management as a process.
Diversity	Diversity as differences and commonalities. Diversity as a potential for project work.
Innovation	Projects promote learning and innovation. Encouraging co-production of knowledge with suppliers and partners.
Change orientation	Encouraging continuous and discontinuous organizational change. Being able to deal with uncertainty and contradictions.

The remainder of this chapter is dedicated to the HRM as one of the functions that needs considerable adaptation to fit and support project orientation. In many organizations, HRM departments organize for training and education of project managers. Thus they realize that new competencies are necessary to perform projects, but often they are quite narrow-minded (Turner et al., 2008). The HRM support for project orientation is often limited to the perspective of developing adequate project managers, without understanding.

First, it is not only the project manager, who needs project management competencies including social competencies as a basis for leadership tasks. It is also the project team members as well as the project owner, who need to understand projects and project management to contribute to the project in their roles adequately.

Secondly, there are structural and cultural consequences that projects bring to the organization. Thus the HRM system as such needs adapting and needs to become more decentralized and flexible to better support this rather decentralized type of organization.

One of the main issues is the extension of the HRM system from the line organization into projects. Because projects as temporary organizations constitute a secondary organizational layer, the HRM system has to cover the permanent part of the organization and extend into the temporary projects. Not only does this mean that HRM needs to take place on projects, but it also questions how HRM on the project is linked to the HRM in the permanent line organization, as project personnel may spend most of their working hours on projects and not in the line structures such as departments and expert pools. The link between on-project HRM and in-line HRM needs to be mutual as shown in Table 39.5.

Project careers and career paths

While HRM on a project primarily serves the project performance, as projects are temporary, there is a distinction to be made between the temporary project HRM and the HRM that takes place in the permanent organization. Difficulties in linking them arise mainly because of the different management logics as described in Table 39.3. For example, the time horizon of a project is per definition short-term, while the development and career aspirations of the project personnel need

Table 39.5 Linking project and HRM in the permanent organization (after Huemann, 2015)

Line HRM	*How line HRM needs to support project HRM*	*How project HRM supports line HRM*	*Project HRM*
Recruiting	Recruiting appropriate personnel Recruiting personnel quickly enough to meet the needs of project mobilization Ensure all project team members have the same terms and conditions Ensure project team members adhere to policies Project categorization system to differentiate competencies required by the project manager	Forecast future requirements Maintain a resource management system within the project Take account of individual and organizational development needs	Assigning
Developing	Develop personnel competent to work on projects Ensure successful planning for future project and program managers Ensure good people are not held in inferior line jobs to the detriment of the organization's needs and the individual's career development Provide adequate careers	Ensure development on the project fits with the line career development plans Ensure project assignments meet organizational and individual development needs	Developing
Appraising	Incorporate project appraisals for the motivation of project personnel	i. Do appraisals/assessments on the project to provide data for the annual line appraisal	Appraising
Rewarding	Ensure rewards reflect project performance so personnel are motivated to work on projects Ensure people from different departments working on the same project are rewarded in the same way for the cohesiveness of the team	Ensure that project rewards and bonuses fit with the organization's policies and the line reward system	Rewarding
Releasing	Capture knowledge from temporary workers leaving the organization Retain a network with temporary workers	Capture knowledge at the end of the project, particularly from temporary workers Ensure project personnel are returned promptly to the line so they can be reassigned quickly to other projects Ensure project personnel are moved to projects where their skills are best used	Dispersing

long-term consideration. This long-term consideration cannot be handled on a particular project but must remain in the line organization, which has a more long-term oriented interest in keeping the project personnel committed to the organization. This has several consequences.

As project management is not only a tool and method but also a strategic management approach for managing temporary organizations, project managers need to have an understanding of leading a project and its stakeholders. Therefore project-oriented organizations need to develop their project managers by letting them grow into the role and assigning them increasingly complex projects as part of their competency and career development. Thus, if managing projects is considered important in an organization, this organization requires a project management career path. Success factors identified for designing a project management career path include aligning the competency and qualification of the project manager with the career path level, adequate organizational recognition of the role of project manager and the necessity for according salary and promotion policy, a project classification system to be able to assign the adequate project manager to a particular class of project (Hölzle, 2010).

Project careers are rather fragmented. This includes not just the project managers, but all project professionals. The project career is characterized by a series of projects in different contractual arrangements; periods of permanent employment contracts and temporary employment contracts are interleaved. Thus, the careers of most of the project professionals in the project-oriented organization – not only of the project manager – relate more or less to project work. Consequently, the management career path and expert career path in the project-oriented organization need to consider projects.

Mentoring is gaining importance especially for young project professionals to develop a project career and allow them to grow in the projects assigned to them (Huemann et al., 2019).

Conclusion

I introduced the project-oriented organization as a contemporary form of organization and discussed its specific features. Table 39.6. summarizes these specific features of the project-oriented organization, which have consequences for all functions of the organization, especially HRM needs to be designed differently to better support projects and the project professionals.

Table 39.6 Features of the project-oriented organization (after Huemann, 2015)

	Description	*Consequence*
Strategy	Managing by Projects as making adequate choices for the organization to perform business processes	A highly differentiated organization which requires a balancing of centralization and decentralization
Structures	Temporary projects in addition to permanent structures	Projects constitute an additional secondary organization consisting of temporary organizations as coupled sub-systems of the project-oriented organization Tensions between permanent and temporary structures for example different management logics between temporary and permanent structures Requires specific governance structures for the managing of projects as well as specific integrative structures such as PPG, PMO, and expert pool Possibility to build up adequate complexity in the organization to deal with the complexity of the environment and to suit different contexts
Culture	Project-oriented culture	Values that fit project orientation enable one to deal with uncertainty, contradictions, and change

References and further reading

Akkermans, J., Keegan, A., Huemann, M., & Ringhofer, C. (2020). Crafting Project Managers' Careers: Integrating the Fields of Careers and Project Management, *Project Management Journal*, 51(2), 135–153.

Gareis, R. (1989). "Managing by Projects": The Management Approach for the Future, *International Journal of Project Management*, 7(4), 243–249.

Gareis, R. (2005). *Happy Projects!*, Vienna: Manz.

Gareis, R. & Stummer, M. (2008). *Processes & Projects*, Vienna: Manz.

Hölzle, K. (2010). Designing and Implementing a Career Path for Project Managers, *International Journal of Project Management*, 28(8), 779–786.

Huemann, M. (2015). *Human Resource Management in the Project-Oriented Organization: Towards a Viable System for Project Personnel*, Aldershot: Gower.

Huemann, M., Ringhofer, C., & Keegan, A. (2019). Who Supports Project Careers? Leveraging the Compensatory Roles of Line Managers, *Project Management Journal*, 50(4), 476–486.

Midler, C. (1995). "Projectification" of the Firm: The Renault Case, *Scandinavian Journal of Management*, 11(4, December 1995), 363–375.

Turner, J.R., & Keegan, A.E. (2001). Mechanisms of Governance in the Project-based Organization: The Role of the Broker and Steward, *European Management Journal*, 19(3), 254–267.

Turner, J.R., Huemann, M., & Keegan, A.E. (2008). Human Resource Management in the Project Oriented Company: Employee Well-being and Ethical Treatment, *International Journal of Project Management, Special Issue: IRNOP X, Innovation in Projects,* 26(5), 577–585.

Woodward, J., (1965). *Industrial Organization; Theory and Practice.* Oxford, Oxford University Press.

Chapter 40

The governance of projects

Ralf Müller

Introduction

Since its first description in the project management literature by Turner and Keegan (1999), the concept of governance has developed into a popular research subject, with steadily increasing numbers of publications and conference presentations.

More recently, professional organizations, like the Project Management Institute (PMI), Association for Project Management (APM), and the International Standardization Organization (ISO), have developed their standards for the governance of projects, making the concept accessible, usable, and popular in practitioner circles as well. These standards reflect the particular governance standards of the countries they originate from in terms of being prescriptive or non-prescriptive. The former suggests a rule-based approach to governance, where processes and tasks are clearly defined and their execution enforced. The corporate governance literature refers to this approach as the 'comply or punished' approach. These standards are typically developed 'bottom-up' as extensions to existing project management methodologies and thus take the prescriptive nature of process compliance and continuous control to the governance level. Examples include the PMI Practice Guide for Governance of Portfolios, Programs, and Projects (PMI, 2016). The complement to this is the non-prescriptive or principles-based approaches to governance. Corporate governance literature refers

DOI: 10.4324/9781003274179-45

to this as 'comply or explain'. These standards outline a series of principles that guide the setup of governance from a corporate perspective, such as ensuring the right number and mix of junior and senior project managers in an organization. These 'top-down' standards do not prescribe any processes or tasks but point to the most crucial aspects of designing a governance system. Examples of that include the APM Guide for the Governance of Project Management (APM, 2011). Mixtures of both approaches can be found in, for example, the ISO 21505 standard (ISO, 2017).

The developments in academia and practice led to various definitions of governance, often triggered by the particular perspectives of the authors, such as economic, management, or ethical perspectives. Most popular are definitions emphasizing that governance provides the structures, processes, policies, and value system, as well as the means and control methods that allow to set and accomplish the objectives of an organization, be it a temporary organization like a project or a permanent organization like a firm. Through this, governance defines the framework within which (project) managers are allowed to do their work, and their performance is evaluated. For example, suppose governance policies do not allow fixed-price contracts in a company's customer delivery projects. In that case, a project manager is held accountable in light of the rule-based or principles-based approach mentioned above when using it without agreement from the governance institution.

At the heart of governance lies the separation of ownership of a task (e.g., managing a project) and the control of the execution of the task by a separate institution. Therefore projects have steering committees as a control institution to oversee the management of the project (i.e., the task). Violations of this 'ground rule' have caused severe damage. For example, the global financial crisis in 2008, where the tasks of investment bankers were insufficiently controlled, led to a chain of bankruptcies, resulting in a global economic downturn.

Governance is present at every layer in the organizational hierarchy or every node of an organizational network. Hence, whenever the frame for the next lower or adjacent layer of management must be defined. Such as from the CEO to the individual directors, from the director to the department manager, or from the depart manager to the project manager. The governance goals, functions, authorities, and roles differ contingent on their particular location in this hierarchy or network. However, they all shall perform the tasks outlined in the above definition of governance. Moreover, all governance systems shall built on the four principles of good governance, which the Organization for Economic Cooperation and Development (OECD) and the World Bank (OECD, 2001) jointly developed. According to them, every governance system (at every layer and node) shall provide for:

Transparency: Provision of accurate and timely information from the managers to the governing institutions

Accountability: Clear definition of roles, rights, and responsibilities within and across organizations. This includes escalation procedures for issue handling.

Responsibility: Use of socially accepted professional working standards in executing tasks, including the training and education for it.

Fairness: Equal, fair, and ethical treatment of persons and institutions inside and outside the organization.

Recently, the OECD added *Sustainability* as a fifth principle. However, due to its conceptual proximity, it is often perceived as a subset of the *Fairness* principle (e.g., being fair to humankind and the planet), as is done in this chapter.

The remainder of this chapter outlines the particularities of governance at the project, program, portfolio, corporate, and megaproject layers. Starting with the nucleus, this chapter deals with the project level, then expands into higher levels of the organizational structure. This chapter finishes by looking at the governance of inter-organizational networks for project delivery, which is popular for implementing large and megaprojects.

Intra-organizational governance of projects

Project governance

Project governance is concerned with the governance of the individual project. This includes (a) governing those aspects of the project that are different from other projects or unique, and (b) overseeing the use of those aspects of governance that are common across projects of similar type or all projects in the organization. The former comprises, for example, the governance of the development, negotiation, and ratification of project-specific contracts or the tailoring of specific processes to effectively meet the project objectives. In other cases, it might include the setup of a project-specific control infrastructure, considering the specific information needs of the particular mix of stakeholder groups in a project. The latter is concerned with the use of governance items passed on from higher governance levels. This may include using commonly used reporting templates, meeting schedules, or project methodologies for projects of the same type, as imposed by the portfolio-level managers.

The typical institutions for project governance are the:

- Steering committee – consisting of the project owner, representatives from upper management, users, suppliers, and others on demand
- Project Management Office (PMO) – whose representatives are experts consulting the project manager on project management methods and techniques.

The Steering Group (in its control function) and the project manager (as task owner) agree on how the project objectives are defined, the means needed to achieve them, and how to control progress. Here project objectives are typically framed by the project owner and refined through input from the project team. The means to achieve the objectives is subject to the policies and practices of the organization running the project or the agreed-upon contract terms in inter-organizational projects. Means to control progress are typically regular status reports, project reviews, and stage-gate meetings between the project manager and the steering committee. In reviews and stage-gate meetings, governance representatives meet the project manager to identify the project's progress and decide on possible risks and their mitigations, as well as the next steps forward. In practice, the Steering Committee fulfills a dual role of governing and supporting the project, governing by ensuring that the project is executed within the given constraints (such as time, cost, quality, and safety) by following the corporate policies for project management and the implementation of the governance principles mentioned above. Support by the Steering Committee is often done by helping to find resources, like specialists needed in the project, and prevent project delays by ensuring that recipients of project deliveries perform their functional tests on time and sign the relevant delivery documents.

PMO representatives typically get involved in introducing new project management methods or when audits are required to identify the causes for deviations from the project's expected performance.

In projects jointly executed by independent organizations, such as customer delivery projects, many of the governance aspects, like the project objectives, performance criteria, compensation, and escalation processes, are defined in a contract. Traditionally the different contract types are used to distribute the risks among the parties. Such as in fixed-price contracts, where the project delivery organization assumes most of the financial risk for delivery, or time-and-material contracts, where the buying organizations assume the main portion of the risk. In the context of large public projects, Public-Private Partnership (PPP) contracts became popular to balance the risks and benefits of the project across multiple parties.

Governance of projects

Governance of projects is concerned with the governance of groups of projects, such as programs, portfolios, or all projects in an organization. This is done by governing the standardization of commonalities across the projects in each group of projects. Examples include:

- Standardized reporting to enable performance comparisons across projects of similar type. This supports the transparency principle at the level of groups of projects
- Development of escalation procedures and definition of manager roles, authorities, and responsibilities. This supports the accountability principle
- Decisions on the number and types of project management methodologies allowed for the particular projects in a group. This defines the way work is executed and thus supports the responsibility principle
- Setting up criteria for prioritizing projects and their staffing. This supports the fairness and transparency principle.

Setting up the above is done by various governance institutions and roles, whose existence, authority, and staffing vary by organization. Larger organizations often have formal portfolio steering groups staffed with upper management representatives, directors of the business units involved in the portfolio, risk managers, etc. Smaller organizations might concentrate all related decision-making on a particular middle manager, a group of related directors, or a strategic PMO. Common to these approaches is the need for joint decision-making by the participants of these governance teams to balance the organization's priorities and available resources for the most effective and efficient achievement of the strategic objectives.

Through that, the governing institutions set the framework for achieving the planned *results*, *purpose*, and *balance of priorities* within the portfolio.

Another important governance function at this layer between corporate governance and project governance is the formation of the governance paradigm. A paradigm is a theoretical framework that guides the selection and execution of tasks in a given situation. A governance paradigm sets the framework for the management tasks that are deemed appropriate in a project. It combines corporate-level and program/portfolio-level approaches to a particular paradigm under which the governed projects are executed. For that, corporate governance provides the corporation's shareholder or stakeholder orientation. The former applies when corporate governance defines the organization's purpose as predominantly serving one stakeholder group, the shareholders. Here all decisions in the organizations are governed by the desire to maximize the share price and dividends for shareholders. Contrarily, suppose corporate governance defines the organization's purpose as serving many different stakeholder groups, often with conflicting objectives, such as shareholders and environmentalists. In that case, the organization is stakeholder-oriented and needs to balance its benefits across various stakeholder groups. Overlaying this continuum from shareholder to stakeholder orientation with a continuum of the control approach for the projects in a given portfolio, ranging from behavior control to outcome control, identifies four governance paradigms. Behavior control prevails when following the process takes priority over accomplishing defined outcomes. Here the trust is higher in the process than in the project manager's capabilities. This is often found in high-risk industries, like firefighting, aviation etc. Contrarily outcome control prevails when priority is given to accomplishing predefined objectives, not caring too much about the process of getting there. This leads to four governance paradigms shown in Figure 40.1 (Müller & Lecoeuvre, 2014).

The *conformist paradigm* indicates that projects shall create shareholder value by project managers following the existing management processes. The underlying assumption is that cost efficiency is accomplished through process compliance. The paradigm implies that project managers should carefully follow their organization's processes and their project management methodology.

The *flexible economist paradigm* indicates that projects shall create predominantly shareholder value, and project managers are controlled by the project's outcomes (i.e., creating deliverables within time, cost, and quality constraints). The underlying assumption is that cost efficiency is accomplished by giving freedom to the

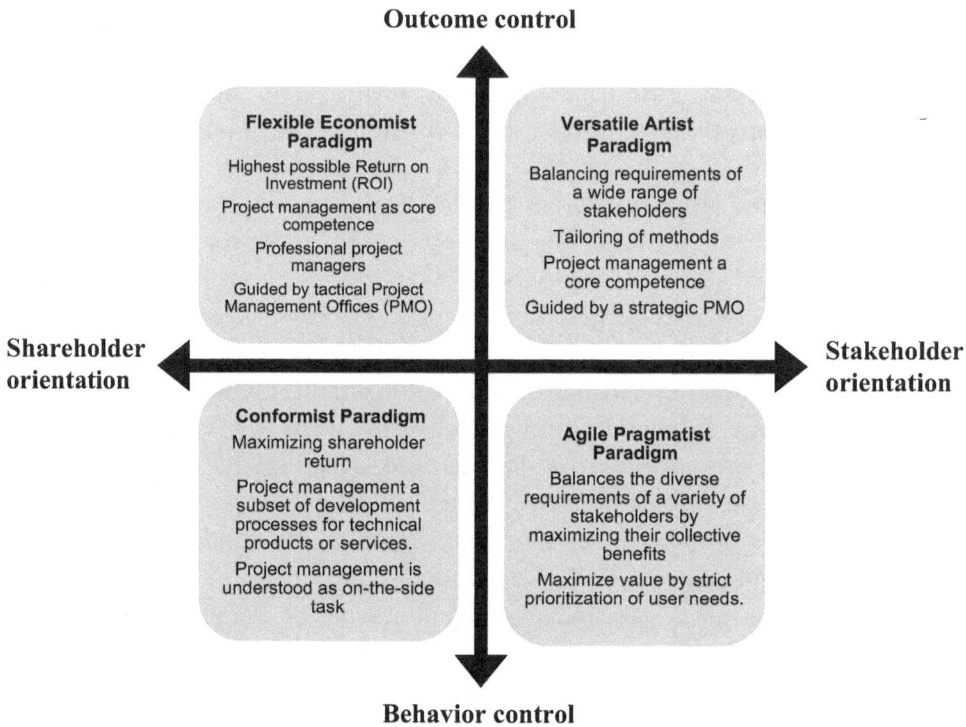

Figure 40.1: Project governance paradigms (after Müller & Lecoeuvre, 2014)

project manager to decide on the most efficient way to run the project. This paradigm implies that project managers are perceived as experts and trusted to manage the project through their experience, often supported by tactical PMOs.

The *versatile artist paradigm* indicates that projects shall create value for multiple stakeholder groups, and project managers are controlled by project outcomes. The underlying assumption is that project managers are closest to the different stakeholder groups and, therefore, can identify the best possible balance of benefits over the different stakeholder groups and their diversity of objectives, including the shareholders. The paradigm implies that project managers are senior experts in both project management and the project's particular industry. They are often supported by strategic PMOs.

The *agile pragmatist paradigm* indicates that projects shall create value for multiple stakeholder groups, accomplished by strictly following given processes. The underlying assumption is that splitting projects into small task groups (sprints), managed through a repetitive process leads to fast and economical delivery in incremental steps. The project sponsor defines the benefits for the stakeholder groups. The paradigm implies that project managers' traditional tasks and decisions are distributed over sponsors, Scrum Masters, and teams.

Each of the four paradigms sets a different framework for decision-making and work priorities for a project. Different paradigms might be applied in different portfolios of projects, like a conformist paradigm in the maintenance department's projects, the agile pragmatist paradigm in the development department, and the versatile artist paradigm in the sales and marketing department.

Corporate governance for projects

Corporate-level governance sets, among other things, the stage and priority for project management in the corporation. Here board or business unit-level decisions are taken to define the extent projects are used as building blocks for the corporation's business. Examples include decisions on how the corporation presents itself in the market by delivering goods and services to customers through individual projects or a repetitive production process. Internal decisions include the number and ratio of junior versus senior project managers, hiring of experienced project managers or developing them in-house, and the need for professional certification for project managers and PMO staff. Organizational decisions include the establishment of related support organizations, like tactical and/or strategic PMOs, their roles, authorities, the scope of their work, and staffing levels.

Corporate governance decisions with a more implicit impact on projects are the shareholder or stakeholder orientation, which trickles down the organization and impacts the project governance paradigm. Similarly, the underlying governance mechanism of the corporate governance system either emphasizes trust or control to govern the corporation. Trust-based approaches to corporate governance often lead to outcome control and control-based governance to behavior control at the project level. Hence, corporate governance sets the stage for project-level governance.

A question frequently discussed is whether project governance of inter-organizational projects is within or outside a corporation's governance. Given that the board of directors of a corporation acts on behalf of the shareholders to control the entire organization, all activities of a corporation must be subordinated to corporate governance. Otherwise, project-based organizations would not be controllable, and shareholders would not invest their money in such organizations. In inter-organizational projects, the contract between the organizations defines the minimum agreed-upon commonality of their different corporate governance systems. Thus, the contract must be in accordance with each corporation's governance system. If a contract is signed that includes terms that are not part of a party's governance system, then the signature extends the governance system of the particular party by the defined term. As such, the contract still falls under the corporation's governance system, and with it, the work done by this party in the project.

Governance of inter-organizational networks for projects

So far, the chapter has discussed the governance of projects from a single organization's perspective. However, many projects, especially large and megaprojects, are implemented using a network of different organizations. Governance of and within these networks is discussed in the following.

Large and megaprojects (further referred to as megaprojects) typically require a large number of different suppliers and other partners, with some of them engaging temporarily to provide products or services, while others engage for the entire duration of the project. The organizational structure of these suppliers is often a mix of a hierarchy and networked entities. We refer to them as networks, a group of three or more organizations connected to achieve a common goal.

These networks for projects are steered by the project owner organizations through their 'ground-rules' for governing the multitude of inter-organizational networks they are involved in. In the following, we follow Unterhitzenberger et al. (2022) and describe this governance in three layers: metagovernance, governance of networks, and network governance, which is summarized in Figure 40.2.

Metagovernance

Metagovernance is set up by project owners (governments or private investors) by issuing (semi)permanent policies as frameworks for the implementation of subordinated governance layers. These define the conditions for forming inter-organizational networks. Metagovernance comprises five dimensions:

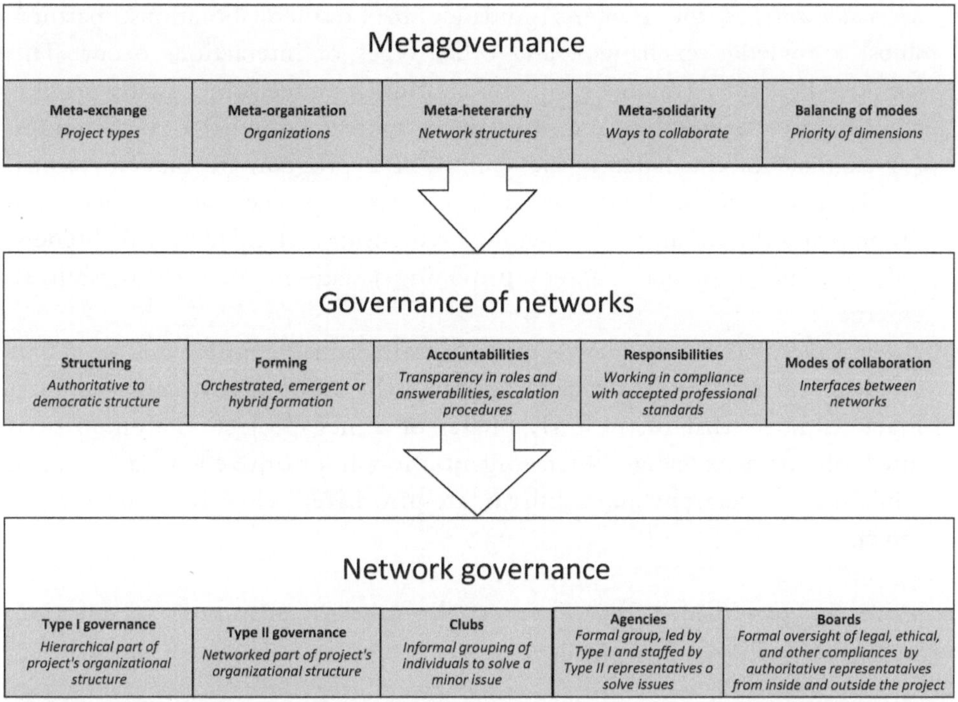

Figure 40.2: Governance framework for inter-organizational project networks (after Müller et al., 2022)

- *Meta-exchange* is the owner's decision for a particular project, whose execution provides the purpose for creating a new network. Through that, the owner steers subsequent governance levels on what (and also on what not) money is spent.
- *Meta-organization* is the owner's criteria for engaging and evaluating organizations to be involved. Examples include issuing policies to prioritize local over international suppliers. This may also include the performance threshold to be met by these organizations to become or remain part of a network.
- *Meta-heterarchy* is the owner's preferred network structure. It guides subsequent governance layers in setting up networks with either more authoritative or more democratic structures. The former is found more often in public projects and the latter in the private industry. This preference reflects the owner's attitude toward the avoidance of governance failures either through formal control structures or through combined knowledge of the participating organizations.

- *Meta-solidarity* is the owner's guidance in how collaborations, partnerships, knowledge exchanges, and other types of interactions occur. This includes bidder conferences for organizations to meet and discuss possible collaborations or building and maintaining specific knowledge communities. An example of the latter is the CONCEPT program by the Norwegian government, which funds research on large project governance, and disseminates the findings at a bi-annual symposium attended by stakeholders, industry, and academia. Thereby providing a stage for new partnerships to emerge.
- *Balance the four metagovernance modes* in situational contingency to adjust to changing circumstances and minimize the risk of governance failure. Practice shows that in the early phases of a megaproject, the emphasis is often on meta-exchange. Meta-organization is prioritized in later stages, while meta-heterarchy and solidarity are prioritized when issues need to be solved.

The five metagovernance dimensions set the stage for governing the creation, maintenance, and closure of networks in the realm of the owner or investor.

Governance of networks

Owners are not launching only one network for one project. They are part of and maintain many different networks simultaneously, such as networks for the training of employees and/or suppliers, certification for various professional, legal, or marketing purposes, or development and dissemination of safety and other standards. Hence, owner organizations are part of a network of networks, which needs governance. In some of these networks, the owner is a member of a network governed elsewhere; others are launched and governed by the owner itself.

Governance of networks (GoN) addresses the governance of a network of networks, typically of an owner organization. GoN provides the framework for setting up networks to successfully pursue long-term and short-term objectives through successful project goal accomplishment in the present and the future. GoN contributes to that by defining formation, structure, accountabilities, responsibilities, and modes of collaboration among networks (Figure 40.2).

- *Structuring* takes the meta-heterarchy requirement from the metagovernance layer. It applies it to structure the network of networks to be launched, emphasizing either authoritative or democratic structures for networks that combine many different actors (consulting, training, certification organizations, etc.)
- *Formation* applies meta-organization and meta-solidarity for the setup of a network. Examples include official calls for tender in the public sector, where bidder conferences and clear selection criteria lead to orchestrated networks. Contrarily, informal calls for proposals to a few selected companies and information meetings in the private sector may lead to emerging networks. By way of that, metagovernance's selection criteria are applied, and networking events are created
- *Accountabilities* are set up contingent on the purpose of the network for the clear definition of roles, answerabilities, and escalation procedures to provide transparency in governance
- *Responsibilities* are also set up contingent on the purpose of the network to meet expected quality levels in work. Done by ensuring compliance with accepted professional working standards, such as ISO 21505 for the governance of projects, programs, and portfolios
- *Modes of collaboration* are also set up contingent on the purpose of the network and comprise definitions of interfaces between networks and their ways of collaboration. Examples include setting up a digital infrastructure in a construction project network through the collaboration of organizations from the project execution and the education network.

Network governance

Just as above with projects, we refer to *network governance* as the governance of one network for one project. Research by Unterhitzenberger and colleagues (2022) showed that these complex networks are explained through Multi-Level Governance Theory (Hooghe & Marks, 2001), which distinguishes between:

- *Type I* governance for the hierarchical parts of the network, typically consisting of the hierarchy of owner/sponsor, a temporary client organization, and the Tier One Suppliers. This governance is rooted in institutionalized rules and norms with clearly defined structures, roles, and responsibilities for each party.

The relationship between these units is explained through existing governance theories, such as agency theory for projects (Müller, 2016).
- *Type II* governance, for the non-hierarchical parts, like the many different suppliers that temporarily engage with the project and may help each other out when issues arise. Their governance is rooted in applying knowledge and experience to establish the project's deliverables. This typically includes jointly overcoming sudden issues through informal, non-institutionalized mutual support, independent of formal structures, roles, and responsibilities. The relationship between these organizations is explained through democratic governance theory (Skelcher, 2005).

Governing these two very different structures as a single entity requires a link between the two types of governance. For example, to ensure that the working policies developed by Type I governance institutions (e.g., the prime contractor) reach the individual Type II institutions like Tier 2 and 3 suppliers performing the work in the network. These links are organizational units, often distinguished by their level of formality:

- *Clubs* are an informal ad-hoc collaboration of volunteers to solve an issue. Clubs form based on peoples' mutual trust that they can jointly solve a problem.
- *Agencies* are formal organizational units that meet regularly, often set up for managing a particular theme, like quality or changes to the project. They are typically managed by prime contractor representatives and staffed with subcontractor representatives.
- *Boards* are most formal and often set up by local municipalities to oversee overall correctness in project execution (such as process compliance or safety) for both internal and external governance of the project and its network. Boards are more authoritative and take a broader perspective on governance than clubs and agencies.

Examples of the above governance structures include a school construction project in Scandinavia, where the local municipality formed a *board* for legal, financial, and technical matters, which enforced process and policy compliance and addressed Type I and Type II governance simultaneously. In a railway construction project, ten *agencies* were set up for specific themes and functioned as the link between the group of main beneficiaries of the project (a Type I institution) and the networked suppliers (Type II organizations). More examples can be found in Šimkonis et al. (2021).

The three layers of governance of inter-organizational projects do not only address different tasks, but they also differentiate themselves by time. Metagovernance is often semi-permanent by nature, setting the ground rules for governance for a long time. Within that time, the GoN adjusts itself continuously to metagovernance's requirements to launch and close networks. Finally, network governance is the shortest in duration, as it is limited to the duration of a project, which can still be several years in cases of megaprojects.

Conclusion

This chapter described governance of and for projects, first from an intra-organizational and then from an inter-organizational governance perspective. For that, the chapter introduced the concept of governance, its principles, and underlying assumptions and then described their application at various levels, intern and extern to the organization. Thereby addressing governance institutions, their roles and responsibilities, and their relationships. Practical examples were given to show and guide practitioners on how these concepts are implemented in practice.

References and further reading

Association for Project Management. (2004). *Directing Change: A Gude to Governance of Project Management*, 3rd edition. Prices Risborough: Association for Project Management.

Hooghe, L., & Marks, G. (2001). Types of Multi-Level Governance. *European Integration Online Papers*, *5*(11), 9163–9170. https://doi.org/10.1039/c9sm90238d

International Standards Organization. (2017). *ISO 21505: Project, Programme and Portfolio Management: Guidance on Governance*. Geneva: International Standards Organization

Müller, R. (2016). *Governance Theories. Governance and Governmentality for Projects: Enablers, Practices, and Consequences*. https://doi.org/10.4324/9781315683294

Müller, R., & Lecoeuvre, L. (2014). Operationalizing Governance Categories of Projects. *International Journal of Project Management*, *32*(8). https://doi.org/10.1016/j.ijproman.2014.04.005

Müller, R., Alonderienė, R., Chmieliauskas, A., Drouin, N., Ke, Y., Minelgaite, I., Mongeon, M., Pilkiene, M., Šimkonis, Š., Unterhhitzenberger, C., Vaagaasar, A.

L., Wang, L., & Zhu, F. (2022). *Governance of Interorganizational Project Networks*. Newtown Square, PA, Retrieved from https://www.pmi.org/learning/library/governance-interorganizational-projects-13452

OECD. (2001). *Governance in the 21st Century*. OECD, Paris, Retrieved from http://www.oecd.org/futures/17394484.pdf

Project Management Institute. (2016). Governance of Portfolios, Programs, and Projects: A Practice Guide. Newtown Square, PA: Project Management Institute.

Šimkonis, Š., Müller, R., Alonderienė, R., Chmieliauskas, A., & Pilkienė, M. (2021). Multi-Level Governance in Inter-Organizational Project Settings. In *Proceedings of the British Academy of Management (BAM) Conference in the Cloud, October 31 to September 2, 2021*, Lancaster University (pp. 1–20).

Skelcher, C. (2005). Jurisdictional Integrity, Polycentrism and the Design of Democratic Governance. *Governance*, *18*(1), 89–111. Retrieved from http://scholar.google.com/scholar?q=related:mVjV0OlkLvIJ:scholar.google.com/&hl=en&num=30&as_sdt=0,5%5Cnpapers2://publication/uuid/6675FBEC-91B7-4415-AD78-6A7B0D8D4246

Turner, J. R., & Keegan, A. (1999). The Versatile Project-Based Organization: Governance and Operational Control. *European Management Journal*, *17*(3), 296–309.

Unterhitzenberger, C., Müller, R., Vaagaasar, A. L., Ke, Y., Alonderienė, R., Minelgaite, I., Pilkienė, M., Ang, L., Zhu, f., Drouin, N., Chmieliauskas, A., Šimkonis, Š., & Mongeon, M. (2022). A Multi-Level Governance Model for Inter-Organizational Project Networks. *Project Management Journal*, *54*(1), 88–105.

World Bank. (2022). Governance. Retrieved from https://www.worldbank.org/en/topic/governance

Chapter 41

The PMO

Monique Aubry

Introduction

Project management offices (PMOs) are now part of the organizational landscape for project delivery within the kind of project-based society that we currently live in. PMOs are generally put in place in various economic sectors and in various categories of projects. For example, large banking institutions generally have multiple PMOs at different levels, taking care of hundreds of projects in different departments. PMOs are also encountered in public or private major projects, where they tend to play an integration role both on the client and supplier side. The broad range of PMO situations makes it very difficult to prescribe a fixed and limited number of PMO types (Braun, 2018). Adding to the difficulty of a typology are the frequent changes to the PMO activities and characteristics in a context of uncertainty and ambiguity.

This chapter proposes a toolbox for the benefit of those who are about to design a very first PMO or wish to modify an existing PMO and will be useful for anyone engaging in understanding the fundamentals of PMOs and their implementation. This chapter is based on learning from a multiyear research program dedicated to the study of PMOs in a variety of organizational contexts. This chapter is also the result of learning about designing PMOs in contexts where politics and power systems are at play. The PMO toolbox proposed in this

DOI: 10.4324/9781003274179-46

chapter should support a reflexive approach based on the knowledge of context and its challenges for today and for the future.

The chapter is structured as two sections. The first section is dedicated to the PMO toolbox. Four categories of basic elements included in the toolbox are described. Together, these elements form the basis from which the PMO can be designed and implemented. The second section presents the five fundamentals which serve as meta-rules to guide the PMO design. This chapter closes with concluding remarks.

The PMO toolbox

The main use of the PMO toolbox is to provide the basic components of a PMO, so it can be assembled through design into a wide variety of forms that can answer a variety of needs and situations. The toolbox approach is well adapted to a diversified and changing world. From previous research (Hobbs & Aubry, 2010), four categories of basic elements should be included as "tools" in the toolbox: organizational context characteristics; characteristics of projects; PMO structural characteristics; and PMO activities. Altogether, the toolbox serves as a learning process that informs PMO design.

Organizational context characteristics

As we all know, projects are temporary organizations; therefore, the context, the circumstances surrounding them, and the way they are delivered can be considerably important. Knowing the organizational context, or circumstance, is a fundamental part of PMO design. To paraphrase Engwall (2003), no PMO is an island: organizational history and context should be taken into consideration. Table 41.1 provides a list of ten characteristics to be considered in designing a PMO. While some of these characteristics are easily knowledgeable, others might need interpretation. For example, the identification of the economic sector should be clear, conversely to the level of project management maturity which may need prior investigation.

Project characteristics

Characteristics of projects may have a great influence on the activities that serve the PMO and on its design. There are a variety of ways to categorize

Table 41.1 Organizational context characteristics

Organizational context	Geographic region
	Economic sector
	Private or public sector
	Organizational size
	Number of projects within the organization
	Internal or external project customers
	Single or multiple project customers
	Level of project management maturity
	Localization relative to project personal
	Supportiveness of organizational culture

Table 41.2 Characteristics of projects

Characteristics of projects	Project size (e.g., the number of persons working on a typical project)
	Project duration
	The type of product or service delivered
	The primary project performance criteria
	The inclusion of post-delivery activities within the project scope
	Involvement in outsourcing contracts

projects. The six characteristics presented in Table 41.2 were used to characterize projects in our research on PMOs. Other characteristics can be added if appropriate in the context of PMO design.

PMO structural characteristics

Organizational design refers very often to structural characteristics – these are essential to take into consideration. The PMO is no exception. These

Table 41.3 PMO structural characteristics

PMO structural characteristics	The PMO's name
	Location within organizational structure
	PMO staff: size, experience, background, presence of business analysts or business architects
	Percent of projects within the mandate
	Percent of project managers within PMO
	Decision-making authority of PMO
	Age of PMO
	PM methodology: homegrown, compulsory, actual use
	Adequacy of funding
	Billing for services

characteristics serve to describe *technically* or *factually* the PMO design. Important to note that despite the importance of structural characteristics, they only provide a partial understanding of the overall context. The three other basic elements must also be included in the PMO design thinking (Table 41.3).

PMO activities

What do PMOs do? A single PMO may perform a variety of activities, in the realm of projects, responding to organizational needs and within a specific context. Indeed, a PMO, like any other organizational entity, should contribute to the organizational performance with its own mission and objectives in relation to the organizational governance. The proposed framework organizes PMO activities into nine domains based on:

- Academic research first identifies five groups of functions and three independent ones based on statistics (Hobbs & Aubry, 2010);

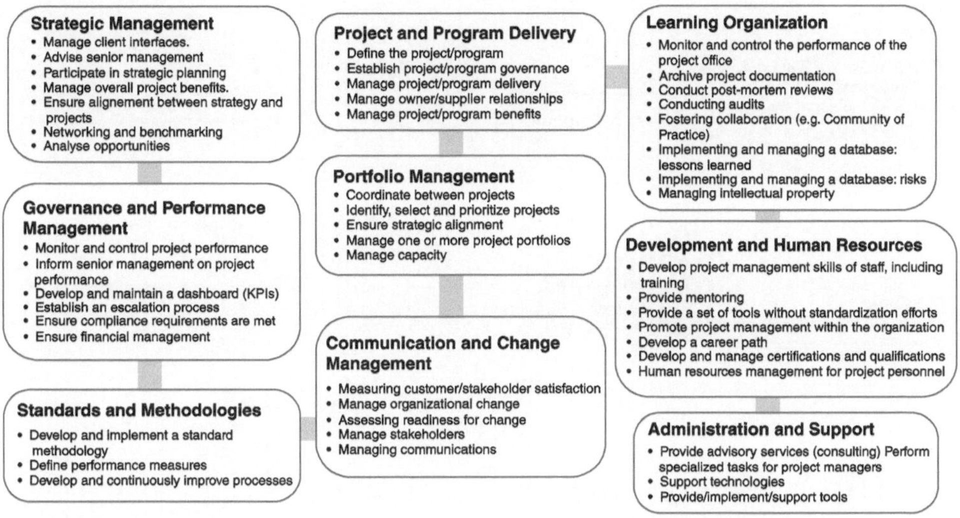

Figure 41.1: The nine domains of PMO activities

- Several workshops with professionals and consultants have given a refined structure of what PMOs do and a framework of PMO activities (e.g., Project Management Institute, 2013);
- Reflection on recent formalization in project-governance structure observed in research.

Figure 41.1 illustrates the nine PMO domains of activities. There is no order of priority in the way activities are presented. Priorities should be given contextually to each specific situation. It is important to keep in mind that rarely does a single PMO perform all the activities identified in the nine domains. Also, these activities are often performed in relation to other PMOs or other entities, internal or external. Care should be taken to ensure a coherent coverage of activities in relation to others.

PMO design fundamentals

We use the term 'fundamentals' deliberately. It refers to research results and attempts to highlight what we have learned about the PMOs' activities and their organizational characteristics (Aubry, Hobbs, Müller, & Blomquist, 2011; Aubry, Müller, & Glückler, 2012; Hobbs & Aubry, 2010). As shown above, with the PMO toolbox, the research program allows us to identify elements that together

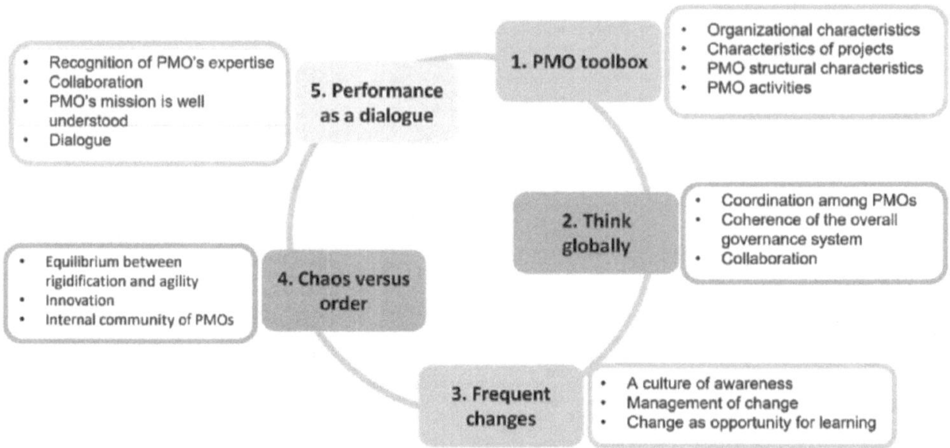

Figure 41.2: The five PMO design fundamentals

form basic knowledge of PMOs. However, knowing these elements does not completely explain the dynamics found in such entities when comes time to engage in PMO design. The PMO design fundamentals provide overall insights into the toolbox. Figure 41.2 illustrates the five fundamental elements of PMO design. Important to note that each one of these elements is not completely isolated nor disconnected: there are some overlaps and strong connections among them.

Fundamental 1: A PMO toolbox instead of "types of PMO"

The search for typology is inherent to the human condition. One only has to think of Linné and his categorization of the animal and vegetal world, published in the 18th century. The question of PMO types emerged early in our research. With a database of over 500 PMO descriptions, several attempts were undertaken, never resulting in a convincing categorization. What we found on PMOs, rather, was extreme variability:

- in their structural characteristics
- in the activities they undertake
- in the perceived value of the PMO

Such variability means that it is difficult to answer important questions with a clear answer, such as, "Should project managers be included in PMO personnel? Is a matrix type of organizing a better fit for our organization?" Results from research show that, the decision to include or not project managers within the PMO represents roughly the same percentage (about 30%) for inclusion and not inclusion. The same diversity is also found concerning the position of the PMO in the organizational hierarchy and its ability to work within a matrix structure.

This variety among PMOs cannot be explained using usual organizational variables, such as industry, geographic regions, public and private sectors, size of the organization (except for the size of PMOs), and internal and external customers. The observed percentage of project managers within the PMO shows a similar distribution in, for example, countries in Europe, the UK, Canada, and the US. Finally, a similar distribution of this variable exists across industries such as those producing tangible products, IT/IS, Telecom, and those offering financial services.

That said, the practical implications highlighted here for professionals in charge of implementing a PMO illustrate the active work to be done, that is, PMO design. In short, the PMO toolbox appears to provide a practical approach to providing basic elements to work on. The toolbox contains four groups of basic elements (see Section "Introduction"), and the design work is all about making decisions on PMO structural characteristics and activities that will form a coherent PMO mandate. The first fundamental emphasizes the PMO design as a real task that takes resources and time. The resulting PMO mandate must contribute to the organization's strategic objectives.

The extreme variability among PMOs found in our research is an indicator that each organizational situation is unique in its context and in its objectives, or strategies, as well as in the organization's history and culture. The PMO design should take all this into account so that it does not copy from one PMO to another. The PMO design task calls for collective sensemaking to transform knowledge into adapted decisions on PMO characteristics and activities.

Fundamental 2: Think globally

Rarely does a PMO exist in a closed environment, whether it be a unique PMO offering services for a major infrastructure project or a PMO in a large project-based organization with multiple PMOs at different organizational levels. More likely, a PMO is an organizational instance embedded in the organizational project management infrastructure (Müller, Drouin, & Sankaran, 2019), defined as the integration of project-related activities of an organization into a cohesive network.

In the case of multiple PMOs within one organization, care should be taken not to reinvent the wheel or to duplicate efforts in one or the other activities. The PMO design should take into consideration the need for coordination among multiple PMOs. This can be done easily by mapping the different activities performed by the PMOs with the list of PMOs. Moreover, other internal or external entities dealing with PMOs might be advantageously considered in the mapping.

One major constraint that must be taken into consideration is the coexistence of a matrix-type organization and hierarchy. Individual projects and programs are often carried out through a matrix-type organization, with multidisciplinary and collective efforts in delivering valuable outcomes. On the one hand, PMO relates to projects and, in this sense, inherits elements from the multidisciplinary and collective approach. On the other hand, there is still a hierarchy in most organizational structures and PMO is often part of it. Together, matrix structure and hierarchy often result in complex structural arrangements creating power struggles, tensions, and other conflicts around the PMO.

The two complementary approaches should overcome the potential for conflicts related to the matrix-type organization: governance and collaboration. First, regarding governance, PMO is part of sound organizational project management, but it represents only one piece of the overall governance system (Müller et al., 2019). Coherence of the overall governance system is crucial to ensure a proper power balance between the PMOs and the other internal and external entities involved in project delivery. The power balance has to be discussed in the case of a new PMO implementation or in its evolution.

The second approach refers to collaboration, a main topic within project studies. In the context of PMO, collaboration is key to overcoming situations of conflict and to optimizing engagement. In this sense, collaboration in the PMO is not simply instrumental in avoiding conflict, but collaboration is also creating value for innovation (Sergeeva & Ali, 2020).

Fundamental 3: Frequent changes

Changes are frequent (probably, too frequent) in organizational life of today. The PMO is no exception. Research shows that 80% of organizations changed their PMOs after three years (Aubry et al., 2011). While reasons for changes vary, the main takeaway gleaned from research is that, for the most part, PMO transformations are not associated with something going wrong. Research shows that, rather, PMOs are dynamic and adapt to their internal and external environments. Just take a look at our natural environment: all living species, including humans, have been evolving for millions of years. In a much shorter period, all organizations do so as well. Not changing could be a sign of organizational inertia and become a barrier to reaching strategic objectives. The best organizational approach regarding PMO transformations is to understand the PMO as in transition, to anticipate the next changes, and to prepare for them.

Preparation for change calls for active awareness of the PMO environment. This might be done in different ways: for example, by building a culture which is alert to any sign of events or emerging tensions in different areas of the organization, such as in the economy, technology, politics of the organization, or social life of the organization, both from within and surrounding it. Another way to prepare for change, or fluctuations, is to stay connected with the strategic thinking within the organization. Yet, any major change in the strategic orientation or objectives will likely bring changes to investments, and, consequently, to the project portfolio. In this situation, PMO characteristics may be adjusted perhaps to maintain the overall alignment in organizational project management (as mentioned in Fundamental 2, 'Think globally').

A point to take into consideration when addressing the question of PMO transformation is the *management* of PMO transformation. Too often organizational changes are not considered as real business changes. Research shows that 50% of PMO transformations do not manage the change even if 71% of these transformations are considered major. There are two main consequences of not taking a PMO transformation seriously as an important organizational change. First, successfully implementing PMO can become so difficult that as a result there is no ultimate execution of the plan. Second, and more importantly, a lack of collaboration emerging from a difficult implementation may greatly disrupt PMO activities.

Changes and transformations represent opportunities for learning, and this is also true in the context of PMO. Learning from experience is often challenging in projects, given their temporary nature (Tshuma, Steyn, & van Waveren, 2022). The PMO provides a good place to access institutional memory and avoid situations of reinventing existing solutions that were previously in place. Learning in situations of PMO transformation, rather, should offer the opportunity to enhance individual and organizational competencies.

Fundamental 4: Chaos versus order

In recent decades, we have all witnessed the evolution of standards, guides, and bodies of knowledge for the management of projects, programs, portfolios, PMOs, risks, and benefits published by professional associations in project management. These documents are recognized as composing the essential knowledge in the project management community. Certifications that apply to standards also contribute to the development of competencies in the management of different aspects of projects in organizations. PMOs benefit from this development, as their role within organizations can rely on well-regarded and standardized processes instead of looking to reinvent the wheel, so to speak.

While bodies of knowledge and standardization are a great contribution to the development of the field of project management, research shows that there may be some rigidification, creating silos in organizations (Aubry et al., 2012). This has been shown despite the recent integration of the concept of agility in most of these standards, guides, and bodies of knowledge. PMOs are generally at the heart of such tension or debate on rigidity and agility. Rigidity refers to the implementation of good practices but with no room for adaptation to evolving needs. In this respect, all this can lead to too much control and *order*. In this section, we use the term "chaos" as a metaphor, and never wish to associate agility with real chaos. Agility brings its own rules and standards but encourages adaptations along the project life cycle. The idea here is to recognize the appropriateness of standardization and control as well as of innovation and agility.

In this regard, we may turn toward the matrix-type of organization. It is essential to remember that the concept of the matrix-type of organization emerged in the 1960s from the field of innovation. With respect to inspiring innovation, this organizational pattern was developed to overcome bureaucratic hierarchies. The assumption was that controlled mechanisms found generally in hierarchies, alongside more formalization and standardization, may hinder the emergence of new ideas. The tension between control and agility can create a general climate of dissatisfaction with respect to agility and may contribute to the overall fear of losing control over projects. PMO design should aspire to reach some point of equilibrium between rigidification and agility, as well as between order and chaos (Geraldi, Söderlund, & Marrewijk, 2021).

Another consequence of rigidification is the "silo" effect between project management instances and particularly between PMOs when there are several of them. Research shows that PMOs in the same organization behave like isolated islands instead of forming a community of practice. Overall, PMOs in the same organization formed a sort of a bagel metaphor, having a central high-level control PMO with other specialized PMOs gravitating around it, with little chance of communication.

Overall, PMO design has a lot to contribute to reaching a point of equilibrium between agility and rigidity, and between control and *laissez-faire*.

Fundamental 5: Performance

PMO performance is often the ultimate measure of its value. It is important to note that the PMO performance should be assessed over the performance of individual projects and programs. Two different research approaches were undertaken to assess the PMO performance. In research using a quantitative approach, results showed that better performance is related to (Hobbs & Aubry, 2010):

- Performing multiple activities, which are viewed as important within specific organizational contexts
- Having a project management organization
- Choosing the structural characteristics of the PMO adapted to the specific organizational context

These results were rather surprising as neither specific activity nor structural characteristics showed up in direct relation to PMO performance. However, the same quantitative research revealed unexpected variables that, together, lead to an interesting explanation for good PMO performance:

- Recognition of PMO's expertise
- Collaboration with other project participants
- PMO's mission being well understood

In a second research approach, we adopted a qualitative and multifaceted approach to allow for a fresh look at PMO performance. With this approach, we found five important elements making up PMO performance (Aubry & Lavoie-Tremblay, 2018):

- Human relations
- Innovation
- Rational goals
- Internal processes
- Quality of the outcome

The foundation of this approach is based on the *value* which each individual and organizational entity offers to the PMO. In this respect, performance is a *construct*, and the best approach to get a proper measurement is to embrace multiple facets of PMO performance: multiple facets that reflect multiple values coexisting in organizations. For example, it is more likely that the finance department will assess the PMO performance with different criteria than the human relations department. Following these results, PMO performance can better be assessed in dialogue to reconcile the different and sometimes paradoxical values seen with respect to PMO performance.

In line with this qualitative approach, our research revealed that different PMO designs may lead to similar PMO performance, in what is defined as 'equifinality' (Aubry, Richer, Lavoie-Tremblay, Fortin, & Fortin Verreault, 2022). There are multiple means of reaching the objectives. This result reinforces the crucial importance of context – internal and external – in PMO design and the care that should be taken to embed the PMO in structural design within the organization.

The different and complementary approaches in this research program on PMO performance suggest that more consideration be given to integration and embeddedness, and probably a bit less emphasis on individual activities and characteristics. Overall, it confirms the dynamic and active work of PMO design in relation to performance. The PMO toolbox presented in this chapter should allow for such work.

Conclusion

This chapter proposes a toolbox approach to PMO design rather than providing specific types of PMO design. Five fundamentals are also proposed to guide the assembly of the basic elements. All this is the fruit of a multiyear research program on PMOs. This chapter recalls the very first findings of the research program as well, even as it makes sense of more recent research results. We have tried to integrate the overall results into a comprehensive whole with respect to PMO design. We also avoid any scientific jargon, to transfer as much of our knowledge as possible on PMOs to the professionals at different organizational levels, and who serve in a variety of roles. Over the years, several workshops and presentations were conducted with professionals all over the world. These rich conversations have doubtlessly refined communication between researchers and professionals.

PMO is not an end in itself. PMO is an organizational entity, and it will evolve within an organization to answer its needs and to aid those in the organization to reach the best potential of every project.

Acknowledgments

We wish to acknowledge the invaluable collaboration and contribution of Brian Hobbs and Ralf Müller, mainly in the first years of the research program on PMOs. Together, we received the 2012 IPMA Research Award for Project Management Office for its contribution to organizational performance. This research program also benefited from the financial support of the Project Management Institute, the Swedish Per and Eivor Wikström Foundation, the Canadian Institutes of Health Research, and the Ministry of Transport in Quebec.

References and further reading

Aubry, M., Hobbs, B., Müller, R., & Blomquist, T. (2011). *Identifying the forces driving the frequent changes in PMOs*. Newtown Square, PA: Project Management Institute.

Aubry, M., & Lavoie-Tremblay, M. (2018). Rethinking Organizational Design for Managing Multiple Projects. *International Journal of Project Management, 36*(1), 12–26.

Aubry, M., Müller, R., & Glückler, J. (2012). *Governance and communities of PMOs*. Newtown Square, PA: Project Management Institute.

Aubry, M., Richer, M.-C., Lavoie-Tremblay, M., Fortin, C., & Fortin Verreault, J.-F. (2022). Revisiting Organizational Design in the Light of Isomorphism and Equifinality: Insights from the Study of Three Major Transformation Projects. *Project Management Journal, 53*(2), 161–180.

Braun, T. (2018). Configurations for Interorganizational Project Networks: The Interplay of the PMO and Network Administrative Organization. *Project Management Journal, 49*(4), 53–61.

Engwall, M. (2003). No Project Is an Island: Linking Projects to History and Context. *Research Policy, 32*(5), 789–808.

Geraldi, J., Söderlund, J., & van Marrewijk, A. (2021). Bright and Dark Spots in Project Studies: Continuing Efforts to Advance Theory Development and Debate. *Project Management Journal, 52*(3), 227–236.

Hobbs, B., & Aubry, M. (2010). *The project management office: A quest for understanding*. Newtown Square, PA: Project Management Institute.

Müller, R., Drouin, N., & Sankaran, S. (2019). Modeling Organizational Project Management. *Project Management Journal, 50*(4), 499–513.

Project Management Institute. (2013). *PMO framework*. Newtown Square, PA: Project Management Institute.

Sergeeva, N., & Ali, S. (2020). The Role of the Project Management Office (PMO) in Stimulating Innovation in Projects Initiated by Owner and Operator Organizations. *Project Management Journal, 51*(4), 440–451.

Tshuma, B., Steyn, H., & van Waveren, C. C. (2022). The Mediation Role of the PMO in the Transfer of Knowledge between Projects – A Case Study of Five PMOs. *International Journal of Managing Projects in Business, 15*(1), 150–174.

Part VI

Perspectives

Chapter 42: Projectification of society

Yvonne Schoper and Helgi Thor Ingason describe the projectification of society. Projectification is defined as the economic trend of an increasing diffusion of projects as a form of business organisation. This development contains many positive but also some negative changes. Organisations, economies and societies become more flexible and innovative, their capability to solve complex problems and transformations is increased by a sufficiently large amount of capable project managers in an organisation or society, they can be able to better deal with changing environments. On the other hand, the projectification trend means that the role of the workplace as a social institution is changing, and that traditional roles of employers and employees need to be redefined when more people work self-employed. This may lead to the loss of labour law rights and increasing insecurity in the work market. Its impact on societies is still to be researched.

Chapter 43: Quality of life in smart cities

Project managers are in a time of enormous potential as *smart cities* emerge around the world. Some cities have become significant leaders in this area: Amsterdam, Barcelona, and various cities in North America, Australia, and Asia are included in this important group. Their progress has created a legacy of experience and insight that can guide younger cities as they evolve toward their own versions of smartness. The central figure, of course, in smart city efforts has to be the citizen. It is certainly easy to lose track of this all-important stakeholder as emphasis remains on a tech-centric view of city life with data acquisition and system efficiency as hallmarks of progress. Beverly Pasian and Aaron Shenhar focus on the citizens, how they are currently profiled, project types that could enhance their quality of life, and the means to engage them.

DOI: 10.4324/9781003274179-47

Chapter 44: A reflection

Throughout its history, project management has faced three dilemmas: whether you view the project as a system or a process; whether you deliver value or achieve the triple constraint, and whether you adopt flexibility or strict control. Rodney reviews the three dilemmas.

Chapter 42

Projectification of society

Yvonne Schoper and Helgi Thor Ingason

Introduction

Modern project management was developed in the 1960s in industrial sectors like aerospace, aeronautics, defence and construction industry. From here, the effective tools and methods were taken to industries like automotive, mechanical engineering, but also IT, insurance or banking. Today the mindset, procedures, tools and vocabulary of project management are applied in education, public administration and politics. The global trend of projectification that comprises all areas of professional and private life is ubiquitous.

Projectification, the amalgam of "project" and "organisational transformation" describes the diffusion of projects as a form of business organisation (Midler, 1995). Projectification is not only observed in typical project-oriented or project-based industries like the construction industry but also in the public sector, in policy implementation, in performing arts or in scientific research. One can observe an expansion of the concept to all parts of private and societal life. As a consequence, we today speak about the "Project Society", sometimes perceived as the fourth industrial revolution or the next Kondratieff cycle. With the creation of the term "projectification" Midler foresaw in 1995 the phenomenon of the transformation of work in organisations, economies and societies. Projectification can also be seen as organisational capability building in which the project logic is spread in organisations, schools, universities,

DOI: 10.4324/9781003274179-48

administrations and governments through the application of PM practices, which again reinforces the organisational project capacities and capabilities.

A projectified society means that more and more organisational members are defined project workers and project managers, which has an effect on their identity. This trend has an impact on all members of society, starting from the micro level (individuals) to the meso level (organisations), the macro level (industries), the mega level (societies, countries, supranational organisations) and finally the meta-level (global social structures). Projectification is leading from the former permanent, long-term stable organisation towards a temporal limitation of temporary organisations, from a formerly retrospective and control-based orientation towards a prospective orientation not only of the management but of all people in the society.

Because of the fundamental impact on all people in the economy, and in all sectors and parts of the society, projectification can be called a paradigm shift. A characteristic of projectification is that it cannot only be observed in typical project-based industries. With the paradigma "projectification of everything" the concept of projectification is expanded to the individual private and societal life of every human being.

Why are there more and more projects?

There are a couple of reasons for the increase in projects in today´s world. First, there is no consistent use of the term "project". Projects are often used to describe any assignment of endeavour. In one organisation, it depends on the duration, e.g. minimum of four weeks. In another organisation it depends on the number of people involved in a project, e.g. minimum of three or five people. In the next organisation, it depends on the uniqueness of the scope, e.g. to build up a vaccination centre within ten days for a capacity of 5,000 people per day.

Second, it can be observed that any assignment called a "project" seems to sound more attractive to many people, as it gives them more individual responsibility than a regular "task". Many bosses know this and frequently use the term "project" to motivate their employees, even if the assignment is just a common task. The role of the "project manager" is sometimes used as a way to place employees in the salary table, even if managing projects is not a part of their job descriptions.

But there are deeper reasons for the real increase of projects in organisations nowadays. An important explanation for this phenomenon is that the amount of routine work is steadily decreasing due to the ongoing standardisation, automatisation and digitalisation of standard processes and the line work in all departments of an organisation, from HR to production, to sales and logistics. Consequently, there is more free capacity left for new, unique tasks as project work.

Another reason is that products and systems that were created once and that are successful in the market need to be further developed, following the motto: "product success leads to follow-up projects". E.g. a smartphone manufacturer has to further develop a new successor phone as the product contributes to a large extent to the turnover of the company. After one year the current model's sales will stagnate, it will be only sold with massive price reductions. The organisation needs a successor model with new innovations that should be as successful as the predecessor model. The success of the previous product forces an organisation to create a further successful product. The production facilities that were built up for the prior model need to be further utilised, the R&D employees need new challenges, marketing and sales need a new product for the markets, and logistics needs to use their complex IT systems. Projects are the engine to keep any organisation running and growing in the best case. Without projects, an organisation stands still, and a standstill means backlog.

The fifth argument is that projects create the future. Projects are the vehicles of transformation and change. A corporate strategy alone is worthless if there is no project undertaken to implement the ideas into something real: a sustainable new product, a new website, an innovative customer service, the acquisition of another company, new office buildings, a new marketing campaign, new supply chain processes or the implementation of new work methods. The creation of any innovation is based on projects. Every corporate strategy needs a project or program to be realised and implemented.

A further argument is that projects are the means to bring diverse experts together, either from different organisations, departments or functional areas. Today's endeavours are so complex that a group of different specialists is needed to cope with all aspects of the tasks in the right way. Diverse project teams ensure diverse thinking and better decisions, generating innovative solutions.

And finally: the more projects an organisation executes effectively, the more successful the organisation will be. Companies with a high level of innovation success show an above-average share of project activity. In other words, less successful companies do less projects.

One can conclude that the application of project management makes organisations more flexible and innovative, and increases their capability to solve complex problems and deal with the changing environment. There is no future success without projects. More and more executives understand this context and implement and foster project management capabilities in their organisations. This is the reason why such a rapid increase in projects can be seen worldwide. The increasing projectification not only has an impact on the competitiveness of individual firms but also reflects the economic development of an entire economy.

Evidence of projectification in economies

A group of researchers analysed the share of project work on the total working hours in Germany, Norway and Iceland and could show that about one-third of all economic activities in these three countries in 2014 were carried out in the form of projects (Schoper et al., 2018). The forecast for the next five years was a clear increase in project work in all kinds of organisations including public administration. Comparing the share of project work five years ago to the forecast for the next five years shows that in all three economies, the share of project work increased and will continue to rise in the future. The study reinforces the hypothesis of increasing projectification over time (Figure 42.1).

The study shows that although differences exist among the three economies of Germany, Norway and Iceland regarding their size and industry structure, the degree of projectification of advanced economies seems to converge on around one-third of all economic activities. This was the first empirical systematic study that measured the degree of projectification of national economies.

Indications of the broader implications of this development have been reported in the context of the European Union, where its policies strongly influence the projectification process – particularly of the social economy sector in the European countries (Bogacz-Wojtanowska & Jalocha, 2016). Further evidence for the projectification of economies can be identified in the discussion about the fourth industrial revolution and the resulting changes in the business environment. Walker and Lloyd-Walker (2019) wrote about the future of the management of projects in the 2030s and contemplated the impact of contemporary trends such as increased digitalisation, robotics, big data, and artificial intelligence e.g. decision-making – to give a few examples. All these forces – associated with the fourth industrial revolution – will in different ways impact the project worker of

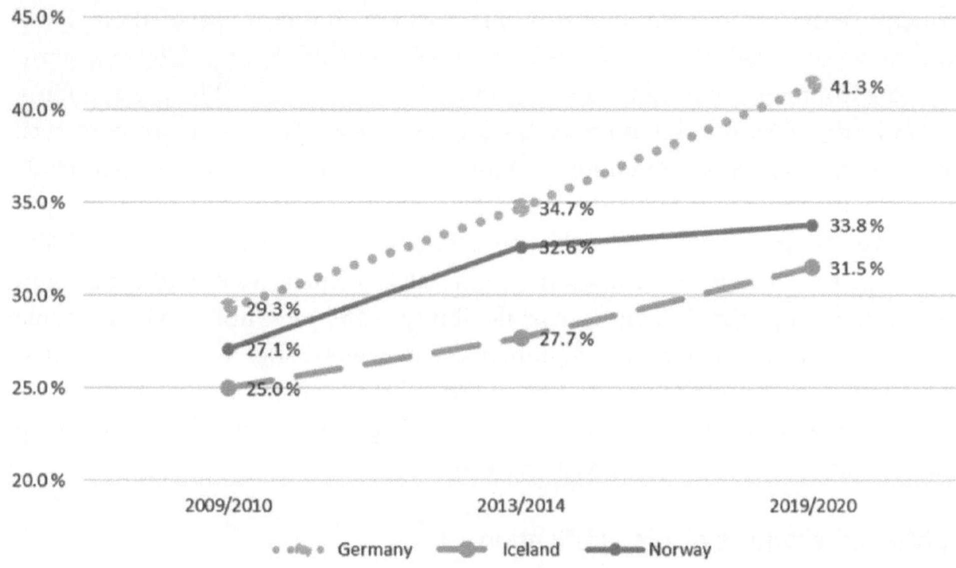

Figure 42.1: Development of projectification in Germany, Norway and Iceland in 2009–2020

the future and in both positive and negative ways affect the work environment. In particular, non-routine roles will become more interesting and rewarding than before whereas routine work is likely to disappear. These are general trends proposed in the reports by the World Economic Forum (2020) on the future of work. The future outlook includes an increased emphasis on the skill sets of the workforce, such as the ability for complex problem solving, critical thinking, creativity and emotional intelligence. It is suggested that major change is on its way for many companies as 45% of businesses plan to reduce their workforce due to technology integration, 41% plan to expand the use of contractors and 34% plan to expand their workforce because of technology integration. Last but not least, many companies plan to change their locations and their value chains. The increased emphasis on contract-based work seems to be aligned with an increased emphasis on distance or remote working. This leads to the need for new skillsets in self-management, active learning, resilience, stress tolerance and flexibility.

The British Association for Project Management (APM) foresees in their future report 2021 that the world is becoming more complex and chaotic and that this calls for more emergent and novel work practices (APM, 2021). A typical representative of this development is the concept of the "gig economy", formerly deriving from the music business where musicians make their living from one paid "gig" to another, which shows the shift from stable, long-term work environments to a short-term, contract-based economy. The gig economy is a projectified economy with project-based, temporary limited work contracts. The evolution of work conditions, economies and societies therefore goes hand-in-hand with the increase of projectification. In today´s times of increasing, partly disruptive transformation, the existence of organisations is based on their ability to manage this change and deliver the right value to their customers at the right cost. In this projectified environment flexibility is the new norm. Many people choose to work on temporary assignments, where networks replace hierarchies, where influence is preferred instead of power, where innovation and creativity are the key to the future and where uncertainty and change are embraced by applying practices that deal with this kind of environment.

Lights and shadows of projectification

Projectification represents a new stage in the evolution of work. This evolution happens fast but silently. It is not managed by a singular force but rather represents the transition of modern societies, where change happens at a fast pace. This evolution can be observed, and it can be monitored and measured, e.g. by its impact on the employee, organisations, national economies and societies.

Projectification is characterised by many positive consequences as it brings great benefits to management e.g. by the optimisation of the economic resources, or to public administration and governments who increasingly define their objectives by annual and multi-annual projects and programs, but it contains also pitfalls and concerns. These are the lights and shadows of projectification for practitioners, organisations and societies.

Although projectification started at the organisation level, it has a great impact on the individual. For individuals working on projects, project work is about high intrinsic motivation, flexibility, a spirit of entrepreneurship and freedom. However, research shows that project work also contains negative aspects such as time pressure to meet the deadlines and the triple constraints, increased stress levels, and excessive control for individuals working on projects. People are not able to separate between work and private life, and as a consequence there are increasing burnout rates which are particularly high among project managers. Increased projectification within the organisations fits well into the enterprise culture since it adapts to prevailing volatile market conditions, but it changes the nature of work for the employees, who are expected to be members of different project teams, in addition to maintaining their more regular roles within the organisations. These factors will become mainstream in the projectified economic environment of modern society. This shows the ambiguous sides of project work for the individual.

A further threat of projectification is the rise of modern slavery in the global economy, and particularly in projects. Modern slavery involves the recruitment, movement, harbouring or receiving of people through any means for the purpose of exploitation. Research by APM in 2020 showed that projects are particularly susceptible to modern slavery as they contain complex flows both of labour and material that need to be reassembled for each project.

Together with projectification goes "projectiflation", a combination of the words "project" and "inflation", introduced by Midler (1995). This means that more and more employees have an education in project management and work as project managers. Project management is thus no distinguishing competence any more.

Projectiflation, neo-liberalism, globalisation, and digitalisation lead to a global economy in which project managers compete for dumping wages without social security. As a consequence, there will be winners and losers of the projectified work, as shown by the classification of "projectocracy" and "projectariat". "Projectocracy" is an amalgam of "project work" and "aristocracy", and means those people involved in projects but enjoying the privileges of stable, unlimited employments (Bogacz-Wojtanowska and Jałocha, 2016). These are experienced project managers, PMO managers or portfolio directors who do not have to hunt for new projects, in comparison to the projectariat, the project workers who are members of the proletariat or precariat class. Indicators for precarious conditions are flexible, instable, non-permanent employment contracts, without the possibility of unionisation, lack of professional identity, many working below their qualification level, those outside normal working hours with limited access to health and unemployment insurance, or a decent pension payment or mortgage loans e.g. for buying an apartment.

In most cases, the training of project managers (if any) consists of attendance of short courses and experimental learning. It can be assumed that the new projectified world needs to be based on a professional approach, and developing training and formal education on different levels will be a challenge in the near future.

On the other hand our perception of the most important knowledge, skills and competencies for project managers is also constantly evolving. Further, emerging challenges for project managers will include the need for a new leadership style, an increase in team members´ emotional management, different communication issues and the motivation of project team members.

But also executives are confronted with projectification. They increasingly understand that projects are the major vehicle to implement corporate strategies. They realise that their success depends on the quality of the projects managed. Research of top executives in Germany´s largest shareholder-based corporations showed that in the sample of executives over 50 years only 30% had their own project management experience, whereas 55% of the top executives below 50 years had their own project expertise as project manager. This demonstrates that project management competence is becoming increasingly important in the boardrooms of corporations.

However, the expansion of project work is challenging traditional organisations. The time aspect of projects contradicts that of traditional calendar planning. A project with its resources is organised to last for a given time. The project timeline relates to a specified goal which is different than the one set by annual company reporting. Furthermore, project work, typically supported by IT, can take place anywhere and most likely in proximity to the customer. This is different from the traditional organisational model, basic conditions for how work is designed and regulated are challenged by this transformation, which leads to stress to central institutions such as labour law and the educational system (Ekstedt, 2018).

The macroeconomic implications of increased project work on the firm level have been studied, there are indications that projectification can have positive implications for production and innovativeness, employment and income. Furthermore, those effects can differ across the sectors of the economy and the increase of projects as vehicles for organising should therefore be applied with care, with an optimal mix of project and non-project work (Henning & Wald 2019).

Conclusion

Projectification and the gig-based economy are not necessarily the same, but both developments are much related. The transformation towards a gig economy includes areas of uncertainty, new dynamics and a redefinition of the traditional roles of employers and employees. The agreement between employee and employer may be changing. More and more people are likely to become self-employed as project workers. Instead of working for an employer, people sell their services to firms and this contractual relationship is based on platforms that are uncertain. In the best case, the gig economy can be a good development as people can choose their projects based on their skills and knowledge.

However, there are many negative consequences of this trend, e.g. the loss of labour law rights, e.g. instance maternity leaves, further payment for sick days, and planning insecurity in the work market where people do not know what happens after they deliver their project. People risk taking on too many projects to avoid being without a job, thus increasing their level of stress. People are forced to take more self-responsibility, e.g. regarding training, professional development and continuous education. The role of the traditional workplace as a social institution is consequently changing. The social and societal consequences of the loss of this institution are still unclear.

Projectification has great means and contains ambivalent aspects for individuals, organisations, societies, social institutions and for nations. The analysis shows that there could be several winners of projectification. The winners could be the projectocracy, the executives in the organisations, the organisations as they are gaining more flexibility and competitiveness, the project management associations, the public sector, the societies and finally the national economies, gaining a higher degree of flexibility, innovativeness and wealth, important competitive factors in the global competition not only between individuals and organisations, but also between national economies. The losers of the projectification trend could be the individuals working in unstable work employment conditions (the projectariat), and the social welfare systems breaking down by the increasing instability and non-predictability. Both sides of the projectification medal need to be reconciled to achieve good conditions for all stakeholders in the future project societies.

We suggest that there should be a stronger influence of the institutions to steer and control this transformation that will have a large impact on all members, and a profound education of the individuals to prevent their exploitation. We finally point out that project management has been criticised as a capitalist masculine management practice. It is therefore the task of the organisations to further develop the discipline so that it becomes a more human-oriented, sustainable management practice, not built upon the exploitation of human and natural resources.

References and further reading

APM (2020). Eliminating modern slavery from projects. URL: https://www.apm.org.uk/media/47794/modern-slavery-final.pdf

APM (2021). Future trends. URL: https://www.apm.org.uk/salary-survey-2021/future-trends/

Bogacz-Wojtanowska, E. & Jałocha, B. (2016). The bright side of the social economy sector's projectification: a study of successful social enterprises, *Project Management Research and Practice*, 3(July–December 2016).

Cicmil, S. & Hodgson, D. (2006). New possibilities for Project Management theory: a critical engagement, *Project Management Journal* (August 2006), 37, pp. 111–122.

Ekstedt, E. (2018). Project work, a challenge to traditional work life institutions, *International Journal of Managing Projects in Business.*

Henning, C. H. & Wald, A. (2019). Toward a wiser projectification: macroeconomic effects of firm-level project work, *International Journal of Project Management*, 37(6), 807–819.

Jensen, A., Thuesen, C. & Geraldi, J. (2016). The projectification of everything: projects as a human condition, *Project Management Journal*, 47(3), pp. 21–34.

Lundin, R. Arvidsson, N., Brady, T., Ekstedt, E., Midler, C. & Sydow, J. (2015). Managing and working in project society: institutional challenges of temporary organizations.

Maylor, H. & Turkulainen, V. (2019). The concept of organisational projectification: past, present and beyond? *International Journal of Managing Projects in Business.*

Midler, C. (1995). "Projectification" of the firm: the Renault case, *Scandinavian Journal of Management*, 11(4, December 1995), pp. 363–375.

Schoper, Y. G., Wald, A., Ingason, H. T. & Fridgeirsson, T. V. (2018). Projectification in Western economies: a comparative study of Germany, Norway and Iceland, *IJPM*, 36, pp. 71–82.

Walker, D. & Lloyd-Walker, B. (2019). The future of the management of projects in the 2030s, *International Journal of Managing Projects in Business*, 12(2), pp. 242–266.

World Economic Forum. (2020, October). *The future of jobs report 2020*. Geneva.

Chapter 43

Quality of life in smart cities

Beverly Pasian and Aaron Shenhar

Introduction

Project managers are in a time of enormous potential as *smart cities* emerge around the world. Despite no universal definition, more than 20 years have passed since the introduction of this unique concept and cities being built. Some cities have become significant leaders in this area: Amsterdam, Barcelona, and various cities in North America, Australia, and Asia are included in this important group. Their progress has created a legacy of experience and insight that can guide younger cities as they evolve toward their own versions of smartness. With books such as this, conferences, and the increasing presence of smart cities in professional associations, project managers have immediate opportunities to learn from their smart city predecessors as they build new cities for the future.

The central figure, of course, in smart city efforts has to be the citizen. It is certainly easy to lose track of this all-important stakeholder as emphasis remains on a tech-centric view of city life with data acquisition and system efficiency as hallmarks of progress. This chapter will focus on the citizen, how they are currently profiled, project types that could enhance their quality of life, and means to engage them. But first, let's set the context.

 DOI: 10.4324/9781003274179-49

What makes a city smart?

Researchers or project managers in the world of smart cities will tell you that there is no universal definition. It's even reasonable to consider 'smart' simply as a media-friendly word that elevates modern urban development to an ideal that, while never achievable, is a helpful guide. Much like project management maturity, the status of a smart city can be mistakenly seen in binary terms when in fact, the state of 'smartness' is an evolving one and dependent on the collaborative interactions of various stakeholders.

Amongst professional associations such as the IPMA (ipma.world), the IEEE (ieee.org) and the ISO (iso.org), definitions are complex and open to wide interpretation. IPMA (Wagner, 2018) defines smart cities as

> A 'Smart City' is one that... dramatically increases the pace at which it improves its social economic and environmental (sustainability) outcomes, responding to challenges such as climate change, rapid population growth, and political and economic instability... by fundamentally improving how it engages society, how it applies collaborative leadership methods, how it works across disciplines and city systems, and how it uses data information and modern technologies... in order to provide better services and quality of life to those in and involved with the city (residents, businesses, visitors), now and for the foreseeable future, without unfair disadvantage of others or degradation of the natural environment.

The International Standards Organization – which has published multiple standards concerning smart and sustainable cities and quality of life – considers a smart city to be one

> that increases the pace at which it provides social, economic and environmental sustainability outcomes and responds to challenges such as climate change, rapid population growth, and political and economic instability by fundamentally improving how it engages society, applies collaborative leadership methods, works across disciplines and city systems, and uses data information and modern technologies to deliver better services and quality of life to those in the city (residents, businesses, visitors), now and for the

> foreseeable future, without unfair disadvantage of others or degradation of the natural environment.
>
> (ISO, 2022)

Such complexity in a definition makes them inherently problematic. What does it mean to remove or adjust a term? Does that, in this case, suggest that a city is less smart? Clarity and simplicity are best and, in the case of a smart city, key principles to which everyone can agree. A clear definition is that... *a smart city is one that continuously improves the quality of life of its citizen*s. And while this is helpful, readers might also benefit from understanding some features of cities that satisfy this definition. Some features include:

- Clear vision statements supplemented by other policies or documents which provide a holistic explanation of a city's planning and development efforts. Progressive cities communicate a holistic approach that shows their understanding of the implications of their smart city choices. The city of Utrecht (The Netherlands) addresses privacy, justice, human dignity, safety, and health (among others) through its *Ethical Value Model.* The city of Bilbao (Spain) released a similar document – *Bilbao Charter Of Values* – which makes clear its commitment to human rights within a smart city context. Among these are social justice, solidarity, diversity and inclusion, social justice, and natural environmental sustainability.
- A single project or program typically dominates a smart city. Often characterised by clear partnerships between researchers, industry partners, and citizen groups, this collaboration (also known as a quadruple helix) lies at the heart of such a project. Many examples can be found throughout Europe and funded by EU funding programs dedicated specifically to smart city development. ***+CityxChange*** *(Positive City Exchange)* is an example of such a marquee project that combines the cities of Limerick, Trondheim, Alba Lulia, Pisek, Sestao, Smolyan and Voru to design and integrate energy solutions. and between the research, industry, and stakeholder collaboration marquee projects often set a smart city apart.
- Leading cities are also characterized by the detailed and comprehensive public release of this information through traditional and social media. Gone are the days when single points of contact (a project manager or public affairs officer)

could provide a full picture of their city's efforts. Project changes are so frequent that websites, YouTube videos, conference presentations, and often high-quality third-party media are reliable sources of detailed information. And as a smart city is intrinsically in the public's interest, the responsibility for ongoing information provision is taken seriously.

- Leadership/management often originates from or is aligned with an innovation office or technology department. They may or may not be project professionals, are typically quite recent to the position, or are staffed according to a funded project. The relative youth of smart city efforts explains these last two characteristics.
- Citizen engagement is necessary and will come in different forms that are often codified and published to demonstrate the transparency of a city's efforts. Trondheim (Norway) provides an excellent example of this through its *City Participation Playbook*. Citizen engagement is, however, particularly vulnerable to criticism. The absence of such bottom-up activities can indicate a top-down approach to a city's planning efforts. Moreover, when participants are particularly adept at technology-centric projects or discussions the absence of people who are less so – likely members of the ageing population or new immigrants to the city – can contribute to a growing divide between technology 'haves' and 'have nots.' The city of Calgary (Canada) shows the sensitivity through its *Digital Equity Strategy* where steps are taken to ensure the absence of technological access or knowledge doesn't contribute to a digital divide in the community.

What is a smart city project?

As with smart cities, a specific or common definition of a smart city project is unavailable. Publications have offered characterizations of a smart city project in organizational or industry scenarios along with specific taxonomies. Van Winden and van den Buuse (2017) focus on the fields of energy and mobility where pilot projects are specifically used to facilitate the upscaling of processes in the rollout, expansion, or replication of city services. They suggest that smart city projects are 'fascinating new arenas where different urban stakeholders engage in coalitions and innovate together.' Yigitcanlar et al. (2018) offer a grander but more critical view by characterizing smart city projects as 'big and expensive capital investments supposed to drive societal and environmental transformations… very hard to deliver.' Meijer and Thaens (2016) emphasize the more 'collaborative and symbolic value of smart city projects, and advocate their evaluation on that basis and not only based on their technological or instrumental value.'

Conversely, Rosati and Conti (2016) use the term smart city project to describe a movement toward a new urban model. It could, they posit, 'allow for a reinvention of its territories (referring to Mediterranean Europe) connecting the concept of smart city and smart land.' They could be 'supported by integrated, forward-looking strategic plans, useful in defining a vision and a methodology for the future development of a city' (Angelidou, 2017). Moving beyond the individual project, attempts have been made to classify smart city projects in taxonomies. On the basis of a relatively small sample with a scope limited to 27 projects, Perboli et al. (2014) classify projects on the basis of their description (as determined by objectives, tools, project initiator, and stakeholders), business model, and purpose. The views of project managers themselves were recently offered but its value is similarly unclear. Bjørner (2021) 'suggests' that a smart city project includes dynamic constructs that are covered in the city [by] taking knowledge, context, interactions, foundation, time, and space into account.

Despite all of these attempts, a smart city project can be defined quite simply… it is an instrument that has a high impact on the quality of life for citizens. It becomes a question of societal value…does the smart city project provide value in the urban environment? The relevance of societal value has been seen beyond smart cities where the success of megaprojects, for example, has been partially based on high societal impact (Shenhar & Holzmann, 2017). The Sydney Opera House, the 2012 Summer Olympic Park, and the Rijks Museum of Amsterdam are just a few examples where the host cities are regularly listed amongst the 'smartest' in the world. But what could project value mean in the specific context of a smart city project?

It's important to make the distinction between these two elements, as both 'project' and 'value' are quite specific and open to numerous interpretations. Martinsuo et al. (2019) recently addressed this by saying that delivering value is meant as

> the activities, processes, and strategies that organizations use to produce benefits at a reasonable cost, either in specific projects or through project business in general…Projects are not merely intended for their immediate deliverables and satisfaction of scope, time and cost goals but are also used to produce benefits and outcomes over the lifecycle of the project deliverable.

Emergent smart city project typology

In the realm of smart cities, one can consider *value in context* where it might be shaped or seen as an extension societal need…or more specifically, quality of life. To this end, a smart city project typology can be proposed characterized by features that maximizes impact on quality of life for all citizens. Several characteristics are described below (Table 43.1):

Current smart city project activity around the world indicates the emergence of certain themes that support quality of life on the basis of one or more of the above characteristics. These themes are provided below along with examples. Such themes serve as the basis for a *smart city project typology* (Table 43.2).

Such projects need coalitions of support from the time of their conception and design. Ideas can come from anywhere but it's only when the diverse collaboration of some or all of the groups below can success occur.

Smart city project stakeholders

While there will be greater or lesser presence depending on the city, the following categories are offered along with examples of their influence, risks and suggestions for working with them.

Elected officials

The visibility an elected official can bring to a smart city project can be enormous. They are often responsible for financial allocations and are the final decision-makers in policy discussions or implementations. Even more important than these operational tasks is the public awareness that they can bring to a smart city project. A politician who is also an advocate for active urban development is invaluable.

Civil servants

Has anyone who has worked in government can attest that while elected officials can make headlines it is really the civil servants that manage City Hall. A candidate or elected official can promise all manner of projects, but without the direct support of social servants promises are hollow. These roles often take the

Table 43.1 Characteristics

Feature	*Explanation*	*Example*
Timing of impact	The temporal impact of some projects might be immediate while others (typically longer to implement) also have a longer influence on quality of life.	Tree planting along a cycling or pedestrian path will likely have an immediate impact on citizens (within days or weeks). A new bridge, road, or other transportation infrastructure will take longer to implement but longer impact on users (years).
Directness to user	Not all projects are directly connected to a citizen or other user.	Street lighting is pervasive and available without any intermediary element. Housing developments, while of universal relevance, are subject to multiple conditions for acquisition.
Potential for secondary outcomes	Smart city projects have the potential for enormous ranges of secondary outcomes beyond their stated purpose.	Facilitating government access, improving learning opportunities, monitoring weather impacts, and maximizing employment possibilities are just a few associated with Wi-Fi installations. Conversely, a street festival or other cultural events might appear to have a single goal in mind (of providing a leisurely activity) when in fact the cultivation of goodwill between the city and entire communities is the ultimate outcome.
Gender sensitivity	A project should be designed to reflect gender realities associated with everyday life within urban spaces.	Neighbourhood safety projects could benefit certain genders more than others.

(Continued)

Table 43.1 (Continued)

Feature	*Explanation*	*Example*
User fee	Some projects are dependent on a fee, membership, or other subscription type. Others are made widely available with no user-based associated fee. One could argue that introducing mandatory requirements negatively impacts quality of life given questions of affordability.	The provision of electric cars reflects a city's growing responsibility towards aggregated environmental sustainability. Specific usage however is entirely dependent on a citizen or visitor's ability to pay the associated expenses.

Table 43.2 Themes

Quality-of-life theme	*Project examples*
Housing	Availability of affordable new residential housing for purchase and renting
Work and economic value	Employment and business offerings and potential
Transportation and mobility	Accessible and quick transportation options, buses, trains, bike routes, roads and parking
Health	Health facilities and services (across ages, genders, residency status)
Education and learning	High-quality schools, teachers, and educational facilities; adult education
Safety	Safe neighbourhoods and low crime rates
Environment	Clean air, water, and any initiatives in support of the United Nations SDG
Leisure	Recreational facilities, beaches, Parks, shopping malls, cinemas, fitness clubs, zoos, amusement parks, Walking trails

(Continued)

Table 43.2 (Continued)

Quality-of-life theme	*Project examples*
Beauty	Landscaping, decorative lighting, and sidewalk treatments
Culture	Agreements with museums, galleries, theatres or historical organizations
Social justice	Support to or protect underprivileged communities, LGBTQ recognition, and support
Spirituality	Activities that provide spiritual guidance and/or contribute to the maintenance of the faith-based built environment
Civic engagement	Information, facilities, and systems that maximize access to and transparency of government services

form of the chief information officer, the chief technology officer, and smart city program manager. In fact, it is often the smart city manager that emerges from a relationship with the CIO.

The institutional memory contained within the civil service is of enormous influence. Understanding successes and failures of the past, case constituencies, and the political landscape can make the top of a servant arguably more influential than the elected official. Cultivating relationships independent of an election cycle is a strategic move that can occur at any time and with long-term benefits.

Neighbourhood associations

A committed group of citizens organized to the point of an association or lobbying group is a formidable instrument. It can be (and has been) in smart city projects to halt or encourage progress. In Amsterdam, for example, the Fietsersbond (Dutch Cycling Union) successfully protected the historic bike path despite its presence literally *in the middle* of the renovation project of the Rijksmuseum (Higgins, 2013).

A different story can be seen in the City of Toronto, however, where the ambitious 'smart city experiment' led by Sidewalk Labs (a firm within Google) has been abandoned. While justifying its decision as a consequence of the economic uncertainty during the current coronavirus pandemic (Carter et al., 2020), the criticism of citizen groups has been influential throughout the 2.5 years of the project (Oliveira, 2018). Assessing the role of citizen-as-end-user smart city projects is one of the clearest examples of seeing the true impact of responsible project management.

University partners

Typically, neighbours to smart city residents, universities, or technical colleges are often essential partners to City Hall smart city projects. Beyond educating generations of technical and socially oriented students who can influence smart city development, universities can offer a neutral location for stakeholder interaction, provide researchers to push the boundaries of innovation, and serve as funding partners. Along with public authorities, industry, and citizens, universities are a key element of the 'quadruple helix' framework (Carayannis & Campbell, 2009) often seen in the innovation projects of climate change and smart cities.

Public-private partnerships

The world of smart cities is populated by many examples of public-private collaborations that often manifest in an agency or a form of third-party corporation. These can be owned by the city or municipality, and always include partnerships across multiple government departments, industry or business partners, and local research institutes. In Europe, the cities of Vienna, Amsterdam, and Barcelona are stellar examples of this practice, along with Chicago and New York in the US. Readers are encouraged to visit their official city websites for more information.

Industry partners

The building of smart cities has brought new challenges to traditional industry while at the same time introducing new players. Infrastructure partners, construction firms, and engineering and architecture firms are all ongoing and active project team players. The advantages they bring to the table are rooted largely in the depth of their experience managing projects, the relationships they might have with City Hall, and their realistic understanding of the demands of the built environment. On the other hand, such depth of knowledge can create an unwillingness to be innovative. Supporting developmental housing projects, for example, might not occur with some construction firms unwilling to participate in social justice projects.

New partners have entered smart city relationships which can often serve as neutral third parties and advocates for open science. *Eurocities*, for example, has been building a network of cities for the sole purpose of supporting quality-of-life projects. While strictly speaking not a government agency their influence since the mid-80s can be seen across Europe as a networking platform that brings commercial and speciality players from across the smart city development spectrum.

Professional associations

The project management community benefits from decades-old professional associations whose sole purpose is to raise the quality skills and knowledge of their professional members. The *International Project Management Association*, for example, created a special interest group in 2018 which focuses entirely on smart cities. Similarly, the Institute of Electric and Electronics Engineers (ieee.org) has a 'society' entirely devoted to smart cities ('IEEE Smart Cities'). Both organizations take a holistic and increasingly human view of the nature of smart city projects. They are both technically oriented associations, but understand that both the city and its projects are ultimately meant to improve citizens' lives. (At the time of this writing, the Project Management Institute did not have a specific smart city focus.)

Citizens: project and smart

Of course, the citizen is the primary stakeholder of any smart city project and deserves special attention in this chapter. The notion of a citizen in a project context has recently been highlighted as a 'bright spot' in need of greater attention (Geraldi et al., 2021). As 'someone who lives within and through projects,' project citizens differ from smart citizens in two important ways. The first concerns involvement or engagement (discussed above) and the second concerns project value where, in a smart city context, the value has to be found in the quality-of-life impact of the project. In a smart city, the citizen-as-end-user is impossible to ignore and often not fully understood (Vanolo, 2016) but sufficient research and project experiences have been documented, however, to see the emergence of some citizen profiles.

Engagement can be drastically influenced by the perception one might have of the citizen. Research on smart city projects shows different characterizations or categories of this broader group. Some are understandably hopeful, while others are surprisingly negative. Table 43.3 below contains the exact language used to describe citizen participants from projects around the world. Each word has been used to finish the phrase 'citizen as...'

What can a project manager do in situations where the personality of the key stakeholder can vary so widely? Being aware of the possibilities is the first step and understanding the dynamics affecting these personality types is another. It's only from a position of understanding that specific and meaningful action can occur. Considering stakeholder (citizen) engagement and project impact on QoL (the differences noted earlier), these citizen types can be positioned in a matrix for further understanding and possible action. Figure 43.1 below combines citizen types in a unique model that reflects this.

With these possibilities, the question becomes... what can project managers do to move their citizens to the highest quadrant of this matrix and become an advocate for their smart city projects? An influential and leading smart city experience is described below.

Table 43.3 Collection of smart citizen descriptors (author)

Absentee	Creative city dweller	Problem-solver
Active party	Educator	Rights' advocate
Client	Entrepreneur	Sensor
Collaborator	Expert	Service user
Commuter	Foil	Student
Consumer	'Have-not'	Subject
Container	Host	Tourist
Contributor	Innovator	User
Cosmopolitan	Participant	Victim

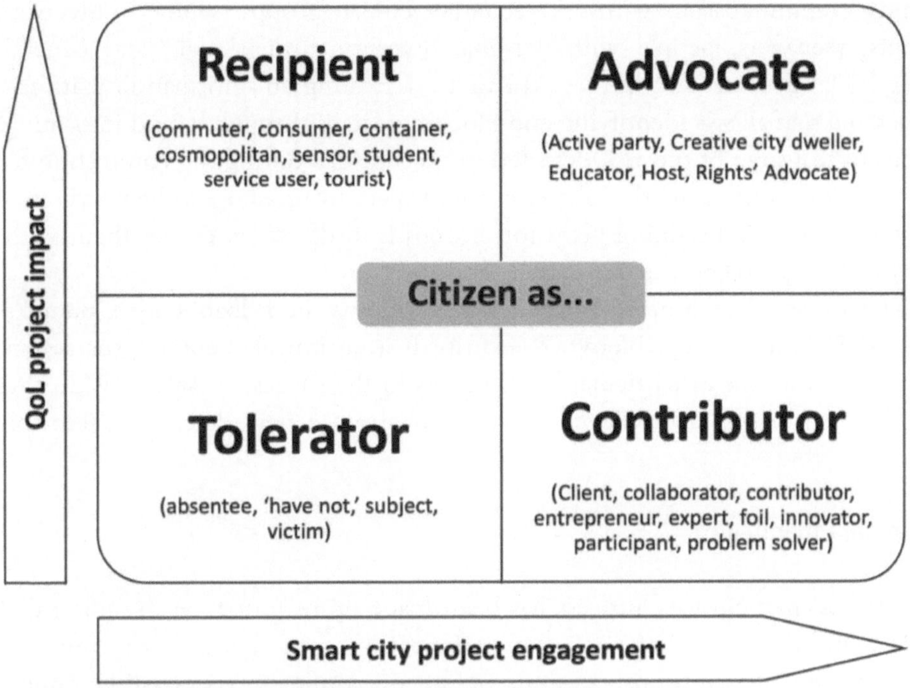

Figure 43.1: Citizen impact-engagement matrix (authors)

Bilbao: an example of robust citizen engagement

The Bilbao smart city approach included a range of engagement opportunities and techniques that have directly supported its mission to increase quality of life. Examples of critical city actions show that through consistent, long-term, and transparent activities, citizens can be turned into advocates of smart city innovation.

Cybersecurity for citizens

In the 'Cybersecurity for Citizens' project, citizens participated from the beginning. From the design, problem clarification and the technological solution citizens incorporated their vision as the end user of the service. In addition, they contrasted this project with agents such as the cybersecurity centre, and policy offices via multiple workshops to identify the key elements of the project.

Coming communication with several target citizen groups: seniors, university students, teenagers, people with personal diversity, professionals, and general citizens. The cybersecurity project is based on creating an information platform in real time that allows identifying and blocking details through it, and informing citizens in real time of this risk detected in their device during the connection to the municipal Wifi network. Likewise, the project integrated excellent cybersecurity awareness and training plans for citizens in order to empower them with tools for their protection in the digital world.

The cybersecurity project became a key priority in Bilbao City Council's Citizens' Security Policy. Network security is a critical element for society in general, and citizens in particular, and, thanks to the success of Bilbao Wifi, the City Council was in a privileged position to create a new defence system for citizens.

Bilbao data manifesto

The citizens' participatory process has been made up of four facets: sending the Bilbao Data Manifesto draft to agents participating in the participatory process; designing, sending, and analyzing an online questionnaire; contrasting online workshops; and face-to-face co-creation workshops. Regarding the online questionnaire, multiple agents were involved who had a significant interest in part of the participatory process including external organizations, municipal entities of Bilbao City Council, and the staff of the Technological Society of Bilbao City Council. Additionally, three online contrast workshops were carried out along with two workshops with external organizations and one workshop with municipal entities. The weaknesses detected by citizens were of special interest to the Bilbao City Council specifically the use of their data (privacy) and the use of ambiguous language. The visual design of the document was considered unattractive with long paragraphs that demand to be more precise in the wording. As it is the Manifesto of Bilbao, it had to be consistent with the character and the identity of the city and of the people who live in it.

Participatory budget

The participatory budget of Bilbao was an open process through which the residents of Bilbao could make their proposal on how to spend a part of the municipal budget. Participants included any person registered in Bilbao over 16 years of age, along with any entity registered in the 'Municipal Register of Citizen Participation Entities' (including but not limited to unions, business associations, professional associations, and public law corporations). Relevant proposals of general interest could be submitted at the city or district level (with some stipulations including that the content was legal, not defamatory or discriminatory, and associated with an area of action or municipal competencies in matters of public expansion). The amount associated with each proposal could not exceed 500,000 euros. Proposals were submitted through a form established on this municipal website and presentation opportunities were offered to many.

Principles of engagement

For cities still in the early stages of smart city development and smart city project definition, it has been shown that key engagement principles can have an enormous impact. Platforms or working groups can be truly facilitative but not all city managers can achieve such formal activity. Having said that, project managers can cultivate an environment where the ethos of facilitation is present even in the absence of a formal mechanism. Some steps to achieve this include:

- Values promotion: The creation and use of communication tools that reflect a city's values and principles. In smart city environments and initiatives, engagement should reflect the traits that citizens hold most dear about their city and life within it. Project managers should take every opportunity to remind them that these are motivating factors in all project work.
- Representative diversity: Beyond obvious demographic and economic categories, project managers need to see true representation at their project tables of population diversity. The notion of a "general public" is inaccurate and inappropriate for the smart city project table. Who are the groups on the margins of the city? Who are the anticipated arrivals? Who may not have technological access and need extra help? These are only some of the basic questions that project managers can ask.
- Transparency: This principle cannot be emphasized enough. From the moment a proposed project is available for public reaction and right on through to the testing and implementation of project deliverables, information about smart city projects needs to be at the fingers or footsteps of the impacted citizens.

- Multilingualism: naturally the dominant language of the city must be reflected, but a project manager must also consider stakeholders beyond the 'typical citizen.' Ask yourself what languages are spoken by immigrants to your city? Or are they members of the ageing population?
- In-person information delivery: relying on the digital delivery of information will unavoidably exclude some citizens from understanding the cities' developments. Traditional, in-person delivery of information should always be a part of project activities. Why? Because the need for human contact will never go away.

Conclusion

The world of smart cities is growing daily and without clarity around its definition or project focus. Despite this, the richness of experiences from some leading cities shows certain key truths: improving quality of life is the most important goal and citizens need to be engaged to achieve this. This chapter provides insights, examples, and specific tools to do this.

References and further reading

Angelidou, M. (2017). The Role of Smart City Characteristics in the Plans of Fifteen Cities. *Journal of Urban Technology*, *24*(4), 3–28. https://doi.org/10.1080/10630732.2017.1348880

Bjørner, T. (2021). The Advantages of and Barriers to being Smart in a Smart City: The Perceptions of Project Managers within a Smart City Cluster Project in Greater Copenhagen. *Cities*, *114*, 103187. https://doi.org/10.1016/j.cities.2021.103187

Carayannis, E., & Campbell, D. F. (2009). 'Mode 3' and 'Quadruple Helix': Toward a 21st Century Fractal Innovation Ecosystem. *International Journal of Technology Management*, *46*, 201–234.

Carter, A., & Rieti, J. (2020). Sidewalk Labs Cancels Plan to Build High-Tech Neighbourhood in Toronto Amid COVID-19. | *CBC News*. 10:31 AM ET | Last Updated (2020, May 7). https://www.cbc.ca/news/canada/toronto/sidewalk-labs-cancels-project-1.5559370

Geraldi, J., Söderlund, J., & van Marrewijk, A. (2021). Bright and Dark Spots in Project Studies: Continuing Efforts to Advance Theory Development and Debate. *Project Management Journal*, *52*(3), 227–236. https://doi.org/10.1177/87569728211004064

Higgins, Charlotte. (2013, April 5). Rijksmuseum to Reopen after Dazzling Refurbishment and Rethink. *The Guardian*. https://www.theguardian.com/culture/2013/apr/05/rijksmuseum-reopens-long-refurbishment-rethink

ISO, (2022). Smart City Definition (ISO). In *Online Browsing Platform*. International Standards Organisation. https://www.iso.org/obp/ui/#iso:std:iso:37122:ed-1:v1:en

Martinsuo, M., Klakegg, O. J., & van Marrewijk, A. (2019). Editorial: Delivering Value in Projects and Project-Based Business. *Delivering Value in Projects and Project-Based Business*, *37*(5), 631–635. https://doi.org/10.1016/j.ijproman.2019.01.011

Meijer, A., & Thaens, M. (2016). Urban Technological Innovation: Developing and Testing a Sociotechnical Framework for Studying Smart City Projects. *Urban Affairs Review*, *54*(2), 363–387. https://doi.org/10.1177/1078087416670274

Oliveira, M. (2018, May 2). *Critics Decry Lack of 'Democratic Participation' Over Sidewalk Labs' Proposed Neighbourhood*. Thestar.Com. https://www.thestar.com/news/gta/2018/05/02/critics-decry-lack-of-democratic-participation-over-sidewalk-labs-proposed-neighbourhood.html

Perboli, G., De Marco, A., Perfetti, F., & Marone, M. (2014). A New Taxonomy of Smart City Projects. *Transportation Research Procedia*, *3*, 470–478.

Rosati, U., & Conti, S. (2016). What Is a Smart City Project? An Urban Model or a Corporate Business Plan? *Procedia Social and Behavioral Sciences*, *223*, 968–973.

Shenhar, A., & Holzmann, V. (2017). The Three Secrets of Megaproject Success: Clear Strategic Vision, Total Alignment, and Adapting to Complexity. *Project Management Journal*, *48*(6), 29–46. https://doi.org/10.1177/875697281704800604

van Winden, W., & van den Buuse, D. (2017). Smart City Pilot Projects: Exploring the Dimensions and Conditions of Scaling Up. *Journal of Urban Technology*, *24*(4), 51–72. https://doi.org/10.1080/10630732.2017.1348884

Vanolo, A. (2016). Is There Anybody Out There? The Place and Role of Citizens in Tomorrow's Smart Cities. *Futures*, *82*. https://doi.org/10.1016/j.futures.2016.05.010

Wagner, R. (2018). *Realizing Smart Cities through Professional Project, Programme and Portfolio Management* (No. 01; IPMA Insights, p. 51). Zurich: IPMA.

Yigitcanlar, T., Kamruzzaman, Md., Buys, L., Ioppolo, G., Sabatini-Marques, J., da Costa, E. M., & Yun, J. J. (2018). Understanding 'Smart Cities': Intertwining Development Drivers with Desired Outcomes in a Multidimensional Framework. *Cities*, *81*, 145–160. https://doi.org/10.1016/j.cities.2018.04.003

Chapter 44

A reflection

Rodney Turner

Introduction

In this chapter, I consider three alternative perspectives of project management that have developed throughout its history

- Systems versus process
- Delivering value versus the triple constraint
- Flexibility versus control

This reflection was stimulated by the Association of Project Management's much-delayed 50th anniversary, which was eventually held at the University of Leeds in April 2003.

Systems versus process

The first pair of perspectives is the systems approach versus the process approach. As the theory of project management initially developed in the United States, they took a systems approach, reflected in the book by David Cleland and Bill King (1983), and the work of Harold Kerzner (2017). A project was viewed as a system, and a systems analysis approach was taken to their management. In Europe

DOI: 10.4324/9781003274179-50

we viewed a project as a process (Gareis, and Stummer, 2008; Turner, 2014, first edition 1993). We describe the process approach in Chapter 19. There are three main types of processes on a project:

- The investment process, focused on delivering project success, to deliver the investment the project makes, and the value and benefit it produces.
- The project process, applying the methodology to its delivery.
- The project management process, focused on delivering project management success, doing the work of the project to deliver the desired project output to time and cost.

Rodney was somewhat surprised when the Project Management Institute in their Guide to the Project Management Body of Knowledge, from the pre-edition (1987) to the sixth edition (2017), took a process approach. They mainly focused on the project management process, describing what needed to be done for each of the nine body of knowledge areas at the five steps in the process. However, in the seventh edition, they have reverted to a systems approach. As we shall say below, they now focus more on delivering value than finishing on time, cost, and performance, so they focus more on the investment process. But primarily they describe a systems analysis approach to achieving value on projects.

Delivering value versus the triple constraint

The second pair of perspectives is delivering value and benefit versus finishing the work of the project in accordance with the triple constraint, of time cost, and performance. In Chapter 2 we give three definitions of projects. The first is from the seventh edition of PMI's Guide to the Body of Knowledge (2021):

> A project is a temporary effort to create value through a unique product, service or result.

This says the primary purpose of the project is to deliver value, and it leads them to emphasise the investment process. It is about achieving project success, delivering the project outcome, and the benefits desired from the project. On the other hand, the Association for Project Management in its body of knowledge (2019) says:

> A project is an endeavour to deliver specific objectives subject to defined acceptance criteria, and those objectives should be delivered within constraints of time and cost.

So it is about delivering the desired project outcome to time and cost targets, achieving the triple constraint. This is project management success. The emphasis will be on the project management process to manage the work. The third definition we give in Chapter 2 is by Rodney Turner and Ralf Müller (2003):

> A project is a temporary organization to which resources are assigned to deliver beneficial change.

The middle of this definition talks about managing resources to do the work of the project to deliver the desired output, the change, but the end talks about delivering the outcome to achieve the benefit. It does not specifically talk about finishing on time cost and quality, but it does mention the management of the resources, and cost.

So since the early 1960s, the primary emphasis of project management has been on delivering the desired project output to time and cost constraints. During the 1950s the emphasis was on getting the work done to achieve the desired objectives. Time was important because the Americans were in an arms race. But the cost suffered somewhat. In the early 1960s, as we will see again below, the new Defence Secretary, Robert McNamara, insisted on achieving the triple constraint. What is ignored is it is usually possible to achieve two of the three. Achieving all three is in your dreams. However, the focus, as illustrated by the seventh edition of the PMI Guide to the Body of Knowledge, the emphasis is moving towards delivering value and benefit. Time and cost are important, because the project must make a profit. But it is acceptable to finish late and overspend if the project still makes a profit. People also now take much greater account of non-financial benefits. We use the example of the Gotthard Base Tunnel. Because of problems with the geology, the project was 25% late and 25% overspent. But it delivered a very worthwhile outcome. It reduced the journey time between Milan and Zurich, made for a much more comfortable ride, and enabled freight the be shifted from road to rail. The project made a profit so it was an investment success, though it was late and overspent.

Flexibility versus control

The third perspective is the difference between adopting a flexible approach and requiring greater control. As we said above, during the 1940s and 1950s, during times of war and the arms race, the emphasis was on getting the project finished to deliver the desired output. Cost suffered. Barry Klein and William Meckling (1958) wrote a now-famous paper about weapons systems development. They identified two people whom they labelled the Optimist and the Sceptic. The optimist assumes they know what the outcome of the project will be and how it will be achieved. Quickly closes down all other options and works towards the assumed output. Klein and Meckling say that will lead to the cheapest outcome if Optimists are right, but they are usually somewhat off the mark. Change and scope creep will lead to inflating costs. The Sceptic on the other hand, assumes the precise nature of the output is not known, and so maintains several options. As work is done, options can be closed and merged, as they work towards the actual result. If the Optimist is right, this will lead to a more expensive outcome but will lead to less change and scope creep, so will usually be cheaper.

When he became Secretary of Defence under President Kennedy in the early 1960s, Robert McNamara said there must be much greater control of cost. The emphasis became to follow the route of the Optimist. Define the project output as quickly as possible and freeze the design. And define how it will be achieved. This was thought to be necessary on fixed-price contracts. The emphasis was on achieving time, cost, and performance, and it was what the project management professional associations preached. T was about achieving the triple constraint.

However, as suggested by Klein and Meckling, the evidence was it didn't achieve the desired outcome. If you move quickly to design freeze, you lock yourself into expensive solutions. In the 1990s, the evidence was that if you leave uncertainty open for longer, you can achieve outcomes that are 30%–50% cheaper. Sir Michael Latham (1994) suggested this in his report to the UK government on the construction industry. It was also the thinking behind the contract approach partnering and alliancing. By leaving the uncertainty open, the client and contractor could work together to find cheaper solutions and reduce risk. It was also the thinking behind an approach adopted in the development of oil rigs in the North Sea, called CRINE, Cost Reduction in a New Era.

So the view is that leaving the flexibility and uncertainty open for longer, rather than freezing the design as quickly as possible leads to cheaper outcomes for projects, though how this is achieved is under discussion. Klein and Meckling said it was because it avoided change and rework. Partnering and alliancing contracts, Sir Michael Latham and CRINE say it is because it allows for innovation, and you can find cheaper designs, cheaper ways of doing things, and better manage the risk.

References and further reading

Cleland, DI & King, WR. (1983). *Systems Analysis and Project Management*, 2nd Edition. New York: McGraw-Hill.

Gareis, R & Stummer, M. (2008). *Projects & Processes*. Vienna: Mainz.

Kerzner, H. (2017). *Project Management: A Systems Approach to Planning, Scheduling, and Controlling*, 12th Edition. New York, Chichester and Indianapolis, IN: Wiley.

Klein, B & Meckling, W. (1958). Application of Operations Research to Development Decisions. *Operations Research*, 6(3): 352–363.

Latham, M. (1994). *Constructing the Team: Joint Review of Procurement and Contractual Arrangements*. London: Her Majesty's Stationery Office.

Murray-Webster, R & Dalcher, D. (2022). *APM Body of Knowledge*, 7th Edition. Prince Risborough: Association for Project Management.

Project Management Institute. (2017). *A Guide to the Project Management Body of Knowledge (PMBOK® Guide)*, 6th Edition. Newtown Square, PA: Project Management Institute.

Project Management Institute. (2021). *A Guide to the Project Management Body of Knowledge (PMBOK® Guide)*, 7th Edition. Newtown Square, PA: Project Management Institute.

Turner, JR. (2014). *The Handbook of Project-Based Management: Leading Strategic Change in organizations*, 4th Edition. New York: McGraw-Hill.

Turner, JR & Müller, R. (2003). On the Nature of the Project as a Temporary Organization. *International Journal of Project Management,* 21(1), 1–8.